CONTEMPORARY AUDITING

REAL ISSUES & CASES   MICHAEL C. KNAPP   SEVENTH EDITION

MAKE IT YOURS!
SELECT JUST THE CASES YOU NEED

Through Cengage Learning's **Make It Yours**, you can — simply, quickly, and affordably — create a quality auditing text that is tailored to your course.

- Pick your coverage and only pay for the cases you use.
- Add cases from a prior edition of Knapp's **Contemporary Auditing**.
- Add your course materials and assignments.
- Pick your own unique cover design.

We recognize that not every program covers the same cases and topics in your auditing course. Chris Knapp wrote his case book for people to use either as a core book or as a supplement to an existing book.

If you would like to use a custom auditing case book or supplement the South-Western accounting book you are currently using, simply check the cases you want to include, indicate if there are other course materials you would like to add, and click submit. A Cengage Learning representative will contact you to review and confirm your order.

Visit **www.custom.cengage.com/makeityours/knapp7e** to make your selections and provide details on anything else you would like to include.

Prefer to use pen and paper? No problem. Fill out questions 1-4 and fax this form to **1.800.270.3310**.
A Custom Solutions editor will contact you within 2-3 business days to discuss the options you have selected.

1. Which of the following cases would you like to include?

Section 1: Comprehensive Cases

- ○ 1.1 Enron Corporation
- ○ 1.2 Just for FEET, Inc.
- ○ 1.3 Jamaica Water Properties
- ○ 1.4 Health Management, Inc.
- ○ 1.5 The Leslie Fay Companies
- ○ 1.6 Star Technologies, Inc.
- ○ 1.7 Lincoln Savings and Loan Association
- ○ 1.8 Crazy Eddie, Inc.
- ○ 1.9 ZZZZ Best Company, Inc.
- ○ 1.10 United States Surgical Corporation
- ○ 1.11 New Century Financial Corporation
- ○ 1.12 AMRE, Inc.*

Section 2: Audits of High-Risk Accounts

- ○ 2.1 Jack Greenberg, Inc.
- ○ 2.2 Golden Bear Golf, Inc.
- ○ 2.3 Happiness Express, Inc.
- ○ 2.4 CapitalBanc Corporation
- ○ 2.5 SmarTalk Teleservices, Inc.
- ○ 2.6 CBI Holding Company, Inc.
- ○ 2.7 Campbell Soup Company
- ○ 2.8 Rocky Mount Undergarment Company, Inc.
- ○ 2.9 General Technologies Group Ltd.*
- ○ 2.10 Perry Drug Stores*

Section 3: Internal Control Issues

- ○ 3.1 The Trolley Dodgers
- ○ 3.2 Howard Street Jewelers, Inc.
- ○ 3.3 Saks Fifth Avenue
- ○ 3.4 Triton Energy Ltd.
- ○ 3.5 Goodner Brothers, Inc.
- ○ 3.6 Troberg Stores

continued on back side

NEW SUBPRIME MORTGAGE CASE: Case 1.11 New Century Financial Corporation

Section 4: Ethical Responsibilities of Accountants

- ○ 4.1   Creve Couer Pizza, Inc.
- ○ 4.2   F&C International, Inc.
- ○ 4.3   Suzette Washington, Accounting Major
- ○ 4.4   Oak Industries, Inc.
- ○ 4.5   Wiley Jackson, Accounting Major
- ○ 4.6   Arvel Smart, Accounting Major
- ○ 4.7   David Quinn, Tax Accountant
- ○ 4.8   Jack Bass, Accounting Professor
- ○ 4.9   Thomas Forehand, CPA
- ○ 4.10 Laurel Valley Estates*

Section 5: Ethical Responsibilities of Independent Auditors

- ○ 5.1   Cardillo Travel Systems, Inc.
- ○ 5.2   Mallon Resources Corporation
- ○ 5.3   The North Face, Inc.
- ○ 5.4   NextCard, Inc.
- ○ 5.5   Koger Properties, Inc.
- ○ 5.6   American Fuel & Supply Company, Inc.
- ○ 5.7   The PTL Club*
- ○ 5.8   Zaveral Boosalis Raisch*

Section 6: Professional Roles

- ○ 6.1   Leigh Ann Walker, Staff Accountant
- ○ 6.2   Bill DeBurger, In-Charge Accountant
- ○ 6.3   David Myers, WorldCom Controller
- ○ 6.4   Tommy O'Connell, Audit Senior
- ○ 6.5   Avis Love, Staff Accountant
- ○ 6.6   Charles Tollison, Audit Manager
- ○ 6.7   Hamilton Wong, In-Charge Accountant

Section 7: Professional Issues

- ○ 7.1   PricewaterhouseCoopers Securities, LLC
- ○ 7.2   Stephen Gray, CPS
- ○ 7.3   Scott Fane, CPA
- ○ 7.4   *Hopkins v. Price Waterhouse*
- ○ 7.5   Sarah Russell, Staff Accountant
- ○ 7.6   Bud Carriker, Audit Senior
- ○ 7.7   National Medical Transportation Network
- ○ 7.8   Fred Stern & Company, Inc.
        (*Ultramares Corporation v. Touche et al.*)
- ○ 7.9   First Securities Company of Chicago
        (*Ernst & Ernst v. Hochfelder et al.*)

Section 8: International Cases

- ○ 8.1   Livent, Inc.
- ○ 8.2   Royal Ahold, N.V.
- ○ 8.3   *Kansayaku*
- ○ 8.4   Registered Auditors, South Africa
- ○ 8.5   *Zuan Yan*
- ○ 8.6   Kaset Thai Sugar Company
- ○ 8.7   Australian Wheat Board
- ○ 8.8   OAO Gazprom
- ○ 8.9   Tata Finance Limited
- ○ 8.10 Baan Company, N.V.
- ○ 8.11 Institute of Chartered Accountants of India

Section 9: Classic Litigation Cases

- ○ 9.1   Equity Funding Corporation of America*
- ○ 9.2   National Student Marketing Corporation*

** Cases drawn from **Knapp's Contemporary Auditing, 6e** that are not available in the 7th edition.*

---

2. Would you like to include your own materials? Consider adding your own content such as a course syllabus, regional material, or sample exam.

- ○ **Yes,** I plan to add additional materials.   ○   **No,** I do not wish to add additional materials.
- ○ I am not sure at this time if I would like to add additional materials.

---

3. Are you considering using these cases along with a South-Western Accounting text?

- ○ No
- ○ Yes
- ○ If yes, which text? _____

---

4. You will be able to create an original cover design that will include items such as your name and course title on the front. You may even add your own school photo or logo. Please fill out the information below so that we may contact you regarding the additional details of your inquiry.

Instructor _____

Email _____

Department _____

School _____

City, State, Zip _____

Phone _____

Course Number and Title _____

Projected Quantity _____

Course Start Date _____

COMMENTS:
_____
_____
_____
_____
_____
_____

Please submit your inquiry at least six weeks prior to the start of your course.

CONTEMPORARY AUDITING
REAL ISSUES AND CASES

Seventh Edition

Michael C. Knapp
University of Oklahoma

SOUTH-WESTERN
CENGAGE Learning™

Australia • Brazil • Japan • Korea • Mexico • Singapore • Spain • United Kingdom • United States

CONTEMPORARY AUDITING
REAL ISSUES AND CASES

Seventh Edition

Contemporary Auditing: Real Issues and Cases, 7e

Michael C. Knapp

VP/Editorial Director:
  Jack W. Calhoun

VP/Editor-in-Chief:
  Rob Dewey

Acquisitions Editor:
  Matt Filmonov

Developmental Editor:
  Heather McAuliffe

Marketing Manager:
  Kristen Hurd

Content Project Manager:
  Lysa Oeters

Senior Media Editor:
  Scott Hamilton

Manufacturing Coordinator:
  Doug Wilke

Production Service:
  Macmillan Publishing Solutions

Art Director:
  Stacy Shirley

Internal Designer:
  Patti Hudepohl

Cover Designer:
  Patrick DeVine

Cover Image:
  Getty Images/iStock Images

Library of Congress Control Number: 2009923268
ISBN-13: 978-1-439-07819-8
ISBN-10: 1-439-07819-X

South-Western Cengage Learning
5191 Natorp Boulevard
Mason, OH 45040
USA

Cengage Learning products are represented in Canada by Nelson Education, Ltd.

For your course and learning solutions, visit **www.cengage.com.**

Purchase any of our products at your local college store or at our preferred online store: **www.ichapters.com.**

Printed in the United States
1 2 3 4 5 6 7 13 12 11 10 09

DEDICATION

To Carol, Johnny, Lindsay, Jessi, and Emmie

BRIEF CONTENTS

CONTENTS

Arthur Edward Andersen established a simple motto that he required his subordinates and clients to invoke: "Think straight, talk straight." For decades, that motto served Arthur Andersen & Co. well. Unfortunately, the firm's association with one client, Enron Corporation, abruptly ended Andersen's long and proud history in the public accounting profession.

KEY TOPICS: history of the public accounting profession in the United States, scope of professional services provided to audit clients, auditor independence, and retention of audit workpapers.

In the fall of 1999, just a few months after reporting a record profit for fiscal 1998, Just for Feet collapsed and filed for bankruptcy. Subsequent investigations by law enforcement authorities revealed a massive accounting fraud that had grossly misrepresented the company's reported operating results. Key features of the fraud were improper accounting for "vendor allowances" and intentional understatements of the company's inventory valuation allowance.

KEY TOPICS: applying analytical procedures, identifying inherent risk and control risk factors, need for auditors to monitor key developments within the client's industry, assessing the health of a client's industry, and receivables confirmation procedures.

Shortly after accepting an executive position with JWP, David Sokol discovered several suspicious items in the company's accounting records. Sokol insisted on thoroughly investigating those items. When that investigation uncovered evidence of a pervasive fraud, Sokol resigned and turned over that evidence to the company's board of directors.

KEY TOPICS: ethical responsibilities of corporate management, control environment issues, and auditor independence.

The Private Securities Litigation Reform Act (PSLRA) of 1995 amended the Securities Exchange Act of 1934. This new federal statute was projected to have a major impact on auditors' legal liability under the 1934 Act. The first major test of the PSLRA was triggered by a class-action lawsuit filed against BDO Seidman for its 1995 audit of Health Management, Inc., a New York–based pharmaceuticals distributor.

KEY TOPICS: inventory audit procedures, auditor independence, audit workpapers, inherent risk factors, and auditors' civil liability under the federal securities laws.

In January 2002, Paul Polishan, the former chief financial officer of The Leslie Fay Companies, began serving a nine-year prison sentence for fraudulently misrepresenting Leslie

Like the United States, Japan has recently made significant changes in the regulatory infrastructure for its financial reporting system. Many of these changes have directly impacted Japan's accounting profession and independent audit function. An accounting and auditing scandal involving a large cosmetics and apparel company, Kanebo Limited, posed the first major challenge of that new regulatory framework.

The South African economy was rocked in recent years by a series of financial reporting scandals. To restore the credibility of the nation's capital markets, the South African Parliament passed a controversial new law, the Auditing Profession Act (APA). The APA established a new auditing regulatory agency and a new professional credential for independent auditors. The APA also mandated that independent auditors immediately disclose to the new auditing agency any "reportable irregularities" committed by an audit client.

The Big Four accounting firms view China as one of the most lucrative markets for accounting and auditing services worldwide. However, those firms face major challenges in that market. Among these challenges are an increasing litigation risk and the difficulty of coping with the often heavy-handed tactics of China's authoritarian central government.

This case focuses on the 1999 murder of Michael Wansley, a partner with Deloitte Touche Tohmatsu. Wansley was supervising a debt-restructuring engagement in a remote region of Thailand when he was gunned down by a professional assassin.

During the United Nations (U.N.) embargo imposed on Iraq following that nation's invasion of Kuwait, this large Australian company paid $300 million in bribes to secure lucrative Iraqi wheat contracts administered through the U.N. Oil-for-Food program. After the bribes were discovered in 2005 by a U.N. task force, two major international accounting firms became involved in the ensuing controversy.

Business Week referred to the huge Gazprom debacle as "Russia's Enron." For the first time in the history of the new Russian republic, a Big Four accounting firm faced a lawsuit for allegedly issuing improper audit opinions on a Russian company's financial statements.

A financial reporting fraud involving this large Indian company became known as "India's Enron." Company executives retained one of India's most prominent accounting firms to investigate the fraud. The report filed by that accounting firm implicated those same executives. Shortly after the report was released, the accounting firm retracted the report and fired the three partners responsible for it.

For the first time in its history, the Securities and Exchange Commission (SEC) sanctioned a foreign audit firm. Moret Ernst & Young Accountants, a Dutch affiliate of Ernst & Young, was sanctioned for having a "joint business relationship" with Baan, a Dutch company with a large U.S. subsidiary. This case also examines a similar situation involving Ernst & Young and one of its audit clients, PeopleSoft Corporation.

The Institute of Chartered Accountants of India (ICAI) is the federal agency that oversees India's accounting profession. In 2002, the ICAI commissioned a study of the alleged takeover of that profession by the major international accounting firms. The resulting 900-page report charged that those firms had used a variety of illicit and even illegal methods to "colonize" India's market for accounting, auditing, and related services to the detriment of the nation's domestic accounting firms.

PREFACE

Who could have foreseen the dramatic circumstances and events that impacted the public accounting profession during the past decade? A series of high-profile scandals focused the attention of the investing public, the press, Wall Street, and, eventually, Congress on our profession. Most of this attention centered on independent auditors and the profession's major international accounting firms. Those scandals cost our profession much of its hard-earned respect.

The spiraling financial crisis that began to unravel in a series of cascading bank and business failures again places the accounting profession and the role of auditing front and center. The new case, The New Century Financial Corporation, is the story of the one firm mired in the subprime crisis and provides much needed perspective for today's turbulent markets.

Many trade and academic publications have maintained that accounting educators are at least partially responsible for our profession's recent problems. Whether or not that is true, we have a responsibility to help shepherd our profession through the turbulent transitional period it now faces. What then can we, as educators, do to help restore the credibility of the critically important, if long underappreciated, independent audit function? One strategy is to make a stronger effort to embrace the litany of reforms recommended several years ago by the Accounting Education Change Commission (AECC). Among the AECC's recommendations is that accounting educators should employ a broader array of instructional resources, particularly experiential resources, designed to stimulate active learning by students. In fact, the intent of my casebook is to provide auditing instructors with a source of such materials that can be used in both undergraduate and graduate auditing courses.

This casebook stresses the "people" aspect of independent audits. If you review a sample of recent "audit failures," you will find that problem audits seldom result from inadequate audit technology. Instead, deficient audits typically result from the presence of one, or both, of the following two conditions: client personnel who intentionally subvert an audit and auditors who fail to carry out the responsibilities assigned to them. Exposing students to problem audits will help them recognize the red flags that often accompany audit failures. An ability to recognize these red flags and the insight gained by discussing and dissecting problem audits will allow students to cope more effectively with the problematic situations they are certain to encounter in their own careers. In addition, this experiential approach provides students with context-specific situations that make it much easier for them to grasp the relevance of important auditing topics, concepts, and procedures.

The cases in this text also acquaint students with the work environment of auditors. After studying these cases, students will better appreciate how client pressure, peer pressure, time budgets, and related factors complicate the work roles of independent auditors. Also embedded in these cases are the ambiguity and lack of structure that auditors face each day. Missing documents, conflicting audit evidence, auditors' dual obligations to the client and to financial statement users, and the lack of definitive professional standards for many situations are additional aspects of the audit environment woven into these cases.

The seventh edition of my casebook contains the following eight sections of cases: Comprehensive Cases, Audits of High-Risk Accounts, Internal Control Issues, Ethical Responsibilities of Accountants, Ethical Responsibilities of Independent Auditors, Professional Roles, Professional Issues, and International Cases. This organizational structure is intended to help adopters readily identify cases best suited for their particular needs.

In preparing this edition, I retained those cases that have been most popular with adopters. These cases include, among many others, Cardillo Travel Systems, Crazy Eddie, Golden Bear Golf, Leigh Ann Walker, Lincoln Savings and Loan Association, The Trolley Dodgers, and ZZZZ Best Company. You will find that many of the "returning" cases have been updated for relevant circumstances and events that have occurred since the publication of the previous edition.

This edition also features 16 new cases. Eight of these cases are included in the new international section. Easily the most dramatic trend in the business world over the past few decades has been the "globalization" of markets, including the market for professional accounting services. Business schools have responded to this dramatic trend by establishing new international majors, study-abroad programs, and a slew of international courses across all business disciplines. Accounting may very well be the business discipline that has been the slowest to "internationalize" its curriculum. The international cases in this edition provide auditing instructors with an efficient and cost-effective way to introduce their students to a wide range of important issues within the global accounting profession that will have far-reaching implications for their careers.

Four of the international cases focus on the history of, and recent developments within, the public accounting professions of the Republic of China (*Zuan Yan*), India (Institute of Chartered Accountants of India), Japan (*Kansayaku*), and Russia (OAO Gazprom). The future of the public accounting profession in the United States will almost certainly be impacted by developments within the public accounting professions of those four very important countries. Consequently, it is important that our students understand the similarities and differences between the U.S. accounting profession and the accounting professions of those four nations.

The Royal Ahold case, which examines the accounting and reporting scandal often referred to as "Europe's Enron," documents many of the challenges that must be overcome when auditing a multinational corporation that operates in dozens of countries. Registered Auditors, South Africa, is a case that focuses on a controversial new law passed in 2006 by the South African Parliament—a law establishing a new professional credential for independent auditors in that country. The most controversial feature of this new law is a requirement that auditors immediately report to a federal agency all potential fraudulent acts they discover during any professional services engagement.

Another of the new international cases, Kaset Thai Sugar Company, documents the tragic murder of Michael Wansley, a Deloitte Touche Tohmatsu partner. Wansley was assassinated in a remote region of Thailand while completing a tense engagement involving a bankrupt client. The Australian Wheat Board case demonstrates that independent auditors can find themselves involved in international events with far-reaching political and economic consequences. This case revolves around the $300 million of bribes paid by a large Australian company to secure lucrative Iraqi wheat contracts administered through the United Nations' Oil-for-Food Program. The Oil-for-Food program provided humanitarian relief to Iraqi citizens during the lengthy trade embargo imposed on Iraq by the United Nations following that country's invasion of Kuwait.

Several of the other new cases in this edition highlight important ethical issues and dilemmas that your students may ultimately face. In fact, two of these new cases involve ethical dilemmas facing accounting majors, meaning that these cases may "strike close to home" for many of your students. In the Wiley Jackson case, a soon-to-graduate accounting major must decide whether to disclose in a pre-employment document a minor-in-possession charge filed against him by the local police.

The Arvel Smart case focuses on a topic with which your students will be particularly familiar, namely, internships. Like many students in five-year programs, Arvel Smart had two internship opportunities: one each during the final two summers of his five-year program. While considering the second internship opportunity, Arvel all but decided to accept a job offer for a permanent position that had been extended to him by the firm with which he had served his first internship. The ethical dilemma facing Arvel was whether it would be inappropriate (unethical) for him to accept the second internship offer when there was almost no chance that he would consider a permanent position with the firm that had offered him that internship.

Other new cases in this edition include Just for Feet; David Quinn, Tax Accountant; Jack Bass, Accounting Professor; Thomas Forehand, CPA; and Tata Finance Limited. Just for Feet is a new comprehensive case that requires students to identify key inherent and control risk factors during the planning phase of an audit. Client confidentiality is the focal issue in the David Quinn case, while the Jack Bass case involves another student-oriented ethical issue, namely, cheating. The Thomas Forehand case documents the tragic series of events involving the sole proprietor of an accounting firm who was goaded by a dishonest client into participating in a money-laundering scheme. Finally, the Tata Finance Limited case examines another Enron-esque accounting scandal. The Tata Finance scandal has been referred to as "India's Enron."

This casebook can be used in several different ways. Adopters can use the casebook as a supplemental text for the undergraduate auditing course or as a primary text for a graduate-level seminar in auditing. The instructor's manual contains a syllabus for a graduate auditing course organized around this text. As a point of information, this latter course satisfies the three-hour ethics requirement that the Texas State Board of Public Accountancy has established for CPA candidates in the state of Texas. Finally, this casebook can be used in the capstone professional practice course incorporated in many five-year accounting programs.

Listed next are brief descriptions of the eight groups of cases included in this text. The casebook's Table of Contents presents an annotated description of each case.

Comprehensive Cases Most of these cases deal with highly publicized problem audits performed by large, international accounting firms. Among the clients involved in these audits are Enron Corporation, The Leslie Fay Companies, Lincoln Savings and Loan Association, United States Surgical Corporation, and ZZZZ Best Company. Each of these cases addresses a wide range of auditing, accounting, and ethical issues.

Audits of High-Risk Accounts In contrast to the cases in the prior section, these cases typically highlight contentious accounting and auditing issues posed by a single account or group of accounts. For example, the Jack Greenberg case focuses primarily on inventory audit procedures. The CapitalBanc case raises audit issues relevant to cash, while the Campbell Soup case examines a series of revenue recognition issues.

Internal Control Issues In recent years, leading authorities in the public accounting profession have emphasized the need for auditors to thoroughly understand their clients' internal control policies and procedures. The cases in this section introduce students to control issues in a variety of contexts. Goodner Brothers, Inc., raises control issues for a wholesaler, while both Saks Fifth Avenue and Howard Street Jewelers examine important control issues for retail businesses.

Ethical Responsibilities of Accountants Integrating ethics into an auditing course requires much more than simply discussing the *AICPA Code of Professional Conduct*. This section presents specific scenarios in which accountants or future accountants have faced perplexing ethical dilemmas. By requiring students to study actual situations in which important ethical issues have arisen, they will be better prepared to resolve similar situations in their own professional careers. One of the cases in this section, Rocky Mount Undergarment Company, focuses on the accountants of a company who had to face the eternal question of whether the end justifies the means. Another case in this section, F&C International, profiles three corporate executives who had to decide whether to compromise their personal code of ethics in the face of a large-scale fraud masterminded by their company's chief executive.

Ethical Responsibilities of Independent Auditors The cases in this section highlight ethical dilemmas faced by independent auditors. Consider the situation faced by Michael Goodbread, an audit partner with a major accounting firm. His firm acquires an audit client in which he has a small but direct financial interest. What should he do? No doubt, any auditing textbook will provide the easy answer to that question. But auditors in public practice don't always "go by the book."

Professional Roles Cases in this section examine specific work roles in the accounting profession. These cases explore the responsibilities associated with those roles and related challenges that professionals occupying them commonly encounter. The Tommy O'Connell case involves a young auditor recently promoted to audit senior. Shortly following his promotion, Tommy finds himself assigned to supervise a small but challenging audit. Tommy's sole subordinate on that engagement happens to be a young man whose integrity and work ethic have been questioned by seniors he has worked for previously. Two cases in this section spotlight the staff accountant work role, which many of your students will experience firsthand following graduation.

Professional Issues The dynamic nature of the public accounting profession continually impacts the work environment of public accountants and the nature of the services they provide. The cases in this section explore this changing work environment. For example, the *Hopkins v. Price Waterhouse* case discusses the unique problems faced by women pursuing careers in public accounting. The Scott Fane and Stephen Gray cases address ethical rules that have important implications for accounting practitioners. Both of these young CPAs became involved in legal disputes with their state boards. These disputes centered on the types of marketing efforts CPAs are allowed to use and the types of services CPAs are permitted to offer to clients. Finally, the Fred Stern and First Securities cases examine the most important legal liability issues that accounting firms currently face.

International Cases Again, the purpose of these cases is to provide your students with an introduction to important issues facing the global accounting profession and auditing discipline. After studying these cases, students will discover that most of the technical, professional, and ethical challenges facing U.S. practitioners are shared by auditors and accountants across the globe. Then again, some of these cases document unique challenges that must be dealt with by auditors and accountants in certain countries or regions of the world. For example, the Chinese case (*Zuan Yan*) demonstrates the problems that an authoritarian central government can pose for independent auditors and accounting practioners. Likewise, the Kaset Thai Sugar Company case vividly demonstrates that auditors and accountants can face hostile and sometimes dangerous assignments in developing countries where their professional roles and resposibilities are not well understood or appreciated.

Customize Your Own Casebook To maximize your flexibility in using these cases, Cengage Learning/South-Western has included *Contemporary Auditing: Real Issues and Cases* in its customized publishing program. Adopters have the option of creating a customized version of this casebook ideally suited for their specific needs. For example, at the University of Oklahoma a customized selection of my cases is used to add an ethics component to the undergraduate managerial accounting course. In fact, since the cases in this text examine ethical issues across a wide swath of different contexts, adopters can develop a customized ethics casebook to supplement almost any accounting course.

This casebook is ideally suited to be customized for the undergraduate auditing course. For example, auditing instructors who want to add a strong international component to their courses could develop a customized edition of this text that includes a series of the international cases. Likewise, to enhance the coverage of ethical issues in the undergraduate auditing course, instructors could choose a series of cases from this text that highlight important ethical issues. Following are several examples of customized versions of this casebook that could be easily integrated into the undergraduate auditing course.

International Focus: Kansayaku (8.3), Registered Auditors, South Africa (8.4), *Zuan Yan* (8.5), Australian Wheat Board (8.7), OAO Gazprom (8.8), Institute of Chartered Accountants of India (8.11). This custom casebook would provide your students with an in-depth understanding of the current state of the auditing discipline in four of the world's most important countries. This series of cases would also acquaint your students with the controversial "reportable irregularities" rule in South Africa and expose them to several important issues related to the Foreign Corrupt Practices Act that are dealt with in the Australian case.

Ethics Focus (I): Suzette Washington, Accounting Major (4.3), Wiley Jackson, Accounting Major (4.5), Arvel Smart, Accounting Major (4.6), Jack Bass, Accounting Professor (4.8), Leigh Ann Walker, Staff Accountant (6.1), Avis Love, Staff Accountant (6.5). The first four of these cases give your students an opportunity to discuss and debate ethical issues directly pertinent to them as accounting majors. The final two cases expose students to important ethical issues they may encounter shortly after graduation if they choose to enter public accounting.

Ethics Focus (II): Creve Couer Pizza, Inc. (4.1), F&C International, Inc. (4.2), David Quinn, Tax Accountant (4.7), Thomas Forehand, CPA (4.9), Koger Properties, Inc. (5.5), Hamilton Wong, In-Charge Accountant (6.7), PricewaterhouseCoopers Securities, LLC (7.1), Stephen Gray, CPA (7.2). This selection of cases is suitable for auditing instructors who have a particular interest in covering a variety of ethical topics relevant to the *AICPA Code of Professional Conduct,* several of which are not directly or exclusively related to auditing.

Applied Focus: Enron Corporation (1.1), ZZZZ Best Company, Inc. (1.9), Golden Bear Golf, Inc. (2.2), CapitalBanc Corporation (2.4), Cardillo Travel Systems, Inc. (5.1), American Fuel & Supply Company, Inc. (5.6), Livent, Inc. (8.1). This series of cases will provide students with a broad-brush introduction to the *real world* of independent auditing. These cases raise a wide range of technical, professional, and ethical issues in a variety of different client contexts.

Professional Roles Focus: Leigh Ann Walker, Staff Accountant (6.1), Bill DeBurger, In-Charge Accountant (6.2), Tommy O'Connell, Audit Senior (6.4), Avis Love, Staff Accountant (6.5), Charles Tollison, Audit Manager (6.6), Hamilton Wong, In-Charge Accountant (6.7), Bud Carriker, Audit Senior (7.6). This custom casebook would be useful for auditing instructors who choose to rely on a standard textbook to cover key technical topics in auditing—but who also want to expose their students to the everyday ethical and professional challenges faced by individuals occupying various levels of the employment hierarchy within auditing firms.

High-Risk Accounts Focus: Each of the cases in Section 2, Audits of High-Risk Accounts. This series of cases will provide your students with relatively intense homework assignments that focus almost exclusively on the financial-statement line items that pose the greatest challenges for auditors.

Of course, realize that you are free to choose any "mix" of my cases to include in a customized casebook for an undergraduate auditing course that you teach. For more information on how to design your customized casebook, please contact your Cengage Learning/South-Western sales representative.

Acknowledgements I greatly appreciate the insight and suggestions provided by the following reviewers of earlier editions of this text: Alex Ampadu, University at Buffalo; Barbara Apostolou, Louisiana State University; Jane Baird, Mankato State University; James Bierstaker, Villanova University; Ed Blocher, University of North Carolina; Susan Cain, Southern Oregon University; Kurt Chaloupecky, Southwest Missouri State University; Ray Clay, University of North Texas; Jeffrey Cohen, Boston College; Mary Doucet, University of Georgia; Rafik Elias, California State University, Los Angeles; Ruth Engle, Lafayette College; Chrislynn Freed, University of Southern California; Carolyn Galantine, Pepperdine University; Michele C. Henney, University of Oregon; Laurence Johnson, Colorado State University; Donald McConnell, University of Texas at Arlington; Heidi Meier, Cleveland State University; Don Nichols, Texas Christian University; Marcia Niles, University of Idaho; Robert J. Ramsay, Ph.D., CPA, University of Kentucky; John Rigsby, Mississippi State University; Dr. Gene Smith, Eastern New Mexico University; Rajendra Srivastava, University of Kansas; Richard Allen Turpen, University of Alabama at Birmingham; T. Sterling Wetzel, Oklahoma State University; and Jim Yardley, Virginia Polytechnic University. This project also benefitted greatly from the editorial assistance of my sister, Paula Kay Conatser; my wife, Carol Ann Knapp; and my son, John William Knapp. I would also like to thank Glen McLaughlin for his continuing generosity in funding the development of instructional materials that highlight important ethical issues. Finally, I would like to acknowledge the contributions of my students, who have provided invaluable comments and suggestions on the content and use of these cases.

Michael C. Knapp
McLaughlin Chair in Business
Ethics and Professor of Accounting
University of Oklahoma

SECTION 1

COMPREHENSIVE CASES

Enron Corporation

John and Mary Andersen immigrated to the United States from their native Norway in 1881. The young couple made their way to the small farming community of Plano, Illinois, some 40 miles southwest of downtown Chicago. Over the previous few decades, hundreds of Norwegian families had settled in Plano and surrounding communities. In fact, the aptly named Norway, Illinois, was located just a few miles away from the couple's new hometown. In 1885, Arthur Edward Andersen was born. From an early age, the Andersens' son had a fascination with numbers. Little did his parents realize that Arthur's interest in numbers would become the driving force in his life. Less than one century after he was born, an accounting firm bearing Arthur Andersen's name would become the world's largest professional services organization with more than 1,000 partners and operations in dozens of countries scattered across the globe.

Think Straight, Talk Straight

Discipline, honesty, and a strong work ethic were three key traits that John and Mary Andersen instilled in their son. The Andersens also constantly impressed upon him the importance of obtaining an education. Unfortunately, Arthur's parents did not survive to help him achieve that goal. Orphaned by the time he was a young teenager, Andersen was forced to take a full-time job as a mail clerk and attend night classes to work his way through high school. After graduating from high school, Andersen attended the University of Illinois while working as an accountant for Allis-Chalmers, a Chicago-based company that manufactured tractors and other farming equipment. In 1908, Andersen accepted a position with the Chicago office of Price Waterhouse. At the time, Price Waterhouse, which was organized in Great Britain during the early nineteenth century, easily qualified as the United States' most prominent public accounting firm.

At age 23, Andersen became the youngest CPA in the state of Illinois. A few years later, Andersen and a friend, Clarence Delany, established a partnership to provide accounting, auditing, and related services. The two young accountants named their firm Andersen, Delany & Company. When Delany decided to go his own way, Andersen renamed the firm Arthur Andersen & Company.

In 1915, Arthur Andersen faced a dilemma that would help shape the remainder of his professional life. One of his audit clients was a freight company that owned and operated several steam freighters that delivered various commodities to ports located on Lake Michigan. Following the close of the company's fiscal year but before Andersen had issued his audit report on its financial statements, one of the client's ships sank in Lake Michigan. At the time, there were few formal rules for companies to follow in preparing their annual financial statements and certainly no rule that required the company to report a material "subsequent event" occurring after the close of its fiscal year—such as the loss of a major asset. Nevertheless, Andersen insisted that his client disclose the loss of the ship. Andersen reasoned that third parties who would use the company's financial statements, among them the company's banker, would want to be informed of the loss. Although unhappy with Andersen's position, the client eventually acquiesced and reported the loss in the footnotes to its financial statements.

Two decades after the steamship dilemma, Arthur Andersen faced a similar situation with an audit client that was much larger, much more prominent, and much more profitable for his firm. Arthur Andersen & Co. served as the independent auditor for the giant chemical company, du Pont. As the company's audit neared completion one year, members of the audit engagement team and executives of du Pont quarreled over how to define the company's operating income. Du Pont's management insisted on a liberal definition of operating income that included income earned on certain investments. Arthur Andersen was brought in to arbitrate the dispute. When he sided with his subordinates, du Pont's management team dismissed the firm and hired another auditor.

Throughout his professional career, Arthur E. Andersen relied on a simple, four-word motto to serve as a guiding principle in making important personal and professional decisions: "Think straight, talk straight." Andersen insisted that his partners and other personnel in his firm invoke that simple rule when dealing with clients, potential clients, bankers, regulatory authorities, and any other parties they interacted with while representing Arthur Andersen & Co. He also insisted that audit clients "talk straight" in their financial statements. Former colleagues and associates often described Andersen as opinionated, stubborn, and, in some cases, "difficult." But even his critics readily admitted that Andersen was point-blank honest. "Arthur Andersen wouldn't put up with anything that wasn't complete, 100% integrity. If anybody did anything otherwise, he'd fire them. And if clients wanted to do something he didn't agree with, he'd either try to change them or quit."[1]

As a young professional attempting to grow his firm, Arthur Andersen quickly recognized the importance of carving out a niche in the rapidly developing accounting services industry. Andersen realized that the nation's bustling economy of the 1920s depended heavily on companies involved in the production and distribution of energy. As the economy grew, Andersen knew there would be a steadily increasing need for electricity, oil and gas, and other energy resources. So he focused his practice development efforts on obtaining clients involved in the various energy industries. Andersen was particularly successful in recruiting electric utilities as clients. By the early 1930s, Arthur Andersen & Co. had a thriving practice in the upper Midwest and was among the leading regional accounting firms in the nation.

The U.S. economy's precipitous downturn during the Great Depression of the 1930s posed huge financial problems for many of Arthur Andersen & Co's audit clients in the electric utilities industry. As the Depression wore on, Arthur Andersen personally worked with several of the nation's largest metropolitan banks to help his clients obtain the financing they desperately needed to continue operating. The bankers and other leading financiers who dealt with Arthur Andersen quickly learned of his commitment to honesty and proper, forthright accounting and financial reporting practices. Andersen's reputation for honesty and integrity allowed lenders to use with confidence financial data stamped with his approval. The end result was that many troubled firms received the financing they needed to survive the harrowing days of the 1930s. In turn, the respect that Arthur Andersen earned among leading financial executives nationwide resulted in Arthur Andersen & Co. receiving a growing number of referrals for potential clients located outside of the Midwest.

During the later years of his career, Arthur Andersen became a spokesperson for his discipline. He authored numerous books and presented speeches throughout the nation regarding the need for rigorous accounting, auditing, and ethical standards

1. R. Frammolino and J. Leeds, "Andersen's Reputation in Shreds," *Los Angeles Times* (online), 30 January 2002.

for the emerging public accounting profession. Andersen continually urged his fellow accountants to adopt the public service ideal that had long served as the motivating premise of the more mature professions such as law and medicine. He also lobbied for the adoption of a mandatory continuing professional education (CPE) requirement. Andersen realized that CPAs needed CPE to stay abreast of rapid developments in the business world that had significant implications for accounting and financial reporting practices. In fact, Arthur Andersen & Co. made CPE mandatory for its employees long before state boards of accountancy adopted such a requirement.

By the mid-1940s, Arthur Andersen & Co. had offices scattered across the eastern one-half of the United States and employed more than 1,000 accountants. When Arthur Andersen died in 1947, many business leaders expected that the firm would disband without its founder, who had single-handedly managed its operations over the previous four decades. But, after several months of internal turmoil and dissension, the firm's remaining partners chose Andersen's most trusted associate and protégé to replace him.

Like his predecessor and close friend who had personally hired him in 1928, Leonard Spacek soon earned a reputation as a no-nonsense professional—an auditor's auditor. He passionately believed that the primary role of independent auditors was to ensure that their clients reported fully and honestly regarding their financial affairs to the investing and lending public. Spacek continued Arthur Andersen's campaign to improve accounting and auditing practices in the United States during his long tenure as his firm's chief executive. "Spacek openly criticized the profession for tolerating what he considered a sloppy patchwork of accounting standards that left the investing public no way to compare the financial performance of different companies."[2] Such criticism compelled the accounting profession to develop a more formal and rigorous rule-making process. In the late 1950s, the profession created the Accounting Principles Board (APB) to study contentious accounting issues and develop appropriate new standards. The APB was replaced in 1973 by the Financial Accounting Standards Board (FASB). Another legacy of Arthur Andersen that Leonard Spacek sustained was requiring the firm's professional employees to continue their education throughout their careers. During Spacek's tenure, Arthur Andersen & Co. established the world's largest private university, the Arthur Andersen & Co. Center for Professional Education located in St. Charles, Illinois, not far from Arthur Andersen's birthplace.

Leonard Spacek's strong leadership and business skills transformed Arthur Andersen & Co. into a major international accounting firm. When Spacek retired in 1973, Arthur Andersen & Co. was arguably the most respected accounting firm not only in the United States, but also worldwide. Three decades later, shortly after the dawn of the new millennium, Arthur Andersen & Co. employed more than 80,000 professionals, had practice offices in more than 80 countries, and had annual revenues approaching $10 billion. However, in late 2001, the firm, which by that time had adopted the one-word name "Andersen," faced the most significant crisis in its history since the death of its founder. Ironically, that crisis stemmed from Andersen's audits of an energy company, a company founded in 1930 that, like many of Arthur Andersen's clients, had struggled to survive the Depression.

The World's Greatest Company

Northern Natural Gas Company was founded in Omaha, Nebraska, in 1930. The principal investors in the new venture included a Texas-based company, Lone Star Gas Corporation. During its first few years of existence, Northern wrestled with the problem

2. *Ibid.*

of persuading consumers to use natural gas to heat their homes. Concern produced by several unfortunate and widely publicized home "explosions" caused by natural gas leaks drove away many of Northern's potential customers. But, as the Depression wore on, the relatively cheap cost of natural gas convinced increasing numbers of cold-stricken and shallow-pocketed consumers to become Northern's customers.

The availability of a virtually unlimited source of cheap manual labor during the 1930s allowed Northern to develop an extensive pipeline network to deliver natural gas to the residential and industrial markets that it served in the Great Plains states. As the company's revenues and profits grew, Northern's management launched a campaign to acquire dozens of its smaller competitors. This campaign was prompted by management's goal of making Northern the largest natural gas supplier in the United States. In 1947, the company, which was still relatively unknown outside of its geographical market, reached a major milestone when its stock was listed on the New York Stock Exchange. That listing provided the company with greater access to the nation's capital markets and the financing needed to continue its growth-through-acquisition strategy over the following two decades.

During the 1970s, Northern became a principal investor in the development of the Alaskan pipeline. When completed, that pipeline allowed Northern to tap vast natural gas reserves it had acquired in Canada. In 1980, Northern changed its name to InterNorth, Inc. Over the next few years, company management extended the scope of the company's operations by investing in ventures outside of the natural gas industry, including oil exploration, chemicals, coal mining, and fuel-trading operations. But the company's principal focus remained the natural gas industry. In 1985, Inter-North purchased Houston Natural Gas Company for $2.3 billion. That acquisition resulted in InterNorth controlling a 40,000-mile network of natural gas pipelines and allowed it to achieve its long-sought goal of becoming the largest natural gas company in the United States.

In 1986, InterNorth changed its name to Enron. Kenneth Lay, the former chairman of Houston Natural Gas, emerged as the top executive of the newly created firm that chose Houston, Texas, as its corporate headquarters. Lay quickly adopted the aggressive growth strategy that had long dominated the management policies of InterNorth and its predecessor. Lay hired Jeffrey Skilling to serve as one of his top subordinates. During the 1990s, Skilling developed and implemented a plan to transform Enron from a conventional natural gas supplier into an energy-trading company that served as an intermediary between producers of energy products, principally natural gas and electricity, and end users of those commodities. In early 2001, Skilling assumed Lay's position as Enron's chief executive officer (CEO), although Lay retained the title of chairman of the board. In the management letter to shareholders included in Enron's 2000 annual report, Lay and Skilling explained the metamorphosis that Enron had undergone over the previous 15 years:

> Enron hardly resembles the company we were in the early days. During our 15-year history, we have stretched ourselves beyond our own expectations. We have metamorphosed from an asset-based pipeline and power-generating company to a marketing and logistics company whose biggest assets are its well-established business approach and its innovative people.

Enron's 2000 annual report discussed the company's four principal lines of business. Energy Wholesale Services ranked as the company's largest revenue producer. That division's 60 percent increase in transaction volume during 2000 was fueled by the rapid development of EnronOnline, a B2B (business-to-business) electronic marketplace for the energy industries created in late 1999 by Enron. During fiscal 2000 alone, EnronOnline processed more than $335 billion of transactions, easily

EXHIBIT 1

ENRON CORPORATION 2000 ANNUAL REPORT FINANCIAL HIGHLIGHTS TABLE (IN MILLIONS EXCEPT FOR PER SHARE AMOUNTS)

	2000	1999	1998	1997	1996
Revenues	$100,789	$40,112	$31,260	$20,273	$13,289
Net Income:					
Operating Results	1,266	957	698	515	493
Items Impacting Comparability	(287)	(64)	5	(410)	91
Total	979	893	703	105	584
Earnings Per Share:					
Operating Results	1.47	1.18	1.00	.87	.91
Items Impacting Comparability	(.35)	(.08)	.01	(.71)	.17
Total	1.12	1.10	1.01	.16	1.08
Dividends Per Share:	.50	.50	.48	.46	.43
Total Assets:	65,503	33,381	29,350	22,552	16,137
Cash from Operating Activities:	3,010	2,228	1,873	276	742
Capital Expenditures and Equity Investments:	3,314	3,085	3,564	2,092	1,483
NYSE Price Range:					
High	90.56	44.88	29.38	22.56	23.75
Low	41.38	28.75	19.06	17.50	17.31
Close, December 31	83.12	44.38	28.53	20.78	21.56

making Enron the largest e-commerce company in the world. Enron's three other principal lines of business included Enron Energy Services, the company's retail operating unit; Enron Transportation Services, which was responsible for the company's pipeline operations; and Enron Broadband Services, a new operating unit intended to be an intermediary between users and suppliers of broadband (Internet access) services. Exhibit 1 presents the five-year financial highlights table included in Enron's 2000 annual report.

The New Economy business model that Enron pioneered for the previously staid energy industries caused Kenneth Lay, Jeffrey Skilling, and their top subordinates to be recognized as skillful entrepreneurs and to gain superstar status in the business world. Lay's position as the chief executive of the nation's seventh-largest firm gave him direct access to key political and governmental officials. In 2001, Lay served on the "transition team" responsible for helping usher in the administration of President-elect George W Bush. In June 2001, Skilling was singled out as "the No. 1 CEO in the entire country," while Enron was hailed as "America's most innovative company."[3] Enron's chief financial officer (CFO) Andrew Fastow was recognized for his efforts in helping to create the financial structure for one of the nation's largest and most complex companies. In 1999, *CFO Magazine* presented Fastow the Excellence Award for Capital Structure Management for his "pioneering work on unique financing techniques."[4]

---

3. K. Eichenwald and D. B. Henriques, "Web of Details Did Enron In as Warnings Went Unheeded," *The New York Times* (online), 10 February 2002.

4. E. Thomas, "Every Man for Himself," *Newsweek*, 18 February 2002, 25.

Throughout their tenure with Enron, Kenneth Lay and Jeffrey Skilling continually focused on enhancing their company's operating results. In the letter to shareholders in Enron's 2000 annual report, Lay and Skilling noted that "Enron is laser-focused on earnings per share, and we expect to continue strong earnings performance." Another important goal of Enron's top executives was increasing their company's stature in the business world. During a speech in January 2001, Lay revealed that his ultimate goal was for Enron to become "the world's greatest company."[5]

As Enron's revenues and profits swelled, its top executives were often guilty of a certain degree of chutzpah. In particular, Skilling became known for making brassy, if not tacky, comments concerning his firm's competitors and critics. During the crisis that gripped California's electric utility industry during 2001, numerous elected officials and corporate executives criticized Enron for allegedly profiteering by selling electricity at inflated prices to the Golden State. Skilling brushed aside such criticism. During a speech at a major business convention, Skilling asked the crowd if they knew the difference between the state of California and the Titanic. After an appropriate pause, Skilling provided the punch line: "At least when the Titanic went down, the lights were on."[6]

Unfortunately for Lay, Skilling, Fastow, and thousands of Enron employees and stockholders, Lay failed to achieve his goal of creating the world's greatest company. In a matter of months during 2001, Enron quickly unraveled. Enron's sudden collapse panicked investors nationwide, leading to what one *Newsweek* columnist described as the "the biggest crisis investors have had since 1929."[7] Enron's dire financial problems were triggered by public revelations of questionable accounting and financial reporting decisions made by the company's accountants. Those decisions had been reviewed, analyzed, and apparently approved by Andersen, the company's independent audit firm.

Debits, Credits, and Enron

Throughout 2001, Enron's stock price drifted lower. Publicly, Enron executives blamed the company's slumping stock price on falling natural gas prices, concerns regarding the long-range potential of electronic marketplaces such as EnronOnline, and overall weakness in the national economy. By mid-October, the stock price had fallen into the mid-$30s from a high in the lower $80s earlier in the year. On October 16, 2001, Enron issued its quarterly earnings report for the third quarter of 2001. That report revealed that the firm had suffered a huge loss during the quarter. Even more problematic to many financial analysts was a mysterious $1.2 billion reduction in Enron's owners' equity and assets that was disclosed seemingly as an afterthought in the earnings press release. This write-down resulted from the reversal of previously recorded transactions involving the swap of Enron stock for notes receivable. Enron had acquired the notes receivable from related third parties who had invested in limited partnerships organized and sponsored by the company. After studying those transactions in more depth, Enron's accounting staff and its Andersen auditors concluded that the notes receivable should not have been reported in the assets section of the company's balance sheet but rather as a reduction to owners' equity.

The October 16, 2001, press release sent Enron's stock price into a free fall. Three weeks later on November 8, Enron restated its reported earnings for the previous five

5. Eichenwald and Henriques, "Web of Details."

6. *Ibid.*

7. N. Byrnes, "Paying for the Sins of Enron," *Newsweek*, 11 February 2002, 35.

years, wiping out approximately $600 million of profits the company had reported over that time frame. That restatement proved to be the death knell for Enron. On December 2, 2001, intense pressure from creditors, pending and threatened litigation against the company and its officers, and investigations initiated by law enforcement authorities forced Enron to file for bankruptcy. Instead of becoming the nation's greatest company, Enron instead laid claim to being the largest corporate bankruptcy in U.S. history, imposing more than $60 billion of losses on its stockholders alone. Enron's "claim to fame" would be eclipsed the following year by the more than $100 billion of losses produced when another Andersen client, WorldCom, filed for bankruptcy.

The massive and understandable public outcry over Enron's implosion during the fall of 2001 spawned a mad frenzy on the part of the print and electronic media to determine how the nation's seventh-largest public company, a company that had posted impressive and steadily rising profits over the previous few years, could crumple into insolvency in a matter of months. From the early days of this public drama, skeptics in the financial community charged that Enron's earnings restatement in the fall of 2001 demonstrated that the company's exceptional financial performance during the late 1990s and 2000 had been a charade, a hoax orchestrated by the company's management with the help of a squad of creative accountants. Any doubt regarding the validity of that theory was wiped away—at least in the minds of most members of the press and the general public—when a letter that an Enron accountant had sent to Kenneth Lay in August 2001 was discovered and reported by the press. The contents of that letter were posted on numerous websites and lengthy quotes taken from it appeared in virtually every major newspaper in the nation.

Exhibit 2 contains key excerpts from the letter that Sherron Watkins wrote to Kenneth Lay in August 2001. Watkins' job title was vice president of corporate development, but she was an accountant by training, having worked previously with Andersen, Enron's audit firm. The sudden and unexpected resignation of Jeffrey Skilling as Enron's CEO after serving in that capacity for only six months had prompted Watkins to write the letter to Lay. Before communicating her concerns to Lay, Watkins had attempted to discuss those issues with one of Lay's senior subordinates. When Watkins offered to show that individual a document that identified significant problems in accounting decisions made previously by Enron, Watkins reported that he rebuffed her. "He said he'd rather not see it."[8]

Watkins was intimately familiar with aggressive accounting decisions made for a series of large and complex transactions involving Enron and dozens of limited partnerships created by the company. These partnerships were so-called SPEs or special-purpose entities that Enron executives had tagged with a variety of creative names, including Braveheart, Rawhide, Raptor, Condor, and Talon. Andrew Fastow, Enron's CFO who was involved in the creation and operation of several of the SPEs, named a series of them after his three children.

SPEs—sometimes referred to as SPVs (special purpose vehicles)—can take several legal forms but are commonly organized as limited partnerships. During the 1990s, hundreds of large corporations began establishing SPEs. In most cases, SPEs were used to finance the acquisition of an asset or fund a construction project or related activity. Regardless, the underlying motivation for creating an SPE was nearly always "debt avoidance." That is, SPEs provided large companies with a mechanism to raise needed financing for various purposes without being required to report the

---

8. T. Hamburger, "Watkins Tells of 'Arrogant' Culture; Enron Stifled Staff Whistle-Blowing," *The Wall Street Journal* (online), 14 February 2002.

EXHIBIT 2

SELECTED EXCERPTS
FROM SHERRON
WATKINS' AUGUST
2001 LETTER TO
KENNETH LAY

Dear Mr. Lay,

Has Enron become a risky place to work? For those of us who didn't get rich over the last few years, can we afford to stay?

Skilling's abrupt departure will raise suspicions of accounting improprieties and valuation issues. Enron has been very aggressive in its accounting—most notably the Raptor transactions and the Condor vehicle. . . .

We have recognized over $550 million of fair value gains on stocks via our swaps with Raptor, much of that stock has declined significantly. . . . The value in the swaps won't be there for Raptor, so once again Enron will issue stock to offset these losses. Raptor is an LJM entity. It sure looks to the layman on the street that we are hiding losses in a related company and will compensate that company with Enron stock in the future.

I am incredibly nervous that we will implode in a wave of scandals. My 8 years of Enron work history will be worth nothing on my resume, the business world will consider the past successes as nothing but an elaborate accounting hoax. Skilling is resigning now for "personal reasons" but I think he wasn't having fun, looked down the road and knew this stuff was unfixable and would rather abandon ship now than resign in shame in 2 years.

Is there a way our accounting gurus can unwind these deals now? I have thought and thought about how to do this, but I keep bumping into one big problem—we booked the Condor and Raptor deals in 1999 and 2000, we enjoyed a wonderfully high stock price, many executives sold stock, we then try and reverse or fix the deals in 2001 and it's a bit like robbing the bank in 1 year and trying to pay it back 2 years later. . . .

I realize that we have had a lot of smart people looking at this and a lot of accountants including AA & Co. have blessed the accounting treatment. None of this will protect Enron if these transactions are ever disclosed in the bright light of day. . . .

The overriding basic principle of accounting is that if you explain the "accounting treatment" to a man on the street, would you influence his investing decisions? Would he sell or buy the stock based on a thorough understanding of the facts?

My concern is that the footnotes don't adequately explain the transactions. If adequately explained, the investor would know that the "Entities" described in our related-party footnote are thinly capitalized, the equity holders have no skin in the game, and all the value in the entities comes from the underlying value of the derivatives (unfortunately in this case, a big loss) AND Enron stock and N/P. . . .

The related-party footnote tries to explain these transactions. Don't you think that several interested companies, be they stock analysts, journalists, hedge fund managers, etc., are busy trying to discover the reason Skilling left? Don't you think their smartest people are pouring [sic] over that footnote disclosure right now? I can just hear the discussions—"It looks like they booked a $500 million gain from this related-party company and I think, from all the undecipherable 1/2 page on Enron's contingent contributions to this related-party entity, I think the related-party entity is capitalized with Enron stock." . . . "No, no, no, you must have it all wrong, it can't be that, that's just too bad, too fraudulent, surely AA & Co. wouldn't let them get away with that?"

debt in their balance sheets. *Fortune* magazine charged that corporate CFOs were using SPEs as scalpels "to perform cosmetic surgery on their balance sheets."[9] During the early 1990s, the Securities and Exchange Commission (SEC) and the FASB had wrestled with the contentious accounting and financial reporting issues posed by SPEs. Despite intense debate and discussions, the SEC and the FASB provided little in the way of formal guidance for companies and their accountants to follow in accounting and reporting for SPEs.

The most important guideline that the authoritative bodies implemented for SPEs, the so-called 3 percent rule, proved to be extremely controversial. This rule allowed a company to omit an SPE's assets and liabilities from its consolidated financial statements as long as parties independent of the company provided a minimum of 3 percent of the SPE's capital. Almost immediately, the 3 percent threshold became both a technical minimum and a practical maximum. That is, large companies using the SPE structure arranged for external parties to provide exactly 3 percent of an SPE's total capital. The remaining 97 percent of an SPE's capital was typically contributed by loans from external lenders, loans arranged and generally collateralized by the company that created the SPE.

Many critics charged that the 3 percent rule undercut the fundamental principle within the accounting profession that consolidated financial statements should be prepared for entities controlled by a common ownership group. "There is a presumption that consolidated financial statements are more meaningful than separate statements and that they are usually necessary for a fair presentation when one of the companies in the group directly or indirectly has a controlling financial interest in the other companies."[10] *Business Week* chided the SEC and FASB for effectively endorsing the 3 percent rule:

> Because of a gaping loophole in accounting practice, companies can create arcane legal structures, often called special-purpose entities (SPEs). Then, the parent can bankroll up to 97 percent of the initial investment in an SPE without having to consolidate it. . . . The controversial exception that outsiders need invest only 3 percent of an SPE's capital for it to be independent and off the balance sheet came about through fumbles by the Securities and Exchange Commission and the Financial Accounting Standards Board.[11]

Throughout the 1990s, many companies took advantage of the minimal legal and accounting guidelines for SPEs to divert huge amounts of their liabilities to off-balance sheet entities. Among the most aggressive and innovative users of the SPE structure was Enron, which created hundreds of SPEs. Unlike most companies, Enron did not limit its SPEs to financing activities. In many cases, Enron used SPEs for the sole purpose of downloading underperforming assets from its financial statements to the financial statements of related but unconsolidated entities. For example, Enron would arrange for a third party to invest the minimum 3 percent capital required in an SPE and then sell assets to that SPE. The SPE would finance the purchase of those assets by loans collateralized by Enron common stock. In some cases, undisclosed side agreements made by Enron with an SPE's nominal owners insulated those individuals from any losses on their investments and, in fact, guaranteed them a windfall profit. Even more troubling, Enron often sold assets at grossly inflated

---

9. J. Kahn, "Off Balance Sheet—And Out of Control," *Fortune*, 18 February 2002, 84.

10. *Accounting Research Bulletin No. 51*, "Consolidated Financial Statements" (New York: AICPA, 1959).

11. D. Henry, H. Timmons, S. Rosenbush, and M. Arndt, "Who Else Is Hiding Debt?" *Business Week*, 28 January 2002, 36–37.

prices to their SPEs, allowing the company to manufacture large "paper" gains on those transactions.

Enron made only nominal financial statement disclosures for its SPE transactions and those disclosures were typically presented in confusing, if not cryptic, language. One accounting professor observed that the inadequate disclosures that companies such as Enron provided for their SPE transactions meant "the nonprofessional [investor] has no idea of the extent of the [given firm's] real liabilities."[12] *The Wall Street Journal* added to that sentiment when it suggested that Enron's brief and obscure disclosures for its off-balance sheet liabilities and related-party transactions "were so complicated as to be practically indecipherable."[13]

Just as difficult to analyze for most investors was the integrity of the hefty profits reported each successive period by Enron. As Sherron Watkins revealed in the letter she sent to Kenneth Lay in August 2001, many of Enron's SPE transactions resulted in the company's profits being inflated by unrealized gains on increases in the market value of its own common stock. In the fall of 2001, Enron's board of directors appointed a Special Investigative Committee chaired by William C. Powers, dean of the University of Texas Law School, to study the company's large SPE transactions. In February 2002, that committee issued a lengthy report of its findings, a document commonly referred to as the Powers Report by the press. This report discussed at length the "Byzantine" nature of Enron's SPE transactions and the enormous and improper gains those transactions produced for the company.

> *Accounting principles generally forbid a company from recognizing an increase in the value of its capital stock in its income statement. . . . The substance of the Raptors [SPE transactions] effectively allowed Enron to report gains on its income statement that were . . . [attributable to] Enron stock, and contracts to receive Enron stock, held by the Raptors.*[14]

The primary motivation for Enron's extensive use of SPEs and the related accounting machinations was the company's growing need for capital during the 1990s. As Kenneth Lay and Jeffrey Skilling transformed Enron from a fairly standard natural gas supplier into a New Economy intermediary for the energy industries, the company had a constant need for additional capital to finance that transformation. Like most new business endeavors, Enron's Internet-based operations did not produce positive cash flows immediately. To convince lenders to continue pumping cash into Enron, the company's management team realized that their firm would have to maintain a high credit rating, which, in turn, required the company to release impressive financial statements each succeeding period.

A related factor that motivated Enron's executives to window dress their company's financial statements was the need to sustain Enron's stock price at a high level. Many of the SPE loan agreements negotiated by Enron included so-called price "triggers." If the market price of Enron's stock dropped below a designated level (trigger), Enron was required to provide additional stock to collateralize the given loan, to make significant cash payments to the SPE, or to restructure prior transactions with the SPE. In a worst-case scenario, Enron might be forced to dissolve an SPE and merge its assets and liabilities into the company's consolidated financial statements.

---

12. *Ibid.*

13. J. Emshwiller and R. Smith, "Murky Waters: A Primer on the Enron Partnerships," *The Wall Street Journal* (online), 21 January 2002.

14. W. C. Powers, R. S. Troubh, and H. S. Winokur, "Report of Investigation by the Special Investigative Committee of the Board of Directors of Enron Corporation," 1 February 2002, pp. 129–130.

What made Enron's stock price so important was the fact that some of the company's most important deals with the partnerships [SPEs] run by Mr. Fastow—deals that had allowed Enron to keep hundreds of millions of dollars of potential losses off its books—were financed, in effect, with Enron stock. Those transactions could fall apart if the stock price fell too far.[15]

As Enron's stock price drifted lower throughout 2001, the complex labyrinth of legal and accounting gimmicks underlying the company's finances became a shaky house of cards. Making matters worse were large losses suffered by many of Enron's SPEs on the assets they had purchased from Enron. Enron executives were forced to pour additional resources into many of those SPEs to keep them solvent. Contributing to the financial problems of Enron's major SPEs was alleged self-dealing by Enron officials involved in operating those SPEs. Andrew Fastow realized $30 million in profits on his investments in Enron SPEs that he oversaw at the same time he was serving as the company's CFO. Several of his friends also reaped windfall profits on investments in those same SPEs. Some of these individuals "earned" a profit of as much as $1 million on an initial investment of $5,800. Even more startling was the fact that Fastow's friends realized these gains in as little as 60 days.

By October 2001, the falling price of Enron's stock, the weight of the losses suffered by the company's large SPEs, and concerns being raised by Andersen auditors forced company executives to act. Enron's management assumed control and ownership of several of the company's troubled SPEs and incorporated their dismal financial statement data into Enron's consolidated financial statements. This decision led to the large loss reported by Enron in the fall of 2001 and the related restatement of the company's earnings for the previous five years. On December 2, 2001, the transformed New Age company filed its bankruptcy petition in New Age fashion—via the Internet. Only six months earlier, Jeffrey Skilling had been buoyant when commenting on Enron's first-quarter results for 2001. "So in conclusion, first-quarter results were great. We are very optimistic about our new businesses and are confident that our record of growth is sustainable for many years to come."[16]

As law enforcement authorities, Congressional investigative committees, and business journalists rifled through the mass of Enron documents that became publicly available during early 2002, the abusive accounting and financial reporting practices that had been used by the company surfaced. Enron's creative use of SPEs became the primary target of critics; however, the company also made extensive use of other accounting gimmicks. For example, Enron had abused the mark-to-market accounting method for its long-term contracts involving various energy commodities, primarily natural gas and electricity. Given the nature of their business, energy-trading firms regularly enter into long-term contracts to deliver energy commodities. Some of Enron's commodity contracts extended over periods of more than 20 years and involved massive quantities of the given commodity. When Enron finalized these deals, company officials often made tenuous assumptions that inflated the profits booked on the contracts.

Energy traders must book all the projected profits from a supply contract in the quarter in which the deal is made, even if the contract spans many years. That means companies can inflate profits by using unrealistic price forecasts, as Enron has been accused of doing. If a company contracted to buy natural gas through 2010 for $3 per thousand cubic feet, an energy-trading desk could aggressively assume it would be able to supply gas in each year at a cost of just $2, for a $1 profit margin.[17]

15. Eichenwald and Henriques, "Web of Details."

16. *Ibid.*

17. P. Coy, S. A. Forest, and D. Foust, "Enron: How Good an Energy Trader?" *Business Week*, 11 February 2002, 42–43.

The avalanche of startling revelations regarding Enron's aggressive business, accounting, and financial reporting decisions reported by the business press during the early weeks of 2002 created a firestorm of anger and criticism directed at Enron's key executives, principally Kenneth Lay, Jeffrey Skilling, and Andrew Fastow. A common theme of the allegations leveled at the three executives was that they had created a corporate culture that fostered, if not encouraged, "rule breaking." *Fortune* magazine observed that "if nothing else, Lay allowed a culture of rule breaking to flourish,"[18] while Sherron Watkins testified that Enron's corporate culture was "arrogant" and "intimidating" and discouraged employees from reporting and investigating ethical lapses and questionable business dealings.[19] Finally, a top executive of Dynegy, a company that briefly considered merging with Enron during late 2001, reported that "the lack of internal controls [within Enron] was mindboggling."[20]

Both Kenneth Lay and Andrew Fastow invoked their Fifth Amendment rights against self-incrimination when asked to testify before Congress in early 2002. Jeffrey Skilling did not. While being peppered by Congressional investigators regarding Enron's questionable accounting and financial reporting decisions, Skilling replied calmly and repeatedly: "I am not an accountant." A well-accepted premise in the financial reporting domain is that corporate executives and their accountants are ultimately responsible for the integrity of their company's financial statements. Nevertheless, frustration stemming from the lack of answers provided by Enron insiders to key accounting and financial reporting–related questions eventually caused Congressional investigators, the business press, and the public to focus their attention, their questions, and their scorn on Enron's independent audit firm, Andersen. These parties insisted that Andersen representatives explain why their audits of Enron had failed to result in more transparent, if not reliable, financial statements for the company. More pointedly, those critics demanded that Andersen explain how it was able to issue unqualified audit opinions on Enron's financial statements throughout its 15-year tenure as the company's independent audit firm.

Say It Ain't So Joe

Joseph Berardino became Andersen's chief executive shortly before the firm was swamped by the storm of criticism surrounding the collapse of its second-largest client, Enron Corporation. Berardino launched his business career with Andersen in 1972 immediately after graduating from college and just a few months before Leonard Spacek ended his long and illustrious career with the firm. Throughout its history, the Andersen firm had a policy of speaking with one voice, the voice of its chief executive. So, the unpleasant task of responding to the angry and often self-righteous accusations hurled at Andersen following Enron's demise fell to Berardino, although he had not been a party to the key decisions made during the Enron audits.

A common question directed at Berardino was whether his firm had been aware of the allegations Sherron Watkins made during August 2001 and, if so, how had Andersen responded to those allegations. Watkins testified before Congress that shortly after she communicated her concerns regarding Enron's questionable accounting and financial reporting decisions to Kenneth Lay, she had met with a member of the Andersen firm with whom she had worked several years earlier. In an

---

18. B. McLean, "Monster Mess," *Fortune*, 4 February 2002, 94.

19. Hamburger, "Watkins Tells of 'Arrogant' Culture."

20. N. Banjeree, D. Barboza, and A. Warren, "At Enron, Lavish Excess Often Came before Success," *The New York Times* (online), 26 February 2002.

internal Andersen memorandum, that individual relayed Watkins' concerns to several colleagues, including the Enron audit engagement partner, David Duncan. At that point, Andersen officials in the firm's Chicago headquarters began systematically reviewing previous decisions made by the Enron audit engagement team.

In fact, several months earlier, Andersen representatives had become aware of Enron's rapidly deteriorating financial condition and become deeply involved in helping the company's executives cope with that crisis. Andersen's efforts included assisting Enron officials in restructuring certain of the company's SPEs so that they could continue to qualify as unconsolidated entities. Subsequent press reports revealed that in February 2001, frustration over the aggressive nature of Enron's accounting and financial reporting decisions caused some Andersen officials to suggest dropping the company as an audit client.[21]

On December 12, 2001, Joseph Berardino testified before the Committee on Financial Services of the U.S. House of Representatives. Early in that testimony, Berardino freely admitted that members of the Enron audit engagement team had made one major error while analyzing a large SPE transaction that occurred in 1999. "We made a professional judgment about the appropriate accounting treatment that turned out to be wrong."[22] According to Berardino, when Andersen officials discovered this error in the fall of 2001, they promptly notified Enron's executives and told them to "correct it." Approximately 20 percent of the $600 million restatement of prior earnings announced by Enron on November 8, 2001, was due to this item.

Berardino pointed out that the remaining 80 percent of the earnings restatement involved another SPE that Enron created in 1997. Unknown to Andersen auditors, one-half of that SPE's minimum 3 percent "external" equity had been effectively contributed by Enron. As a result, that entity did not qualify for SPE treatment, meaning that its financial data should have been included in Enron's consolidated financial statements from its inception. When Andersen officials discovered this violation of the 3 percent rule in the fall of 2001, they immediately informed Enron's accounting staff. Andersen also informed the company's audit committee that the failure of Enron officials to reveal the source of the SPE's initial funding could possibly be construed as an illegal act under the Securities Exchange Act of 1934. Berardino implied that the client's lack of candor regarding this SPE exempted Andersen of responsibility for the resulting accounting and financial reporting errors linked to that entity.

Berardino also explained to Congress that Andersen auditors had been only minimally involved in the transactions that eventually resulted in the $1.2 billion reduction of owners' equity reported by Enron on October 16, 2001. The bulk of those transactions had occurred in early 2001. Andersen had not audited the 2001 quarterly financial statements that had been prepared following the initial recording of those transactions—public companies are not required to have their quarterly financial statements audited.

Berardino's testimony before Congress in December 2001 failed to appease Andersen's critics. Over the next several months, Berardino continually found himself defending Andersen against a growing torrent of accusations. Most of these accusations centered on three key issues. First, many critics raised the controversial and longstanding "scope of services" issue when criticizing Andersen's role in the Enron

21. S. Labaton, "S.E.C. Leader Sees Outside Monitors for Auditing Firms," *The New York Times* (online), 18 January 2002.

22. J. Kahn and J. D. Glater, "Enron Auditor Raises Specter of Crime," *The New York Times* (online), 13 December 2001.

debacle. Over the final few decades of the twentieth century, the major accounting firms had gradually extended the product line of professional services they offered to their major audit clients. A research study focusing on nearly 600 large companies that released financial statements in early 1999 revealed that for every $1 of audit fees those companies had paid their independent auditors, they had paid those firms $2.69 for nonaudit consulting services.[23] These services included a wide range of activities such as feasibility studies of various types, internal auditing, design of accounting systems, development of e-commerce initiatives, and a varied assortment of other information technology (IT) services.

In an interview with *The New York Times* in March 2002, Leonard Spacek's daughter revealed that her father had adamantly opposed accounting firms providing consulting services to their audit clients. "I remember him ranting and raving, saying Andersen couldn't consult and audit the same firms because it was a conflict of interest. Well, now I'm sure he's twirling in his grave saying, 'I told you so.'"[24] In the late 1990s, Arthur Levitt, the chairman of the SEC, had led a vigorous, one-man campaign to limit the scope of consulting services that accounting firms could provide to their audit clients. In particular, Levitt wanted to restrict the ability of accounting firms to provide IT and internal audit services to their audit clients. An extensive and costly lobbying campaign that the Big Five firms carried out in the press and among elected officials allowed those firms to defeat the bulk of Levitt's proposals.

Public reports that Andersen earned approximately $52 million in fees from Enron during 2000, only $25 million of which was directly linked to the 2000 audit, caused the scope of services issue to resurface. Critics charged that the enormous consulting fees accounting firms earned from their audit clients jeopardized those firms' independence. "It's obvious that Andersen helped Enron cook the books. Andersen's Houston office was pulling in $1 million a week from Enron—their objectivity went out the window."[25] These same critics reiterated an allegation that had widely circulated a few years earlier, namely, that the large accounting firms had resorted to using the independent audit function as "a loss leader, a way of getting in the door at a company to sell more profitable consulting contracts."[26] One former partner of a Big Five accounting firm provided anecdotal evidence corroborating that allegation. This individual revealed that he had been under constant pressure from his former firm to market various professional services to his audit clients. So relentless were his efforts that at one point a frustrated client executive asked him, "Are you my auditor or a salesperson?"[27]

A second source of criticism directed at Andersen stemmed from the firm's alleged central role in Enron's aggressive accounting and financial reporting treatments for its SPE-related transactions. The Powers Report released to the public in February 2002 spawned much of this criticism. That lengthy report examined in detail several of Enron's largest and most questionable SPE transactions. The Powers Report pointedly and repeatedly documented that Andersen personnel had been deeply involved in those transactions. Exhibit 3 contains a sample of selected excerpts from the Powers Report that refers to Andersen's role in "analyzing" and "reviewing" Enron's SPE transactions.

---

23. N. Byrnes, "Accounting in Crisis," *Business Week*, 28 January 2002, 46.

24. D. Barboza, "Where Pain of Arthur Andersen Is Personal," *The New York Times* (online), 13 March 2002.

25. *SmartPros.com*, "Lawsuit Seeks to Hold Andersen Accountable for Defrauding Enron Investors, Employees," 4 December 2001.

26. J. Kahn, "One Plus One Makes *What?*" *Fortune*, 7 January 2002, 89.

27. I. J. Dugan, "Before Enron, Greed Helped Sink the Respectability of Accounting," *The Wall Street Journal* (online), 14 March 2002.

Page 5: In virtually all of the [SPE] transactions Enron's accounting treatment was determined with the extensive participation and structuring advice from Andersen, which reported to the Board.

Page 17: Various disclosures [regarding Enron's SPE transactions] were approved by one or more of Enron's outside [Andersen] auditors and its inside and outside counsel. However, these disclosures were obtuse, did not communicate the essence of the transactions completely or clearly, and failed to convey the substance of what was going on between Enron and the partnerships.

Page 24: The evidence available to us suggests that Andersen did not fulfill its professional responsibilities in connection with its audits of Enron's financial statements, or its obligation to bring to the attention of Enron's Board (or the Audit and Compliance Committee) concerns about Enron's internal controls over the related-party [SPE] transactions.

Page 24: Andersen participated in the structuring and accounting treatment of the Raptor transactions, and charged over $1 million for its services, yet it apparently failed to provide the objective accounting judgment that should have prevented these transactions from going forward.

Page 25: According to recent public disclosures, Andersen also failed to bring to the attention of Enron's Audit and Compliance Committee serious reservations Andersen partners voiced internally about the related-party transactions.

Page 25: The Board appears to have reasonably relied upon the professional judgment of Andersen concerning Enron's financial statements and the adequacy of controls for the related-party transactions. Our review indicates that Andersen failed to meet its responsibilities in both respects.

Page 100: Accountants from Andersen were closely involved in structuring the Raptors [SPE transactions]. . . . Enron's records show that Andersen billed Enron approximately $335,000 in connection with its work on the creation of the Raptors in the first several months of 2000.

Page 107: Causey [Enron's chief accounting officer] informed the Finance Committee that Andersen "had spent considerable time analyzing the Talon structure and the governance structure of LJM2 and was comfortable with the proposed [SPE] transaction."

Page 126: At the time [September 2001], Enron accounting personnel and Andersen concluded (using qualitative analysis) that the error [in a prior SPE transaction] was not material and a restatement was not necessary.

Page 129: Proper financial accounting does not permit this result [questionable accounting treatment for certain of Enron's SPE transactions]. To reach it, the accountants at Enron and Andersen—including the local engagement team and, apparently, Andersen's national office experts in Chicago—had to surmount numerous obstacles presented by pertinent accounting rules.

Page 132: It is particularly surprising that the accountants at Andersen, who should have brought a measure of objectivity and perspective to these transactions, did not do so. Based on the recollections of those involved in the transactions and a large collection of documentary evidence, there is no question that Andersen accountants were in a position to understand all the critical features of the Raptors and offer advice on the appropriate

EXHIBIT 3

SELECTED EXCERPTS FROM THE POWERS REPORT REGARDING ANDERSEN'S INVOLVEMENT IN KEY ACCOUNTING AND FINANCIAL REPORTING DECISIONS FOR ENRON'S SPE TRANSACTIONS

(continued)

EXHIBIT 3 —
continued

SELECTED EXCERPTS
FROM THE POWERS
REPORT REGARDING
ANDERSEN'S
INVOLVEMENT IN
KEY ACCOUNTING
AND FINANCIAL
REPORTING
DECISIONS FOR
ENRON'S SPE
TRANSACTIONS

accounting treatment. Andersen's total bill for Raptor-related work came to approximately $1.3 million. Indeed, there is abundant evidence that Andersen in fact offered Enron advice at every step, from inception through restructuring and ultimately to terminating the Raptors. Enron followed that advice.

Page 202: While we have not had the benefit of Andersen's position on a number of these issues, the evidence we have seen suggests Andersen accountants did not function as an effective check on the disclosure approach taken by the company. Andersen was copied on drafts of the financial statement footnotes and the proxy statements, and we were told that it routinely provided comments on the related-party transaction disclosures in response. We also understand that the Andersen auditors closest to Enron Global Finance were involved in drafting of at least some of the disclosures. An internal Andersen e-mail from February 2001 released in connection with recent Congressional hearings suggests that Andersen may have had concerns about the disclosures of the related-party transactions in the financial statement footnotes. Andersen did not express such concerns to the Board. On the contrary, Andersen's engagement partner told the Audit and Compliance Committee just a week after the internal e-mail that, with respect to related-party transactions, "'[r]equired disclosure [had been] reviewed for adequacy,' and that Andersen would issue an unqualified audit opinion on the financial statements."

Source: W. C. Powers, R. S. Troubh, and H. S. Winokur, "Report of Investigation by the Special Investigative Committee of the Board of Directors of Enron Corporation," 1 February 2002.

Among the parties most critical of Andersen's extensive involvement in Enron's accounting and financial reporting decisions for SPE transactions was former SEC Chief Accountant Lynn Turner. During his tenure with the SEC in the 1990s, Turner had participated in the federal agency's investigation of Andersen's audits of Waste Management Inc. That investigation culminated in sanctions against several Andersen auditors and in a $1.4 billion restatement of Waste Management's financial statements, the largest accounting restatement in U.S. history at that time. Andersen eventually paid a reported $75 million in settlements to resolve various civil lawsuits linked to those audits and a $7 million fine to settle charges filed against the firm by the SEC.

In an interview with *The New York Times*, Turner suggested that the charges of shoddy audit work that had plagued Andersen in connection with its audits of Waste Management, Sunbeam, Enron, and other high-profile public clients was well-deserved. Turner compared Andersen's problems with those experienced several years earlier by Coopers & Lybrand, a firm for which he had been an audit partner. According to Turner, a series of "blown audits" was the source of Coopers' problems. "We got bludgeoned to death in the press. People did not even want to see us at their doorsteps. It was brutal, but we deserved it. We had gotten into this mentality in the firm of making business judgment calls." [28] Clearly, the role of independent auditors does not include "making business judgments" for their clients. Instead, auditors have a responsibility to provide an objective point of view regarding the proper accounting and financial reporting decisions for those judgments.

Easily the source of the most embarrassment for Berardino and his Andersen colleagues was the widely publicized effort of the firm's Houston office to shred a large

---

28. F. Norris, "From Sunbeam to Enron, Andersen's Reputation Suffers," *The New York Times* (online), 23 November 2001.

quantity of documents pertaining to various Enron audits. In early January 2002, Andersen officials informed federal investigators that personnel in the Houston office had "destroyed a significant but undetermined number of documents relating to the company [Enron] and its finances."[29] That large-scale effort began in September 2001 and apparently continued into November after the SEC revealed it was conducting a formal investigation of Enron's financial affairs. The report of the shredding effort immediately caused many critics to suggest that Andersen's Houston office was attempting to prevent law enforcement authorities from obtaining potentially incriminating evidence regarding Andersen's role in Enron's demise. Senator Joseph Lieberman, chairman of the U.S. Senate Governmental Affairs Committee that would be investigating the Enron debacle, warned that the effort to dispose of the Enron-related documents might be particularly problematic for Andersen.

> It [the document-shredding] came at a time when people inside, including the executives of Arthur Andersen and Enron, knew that Enron was in real trouble and that the roof was about to collapse on them, and there was about to be a corporate scandal. ... [This] raises very serious questions about whether obstruction of justice occurred here. The folks at Arthur Andersen could be on the other end of an indictment before this is over. This Enron episode may end this company's history.[30]

The barrage of criticism directed at Andersen continued unabated during the early months of 2002. Ironically, some of that criticism was directed at Andersen by Enron's top management. On January 17, 2002, Kenneth Lay issued a press release reporting that his company had decided to discharge Andersen as its independent audit firm.[31]

> As announced on Oct. 31, the Enron Board of Directors convened a Special Committee to look into accounting and other issues relating to certain transactions. While we had been willing to give Andersen the benefit of the doubt until the completion of that investigation, we can't afford to wait any longer in light of recent events, including the reported destruction of documents by Andersen personnel and the disciplinary actions against several of Andersen's partners in its Houston office.[32]

Throughout the public relations nightmare that besieged Andersen following Enron's bankruptcy filing, a primary tactic adopted by Joseph Berardino was to insist repeatedly that poor business decisions, not errors on the part of Andersen, were responsible for Enron's downfall and the massive losses that ensued for investors, creditors, and other parties. "At the end of the day, we do not cause companies to fail."[33] Such statements failed to generate sympathy for Andersen. Even the editor-in-chief of *Accounting Today*, one of the accounting profession's leading publications, was unmoved by Berardino's continual assertions that his firm was not responsible for the Enron fiasco. "If you accept the audit and collect the fee, then be prepared to accept the blame. Otherwise you're not part of the solution but rather, part of the problem."[34]

29. K. Eichenwald and F. Norris, "Enron Auditor Admits It Destroyed Documents," *The New York Times* (online), 11 January 2002.

30. R. A. Oppel, "Andersen Says Lawyer Let Its Staff Destroy Files," *The New York Times* (online), 14 January 2002.

31. Kenneth Lay resigned as Enron's chairman of the board and CEO on January 23, 2002, one day after a court-appointed "creditors committee" had requested him to step down.

32. M. Palmer, "Enron Board Discharges Arthur Andersen in All Capacities," *Enron.com*, 17 January 2002.

33. M. Gordon, "Labor Secretary to Address Enron Hearings," *Associated Press* (online), 6 February 2002.

34. B. Carlino, "Enron Simply Newest Player in National Auditing Crisis," *The Electronic Accountant* (online), 17 December 2001.

Ridicule and Retrospection

As 2001 came to a close, *The New York Times* reported that the year had easily been the worst ever for Andersen, "the accounting firm that once deserved the title of the conscience of the industry."[35] The following year would prove to be an even darker time for the firm. During the early months of 2002, Andersen faced scathing criticism from Congressional investigators, enormous class-action lawsuits filed by angry Enron stockholders and creditors, and a federal criminal indictment stemming from the shredding of Enron-related documents.

In late March 2002, Joseph Berardino unexpectedly resigned as Andersen's CEO after failing to negotiate a merger of Andersen with one of the other Big Five firms. During the following few weeks, dozens of Andersen clients dropped the firm as their independent auditor out of concern that the firm might not survive if it was found guilty of the pending criminal indictment. The staggering loss of clients forced Andersen to lay off more than 25 percent of its workforce in mid-April. Shortly after that layoff was announced, U.S. Department of Justice officials revealed that David Duncan, the former Enron audit engagement partner, had pleaded guilty to obstruction of justice and agreed to testify against his former firm. Duncan's plea proved to be the death knell for Andersen. In June 2002, a federal jury found the firm guilty of obstruction of justice. That conviction forced the firm to terminate its relationship with its remaining public clients, effectively ending Andersen's long and proud history within the U.S. accounting profession.

Three years later, the U.S. Supreme Court unanimously overturned the felony conviction handed down against Andersen. In an opinion written by Chief Justice William Rehnquist, the high court ruled that federal prosecutors did not prove that Andersen had *intended* to interfere with a federal investigation when the firm shredded the Enron audit workpapers. The Supreme Court's decision was little consolation to the more than 20,000 Andersen partners and employees who had lost their jobs when the accounting firm was forced out of business by the felony conviction.

Numerous Enron officials faced criminal indictments for their roles in the Enron fraud, among them Andrew Fastow, Jeffrey Skilling, and Kenneth Lay. Fastow pleaded guilty to conspiracy to commit securities fraud as well as to other charges. The former CFO received a 10-year prison term, which was reduced to 6 years after he testified against Skilling and Lay. Fastow was also required to forfeit nearly $25 million of personal assets that he had accumulated during his tenure at Enron. Largely as a result of Fastow's testimony against them, Skilling and Lay were convicted on multiple counts of fraud and conspiracy in May 2006. In September 2006, Skilling was sentenced to 24 years in prison. Kenneth Lay, who was to be sentenced at the same time, died of a massive heart attack in July 2006. Three months later, a federal judge overturned Lay's conviction since Lay was no longer able to pursue his appeal of that conviction.

The toll taken on the public accounting profession by the Enron debacle was not limited to Andersen, its partners, or its employees. An unending flood of jokes and ridicule directed at Andersen tainted and embarrassed practically every accountant in the nation, including both accountants in public practice and those working in the private sector. The Enron nightmare also prompted widespread soul-searching within the profession and a public outcry to strengthen the independent audit function and improve accounting and financial reporting practices. Legislative and regulatory authorities quickly responded to the public's demand for reforms.

---

35. Norris, "From Sunbeam to Enron."

The FASB imposed stricter accounting and financial reporting guidelines on SPEs as a direct result of the Enron case. Those new rules require many companies to include the financial data for those entities—now referred to as VIEs (variable interest entities)—in their consolidated financial statements. In 2002, Congress passed the Sarbanes-Oxley Act to strengthen financial reporting for public companies, principally by improving the rigor and quality of independent audits. Among other requirements, the Sarbanes-Oxley Act limits the types of consulting services that independent auditors can provide to their clients and requires public companies to prepare annual reports on the quality of their internal controls. The most sweeping change in the profession resulting from the Enron fiasco was the creation of a new federal agency, the Public Company Accounting Oversight Board, to oversee the rule-making process for the independent audit function.

Among the prominent individuals who commented on the challenges and problems facing the accounting profession was former SEC Chairman Richard Breeden when he testified before Congress in early 2002. Chairman Breeden observed that there was a simple solution to the quagmire facing the profession. He called on accountants and auditors to adopt a simple rule of thumb when analyzing, recording, and reporting on business transactions, regardless of whether those transactions involved "New Economy" or "Old Economy" business ventures. "When you're all done, the result had better fairly reflect what you see in reality."[36]

In retrospect, Commissioner Breeden's recommendation seems to be a restatement of the "Think straight, talk straight" motto of Arthur E. Andersen. Andersen and his colleagues insisted that their audit clients adhere to a high standard of integrity when preparing their financial statements. An interview with Joseph Berardino by *The New York Times* in December 2001 suggests that Mr. Berardino and his contemporaries may have had a different attitude when it came to dealing with cantankerous clients such as Enron: "In an interview yesterday, Mr. Berardino said Andersen had no power to force a company to disclose that it had hidden risks and losses in special-purpose entities. 'A client says: "There is no requirement to disclose this. You can't hold me to a higher standard."'"[37]

Berardino is certainly correct in his assertion. An audit firm cannot force a client to adhere to a higher standard. In fact, even Arthur Edward Andersen did not have that power. But Mr. Andersen did have the resolve to tell such clients to immediately begin searching for another audit firm.

Questions

1. The Enron debacle created what one public official reported was a "crisis of confidence" on the part of the public in the accounting profession. List the parties whom you believe are most responsible for that crisis. Briefly justify each of your choices.

2. List three types of consulting services that audit firms have provided to their audit clients in recent years. For each item, indicate the specific threats, if any, that the provision of the given service can pose for an audit firm's independence.

3. For purposes of this question, assume that the excerpts from the Powers Report shown in Exhibit 3 provide accurate descriptions of Andersen's involvement in

---

36. R. Schlank, "Former SEC Chairmen Urge Congress to Free FASB," *AccountingWeb* (online), 15 February 2002.

37. F. Norris, "The Distorted Numbers at Enron," *The New York Times* (online), 14 December 2001.

Enron's accounting and financial reporting decisions. Given this assumption, do you believe that Andersen's involvement in those decisions violated any professional auditing standards? If so, list those standards and briefly explain your rationale.

4. Briefly describe the key requirements included in professional auditing standards regarding the preparation and retention of audit workpapers. Which party "owns" audit workpapers: the client or the audit firm?

5. Identify and list five recommendations that have been made recently to strengthen the independent audit function. For each of these recommendations, indicate why you support or do not support the given measure.

6. Do you believe that there has been a significant shift or evolution over the past several decades in the concept of "professionalism" as it relates to the public accounting discipline? If so, explain how you believe that concept has changed or evolved over that time frame and identify the key factors responsible for any apparent changes.

7. As pointed out in this case, the SEC does not require public companies to have their quarterly financial statements audited. What responsibilities, if any, do audit firms have with regard to the quarterly financial statements of their clients? In your opinion, should quarterly financial statements be audited? Defend your answer.

Just for FEET, Inc.

*Life is so fragile. A single bad choice in a single
moment can cause a life to turn irrevocably 180 degrees.*

U.S. District Judge C. Lynwood Smith, Jr.

In 1971, 25-year-old Thomas Shine founded a small sporting goods company, Logo 7, that would eventually become known as Logo Athletic. Shine's company manufactured and marketed a wide range of shirts, hats, jackets, and other apparel items that boldly displayed the logos of the Minnesota Vikings, New York Islanders, St. Louis Cardinals, and dozens of other professional sports teams. In 2001, Shine sold Logo to Reebok and became that company's senior vice president of sports and entertainment marketing. In that position, Shine wined and dined major sports stars with the intent of persuading them to sign exclusive endorsement contracts with Reebok.

During his long career, Thomas Shine became one of the most well-known and respected leaders of the sporting goods industry. Shine's prominence and credibility in that industry took a severe blow in February 2004 when he pleaded guilty to a criminal indictment filed against him by the U.S. Department of Justice. The Justice Department charged that Shine had signed a false audit confirmation sent to him in early 1999 by one of Logo's largest customers. The confirmation indicated that Logo owed that customer approximately $700,000. Although Shine knew that no such debt existed, he signed the confirmation and returned it to the customer's independent audit firm, Deloitte & Touche, after being pressured to do so by an executive of the customer. As a result of his guilty plea, Shine faced a possible sentence of five years in federal prison and a fine of up to $250,000.

Out of South Africa

At approximately the same time that Thomas Shine was launching his business career in the retail industry in the United States, Harold Ruttenberg was doing the same in South Africa. Ruttenberg, a native of Johannesburg, paid for his college education by working nights and weekends as a sales clerk in an upscale men's clothing store. After graduation, he began importing Levi's jeans from the United States and selling them from his car, his eventual goal being to accumulate sufficient capital to open a retail store. Ruttenberg quickly accomplished that goal. In fact, by the time he was 30, he owned a small chain of men's apparel stores.

Mounting political and economic troubles in his home country during the early and mid-1970s eventually convinced Ruttenberg to move his family to the United States. South Africa's strict emigration laws forced Ruttenberg to leave practically all of his net worth behind. When he arrived in California in 1976 with his spouse and three small children, Ruttenberg had less than $30,000. Despite his limited financial resources and unfamiliarity with U.S. business practices, the strong-willed South African was committed to once again establishing himself as a successful entrepreneur in the retailing industry.

Ruttenberg soon realized that the exorbitant rents for commercial retail properties in the major metropolitan areas of California were far beyond his reach. So, he moved his family once more, this time to the more affordable business environment of Birmingham, Alabama. Ruttenberg leased a vacant storefront in a Birmingham mall and a few months later opened Hang Ten Sports World, a retail store that marketed children's sportswear products. Thanks largely to his work ethic and intense desire to succeed, Ruttenberg's business prospered over the next decade.

In 1988, Ruttenberg decided to take a gamble on a new business venture. Ruttenberg had come to believe that there was an opportunity to make large profits in the retail shoe business. At the time, the market for high-priced athletic shoes—basketball shoes, in particular—was growing dramatically and becoming an ever-larger segment of the retail shoe industry. The principal retail outlets for the shoes produced by Adidas, Nike, Reebok, and other major athletic shoe manufacturers were relatively small stores located in thousands of suburban malls scattered across the country, meaning that the retail athletic shoe "subindustry" was highly fragmented. The five largest retailers in this market niche accounted for less than 10 percent of the annual sales of athletic shoes.

Ruttenberg realized that the relatively small floor space of retail shoe stores in suburban malls limited a retailer's ability to display the wide and growing array of products being produced by the major shoe manufacturers. Likewise, the high cost of floor space in malls with heavy traffic served to limit the profitability of shoe retailers. To overcome these problems, Ruttenberg decided that he would build freestanding shoe "superstores" located near malls. To lure consumers away from mall-based shoe stores, Ruttenberg developed a three-pronged business strategy focusing on "selection," "service," and "entertainment."

The business plan Ruttenberg developed for his superstores involved a stores-within-a-store concept; that is, he intended to create several mini-stores in his large retail outlets, each of which would be devoted exclusively to the products of individual shoe manufacturers. He believed this store design would appeal to both consumers and vendors. Consumers who were committed to one particular brand would not have to search through store displays that included a wide assortment of branded products. Likewise, his proposed floor design would provide major vendors an opportunity to participate in marketing their products. Ruttenberg hoped that his planned floor design would spur the major vendors to compete with each other in providing so-called vendor allowances to his superstores to make their individual displays more attractive than those of competitors.

Customer service was the second major element of Ruttenberg's business plan for his shoe superstores. Ruttenberg planned to staff his stores so that there would be an unusually large ratio of sales associates to customers. Sales associates would be required to complete an extensive training course in "footwear technology" so that they would be well equipped to answer any questions posed by customers. When a customer chose to try on a particular shoe product, he or she would have to ask a sales associate to retrieve that item from the "back shop." Sales associates were trained to interact with customers in such a way that they would earn their trust and thus create a stronger bond with them.

Just for Feet's 1998 Form 10-K described the third feature of Harold Ruttenberg's business plan as creating an "Entertainment Shopping Experience." Rock and roll music and brightly colored displays greeted customers when they entered the superstores. When they were tired of shopping, customers could play a game of "horse" on an enclosed basketball half-court located near the store's entrance or sit back and enjoy a multiscreen video bank in the store's customer lounge. Frequent promotional events included autograph sessions with major sports celebrities such as Bart Starr, the former Green Bay Packers quarterback who was also on the company's board of directors.

Ruttenberg would eventually include two other key features in the floor plans of his superstores. Although Just for Feet did not target price-conscious customers, Ruttenberg added a "Combat Zone" to each superstore where such customers could rummage through piles of discontinued shoe lines, "seconds," and other discounted items. For those customers who simply wanted a pair of shoes and did not have a strong preference for a given brand, Ruttenberg developed a "Great Wall" that contained a wide array of shoes sorted not by brand but rather by function. In this large display, customers could quickly compare and contrast the key features of dozens of different types of running shoes, walking shoes, basketball shoes, cross-trainers, etc.

Quite a FEET

Just for Feet's initial superstore in Birmingham proved to be a huge financial success. That success convinced Harold Ruttenberg to open similar retail outlets in several major metropolitan areas in the southern United States and to develop a showcase superstore within the glitzy Caesar's Forum shopping mall on the Las Vegas Strip. By 1992, Just for Feet owned and operated five superstores and had sold franchise rights for several other stores. The company's annual sales were approaching $20 million, but that total accounted for a nominal proportion of the retail shoe industry's estimated $15 billion of annual sales.

To become a major force in the shoe industry, Ruttenberg knew that he would have to expand his retail chain nationwide, which would require large amounts of additional capital. To acquire that capital, Ruttenberg decided to take his company public. On March 9, 1994, Just for Feet's common stock began trading on the NASDAQ exchange under the ticker symbol FEET. The stock, which sold initially for $6.22 per share, would quickly rise over the next two years to more than $37 per share.

Ruttenberg used the funds produced by Just for Feet's initial public offering (IPO) to pursue an aggressive expansion program. The company opened dozens of new superstores during the mid-1990s and acquired several smaller competitors, including Athletic Attic in March 1997 and Sneaker Stadium in July 1998. For fiscal 1996, which ended January 31, 1997, the company reported a profit of $13.9 million on sales of $250 million. Two years later, the company earned a profit of $26.7 million on sales of nearly $775 million. By the end of 1998, Just for Feet was the second largest athletic shoe retailer in the United States with 300 retail outlets.

During the mid-1990s, Just for Feet's common stock was among the most closely monitored and hyped securities on Wall Street. Analysts and investors tracking the stock marveled at the company's ability to consistently outperform its major competitors. By the late 1990s, market saturation and declining profit margins were becoming major concerns within the athletic shoe segment of the shoe industry. Despite the lackluster profits and faltering revenue growth trends of other athletic shoe retailers, Harold Ruttenberg continued to issue press releases touting his company's record profits and steadily growing sales. Most impressive was the company's 21 straight quarterly increases in same-store sales through the fourth quarter of fiscal 1998.

In November 1997, Delphi Investments released a lengthy analytical report focusing on Just for Feet's future prospects. In that report, which included a strong "buy" recommendation for the company's common stock, Delphi commented on the "Harold Ruttenberg factor." The report largely attributed the company's financial success and rosy future to "the larger-than-life founder and inventor of the Just for Feet concept."

In frequent interviews with business journalists, Harold Ruttenberg was not timid in discussing the huge challenges that he had personally overcome to establish himself as one of the leading corporate executives in the retail apparel industry. Nor was Ruttenberg reluctant to point out that he had sketched out the general framework of Just for Feet's successful business plan over a three-day vacation in the late 1980s. After being named one of 1996's Retail Entrepreneurs of the Year, Ruttenberg noted that Just for Feet had succeeded principally because of the unique marketing strategies he had developed for the company. "Customers love our stores because they are so unique. We are not a copycat retailer. Nobody does what we do, the way we do it. The proof is in our performance."[1] In this same interview, Ruttenberg reported that he had never been tempted to check out a competitor's store. "I have nothing to learn from them. I'm certainly not going to copy anything they are doing."[2] Finally, Ruttenberg did not dispute, or apologize for, his reputation as a domineering, if not imposing, superior. "I can be a very demanding, difficult boss. But I know how to build teams. And I have made a lot of people very rich."[3]

Ruttenberg realized that one of his primary responsibilities was training a new management team to assume the leadership of the company following his retirement. "As the founder, my job is to put the right people in place for the future. I'm preparing this company for 25 years down the road when I won't be here."[4] One of the individuals who Ruttenberg handpicked to lead the company into the future was his son, Don-Allen Ruttenberg, who shared his father's single-minded determination and tenacious business temperament. In 1997, at the age of 29, Don-Allen Ruttenberg was named Just for Feet's Vice President of New Store Development. Two years later, the younger Ruttenberg was promoted to the position of Executive Vice President.

Similar to most successful companies, Just for Feet's path to success was not without occasional pitfalls. In 1995, Wall Street's zeal for Just for Feet's common stock was tempered somewhat by an accounting controversy involving "store opening" costs. Throughout its existence, Just for Feet had accumulated such costs for each new store in an asset account and then amortized the costs over the 12-month period following the store's grand opening. A more common practice within the retail industry was to expense such costs in the month that a new store opened. Criticism of Just for Feet's accounting for store opening costs goaded company management to adopt the industry convention, which resulted in the company recording a $2.1 million cumulative effect of a change in accounting principle during fiscal 1996.

In the summer of 1996, Wall Street took notice when Harold Ruttenberg, his wife, Pamela, and their son, Don-Allen, sold large blocks of their Just for Feet common stock in a secondary offering to the general public. Collectively, the three members of the Ruttenberg family received nearly $49.5 million from the sale of those securities. Major investors and financial analysts questioned why the Ruttenbergs would dispose of much of their Just for Feet stock while, at the same time, the senior Ruttenberg was issuing glowing projections of the company's future prospects.

Clay Feet

No one could deny the impressive revenue and profit trends that Just for Feet established during the mid- and late 1990s. Exhibit 1 and Exhibit 2, which present the company's primary financial statements for the three-year period fiscal 1996 through fiscal 1998, document those trends. However, hidden within the company's financial data for that three-year period was a red flag. Notice in the statements of cash flows shown in Exhibit 2 that, despite the rising profits Just for Feet reported in the late 1990s, the company's operating cash flows during that period were negative. By early 1999, these negative operating cash flows posed a huge liquidity problem for the

1. *Chain Store Age*, "Retail Entrepreneurs of the Year: Harold Ruttenberg," December 1996, 68.

2. *Ibid.*

3. *Ibid.*

4. *Ibid.*

EXHIBIT 1

JUST FOR FEET,
INC., 1996–1998
BALANCE SHEETS

JUST FOR FEET, INC.
BALANCE SHEETS (000s omitted)

	1999	January 31, 1998	1997
Current assets:			
Cash and cash equivalents	$ 12,412	$ 82,490	$138,785
Marketable securities available for sale	—	—	33,961
Accounts receivable	18,875	15,840	6,553
Inventory	399,901	206,128	133,323
Other current assets	18,302	6,709	2,121
Total current assets	449,490	311,167	314,743
Property and equipment, net	160,592	94,529	54,922
Goodwill, net	71,084	36,106	—
Other	8,230	6,550	6,169
Total assets	$689,396	$448,352	$375,834
Current liabilities:			
Short-term borrowings	$ —	$ 90,667	$100,000
Accounts payable	100,322	51,162	38,897
Accrued expenses	24,829	9,292	5,487
Income taxes payable	902	1,363	425
Current maturities of long-term debt	6,639	3,222	2,105
Total current liabilities	132,692	155,706	146,914
Long-term debt and obligations	230,998	24,562	10,364
Total liabilities	$363,690	$180,268	$157,278
Shareholders' equity:			
Common stock	3	3	3
Paid-in capital	249,590	218,616	190,492
Retained earnings	76,113	49,465	28,061
Total shareholders' equity	325,706	268,084	218,556
Total liabilities and shareholders' equity	$689,396	$448,352	$375,834

company. To address this problem, Just for Feet sold $200 million of high-yield or so-called "junk" bonds in April 1999.

A few weeks after selling the junk bonds, Just for Feet issued an earnings warning. This press release alerted investors that the company would likely post its first-ever quarterly loss during the second quarter of fiscal 1999. One month later, Just for Feet shocked its investors and creditors when it announced that it might default on its first interest payment on the $200 million of junk bonds. Investors received more disturbing news in July 1999 when Harold Ruttenberg unexpectedly resigned as Just for Feet's CEO. The company replaced Ruttenberg with a corporate turnaround specialist, Helen Rockey. Upon resigning, Ruttenberg insisted that Just for Feet's financial problems were only temporary and that the company would likely post a profit during the third quarter of fiscal 1999.

Harold Ruttenberg's statement did not reassure investors. The company's stock price went into a freefall during the spring and summer of 1999, slipping to near $4 per share by the end of July. In September, the company announced that it had lost $25.9 million during the second quarter of fiscal 1999, a much larger loss than had been expected by Wall Street. Less than two months later, on November 2, 1999, the company shocked its investors and creditors once more when it filed for Chapter 11 bankruptcy protection in the federal courts.

Just for Feet's startling collapse over a period of a few months sparked a flurry of lawsuits against the company and its executives. Allegations of financial mismanagement and accounting irregularities triggered investigations of the company's financial affairs by state and federal law enforcement authorities, including the Alabama Securities Commission, the FBI, the Securities and Exchange Commission (SEC), and the U.S. Department of Justice. In May 2003, the Justice Department announced that a former Just for Feet executive, Adam Gilburne, had pleaded guilty to conspiracy to commit wire and securities fraud. Gilburne, who had served in various executive positions with Just for Feet, revealed that he and other members of the company's top management had conspired to inflate the company's reported earnings from 1996 through 1999.

EXHIBIT 2

JUST FOR FEET, INC., 1996–1998 INCOME STATEMENTS AND STATEMENTS OF CASH FLOWS

JUST FOR FEET, INC.
CONSOLIDATED STATEMENTS OF EARNINGS (000s omitted)

	Year Ended January 31,		
	1999	1998	1997
Net sales	$774,863	$478,638	$256,397
Cost of sales	452,330	279,816	147,526
Gross profit	322,533	198,822	108,871
Other revenues	1,299	1,101	581
Operating expenses:			
Store operating	232,505	139,659	69,329
Store opening costs	13,669	6,728	11,240
Amortization of intangibles	2,072	1,200	180
General and administrative	24,341	18,040	7,878
Total operating expenses	272,587	165,627	88,627
Operating income	51,245	34,296	20,825
Interest expense	(8,059)	(1,446)	(832)
Interest income	143	1,370	4,750
Earnings before income taxes and cumulative effect of change in accounting principle	43,329	34,220	24,743
Provision for income taxes	16,681	12,817	8,783
Earnings before cumulative effect of a change in accounting principle	26,648	21,403	15,960
Cumulative effect on prior years of change in accounting principle	—	—	(2,041)
Net earnings	$ 26,648	$ 21,403	$ 13,919

JUST FOR FEET, INC.
CONSOLIDATED STATEMENTS OF CASH FLOWS (000s omitted)

	Year Ended January 31,		
	1999	1998	1997
Operating activities:			
Net earnings	$ 26,648	$ 21,403	$ 13,919
Adjustments to reconcile net earnings to net cash used by operating activities:			
Cumulative effect of a change in accounting principle	—	—	2,041
Depreciation and amortization	16,129	8,783	3,971
Deferred income taxes	12,100	2,194	(744)
Deferred lease rentals	2,655	2,111	1,456
Changes in assets and liabilities providing (using) cash, net of effects of acquisitions:			
(Increase) decrease in accounts receivable	(2,795)	(8,918)	(3,143)
(Increase) decrease in inventory	(170,169)	(56,616)	(76,685)
(Increase) decrease in other assets	(8,228)	(5,643)	271
Increase (decrease) in accounts payable	34,638	7,495	16,628
Increase (decrease) in accrued expenses	7,133	2,264	2,709
Increase (decrease) in income taxes payable	(181)	543	(2,506)
Net cash used by operating activities	(82,070)	(26,384)	(42,083)
Investing activities:			
Purchases of property and equipment, net of disposals	(78,984)	(43,446)	(33,206)
Acquisitions, net of cash acquired	(199)	(25,548)	—
Purchases of marketable securities	—	(14,726)	(44,778)
Maturities and sales of marketable securities	—	51,653	63,132
Net cash used for investing activities	(79,183)	(32,067)	(14,852)
Financing activities:			
Borrowings (repayments) under credit facilities, net	(90,667)	(9,333)	45,000
Borrowings of long-term obligations	291,076	12,739	479
Principal payments on long-term obligations	(132,290)	(2,054)	(1,335)
Proceeds from issuance of common stock, net	20,000	—	52,900
Proceeds from exercise of options	3,056	804	1,822
Net cash provided by financing activities	91,175	2,156	98,866
Net increase (decrease) in cash and equivalents	(70,078)	(56,295)	41,931
Cash and equivalents, beginning of year	82,490	138,785	96,854
Cash and equivalents, end of year	$ 12,412	$ 82,490	$138,785

EXHIBIT 2—
continued

Just for FEET, Inc., 1996–1998 Income Statements and Statements of Cash Flows

The information [testimony provided by Gilburne] alleges that beginning in about 1996, Just for Feet's CEO [Harold Ruttenberg] would conduct meetings at the end of every quarter in which he would lay out analysts' expectations of the company's earnings, and then draw up a list of "goods"—items which produced or added income—and "bads"—those which reduced income. The information alleges that the CEO directed Just for Feet's employees to increase the "goods" and decrease the "bads" in order to meet his own earnings expectations and those of Wall Street analysts.[5]

5. U.S. Department of Justice, "Former 'Just for Feet, Inc.' Executive Pleads Guilty to Conspiracy to Commit Wire, Securities Fraud," http://www.usdoj.gov, 12 May 2003.

Approximately two years following Gilburne's guilty plea, the SEC issued a series of enforcement releases that documented the three key facets of the fraudulent scheme perpetrated by Just for Feet's management team. "Just for Feet falsified its financial statements by (1) improperly recognizing unearned and fictitious receivables from its vendors, (2) failing to properly account for excess inventory, and (3) improperly recording as income the value of display booths provided by its vendors."[6]

As noted earlier, the stores-within-a-store floor plan developed by Harold Ruttenberg provided an opportunity for Just for Feet's vendors to become directly involved in the marketing of their products within the company's superstores. Each year, Just for Feet received millions of dollars of "vendor allowances" or "advertising co-op" from Adidas, Converse, Nike, Reebok, and its other major suppliers. These allowances were intended to subsidize Just for Feet's advertising expenditures for its superstores.

Despite the large size of the vendor allowances, there was typically not a written agreement that documented the conditions under which Just for Feet was entitled to an allowance. Instead, an account manager of each vendor generally had considerable discretion in determining the size and timing of the allowances to be granted to Just for Feet. After Just for Feet had run a series of advertisements or other promotional announcements for a vendor's product, copies of the advertising materials would be submitted to the vendor. The vendor would then pay Just for Feet an allowance based largely upon the amount of the advertised products that the company had purchased.

Generally accepted accounting principles (GAAP) dictated that vendor allowances not be offset against advertising expenses until the given advertisements had been run or other promotional efforts had been completed. However, Just for Feet began routinely recording *anticipated* vendor allowances as receivables and advertising expense offsets well before the related advertising or promotional programs had been completed. Just for Feet's management team was particularly aggressive in "frontloading" vendor allowances during fiscal 1998. At the end of fiscal 1997, Just for Feet had slightly more than $400,000 of outstanding vendor allowance receivables; 12 months later, at the end of fiscal 1998, that total had soared to almost $29 million.[7]

During fiscal 1998, Just for Feet's merchandise inventory nearly doubled, rising from $206 million on January 31, 1998, to almost $400 million on January 31, 1999. Although Just for Feet had a large amount of slow-moving inventory, the company's management team refused to properly apply the lower of cost or market rule in arriving at a year-end valuation reserve for that important asset. As a result, at the end of both fiscal 1997 and fiscal 1998, the company's allowance for inventory obsolescence stood at a nominal $150,000.

The major athletic shoe vendors frequently erected promotional displays or booths in the Just for Feet superstores. These booths were maintained by sales representatives of the vendors and were the property of those vendors. In early 1998, Don-Allen Ruttenberg concocted a fraudulent scheme to produce millions of dollars of "booth income" for Just for Feet. Without the knowledge of its vendors, Just for Feet began recording in its accounting records monthly booth income amounts allegedly earned from those vendors. The offsets to these revenue amounts for accounting

---

6. U.S. Securities and Exchange Commission, "SEC Charges Deloitte & Touche and Two of Its Personnel for Failures in Their Audits of Just for Feet," http://www.sec.gov, 26 April 2005.

7. Although technically receivables, the vendor allowances purportedly due to Just for Feet were netted against the given vendor's accounts payable balance, which explains why these receivables do not appear explicitly in the company's balance sheets shown in Exhibit 1.

purposes were booked (debited) to a booth assets account.[8] By the end of fiscal 1998, Just for Feet had recorded $9 million of bogus assets and related revenues as a result of this scheme. More than 80 percent of these bogus transactions were recorded during the final two quarters of fiscal 1998, ostensibly to allow Just for Feet to reach its previously announced earnings targets for those two periods.

An important feature of the Just for Feet accounting fraud was Don-Allen Ruttenberg's close relationships with key executives of the major athletic shoe vendors. Since Just for Feet was among the largest customers of each of these vendors, the company had a significant amount of economic leverage on those executives. The younger Ruttenberg used this leverage to persuade those executives to return false confirmations to Just for Feet's independent audit firm, Deloitte & Touche. Those confirmations were sent to Just for Feet's vendors to confirm bogus receivables that were a product of the company's fraudulent accounting scheme. In most cases, the bogus receivables resulted from inflated or otherwise improper vendor allowances booked by Just for Feet. One of the five vendor executives who capitulated to Don-Allen Ruttenberg's demands was Thomas Shine, the senior executive of Logo Athletic. Executives of four Just for Feet vendors steadfastly refused to provide false confirmations to Deloitte. Those executives were employed by Asics-Tiger, New Balance, Reebok, and Timberland. Ironically, in 2001, Thomas Shine became an executive of Reebok when that company purchased Logo Athletic.

Footing & Cross-Footing

Deloitte & Touche served as Just for Feet's independent audit firm from 1992 through early December 1999, one month after the company filed for Chapter 11 bankruptcy. Deloitte issued unqualified audit opinions each year on Just for Feet's financial statements, including the financial statements in the S-1 registration statement the company filed with the SEC when it went public in 1994.

Steven Barry served as Just for Feet's engagement partner for the fiscal 1998 audit. Barry was initially an employee of Touche Ross & Co. and was promoted to partner with that firm in 1988. The next year, Barry became a Deloitte & Touche partner following the merger of Touche Ross with Deloitte, Haskins, & Sells. In 1996, Barry was promoted to managing partner of Deloitte's Birmingham, Alabama office. Barry's principal subordinate on the 1998 Just for Feet audit was Karen Baker, who had been assigned to the company's audit engagement team since 1993. Initially the audit senior on that engagement team, she became the engagement audit manager after being promoted to that rank in 1995.

Deloitte assigned a "greater than normal" level of audit risk to the fiscal 1998 Just for Feet audit during the planning phase of that engagement. To help monitor high-risk audit engagements, Deloitte had established a "National Risk Management Program." In both 1997 and 1998, Just for Feet was included in that program. Each client involved in this program was assigned a "National Review Partner." This partner's duties included "discussing specific risk areas and plans to respond to them, . . . reviewing the audit workpapers concerning risk areas of the engagement, and reviewing the financial statements and Deloitte's audit reports with an emphasis on the identification of specific risk areas as well as the adequacy of the audit report and disclosures regarding these risk areas."[9]

8. This fraudulent scheme actually replaced a similar but smaller-scale scam that the younger Ruttenberg had used since December 1996 to inflate Just for Feet's operating results.

9. Securities and Exchange Commission, *Accounting and Auditing Enforcement Release No. 2238*, 26 May 2005. Unless noted otherwise, the remaining quotations in this case were taken from this source.

The audit workpapers for the fiscal 1997 audit identified several specific audit risk factors. These factors included "management accepts high levels of risk," "places significant emphasis on earnings," and "has historically interpreted accounting standards aggressively." Another 1997 workpaper noted that the company's management team placed a heavy emphasis on achieving previously released earnings targets, expressed an "excessive" interest in maintaining the company's stock price at a high level, and engaged in "unique and highly complex" transactions near fiscal year-end. A summary 1997 workpaper entitled "Risk Factors Worksheet" also noted that Harold Ruttenberg exercised "one man (autocrat) rule" over Just for Feet and that the company practiced "creative accounting."

For both the 1997 and 1998 audit engagements, Deloitte personnel prepared a "Client Risk Profile." This workpaper for those two audits identified vendor allowances and inventory valuation as key audit risk areas. In 1996, Deloitte's headquarters office had issued a firm-wide "Risk Alert" informing practice offices that vendor allowances should be considered a "high-risk area" for retail clients.

During the 1998 audit, the Deloitte engagement team identified several factors that, according to the SEC, should have caused both Barry and Baker to have "heightened professional skepticism" regarding Just for Feet's vendor allowances. The most important of these factors was the huge increase in the vendor allowance receivables between the end of fiscal 1997 and fiscal 1998. In the final few weeks of fiscal 1998, Just for Feet recorded $14.4 million of vendor allowances, accounting for almost one-half of the year-end balance of that account. Deloitte was never provided with supporting documentation for $11.3 million of those vendor allowances, although a Just for Feet executive had promised to provide that documentation. Deloitte completed its fieldwork for the fiscal 1998 audit on April 23, 1999, almost three months following the fiscal year-end. As of that date, Just for Feet had not received any payments from its suppliers for the $11.3 million of undocumented vendor allowances.

In March 1999, Deloitte mailed receivables confirmations to 13 of Just for Feet's suppliers. Collectively, those vendors accounted for $22 million of the $28.9 million of year-end vendor allowances. Again, Don-Allen Ruttenberg persuaded executives of five Just for Feet vendors to sign and return confirmations to Deloitte even though the vendor allowance receivables listed on those confirmations did not exist or were grossly inflated. The confirmations returned by the other eight vendors were generally "nonstandard," according to the SEC. That is, these confirmations included caveats, disclaimers, or other statements that should have alerted Deloitte to the possibility that the given receivable balances were unreliable. "Five vendors returned nonstandard letters that, instead of unambiguously confirming amounts owed to Just for Feet at the *end* of the fiscal 1998 year, as requested by the auditors, provided ambiguous information on amounts of co-op [vendor allowances] that the Company had earned, accrued, or had available *during* the year" [emphasis added by SEC]. Another of the returned confirmations explicitly noted that "no additional funds" were due to Just for Feet.

The eight nonstandard confirmations accounted for approximately $16 million of the $22 million of vendor allowance receivables that Deloitte attempted to confirm at year-end. "Despite these and other flaws, the Respondents [Deloitte, Barry, and Baker] nonetheless accepted these letters as confirming approximately $16 million in receivables claimed by Just for Feet." The SEC's investigation of Deloitte's Just for Feet audits revealed that although Barry and Baker accepted these flawed confirmations, two subordinates assigned to the 1998 engagement team continued to investigate the obvious discrepancies in those confirmations well after the completion of that audit. These two individuals, who were audit seniors, twice contacted a Just for Feet executive in the months following the completion of the 1998 audit in an attempt to obtain plausible explanations for the eight nonstandard and suspicious confirmations. That executive did not respond to the audit seniors and neither Barry, nor Baker, apparently, insisted that he provide appropriate documentation and/or explanations regarding the amounts in question.

Just for Feet's large increase in inventory during fiscal 1998 presented several obvious issues for the Deloitte auditors to consider during the 1998 audit, the most important being whether the client's reserve for inventory obsolescence was sufficient. The primary audit procedure used by Deloitte during the 1998 audit to assess the reasonableness of the client's inventory valuation reserve was to obtain and test an inventory "reserve analysis" prepared by a company vice president. This latter document was supposed to include the three classes of inventory items to which company policy required the lower of cost or market rule to be applied: (1) shoe styles for which the company had four or fewer pairs, (2) shoes and other apparel that were selling for less than cost, and (3) any inventory styles for which no items had been sold during the previous 12 months. However, the reserve analysis for 1998 excluded those inventory styles for which no sales had been made during the previous 12 months, an oversight that the Deloitte auditors never questioned or investigated. The Deloitte auditors also discovered that a large amount of inventory included in a Just for Feet warehouse had been excluded from the reserve analysis prepared by the company vice president. Again, the auditors chose not to question client personnel regarding this oversight.

After completing their inventory audit procedures, the Deloitte auditors concluded that Just for Feet's year-end reserve for inventory obsolescence was significantly understated. The SEC noted that this conclusion was reached by the Deloitte auditors despite the obvious deficiencies in audit procedures applied to Just for Feet's reserve for inventory obsolescence:

> Even using the flawed inventory analysis provided by the Vice President and the deficient inventory information that excluded the goods from the New Jersey warehouse, the Respondents concluded that Just for Feet's obsolescence reserve should have been in the range of $441,000 to over $1 million.

The Deloitte audit team prepared a proposed audit adjustment to increase the reserve for inventory obsolescence by more than $400,000; however, the client rejected that audit adjustment, meaning that the year-end balance of that account remained at a meager $150,000.

Although not specifically identified as a "key audit risk area" during the 1998 audit, the Deloitte auditors focused considerable attention on Just for Feet's accounting decisions for the approximately $9 million of "booth income" the company recorded during that year. The Deloitte auditors discovered the monthly booth income journal entries recorded by Just for Feet during fiscal 1998 and prepared a workpaper documenting those entries. "An analysis at the end of the workpaper, which Baker reviewed, showed that the net effect of Just for Feet's booth-related journal entries was to increase assets with a corresponding increase in income. The Respondents [Deloitte, Barry, and Baker] performed no further analysis to determine the basis and propriety of these journal entries."

Instead of independently investigating these entries, the Deloitte auditors accepted the representation of a Just for Feet executive who insisted that the entries had no effect on the company's net income. According to this executive, the monthly booth income amounts were offset by preexisting "co-op" or advertising credits that had been granted to Just for Feet by its major vendors. In other words, instead of using those advertising credits to reduce reported advertising expenses, Just for Feet was allegedly converting those credits into booth income or revenue amounts.

By the end of 1998, the bogus booth income journal entries had produced $9 million of nonexistent "booth assets" in Just for Feet's accounting records. Since "neither the Company nor the auditors had internal evidence supporting the recording of $9 million of booth assets," the Deloitte engagement team decided to corroborate the existence and ownership assertions for those assets by obtaining confirmations from the relevant Just for Feet vendors. These confirmations were prepared with the assistance of certain Just for Feet executives who were aware of the fraudulent nature of the booth income/booth assets amounts. Apparently, these executives contacted the vendor representatives to whom the confirmations were mailed and told them how to respond to the confirmations. The booth assets confirmations returned by the vendors to Deloitte were replete with errors and ambiguous statements. A frustrated audit senior who reviewed the confirmations brought this matter to the attention of both Barry and Baker.

> An audit senior reviewed these confirmations and informed Barry and Baker that she was in some cases sending multiple confirmation requests to the vendors because many of their initial requests came back in forms different from that requested. The Respondents failed to discover from these indications that Just for Feet might not actually ... [own] the booths as claimed.

EPILOGUE

In February 2000, after realizing that Just for Feet was no longer salvageable, Helen Rockey began the process of liquidating the company under Chapter 7 of the federal bankruptcy code. Over the next few years, settlements were announced to a number of large lawsuits linked to the Just for Feet accounting fraud and the company's subsequent bankruptcy. Just for Feet's former executives and Deloitte were among the principal defendants in those lawsuits. One of those cases, a class-action lawsuit filed by Just for Feet's former stockholders, was settled for a reported $32.4 million in 2002.

Several of Just for Feet's former executives pleaded guilty to criminal charges for their roles in the company's massive accounting fraud. Among these individuals was Don-Allen Ruttenberg. In April 2005, a federal judge sentenced Ruttenberg to 20 months in federal prison and fined him $50,000. At the same time

that the younger Ruttenberg's sentence was announced, a Department of Justice official reported that Harold Ruttenberg, who was gravely ill with brain cancer, would not be charged in the case. In January 2006, Harold Ruttenberg died at the age of 63.

Five executives of Just for Feet's former vendors also pleaded guilty to various criminal charges for providing false confirmations to the company's auditors. Most of these individuals, including Thomas Shine, received probationary sentences. An exception was Timothy McCool, the former director of apparel sales for Adidas, who received a four-month "noncustodial" sentence. While sentencing McCool, U.S. District Judge C. Lynwood Smith, Jr., noted, "Life is so fragile. A single bad choice in a single moment can cause a life to turn irrevocably 180 degrees. I think that is where you find yourself."[10]

---

10. *The Associated Press State & Local Wire*, "Adidas America Executive Sentenced in Just for Feet Case," 22 March 2004.

Arguably, the party to the Just for Feet scandal that received the most condemnation from the courts and the business press was Deloitte. In April 2005, the SEC berated the prominent accounting firm for the poor quality of its Just for Feet audits in *Accounting and Auditing Enforcement Release No. 2238*. In that same enforcement release, the SEC fined Deloitte $375,000 and suspended Steven Barry from serving on audit engagements involving SEC registrants for two years; Karen Baker received a one-year suspension.

On the same date that the SEC announced the sanctions that it had imposed on Deloitte for its Just for Feet audits, the federal agency also revealed the sanctions that Deloitte received for its allegedly deficient audits of a large telecommunications company, Adelphia Communications. Similar to Just for Feet, the once high-flying Adelphia had suddenly collapsed in 2002 following revelations that its previously issued financial statements that had been audited by Deloitte were riddled with errors. The SEC stunned the public accounting profession by fining Deloitte $50 million for its role in the huge Adelphia scandal, which was easily the largest fine ever imposed on an accounting firm by the federal agency.

Shortly after the SEC announced the sanctions that it had levied on Deloitte for its Just for Feet and Adelphia Communications audits, James Quigley, Deloitte's CEO, issued a press release responding to those sanctions. Quigley noted in his press release that, "Among our most significant challenges is the early detection of fraud, particularly when the client, its management and others collude specifically to deceive a company's auditors."[11] This statement infuriated SEC officials. An SEC spokesperson responded to Quigley's press release by stating that, "Deloitte was not deceived in this case. The findings in the order show that the relevant information was right in front of their eyes. Deloitte just didn't do its job, plain and simple. They didn't miss red flags. They pulled the flag over their head and claimed they couldn't see."[12]

The SEC also suggested that Quigley's press release violated the terms of the agreement that the agency had reached with Deloitte in settling the Just for Feet and Adelphia cases. Under the terms of that agreement, Deloitte was not required to "admit" to the SEC's findings, nor was it allowed to "deny" those findings. Deloitte subsequently rescinded Quigley's press release and issued another that eliminated some, but not all, of the statements that had offended the SEC.

Questions

1. Prepare common-sized balance sheets and income statements for Just for Feet for the period 1996–1998. Also compute key liquidity, solvency, activity, and profitability ratios for 1997 and 1998. Given these data, comment on what you believe were the high-risk financial statement items for the 1998 Just for Feet audit.

2. Just for Feet operated large, high-volume retail stores. Identify internal control risks common to such businesses. How should these risks affect the audit planning decisions for such a client?

3. Just for Feet operated in an extremely competitive industry, or subindustry. Identify inherent risk factors common to businesses facing such competitive

11. Stephen Laub, "Deloitte Statement Irks SEC," *CFO.com*, 28 April 2005.

12. Siobhan Hughes, "SEC Rebukes Deloitte over Spin of Adelphia Audit," *The Associated Press State & Local Wire*, 27 April 2005.

conditions. How should these risks affect the audit planning decisions for such a client?

4. Prepare a comprehensive list, in a bullet format, of the audit risk factors present for the 1998 Just for Feet audit. Identify the five audit risk factors that you believe were most critical to the successful completion of that audit. Rank these risk factors from least to most important and be prepared to defend your rankings. Briefly explain whether or not you believe that the Deloitte auditors responded appropriately to the five critical audit risk factors that you identified.

5. Put yourself in the position of Thomas Shine in this case. How would you have responded when Don-Allen Ruttenberg asked you to send a false confirmation to Deloitte & Touche? Before responding, identify the parties who will be affected by your decision.

Jamaica Water Properties

*If you ever obtain something by lying, it's
worthless. Integrity is the highest order of the day.*

David Sokol

In 1990, David Sokol faced a problem that has stymied the careers of many business executives.[1] At the time, Sokol served as president of Ogden Projects, Inc., an environmental services company. Sokol had his sights set on becoming the company's chief executive officer (CEO), but something, or rather someone, stood in his way, namely, the boss's son. Many company insiders believed that the chairman of Ogden Corporation, the parent company of Ogden Projects, had already decided to appoint his son as the next CEO of Ogden Projects. Rather than provoke an unpleasant "scene," Sokol graciously resigned and returned to his hometown of Omaha, Nebraska, to search for another position.

A few months later, in early 1991, Sokol landed a job with a large Omaha construction and mining company. That firm owned a controlling interest in California Energy, a public company based in San Francisco that was struggling financially. Sokol's new employer gave him the difficult task of "turning around" CalEnergy by appointing him the company's CEO. Sokol, who majored in civil engineering, not business, at the University of Nebraska, spent his first several weeks in his new position scrutinizing CalEnergy's accounting records. He quickly decided that the company's financial problems stemmed from poor cost control and inefficiencies in its operations. Within a few months, Sokol had implemented an austerity program for CalEnergy. That program included eliminating executive perks such as private jets and limos, slashing the company's bloated payroll by 25 percent, and moving CalEnergy's corporate headquarters from the pricey San Francisco Bay area to the more modest and economical outskirts of Omaha.

The rapid and dramatic impact that Sokol's turnaround program had on CalEnergy's operations caught the attention of corporate boards across the nation. In early 1992, Sokol was offered the position of president and chief operating officer (COO) of JWP Inc., a large, New York–based conglomerate. JWP had an impressive history of sustained profitability and revenue growth that was being threatened by its sprawling operations and heavy administrative burden. In early 1992, the company had 117 offices and 23 subsidiaries scattered across the country, several overseas operating units, and a huge new division that was competing in a lucrative and rapidly developing market. JWP's CEO, Andrew Dwyer, knew that despite being soft-spoken and thoughtful, Sokol had a well-deserved reputation of being an effective corporate manager who could quickly "whip" a company into shape. Sokol eventually succumbed to Dwyer's persistent recruiting efforts and agreed to assume responsibility for directing JWP's day-to-day operations.

From Queens to Computers

The Jamaica Water Supply Company began operations in 1886 as a small business that delivered water to a few neighborhoods in the Queens borough of New York

---

1. The development of this case was funded by the 2002 McLaughlin Curriculum Development Grant. I would like to thank Glen McLaughlin for his generous and continuing support of efforts to integrate ethics into business curricula.

City. Gradually, the company expanded its geographic market and eventually became one of New York State's largest water utilities. In the mid-1960s, Martin Dwyer took control of the company. Dwyer realized that the heavily regulated water utility industry limited his company's profit potential, so he decided to branch out into other businesses. Because of his familiarity with governmental agencies, Dwyer began offering various contracting and construction services to local municipalities. Soon, Dwyer's company was installing telephone lines, working on street lighting projects, and developing traffic control systems. Over the next several years, the company expanded into other lines of business by acquiring a varied assortment of small firms in the New York City metropolitan area.

Throughout its long existence, Jamaica Water Supply had been characterized by financial stability, slow but steady growth, and modest profits. That all changed under Dwyer's leadership. During the 1960s and 1970s, the company grew rapidly, while its profits—and losses—vacillated sharply from year to year. To finance the company's expansion program, Dwyer borrowed heavily from banks and other lenders. By the mid-1970s, high interest rates, a severe nationwide recession, and a series of poor decisions by Dwyer and his management team had driven the company to the verge of bankruptcy. To salvage the company, Martin Dwyer stepped down as its top executive in 1978 and placed his 30-year-old son, Andrew, in charge.

The younger Dwyer quickly disposed of the company's weakest divisions, paid off much of its debt, and developed a new, more focused business plan. This business plan called for the company to become the "premier technical services" firm in the world.[2] By the mid-1980s, the company, renamed JWP (Jamaica Water Properties) Inc. by that time, offered a wide range of services involving the design, development, and maintenance of complex mechanical, electrical, and computer systems. JWP targeted its services to high-tech industries, including the financial services industry. The company developed sophisticated control systems that helped major Wall Street firms, such as Merrill Lynch and Goldman Sachs, more efficiently and cost-effectively manage their operations.

By the early 1990s, Andrew Dwyer's new business model for JWP had converted the company into a multibillion-dollar firm with a workforce of more than 20,000 employees. The company's stock was listed on the New York Stock Exchange and included in the Standard & Poor's 500. Probably most impressively, the company reported increased revenues each quarter over a 12-year period from 1979 through 1991. Although JWP still had a water utility division, that division accounted for only 2 percent of the firm's annual revenues.

In early 1991, Dwyer made a key decision that he hoped would catapult JWP to among the largest and most prominent companies in the nation. Dwyer purchased the large computer retailer Businessland, Inc. Businessland's operations were integrated into a new division of JWP that marketed computer hardware, business software applications, and information systems development services. Dwyer believed the new division would provide JWP with the means to compete with companies such as IBM and Microsoft that were profiting enormously from the computer revolution sweeping through the business world.

Despite Dwyer's lofty plans for his new division, he realized that it only worsened a problem that JWP had been battling over the previous few years. The company's rapid growth during the 1980s had resulted in a far-flung and unwieldy organization that was difficult to manage and weighted down by disproportionately high

---

2. Unless indicated otherwise, the remaining quotations appearing in this case were taken from the following legal opinion: *AUSA Life Insurance Company et al. v. Ernst & Young*, 1997 U.S. Dist. LEXIS 21357.

administrative expenses. To remedy this problem, Andrew Dwyer went in search of an individual with a proven track record of managing companies facing difficult circumstances. In a matter of weeks, Dwyer identified David Sokol as the top candidate for JWP's COO position.

Dark Secrets

David Sokol accepted Andrew Dwyer's offer to become JWP's COO in January 1992 because he enjoyed tackling challenging assignments. But Sokol was unaware of the biggest challenge he would face at JWP. Over the previous several years, the company's financial data had been embellished by a pervasive accounting fraud. The abusive accounting practices included misapplying the purchase method of accounting for acquisitions, recording fictitious assets, improper accounting for net operating loss (NOL) carryforwards, failing to record appropriate allowances for uncollectible receivables, and misapplying the percentage-of-completion method of accounting for long-term contracts. Collectively, these accounting abuses had a significant impact on JWP's reported profits. For example, in 1991, JWP reported a net income of $60.1 million. A subsequent investigation by the Securities and Exchange Commission (SEC) revealed that the company's actual profit for that year was $28.9 million.

The principal architect of JWP's accounting fraud was Ernest Grendi, JWP's chief financial officer (CFO). Three of the company's senior accountants helped him carry out and conceal the fraud. Each of the four individuals was a CPA and a former employee of JWP's audit firm, Ernst & Young. Similar to most accounting frauds, simple greed was the factor that apparently motivated Grendi and his three lieutenants. Over the course of the JWP fraud, the four individuals received sizable bonuses linked to the company's overstated earnings and cashed in large gains in the stock market by selling JWP securities at prices inflated by the fraudulent earnings figures. Although they benefited financially from Grendi's scam, Andrew Dwyer and the company's other top executives were never implicated in the fraud.

Grendi's subordinates often joked that rather than applying generally accepted accounting principles, or GAAP, their company applied EGAAP—Ernest Grendi's Accepted Accounting Principles. These subordinates used another distinctive phrase in referring to the unusual revenue pattern apparent in JWP's internal financial reports. Near the end of a quarterly accounting period, JWP's accounting staff often "front-loaded" the revenue recognized on long-term construction contracts to ensure that the company sustained its unbroken chain of quarterly revenue increases. The resulting accounting entries produced sharp spikes in JWP's revenue charts near the end of quarterly accounting periods. These recurring spikes became known as the "High Sierras" by Grendi's co-conspirators.

Prior to David Sokol's arrival at JWP, Grendi relied on the far-reaching authority granted to him by Andrew Dwyer and on his "intransigent and intimidating"[3] personality to establish complete control over JWP's accounting function. He also used his menacing personality to neutralize JWP's various control functions, particularly the company's internal audit staff. A JWP internal auditor subsequently reported that fear of being fired had deterred him from challenging the company's improper accounting treatments. Another JWP internal auditor expressed a similar sentiment when he reported that he had feared being "crushed like a flea" if he questioned the company's improper accounting decisions.

---

3. *AUSA Life Insurance Company et al. v. Ernst & Young*, 119 F. Supp. 2d 394; 2000 U.S. Dist. LEXIS 14298.

Secrets Revealed

Court records document that Ernest Grendi was concerned that David Sokol would prove to be a "hands-on" COO when Andrew Dwyer hired him in January 1992. Grendi was right. Just as he had done after being appointed CalEnergy's CEO, Sokol immediately immersed himself in his new employer's accounting records. By the early summer of 1992, Sokol had uncovered several suspicious items, including a $46 million receivable in JWP's corporate general ledger that had gone uncollected for an extended period of time. Sokol determined that the large receivable was actually a series of smaller receivables that had originated within one of the company's divisions. Shortly before Sokol arrived at JWP, Grendi had attempted to conceal the past-due receivables from the new COO by transferring them to JWP's corporate general ledger. In the given division's accounting records, Grendi had replaced the collective dollar amount of the transferred receivables with a large intercompany receivable.

After discovering the series of accounting entries involving the long overdue receivables, Sokol met with the CFO of the division to which the receivables actually belonged. That individual explained to Sokol that his division's impressive profits in previous years had been inflated by aggressive revenue recognition policies, which, in turn, had overstated the division's receivables and total assets. Sokol then arranged a meeting involving himself, the divisional CFO, and attorneys representing the law firm that JWP used to help collect overdue receivables. The attorneys informed Sokol that they had previously told Grendi that the past-due receivables in question should be written off as bad debts. The relentless Sokol then met with the CFOs of several other JWP divisions. These individuals reported similar problems in their accounting records.

In July 1992, David Sokol met with Andrew Dwyer to discuss the troubling items he had uncovered. During that meeting, Sokol told Dwyer that he believed JWP needed to record $125 million in write-offs to correct the company's accounting records. Sokol also told Dwyer that he wanted to delve further into those records. To help him complete his investigation, he requested that Dwyer authorize him to retain an accounting firm other than Ernst & Young, which had issued unqualified audit opinions on JWP's financial statements the previous six years. Sokol was apparently concerned by the close relationships between and among members of the Ernst & Young audit team and JWP's senior accountants, which included Ernest Grendi and his three accomplices. Many of these relationships had been formed years earlier when the JWP accountants had been Ernst & Young employees. "I insisted that I wanted a different auditing firm brought in to assist me in the process, because I seriously questioned whether or not I was receiving accurate information from Ernie Grendi. . . . Also I was not comfortable that I could trust Ernst & Young, and I wanted an outside auditing firm brought in to help me."

Dwyer agreed to retain Deloitte & Touche to carry out a large-scale investigation of JWP's accounting records. While Deloitte & Touche mapped out its planned investigation, Sokol continued his intense and persistent one-man effort to determine the extent to which JWP's financial statement data had been misrepresented. In early September, Sokol interviewed two of Ernest Grendi's subordinates. These individuals showed Sokol the "High Sierras" charts that documented the unusual fluctuations in JWP's revenues. Sokol realized at this point that JWP's financial data had been intentionally distorted.

> Up until this time, Mr. Sokol had been trying to convince [himself], as these things kept coming up, that these items . . . these accounting issues . . . were just a series of bad judgments and things of that nature. But with the "High Sierras," David Sokol learned that "these were not accidents."

After Sokol reviewed the High Sierras charts he sought and obtained further evidence from Grendi's subordinates that JWP's financial data had been systematically manipulated. Sokol then called another meeting with Andrew Dwyer. Sokol told Dwyer that he had been misled prior to joining JWP and was considering leaving the company. Dwyer pleaded with Sokol not to leave, at least until the extent of the restatements that would be necessary to JWP's financial data had been determined. If Sokol left before the investigation was completed, Dwyer insisted that the impact on JWP would be "devastating." To persuade him to remain, Dwyer offered Sokol a $1 million "stay bonus."

Sokol was unmoved by Dwyer's offer. Shortly after meeting with Dwyer, he met with JWP's board and turned over all of the information he had collected regarding the company's accounting irregularities. The following day, David Sokol resigned as JWP's president and COO and terminated all ties with the company.

Implosion, Embarrassment . . . Emcor

Deloitte & Touche's investigation continued for several months. When the investigation was completed, JWP restated (reduced) its previously reported earnings for 1990 and 1991 by approximately $40 million.[4] The investigation also resulted in a $653 million write-down of the company's assets. In April 1993, Andrew Dwyer resigned as JWP's CEO; three months later, he resigned as the company's chairman of the board. Ernest Grendi had been forced to resign as JWP's CFO in late 1992. JWP filed for bankruptcy in October 1993. The reorganization plan subsequently approved by the federal bankruptcy courts wiped out the common stockholders' equity and resulted in the creation of a new company known as Emcor Group Inc. JWP's former creditors became the principal owners of this company when it emerged from the bankruptcy courts in December 1994.

In 1995 and 1996, the SEC issued a series of accounting and auditing enforcement releases focusing on Ernest Grendi and the three other senior JWP accountants involved in the accounting fraud. The SEC dealt with Grendi's subordinates first. Each of those individuals agreed to repay the bonuses they had received due to JWP's overstated net income for 1991. These amounts ranged from $20,000 to $51,000. Two of the individuals forfeited profits of approximately $165,000 that they had earned by selling JWP's common stock in the early 1990s. Finally, two of the three individuals agreed to pay civil fines totaling approximately $90,000. None of the individuals admitted or denied the allegations that the SEC had filed against them but did agree not to violate federal securities laws in the future.

The SEC permanently banned Ernest Grendi from being involved as an accountant with any future registration statements filed with the agency. Grendi also agreed to pay restitution of approximately $700,000, which represented his 1991 bonus and the trading profits that he had earned on the company's stock during the early 1990s. The SEC waived additional civil fines and repayments totaling nearly $250,000 because of Grendi's inability to pay those amounts. In agreeing to the sanctions, Grendi neither admitted nor denied the allegations that the SEC had filed against him.

Accommodating Auditors

The SEC did not sanction or even criticize Ernst & Young in the various enforcement releases that focused on the JWP accounting fraud. But Ernst & Young was not so fortunate in the courts. JWP's former stockholders and creditors, who suffered huge

---

4. The impact of the abusive accounting practices on JWP's pre-1990 earnings could not be determined.

losses as a result of the company's bankruptcy, targeted the "deep pockets" of Ernst & Young in their efforts to recover those losses. No doubt, David Sokol's candid admission that he lost trust in Ernst & Young during his investigation of the massive accounting fraud buoyed the plaintiffs' hopes that they would be successful in their lawsuits filed against the prominent accounting firm.

Ernst & Young officials agreed to settle the lawsuits filed by JWP's former stockholders. In total, Ernst & Young paid those plaintiffs a reported $23 million. The other major class of plaintiffs that sued Ernst & Young was a group of insurance companies that had incurred approximately $100 million of losses on loans made to JWP. For years, these insurance companies doggedly pursued Ernst & Young in the federal courts. Finally, in October 2000, the claims of the insurance companies against Ernst & Young were resolved. The federal magistrate who presided over this lawsuit was Judge William C. Conner. The series of legal opinions that Judge Conner handed down in the case provide a colorful and insightful history of Ernst & Young's tenure as JWP's independent audit firm.

In 1985, Ernest Grendi dismissed Arthur Andersen & Co. as JWP's audit firm, claiming that the firm's audit fee was too high. Grendi then contacted a close friend and former colleague at Ernst & Young who was an audit partner. After JWP retained Ernst & Young as its new audit firm, Grendi's friend was appointed JWP's audit engagement partner. In 1988, Grendi negotiated a three-year "retention agreement" with Ernst & Young. This agreement capped the audit fee JWP would be required to pay for the 1988, 1989, and 1990 audits. Judge Conner was surprised that Ernst & Young agreed to this arrangement "without knowing what those future audits would entail."

Judge Conner documented repeatedly that the close relationship between Grendi and the JWP engagement partner appeared to have influenced judgments made by Ernst & Young personnel on the annual JWP audits. The judge's legal opinions in the case contrasted the intense efforts of David Sokol to pursue and uncover the fraud despite the intimidating persona of Ernest Grendi with Ernst & Young's "willingness to accommodate Mr. Grendi." The Ernst & Young auditors frequently uncovered improper entries in the company's accounting records but failed to persuade Grendi and his subordinates to make the appropriate adjustments for those items. Judge Conner attributed the deficient JWP audits to the "spinelessness" of the Ernst & Young auditors.

> *E&Y's deficiency was not in the planning or execution of its annual audits. They were sufficiently thorough and effective to uncover virtually all of the violations of GAAP which were ultimately corrected in the restatements. Instead, E&Y's failure lay in the seeming spinelessness of [the audit engagement partner] and the other E&Y accountants in their dealings with JWP, and particularly with its CFO, Ernest Grendi. When they met to discuss E&Y's annual Summary of Audit Differences, Grendi almost invariably succeeded in either persuading or bullying them to agree that JWP's books required no adjustment. . . . Obviously, an audit becomes a pointless exercise if the auditor, after discovering substantial errors in a publicly owned company's financial statements, supinely acquiesces in the client's refusal to correct the errors and certifies the statements anyway.*[5]

Judge Conner concluded that Ernst & Young "knew about the accounting irregularities that were pervasive at JWP," irregularities that had materially inflated the company's profits. "In the face of this knowledge, Ernst & Young abandoned its 'watchdog' obligations to bark an alarm. Instead, Ernst & Young issued clean audit opinions and

---

5. *AUSA Life Insurance Company et al. v. Ernst & Young*, 991 F. Supp. 234; 1997 U.S. Dist. LEXIS 19290; Fed. Sec. L. Rep. (CCH) P90,140.

no-default certificates, thereby lending the considerable prestige of Ernst & Young's imprimatur to JWP's erroneous financial statements." Despite this conclusion and despite the caustic tirades he directed at the Ernst & Young auditors, Judge Conner ruled in late 2000 that the insurance companies that had sued Ernst & Young could *not* recover their losses from the accounting firm. He reached this decision after determining that JWP's bankruptcy in 1993 and the resulting losses suffered by the insurance companies were not due to Ernst & Young's malfeasance but rather to poor management decisions on the part of Andrew Dwyer and other JWP executives. Those management decisions had undermined JWP's financial health even as the company continued to release impressive (but bogus) financial statements to the public.

Sokol Returns Home

Following his short and unpleasant tenure as JWP's COO, David Sokol returned once more to his native Nebraska. In April 1993, CalEnergy's board of directors reappointed Sokol as the company's president and CEO. Under Sokol's leadership, CalEnergy grew steadily during the remainder of the 1990s. In the late 1990s, Sokol, with the financial backing of billionaire investor Warren Buffett, Omaha's most famous resident, orchestrated CalEnergy's $9 billion dollar takeover of MidAmerican Energy Holdings, a company that supplied electricity and natural gas to three million residential customers in several Midwestern states. Although CalEnergy was the acquiring company, following the acquisition the new entity retained MidAmerican's name.

The rapid growth of CalEnergy and, subsequently, MidAmerican Energy Holdings, resulted in more accolades for David Sokol. In 2000, the *Financial Times* selected Sokol as the chief executive of the year within the energy industries. Among the many lessons that Sokol has learned during his tumultuous career is the critical importance of personal integrity, the importance of simply "doing the right thing" when problematic circumstances arise. Several years after he left JWP, Sokol commented on how difficult it is in the current business environment for even high-ranking corporate executives to expose an ongoing fraud. "I was president, chief operating officer, and a director. And yet this was incredibly difficult to get to the surface. What would happen to a guy making $50,000 in the accounting department? How does he have the courage to put his whole career on the line?"[6]

In March 2002, Congress invited Sokol to testify regarding the spectacular collapse of Enron Corporation. The following month, Sokol shared some of that testimony in an interview he granted to his hometown newspaper, the *Omaha World-Herald*. In that interview, Sokol commented on the critical importance of proper accounting by corporations and the need for more severe punishment to be meted out to corporate executives who condone, encourage, or insist upon improper accounting.

Accounting rules have to be followed, and if they aren't, people should be severely penalized for that. . . . Historically, executives have not been held responsible for breaking the rules. They settle and pay a fine. But in some cases the fine that they pay is less than half of the money they made misleading the public. We don't tell an 18-year-old when he robs a convenience store, "If you give half of it back, we'll let you go." But we have allowed that kind of mentality at the white-collar crime level.[7]

6. F. Norris, "Fraud Can Occur at a Company, Even with Auditors Checking," *The New York Times*, 22 September 1995, D6.

7. S. Jordon, "Businesses Can Avoid Trouble by Telling the Truth, Sokol Says," *Omaha World-Herald*, 17 March 2002, 1D.

Questions

1. Place yourself in David Sokol's position. After discovering the suspicious items in JWP's accounting records, would you have taken a different course of action than he did? Why or why not?

2. What measures can and should be taken to make it easier for corporate employees to "blow the whistle" on a fraudulent scheme they uncover within their firm?

3. Should businesses, accounting firms, and other organizations explicitly reward ethical behavior by their employees and executives? Defend your answer.

4. List several measures accounting firms can take to reduce the risk that personal relationships between client personnel and members of an audit engagement team will adversely affect the quality of an audit.

5. Do you believe the 1988 "retention agreement" that Ernst & Young made with JWP was appropriate? Defend your answer.

6. Why do you believe that Ernst & Young agreed to pay a large settlement to JWP's stockholders but chose to contest the lawsuit filed against it by the insurance companies?

Health Management, Inc.

Clifford Hotte had a problem. His company had come up short of its earnings target. For the fiscal year ended April 30, 1995, financial analysts had projected that Health Management, Inc. (HMI), a New York–based pharmaceuticals distributor, would post earnings per share of $0.74. Following the close of fiscal 1995, Drew Bergman, HMI's chief financial officer (CFO) informed Hotte, the company's founder and chief executive officer (CEO), that the actual earnings figure for fiscal 1995 would be approximately $0.54 per share. According to Bergman, Hotte refused to "take the hit," that is, the almost certain drop in HMI's stock price that would follow the announcement of the disappointing earnings.[1] Instead, Hotte wanted HMI to report 1995 earnings in line with analysts' predictions.[2]

Bergman altered HMI's accounting records to allow the company to reach its 1995 earnings target. To lower cost of sales and increase HMI's gross profit and net income, Bergman inflated the company's year-end inventory by approximately $1.8 million. Bergman also posted a few other smaller "adjustments" to HMI's accounting records. Both Bergman and Hotte realized that the company would have to take elaborate measures to conceal the accounting fraud from its audit firm. Bergman was very familiar with BDO Seidman and its audit procedures since he had been employed by that accounting firm several years earlier. In fact, Bergman had supervised BDO Seidman's 1989 and 1990 audits of HMI.

HMI's inventory fraud was not particularly innovative. Corporate executives who want to embellish their company's operating results are aware that the easiest method of achieving that goal is to overstate year end inventory. What was unique about HMI's inventory hoax was that it triggered one of the first major tests of an important and controversial new federal law, the 1995 Private Securities Litigation Reform Act (PSLRA). The PSLRA was the only law passed by Congress during President Clinton's first administration that overcame a presidential veto.

Among the parties most pleased by the passage of the PSLRA were the large, international accounting firms. These firms' mounting litigation losses in the latter decades of the twentieth century had prompted them to lobby Congress to reform the nation's civil litigation system. In particular, the firms argued that they were being victimized unfairly by the growing number of class-action lawsuits. The bulk of these lawsuits were being filed under the Securities Exchange Act of 1934, one of the federal statutes that helped create the regulatory infrastructure for the nation's securities markets in the early 1930s. Top officials of the major accounting firms believed that the PSLRA, which amended key provisions of the 1934 Act, would make it much more difficult for plaintiff attorneys to extract large legal judgments or settlements from their firms. The jury's verdict in favor of BDO Seidman in the HMI lawsuit seemed to support that conclusion. HMI's stockholders filed suit against BDO

---

1. Unless indicated otherwise, the quotations in this case were drawn from court transcripts obtained for the *In Re Health Management, Inc. Securities Litigation* case that was tried in U.S. District Court (Eastern District of New York) in October 1999.

2. I would like to acknowledge a former student of mine, Amy Hollis, for her excellent research that contributed to this case. I would also like to acknowledge the kind assistance of Michael Young.

Seidman for failing to detect the inventory fraud masterminded by Drew Bergman and Clifford Hotte. Michael Young, a prominent New York attorney who headed up BDO Seidman's legal defense team, predicted that the case would become a "watershed event" in the accounting profession's struggle to curb its litigation losses.[3]

Thinly Veiled Extortion

The federal securities laws passed by Congress in the early 1930s not only established a formal regulatory structure for the securities markets, they also strengthened an informal control mechanism that had long served to promote and preserve the integrity of the capital markets. That control mechanism was private securities litigation. The federal securities laws make it unlawful for companies registered with the SEC to issue financial statements that misrepresent their financial condition and operating results. However, the courts have also permitted those statutes to be used as the basis for civil actions. Investors and creditors can file tort actions to recover damages they suffer at the hands of parties who prepare or are otherwise associated with misrepresented financial statements of SEC registrants.

Prior to the passage of the federal securities laws and for several decades thereafter, major institutional investors and large creditors, such as metropolitan banks, filed most private securities lawsuits. Individual investors and creditors who suffered damages as a result of relying on misrepresented financial statements generally found that it was not economically feasible to use the courts to recover their losses. During the 1970s, resourceful attorneys cured this "problem" by employing the concept of a "class- action" lawsuit. In such lawsuits, the legal claims of a large number of individual plaintiffs are consolidated into one joint claim. In exchange for representing these joint plaintiffs, attorneys receive a contingent fee equal to a percentage of any collective judgment or settlement awarded to the plaintiffs.

Thanks to their newfound ability to file class-action lawsuits, attorneys specializing in private securities litigation began vigorously suing parties directly or indirectly linked to allegedly false or misleading financial statements filed with the SEC. Most of these lawsuits claimed one or more violations of Rule 10b-5 of the Securities Exchange Act of 1934. That section of the 1934 Act prohibits the "employment of manipulative and deceptive devices" in connection with the preparation and distribution of the financial statements of SEC-registered companies.[4]

By the late 1970s, class-action lawsuits predicated on Rule 10b-5 violations were commonplace. One legal scholar observed that the "low transaction cost" of filing a class-action lawsuit under the federal securities laws invited abuse of this legal maneuver or tactic by plaintiff attorneys.[5] Former SEC Chairman Richard Breeden frequently spoke out against the epidemic of class-action securities lawsuits plaguing corporations, their executives, and related parties. Breeden characterized the securities class-action system "as a legal regime disconnected from principles of right and wrong that is riddled with abuse and that involves nothing less than thinly veiled extortion."[6]

---

3. G. Cheney, "BDO Wins Landmark Case under New Tort Reform Law," *Accounting Today*, November 22–December 12, 1999, 3.

4. Case 7.9, "First Securities Company of Chicago," presents the complete text of Rule 10b-5.

5. H. E. Milstein, "Recent Developments in the Private Securities Litigation Reform Act," *Securities Litigation & Regulation Reporter*, 12 January 2000, 12.

6. R. M. Phillips and G. C. Miller, "The Private Securities Litigation Reform Act of 1995: Rebalancing Litigation Risks and Rewards for Class Action Plaintiffs, Defendants, and Lawyers," *The Business Lawyer*, August 1996, 51 Bus. Law. 1009.

Class-action securities lawsuits proved to be particularly problematic for the large accounting firms that audit the financial statements of most major public companies. An unavoidable facet of these firms' primary line of business is being burdened occasionally with a client whose executives choose to use "creative" or even blatantly fraudulent accounting methods. An audit firm that fails to detect irregularities in a public client's financial statements faces a considerable risk of being named a defendant in a class-action lawsuit if those irregularities eventually surface. An accounting firm that issues an unqualified opinion on financial statements later proven to contain material errors may only be guilty of accepting a client whose management is inept and/or unethical. Nevertheless, the financial resources of the large accounting firms make them inviting targets for investors and creditors who have relied to their detriment on misleading financial statements.

The executives of many large accounting firms decided that the most rational approach to dealing with class-action lawsuits filed against them was to settle those lawsuits out of court as quickly and quietly as possible. Michael Cook, former CEO of Deloitte & Touche, testified before Congress that his firm often used that strategy because of the leverage plaintiff attorneys had on his firm. That leverage stemmed from the enormous judgments Deloitte & Touche potentially faced if it allowed class-action lawsuits in which it was named as a defendant to go to trial. Most frustrating to Cook and his colleagues at other accounting firms was the need to pay large sums to settle cases in which they were convinced their firms were not at fault. According to Cook, "I am forced to settle cases in which I believe our firm did nothing wrong."[7]

Skeptics questioned the veracity of such statements by Cook and other top executives of major accounting firms. However, empirical research by Professor Zoe-Vonna Palmrose, an authority on audit-related litigation, suggested that the large accounting firms were often named as defendants in class-action lawsuits because of their "deep pockets" rather than because they were at fault.[8] The ability of plaintiff attorneys to goad defendants into settling was borne out by a study of class-action securities lawsuits filed prior to the mid-1990s. Only 2 percent of those lawsuits went to trial, while 20 percent were dismissed. In the remaining 78 percent of those cases the plaintiffs received out-of-court settlements, often multimillion-dollar settlements, from the defendants.[9]

"Relief" Is Spelled . . . PSLRA

In 1991, the Big Six accounting firms launched a costly and coordinated campaign to persuade Congress to reform the nation's private securities litigation system. Congress finally took up that cause during the mid-1990s. The resulting congressional debate was heated, far-reaching, and drew extensive coverage by the media. The most contentious issue addressed in this debate was what "pleading standard" federal judges should invoke when deciding whether a given lawsuit should be allowed to proceed to trial. The Big Six firms wanted Congress to raise the pleading standard, making it more likely that class-action securities lawsuits would be dismissed shortly after being filed.

Congress sided with the Big Six firms when it enacted the PSLRA in December 1995 after overriding President Clinton's veto of the bill. President Clinton vetoed the

7. *Ibid.*

8. Z.-V. Palmrose, "The Joint and Several vs. Proportionate Liability Debate: An Empirical Investigation of Audit-Related Litigation," *Stanford Journal of Law, Business and Finance*, 1994 (Vol.1), 53–72.

9. W. Hamilton, "Stock-Fraud Suits Increase Despite '95 Law," *Los Angeles Times*, 1 July 1998, D1.

bill because he believed the PSLRA's tough pleading standard would make it too difficult for plaintiffs with legitimate claims to have their day in court. Generally, the federal courts have interpreted the PSLRA to require plaintiffs to allege that a defendant was at least "reckless" for a case to proceed to trial. Among other requirements, the law mandates that plaintiffs identify or plead specific facts to support their allegations against defendants. No longer do the federal courts allow "fishing expeditions" by plaintiff attorneys. For example, plaintiff attorneys are now barred from making general, broad-brush allegations of professional misconduct when filing class-action lawsuits against accounting firms, a tactic they commonly used prior to the PSLRA.[10]

Congress's inclusion of a proportionate liability rule in the PSLRA was also a major victory for accounting firms. Previously, the federal courts had imposed joint and several liability on defendants proven to have violated federal securities laws in a civil case. Under this standard, each such defendant was responsible for the entire judgment awarded to the plaintiff. If one or more defendants could not pay their share of a judgment, their portion had to be paid by any remaining defendants that were solvent. The joint and several liability rule served to punish accounting firms since they were often the only solvent defendant in a class-action lawsuit. The PSLRA imposes joint and several liability only on defendants that knowingly participated in a fraud. A defendant guilty of no more than "recklessness" is generally responsible for only a percentage of the plaintiffs' losses. This percentage is equal to the defendant's percentage of responsibility or fault for the given series of events that produced those losses.

Another important feature of the PSLRA for the accounting profession is a clause permitting federal judges to fine plaintiff attorneys who file frivolous securities lawsuits. The PSLRA also contains several clauses that relate directly to the independent audit function, some of which were adapted from the profession's own technical standards. The statute requires audit firms to design audits to provide reasonable assurance of detecting illegal acts that have a material and direct effect on a client's financial statements. Likewise, the law mandates that auditors use appropriate procedures to identify a client's related party transactions and to assess the client's ability to remain a going concern over the following 12 months. A new requirement that the PSLRA imposed on auditors is reporting to the SEC any illegal acts by a client that have a material effect on the client's financial statements—assuming the client refuses to report such items to the SEC.

Following the passage of the PSLRA, members of the accounting profession, trial attorneys, and other interested parties waited anxiously for a major litigation case to test the new statute's key features. That test would ultimately be provided by the class-action lawsuit filed by HMI's stockholders against BDO Seidman.

Hotte Inventory

Clifford Hotte, a licensed pharmacist with a Ph.D. in nuclear pharmacology and a former president of the New York State Board of Pharmacy, founded Homecare Management in 1986. This small company sold medical supplies and equipment to the public and to individuals and firms that provided in-home medical services. Hotte's company grew rapidly and expanded into other lines of business. By the mid-1990s, Hotte had taken his company public and renamed it Health Management, Inc. (HMI). At this point, the company's principal line of business was "chronic disease

---

10. Recognize that since the PSLRA served as an amendment to the Securities Exchange Act of 1934, this statute applies only to lawsuits involving the financial statements of public companies, that is, companies that file periodic financial statements with the SEC.

management." The company specialized in marketing expensive drugs needed by individuals suffering from a wide range of chronic illnesses including AIDS, Alzheimer's, Parkinson's, and schizophrenia.

Hotte retained BDO Seidman as his company's audit firm in 1989. According to subsequent court testimony, the company's prior audit firm resigned because of concerns it had regarding HMI's inventory accounting procedures. One of the auditors assigned to the 1989 and 1990 HMI audit engagement teams was Drew Bergman. Bergman graduated from Queens College in 1979 and accepted an entry-level position with a small accounting firm that later merged with BDO Seidman's predecessor. In 1987, Bergman was transferred to BDO Seidman's Long Island office. Bergman served as the senior audit manager on the 1989 and 1990 HMI audits. In court testimony, Bergman provided the following description of his responsibilities as a senior audit manager:

> In that position, I was responsible for running the engagement from the time that we started working on a particular job, making sure that the staffing was accurate [sic], that we had the appropriate levels of people to do the work that was necessary, and accumulate the work product necessary to support the conclusions that we needed to reach before reaching an opinion on the financial statements.

One of Bergman's subordinates on the 1989 and 1990 HMI audits was Mei-ya Tsai. During the three years Bergman worked for BDO Seidman's Long Island office, Tsai was assigned to approximately 20 engagements he supervised. On the 1989 and 1990 HMI audits, Tsai served as the audit senior. When Drew Bergman resigned from BDO Seidman, Tsai was promoted to audit manager and assumed Bergman's responsibilities on subsequent HMI audits. After Bergman left BDO Seidman, he and Tsai maintained the friendship they had developed while working together at the audit firm. That friendship was strengthened by a relationship that developed between Tsai and Bergman's wife, Nancy. From 1986 through the mid-1990s, Nancy Bergman was the marketing director and administrative office manager for BDO Seidman's Long Island office. Nancy Bergman and Mei-ya Tsai became close friends during that time. The two women, their spouses, and their children frequently visited each other and occasionally spent holidays together.

Clifford Hotte hired Drew Bergman away from BDO Seidman in 1990 and appointed him HMI's CFO. Bergman testified that he was "ultimately responsible" for HMI's accounting records and for "generating financial statements which then were sent to various governmental agencies." In his role as CFO, Bergman met frequently with Hotte to discuss important accounting and financial matters for HMI. During the first week of June 1995, Bergman delivered the unpleasant news to Hotte that HMI's net income for the fiscal year ended April 30, 1995, had fallen short of the company's forecasted profit for that period. After scouring HMI's accounting records with Bergman and confirming the earnings shortfall, Hotte told his CFO that HMI would not report an earnings figure significantly lower than the $0.74 per share financial analysts had predicted the company would earn during fiscal 1995. A flabbergasted Bergman responded, "We are already at the end of the year . . . we're in June. April ended already, sales are done. Inventories have been taken." Following an awkward period of silence, Hotte made himself even more clear to Bergman when he stated that reporting disappointing earnings was "not an option." At this point, Bergman finally realized what Hotte was implying.

After "stewing over" the predicament he found himself in, Bergman went to Hotte's office later that same day with a proposition. "I went back into Dr. Hotte, and I said, 'Dr. Hotte,' I said, 'listen, recruiting people for this, I don't want anything to do with it . . . [but] if you can go out and get them [other subordinates] to go along with this, then I'd be willing to make the [accounting] adjustments.'" Over the next two weeks, Bergman and Hotte worked on their plan. Eventually, Bergman decided to increase the company's April 30, 1995, inventory by approximately $1.8 million. His justification for this increase? He had overlooked $1.8 million of inventory in transit on April 30 when compiling the results of the company's year-end physical inventory. Bergman and Hotte invented a series of bogus events and fabricated several documents to support the in-transit inventory tale. Bergman later admitted in court that these efforts were intended to "fool BDO Seidman," in other words, to conceal the inventory fraud from the auditors.

The centerpiece of the in-transit inventory hoax was a $1.3 million inventory transfer that had supposedly taken place between HMI's Pittsburgh warehouse and another HMI warehouse in New York City. An HMI truck driver had allegedly left the company's Pittsburgh facility on Friday, April 28, 1995, in a company van that contained nearly $1.3 million of drugs. (These drugs were among the most expensive marketed by HMI, which explained why such a sizable dollar value of inventory could plausibly be transported in a relatively small vehicle.) Since the driver left the Pittsburgh warehouse before the inventory counting procedures were begun at that location, the drugs in the van were not included in that site's year-end physical inventory. When the truck driver arrived at the New York warehouse on the afternoon of Monday, May 1, 1995, the inventory counting had been completed at that facility.[11] So the $1.3 million of drugs were also excluded from the year-end physical inventory of the New York warehouse.

Another bogus inventory transfer of more than $500,000 accounted for the remaining portion of the year-end in-transit inventory conjured up by Bergman. These drugs had allegedly been segregated from the other pharmaceuticals in the New York warehouse and intentionally excluded from that site's year-end physical inventory. On his return trip to Pittsburgh, the truck driver had supposedly transported this $500,000 of inventory to HMI's Pittsburgh warehouse. According to Bergman's yarn, this inventory had arrived at the Pittsburgh site too late to be included in its physical inventory.

The seven HMI employees who served as accomplices in the inventory hoax included the truck driver, pharmacists who worked at the HMI warehouses, and the company controller who reported directly to Bergman. These employees were given specific instructions on what they should tell the BDO Seidman auditors regarding the year-end inventory transfers, the objective being to ensure that each conspirator's "story" was consistent with the scam as laid out by Bergman. HMI's controller subsequently testified that Tom Boyle, the audit senior who supervised the fieldwork on the 1995 HMI audit, asked him why the $1.3 million year-end inventory transfer had been necessary. "Drew Bergman basically told me what I had to tell the auditors, and I just reiterated [to Boyle] what he [Bergman] had told me."

Bergman realized that HMI's lack of a perpetual inventory system would make it difficult for BDO Seidman's auditors to uncover the inventory scam that he and Hotte had masterminded. Nevertheless, he was very concerned that BDO Seidman would perform an "inventory rollback" to substantiate the existence assertion for the in-transit inventory. In responding to a question posed by the federal judge who

---

11. The truck driver, who was a relative of Hotte, spent the weekend (supposedly) visiting his aunt in New Jersey, meaning that the $1.3 million of inventory was (supposedly) left unguarded in a residential driveway for more than two days.

presided over the HMI lawsuit, Bergman explained why he was so concerned by this possibility.

> *Your Honor, assuming again that I had all the information, all of the units that were sold and all of the units that were purchased for that period of time, I—you would know conclusively what the ending inventory would have been and whether this inventory in transit would have existed or did not exist.*

"Oh, by the way . . ."

Mei-ya Tsai planned to begin the 1995 audit of HMI in mid-June 1995. But Drew Bergman insisted that the auditors arrive one week later than originally planned. Bergman and his confederates needed the extra week to finalize and shore up the details of the in-transit inventory ruse. The BDO Seidman audit team finally arrived at HMI's headquarters during the latter part of June. On that first day at the client's office, Tsai received a rude shock from her old friend. During a meeting with Tsai, Bergman informed her of the $1.8 million of in-transit inventory at year-end. According to Bergman, Tsai responded to that revelation with a rhetorical question: "Inventory in transit of $1,800,000?"[12] Tsai, no doubt, was alarmed by that figure since it represented nearly 20 percent of HMI's year-end inventory of $9.8 million and approximately one-half of the year-end inventory of HMI's New York warehouse. The company typically had no, or only negligible amounts of, inventory in transit at year-end. Another unusual feature of the year-end inventory transfers was that they had been transported in an HMI vehicle. The company typically used common carriers, such as United Parcel Service (UPS), to transfer significant amounts of inventory from one location to another.

Bergman testified that he only discussed the in-transit inventory on one other occasion with members of the audit engagement team. This second discussion involved Tsai and two BDO Seidman audit partners. One of those partners was Fred Bornstein, the HMI audit engagement partner, while the other partner was Warren Fisk, who served as the concurring review partner on the engagement. During this second meeting, which took place on approximately July 15, 10 days or so before the completion of the audit, Fred Bornstein chastised his former subordinate. "I [Bornstein] said, how could you ever have let this happen? I said, you are an accountant, and you have been an accountant for 20 years, and you know that something like this never should have happened." Warren Fisk, who was scheduled to replace Bornstein as the HMI audit partner in 1996, told Bergman that the in-transit inventory made him "uncomfortable." Fisk informed Bergman that he and his colleagues were considering various additional tests to verify the in-transit inventory and would likely require HMI officials to sign a separate management representation letter confirming that item. Bergman recalled telling Fisk that "you have to do what you have to do."

The in-transit inventory was a key focus of the month-long 1995 audit of HMI. During the engagement, several BDO Seidman auditors questioned, investigated, and fretted over that item. Those individuals included Warren Fisk, Fred Bornstein, Mei-ya Tsai, Tom Boyle, and Jill Karnick, the semi-senior who had been assigned the primary responsibility for auditing inventory. Exhibit 1 lists the principal audit procedures BDO Seidman applied to the in-transit inventory.

---

12. The trial in the HMI case took place in October 1999, more than four years after the 1995 audit was completed. Not surprisingly, the witnesses in the case often had differing recollections of key events that occurred during that audit. Mei-ya Tsai testified that she first learned of the in-transit inventory from Tom Boyle, the audit senior assigned to the 1995 HMI audit. According to Tsai's testimony, early in the audit Boyle called her at BDO Seidman's Long Island office and informed her of the in-transit inventory.

EXHIBIT 1

AUDIT PROCEDURES
APPLIED BY BDO
SEIDMAN TO HMI'S
IN-TRANSIT
INVENTORY

1. Requested the usual documentation that HMI prepared for all inventory transfers.

2. Verified that the inventory transfer documents were signed by both the shipping and receiving pharmacists, identified on the documents the pharmaceuticals reportedly included in the transfers, confirmed that the quantities and per unit prices of those pharmaceuticals agreed with the information previously provided to the auditors by HMI management.

3. Interviewed the truck driver who allegedly transported the year-end inventory transfers. Compared his chronology of the relevant events with the inventory transfer documents and found no inconsistencies.

4. Examined the expense report filed by the truck driver and found it consistent with his chronology of the relevant events and the chronology of those events provided by other HMI personnel.

5. Discussed the inventory transfers with HMI's controller who provided a credible explanation for why the transfers were necessary.

6. Discussed the inventory transfers with HMI's CFO (Bergman) who indicated that he had not been able to prevent the transfers because he had not learned of them until after the fact.

7. Used various mathematical tests, including a gross profit percentage test, to challenge the reasonableness of the company's total year-end inventory; these tests suggested that the year-end inventory was reasonable.

8. Obtained a standard management representations letter and a separate representation letter from company officials focusing exclusively on the in-transit inventory; each of these letters confirmed the existence of the in-transit inventory.

Source: Trial brief prepared for BDO Seidman *In Re Health Management, Inc. Securities Litigation*, U.S. District Court, Eastern District of New York, Civil Action No. 96-CV-889 (ADS) (ARL).

Despite the inordinate time and effort BDO Seidman focused on HMI's inventory account, the audit team also wrestled with several other contentious issues during the 1995 audit. Near the end of the audit, a dispute arose between HMI management and the auditors regarding the adequacy of the allowance for doubtful accounts for the company's more than $30 million of accounts receivable. The auditors proposed an adjusting entry to increase the year-end balance of the allowance account by $1.2 million. Management insisted that an increase of only one-half of that amount was necessary. Complicating BDO Seidman's decision regarding whether to accept the client's proposed adjustment was a letter of inquiry the audit firm had received from the SEC several months earlier. In that letter, the SEC had expressed concern and requested information concerning the method HMI was using to arrive at its allowance for doubtful accounts. Despite the unusual nature of that inquiry, an expert witness for the plaintiffs testified that he found no reference to it in BDO Seidman's 1995 workpapers, nor any evidence that the auditors had modified their audit procedures for the allowance account as a result of the inquiry.

After considerable discussion with HMI's officers, Fred Bornstein decided to accept the client's proposed adjustment of $600,000 for the allowance account. Bornstein provided the following justification for that decision during testimony in the HMI lawsuit: "First of all, it is the client's financial statements. It is not our financial statements. Secondly, we may not be right all the time. The client looks at them [proposed audit adjustments] and decides which ones he agrees with and which ones he doesn't agree with. It is a give and take. And as long as we are satisfied with the client's explanation . . . [we accept the client's decisions regarding those adjustments]."

Another problem the HMI audit team faced during the 1995 engagement was an earnings release issued by the company approximately one week prior to the date that the fieldwork was begun. That press release reported HMI's anticipated, post-audit net income, a figure that had been materially inflated by the fraudulent inventory scheme. This earnings release distressed Mei-ya Tsai and her superiors. Although not required to do so, client executives customarily delay such press releases until their auditors are fairly certain that the anticipated earnings figure is a "firm" number. A company that reports its earnings before the completion of the annual audit exerts subtle but significant pressure on the auditors to "pass" on proposed adjustments that would materially reduce the prematurely released earnings figure. If the auditors insist that a lower earnings figure be included in the audited financial statements, the resulting "earnings surprise" may cause a sharp drop in the client's stock price.

Apparently even more distressing to BDO Seidman than the SEC's inquiry regarding HMI's allowance for doubtful accounts and the client's premature earnings release was an anonymous letter the audit firm received in May 1995. That letter criticized certain HMI accounting procedures and suggested the company was misleading financial analysts tracking the company's stock. The letter also charged that BDO Seidman's independence was being undermined by a close friendship involving Drew Bergman and an undisclosed member of the audit engagement team. (As discussed during the trial, Mei-ya Tsai was the auditor alluded to by the letter.) During subsequent court testimony, Fred Bornstein revealed that in his 30 years of professional audit experience he had never received such a letter. Bornstein reported that he discussed the letter's contents during a meeting with the individuals assigned to the 1995 HMI audit. But neither during that meeting nor afterwards did Bornstein directly ask individual members of the audit team whether they had a relationship with Bergman that would impair their independence.

BDO Seidman completed the 1995 HMI audit in late July. Similar to the audit opinions issued by the firm in previous years on HMI's financial statements, the 1995 audit opinion was unqualified. In December 1995, Drew Bergman was given a new title at HMI, Corporate Development Officer.[13] Paul Jurewicz, an individual with considerable accounting experience in the healthcare industry, was hired to replace Bergman as HMI's CFO. Shortly after he joined HMI, Jurewicz was having a casual conversation with the company's controller, one of Bergman and Hotte's co-conspirators. During that conversation, the controller matter-of-factly referred to the inventory fraud, believing Jurewicz was aware of it. According to the controller, Jurewicz "turned white as a ghost" and abruptly ended the conversation. Immediately, the controller knew the "gig was up."

Jurewicz informed Clifford Hotte of the information he had accidentally obtained from the controller. Hotte denied any knowledge of the inventory fraud and refused to refer the matter to other members of HMI's board or the company's legal counsel. Jurewicz then took matters into his own hands and informed the company's legal counsel. In short order, the company's board retained the services of a former federal

---

13. Effective May 1, 1995, HMI's board of directors had more than doubled Bergman's annual salary to $200,000.

prosecutor to investigate the alleged inventory fraud. In February 1996, HMI issued a press release indicating that irregularities had been discovered in the company's accounting records. That press release sent HMI's stock price spiraling downward and prompted BDO Seidman to withdraw its audit opinion on the company's 1995 financial statements. Next, a flurry of lawsuits and criminal indictments swamped HMI, its corporate officers, and other parties associated with the 1995 financial statements.

Federal prosecutors filed a litany of fraud charges against Clifford Hotte and his co-conspirators. In exchange for agreeing to testify against Hotte and the other conspirators, Drew Bergman was granted immunity from prosecution.[14] Hotte's initial trial ended in a hung jury. Throughout that first trial, Hotte insisted that Bergman had been responsible for the fraudulent inventory scheme. But, in a second trial, a jury convicted Hotte of 14 counts of conspiracy and securities fraud. The former CEO was sentenced to nine years in federal prison, ordered to pay a $250,000 fine, and to make $9.6 million of restitution to the victims of the inventory hoax. HMI never recovered from the trauma inflicted on it by Bergman and Hotte. In October 1997, another healthcare firm acquired HMI for a nominal amount.

The class-action securities lawsuit filed against BDO Seidman by more than 4,000 HMI stockholders initially included several defendants, most of whom were Hotte and Bergman's co-conspirators. Those co-conspirators reached out-of-court settlements and were dismissed from the lawsuit. Bergman was also dismissed from the lawsuit after agreeing to testify truthfully regarding the HMI inventory fraud and other relevant events and circumstances during his tenure at HMI. The two remaining defendants were Hotte and BDO Seidman. Judge Arthur Spatt, who presided over the HMI case, ordered a "directed verdict" against Hotte, who refused to participate in the trial after invoking his Fifth Amendment rights against self-incrimination. As a result, BDO Seidman took center stage as the sole defendant in the class-action lawsuit. The attorneys for HMI's stockholders claimed that the inventory fraud had cost their clients approximately $37 million and that BDO Seidman was responsible for 75 percent of those damages.

As suggested earlier, prior to the passage of the PSLRA, large accounting firms were reluctant to "gamble" that a jury would resolve a class-action lawsuit in their favor. But the team of attorneys retained by BDO Seidman believed the PSLRA gave their client a very reasonable chance of prevailing in court. BDO Seidman followed those attorneys' advice and "rolled the dice." The large accounting firm lost its first gamble when Judge Spatt ruled that the plaintiffs had made sufficiently credible and specific allegations to allow the case to proceed to trial.

Red Flags & Crooks

The skilled teams of attorneys retained by the plaintiffs and defendants in the HMI lawsuit faced many challenges in representing their clients. One of those challenges was shared by both teams of attorneys. The jury that would decide the outcome of the case was composed principally of individuals from blue-collar backgrounds: individuals who had little familiarity with the complex accounting issues, financial reporting matters, and capital market phenomena that would be discussed during the trial. To clarify and strengthen their arguments, each team of attorneys retained prominent expert witnesses to testify during the trial. Plaintiff counsel hired a CPA specializing in forensic services to identify and explain alleged deficiencies in BDO

---

14. Drew Bergman was sanctioned by the SEC. The federal agency barred him from serving as an officer or director of a public company and fined him approximately $75,000.

Seidman's audit procedures. To refute much of that individual's testimony, the defense attorneys relied on a former member of the Auditing Standards Board. Each team of attorneys also hired a damages expert to estimate the losses suffered by the HMI stockholders who had filed the lawsuit. According to the trial transcripts, the two teams paid these expert witnesses approximately $600,000 in total. That amount was four times larger than the approximately $140,000 BDO Seidman received for performing the 1995 HMI audit.

Each team of attorneys went into the trial with a well-rehearsed "game plan." The principal objective of the plaintiff attorneys was to convince the jury that the auditors, at a minimum, had recklessly ignored the auditing profession's technical standards during the 1995 audit and that this reckless conduct had prevented them from uncovering the inventory fraud. To paint a "reckless" image of the auditors in the minds of the jurors, the plaintiff attorneys repeatedly drew attention to the red flags the auditors had allegedly overlooked or, at least, slighted during the 1995 HMI audit. These red flags included, among other items, the SEC's inquiry regarding HMI's allowance for doubtful accounts, the premature press release reporting the company's 1995 earnings, the allegations included in the anonymous letter that BDO Seidman received before the beginning of the 1995 audit, and the suspicious circumstances surrounding the in-transit inventory at year-end.

The plaintiff attorneys faced two major problems in presenting their case to the jury. First, they were forced to use Drew Bergman as their principal witness to attack the credibility and professionalism of the BDO Seidman auditors. Since Bergman admitted on the stand that he had been a primary architect of HMI's inventory fraud, the jury had an obvious reason to question his credibility.

A second and related challenge facing plaintiff counsel was diverting the jury's attention away from the flagrantly criminal conduct of Bergman, Hotte, and the other conspirators who had carried out the inventory fraud. Because of the PSLRA's proportionate liability rule, the plaintiff attorneys had to convince the jury that the BDO Seidman auditors had been reckless during the 1995 HMI audit *and* that they were responsible for a large proportion of the losses suffered by HMI's stockholders. A possible outcome of the trial would be the jury finding the auditors reckless but then concluding that they were responsible for only a negligible percentage of the stockholder losses. Throughout the trial, the plaintiff attorneys struggled with the awkward task of having Bergman describe the fraud that he had designed, while attempting to convince the jury that BDO Seidman was responsible for the bulk of the stockholder losses resulting from that fraud.

The team of defense attorneys led by Michael Young used a three-prong strategy during the trial to help their client prevail. First, at every opportunity, Young and his colleagues attempted to portray the auditors as victims of the inventory fraud rather than as "reckless," if unwitting, accomplices of Bergman and Hotte. Young and the other defense attorneys drew repeated and stark contrasts between the BDO Seidman auditors and the HMI conspirators. In his opening statement, Michael Young introduced the jury one by one to the four BDO Seidman auditors seated in the courtroom who had been deeply involved in the 1995 audit. "Next, I would like to introduce Mei-ya Tsai ... [She] lives in Bellmore with her husband and two children." This tactic was apparently meant to convey to the jury members that the auditors were similar to themselves: hard working, family-oriented individuals who lived in local communities. In contrast, when referring to the participants in the HMI fraud, the defense counsel often invoked derisive epithets such as "those crooks" or "those liars." Near the end of the trial, one of the defense attorneys told the jury members that they had to "distinguish between the liars, and those who were lied to."

A second strategy of the defense counsel was to repeatedly "thump the bible" of the auditing profession, that is, the professional auditing standards. Young and his cohorts constantly challenged the plaintiff attorneys and their witnesses to identify specific requirements in the professional standards that the auditors had violated. The defense attorneys charged that the allegations filed against the auditors were based upon abstract and largely indefensible interpretations of those standards.

The final feature of the defense counsel's trial strategy was intended to blunt the repeated allegations of the plaintiff attorneys that BDO Seidman had failed to properly investigate the $1.8 million of in-transit inventory. Throughout the trial, the defense attorneys used a phrase to characterize the auditors' consideration of that item: "But they didn't stop there." On several occasions when the plaintiff attorneys focused the jurors' attention on the bogus in-transit inventory, the defense attorneys responded by using a flip chart to sequentially and forcefully list the series of audit tests and other procedures (shown in Exhibit 1) that the auditors had used to corroborate the year-end inventory transfers. After each audit test or procedure was explained, the defense attorneys would typically turn to the jury and remark, "But they didn't stop there"—before proceeding to a discussion of the next item.

The Trial: Rollbacks and Relationships

The two most contentious issues that arose during the trial centered on whether the auditors should have completed an inventory rollback during the 1995 HMI audit and whether the relationship between Drew Bergman and Mei-ya Tsai impaired BDO Seidman's independence. As noted earlier, Bergman feared that the auditors would perform an inventory rollback to test the reasonableness of the $1.8 million of in-transit inventory. The CPA who testified as an expert witness for the plaintiff attorneys insisted that had the auditors completed an inventory rollback, they would have determined that the in-transit inventory had never existed.

> Mr. Fox (plaintiff attorney):   *Have you seen any evidence that BDO Seidman even attempted to do any tests which resemble an inventory rollback?*
>
> Mr. Moore (plaintiff expert witness):   *Not that was included in the workpapers, no.*
>
> Mr. Fox: *And do you have an opinion about whether BDO Seidman could have done an inventory rollback in this case?*
>
> Mr. Moore: *Yes, I do.*
>
> Mr. Fox: *And what is that opinion?*
>
> Mr. Moore: *I think it would have been very easy to do. They could have done a rollback. And it was the only test that would have substantiated without a doubt whether or not the in-transit inventory existed.*
>
> Mr. Fox: *If an inventory rollback was performed by BDO Seidman, what would it have shown?*
>
> Mr. Moore: *It would have shown that the in-transit inventory didn't exist and couldn't have existed.*

The expert witness then used a flip chart presentation to walk the jury through an example of how an inventory rollback is performed. Instead of completing an inventory rollback, the expert witness charged BDO Seidman with applying an "audit by conversation" approach to the in-transit inventory. That is, the expert charged that the auditors relied heavily on client representations to support the existence of that inventory.

Michael Young bluntly contested the expert witness's assertion that BDO Seidman should have performed an inventory rollback. Young began by getting the witness to agree that generally accepted auditing standards are the accepted benchmark for assessing the work of independent auditors. Young then produced a bound copy of those standards.

Mr. Young: *This is the bible?*

Mr. Moore: *Basically for auditors, yes.*

Mr. Young: *Okay. There is no section of this book—there is no section of generally accepted auditing standards entitled "in-transit inventory," is there?*

Mr. Moore: *No. There is only a section entitled "inventory" that we have already discussed.*

Mr. Young: *Right. It doesn't tell you exactly how to go about testing in-transit inventory, does it?*

Following these exchanges, Young quoted the following section of the auditing standards: "The independent auditor must exercise his judgment in determining which auditing procedures to apply." Young maintained that this statement demonstrated that the members of the HMI engagement team were well within their rights as professional auditors to decide whether or not to perform an inventory rollback during the 1995 audit. Young was still not satisfied the jury recognized that the expert witness's opinion regarding the need for an inventory rollback during the 1995 audit was just that—one man's opinion. So, in a subsequent exchange, Young pointedly asked the witness: "Now, is it fair to say that this notion that generally accepted auditing standards required an inventory rollback is just something you made up?" The witness responded with a firm "No." Young then handed the witness a copy of the bound auditing standards and asked him to identify the phrase "inventory rollback" in the alphabetical index of those standards. Of course, Young realized that phrase was not included in the index.

Mr. Young: *Is it fair to say that the reference to rollback appears nowhere in the "bible"?*

Mr. Moore: *Yes.*

Mr. Young: *So, basically, it all boils down to your opinion that the auditors should have done more [that is, an inventory rollback]; is that correct?*

Mr. Moore: *Yes.*

Later in the trial, Jill Karnick, the BDO Seidman semi-senior who had been assigned the primary responsibility for auditing HMI's inventory account, took the witness stand. Karnick surprised the jury when she revealed that, in fact, she had attempted during the audit to perform an inventory roll forward, which is essentially equivalent to an inventory rollback.[15] After spending three days on this task, Karnick became frustrated and decided not to continue. She testified that the volume of inventory purchases and sales was simply too large to allow her to complete the roll forward. Karnick was then asked why there was no indication in the audit workpapers that an inventory roll forward had been attempted. She replied that it was "normal practice" to discard the results of "inconclusive" audit tests.

Another surprising revelation made by Karnick during her testimony was that she never spoke directly to either Mei-ya Tsai, the audit manager on the 1995 HMI audit, or Fred Bornstein, the audit engagement partner, regarding the in-transit inventory.

---

15. Ms. Karnick attempted to roll the April 30, 1994, inventory forward to April 30, 1995. The inventory rollback procedure would have involved using purchases and sales data for the first several weeks of fiscal 1996 to "back into" the inventory value as of April 30, 1995.

Mr. Strauss (plaintiff attorney):   *Ms. Karnick, isn't it true you never spoke to your superior, Mei-ya Tsai, about the in-transit inventory?*

Ms. Karnick: *Face to face verbally, no, that's true.*

Mr. Strauss: *In fact, isn't it true that Mei-ya Tsai never even asked you to do anything concerning inventory in transit?*

Ms. Karnick: *Not directly, no.*

Mr. Strauss: *And Mr. Bornstein never instructed you to do anything relating to inventory in transit either, did he?*

Ms. Karnick: *Not directly, no.*

Mr. Strauss: *So, the two most senior people on the audit, the partner and the senior manager, never spoke to you about, or instructed you to do anything concerning, inventory in transit. Correct?*

Ms. Karnick: *Yes.*

On cross-examination, Michael Young had Karnick clarify that it was BDO Seidman's policy for semi-seniors to receive their work instructions and be supervised by their immediate superior on an audit engagement. During the 1995 HMI audit, Tom Boyle, the audit senior assigned to that engagement, had supervised Karnick. In his brief time on the witness stand, Boyle reported that he had only a "limited role" in auditing inventory during the HMI audit. "Jill [Karnick] dealt mostly directly with Mei-ya Tsai on that, as I was out in the field being Jill's supervisor. . . . I would provide guidance basically as to the questions she had." This testimony seemed at odds with Karnick's assertion that she never spoke directly to Tsai regarding the in-transit inventory.

Of all the issues raised during the trial, the one that had the most pervasive implications was the question of whether the close friendship between Drew Bergman and Mei-ya Tsai had impaired BDO Seidman's independence during the 1995 HMI audit. The auditing profession has long maintained that independence is the cornerstone of the independent audit function. If a key member of an audit team loses his or her independence, then all other issues or questions regarding the quality or integrity of the given audit become moot.

The CPA who served as an expert witness for the plaintiffs testified that he believed the social relationship between Bergman and Tsai violated the independence standard included in GAAS: "In all matters relating to the assignment, an independence of mental attitude is to be maintained by the auditor or auditors." According to the expert witness, the Bergman-Tsai friendship "made it extremely difficult to maintain a real level of professional skepticism on the part of the auditor [Ms. Tsai] in looking at the financial statements of HMI." More to the point, the expert witness believed the friendship of the two individuals would have prevented Tsai from going to Bergman after uncovering the inventory scam and telling him, "I think you are a thief, I think you are a fraud."

During her testimony, Mei-ya Tsai acknowledged that BDO Seidman's policy and procedures manual commented on independence concerns posed by social or personal relationships between auditors and officers of a client. A related issue arising during her testimony was that at some point during 1995 she had been offered the position of chief accounting officer (CAO) at HMI, an offer she eventually turned down. Tsai testified that she was unclear regarding the timing of the offer.

Mr. Strauss (plaintiff attorney):   *Isn't it true, Ms. Tsai, that during the 1995 audit, you were being considered for the chief accounting officer position at Health Management?*

Ms. Tsai: *At one time. I don't remember exactly when the job offer was made to me.*

Mr. Strauss: *And you were being considered for that job during the 1995 audit; isn't that correct?*

Ms. Tsai: *I don't know the timing.*

Mr. Strauss: *Isn't it—*

Ms. Tsai: *Definitely not during the audit, no.*

Mr. Strauss: *Isn't it true that your friend, Drew Bergman, recommended you for that job during the 1995 audit?*

Ms. Tsai: *As I said, I don't know the timing. But it can't be during the audit.*

Mr. Strauss: *You are sure of that?*

Ms. Tsai: *I don't believe it's during the audit.*

Later in the trial, the plaintiff attorneys introduced evidence indicating that Drew Bergman apparently recommended that Tsai be offered the CAO position during an HMI board meeting that took place on July 20, 1995. That was one week prior to the date of the audit report issued by BDO Seidman on HMI's 1995 financial statements.

Michael Young resorted to one of his key defense strategies when tackling the contentious question of whether the Bergman-Tsai friendship impaired BDO Seidman's independence. While cross-examining Mr. Moore, the plaintiff's expert witness, Young once more handed him a bound copy of the profession's auditing standards and a copy of the *AICPA Code of Professional Conduct*. "Would you please read to the jury the part where it says that an auditor may not be friends with an audit client?" Moore replied that those "specific words" were not included in either item. Young then asked Moore another question: "Isn't is possible for a representative of an audit firm to be social friends with a representative of a client company and for the audit firm to still be independent? Is that possible, Mr. Moore?" Moore grudgingly replied, "It's possible."

Once the testimony in a jury trial is complete, the presiding judge must give the jury detailed instructions for them to follow during their deliberations. Near the completion of the HMI trial, the two teams of attorneys spent three days debating before Judge Spatt—in the absence of the jury—the information that should be included in the jury instructions. The key issue facing Judge Spatt was how to define "recklessness" in the jury instructions. Both sets of attorneys realized that the outcome of the trial might hinge on Judge Spatt's definition of that critical term. Judge Spatt eventually settled on the following description of recklessness: "The plaintiff must prove that there was an egregious refusal to see the obvious or to investigate the doubtful, or that the auditing judgments made were such that no reasonable auditor would have made the same decision if confronted with the same facts."

The Verdict

During the jury deliberations, the jury foreman sent a note to Judge Spatt asking for further clarification of the term "recklessness." Judge Spatt then brought the jury members back into the courtroom and gave them additional instructions. Judge Spatt reiterated the important distinction between negligence and recklessness. "I want to make clear that an auditor is not liable under Section 10(b) and Rule 10b-5 [of the Securities Exchange Act of 1934] merely because he or she made a mistake or was merely negligent. I repeat, recklessness is more than mere negligence. Reckless conduct represents grossly unreasonable or rash behavior."

Shortly after being sequestered once more, the jury arrived at its verdict in favor of BDO Seidman. In celebrating the victory, Michael Young commented on the PSLRA's impact on the case. "It is questionable whether an accounting firm could muster the courage to take a case like this to trial absent the innovations under the Reform

Act."[16] Young went on to explain that the PSLRA's elimination of joint and several liability for auditors guilty of no more than recklessness was the source of BDO Seidman's "courage" to defend itself in court.

Jeffrey Zwerling, one of the plaintiff attorneys, spoke with several of the jurors following the trial.[17] Zwerling reported that the jurors had difficulty grasping the legal definition of recklessness even after asking Judge Spatt to clarify that term. Zwerling implied that confusion might have predisposed the jury to rule in favor of the auditors. BDO Seidman's general legal counsel put a different "spin" on the outcome of the trial. He maintained that the plaintiff attorneys' strategy of relying on Drew Bergman's testimony "blew up in their faces" since Bergman admitted during the trial that he had specifically designed the fraud to deceive the auditors.[18]

Despite the favorable outcome of the HMI lawsuit for BDO Seidman, the post-PSLRA litigation trends have been mixed for the public accounting profession. Since 1995, class-action securities lawsuits have generally declined on an annual basis when expressed as a percentage of the total number of public companies.[19] However, the percentage of such lawsuits predicated on accounting irregularities has steadily increased since 1995. This is bad news for auditors since they are more likely to be named as defendants in a class-action securities lawsuit when a client is charged with manipulating its accounting records. More bad news for audit firms: the average settlement paid to resolve class-action lawsuits involving charges of accounting irregularities has also been rising.[20]

Questions

1. BDO Seidman's attorneys pointed out correctly that professional standards do not prohibit auditors and client personnel from being "friends." At what point do such relationships result in violations of the auditor independence rules and guidelines? Provide hypothetical examples to strengthen your answer.

2. According to court testimony, on July 20, 1995, Drew Bergman recommended to HMI's board of directors that Mei-ya Tsai be hired as the company's chief accounting officer (CAO). One week later, BDO Seidman issued its audit report on HMI's 1995 financial statements. Under presently existing professional standards would this situation have presented an independence "problem" for BDO Seidman? Defend your answer.

3. Under what circumstances is an inventory rollback typically performed? How valid is the evidence yielded by this audit procedure? Explain.

16. M. Riccardi, "Accounting Fraud Trial Breaks New Ground," *New York Law Journal*, 29 October 1999, 1.

17. E. L. Rosen, "Defendants Heartened by the First Trial of PSLRA Case," *The National Law Journal*, 15 November 1999, B5.

18. E. MacDonald, "Federal Jury Exonerates BDO Seidman in Accounting Suit over Audit of Firm," *The Wall Street Journal*, 28 October 1999, B2.

19. An exception to this trend was 2001. The bursting of the "dot-com" bubble in the stock market triggered an usually large number of class-action securities lawsuits in that year.

20. In August 2007, a Florida jury ordered BDO Seidman to pay more than $500 million in damages to a plaintiff in a civil case. A spokesperson for BDO Seidman reported that the firm intended to appeal the jury's decision. Many parties within the accounting profession believed that if BDO Seidman was ultimately forced to pay the large jury award, the firm's economic viability might be threatened.

4. Jill Karnick abandoned her attempt to complete an inventory roll forward because of the considerable amount of work the procedure involved. Do you believe she made an appropriate decision given the circumstances she faced? How should auditors weigh the cost of an audit procedure, in terms of time and other resources, against the quantity and quality of evidence that it yields?

5. Should the results of inconclusive audit tests be included in audit workpapers? Defend your answer.

6. A major focus of the trial in this case was BDO Seidman's consideration of, and response to, the "red flags" apparent during the 1995 HMI audit. Define or describe the phrase "red flags." Explain the impact of red flags identified by auditors on each major phase of an audit.

7. The PSLRA requires auditors to report to the SEC illegal acts "that would have a material effect" on a client's financial statements, assuming client management refuses to do so. Briefly describe three hypothetical situations involving potential illegal acts discovered by auditors. Indicate whether the auditors involved in these situations should insist that client management report the given item to the SEC. Defend your decision for each item.

The Leslie Fay Companies

Paul Polishan graduated with an accounting degree in 1969 and immediately accepted an entry-level position in the accounting department of The Leslie Fay Companies, a women's apparel manufacturer based in New York City. Fred Pomerantz, Leslie Fay's founder, personally hired Polishan. Company insiders recall that Pomerantz saw in the young accounting graduate many of the same traits that he possessed. Both men were ambitious, hard driving, and impetuous by nature.

After joining Leslie Fay, Polishan quickly struck up a relationship with John Pomerantz, the son of the company's founder. John had joined the company in 1960 after earning an economics degree from the Wharton School at the University of Pennsylvania. In 1972, the younger Pomerantz became Leslie Fay's president and assumed responsibility for the company's day-to-day operations. Over the next few years, Polishan would become one of John Pomerantz's most trusted allies within the company. Polishan quickly rose through the ranks of Leslie Fay, eventually becoming the company's chief financial officer (CFO) and senior vice president of finance.

Leslie Fay's corporate headquarters were located in the heart of Manhattan's bustling garment district. However, the company's accounting offices were 100 miles to the northwest in Wilkes-Barre, Pennsylvania. During Polishan's tenure as Leslie Fay's top accounting and finance officer, the Wilkes-Barre location was tagged with the nickname "Poliworld." The strict and autocratic Polishan ruled the Wilkes-Barre site with an iron fist. When closing the books at the end of an accounting period, Polishan often required his subordinates to put in 16-hour shifts and to work through the weekend. Arriving two minutes late for work exposed Poliworld inhabitants to a scathing reprimand from the CFO. To make certain that his employees understood what he expected of them, Polishan posted a list of rules within the Wilkes-Barre offices that documented their rights and privileges in minute detail. For example, they had the right to place one, and only one, family photo on their desks. Even Leslie Fay personnel in the company's Manhattan headquarters had to cope with Polishan's domineering manner. When senior managers in the headquarters office requested financial information from Wilkes-Barre, Polishan often sent them a note demanding to know why they needed the information.

Polishan's top lieutenant at the Wilkes-Barre site was the company controller, Donald Kenia. On Polishan's frequent trips to Manhattan, Kenia assumed control of the accounting offices. Unlike his boss, Kenia was a soft-spoken individual who apparently enjoyed following orders much more than giving them. Because of Kenia's meek personality, friends and coworkers were stunned in early February 1993 when he took full responsibility for a large accounting fraud revealed to the press by John Pomerantz. Investigators subsequently determined that Leslie Fay's earnings had been overstated by approximately $80 million from 1990 through 1992.

Following the public disclosure of the large fraud, John Pomerantz repeatedly and adamantly insisted that he and the other top executives of Leslie Fay, including Paul Polishan, had been unaware of the massive accounting irregularities perpetrated by Kenia. Nevertheless, many parties inside and outside the company expressed doubts regarding Pomerantz's indignant denials. Kenia was not a major stockholder and did not have an incentive-based compensation contract tied to the company's earnings, meaning that he had not benefited directly from the grossly inflated earnings figures he had manufactured. On the other hand, Pomerantz, Polishan, and several other Leslie Fay executives held large blocks of the company's stock and had received substantial year-end bonuses, in some cases bonuses larger than their annual salaries, as a result of Kenia's alleged scam. Even after Kenia pleaded guilty to fraud charges, many third parties remained unconvinced that he had directed the fraud. When asked by a reporter to comment on Kenia's confession, a Leslie Fay employee and close friend of Kenia indicated that he was a "straight arrow, a real decent guy" and then went on to observe that, "something doesn't add up here."[1]

Lipstick-Red Rolls Royces and the Orient Express

Similar to many of his peers, Fred Pomerantz served his country during World War II. But instead of storming the beaches of Normandy or pursuing Rommel across North Africa, Pomerantz served his country by making uniforms, uniforms for the Women's Army Corps. Following the war, Pomerantz decided to make use of the skills he had acquired in the military by creating a company to manufacture women's dresses. He named the company after his daughter, Leslie Fay. His former subordinates and colleagues in the industry recall that Pomerantz was a "character." Over the years, he reportedly developed a strong interest in gambling, enjoyed throwing extravagant parties, and reveled in shocking new friends and business associates by pulling up his shirt to reveal knife scars he had collected in encounters with ruffians in some of New York's tougher neighborhoods. Adding to Pomerantz's legend within the top rung of New York's high society was his lipstick-red Rolls Royce that he used to cruise up and down Manhattan's crowded streets.

Pomerantz's penchant for adventure and revelry did not prevent him from quickly establishing his company as a key player in the volatile and intensely competitive women's apparel industry. From the beginning, Pomerantz focused Leslie Fay on one key segment of that industry. He and his designers developed moderately priced and stylishly conservative dresses for women aged 30 through 55. Leslie Fay's principal customers were the large department store chains that flourished in major metropolitan areas in the decades following World War II. By the late 1980s, Leslie Fay was the largest supplier of women's dresses to department stores. At the time, Leslie Fay's principal competitors included Donna Karan, Oscar de la Renta, Nichole Miller, Jones New York, and Albert Nipon. But, in the minds of most industry observers, Liz Claiborne, an upstart company that had been founded in 1976 by an unknown designer and her husband, easily ranked as Leslie Fay's closest and fiercest rival. Liz Claiborne was the only publicly owned women's apparel manufacturer in the late 1980s that had larger annual sales than Leslie Fay.

Fred Pomerantz took his company public in 1952. In the early 1980s, the company went private for a period of several years via a leveraged buyout orchestrated by John Pomerantz, who became the company's chief executive officer (CEO) and chairman of the board following his father's death in 1982. The younger Pomerantz pocketed $40 million and a large bundle of Leslie Fay stock when the firm reemerged as a public company in 1986. Like his father before him, John Pomerantz believed that the top executive of a company involved in the world of fashion should exhibit a certain amount of panache. As a result, the popular and outgoing businessman invested in several Broadway shows and became a mainstay on Manhattan's celebrity circuit. The windfall that Pomerantz realized in the early 1980s

---

1. S. Strom, "Accounting Scandal at Leslie Fay," *The New York Times*, 2 February 1993, D1.

allowed him to buy an elegant, Mediterranean-style estate in Palm Beach, Florida, where he often consorted during the winter months with New York City's rich and famous. To reward his company's best clients, he once rented the legendary Orient Express for an extended and festive railway jaunt across northern Europe and Asia.

Despite Leslie Fay's size and prominence in the apparel industry, John Pomerantz continued operating the company much like his father had for decades. Unlike his competitors, Pomerantz shunned extensive market testing to gauge women's changing tastes in clothes. Instead, he relied on his and his designers' intuition in developing each season's new offerings. Pomerantz was also slow to integrate computers into his company's key internal functions. Long after most women apparel manufacturers had developed computer linkages to monitor daily sales of their products at major customer outlets, Leslie Fay officials continued to track the progress of their sales by telephoning large customers on a weekly basis. Pomerantz's insistence on doing business the "old-fashioned way" also meant that the company's Wilkes-Barre location was slow to take advantage of the speed and efficiency of computerized data processing.

Management's aversion to modern business practices and the intense competition within the women's apparel industry did not prevent Leslie Fay from prospering after John Pomerantz succeeded his father. Thanks to the younger Pomerantz's business skills, Leslie Fay's annual revenues and earnings grew robustly under his leadership.

Fashion Becomes Unfashionable

By the late 1980s, a trend that had been developing within the women's apparel industry for several years became even more evident. During that decade, fashion gradually became unfashionable. The so-called "casualization" of America meant that millions of consumers began balking at the new designs marketed by apparel manufacturers, opting instead for denims, t-shirts, and other more comfortable attire, including well-worn, if not tattered, garments that they had purchased years earlier. Initially, this trend had a much more pronounced impact on the buying habits of younger women. But, gradually, even women in the 30- to 55-year-old age bracket, the consumers targeted by Leslie Fay, decided that casual was the way to go.

The trend toward casual clothing had the most dramatic impact on women's dress sales. Since Leslie Fay's inception, the company had concentrated its product offerings on dresses, even after pantsuits became widely recognized as suitable and stylish for women of all ages during the 1970s. In the early 1970s, annual dress sales began gradually declining. Most corporate executives in the women's apparel industry believed this trend would eventually reverse. However, the preference for more casual apparel that developed during the 1980s resulted in declining dress sales throughout the end of the century.

The recession of the late 1980s and early 1990s compounded the problems facing the women's apparel industry. That recession caused many consumers to curtail their discretionary expenditures, including purchases of new clothes. The economy-wide decline in retail spending had far-reaching implications for the nation's major department store chains, Leslie Fay's principal customers. Even as other segments of the economy improved, continued weakness in the retail sector cut deeply into the sales and earnings of department stores. Eventually, several large chains were forced to merge with competitors or to liquidate. In late 1989, Leslie Fay incurred a substantial loss when it wrote off a receivable from Allied/Federated Department Stores after the large retailer filed for bankruptcy. Many of the department store chains that survived wrangled financial concessions from their suppliers. These concessions included longer payment terms, more tax return policies, and increased financial assistance to develop and maintain in-store displays, kiosks, and apparel boutiques.

The structural and economic changes affecting the women's apparel industry during the late 1980s and early 1990s had a major impact on most of its leading companies. Even Liz Claiborne, whose revenues had zoomed from $47 million in 1979 to more than $1 billion by 1987, faced slowing sales from its major product lines and was eventually forced to take large inventory write-downs. Occasionally, industry publications reported modest quarterly sales increases. But the companies that benefited the most from those increases were not the leading apparel manufacturers but rather firms such as Clothestime that marketed their wares to discount merchandisers.

Despite the trauma being experienced by its key competitors, Leslie Fay reported impressive sales and earnings throughout the late 1980s and early 1990s. Leslie Fay's typical quarterly earnings release during that time frame indicated that the company had posted record earnings and sales for the just completed period. For example, in October 1991, John Pomerantz announced that Leslie Fay had achieved record earnings for the third quarter of the year despite the "continued sluggishness in retail sales and consumer spending."[2] Exhibit 1 presents Leslie Fay's consolidated balance sheets and income statements for 1987 through 1991. For comparison purposes, Exhibit 2 presents norms for key financial ratios within the women's apparel industry in 1991. These benchmark ratios are composite amounts derived from data reported by the investment services that publish financial ratios and other financial measures for major industries.

The gregarious John Pomerantz remained upbeat to the business press regarding his company's future prospects even as Leslie Fay's competitors questioned how the company was able to sustain strong sales and earnings in the face of the stubborn recession gripping the retail sector. Privately, though, Pomerantz was worried. Pomerantz realized that retailers were increasingly critical of Leslie Fay's product line. "Old-fashioned," "matronly," "drab," and "overpriced" were adjectives that the company's sales reps routinely heard as they made their sales calls. To keep his major customers happy, Pomerantz had to approve significant markdowns in Leslie Fay's wholesale prices and grant those customers large rebates when they found themselves "stuck" with excess quantities of the company's products. To keep investors happy, Pomerantz lobbied financial analysts tracking Leslie Fay's stock. One analyst reported that an "irate" Pomerantz called her in 1992 and chastised her for issuing an earnings forecast for Leslie Fay that was too "pessimistic."[3]

"Houston, We Have a Problem"

On Friday morning, January 29, 1993, Paul Polishan called John Pomerantz, who was on a business trip in Canada. Polishan told Pomerantz, "We got a problem . . . maybe a little more than just a problem."[4] Polishan then informed his boss of the enormous accounting hoax that Donald Kenia had secretly carried out over the past several years. According to Polishan, Kenia had admitted to masterminding the fraud, although some of his subordinates had helped him implement and conceal the various scams. Pomerantz's first reaction to the startling news? Disbelief. "I thought it was a joke."[5]

---

2. *Business Wire*, "Leslie Fay Announces Record Earnings," 17 October 1991.

3. T. Agins, "Dressmaker Leslie Fay Is an Old-Style Firm That's in a Modern Fix," *The Wall Street Journal*, 23 February 1993, A8.

4. Strom, "Accounting Scandal at Leslie Fay."

5. T. Agins, "Leslie Fay Says Irregularities in Books Could Wipe Out '92 Profit; Stock Skids," *The Wall Street Journal*, 2 February 1993, A5.

EXHIBIT 1

THE LESLIE FAY
COMPANIES
1987–1991
BALANCE SHEETS

The Leslie Fay Companies
Consolidated Balance Sheets 1987–1991
(in millions)

ASSETS	1991	1990	1989	1988	1987
Current Assets:					
Cash	$ 4.7	$ 4.7	$ 5.5	$ 5.5	$ 4.1
Receivables (net)	118.9	139.5	117.3	109.9	82.9
Inventories	126.8	147.9	121.1	107.0	83.0
Prepaid Expenses & Other Current Assets	19.7	22.5	19.5	16.4	15.9
Total Current Assets	270.1	314.6	263.4	238.8	185.9
Property, Plant, and Equipment	39.2	30.0	27.2	25.9	24.1
Goodwill	81.3	88.1	91.2	94.1	90.3
Deferred Charges and Other Assets	5.2	6.2	5.5	4.2	5.1
Total Assets	$395.8	$438.9	$387.3	$363.0	$305.4
LIABILITIES AND STOCKHOLDERS' EQUITY					
Current Liabilities:					
Notes Payable	35.0	48.0	23.0	29.0	15.5
Current Maturities of Long-term Debt	.3	.3	.3	.3	1.4
Accounts Payable	31.9	43.3	38.6	45.6	31.6
Accrued Interest Payable	3.0	3.8	4.1	3.9	3.7
Accrued Compensation	16.9	14.9	19.5	16.6	10.6
Accrued Expenses & Other	4.3	6.4	5.8	7.2	7.4
Income Taxes Payable	1.4	2.3	4.6	6.1	1.8
Total Current Liabilities	92.8	119.0	95.9	108.7	72.0
Long-term Debt	84.4	129.7	129.0	116.3	116.6
Deferred Credits & Other Noncurrent Liabilities	2.8	2.6	2.7	4.2	4.9
Stockholders' Equity:					
Common Stock	20.0	20.0	20.0	20.0	20.0
Capital in Excess of Par Value	82.2	82.2	82.1	82.2	82.2
Retained Earnings	156.9	127.6	98.5	72.8	50.5
Other	(34.3)	(31.5)	(31.9)	(32.0)	(31.7)
Treasury Stock	(9.0)	(10.7)	(9.0)	(9.1)	(9.1)
Total Stockholders' Equity	215.8	187.6	159.7	133.8	111.9
Total Liabilities and Stockholders' Equity	$395.8	$438.9	$387.3	$363.0	$305.4

(continued)

When revealing the fraud to the press the following Monday, Pomerantz denied having any clue as to what might have motivated Kenia to misrepresent Leslie Fay's financial data. Pomerantz also denied that he and the other top executives of Leslie Fay had suspected Kenia of any wrongdoing. He was particularly strident in defending his close friend Paul Polishan who had supervised Kenia and who was directly responsible for the integrity of Leslie Fay's accounting records. Pomerantz firmly told a reporter that Polishan "didn't know anything about this."[6]

6. *Ibid.*

EXHIBIT 1—
continued

THE LESLIE FAY
COMPANIES
1987–1991
INCOME STATEMENTS

The Leslie Fay Companies
Consolidated Income Statements 1987–1991
(in millions)

	1991	1990	1989	1988	1987
Net Sales	$836.6	$858.8	$786.3	$682.7	$582.0
Cost of Sales	585.1	589.4	536.8	466.3	403.1
Gross Profit	251.5	269.4	249.5	216.4	178.9
Operating Expenses:					
Selling, Warehouse, General and					
Administrative	186.3	199.0	183.8	156.2	132.5
Amortization of Intangibles	2.7	2.9	2.6	3.3	3.8
Total Operating Expenses	189.0	201.9	186.4	159.5	136.3
Operating Income	62.5	67.5	63.1	56.9	42.6
Interest Expense	18.3	18.7	19.3	18.2	16.4
Income Before Non-recurring Charges					
(Credits)	44.2	48.8	43.8	38.7	26.2
Non-recurring Charges (Credits)	—	—	—	—	(5.0)
Income Before Taxes on Income	44.2	48.8	43.8	38.7	31.2
Income Taxes	14.8	19.7	18.0	16.4	11.5
Net Income	$ 29.4	$ 29.1	$ 25.8	$ 22.3	$ 19.7
Net Income per Share	$ 1.55	$ 1.53	$ 1.35	$ 1.17	$ 1.03

EXHIBIT 2

THE LESLIE FAY
COMPANIES 1991
INDUSTRY NORMS
FOR KEY FINANCIAL
RATIOS

Liquidity:

Current Ratio	1.8
Quick Ratio	.9

Solvency:

Debt to Assets	.53
Times Interest Earned	4.2
Long-term Debt to Equity	.14

Activity:

Inventory Turnover	6.7
Age of Inventory	53.7 days
Accounts Receivable Turnover	8.0
Age of Accounts Receivable	45.5 days
Total Asset Turnover	3.1

Profitability:

Gross Margin	31.5%
Profit Margin on Sales	2.2%
Return on Total Assets	6.0%
Return on Equity	14.0%

During the following weeks and months, an increasingly hostile business press hounded Pomerantz for more details of the fraud, while critics openly questioned whether he was being totally forthcoming regarding his lack of knowledge of Kenia's accounting scams. Responding to those critics, the beleaguered CEO maintained that rather than being involved in the fraud, he was its principal victim. "Do I hold myself personally responsible? No. In my heart of hearts, I feel that I'm a victim. I know there are other victims. But I'm the biggest victim."[7] Such protestations did not prevent critics from questioning why Pomerantz had blithely accepted Leslie Fay's impressive operating results while many of the company's competitors were struggling financially.

Shortly after Pomerantz publicly disclosed Kenia's fraud, Leslie Fay's audit committee launched an intensive investigation of its impact on the company's financial statements for the previous several years. The audit committee retained Arthur Andersen & Co. to help complete that study. Pending the outcome of the investigation, Pomerantz reluctantly placed Polishan on temporary paid leave. BDO Seidman had served as Leslie Fay's audit firm since the mid-1970s and issued unqualified opinions each year on the company's financial statements. Following Pomerantz's disclosure of the fraud, BDO Seidman withdrew its audit opinions on the company's 1990 and 1991 financial statements. In the ensuing weeks, Leslie Fay stockholders filed several large lawsuits naming the company's management team and BDO Seidman as defendants. In April 1993, BDO Seidman officials contacted the Securities and Exchange Commission (SEC) and inquired regarding the status of their firm's independence from Leslie Fay given the pending lawsuits. The SEC informed BDO Seidman that its independence was jeopardized by those lawsuits, which forced the firm to resign as Leslie Fay's auditor in early May 1993. Company management immediately appointed Arthur Andersen as Leslie's Fay new auditor.

In September 1993, Leslie Fay's audit committee completed its eight-month investigation of the accounting fraud. The resulting 600-page report was reviewed by members of Leslie Fay's board and then submitted to the SEC and federal prosecutors. Although the report was not released publicly, several of its key findings were leaked to the press. The most startling feature of the fraud was its pervasive nature. According to a company insider who read the report, "There wasn't an entry on the cost side of the company's ledgers for those years that wasn't subject to some type of rejiggering."[8] The key focus of the fraudulent activity was Leslie Fay's inventory. Kenia and his subordinates had inflated the number of dresses manufactured each quarterly period to reduce the per unit cost of finished goods and increase the company's gross profit margin on sales. During period-ending physical inventories, the conspirators "manufactured" the phantom inventory they had previously entered in the company's accounting records. Forging inventory tags for nonexistent products, inflating the number of dresses of a specific style on hand, and fabricating large amounts of bogus in-transit inventory were common ruses used to overstate inventory during the period-ending counts.

Other accounting gimmicks used by Kenia included failing to accrue period-ending expenses and liabilities, "prerecording" orders received from customers as consummated sales to boost Leslie Fay's revenues near the end of an accounting period, failing to write off uncollectible receivables, and ignoring discounts on outstanding receivables granted to large customers experiencing slow sales of the company's products. Allegedly, Kenia decided each period what amount of profit Leslie Fay should report. He and his subordinates then adjusted Leslie Fay's key financial numbers until that profit figure was achieved. From 1990 through the end of 1992, approximately $130 million of bogus entries were made in Leslie Fay's accounting records. These fraudulent entries overstated the company's profits by approximately $80 million.

---

7. E. Lesly, "Who Played Dress-up with the Books?" *Business Week*, 15 March 1993, 34.

8. T. Agins, "Report Is Said to Show Pervasive Fraud at Leslie Fay," *The Wall Street Journal*, 27 September 1993, B3.

Kenia and his co-conspirators molded Leslie Fay's financial statements so that key financial ratios would be consistent with historical trends. The financial ratio that the fraudsters paid particular attention to was Leslie Fay's gross profit percentage. For several years, the company's gross profit percentage had hovered near 30 percent. Leslie Fay's actual gross profit percentage was approximately 20 percent by the early 1990s, but Kenia relied on his assorted bag of accounting tricks to inflate that financial ratio to near its historical norm.

Excerpts released to the press from the audit committee's report largely exonerated John Pomerantz of any responsibility for Leslie Fay's accounting irregularities. The report indicated that there was no evidence that he and other members of Leslie Fay's headquarters management team had been aware of those irregularities but did criticize those executives for failing to aggressively pursue unusual and suspicious circumstances they had encountered during the course of Kenia's fraud. If those circumstances had been vigorously investigated, the audit committee concluded that the fraud might have been uncovered much earlier than January 1993. In particular, the audit committee questioned why Pomerantz had not investigated Leslie Fay's remarkably stable gross profit percentage in the early 1990s given the significant problems facing other women's dress manufacturers and the apparently poor response to many of the company's new product offerings during that period.

Following the completion of the audit committee's investigation in September 1993, Leslie Fay's board of directors allowed John Pomerantz to remain as the CEO but relieved him of all financial responsibilities related to the company's operations. The board created a committee of outside directors to oversee the company's operations while Leslie Fay dealt with the aftermath of the large-scale fraud. The board also dismissed Paul Polishan as Leslie Fay's CFO and senior vice president of finance and replaced him with an Arthur Andersen partner who had been involved in the audit committee investigation.

BDO Seidman: Odd Man Out

In April 1993, Leslie Fay filed for protection from its creditors under Chapter 11 of the federal bankruptcy code. Press reports of Kenia's fraudulent scheme had cut off the company's access to the additional debt and equity capital that it needed to continue normal operations. By early April 1993, the price of Leslie Fay's stock had dropped by nearly 85 percent since the first details of the fraud had become public two months earlier. The company's plummeting stock price and the mounting criticism of its officers in the business press triggered additional lawsuits by angry stockholders against Pomerantz, other Leslie Fay executives, and the company's longtime auditor, BDO Seidman.

The lawsuits that named BDO Seidman as a defendant charged that the firm had been at least reckless in auditing Leslie Fay's periodic financial statements during the early 1990s. Howard Schilit, an accounting professor and forensic accounting specialist, suggested in the business press that Leslie Fay's financial data had been replete with red flags. These red flags included implausible trend lines in the company's financial data, implausible relationships between key financial statement items, and unreasonably generous bonuses paid to top executives, bonuses linked directly to the record earnings Leslie Fay reported each successive period. For 1991, John Pomerantz had received total salary and bonuses of $3.6 million, three times more than the 1991 compensation of Liz Claiborne's CEO, whose company reported sales more than double those of Leslie Fay's.

BDO Seidman officials chafed at published reports criticizing their firm's Leslie Fay audits. Those officials insisted that BDO Seidman was being indicted in the press on the basis of innuendo and incomplete information since the full details of the investigative report issued by Leslie Fay's audit committee had not been released to the public. These same individuals also maintained that Leslie Fay's top management, principally John Pomerantz, should shoulder the bulk of the responsibility for not discovering the massive fraud.

During various court proceedings following the disclosure of the Leslie Fay fraud, many parties questioned the objectivity of the forensic investigation supervised by Leslie Fay's audit committee that had largely vindicated Pomerantz and other top company executives. These skeptics suggested that the members of the audit committee had been reluctant to criticize the company's top executives who were their colleagues. To squelch such criticism, the federal judge presiding over Leslie Fay's bankruptcy filing appointed an independent examiner, Charles Stillman, to prepare another report on the details of the fraud. Stillman was also charged with identifying the individuals responsible for the fraud and those responsible for failing to discover it.

In August 1994, the U.S. Bankruptcy Court released the so-called Stillman Report. This document corroborated the key findings of the audit committee investigation. Similar to the audit committee report, the Stillman Report largely exonerated Leslie Fay's top executives, including John Pomerantz, of any responsibility for the fraud. "The examiner's report concludes there is no evidence to suggest that viable claims exist against any members of Leslie Fay's current management or its board of directors."[9] The Stillman Report went on to suggest that although there were likely "viable claims" against Kenia and Polishan based upon "presently available information,"[10] the limited assets of those individuals made it economically infeasible for the bankruptcy court to pursue those claims. Finally, the Stillman Report indicted the quality of BDO Seidman's audits of Leslie Fay by asserting that there may be "claims worth - pursuing against . . . BDO Seidman,"[11] and that "it is likely BDO Seidman acted negligently in performing accounting services for Leslie Fay."[12]

Following the release of the Stillman Report, Leslie Fay's stockholders filed a large civil lawsuit against BDO Seidman in the federal bankruptcy courts. At approximately the same time, BDO Seidman filed a lawsuit against Leslie Fay's principal officers, including John Pomerantz. In commenting on this latter lawsuit, BDO Seidman officials reported that "Leslie Fay's upper management not only tolerated fraud to bolster reported financial results but they benefited directly from its execution. As BDO Seidman has said from the beginning, we are victims of this fraud. As Leslie Fay's outside auditors, we were deceived by the company. Our reputation has suffered needlessly as a result of Leslie Fay's deliberate deception."[13]

Leslie Fay's management responded immediately to the news that BDO Seidman had named John Pomerantz and his fellow officers as defendants in a large civil lawsuit. "The unsubstantiated and unfounded allegations made today by BDO Seidman are a classic example of 'revisionist history' and are clearly an attempt by the accounting firm to divert attention from its own apparent negligence by blaming others."[14]

9. *Business Wire*, "Independent Examiner Confirms Findings of Leslie Fay's Audit Committee Investigation," 16 August 1994.

10. *Ibid.*

11. *Ibid.*

12. *Business Wire*, "Leslie Fay Responds to Unfounded Allegations by BDO Seidman," 29 March 1995.

13. *PR Newswire*, "BDO Seidman Announces Cross-Claims and Third Party Complaints against Key Leslie Fay Figures," 29 March 1995.

14. *Business Wire*, "Leslie Fay Responds to Unfounded Allegations."

EPILOGUE

In July 1997, a federal judge approved a $34 million settlement to the large number of lawsuits filed by Leslie Fay's stockholders and creditors against the company, its executives, and BDO Seidman. BDO Seidman contributed $8 million to the settlement pool, although the firm reported that it was agreeing to the settlement only because it was the most economical and expeditious way to "put this matter behind us."[15] In June 1997, Leslie Fay emerged from federal bankruptcy court. Over the next several years, the much smaller company returned to a profitable condition before being purchased in late 2001 by a large investment fund. A few months later, in April 2002, John Pomerantz received a lifetime achievement award at the annual American Image Awards, a glitzy event sponsored by the major companies and organizations in the fashion industries.

On October 31, 1996, federal prosecutors filed a 21-count fraud indictment against Paul Polishan. The specific charges included conspiracy, making false statements to the SEC, bank fraud, and wire fraud. Unknown to the public, three years earlier, Donald Kenia had broken down under relentless questioning by federal investigators and admitted that Polishan, his former boss, had been the architect of the Leslie Fay fraud. According to Kenia's testimony, Polishan had overseen and directed every major facet of the fraud. Because of Polishan's intimidating personality, Kenia and several of his subordinates had agreed to make the enormous number of fraudulent entries in Leslie Fay's accounting records that he had demanded. Polishan had also compelled Kenia to accept full responsibility for the accounting irregularities when it became apparent in late January 1993 that the fraud would soon be exposed.

Following a series of lengthy and fiercely contested pretrial hearings, Polishan's criminal case was finally heard in federal court in the summer of 2000. Polishan was convicted on 18 of the 21 fraud counts filed against him. His attorneys immediately appealed the guilty verdict. The attorneys' principal contention during the appeal was that there was almost no physical evidence to link their client to the fraud. Instead, they maintained that Polishan's conviction had hinged almost entirely upon the veracity of Kenia's testimony.

The federal judge who presided over Polishan's appeal did not dispute his attorneys' principal contention. Throughout the fraud, the former CFO had painstakingly avoided leaving incriminating physical evidence that linked him directly to the accounting irregularities. Despite that fact, the judge denied Polishan's appeal. The judge observed that a substantial amount of circumstantial evidence had been presented during the trial. After studying the evidence in painstaking detail, the judge ruled that it was much more consistent with Kenia's testimony than that of Polishan.

A key factor contributing to the judge's decision was the unusual relationship that had existed between Polishan and Kenia during their long tenure with Leslie Fay, a relationship that had been documented and discussed at length during the trial. The judge noted that Polishan had "dominated" Kenia through intimidation and fear. In the opinion he issued in the case, the judge referred on multiple occasions to an episode that had occurred during 1992 to demonstrate how completely Polishan had controlled Kenia. In forcing Kenia to take responsibility for an accounting error that had been discovered in Leslie Fay's accounting records, Polishan had required Kenia to tell another company executive, "I am a _____ idiot."[16]

On January 21, 2002, almost exactly nine years after the news of the Leslie Fay fraud

---

15. *The Electronic Accountant* (online), "BDO to Pay $8 Million to Settle Leslie Fay Lawsuit," 10 March 1997. As a point of information, there is no public report of any resolution to the lawsuit filed against John Pomerantz *et al.* by BDO Seidman. Most likely, that lawsuit was dropped by BDO Seidman following the settlement approved by the federal judge.

16. *United States of America v. Paul Polishan*, 2001 U.S. Dist. LEXIS 10662.

surfaced in the press, Paul Polishan was sentenced to serve nine years in federal prison for his role in plotting and overseeing that fraud.[17] Polishan, who filed for personal bankruptcy in 1999 claiming assets of only $17,000, was also fined $900. After losing an appeal to overturn his conviction, Polishan reported to the federal correctional facility in Schuylkill County, Pennsylvania, in early September 2003 to begin serving his nine-year sentence. In exchange for his testimony against Polishan, Donald Kenia was allowed to plead guilty to two counts of making false statements to the SEC. In 2001, Kenia was sentenced to two years in the Allenwood Federal Prison Camp in Montgomery, Pennsylvania.

Questions

1. Prepare common-sized financial statements for Leslie Fay for the period 1987–1991. For that same period, compute for Leslie Fay the ratios shown in Exhibit 2. Given these data, which financial statement items do you believe should have been of particular interest to BDO Seidman during that firm's 1991 audit of Leslie Fay? Explain.

2. In addition to the data shown in Exhibit 1 and Exhibit 2, what other financial information would you have obtained if you had been responsible for planning the 1991 Leslie Fay audit?

3. List nonfinancial variables or factors regarding a client's industry that auditors should consider when planning an audit. For each of these items, briefly describe their audit implications.

4. Paul Polishan apparently dominated Leslie Fay's accounting and financial reporting functions and the individuals who were his subordinates. What implications do such circumstances pose for a company's independent auditors? How should auditors take such circumstances into consideration when planning an audit?

5. Explain why the SEC ruled that BDO Seidman's independence was jeopardized by the lawsuits that named the accounting firm, Leslie Fay, and top executives of Leslie Fay as codefendants.

---

17. Polishan's attorneys asked the presiding judge to reduce their client's sentence because Polishan allegedly suffered from a narcissistic personality disorder. The judge denied that request.

CASE 1.6

Star Technologies, Inc.

Economic ups and downs are a fact of life for companies in high-tech industries. Take the case of Star Technologies, Inc., a Virginia-based computer manufacturer incorporated in 1981 that went public in 1984.[1] In its early years, Star marketed scientific computers or "supercomputers" for highly specialized uses, including military surveillance and petroleum exploration. Star's operating results gyrated wildly during the 1980s. Exhibit 1 presents Star's key financial data for the five-year period 1985–1989. Notice that in 1985 Star reported a net loss exceeding $8 million on revenues of $21.2 million. The following year's results were even worse. In 1987, Star's revenues vaulted to $44 million, allowing the company to earn an after-tax profit of $1.4 million. Two years later, more bad news. Star's revenues fell to $39 million in 1989, resulting in a loss of $4.4 million.

Like many firms in the highly competitive computer industry, Star found itself trapped in a vicious cycle during the 1980s, a cycle that accounted for the large swings in its operating results. Star's 1989 annual report declared that the company was committed to staying "in the forefront of technological innovation" in the computer industry. Because of this commitment, Star's 1989 R&D (research and development) expenditures consumed 20 percent of its revenues. Unfortunately, rapid changes in technology within the computer industry rendered many of Star's impressive products obsolete shortly after they were introduced. This short product life cycle forced Star's executives to repeatedly "go back to the drawing board" and incur heavy R&D expenditures. As history later proved, only a few computer manufacturers could prosper under such conditions. Star Technologies was not among those firms.

A Fallen Star

By the end of fiscal 1989—March 31, 1989—Star faced a financial crisis. Among the company's major products was a computer designed for use in petroleum exploration. Company officials forecast that Star would sell 29 of the computers during 1989. Because of changes in computer technology and a slowdown in petroleum exploration activities, Star sold only one of these computers during 1989 and had no outstanding sales orders for the product at year-end. Star's poor operating results for 1989 caused the company to violate several covenants of a lending agreement with its principal bank. That bank had extended Star a $5.8 million long-term loan. The debt covenant violations accelerated the maturity date of the loan, making it immediately due and payable at the end of fiscal 1989.

Price Waterhouse audited Star's financial statements throughout the late 1980s. During the fiscal 1989 audit, several contentious issues arose between Price Waterhouse and Star's top executives. Among these issues were the refusal of Star's management to reclassify the $5.8 million bank loan as a current liability, disagreements over the adequacy of Star's reserves for bad debts and inventory obsolescence, and

---

1. Two enforcement releases issued by the Securities and Exchange Commission (SEC) and various annual reports of Star Technologies, Inc., provided the background facts for this case. The parties involved in this case neither admitted nor denied the SEC's reported findings and conclusions. Unless indicated otherwise, the quotations in this case were drawn from the following source: Securities and Exchange Commission, *Accounting and Auditing Enforcement Release No. 455,* 24 June 1993.

EXHIBIT 1

SELECTED FINANCIAL
DATA REPORTED
BY STAR
TECHNOLOGIES,
1985–1989
(000S OMITTED)

	1989	1988	1987	1986	1985
Revenue	$39,004	$35,689	$44,050	$15,050	$21,298
Operating income	(2,614)	3,830	4,729	(17,946)	(6,983)
Net income	(4,393)	2,218	1,374	(19,971)	(8,092)
Working capital	13,855	13,217	8,621	3,946	22,328
Total assets	31,277	25,025	28,528	35,908	44,957
Total debt	19,796	12,976	16,294	26,134	18,866

EXHIBIT 2

STAR
TECHNOLOGIES,
INC., 1988–1989
BALANCE SHEETS

STAR TECHNOLOGIES, INC.
BALANCE SHEETS (000s omitted)

	March 31,	
	1989	1988
Current assets:		
Cash and equivalents	$ 1,444	$ 1,651
Accounts receivable	5,025	4,063
Inventory	12,962	10,732
Other current assets	1,952	582
Total current assets	21,383	17,028
Property and equipment, net	6,917	5,033
Other assets	2,977	2,964
Total assets	$31,277	$25,025
Current liabilities:		
Accounts payable	$ 4,739	$ 1,524
Accrued payroll and related		
benefits	1,156	926
Other accrued liabilities	277	747
Deferred revenue	266	381
Notes payable	1,090	233
Total current liabilities	7,528	3,811
Notes payable, net of current portion	18,706	12,743
Total liabilities	26,234	16,554
Stockholders' equity:		
Convertible preferred stock	2	2
Common stock	161	155
Additional paid-in capital	49,299	48,340
Retained earnings (deficit)	(44,419)	(40,026)
Total stockholders' equity	5,043	8,471
Total liabilities and		
stockholders' equity	$31,277	$25,025

the capitalization of R&D expenditures by the company. Eventually, the company's
management team and the Price Waterhouse partner who oversaw the 1989 Star
audit resolved these issues to their mutual satisfaction, allowing Price Waterhouse to
issue an unqualified opinion on Star's 1989 financial statements. Exhibit 2 contains
the company's 1988 and 1989 balance sheets. Exhibit 3 presents the company's income statements and statements of cash flows for the period 1987–1989.

EXHIBIT 3

STAR
TECHNOLOGIES,
INC., 1987–1989
INCOME STATEMENTS
AND STATEMENTS OF
CASH FLOWS

STAR TECHNOLOGIES, INC.
CONSOLIDATED STATEMENTS OF OPERATIONS (000s omitted)

	Year Ended March 31,		
	1989	1988	1987
Revenue	$39,004	$35,689	$44,050
Costs and expenses:			
Cost of revenue	22,498	17,343	25,437
Research and development	7,945	4,684	5,031
Marketing and sales	8,206	7,363	6,118
General and administrative	2,969	2,469	2,410
Provision for restructuring	—	—	325
Operating income (loss)	(2,614)	3,830	4,729
Interest expense	(1,597)	(1,453)	(1,971)
Other income (expense)	(182)	(93)	(84)
Income (loss) before income taxes and extraordinary items	(4,393)	2,284	2,674
Provision for income taxes	—	(1,286)	(1,230)
Income (loss) before extraordinary items	(4,393)	998	1,444
Extraordinary items:			
Utilization of NOL carryforward	—	1,220	1,230
Provision for stockholder suit settlement	—	—	(1,300)
Net income (loss)	$(4,393)	$ 2,218	$ 1,374

STAR TECHNOLOGIES, INC.
CONSOLIDATED STATEMENTS OF CASH FLOWS (000s omitted)

	Year Ended March 31,		
	1989	1988	1987
Cash flows from (used for) operating activities:			
Net income (loss) before extraordinary items	$(4,393)	$ 998	$ 1,444
Extraordinary items	—	1,220	(70)
Adjustments to reconcile net income to net cash from operating activities:			
Depreciation and amortization	3,758	2,976	3,872
Stock issued for services	—	—	68
(Increase) decrease in accounts receivable	(867)	(896)	174
(Increase) decrease in inventory	(1,094)	4,090	1,689
Increase (decrease) in accounts payable	3,215	(3,241)	2,465
Increase (decrease) in accrued liabilities	(240)	(356)	(370)
Increase (decrease) in deferred revenue	(115)	232	(1,513)
Net cash from operating activities	264	5,023	7,759
Cash flows from (used for) investing activities:			
Deferred software and contract costs	(452)	(893)	—
Capital expenditures and other	(4,654)	(563)	130
Advances to Culler	(800)	—	—
Acquisition of Graphicon	(611)	—	—
Net cash from (used for) investing activities	(6,517)	(1,456)	130
Cash flows from (used for) financing activities:			
(Decrease) increase in notes payable	6,023	(3,318)	(9,840)
Proceeds from stock option exercises	—	873	337
Proceeds from stock issuances	23	—	—
Net cash from (used for) financing activities	6,046	(2,445)	(9,503)
Net increase (decrease) in cash and equivalents	(207)	1,122	(1,614)
Cash and equivalents, beginning of year	1,651	529	2,143
Cash and equivalents, end of year	$ 1,444	$1,651	$ 529

In January 1990, Price Waterhouse's national office received an anonymous letter alleging that the 1989 audit of Star Technologies was an "audit failure." After a brief investigation, the national office deemed the allegation unfounded. An executive partner in Price Waterhouse's Washington, D.C., office, which had issued the 1989 Star audit opinion, was not satisfied with the national office's investigation and decided to pursue the matter further. Following a lengthy discussion with the individual who served as the audit manager on the 1989 Star audit, the executive partner concluded that the audit had been inadequate and reported this finding to the national office. In early 1990, Price Waterhouse notified Star that it was withdrawing the audit opinion issued on the company's 1989 financial statements. Price Waterhouse also informed Star that those financial statements contained material errors. Although Star's executives initially disagreed with the audit firm's conclusion, they later accepted that decision and issued restated financial statements for 1989.

Price Waterhouse's 1989 Audit of Star Technologies

Clark Childers, an audit partner with Price Waterhouse since 1984, served as the engagement partner on the annual audits of Star's financial statements from 1987 through 1989. Childers' principal subordinate during the 1989 Star audit was Paul Argy, a senior audit manager who was to be considered for promotion to partner the following year. Argy assumed responsibility for planning and coordinating the 1989 audit, supervising the staff assigned to the engagement, and serving as Price Waterhouse's on-site liaison with Star's executives.

The Star audit proved to be a difficult engagement for Argy. Throughout the audit, he clashed with client management over several accounting and financial reporting issues. During one of those confrontations, Star's management demanded that Argy be removed from the audit. Childers refused to remove Argy—but from that point assumed a larger role in dealing with client officials when disputes arose. Following one particularly heated encounter between Childers and Star management, the company's executives decided to dismiss Price Waterhouse. A subsequent investigation by the SEC revealed that Star's audit committee interceded and vetoed that decision. The disagreements between the Price Waterhouse auditors and client executives during the 1989 audit involved the following items: R&D expenditures, the reserve for inventory obsolescence, the reserve for bad debts, certain "mystery assets" included in Star's accounting records, and the balance sheet classification of a large note payable.

R&D Expenditures

In 1989, Star established a joint R&D effort with Glen Culler & Associates, a small company that developed supercomputers. Star advanced nearly $900,000 to Culler during fiscal 1989. The agreement between the two companies required those funds to be repaid in 10 years and obligated Culler to use the funds to develop a new computer that Star would have an exclusive right to manufacture. Culler pledged all of its assets as collateral for the $900,000 advance. This stipulation of the agreement was inconsequential since Culler had no source of revenue or working capital other than Star, its sole customer; had a negative net worth of nearly $200,000; and had few tangible assets. Finally, the agreement between the two companies granted Star the right to acquire Culler.

Star's management maintained that the $900,000 advanced to Culler during 1989 qualified as a note receivable and included it in "other" assets on Star's 1989 balance sheet. Childers agreed with this decision. As required by Price Waterhouse, a second audit partner reviewed the 1989 Star workpapers before Childers released the audit opinion on the company's financial statements. This partner questioned the decision to report the $900,000 advance to Culler as an asset in Star's 1989 balance sheet and suggested instead writing off the advance as R&D expense in Star's 1989 income statement. The review partner then referred Childers to paragraphs 11 and 12 of *Statement on Financial Accounting Standards No. 2*, "Accounting for Research and Development Costs." Listed next are excerpts from those two paragraphs.

> *The costs of services performed by others in connection with the research and development activities of an enterprise, including research and development conducted by others on behalf of the enterprise, shall be included in research and development costs. If repayment to the enterprise of any loan or advance by the enterprise to the other parties depends solely on the results of the research and development having future economic benefit, the loan or advance shall be accounted for as costs incurred by the enterprise. The costs shall be charged to research and development expense. . . .*

To provide additional support for his position that the $900,000 advance to Culler should be expensed, the review partner cited the description of the agreement between Star and Culler that was included in the draft of Star's 1989 financial statement footnotes. That description specifically referred to the arrangement as a "joint research and development agreement."

After meeting with the review partner, Childers consulted with Star's chief financial officer (CFO). Childers told the CFO that the description of the Star–Culler agreement included in the draft of the financial statement footnotes suggested that the $900,000 advance should be treated as R&D expense by Star.

> *Following that conversation, Star's CFO caused all references to the transaction as a research and development agreement to be deleted from the final version of the financial statements. The final version described the agreement as a "working capital agreement."*

Childers accepted this revision without referring to the actual contract between the two parties. An inspection of that document would have revealed that the CFO's updated description of the Star–Culler relationship was misleading. The change in the footnote description of the Star–Culler agreement apparently satisfied the review partner, causing him to drop his objection to Star's financial statement treatment of the $900,000 advance to Culler.

During fiscal 1990, Star acquired Culler. While reviewing this transaction, Childers and Argy discovered that Star's 1989 financial statement footnotes had not accurately described the Star–Culler agreement. Childers and Argy contacted Price Waterhouse's national office for advice on this matter. To provide a clear understanding of the Star–Culler agreement, Argy forwarded to the national office copies of relevant documents pertaining to that agreement. After studying those documents, a Price Waterhouse partner in the firm's national office concluded that, at a minimum, $400,000 of the $900,000 advanced to Culler by Star during fiscal 1989 should have been treated as R&D expense by Star.[2]

The national office partner then addressed the issue of whether Star's 1989 financial statements should be restated. The partner asked Childers if an adjustment to write off $400,000 of the Culler receivable to R&D expense would have materially impacted Star's 1989 financial statements. Childers convinced the national partner that

---

2. The $400,000 amount represented the funds Star advanced to Culler after signing the agreement giving it the right to acquire that company. The national office partner maintained that since Star essentially had *de facto* control of Culler after the agreement was signed, the funds subsequently advanced to Culler should have been treated as an operating expense by Star.

such an adjustment would have had an immaterial effect on Star's financial statements. Childers also told the national partner that an adjustment had been proposed during the 1989 audit to write off a portion of the $900,000 Culler receivable to expense. According to Childers, that adjustment had been waived due to its immaterial effect on Star's financial statements.

The SEC's subsequent investigation found no evidence of the proposed adjustment in Price Waterhouse's 1989 workpapers. Following his interaction with the national partner, Childers had instructed a subordinate to include such a proposed adjustment in the 1989 Star workpapers. Despite that explicit instruction, the subordinate had refused to change the workpapers.

Reserve for Inventory Obsolescence

One of Star's original products was the ST-100 computer. Although a state-of-the-art computer when first marketed in 1982, by 1989 the ST-100 was outmoded. During 1989, Star added $3.5 million to the reserve for inventory obsolescence for its remaining inventory of ST-100s, reducing that inventory to a net book value of $2 million. Argy and other members of the Star engagement team believed that the ST-100 inventory was still overvalued. Argy recommended an additional $1.5 million write-down for that inventory.

Star's management resisted Argy's suggestion to write the ST-100 inventory down to a net book value of $500,000. The client's executives persuaded Childers that the company would sell ST-100s in the future despite not having any existing orders for that product and despite having sold only one ST-100 during 1989. Star's management also provided Childers with a list of $1 million of spare parts included in the ST-100 inventory that would allegedly be needed by Star to service previously sold ST-100s.

> *Childers accepted the $1 million spare parts requirement at face value and failed to perform any procedures or make additional inquiries to support the value. With regard to the remaining $1 million of obsolete ST-100 inventory, Childers agreed, apparently in a compromise with Star's management, to an arbitrary reserve increase of $350,000 without any documentation as to the basis for, or the rationale behind, the adjustment.*

Reserve for Bad Debts

Star reported slightly more than $5 million of net accounts receivable at the end of fiscal 1989. Two of Star's largest receivables had been outstanding for more than four years. These receivables, both in litigation at the time, totaled $1,062,000 and resulted from earlier sales of ST-100 computers. Before year-end adjusting entries, Star's allowance for doubtful accounts totaled $673,000. After analyzing Star's receivables, Argy determined that the allowance should be increased by approximately $400,000. That figure roughly equaled the total of the two disputed receivables less the existing balance of the allowance account.

In previous years, Price Waterhouse had reduced any proposed adjustment to the allowance account by the value of the collateral for potentially uncollectible receivables. Since the collateral for the disputed receivables, two ST-100 computers, was minimal, Argy decided that the proposed adjustment for uncollectible receivables should not be reduced.

Childers advised Star's management that he agreed with Argy's analysis of the allowance for doubtful accounts. The client's executives balked at making the $400,000 addition to the allowance and instead referred Childers to the company's attorneys. Those attorneys insisted that the proposed adjustment was excessive. As a compromise,

Star's chief executive officer (CEO) recommended increasing the allowance account $65,000 at the end of fiscal 1989. Childers agreed to that adjustment. The SEC later challenged Childers' decision to accept the modest increase in the allowance account.

> Childers had an inadequate basis to accept the CEO's proposition to increase the bad debt reserve by only $65,000. There was insufficient audit evidence to suggest that the remaining $335,000 of the receivables in question were collectible. In circumstances such as these, opinions of counsel are not dispositive evidence of collectibility.

"Mystery" Assets

During the 1989 Star audit, a Price Waterhouse staff auditor discovered an account entitled "Assets in Process" having a balance of approximately $435,000. A Star official told the staff auditor that the assets represented by that account involved computer equipment purchased and placed in service in 1985. However, Star could not provide invoices or other documentation to support the existence or valuation of these assets, nor were any depreciation records available for the assets.[3] In fact, the client could not locate the assets or describe them in detail to the Price Waterhouse audit team. Star's CFO claimed that the equipment could not be identified because it had been fully integrated into the company's existing computer facilities.

The staff auditor who uncovered the Assets in Process account noted in the 1989 workpapers that Star depreciated computer equipment over five years and began depreciating such assets in the year they were placed into service. Since the equipment purportedly represented by the account had been placed in service in 1985, the staff auditor reasoned that it should have been fully depreciated by the end of fiscal 1989. Argy agreed with his subordinate's analysis and concluded that the mystery assets should be immediately written off to expense.

When Childers brought the Assets in Process account to the attention of Star's CFO, the CFO refused to accept the proposed adjustment to write off the balance of the account. At this point, the CFO claimed that the assets had actually been placed in service in 1987 rather than 1985, although he could provide no evidence to support that assertion. Instead of accepting the proposed $435,000 adjustment, the CFO offered to record $100,000 of depreciation expense on the assets in 1989 and write off the remaining $335,000 cost of those assets over the following four years. Childers accepted the CFO's proposal.

Classification of Note Payable

Star's poor operating results for fiscal 1989 resulted in the company violating seven debt covenants included in the loan agreement with its principal bank. These debt covenant violations caused a $5.8 million bank loan to be immediately due and payable, as noted earlier. On June 15, 1989, Price Waterhouse completed the 1989 Star audit; however, Childers refused to issue an audit report on Star's financial statements until the company's bank waived the debt covenant violations. On June 29, 1989, Star faxed Price Waterhouse a waiver obtained two days earlier from its bank.

> The waiver covered only a five-month period, but also stated that it was not the bank's intention to accelerate the loans by virtue of defaults existing at the 1989 fiscal year-end. After reviewing the waiver, the audit senior told Childers that in his opinion the waiver was not adequate to classify the loans as a long-term liability.

---

3. Price Waterhouse had identified this account in earlier audits but apparently made no effort to corroborate the given assets' existence or valuation.

Childers disagreed with the audit senior's conclusion. Because the bank stated that it had no intention of making the $5.8 million loan immediately due and payable, Childers believed the loan qualified as a long-term liability. Shortly after receiving the bank waiver, Childers signed the unqualified audit opinion on Star's 1989 financial statements, dating the opinion as of June 15. Star included that opinion in its 1989 Form 10-K filed with the SEC.

Where Was Argy?

Paul Argy left the Star audit engagement approximately one week before the 1989 audit was completed to begin work on a new assignment in another city. Argy returned to Price Waterhouse's Washington, D.C., office on July 10, more than 10 days after Childers issued the unqualified opinion on Star's 1989 financial statements.

Upon Argy's return, Childers instructed him to complete his review of the workpapers for the Star audit and to sign off on the "audit summary" for the engagement. A Price Waterhouse policy required the audit manager on an engagement to sign off on the audit summary document after completing his or her review of the workpapers. Argy initially refused to sign off on the Star audit. Argy had contested several of the questionable decisions made by Childers during the 1989 Star audit and believed that the 1989 workpapers contained "materially incorrect" conclusions. Finally, after several confrontations with Childers, Argy capitulated and signed off on the Star workpapers and the audit summary.

EPILOGUE

Price Waterhouse recalled its opinion on Star's 1989 financial statements on March 9, 1990. The following month, the company's management issued financial statements for fiscal 1989 that contained appropriate adjustments for the items discussed earlier. Star's amended 1989 income statement reported a net loss of $7.4 million rather than the $4.4 million loss originally reported. On March 28, 1990, Price Waterhouse issued an unqualified audit opinion on Star's restated 1989 financial statements. One week later, Star dismissed Price Waterhouse and retained Coopers & Lybrand as its independent audit firm.

The SEC's investigation of Star's original 1989 financial statements and its 1989 audit culminated in sanctions being imposed on both Star and the two key members of the 1989 audit engagement team. The SEC issued a cease and desist order against Star that prohibited the company from future violations of the federal securities laws. Paul Argy received an 18-month suspension from practicing before the SEC, while Clark Childers received a five-year suspension.[4]

In commenting on Argy's involvement in the 1989 Star audit, the SEC complimented him for recommending that Star make several large and necessary adjustments to its 1989 financial statements.

Argy acted properly in insisting on material adjustments to Star's financial statements, notwithstanding strong opposition to those proposed adjustments by Star's CFO. He properly recognized and confronted Childers with his belief that the audit conclusions were improper and the audit evidence was insufficient.

---

4. In 1999, Paul Argy's application to regain his right to practice before the SEC was approved by the federal agency. See Securities and Exchange Commission, *Accounting and Auditing Enforcement Release No. 1130*, 22 April 1999.

The SEC went on to chastise Argy for signing off on the 1989 Star audit workpapers when he believed they contained materially incorrect conclusions.

Instead of signing off on the Star workpapers, the SEC maintained that Argy should have dissociated himself from the Star audit. That option was available to him since Price Waterhouse had a "disagreement procedure" allowing auditors on an engagement to explicitly dissociate themselves from any decision with which they did not agree. The SEC suggested that Argy may have allowed his desire to be promoted to partner cloud his professional judgment.

> *An independent accountant, including an audit manager, cannot excuse his failure to comply with GAAS because of a sense of futility after his proposed approaches to certain accounting issues are repeatedly rejected. . . . The audit manager may encounter pressure to compromise audit standards and may encounter frustration in dealing with partners and clients. The audit manager may also sense that his response to those pressures may adversely affect his opportunity for advancement. However, in fulfilling his responsibilities, the audit manager plays a crucial role in ensuring that an audit report is issued only when the audit was in fact conducted in accordance with GAAS.*

By imposing a five-year suspension on Childers, the SEC affirmed that the audit partner shouldered a greater degree of responsibility for the 1989 Star audit than did his subordinate, Argy. Following are the specific allegations of misconduct that the SEC filed against Childers.

1. Failing to ensure that sufficient competent evidential matter was obtained to afford a reasonable basis for his conclusions
2. Failing to exercise due professional care and sufficient professional skepticism in the performance of the audit
3. Failing to assure that the financial statements on which Price Waterhouse issued an unqualified opinion were prepared in accordance with GAAP
4. Responding without an adequate basis to the questions of the second partner reviewer when issues were raised about the agreement with Culler
5. Instructing Argy to sign off on the audit regardless of Argy's stated disagreement with the conclusions reached by Childers
6. Making misleading statements to the Price Waterhouse national office concerning its investigation of Star's agreement with Culler
7. Instructing a Price Waterhouse audit manager to make inappropriate alterations to workpapers

Star Technologies' financial condition steadily worsened in the years following its unpleasant encounter with the SEC. The company's computer manufacturing operations never became economically viable. At last report, the company had fewer than two dozen employees and its principal line of business was the development of computer software.

Questions

1. Explain why "industry knowledge" is so important to an audit engagement team. Identify risk factors commonly posed by companies in high-tech industries.

2. Review Star Technologies' financial statements included in Exhibit 2 and Exhibit 3. What changes in Star's financial status between fiscal year-end 1988 and 1989 should have been of concern to the company's independent auditors? How should these changes have affected key audit planning decisions for the 1989 Star audit?

3. Review Star's statements of cash flows shown in Exhibit 3. What information can auditors obtain from a client's cash-flow data that is relevant to the audit plan developed for the client?

4. *SAS No. 106*, "Audit Evidence," identifies the "management assertions" that may be explicit or implicit in a set of financial statements and accompanying footnotes. What management assertions were invalid in Star's original 1989 financial statements? Explain.

5. Star's bank indicated in the waiver of the debt covenant violations that it did not intend to accelerate the maturity date of the $5.8 million loan. Was that statement a sufficient basis for classifying the loan as a long-term liability rather than as a current liability? Defend your answer.

6. Briefly describe the nature and purpose of the audit review process. Identify any breakdowns that occurred in the audit review process during the 1989 Star audit.

7. How should disagreements between members of an audit engagement team be resolved? What mistakes, if any, were made by Childers and/or Argy in resolving the conflicts that arose between them during the 1989 Star audit?

CASE 1.7

Lincoln Savings and Loan Association

Charles Keating, Jr., was a scholar-athlete at the University of Cincinnati during the mid-1940s. In 1946, Keating won an NCAA individual championship in the 200-yard butterfly, a swimming event, and two years later graduated from the University of Cincinnati Law School. Over the next 30 years, Keating established himself as the nation's leading critic of the pornography industry. In 1960, he founded the Citizens for Decency through Law, an organization dedicated to "stamping out smut." A decade later, Keating was appointed to President Nixon's Commission on Pornography. Keating became best known nationally for his successful effort to help law enforcement authorities prosecute magazine publisher Larry Flynt, another native of Cincinnati, on obscenity charges.

In 1978, Keating began focusing his time and energy on his business endeavors when he founded the real estate firm, American Continental Corporation (ACC). Six years later, ACC acquired Lincoln Savings and Loan Association, which was headquartered in Phoenix, although its principal operations were in California. In his application to purchase Lincoln, Keating pledged to regulatory authorities that he would retain the Lincoln management team, that he would not use brokered deposits to expand the size of the savings and loan, and that residential home loans would remain Lincoln's principal line of business. After gaining control of Lincoln, Keating replaced the management team; began accepting large deposits from money brokers, which allowed him to nearly triple the size of the savings and loan in two years; and shifted the focus of Lincoln's lending activity from residential mortgage loans to land development projects.

On April 14, 1989, the Federal Home Loan Bank Board (FHLBB) seized control of Lincoln Savings and Loan, alleging that Lincoln was dissipating its assets by operating in an unsafe and unsound manner. On that date, Lincoln's balance sheet reported total assets of $5.3 billion, only 2.3 percent of which were investments in residential mortgage loans. Nearly two-thirds of Lincoln's asset portfolio was invested directly or indirectly in high-risk land ventures and other commercial development projects. At the time, federal authorities estimated that the closure of Lincoln Savings and Loan would cost U.S. taxpayers at least $2.5 billion.

Congressional hearings into the collapse of Lincoln Savings and Loan initially focused on the methods Keating used to circumvent banking laws and on disclosures that five U.S. senators intervened on Keating's behalf with federal banking regulators. Eventually, the hearings centered on the failure of Lincoln's independent auditors to expose fraudulent real estate transactions that allowed the savings and loan to report millions of dollars of nonexistent profits. In summarizing the Lincoln debacle, U.S. Representative Jim Leach laid the blame for the costly savings and loan failure on a number of parties, including Lincoln's auditors and the accounting profession as a whole:

I am stunned. As I look at these transactions, I am stunned at the conclusions of an independent auditing firm. I am stunned at the result. And let me just tell you, I think that this whole circumstance of a potential $2.5 billion cost to the United States taxpayers is a scandal for the United States Congress. It is a scandal for the Texas and

California legislatures. It is a scandal for the Reagan administration regulators. And it is a scandal for the accounting profession.[1]

Creative Accounting, Influence Peddling, and Other Abuses at Lincoln Savings and Loan

Representative Henry Gonzalez, chairman of the U.S. House Committee on Banking, Finance, and Urban Affairs, charged that over the five years Charles Keating owned Lincoln, he employed accounting schemes to divert the savings and loan's federally insured deposits into ACC's treasury. Keating was aware that he would be permitted to withdraw funds from Lincoln and invest them in ACC or use them for other purposes only to the extent that Lincoln reported after-tax profits. Consequently, he and his associates wove together complex real estate transactions involving Lincoln, ACC, and related third parties to manufacture paper profits for Lincoln. Kenneth Leventhal & Company, an accounting firm retained by regulatory authorities to analyze and report on Lincoln's accounting practices, used a few simple examples to explain the saving and loan's fraudulent schemes. Exhibit 1 contains a portion of the

EXHIBIT 1

CONGRESSIONAL TESTIMONY OF KENNETH LEVENTHAL & COMPANY REGARDING LINCOLN'S REAL ESTATE TRANSACTIONS

To illustrate the accounting concepts Lincoln used, let me give you a few simple, hypothetical examples. Suppose you own a house that you paid $100,000 for, and against which you still owe $60,000. Now, suppose you could not find a buyer for your house. Therefore, you go out and find an individual who agrees to pay you the $200,000 you want for your house, but is only willing to give you one dollar in cash and a nonrecourse note for the balance of $199,999. A nonrecourse note means that you cannot get at him personally. If he defaults on the note, your only recourse is to take the house back.

So now you have one dollar in your pocket, and a note for the rest. You very likely have not parted company with your house in this situation, because your so-called buyer may be unable to pay you, or he may simply decide that he does not want to pay you. Economically, he has an option to stick to the deal if the price of the house appreciates, or he can walk away from it if it does not. That is not a sale.

Now, suppose you have the same house again. Your next-door neighbor has a different house, but it is worth the same as yours, and has the same outstanding mortgage balance. You then swap houses and mortgages with your neighbor.

You now have a house which is different, but very similar to the one that you did have. I think that you will agree, there is no profit realized on this exchange. By the accounting theory that Lincoln appears to have followed, you would be able to record a $100,000 profit: the difference between what you originally paid for your house and what you think your neighbor's house is worth.

Really, it could have been more, if you could have found an appraiser to tell you that your neighbor's house was worth $300,000. And it could have been still more if you and your neighbor had simply chosen to agree upon a stated price which was even in excess of these amounts.

As you can see, all sales of real estate are not created equal. Over the years, accountants have had to wrestle with what is economically a sale and what is not. The economic substance of a transaction should of course be the controlling consideration.

---

1. This and all subsequent quotations, unless indicated otherwise, were taken from the following source: U.S. Congress, House, Committee on Banking, Finance and Urban Affairs; *Investigation of Lincoln Savings and Loan Association, Part 4* (Washington, DC: U.S. Government Printing Office, 1990).

Leventhal firm's testimony before Representative Gonzalez's committee, which sponsored the lengthy congressional investigation of Lincoln Savings and Loan.

One of the most scrutinized of Lincoln's multimillion-dollar real estate deals was the large Hidden Valley transaction that took place in the spring of 1987. On March 30, 1987, Lincoln loaned $19.6 million to E. C. Garcia & Company. On that same day, Ernie Garcia, a close friend of Keating and the owner of the land development company bearing his name, extended a $3.5 million loan to Wescon, a mortgage real estate concern owned by Garcia's friend, Fernando Acosta. The following day, Wescon purchased 1,000 acres of unimproved desert land in central Arizona from Lincoln for $14 million, nearly twice the value established for the land by an independent appraiser one week earlier. Acosta used the loan from Garcia as the down payment on the tract of land and signed a nonrecourse note for the balance. Lincoln recorded a profit of $11.1 million on the transaction—profit that was never realized, since the savings and loan never received payment on the nonrecourse note.

In fact, Lincoln never expected to be paid the balance of the nonrecourse note. Lincoln executives arranged the loan simply to allow the savings and loan to book a large paper gain. Garcia later testified that he agreed to become involved in the deceptive Hidden Valley transaction only because he wanted the $19.6 million loan from Lincoln.[2] Recognizing a profit on the Hidden Valley transaction would have openly violated financial accounting standards if Garcia had acquired the property directly from Lincoln and used for his down payment funds loaned to him by the savings and loan.

Fernando Acosta eventually admitted that his company, Wescon, which prior to the Hidden Valley transaction had total assets of $87,000 and a net worth of $30,000, was only a "straw buyer" of the Hidden Valley property. In a *Los Angeles Times* article, Acosta reported that Wescon "was too small to buy the property and that he signed the documents without reading them to help his friend, Ernie Garcia."[3] Exhibit 2 contains a letter that a worried Acosta wrote to Garcia in 1988 regarding the Hidden Valley transaction. In that letter, Acosta encouraged Garcia to assume title to the property so that he could take it off Wescon's books.

Keating and his associates repeatedly used bogus real estate transactions, such as the Hidden Valley charade, to produce enormous gains for Lincoln. In 1986 and 1987 alone, Lincoln recognized more than $135 million of profits on such transactions. That amount represented more than one-half of the savings and loan's total reported profits for the two-year period.

The gains recorded by Lincoln on its real estate transactions allowed ACC to withdraw huge sums of cash from the savings and loan in the form of intercompany dividend payments, funds that were actually federally insured deposits. When the "purchasers" of these tracts of land defaulted on their nonrecourse notes, Lincoln was forced to recognize losses—losses that the savings and loan offset with additional "profitable" real estate transactions. This recurring cycle of events ensured that Lincoln would eventually fail. However, since the Federal Savings and Loan Insurance Corporation (FSLIC) guaranteed Lincoln's liabilities (that is, its deposits), and since ACC had little equity capital invested in Lincoln, Keating was not overly concerned by the inevitable demise of his company's savings and loan subsidiary.

Lincoln's convoluted and contrived real estate transactions appalled members of Representative Gonzalez's congressional committee. One of the Leventhal partners

---

2. K. Kerwin and C. Yang, "Everything Was Fine Until I Met Charlie: The Rise and Stumble of Whiz Kid and Keating Crony Ernie Garcia," *Business Week*, 12 March 1990, 44, 46.

3. J. Granelli, "Firm Says It Was a 'Straw Man' in Lincoln Deal," *Los Angeles Times*, 3 January 1990, D1, D13.

EXHIBIT 2

LETTER FROM
WESCON TO
ERNIE GARCIA
REGARDING HIDDEN
VALLEY PROPERTY

[This letter was addressed to Mr. E. C. Garcia, E. C. Garcia and Company, Inc., and appeared on Wescon letterhead.]

Re: Hidden Valley Project/Property

Dear Ernie:

The time when we should have been out of this project is well past.

For various reasons, our discomfort with continuation in the project is growing. Particularly of late, we have been concerned with how to report this to the IRS. We are convinced that all we can do is report as if the corporation were not the true/beneficial owner, but merely the nominal title holder, which is consistent with the facts and the reality of the situation. Correspondingly, it seems you should have, and report, the real tax burdens and benefits arising from this property.

Also, we are increasingly uncomfortable with showing this property on our company's financial statements (and explaining why it is there). We absolutely need to extract this item.

In order to expedite relief for us on this matter, in line with your repeated assurances, please arrange for the transfer of this property to its rightful owner as soon as possible.

Sincerely,

FRA/Wescon

Fernando R. Acosta

who testified before the congressional committee provided the following overview of his firm's report on Lincoln's accounting schemes:

> *Seldom in our experience have we encountered a more egregious example of misapplication of generally accepted accounting principles. This association [Lincoln] was made to function as an engine, designed to funnel insured deposits to its parent in tax allocation payments and dividends. To do this, it had to generate reportable earnings. It created profits by making loans. Many of these loans were bad. Lincoln was manufacturing profits by giving money away.*

Critics chastised Charles Keating not only for employing creative accounting methods but for several other abusive practices as well. In 1979, Keating signed a consent decree with the Securities and Exchange Commission (SEC) to settle conflict of interest charges the agency had filed against him. In 1985, Keating handpicked his 24-year-old son, Charles Keating III, to serve as Lincoln's president. Along with the impressive job title came an annual salary of $1 million. At the time, the young man's only prior work experience was as a busperson in a country club restaurant. Years later, the younger Keating testified that he did not understand many of the transactions he signed off on as Lincoln's president.

The elder Keating's gaudy lifestyle and ostentatious spending habits were legendary. U.S. taxpayers absorbed many of the outrageous expenses rung up by Keating since he pawned them off as business expenses of Lincoln. The bill for a 1987 dinner Keating hosted at an upscale Washington, D.C., restaurant came to just slightly less than $2,500. One of the guests at that dinner was a former SEC commissioner. In another incident, after inadvertently scuffing a secretary's $30 shoes, Keating wrote her a check for $5,000 to replace them—and the rest of her wardrobe as well, apparently.

Other Keating excesses documented by federal and state investigators included sa-
faris, vacations in European castles, numerous trips to the south of France, and lavish
parties for relatives and government officials.

The most serious charges leveled at Keating involved allegations of influence peddling. Keating contributed heavily to the election campaigns of five prominent senators, including John Glenn of Ohio and John McCain of Arizona. These five senators,
who became known as the Keating Five, met with federal banking regulators and lobbied for favorable treatment of Lincoln Savings and Loan. The key issue in these lobbying efforts was the so-called direct investment rule adopted by the FHLBB in 1985. This
rule limited the amount that savings and loans could invest directly in subsidiaries, development projects, and other commercial ventures to 10 percent of their total assets.
Because such investments were central to Lincoln's operations, the direct investment
rule imposed severe restrictions on Keating—restrictions that he repeatedly ignored.

In 1986, a close associate of Keating's was appointed to fill an unexpired term on the
FHLBB. Following his appointment, this individual proposed an amendment to the direct investment rule that would have exempted Lincoln from its requirements. The
amendment failed to be seconded and thus was never adopted. Shortly before Alan
Greenspan was appointed to the powerful position of chairman of the Federal Reserve
Board, Keating retained him to represent Lincoln before the FHLBB. In a legal brief
submitted to the FHLBB, Greenspan reported that Lincoln's management team was
"seasoned and expert" and that the savings and loan was a "financially strong" institution. Congressional testimony also disclosed that Keating loaned $250,000, with very
favorable payback terms, to a former SEC commissioner, who then lobbied the SEC on
Lincoln's behalf.

The charges of influence peddling failed to concern or distract Keating. In responding to these charges, Keating made the following remarks during a press conference: "One question, among the many raised in recent weeks, has to do with
whether my financial support in any way influenced several political figures to take
up my cause. I want to say in the most forceful way I can: I certainly hope so."[4]

Federal authorities eventually indicted Keating on various racketeering and securities fraud charges. He was also sued by the Resolution Trust Corporation, the federal
agency created to manage the massive savings and loan crisis that threatened the integrity of the nation's banking system during the 1980s. That agency charged Keating
with insider dealing, illegal loans, sham real estate and tax transactions, and the
fraudulent sale of Lincoln securities.

Audit History of Lincoln Savings and Loan

Arthur Andersen served as Lincoln's independent auditor until 1985 when it resigned
"to lessen its exposure to liability from savings and loan audits," according to a *New
York Times* article.[5] That same article described the very competitive nature of the
Phoenix audit market during the mid-1980s when Lincoln was seeking a replacement auditor. Because of the large size of the Lincoln audit, several audit firms pursued the engagement, including Arthur Young & Company.[6] From 1978 through 1984,

4. D. J. Jefferson, "Keating of American Continental Corp. Comes Out Fighting," *The Wall Street Journal*, 18 April 1989, B2.

5. E. N. Berg, "The Lapses by Lincoln's Auditors," *The New York Times*, 28 December 1989, D1, D6.

6. Arthur Andersen and, subsequently, Arthur Young audited both ACC and Lincoln, a wholly owned subsidiary of ACC. However, the Lincoln audit was much more complex and required much more time to 7complete than the ACC audit. Reportedly, the ACC/Lincoln audit accounted for one-fifth of the annual audit revenues of Arthur Young's Phoenix office during 1986 and 1987.

Arthur Young suffered a net loss of 63 clients nationwide.[7] Over the next five years, an intense marketing effort produced a net increase of more than 100 audit clients for the firm. During the 1980s, critics of the accounting profession suggested that the extremely competitive audit market induced many audit firms to accept high-risk clients, such as Lincoln, in exchange for large audit fees.

> *The savings industry crisis has revived questions repeatedly raised in the past about the profession's independence in auditing big corporate clients: whether the accounts need more controls and whether some firms are willing to sanction questionable financial statements in exchange for high fees, a practice called "bottom fishing."*[8]

Before pursuing Lincoln as an audit client, Jack Atchison, an Arthur Young partner in Phoenix, contacted the former Lincoln engagement partner at Arthur Andersen. The Arthur Andersen partner told Atchison that he had no reason to question the integrity of Lincoln's management and that no major disagreements preceded the resignation of his firm as Lincoln's auditor. At the time of Arthur Andersen's resignation, Lincoln was undergoing an intensive examination by FHLBB auditors, who were raising serious questions regarding Lincoln's financial records. Arthur Young was not informed of this investigation by Arthur Andersen. Years later, Arthur Andersen partners denied that they were aware of the examination when they resigned from the audit.

Shortly after accepting Lincoln as an audit client, Arthur Young learned of the FHLBB audit. Among the most serious charges of the FHLBB auditors was that Lincoln had provided interest-free loans to ACC—a violation of federal banking laws—and had falsified loan documents. Three years later, officials from the Office of Thrift Supervision testified before Congress that Arthur Andersen and Lincoln employees had engaged in so-called file-stuffing. These charges resulted in formal inquiries by the Federal Bureau of Investigation and the U.S. Department of Justice.[9] Arthur Andersen officials denied involvement in any illegal activities but did acknowledge that employees of their firm had worked "under the direction of client [Lincoln] personnel to assist them in organizing certain [loan] files."[10] Later, a representative of Lincoln admitted that "memorialization" had been used for certain loan files.

Congressional testimony of several Arthur Young representatives revealed that the 1986 and 1987 Lincoln audits were very complex engagements. William Gladstone, the co-managing partner of Ernst & Young (the firm formed by the 1989 merger of Ernst & Whinney and Arthur Young), testified that the 1987 audit required 30,000 hours to complete. Despite concerns being raised by regulatory authorities, Arthur Young issued an unqualified opinion on Lincoln's financial statements in both 1986 and 1987. Critics contend that these clean opinions allowed Lincoln to continue engaging in illicit activities. Of particular concern to congressional investigators was that during this time Keating and his associates sold ACC's high-yield "junk" bonds in the lobbies of Lincoln's numerous branches. The sale of these bonds, which were destined to become totally worthless, raised more than $250 million for ACC. The marketing campaign for the bonds targeted retired individuals, many of whom believed that the bonds were federally insured since they were being sold on the premises of a savings and loan.

---

7. L. Berton, "Spotlight on Arthur Young Is Likely to Intensify as Lincoln Hearings Resume," *The Wall Street Journal*, 21 November 1989, A20.

8. N. C. Nash, "Auditors of Lincoln On the Spot," *The New York Times*, 14 November 1989, D1, D19.

9. P. Thomas and B. Jackson, "Regulators Cite Delays and Phone Bugs in Examination, Seizure of Lincoln S & L," *The Wall Street Journal*, 27 October 1989, A4; Berg, "The Lapses by Lincoln's Auditors."

10. Thomas and Jackson, "Regulators Cite Delays and Phone Bugs."

When called to testify before the U.S. House committee, SEC Commissioner Richard Breeden was asked to explain why his agency did not force ACC to stop selling the junk bonds in Lincoln's branches.

Congressman Hubbard: *Didn't the SEC have not one, not two, but actually three or more opportunities to stop the sale of the ACC subordinated debt?*

Commissioner Breeden: *We did not have any opportunity—the only way in which the SEC can stop the sale of securities is if we are able to prove those securities are being distributed based on false and misleading information. And we have to prove that in court. We cannot have reasons to be concerned about it, we cannot have suspicions, we cannot just have cause to be concerned; we have to be able to prove that in court.*

And remember that this is a situation in which one of the Big Eight accounting firms is certifying that these accounts comply fully with generally accepted accounting principles, without caveat or limitation in any way. That is an important factor in that kind of decision. *[Emphasis added.]*

Following the completion of the 1987 Lincoln audit, the engagement audit partner, Jack Atchison, resigned from Arthur Young and accepted a position with ACC. Exhibit 3 contains the memorandum Atchison wrote to William Gladstone, who at the time was Arthur Young's managing partner, to inform Gladstone of his resignation. Gladstone later testified that Atchison earned approximately $225,000 annually as an Arthur Young partner before his resignation. ACC records revealed that Atchison's new position came with an annual salary of approximately $930,000.

The close relationship that Atchison developed with Keating before resigning from Arthur Young alarmed congressional investigators. Testimony before the congressional committee disclosed that Atchison, while he was serving as the engagement partner on the Lincoln audit, wrote several letters to banking regulators and U.S. senators vigorously supporting the activities of Keating and Lincoln. "Atchison seemed to drop the auditor's traditional stance of independence by repeatedly defending the practices of Lincoln and its corporate parent to Congress and federal regulators. . . . Since when does the outside accountant —the public watchdog—become a proponent of the client's affairs?"[11]

Congressman Gonzalez's committee also questioned Arthur Young representatives regarding Atchison's relationship with the Arthur Young audit team after he joined ACC. The committee was concerned that Atchison may have been in a position to improperly influence the auditors he had supervised just weeks earlier.

Congressman Lehman: *Did anyone at AY have any contact with Mr. Atchison after he left and went to work for Lincoln?*

Mr. Gladstone: *Yes, sir.*

Congressman Lehman: *In the course of the audit?*

Mr. Gladstone: *Yes.*

Congressman Lehman: *So he went from one side of the table to the other for $700,000 more?*

Mr. Gladstone: *That is what happened.*

Congressman Lehman: *And he—just tell me what his role was in the audits . . . when he was on the other side of the table.*

Mr. Gladstone: *He was a senior vice president for American Continental when he joined them in May 1988.*

11. Berg, "The Lapses by Lincoln's Auditors."

EXHIBIT 3

Memorandum from
Jack Atchison
to William
Gladstone

[This memorandum appeared on Arthur Young letterhead.]

TO: Office of Chairman   FROM: Phoenix Office
    William L. Gladstone   Jack D. Atchison
    Hugh Grant, West Regional Office
    Al Boos, Phoenix Office

SUBJECT:

Several weeks ago, Charles H. Keating, Jr., Chairman of American Continental Corporation, asked me to consider joining his company at a senior executive level. Because we were in the process of conducting an audit, I informed Mr. Keating that any discussions regarding future employment would have to await the conclusion of the audit. I also informed Hugh Grant of Mr. Keating's overtures to me.

Knowing Mr. Keating would raise the subject again at the conclusion of the audit, I began to seriously consider the possibility of leaving Arthur Young to join American Continental. Arthur Young has been my professional home for over 24 years, providing a comfortable source of income and rewarding professional environment. My closest personal friends are also my partners. To even consider no longer being a part of Arthur Young was difficult and traumatic, since serving as a partner in Arthur Young has been my single professional goal since 1962.

On April 8 and 11, 1988, I had discussions with Mr. Keating wherein he presented an employment offer which was very rewarding economically and very challenging professionally. His offer addressed all of my economic, job security and position description requirements and concerns. American Continental offers some unique challenges and potential rewards not presently available in Arthur Young. It also presents some risks not present in the Arthur Young environment.

Based on American Continental's offer and my perception of the future there, I have decided to accept their offer and seek to withdraw from the Arthur Young partnership at the earliest possible date. Since American Continental is an SEC client and active issuer of securities requiring registration, and Arthur Young's consent to the use of its report is needed in such filings, an expedited withdrawal arrangement would protect against any real or apparent conflicts of interest between Arthur Young and American Continental.

Congressman Lehman: *Did the job he had there have anything to do with interfacing with the auditors?*

Mr. Gladstone: *To some extent, yes.*

Congressman Lehman: *What does "to some extent" mean?*

Mr. Gladstone: *On major accounting issues that were discussed in the Form 8-K, we did have conversations with Jack Atchison.*

Congressman Lehman: *So he was the person Mr. Keating had to interface with you in major decisions?*

Mr. Gladstone: *Him, and other officers of American Continental.*

During the summer of 1988, the relationship between Lincoln's executives and the Arthur Young audit team gradually soured. Janice Vincent, who became the Lincoln engagement partner following Atchison's resignation, testified that disagreements arose with client management that summer over the accounting treatment applied to several large real estate transactions. The most serious disagreement involved a proposed exchange of assets between Lincoln and another corporation—a transaction for which Lincoln intended to record a $50 million profit. Lincoln management insisted that the exchange involved dissimilar assets. Vincent, on the other hand, stubbornly maintained that the transaction involved the exchange of similar assets and, consequently, that the gain on the transaction could not be recognized. During the congressional hearings, Vincent described how this dispute and related disputes eventually led to the resignation of Arthur Young as Lincoln's auditor.

> *These disagreements created an adversarial relationship between members of Arthur Young's audit team and American Continental officials, which resulted in Mr. Keating requesting a meeting with Bill Gladstone. . . . While in New York at that meeting, Mr. Keating turned to me at one point and said, "Lady, you have just lost a job." That did not happen. Rather, he had lost an accounting firm.*

Following Arthur Young's resignation in October 1988, Keating retained Touche Ross to audit Lincoln's 1988 financial statements. Touche Ross became ensnared, along with Arthur Andersen and Arthur Young, in the web of litigation following Lincoln's collapse. Purchasers of the ACC bonds sold in Lincoln's branches named Touche Ross as a defendant in a large class-action lawsuit. The suit alleged that had Touche Ross not accepted Lincoln as an audit client, ACC's ability to sell the bonds would have been diminished significantly.

Criticism of Arthur Young Following Lincoln's Collapse

Both Arthur Young and its successor, Ernst & Young, were criticized for the former's role in the Lincoln Savings and Loan debacle. One of the most common criticisms was that Arthur Young readily accepted questionable documentary evidence provided by Lincoln employees to corroborate the savings and loan's real estate transactions. During the congressional hearings into the collapse of Lincoln, William Gladstone commented on the appraisals that Arthur Young obtained to support those transactions. "All appraisals of land [owned by Lincoln] were done by appraisers hired by the company, and we had to rely on them." Certainly, these appraisals were relevant evidence to be used in auditing Lincoln's real estate transactions. However, appraisals obtained by Arthur Young from independent third parties would have been just as relevant and less subject to bias.[12]

Among Arthur Young's most vocal critics during the congressional hearings was the newly appointed SEC commissioner, Richard Breeden. Commissioner Breeden berated Arthur Young for failing to cooperate with an SEC investigation into Lincoln's financial affairs.

> **Commissioner Breeden:**   *We subpoenaed the accountants [Arthur Young] to provide all of their workpapers and their back-up.*
>
> **Congressman Hubbard:**   *Do you know if they were forthcoming and helpful in helping you resolve some of these questions, or helping the SEC resolve some of these questions?*
>
> **Commissioner Breeden:**   *No. I would characterize them as very unhelpful, very unforthcoming, and very resistant to cooperate in any way, shape, or form.*

Earlier, Commissioner Breeden had testified that many of the subpoenaed documents that Arthur Young eventually produced were illegible or obscured: "The firm [Arthur Young] ultimately, after much discussion, produced legible copies of the documents, but not before the Commission [SEC] was forced to prepare court enforcement requests to overcome Arthur Young's uncooperative stance. Unfortunately, a

---

12. Quite possibly, Arthur Young did obtain independent appraisals in certain cases, although Gladstone's testimony suggests otherwise.

substantial amount of staff time and resources was devoted unnecessarily to over-coming this resistance to the Commission's subpoenas."

When given an opportunity to respond to Commissioner Breeden's charges, William Gladstone maintained that the delays in providing the SEC with the re-quested documents were not intentional: "We did not stonewall the SEC. There are Arizona state privilege statutes and ethics rules which prohibit our producing our work papers without a client consent. . . . I also take issue with the allegation that we obliterated some papers. . . . The SEC itself requires a confidentiality stamp on all pa-pers on which confidentiality was requested."

The most stinging criticism of Arthur Young during the congressional hearings was triggered by the report prepared by Kenneth Leventhal & Company on Lincoln's ac-counting decisions for its major real estate transactions. Although the Leventhal re-port served as the basis for much of the criticism directed at Arthur Young, the report did not mention Arthur Young or, in any way, explicitly criticize its Lincoln audits. Nev-ertheless, since Arthur Young had issued unqualified opinions on Lincoln's financial statements, many parties, including Ernst & Young officials, regarded the Leventhal re-port as an indictment of the quality of Arthur Young's audits.

The key finding of the Leventhal report was that Lincoln had repeatedly violated the substance-over-form concept by engaging in "accounting-driven" deals among re-lated parties to manufacture illusory profits. Ernst & Young representatives contested this conclusion by pointing out that Leventhal reviewed only 15 of the hundreds of real estate transactions that Lincoln engaged in during Arthur Young's tenure. The Ernst & Young representatives were particularly upset that, based upon a review of those 15 transactions, Leventhal implied that none of Lincoln's major real estate transactions were accounted for properly. In Leventhal's defense, a congressman noted that the 15 transactions in question were all very large and, collectively, ac-counted for one-half of Lincoln's pretax profits during 1986 and 1987.

At times, the debate over the Leventhal report became very heated. William Glad-stone maligned the report, stating that it was gratuitous; contained broad, sweeping generalizations; in certain cases was "flatly wrong"; and in his opinion, was unprofes-sional. In responding to these charges, Congressman Leach questioned the profes-sionalism of Gladstone's firm.

Congressman Leach: *[addressing William Gladstone] I am going to be very frank with you, that I am not impressed with the professional ethics of your firm vis-à-vis the United States Congress. Several days ago, my office was contacted by your firm and asked if we would be interested in questions to ask of Leventhal. We said, "Surely." The questions you provided were of an offensive nature. They were to request of Leventhal how much they were paid, implying that perhaps based upon their payment from the U.S. Government that their decisions as CPAs would be biased. I consider that to be very offensive.*

Now, in addition, one of the questions that was suggested I might ask of the Leventhal firm was: Could it be that their firm is biased because a partner in their firm did not make partner in your firm?

I consider that exceedingly unprofessional. Would you care to respond to that?

Mr. Gladstone: *I do not know who contacted you, and I certainly do not know how the questions were raised.*

Later in the hearings, the individual who had submitted the questions to Congress-man Leach's office was identified as an Ernst & Young employee.

Congressman Leach also took issue with the contention of Ernst & Young represen-tatives that Leventhal's report contained angry and vengeful comments regarding their firm.

Congressman Leach: *I read that report very carefully, and I found no angry, vengeful sweeping statements. But I did find a conclusion that Arthur Young had erred rather grievously.*

In any regard, what we are looking at is an issue that is anything but an accounting kind of debate. One of the techniques of Lincoln vis-à-vis the U.S. government was to attack the opposition. You are employing the same tactics toward Leventhal. . . . I think that is unprofessional, unethical, and, based upon a very careful reading of their statement, irresponsible.

Now, I would like to ask you if you would care to apologize to the Leventhal firm.

Mr. Gladstone: *First, Mr. Leach, I stated in my opening remarks that I believed that their report was general and sweeping and unprofessional, because what I would call unprofessional about it is the statement that looking at 15 transactions, that therefore they would conclude that nothing Lincoln did had the substance—*

Congressman Leach: *I have carefully read their report, and they note that they have just been allowed to look at 15 transactions. They could not go into more detail, but they were saying that ACC batted 15 for 15, that all 15 transactions were unusual, perplexing, and in their judgment in each case breached ethical standards in terms of generally accepted accounting principles.*

Your firm in effect is saying, "We think that there may be some legal liabilities. Therefore, we are going to stonewall, and we are going to defend each and every one of these transactions."

I believe that you are one of the great firms in the history of accounting. But I also believe that big and great people and institutions can sometimes err. And it is better to acknowledge error than to put one's head in the sand.

I think before our committee you have rather righteously done that.

EPILOGUE

Anthony Elliot, a widower and retired accountant in his 80s, was one of thousands of elderly Californians who invested heavily in the junk bonds of Lincoln Savings and Loan's parent company, ACC. In fact, Elliot invested practically all of his life savings, approximately $200,000, in the ACC bonds. Like many of his friends who had also purchased the bonds—which they, along with Elliot, believed were federally insured—Elliot was forced to scrape by each month on his small Social Security check after ACC defaulted on the bonds. On Thanksgiving Day 1990, Elliot slashed his wrists and bled to death in his bathtub. In a suicide note, he remarked that there was "nothing left for me."[13] Elliot's story is just one of many personal tragedies resulting from the Lincoln Savings and Loan scandal.

The estimated losses linked to the demise of Lincoln Savings and Loan eventually rose to $3.4 billion, making it the most costly savings and loan failure in U.S. history. In March 1991, after posting huge losses—approximately $1 billion in 1989 alone—most of Lincoln's remaining assets were sold to another financial institution by the Resolution Trust Corporation, which had been operating the savings and loan for more than one year. One month later, Lincoln's parent company, ACC, filed for protection from its creditors under the federal bankruptcy laws.

In late 1992, Ernst & Young paid $400 million to settle four lawsuits filed against it by the

---

13. M. Connelly, "Victim of S & L Loss Kills Self," *Los Angeles Times*, 29 November 1990, B1.

federal government. These lawsuits charged Ernst & Young with substandard audits of four savings and loans, including Lincoln Savings and Loan. In a similar settlement reported in 1993, Arthur Andersen paid $85 million to the federal government to settle lawsuits that charged the firm with shoddy audits of five savings and loans, including Lincoln. Finally, although Touche Ross served as Lincoln's auditor for only five months, that firm's successor, Deloitte & Touche, paid nearly $8 million to the federal government to settle charges filed against it for its role in the Lincoln debacle.

In April 1991, Ernst & Young agreed to pay the California State Board of Accountancy $1.5 million to settle negligence complaints that the state agency filed against the firm for Arthur Young's audits of Lincoln. An Ernst & Young spokesman noted that the accounting firm agreed to the settlement to "avoid protracted and costly litigation" and insisted that the settlement did not involve the "admission of any fault by the firm or any partner."[14] In August 1994, Arthur Andersen agreed to pay $1.7 million to the California State Board of Accountancy for its alleged negligence in auditing Lincoln. Andersen personnel were also required to perform 10,000 hours of community service. Like Ernst & Young, Andersen denied any wrongdoing when its settlement with the California State Board was announced.

In October 1990, Ernie Garcia pleaded guilty to fraud for his involvement in the Hidden Valley real estate transaction. His plea bargain agreement with federal prosecutors required him to assist them in their investigation of Charles Keating, Jr. In March 1991, the Lincoln executive who oversaw the sale of ACC's junk bonds through Lincoln's branches pleaded guilty to eight state and federal fraud charges that he had misled the investors who purchased those bonds. Two years later, Charles Keating III was sentenced to eight years in prison after being convicted of fraud and conspiracy charges.

In a California jury trial presided over by Judge Lance Ito, Charles Keating, Jr., was convicted in 1991 on 17 counts of securities fraud for his role in marketing ACC's junk bonds. While serving a 10-year prison term for that conviction, Keating was convicted of similar fraud charges in a federal court and sentenced to an additional 12 years in prison.

In April 1996, a federal appeals court overturned Keating's 1991 conviction. The appellate court ruled that Judge Lance Ito had given improper instructions to the jurors who found Keating guilty of securities fraud. Several months later, a U.S. District judge overturned Keating's federal conviction on fraud charges. The judge ruled that several jurors in the federal trial had been aware of Keating's 1991 conviction. According to the judge, that knowledge had likely prejudiced the federal jury in favor of convicting Keating. For the same reason, the judge overturned the 1993 conviction of Charles Keating III.

With both of his convictions overturned, Charles Keating was released from federal prison in December 1996 after serving four and one-half years. In January 1999, federal prosecutors announced that they would retry the 75-year-old Keating on various fraud charges. Three months later, the federal prosecutors and Keating reached an agreement, an agreement that gave both parties what they wanted most. In federal court, Keating admitted for the first time that he had committed various fraudulent acts while serving as ACC's chief executive. In return, Keating was sentenced to the time he had already served in prison. Even more important to Keating, his plea bargain arrangement required federal prosecutors to drop all charges still outstanding against his son, Charles Keating III.[15]

---

14. "E & Y Pays $1.5M in Lincoln Failure," *Accounting Today*, 13 May 1991, 1, 25.

15. In November 2000, California state prosecutors announced that they would not retry Charles Keating for his role in marketing ACC's junk bonds. This announcement effectively ended Keating's legal problems linked to the collapse of Lincoln Savings and Loan.

Questions

1. Arthur Young was criticized for not encouraging Lincoln to invoke the substance-over-form principle when accounting for its large real estate transactions. Briefly describe the substance-over-form concept and exactly what it requires. What responsibility, if any, do auditors have when a client violates this principle?

2. Explain how the acceptance of large, high-risk audit clients for relatively high audit fees may threaten an audit firm's *de facto* and perceived independence. Under what circumstances should such prospective clients be avoided?

3. How is an auditor's examination affected when a client has engaged in significant related-party transactions? What measures should an auditor take to determine that such transactions have been properly recorded by a client?

4. Professional standards require auditors to consider a client's "control environment." Define *control environment*. What weaknesses, if any, were evident in Lincoln's control environment?

5. What was the significance of Lincoln receiving nonrecourse notes rather than recourse notes as payment or partial payment on many of the properties it sold?

6. *SAS No. 106*, "Audit Evidence," identifies the principal "management assertions" that underlie a set of financial statements. What were the key assertions that Arthur Young should have attempted to substantiate for the Hidden Valley transaction? What procedures should Arthur Young have used for this purpose, and what types of evidence should have been collected?

7. Do you believe that Jack Atchison's close relationship with Lincoln and Charles Keating prior to his leaving Arthur Young was proper? Why or why not? After joining Lincoln's parent company, ACC, should Atchison have "interfaced" with the Arthur Young auditors assigned to the Lincoln and ACC engagements? Again, support your answer.

8. Does the *AICPA Code of Professional Conduct* discuss the collegial responsibilities of CPA firms? In your opinion, were representatives of either Ernst & Young or Kenneth Leventhal & Company unprofessional in this regard during their congressional testimony?

9. What responsibility does an auditor have to uncover fraud perpetrated by client management? Discuss factors that mitigate this responsibility and factors that compound it. Relate this discussion to Arthur Young's audits of Lincoln.

Crazy Eddie, Inc.

In 1969, Eddie Antar, a 21-year-old high school dropout from Brooklyn, opened a consumer electronics store with 150 square feet of floor space in New York City.[1] Despite this modest beginning, Antar would eventually dominate the retail consumer electronics market in the New York City metropolitan area. By 1987, Antar's firm, Crazy Eddie, Inc., had 43 retail outlets, sales exceeding $350 million, and outstanding stock with a collective market value of $600 million. Antar personally realized more than $70 million from the sale of Crazy Eddie stock during his tenure as the company's chief executive.

A classic rags-to-riches story became a spectacular business failure in the late 1980s when Crazy Eddie collapsed following allegations of extensive financial wrongdoing by Antar and his associates. Shortly after a hostile takeover of the company in November 1987, the firm's new owners discovered that Crazy Eddie's inventory was overstated by more than $65 million. This inventory shortage had been concealed from the public in registration statements filed with the Securities and Exchange Commission (SEC). Subsequent investigations by regulatory authorities revealed that Eddie Antar and his subordinates had grossly overstated Crazy Eddie's reported profits throughout its existence.[2]

Eddie Antar: The Man Behind the Legend

Eddie Antar was born into a large, closely knit Syrian family in 1947. After dropping out of high school at the age of 16, Antar began peddling television sets in his Brooklyn neighborhood. Within a few years, Antar and one of his cousins scraped together enough cash to open an electronics store near Coney Island. It was at this tiny store that Antar acquired the nickname "Crazy Eddie." When a customer attempted to leave the store empty-handed, Antar would block the store's exit, sometimes locking the door until the individual agreed to buy something—anything. To entice a reluctant customer to make a purchase, Antar first determined which product the customer was considering and then lowered the price until the customer finally capitulated.

Antar became well known in his neighborhood not only for his unusual sales tactics but also for his unconventional, if not asocial, behavior. A bodybuilder and fitness fanatic, he typically came to work in his exercise togs, accompanied by a menacing German shepherd. His quick temper caused repeated problems with vendors, competitors, and subordinates. Antar's most distinctive trait was his inability to trust anyone outside of his large extended family. In later years, when he needed someone to serve in an executive capacity in his company, Antar nearly always

---

1. This case was coauthored by Carol Knapp, Assistant Professor at the University of Oklahoma.

2. The facts of this case were drawn from numerous articles and SEC enforcement releases published over a period of several years. *The New York Times* and *The Wall Street Journal,* in particular, closely followed the colorful saga of Crazy Eddie and its founder, Eddie Antar. One of the more comprehensive investigative reports that documented the history of Crazy Eddie, Inc., is the following article: G. Belsky and P. Furman, "Calculated Madness: The Rise and Fall of Crazy Eddie Antar," *Crain's New York Business,* 5 June 1989, 21–33. That article provided much of the background information regarding Eddie Antar that is included in this case.

tapped a family member, although the individual seldom had the appropriate training or experience for the position. Eventually, Antar's father, sister, two brothers, uncle, brother-in-law, and several cousins would assume leadership positions with Crazy Eddie, while more than one dozen other relatives would hold minor positions with the firm.

Crazy Eddie's Formula for Success

In the early 1980s, sales in the consumer electronics industry exploded, doubling in the four-year period from 1981 to 1984 alone. As the public's demand for electronic products grew at an ever-increasing pace, Antar converted his Crazy Eddie stores into consumer electronics supermarkets. Antar stocked the shelves of Crazy Eddie's retail outlets with every electronic gadget he could find and with as many different brands of those products as possible. By 1987, the company featured seven product lines. Following are those product lines and their percentage contributions to Crazy Eddie's 1987 sales.

Televisions	53%
Audio products and systems	15
Portable and personal electronics	10
Car stereos	5
Accessories and tapes	4
Computers and games	3
Miscellaneous items—including microwaves, air conditioners, and small appliances	10
Total	100%

Antar encouraged his salespeople to supplement each store's profits by pressuring customers to buy extended product warranties. Many, if not most, of the repair costs that Crazy Eddie paid under these warranties were recovered by the company from manufacturers that had issued factory warranties on the products. As a result, the company realized a 100 percent profit margin on much of its warranty revenue.

As his firm grew rapidly during the late 1970s and early 1980s, Antar began extracting large price concessions from his suppliers. His ability to purchase electronic products in large quantities and at cut-rate prices enabled him to become a "transshipper," or secondary supplier, of these goods to smaller consumer electronics retailers in the New York City area. Although manufacturers frowned on this practice and often threatened to stop selling to him, Antar continually increased the scale of his transshipping operation.

The most important ingredient in Antar's marketing strategy was large-scale advertising. Antar created an advertising "umbrella" over his company's principal retail market that included the densely populated area within a 150-mile radius of New York City. Antar blanketed this region with raucous, sometimes annoying, but always memorable radio and television commercials.

In 1972, Antar hired a local radio personality and part-time actor known as Doctor Jerry to serve as Crazy Eddie's advertising spokesperson. Over the 15 years that the bug-eyed Doctor Jerry hawked products for Crazy Eddie, he achieved a higher "recognition quotient" among the public than Ed Koch, the longtime mayor of New York City. Doctor Jerry's series of ear-piercing television commercials that featured him screaming "Crazy Eddie—His prices are insane!" brought the company national notoriety when they were parodied by Dan Akroyd on *Saturday Night Live*.

Crazy Eddie's discounting policy served as the focal theme of the company's advertising campaigns. The company promised to refund the difference between the selling price of a product and any lower price for that same item that a customer found within 30 days of the purchase date. Despite the advertising barrage intended to convince the public that Crazy Eddie was a deep-discounter, the company's prices on most products were in line with those of its major competitors. Customers drawn to Crazy Eddie outlets by "advertised specials" were routinely diverted by sales staff to higher-priced merchandise.

Crazy Eddie Goes Public

In 1983, Antar decided to sell stock in Crazy Eddie to raise capital to finance his aggressive expansion program. The underwriting firm retained by Antar delayed Crazy Eddie's initial public offering (IPO) for more than one year after discovering that the company's financial records were in disarray. Among other problems uncovered by the underwriter were extensive related-party transactions, interest-free loans to employees, and speculative investments unrelated to the company's principal line of business. The underwriting firm was also disturbed to find that nearly all of the company's key executives were members of the Antar family. Certain of these individuals, including Antar's wife and mother, were receiving salaries approaching $100,000 for little or no work.

To prepare for the IPO, the underwriter encouraged Antar, Crazy Eddie's chairman of the board and president, to clean up the company's accounting records and financial affairs. The underwriter also urged Antar to hire a chief financial officer (CFO) who had experience with a public company and who was not a member of the Antar family. The underwriter warned Antar that investors would question the competence of Crazy Eddie's executives who were his relatives. Despite the underwriter's concern, Antar hired his first cousin, Sam E. Antar, to serve as Crazy Eddie's CFO.

The sale of Crazy Eddie's stock to the public was a tremendous success. Because the IPO was oversubscribed, the company's underwriter obtained permission from the SEC to sell 200,000 more shares than originally planned. Following the public offering, Antar worked hard to convince the investment community, particularly financial analysts, that his firm was financially strong and well managed. At every opportunity, Antar painted a picture of continued growth and increased market share for Crazy Eddie.

One tactic Antar used to convince financial analysts that the company had a rosy future was to invite them to a store and demonstrate in person his uncanny ability to "close" sales. Such tactics worked to perfection as analysts from the most prominent investment firms released glowing reports regarding Crazy Eddie's management team and the company's bright prospects. One analyst wrote, "Crazy Eddie is a disciplined, competently organized firm with a sophisticated management and a well-trained, dedicated staff."[3] Another analyst wrote that Antar is a "brilliant merchant surrounded by a deeply dedicated organization eager to create an important retail business."[4] Because of such reports and continued strong operating results (as reflected by the company's 1984–1987 financial statements shown in Exhibit 1 and Exhibit 2), the price of Crazy Eddie's stock skyrocketed. Many investors who purchased the company's stock in the IPO realized a 1,000 percent increase in the value of their investments.

3. J. E. Tannenbaum, "How Mounting Woes at Crazy Eddie Sank Turnaround Effort," *The Wall Street Journal*, 10 July 1989, A1, A4.

4. G. Belsky and P. Furman, "Calculated Madness: The Rise and Fall of Crazy Eddie Antar," *Crain's New York Business*, 5 June 1989, 26.

EXHIBIT 1

1984–1987
BALANCE SHEETS
OF CRAZY EDDIE

CRAZY EDDIE, INC.
BALANCE SHEETS (000s omitted)

	March 1, 1987	March 2, 1986	March 3, 1985	May 31, 1984
Current assets:				
Cash	$ 9,347	$ 13,296	$22,273	$ 1,375
Short-term investments	121,957	26,840	—	—
Receivables	10,846	2,246	2,740	2,604
Merchandise inventories	109,072	59,864	26,543	23,343
Prepaid expenses	10,639	2,363	645	514
Total current assets	261,861	104,609	52,201	27,836
Restricted cash	—	3,356	7,058	—
Due from affiliates	—	—	—	5,739
Property, plant and equipment	26,401	7,172	3,696	1,845
Construction in process	—	6,253	1,154	—
Other assets	6,596	5,560	1,419	1,149
Total assets	$294,858	$126,950	$65,528	$36,569
Current liabilities:				
Accounts payable	$ 50,022	$ 51,723	$23,078	$20,106
Notes payable	—	—	—	2,900
Short-term debt	49,571	2,254	423	124
Unearned revenue	3,641	3,696	1,173	764
Accrued expenses	5,593	17,126	8,733	6,078
Total current liabilities	108,827	74,799	33,407	29,972
Long-term debt	8,459	7,701	7,625	46
Convertible subordinated debentures	80,975	—	—	—
Unearned revenue	3,337	1,829	635	327
Stockholders' equity:				
Common stock	313	280	134	50
Additional paid-in capital	57,678	17,668	12,298	574
Retained earnings	35,269	24,673	11,429	5,600
Total stockholders' equity	93,260	42,621	23,861	6,224
Total liabilities and stockholders' equity	$294,858	$126,950	$65,528	$36,569

Crazy Eddie Goes . . . Bust

Despite Crazy Eddie's impressive operating results during the mid-1980s and the fact that the company's stock was one of the hottest investments on Wall Street, all was not well within the firm. By 1986, the company was in deep trouble. By the latter part of that year, the boom days had ended for the consumer electronics industry. Although sales of consumer electronics were still increasing, the rate of growth had tapered off considerably as compared with the dramatic growth rates realized by the industry during the early 1980s. Additionally, the industry had become saturated with retailers, particularly in major metropolitan areas such as New York City, Crazy Eddie's

EXHIBIT 2

1984–1987 INCOME
STATEMENTS OF
CRAZY EDDIE

CRAZY EDDIE, INC. INCOME STATEMENTS (000s omitted)				
	Year Ended March 1, 1987	Year Ended March 2, 1986	Nine Months Ended March 3, 1985	Year Ended May 31, 1984
Net sales	$352,523	$262,268	$136,319	$137,285
Cost of goods sold	(272,255)	(194,371)	(103,421)	(106,934)
Gross profit	80,268	67,897	32,898	30,351
Selling, general and administrative expense	(61,341)	(42,975)	(20,508)	(22,560)
Interest and other income	7,403	3,210	1,211	706
Interest expense	(5,233)	(820)	(438)	(522)
Income before taxes	21,097	27,312	13,163	7,975
Pension contribution	(500)	(800)	(600)	—
Income taxes	(10,001)	(13,268)	(6,734)	(4,202)
Net income	$ 10,596	$ 13,244	$ 5,829	$ 3,773
Net income per share	$.34	$.48	$.24	$.18

home base. Increased competition meant smaller profit margins for Crazy Eddie and diminished Antar's ability to extract sweetheart deals from his suppliers.

Besides the problems posed by the increasingly competitive consumer electronics industry, Crazy Eddie faced a corporate meltdown in the late 1980s. The tripling of the company's annual sales volume between 1984 and 1987 and the more complex responsibilities associated with managing a public company imposed an enormous administrative burden on Crazy Eddie's executives. Complicating matters was the disintegration of Antar's inner circle of relatives, who had served as his principal advisers during the first 15 years of his company's existence. Antar forced many of his relatives to leave the firm after they sided with his former wife in a bitter divorce. Even as Crazy Eddie's internal affairs spiraled into chaos and the firm lurched toward financial disaster, Wall Street continued to tout the company's stock as a "can't miss" investment.

In late 1986, Eddie Antar resigned as company president, although he retained the title of chairman of the board. A few weeks later, he simply dropped out of sight. In the absence of Antar, Crazy Eddie's financial condition worsened rapidly. Poor operating results that the company reported for the fourth quarter of fiscal 1987—which ended March 1, 1987—sent Crazy Eddie's stock price into a tailspin from which it never recovered. In November 1987, a takeover group headed by two prominent financiers gained control of the company. A company-wide physical inventory taken by the new owners uncovered the $65 million shortage of inventory alluded to earlier. That inventory shortage, which was larger than the total profits the company had reported since it went public in 1984, would eventually plunge Crazy Eddie into bankruptcy and send regulatory authorities in pursuit of Eddie Antar for an explanation.

Charges of Accounting Irregularities

Extensive investigations of Crazy Eddie's financial records by the new owners and regulatory authorities culminated in fraud charges being filed against Eddie Antar and his former associates. The SEC alleged that after Crazy Eddie went public in 1984, Antar became preoccupied with the price of his company's stock. Antar realized that Crazy Eddie had to keep posting impressive operating results to maintain the upward trend in the stock's price. An SEC investigation revealed that within the first six months after the company went public, Antar ordered a subordinate to overstate inventory by $2 million, resulting in the firm's gross profit being overstated by the same amount. The following year Antar ordered year-end inventory to be overstated by $9 million and accounts payable to be understated by $3 million. Court records documented that Crazy Eddie employees overstated year-end inventory by preparing inventory count sheets for items that did not exist. To understate accounts payable, employees prepared bogus debit memos and entered them in the company's accounting records.

As the economic fortunes of Crazy Eddie began to fade in the late 1980s, Antar became more desperate in his efforts to enhance the company's reported revenues and profits. He ordered company employees to include in inventory consigned merchandise and goods being returned to suppliers. Another fraudulent tactic Antar used to overstate inventory involved transhipping transactions, the large-volume transactions between Crazy Eddie and many of its smaller competitors.

Antar knew that financial analysts closely monitor the annual percentage change in "same store" sales for retailers. A decline in this percentage is seen as a negative indicator of a retailer's future financial performance. As the consumer electronics industry became increasingly crowded, the revenues of Crazy Eddie's individual stores began to fall, although the firm's total revenues continued to climb due to new stores being opened each year. To remedy the drop in same-store sales, Antar instructed his employees to record selected transhipping transactions as retail sales of individual stores. For instance, suppose that Crazy Eddie sold 100 microwaves costing $180 each to another retailer at a per unit price of $200. The $20,000 in sales would be recorded as retail sales with a normal gross profit margin of 30 to 50 percent—meaning that inventory would not be credited for the total number of microwaves actually sold. This practice killed two birds with the proverbial stone. Same-store sales were inflated for selected operating units, and inventory was overstated with a corresponding increase in gross profit from sales.

Where Were the Auditors?

"Where were the auditors?" was a question posed repeatedly by investors, creditors, and other interested parties when the public learned of the Crazy Eddie fraud. Four different accounting firms audited Crazy Eddie's financial statements over its turbulent history. Antar dismissed Crazy Eddie's first accounting firm, a local firm, before he took the company public. The underwriter that managed Crazy Eddie's IPO urged Antar to retain a more prestigious accounting firm to increase the public's confidence in the company's financial statements. As a result, Antar retained Main Hurdman to serve as Crazy Eddie's audit firm. Main Hurdman had a nationwide accounting practice with several prominent clients in the consumer electronics industry. In the mid-1980s, Peat Marwick became Crazy Eddie's audit firm when it merged with Main Hurdman. Following the corporate takeover of Crazy Eddie in 1987, the new owners replaced Peat Marwick with Touche Ross.

Much of the criticism triggered by the Crazy Eddie scandal centered on Main Hurdman and its successor, Peat Marwick. Main Hurdman charged Crazy Eddie comparatively modest fees for the company's annual audits. A leading critic of major accounting firms alleged that Main Hurdman had "lowballed" to obtain Crazy Eddie as an audit client, realizing that it could make up for any lost audit revenue by selling the company consulting services.

> *In one year, Main Hurdman charged only $85,000 to do a complete audit of Crazy Eddie—a business with hundreds of millions of dollars in reported revenues, dozens of retail stores, and two large warehouses. At the very same time that Main Hurdman was charging the bargain basement price of $85,000 for supposedly conducting an audit, its consulting division was charging Crazy Eddie millions of dollars to computerize Crazy Eddie's inventory system.[5]*

This same individual challenged Main Hurdman's ability to objectively audit an inventory system that it had effectively developed. Main Hurdman's independence was also questioned because many of Crazy Eddie's accountants were former members of that accounting firm. Critics charge that a company that hires one or more of its former auditors can more easily conceal fraudulent activities during the course of subsequent audits. That is, a former auditor may help his or her new employer undermine subsequent audits. In fact, Crazy Eddie's practice of hiring its former auditors is not unusual. Many accounting firms actually arrange such "placements" with audit clients.

> *You would think that if an auditor wanted to leave a public accounting firm, he or she would be discouraged from going to work for clients they had audited. Instead, just the opposite is true with big accounting firms encouraging their personnel to work for clients in the apparent belief that it helps cement the accountant–client relationship.[6]*

Most of the criticism directed at Crazy Eddie's auditors stemmed from their failure to uncover the huge overstatement of the company's inventory and the material understatement of accounts payable. Third parties who filed suit against the auditors accused them of "aiding and abetting" the fraud by failing to thoroughly investigate numerous suspicious circumstances they discovered. Of particular concern were several reported instances in which the auditors requested client documents, only to be told that those documents had been lost or inadvertently destroyed.

In Peat Marwick and Main Hurdman's defense, Antar and his associates engaged in a large-scale plan to deceive the auditors. For example, after determining which inventory sites the auditors would be visiting at year-end, Antar shipped sufficient inventory to those stores or warehouses to conceal any shortages. Likewise, Crazy Eddie personnel systematically destroyed incriminating documents to conceal inventory shortages from the auditors. Antar also ordered his employees to "junk" the sophisticated, computer-based inventory system designed by Main Hurdman and to return to the outdated manual inventory system previously used by the company. The absence of a computer-based inventory system made it much more difficult for the auditors to determine exactly how much inventory the firm had at any point in time.

A particularly disturbing aspect of the Crazy Eddie scandal was the involvement of several key accounting employees in the various fraudulent schemes. These parties included the director of the internal audit staff, the acting controller, and the director of accounts payable. Past audit failures demonstrate that a fraud involving the collusion of key accounting personnel is difficult for auditors to uncover.

---

5. M. I. Weiss, "Auditors: Be Watchdogs, Not Just Bean Counters," *Accounting Today*, 15 November 1993, 41.

6. *Ibid.*, 42.

EPILOGUE

In June 1989, Crazy Eddie filed a Chapter 11 bankruptcy petition after losing its line of credit. Later that year, the company closed its remaining stores and liquidated its assets. Meanwhile, Eddie Antar was named as a defendant in several lawsuits, including a large civil suit filed by the SEC and a criminal indictment filed by a *U.S. District Attorney.* In January 1990, a federal judge ordered Antar to repatriate $52 million that he had transferred to foreign bank accounts in 1987.

The following month, federal marshals began searching for Antar after he failed to appear in federal court. A judge had scheduled a hearing to force Antar to account for the funds he had transferred to overseas bank accounts. After Antar surrendered to federal marshals, the judge found him in contempt and released him on his own recognizance. Following this court appearance, Antar became a fugitive. For the next two years, Antar eluded federal authorities despite reported sightings of him in Brooklyn, South America, and Jerusalem.

On June 25, 1992, Israeli police arrested Eddie Antar. At the time, he was living in a small town outside Tel Aviv and posing as an Israeli citizen, David Jacob Levi Cohen. On December 31, 1992, Antar's attorney announced that an extradition agreement had been reached with the U.S. Department of Justice and Israeli authorities. After being extradited, Antar was convicted in July 1993 on 17 counts of financial fraud including racketeering, conspiracy, and mail fraud. In May 1994, a federal judge sentenced Antar to 12½ years in federal prison and ordered him to pay restitution of $121 million to former stockholders and creditors.

A federal appeals court overturned Antar's fraud conviction in April 1995. The appeals court ruled that the judge who had presided over Antar's trial had been biased against him and ordered that a new trial be held under a different judge. In May 1996, Antar's attorneys and federal prosecutors arranged a plea bargain agreement to settle the charges outstanding against him. Under the terms of this agreement, Antar pleaded guilty to one federal charge of racketeering and publicly admitted, for the first time, that he had defrauded investors by manipulating his company's accounting records. Following his admission of guilt, one of the prosecuting attorneys commented that "Crazy Eddie wasn't crazy, he was crooked."[7]

In early 1997, Eddie Antar was sentenced to seven years in federal prison. Antar, who had remained in custody since being extradited to the United States in 1993, received credit for the time he had already spent in prison. As a result, he was required to serve only two years of his seven-year sentence.

Several of Antar's former cohorts have also been convicted or have pleaded guilty to fraud charges, including Sam E. Antar, Crazy Eddie's former CFO. After being released from prison, Sam E. Antar openly described and discussed his role in the fraud masterminded by his cousin. He revealed that Eddie had financed his college degree in accounting because the family needed an expert accountant to help design, manage, and conceal the company's fraudulent schemes. Sam graduated *magna cum laude* in accounting and passed the CPA exam on his first attempt. Upon joining Crazy Eddie, Sam confessed that he became a "thug" and a willing participant in the massive fraud:

> *Crazy Eddie was an empire built on deceit. The company was rotten to its core. Eddie Antar, his father, brothers, brother-in-law, me, and others formed the nucleus of this massive criminal enterprise. In our day, we considered the humanity of others as weaknesses to be exploited in our efforts to commit our crimes. We simply gave investors, creditors, and many customers a raw deal.... We were nothing but cold-hearted and soulless criminals. We were two-bit thugs.*[8]

---

7. F.A. McMorris, "Crazy Eddie Inc.'s Antar Admits Guilt in Racketeering Conspiracy," *The Wall Street Journal,* 9 May 1996, B7.

8. Sam E. Antar, "Crazy Eddie Speaks, Cousin Sam E. Antar Responds," *White Collar Fraud* (http://whitecollarfraud.blogspot.com), 25 June 2007.

In March 1993, an agreement was reached to settle dozens of pending civil lawsuits spawned by the Crazy Eddie fraud. The contributions of the various defendants to the $42 million settlement pool were not disclosed; however, the defendants contributing to that pool included Peat Marwick and the local accounting firm used by Crazy Eddie before the company went public. To date, authorities have recovered more than $150 million from the parties that profited from the fraud. These funds include more than $40 million that a federal judge ordered Sam Antar, Eddie Antar's father, to surrender in August 2002.

In the late 1990s, Eddie Antar's mother purchased the Crazy Eddie logo and the company's former advertising catch phrase, "Crazy Eddie—His prices are insane!" which had been sold in bankruptcy proceedings years earlier. In 1998, two nephews of Eddie Antar revived their uncle's business. The "new" Crazy Eddie operated principally as a mail-order and Internet-based retailer of consumer electronics. In June 2001, a New York business publication reported that the company had hired a former executive in the consumer electronics industry to serve as the "creative force" behind its marketing efforts.[9] That individual was none other than Crazy Eddie Antar.[10]

Questions

1. Compute key ratios and other financial measures for Crazy Eddie during the period 1984–1987. Identify and briefly explain the red flags in Crazy Eddie's financial statements that suggested the firm posed a higher-than-normal level of audit risk.

2. Identify specific audit procedures that might have led to the detection of the following accounting irregularities perpetrated by Crazy Eddie personnel: (a) the falsification of inventory count sheets, (b) the bogus debit memos for accounts payable, (c) the recording of transhipping transactions as retail sales, and (d) the inclusion of consigned merchandise in year-end inventory.

3. The retail consumer electronics industry was undergoing rapid and dramatic changes during the 1980s. Discuss how changes in an audit client's industry should affect audit planning decisions. Relate this discussion to Crazy Eddie.

4. Explain what is implied by the term *lowballing* in an audit context. How can this practice potentially affect the quality of independent audit services?

5. Assume that you were a member of the Crazy Eddie audit team in 1986. You were assigned to test the client's year-end inventory cutoff procedures. You selected 30 invoices entered in the accounting records near year-end: 15 in the few days prior to the client's fiscal year-end and 15 in the first few days of the new year. Assume that client personnel were unable to locate 10 of these invoices. How should you and your superiors have responded to this situation? Explain.

6. Should companies be allowed to hire individuals who formerly served as their independent auditors? Discuss the pros and cons of this practice.

---

9. *Crain's New York Business*, "Week in Review," 11 June 2001, 34.

10. In 2004, the "new" Crazy Eddie failed. The company's trademarks were purchased by a Texas-based firm.

CASE 1.9

ZZZZ Best Company, Inc.

On May 19, 1987, a short article in *The Wall Street Journal* reported that ZZZZ Best Company, Inc., of Reseda, California, had signed a contract for a $13.8 million insurance restoration project. This project was just the most recent of a series of large restoration jobs obtained by ZZZZ Best (pronounced "zee best"). Located in the San Fernando Valley of southern California, ZZZZ Best had begun operations in the fall of 1982 as a small, door-to-door carpet cleaning operation. Under the direction of Barry Minkow, the extroverted 16-year-old who founded the company and initially operated it out of his parents' garage, ZZZZ Best experienced explosive growth in both revenues and profits during the first several years of its existence. In the three-year period from 1984 to 1987, the company's net income surged from less than $200,000 to more than $5 million on revenues of $50 million.

When ZZZZ Best went public in 1986, Minkow and several of his close associates became multimillionaires overnight. By the late spring of 1987, the market value of Minkow's stock in the company exceeded $100 million, while the total market value of ZZZZ Best surpassed $200 million. The youngest chief executive officer in the nation enjoyed the "good life," which included an elegant home in an exclusive suburb of Los Angeles and a fire-engine red Ferrari. Minkow's charm and entrepreneurial genius made him a sought-after commodity on the television talk show circuit and caused the print and visual media to tout him as an example of what America's youth could attain if they would only apply themselves. During an appearance on *The Oprah Winfrey Show* in April 1987, Minkow exhorted his peers with evangelistic zeal to "Think big, be big" and encouraged them to adopt his personal motto, "The sky is the limit."

Less than two years after appearing on *Oprah*, Barry Minkow began serving a 25-year prison sentence. Tried and convicted on 57 counts of securities fraud, Minkow had been exposed as a fast-talking con artist who swindled his closest friends and Wall Street out of millions of dollars. Federal prosecutors estimate that, at a minimum, Minkow cost investors and creditors $100 million. The company that Minkow founded was, in fact, an elaborate Ponzi scheme. The reported profits of the firm were nonexistent and the large restoration contracts, imaginary. As one journalist reported, rather than building a corporation, Minkow created a hologram of a corporation. In July 1987, just three months after the company's stock reached a market value of $220 million, an auction of its assets netted only $62,000.

Unlike most financial frauds, the ZZZZ Best scam was perpetrated under the watchful eye of the Securities and Exchange Commission (SEC). The SEC, a large and reputable West Coast law firm that served as the company's general counsel, a prominent Wall Street brokerage firm, and an international public accounting firm all failed to uncover Minkow's daring scheme. Ultimately, the persistence of an indignant homemaker who had been bilked out of a few hundred dollars by ZZZZ Best resulted in Minkow being exposed as a fraud.

How a teenage flimflam artist could make a mockery of the complex regulatory structure that oversees the U.S. securities markets was the central question posed by a congressional subcommittee that investigated the ZZZZ Best debacle. That subcommittee was headed by Representative John D. Dingell, chairman of the U.S. House Committee on Energy and Commerce. Throughout the investigation,

Representative Dingell and his colleagues focused on the role the company's independent auditors played in the ZZZZ Best scandal.

> *The ZZZZ Best prospectus told the public that revenues and earnings from insurance restoration contracts were skyrocketing but did not reveal that the contracts were completely fictitious. Where were the independent auditors and the others that are paid to alert the public to fraud and deceit?*[1]

Like many other daring financial frauds, the ZZZZ Best scandal caused Congress to reexamine the maze of rules that regulate financial reporting and serve as the foundation of the U.S. system of corporate oversight. However, Daniel Akst, a reporter for *The Wall Street Journal* who documented the rise and fall of Barry Minkow, suggested that another ZZZZ Best was inevitable. "Changing the accounting rules and securities laws will help, but every now and then a Barry Minkow will come along, and ZZZZ Best will happen again. Such frauds are in the natural order of things, I suspect, as old and enduring as human needs."[2]

The Early History of ZZZZ Best Company

Barry Minkow was introduced to the carpet cleaning industry at the age of 12 by his mother, who helped make ends meet by working as a telephone solicitor for a small carpet cleaning firm. Although the great majority of companies in the carpet cleaning industry are legitimate, the nature of the business attracts a disproportionate number of shady characters. There are essentially no barriers to entry: no licensing requirements, no apprenticeships to be served, and only a minimal amount of start-up capital is needed. A 16-year-old youth with a driver's license can easily become what industry insiders refer to as a "rug sucker," which is exactly what Minkow did when he founded ZZZZ Best Company.

Minkow quickly learned that carpet cleaning was a difficult way to earn a livelihood. Customer complaints, ruthless competition, bad checks, and nagging vendors demanding payment complicated the young entrepreneur's life. Within months of striking out on his own, Minkow faced the ultimate nemesis of the small businessperson: a shortage of working capital. Because of his age and the fact that ZZZZ Best was only marginally profitable, local banks refused to loan him money. Ever resourceful, the brassy teenager came up with his own innovative ways to finance his business: check kiting, credit card forgeries, and the staging of thefts to fleece his insurance company. Minkow's age and personal charm allowed him to escape unscathed from his early brushes with the law that resulted from his creative financing methods. The ease with which the "system" could be beaten encouraged him to exploit it on a broader scale.

Throughout his tenure with ZZZZ Best, Minkow recognized the benefits of having an extensive social network of friends and acquaintances. Many of these relationships he developed and cultivated at a Los Angeles health club. After becoming a friend of Tom Padgett, an insurance claims adjuster, Minkow devised a scheme to exploit that friendship. Minkow promised to pay Padgett $100 per week if he would simply confirm over the telephone to banks and any other interested third parties that ZZZZ Best was the recipient of occasional insurance restoration contracts. Ostensibly, Minkow had obtained these contracts to clean and do minor remodeling work on properties damaged by fire, storms, or other catastrophes. Minkow convinced the

1. This and all subsequent quotations, unless indicated otherwise, were taken from the following source: U.S. Congress, House, Subcommittee on Oversight and Investigations of the Committee on Energy and Commerce, *Failure of ZZZZ Best Co.* (Washington, DC: U.S. Government Printing Office, 1988).

2. D. Akst, *Wonder Boy, Barry Minkow—The Kid Who Swindled Wall Street* (New York: Scribner, 1990), 271.

gullible Padgett that the sole purpose of the confirmations was to allow ZZZZ Best to circumvent much of the bureaucratic red tape in the insurance industry.

From this modest beginning, the ZZZZ Best fraud blossomed. Initially, Minkow used the phony insurance restoration contracts to generate the paper profits and revenues he needed to convince bankers to loan him money. Minkow's phony financial statements served their purpose, and he expanded his operations by opening several carpet cleaning outlets across the San Fernando Valley. Minkow soon realized that there was no need to tie his future to the cutthroat carpet cleaning industry when he could literally dictate the size and profitability of his insurance restoration "business." Within a short period of time, insurance restoration, rather than carpet cleaning, became the major source of revenue appearing on ZZZZ Best's income statements.

Minkow's "the sky is the limit" philosophy drove him to be even more innovative. The charming young entrepreneur began using his bogus financial statements to entice wealthy individuals in his ever-expanding social network to invest in ZZZZ Best. Eventually, Minkow recognized that the ultimate scam would be to take his company public, a move that would allow him to tap the bank accounts of unsuspecting investors nationwide.

Going Public with ZZZZ Best

Minkow's decision to take ZZZZ Best public meant that he could no longer completely control his firm's financial disclosures. Registering with the SEC required auditors, investment bankers, and outside attorneys to peruse ZZZZ Best's periodic financial statements.

ZZZZ Best was first subjected to a full-scope independent audit for the 12 months ended April 30, 1986. George Greenspan, the sole practitioner who performed that audit, confirmed the existence of ZZZZ Best's major insurance restoration contracts by contacting Tom Padgett. Padgett served as the principal officer of Interstate Appraisal Services, which reportedly contracted the jobs out to ZZZZ Best. By this time, Padgett was an active and willing participant in Minkow's fraudulent schemes. Minkow established Interstate Appraisal Services and Assured Property Management for the sole purpose of generating fake insurance restoration contracts for ZZZZ Best.

In testimony before the congressional subcommittee that investigated the ZZZZ Best scandal, Greenspan insisted that he had properly audited Minkow's company. Greenspan testified that while planning the 1986 audit he had performed various analytical procedures to identify unusual relationships in ZZZZ Best's financial data. These procedures allegedly included comparing ZZZZ Best's key financial ratios with industry norms. Regarding the insurance contracts, Greenspan testified that he had obtained and reviewed copies of all key documents pertaining to those jobs. However, Greenspan admitted that he had not inspected any of the insurance restoration sites.

> **Congressman Lent:**   *Mr. Greenspan, I am interested in the SEC Form S-1 that ZZZZ Best Company filed with the SEC.... You say in that report that you made your examination in accordance with generally accepted auditing standards and accordingly included such tests of the accounting records and other auditing procedures as we consider necessary in the circumstances.... You don't say in that statement that you made any personal on-site inspections.*

> **Mr. Greenspan:**   *It's not required. Sometimes you do; sometimes you don't. I was satisfied that these jobs existed and I was satisfied from at least six different sources, including payment for the job. What could you want better than that?*

Congressman Lent: *Your position is that you are an honest and reputable accountant.*

Mr. Greenspan: *Yes, sir.*

Congressman Lent: *You were as much a victim as some of the investors in this company?*

Mr. Greenspan: *I was a victim all right. . . . I am as much aghast as anyone. And every night I sit down and say, why didn't I detect this damned fraud.*

Retention of Ernst & Whinney by ZZZZ Best

Shortly after Greenspan completed his audit of ZZZZ Best's financial statements for fiscal 1986, which ended April 30, 1986, Minkow dismissed him and retained Ernst & Whinney to perform the following year's audit. Apparently, ZZZZ Best's investment banker insisted that Minkow obtain a Big Eight accounting firm to enhance the credibility of the company's financial statements. At approximately the same time, and for the same reason, Minkow retained a high-profile Los Angeles law firm to represent ZZZZ Best as its legal counsel.

The congressional subcommittee asked Greenspan what information he provided to Ernst & Whinney regarding his former client. In particular, the subcommittee wanted to know whether Greenspan discussed the insurance restoration contracts with the new auditors.

Congressman Wyden: *Mr. Greenspan, in September 1986, Ernst & Whinney came on as the new independent accountant for ZZZZ Best. What did you communicate to Ernst & Whinney with respect to the restoration contracts?*

Mr. Greenspan: *Nothing. I did—there was nothing because they never got in touch with me. It's protocol for the new accountant to get in touch with the old accountant. They never got in touch with me, and it's still a mystery to me.*

Representatives of Ernst & Whinney later testified that they did, in fact, communicate with Greenspan prior to accepting ZZZZ Best as an audit client. However, Ernst & Whinney did not comment on the nature or content of that communication. (Greenspan was not recalled to rebut Ernst & Whinney's testimony on this issue.)[3]

Exhibit 1 contains the engagement letter signed by Ernst & Whinney and Barry Minkow in September 1986. The engagement letter outlined four services that the audit firm intended to provide ZZZZ Best: a review of the company's financial statements for the three-month period ending July 31, 1986; assistance in the preparation of a registration statement to be filed with the SEC; a comfort letter to be submitted to ZZZZ Best's underwriters; and a full-scope audit for the fiscal year ending April 30, 1987. Ernst & Whinney completed the review, provided the comfort letter to ZZZZ Best's underwriters, and apparently assisted the company in preparing the registration statement for the SEC; however, Ernst & Whinney never completed the 1987 audit. The audit firm resigned on June 2, 1987, amid growing concerns that ZZZZ Best's financial statements were grossly misstated.

The congressional subcommittee investigating the ZZZZ Best fraud questioned Ernst & Whinney representatives at length regarding the bogus insurance restoration contracts—contracts that accounted for 90 percent of ZZZZ Best's reported profits.

---

3. After a lengthy investigation, the American Institute of Certified Public Accountants ruled in 1998 that there was no "prima facie evidence" that Greenspan had violated the organization's *Code of Professional Conduct* during the time that ZZZZ Best was his client. A similar conclusion was reached by two state boards of accountancy with which Greenspan was registered to practice public accounting.

EXHIBIT 1

ERNST & WHINNEY'S
ZZZZ BEST
ENGAGEMENT
LETTER

September 12, 1986

Mr. Barry Minkow
Chairman of the Board
ZZZZ Best Co., Inc.
7040 Darby Avenue
Reseda, California

Dear Mr. Minkow:

This letter is to confirm our understanding regarding our engagement as independent accountants of ZZZZ BEST CO., INC. (the Company) and the nature and limitations of the services we will provide.

We will perform the following services:

1. We will review the balance sheet of the Company as of July 31, 1986, and the related statements of income, retained earnings, and changes in financial position for the three months then ended, in accordance with standards established by the American Institute of Certified Public Accountants. We will not perform an audit of such financial statements, the objective of which is the expressing of an opinion regarding the financial statements taken as a whole, and, accordingly, we will not express an opinion on them. Our report on the financial statements is presently expected to read as follows:

> "We have made a review of the condensed consolidated balance sheet of ZZZZ BEST CO., INC. and subsidiaries as of July 31, 1986, and the related condensed consolidated statements of income and changes in financial position for the three-month period ended July 31, 1986, in accordance with standards established by the American Institute of Certified Public Accountants. A review of the condensed consolidated financial statements for the comparative period of the prior year was not made.
>
> A review of financial information consists principally of obtaining an understanding of the system for the preparation of interim financial information, applying analytical review procedures to financial data, and making inquiries of persons responsible for financial and accounting matters. It is substantially less in scope than an examination in accordance with generally accepted auditing standards, which will be performed for the full year with the objective of expressing an opinion regarding the financial statements taken as a whole. Accordingly, we do not express such an opinion. Based on our review, we are not aware of any material modifications that should be made to the condensed consolidated interim financial statements referred to above for them to be in conformity with generally accepted accounting principles."

Our engagement cannot be relied upon to disclose errors, irregularities, or illegal acts, including fraud or defalcations, that may exist. However, we will inform you of any such matters that come to our attention.

2. We will assist in the preparation of a Registration Statement (Form S-1) under the Securities Act of 1933 including advice and counsel in conforming the financial statements and related information to Regulation S-X.

3. We will assist in resolving the accounting and financial reporting questions which will arise as a part of the preparation of the Registration Statement referred to above.

4. We will prepare a letter for the underwriters, if required (i.e., a Comfort Letter), bearing in mind the limited nature of the work we have done with respect to the financial data.

(continued)

EXHIBIT 1—
continued

Ernst & Whinney's
ZZZZ Best
Engagement
Letter

5. We will examine the consolidated financial statements of the Company as of April 30, 1987, and for the year then ended and issue our report in accordance with generally accepted auditing standards approved by the American Institute of Certified Public Accountants. These standards contemplate, among other things, that (1) we will study and evaluate the Company's internal control system as a basis for reliance on the accounting records and for determining the extent of our audit tests; and (2) that we will be able to obtain sufficient evidential matter to afford a reasonable basis for our opinion on the financial statements. However, it should be understood that our reports will necessarily be governed by the findings developed in the course of our examination and that we could be required, depending upon the circumstances, to modify our reporting from the typical unqualified opinion. We will advise you, as our examination progresses, if any developments indicate that we will be unable to express an unqualified opinion. Because our examination will be performed generally on a test basis, it will not necessarily disclose irregularities, if any, that may exist. However, we will promptly report to you any irregularities which our examination does disclose.

Our fees will be derived from our customary rates for the various personnel involved plus out-of-pocket expenses. Certain factors can have an effect on the time incurred in the conduct of our work. Among these are the general condition of the accounting records, the amount of assistance received from your personnel in the accumulation of data, the size and transaction volume of business, any significant financial reporting issues that arise in connection with the SEC's review of the S-1, as well as unforeseen circumstances. Based upon our current understanding of the situation, the amount of our proposed billing for the various services which we will be providing are estimated to be:

Review of the July 31, 1986 financial statements	$ 5,000–$ 7,500
Assistance in the preparation of the Registration Statement	8,000–30,000
Comfort Letter	4,000–6,000
Audit of financial statements as of April 30, 1987	24,000–29,000

We will invoice you each month for the time charges and expenses incurred in the previous month and such invoices are due and payable upon presentation.

Larry D. Gray, Partner, is the Client Service Executive assigned to the engagement. Peter Griffith, Audit Manager, and Michael McCormick, Tax Manager, have also been assigned.

We greatly appreciate your engagement of our firm; if you have any questions, we shall be pleased to discuss them with you. Please indicate your acceptance of the above arrangements by signing and returning the enclosed copy. This letter constitutes the full understanding of the terms of our engagement.

Very truly yours,
Ernst & Whinney
By Larry D. Gray, Partner
ACCEPTED:
ZZZZ BEST CO., INC.
Barry J. Minkow, Chairman of the Board (signed)
9/16/86

Congressional testimony disclosed that Ernst & Whinney repeatedly insisted on visiting several of the largest of these contract sites, and that Minkow and his associates attempted to discourage such visits. Eventually, Minkow realized that the auditors would not relent and agreed to allow them to visit certain of the restoration sites, knowing full well that none of the sites actually existed.

To convince Ernst & Whinney that the insurance restoration contracts were authentic, Minkow plotted and carried out a series of sting operations that collectively cost millions of dollars. In the late fall of 1986, Larry Gray, the engagement audit partner for ZZZZ Best, told client personnel that he wanted to inspect a restoration site in Sacramento on which ZZZZ Best had reported obtaining a multimillion-dollar contract. Minkow sent two of his subordinates to Sacramento to find a large building under construction or renovation that would provide a plausible site for a restoration contract. Gray had visited Sacramento a few weeks earlier to search for the site that Minkow had refused to divulge. As chance would have it, the building chosen by the ZZZZ Best conspirators was the same one Gray had identified as the most likely site of the insurance restoration job.

Minkow's two confederates posed as leasing agents of a property management firm and convinced the supervisor of the construction site to provide the keys to the building one weekend on the pretext that a large, prospective tenant wished to tour the facility. Prior to the arrival of Larry Gray and an attorney representing ZZZZ Best's law firm, Minkow's subordinates visited the site and placed placards on the walls at conspicuous locations indicating that ZZZZ Best was the contractor for the building renovation. No details were overlooked by the two co-conspirators. They even paid the building's security officer to greet the visitors and demonstrate that he was aware in advance of their tour of the site and its purpose. Although the building had not been damaged and instead was simply in the process of being completed, the sting operation went off as planned. Exhibit 2 presents the memorandum Gray wrote describing his tour of the building—a memorandum included in Ernst & Whinney's ZZZZ Best workpapers.

Congressional investigators quizzed Gray regarding the measures he took to confirm that ZZZZ Best actually had a restoration contract on the Sacramento building. They were particularly concerned that he never discovered the building had not suffered several million dollars in damages a few months earlier, as claimed by ZZZZ Best personnel.

Congressman Lent: *Did you check the building permit or construction permit?*

Mr. Gray: *No, sir. That wouldn't be necessary to accomplish what I was setting out to accomplish.*

Congressman Lent: *And you did not check with the building's owners to see if an insurance claim had been filed?*

Mr. Gray: *Same answer. It wasn't necessary. I had seen the paperwork internally of our client, the support for a great amount of detail. So, I had no need to ask—to pursue that.*

Congressman Lent: *You understand that what you saw was not anything that was real in any sense of the word? . . . You are saying you were duped, are you not?*

Mr. Gray: *Absolutely.*

Before allowing Ernst & Whinney auditors to visit a bogus restoration project, Minkow insisted that the firm sign a standard confidentiality agreement. Exhibit 3 presents a copy of that agreement. Members of the congressional subcommittee were troubled by the following stipulation of the confidentiality agreement: "We will not make any follow-up telephone calls to any contractors, insurance companies, the building owner, or other individuals involved in the restoration contract." This restriction effectively precluded the auditors from corroborating the insurance restoration contracts with independent third parties.

EXHIBIT 2

ERNST & WHINNEY
INTERNAL MEMO
REGARDING VISIT
TO ZZZZ BEST
RESTORATION
PROJECT

TO: ZZZZ Best Co., Inc. File

FROM: Larry D. Gray

RE: Visit to Sacramento Job

At our request, the Company arranged for a tour of the job site in Sacramento on November 23rd [1986]. The site (not previously identified for us because of the confidentiality agreement with their customer) had been informally visited by me on October 27. I knew approximately where the job was, and was able to identify it through the construction activity going on.

On November 23, Mark Morse accompanied Mark Moskowitz of Hughes Hubbard & Reed and myself to Sacramento. We visited first the offices of the Building Manager, Mark Roddy of Assured Property Management, Inc. Roddy was hired by the insurance company (at Tom Padgett's suggestion according to Morse) to oversee the renovation activities and the leasing of the space. Roddy accompanied us to the building site.

We were informed that the damage occurred from the water storage on the roof of the building. The storage was for the sprinkler systems, but the water was somehow released in total, causing construction damage to floors 17 and 18, primarily in bathrooms which were directly under the water holding tower, then the water spread out and flooded floors 16 down through about 5 or 6, where it started to spread out even further and be held in pools.

We toured floor 17 briefly (it is currently occupied by a law firm) then visited floor 12 (which had a considerable amount of unoccupied space) and floor 7. Morse pointed out to us the carpet, painting and clean up work which had been ZZZZ Best's responsibility. We noted some work not done in some other areas (and in unoccupied tenant space). But per Mark, this was not ZZZZ Best's responsibility, rather was work being undertaken by tenants for their own purposes.

Per Morse (and Roddy) ZZZZ Best's work is substantially complete and has passed final inspection. Final sign-off is expected shortly, with final payment due to ZZZZ Best in early December.

Morse was well versed in the building history and in the work scope for ZZZZ Best. The tour was beneficial in gaining insight as to the scope of the damage that had occurred and the type of work that the Company can do.

Resignation of Ernst & Whinney

Ernst & Whinney resigned as ZZZZ Best's auditor on June 2, 1987, following a series of disturbing events that caused the firm to question Barry Minkow's integrity. First, Ernst & Whinney was alarmed by a *Los Angeles Times* article in mid-May 1987 that revealed Minkow had been involved in a string of credit card forgeries as a teenager. Second, on May 28, 1987, ZZZZ Best issued a press release, without consulting or notifying Ernst & Whinney, that reported record profits and revenues. Minkow intended this press release to restore investors' confidence in the company—confidence that had been shaken by the damaging *Los Angeles Times* story. Third, and most important, on May 29, Ernst & Whinney auditors discovered evidence supporting allegations made several weeks earlier by a third-party informant that ZZZZ Best's insurance restoration business was fictitious.

Mr. Barry Minkow, President
ZZZZ Best Co., Inc.
7040 Darby Avenue
Reseda, California

Dear Barry:

In connection with the proposed public offering (the Offering) of Units consisting of common stock and warrants of ZZZZ Best Co., Inc. (the Company), we have requested a tour of the site of the Company's insurance restoration project in Sacramento, California, Contract No. 18886. Subject to the representations and warranties below, the Company has agreed to arrange such a tour, which will be conducted by a representative of Assured Property Management Inc. (the Representative), which company is unaffiliated with Interstate Appraisal Services. The undersigned, personally and on behalf of Ernst & Whinney, hereby represents and warrants that:

1. We will not disclose the location of such building, or any other information with respect to the project or the building, to any third parties or to any other members or employees of our firm;

2. We will not make any follow-up telephone calls to any contractors, insurance companies, the building owner, or other individuals involved in the restoration project;

3. We will obey all on-site safety and other rules and regulations established by the Company, Interstate Appraisal Services and the Representative;

4. The undersigned will be the only representative of this Firm present on the tour.

This Confidentiality Letter is also being furnished for the benefit of Interstate Appraisal Services, to the same extent as if it were furnished directly to such company.

The informant had contacted Ernst & Whinney in April 1987 and asked for $25,000 in exchange for information proving that one of the firm's clients was engaging in a massive fraud. Ernst & Whinney refused to pay the sum, and the individual recanted shortly thereafter, but not until the firm determined that the allegation involved ZZZZ Best. (Congressional testimony disclosed that the individual recanted because of a bribe paid to him by Minkow.) Despite the retraction, Ernst & Whinney questioned Minkow and ZZZZ Best's board of directors regarding the matter. Minkow insisted that he did not know the individual who had made the allegation. On May 29, 1987, however, Ernst & Whinney auditors discovered several cancelled checks that Minkow had personally written to the informant several months earlier.

Because ZZZZ Best was a public company, the resignation of its independent auditor had to be reported to the SEC in an 8-K filing. This requirement alerts investors and creditors of circumstances that may have led to the change in auditors. At the time, SEC registrants were allowed 15 days to file an 8-K auditor change announcement. After waiting the maximum permissible time, ZZZZ Best reported the change in auditors but, despite Ernst & Whinney's insistence, made no mention in the 8-K of the fraud allegation that had been subsequently recanted.

The SEC requires a former audit firm to prepare a letter to be filed as an exhibit to its former client's 8-K auditor change announcement. That exhibit letter must comment on the 8-K's accuracy and completeness. In 1987, former audit firms had 30 days to file an exhibit letter, which was the length of time Ernst & Whinney waited before submitting its exhibit letter to the SEC. In that letter, Ernst & Whinney revealed that ZZZZ Best's insurance contracts might be fraudulent.

The congressional subcommittee was alarmed that 45 days had passed before the charges of fraudulent misrepresentations in ZZZZ Best's financial statements were disclosed to the public. By the time the SEC released Ernst & Whinney's exhibit letter to the public, ZZZZ Best had filed for protection from its creditors under Chapter 11 of the federal bankruptcy code. During the period that elapsed between Ernst & Whinney's resignation and the public release of its 8-K exhibit letter, ZZZZ Best obtained significant financing from several parties, including $1 million from one of Minkow's close friends. These parties never recovered the funds invested in, or loaned to, ZZZZ Best. As a direct result of the ZZZZ Best debacle, the SEC shortened the length of time that registrants and their former auditors may wait before filing auditor change documents.

The congressional subcommittee also quizzed Ernst & Whinney representatives regarding the information they disclosed to Price Waterhouse, the audit firm Minkow retained to replace Ernst & Whinney.[4] Congressman Wyden wanted to know whether Ernst & Whinney had candidly discussed its concerns regarding Minkow's integrity with Price Waterhouse.

> Congressman Wyden: *I am going to insert into the record at this point a memo entitled "Discussion with successor auditor," written by Mr. Gray and dated June 9, 1987. Regarding a June 4 meeting, Mr. Gray, with Dan Lyle of Price Waterhouse concerning the integrity of ZZZZ Best's management, you stated that you had no reportable disagreements and no reservations about management integrity pending the results of a board of directors' investigation. Then you went on to say that you resigned because, and I quote here: "We came to a conclusion that we didn't want to become associated with the financial statements."*
>
> *Is that correct?*
>
> Mr. Gray: *That is correct.*
>
> Mr. Wyden: *. . . Mr. Gray, you told the committee staff on May 29, 1987, that when you uncovered evidence to support allegations of fraud that you decided to pack up your workpapers and leave the ZZZZ Best audit site. How did your leaving without telling anybody except the ZZZZ Best management and board of directors the reasons for leaving help the public and investors?*

A final twist to the ZZZZ Best scandal was an anonymous letter Ernst & Whinney received one week after the firm resigned as ZZZZ Best's auditor. At that time, no one other than Ernst & Whinney and ZZZZ Best's officers was aware of the firm's resignation. The letter, shown in Exhibit 4, contained several allegations suggesting that ZZZZ Best's financial statements were fraudulent. According to the congressional testimony, Ernst & Whinney forwarded this letter to the SEC on June 17, 1987.

Collapse of ZZZZ Best

The *Los Angeles Times* article published in mid-May 1987 that disparaged Barry Minkow ultimately doomed the young entrepreneur and his company. Several years earlier, a homemaker had fallen victim to Minkow's credit card forgeries. Minkow had added a fraudulent charge to a credit charge slip the woman had used to make a

---

4. Price Waterhouse never issued an audit report on ZZZZ Best's financial statements. ZZZZ Best was liquidated less than two months after Price Waterhouse was retained.

EXHIBIT 4

ANONYMOUS LETTER
RECEIVED BY
ERNST & WHINNEY
REGARDING ZZZZ
BEST

June 9, 1987

Mr. Guy Wilson
Ernst & Whinney
515 South Flower
Los Angeles, California 90021

Dear Mr. Wilson:

I am an individual having certain confidential information regarding the financial condition of ZZZZ Best Co., Inc. I have read the prospectus and your Review Report dated October 3, 1986 and recognize you have not done an examination in accordance with generally accepted auditing standards, but that such audit will be forthcoming by you.

I wish to make you aware of the following material facts which require you to confirm or disaffirm:

1. The electric generators which appear on the balance sheet under Note 6 as being purchased for $1,970,000 were purchased for scrap for less than $100,000 thru intermediaries of ZZZZ Best and resold to ZZZZ Best at the inflated value. The sole purpose was to boost the assets on the balance sheet. These generators have never been used and have no utility to the company.

2. Note 5 of the balance sheet discusses joint ventures and two restoration contracts. These contracts are fictitious as are the bookkeeping entries to support their validity. Interstate Appraisal Service [sic] did not let such contracts although they confirm their existence. The same is true for the alleged $7,000,000 Sacramento contract and the $40–100 million contracts with Interstate.

3. Further, checks made and passed between ZZZZ Best, its joint venturers and some of its vendors are no more than transactions among conspirators to support the validity of these restoration contracts.

4. Earnings reported by ZZZZ Best are being reported as Billings in excess of costs and estimated earnings on restoration contracts. These contracts do not exist nor do the earnings. This can be confirmed directly by contacting the alleged insurance carriers as well as physical inspections as to the existence and extent of the contracts.

5. Billings and Earnings for 1985 and 1986 were fabricated by the company before being presented to other accountants for certification.

Confirmation of these allegations can be accomplished by a careful due diligence. Such due diligence on your behalf is imperative for your protection.

Very truly yours,

B. Cautious
(Signed)

payment on her account. Despite her persistence, Minkow avoided repaying the small amount. The woman never forgot the insult and tracked down, and kept a record of, individuals who had been similarly harmed by Minkow. At the urging of this woman, a reporter for the *Los Angeles Times* investigated her allegations. The woman's diary eventually became the basis for the *Los Angeles Times* article that, for the first time, cast doubt on the integrity of the "boy wonder" who was the talk of Wall Street.

The newspaper article triggered a chain of events that caused ZZZZ Best to collapse and disappear less than three months later. First, a small brokerage firm specializing in newly registered companies with suspicious earnings histories began short-selling ZZZZ Best stock, forcing the stock's price into a tailspin. Second, Ernst & Whinney, ZZZZ Best's law firm, and ZZZZ Best's investment banker began giving more credence to the allegations and rumors of financial wrongdoing by Minkow and his associates. Third, and most important, the article panicked Minkow and compelled him to make several daring moves that cost him even more credibility. The most critical mistake was his issuance of the May 28, 1987, press release that boldly reported record profits and revenues for his firm.

EPILOGUE

Among the parties most vilified for their role in the ZZZZ Best scandal was Ernst & Whinney. The transcripts of the congressional testimony focusing on the ZZZZ Best fraud included a list of 10 "red flags" that the audit firm had allegedly overlooked while examining ZZZZ Best's financial statements (see Exhibit 5). Ernst & Whinney officials flatly rejected assertions that their firm was even partially to blame for the ZZZZ Best fiasco. In his congressional testimony, Leroy Gardner, the West Coast director of accounting and auditing for Ernst & Whinney, maintained that when all the facts were revealed, his firm would be totally vindicated:

The ZZZZ Best situation proves at least one thing: a well-orchestrated fraud will often succeed even against careful, honest, hard-working people.... The facts that have begun to emerge establish that Minkow, along with confederates both inside and outside ZZZZ Best, went to extraordinary lengths to deceive Ernst & Whinney. For example, Thomas Padgett, an alleged conspirator, revealed in a recent televised interview that Minkow spent $4 million to deceive Ernst & Whinney during a visit to one of ZZZZ Best's job sites.... Ernst & Whinney never misled investors about the reliability of ZZZZ Best's financial statements. Ernst & Whinney never even issued an audit opinion for ZZZZ Best.... We are not part of the problem in this case. We were part of the solution.

In one of the largest civil suits stemming from the ZZZZ Best fraud, a court ruled that Ernst & Whinney was not liable to a large California bank that had extended ZZZZ Best a multimillion-dollar loan in 1986. The bank alleged that in granting the loan, it had relied upon the review report issued by Ernst & Whinney on ZZZZ Best's financial statements for the three-month period ending July 31, 1986. However, an appellate judge ruled that the bank was not justified in relying on the review report since Ernst & Whinney had expressly stated in the report that it was not issuing an opinion on the ZZZZ Best financial statements. "Ernst, because it issued only a review report, specifically declined to express an opinion on ZZZZ Best's financial statements. The report expressly disclaimed any right to rely on its content."[5]

In the late 1980s, ZZZZ Best's former stockholders filed a class-action lawsuit against Ernst & Whinney, ZZZZ Best's former law firm, and ZZZZ Best's former investment banker. An Internet publication reported in March 1996 that this lawsuit had been settled privately. The defendants reportedly paid the former ZZZZ Best

---

5. "Ernst & Young Not Liable in ZZZZ Best Case," *Journal of Accountancy*, July 1991, 22.

EXHIBIT 5

TEN RED FLAGS
THAT ZZZZ
BEST'S AUDITORS
ALLEGEDLY
OVERLOOKED

1. The amounts called for by the insurance restoration contracts were unrealistically large.

2. The number of multimillion-dollar insurance restoration contracts reportedly obtained by ZZZZ Best exceeded the total number available nationwide during the relevant time period.

3. The purported contracts failed to identify the insured parties, the insurance companies, or the locations of the jobs.

4. The contracts consisted of a single page which failed to contain details and specifications of the work to be done, such as the square yardage of carpet to be replaced, which were usual and customary in the restoration business.

5. Virtually all of the insurance restoration contracts were with the same party.

6. A large proportion of the ZZZZ Best insurance restoration contracts occurred immediately, and opportunistically, prior to a planned offering of stock.

7. The purported contracts provided for payments to ZZZZ Best or Minkow alone rather than to the insured or jointly with ZZZZ Best and the insured, contrary to the practice of the industry.

8. The purported contracts provided for payments by the insurance adjustor contrary to normal practice in the industry under which payments are customarily made by the insurance company directly to its insured or jointly to its insured and the restorer.

9. ZZZZ Best's purported gross profit margins for its restoration business were greatly in excess of the normal profit margins for the restoration industry.

10. The internal controls at ZZZZ Best were grossly inadequate.

stockholders $35 million. However, the contribution of each defendant to the settlement pool was not disclosed.[6]

Barry Minkow was released from prison in late 1994. Minkow secured the reduction in his 25-year prison sentence for "good behavior and efforts to improve himself."[7] These efforts included earning by correspondence bachelor's and master's degrees in religion from Liberty University. Shortly after being paroled, Minkow married a young woman introduced to him by a fellow inmate. That inmate was a former subordinate of Charles Keating, the principal architect of the massive Lincoln Savings and Loan fraud.

In early 1995, Minkow began serving as the associate pastor of an evangelical church in a community near his hometown of Reseda. Two years later, Minkow was appointed the senior pastor of a large nondenominational church in San Diego. Besides his pastoral duties, Minkow serves as the spokesperson for an Internet company, the Fraud Discovery Institute, which markets various fraud prevention and detection services.

Minkow regularly presents lectures and seminars across the United States that focus on his "experience" with corporate fraud. He has spoken to groups of CPAs, educational institutions, and, most notably, the FBI Academy at Quantico, Virginia. Minkow, who typically delivers his lectures while dressed in an orange prison jumpsuit, often chastises the accountants and auditors in his audience. During one presentation, Minkow noted that, "CPAs are creatures of habit. You're interested in making tick marks and footnotes, not in thinking outside the box."[8] Minkow also chides auditors for being overly

6. C. Byron, "$26 Million in the Hole," *Worth Online*, March 1996.
7. M. Matzer, "Barry Minkow," *Forbes*, 15 August 1994, 134.
8. T. Sickinger, "Ex–Con Artist Helps Find Fraud," *The Kansas City Star*, 18 October 1995, B1.

willing to accept weak forms of audit evidence, such as client representations. He warns auditors, "Don't give up objectivity for convenience."[9]

Journalists frequently interview Minkow and ask for his views on corporate fraud and related issues. In January 2005, Minkow gave the following response when he was asked by *CFO Magazine* whether the Sarbanes-Oxley Act of 2002 would likely serve to mitigate or deter corporate fraud: "Let me tell you why this legislation is brilliant. Sarbox hit at a common denominator of corporate fraud: bypassing systems of internal control. I would not have been able to perpetrate the ZZZZ Best fraud if I had not been able to bypass the internal controls."[10]

Questions

1. Ernst & Whinney never issued an audit opinion on financial statements of ZZZZ Best but did issue a review report on the company's quarterly statements for the three months ended July 31, 1986. How does a review differ from an audit, particularly in terms of the level of assurance implied by the auditor's report?

2. *SAS No. 106*, "Audit Evidence," identifies the principal "management assertions" that underlie a set of financial statements. The occurrence assertion was particularly critical for ZZZZ Best's insurance restoration contracts. ZZZZ Best's auditors obtained third-party confirmations to support the contracts, reviewed available documentation, performed analytical procedures to evaluate the reasonableness of the revenues recorded on the contracts, and visited selected restoration sites. Comment on the limitations of the evidence that these procedures provide with regard to the management assertion of occurrence.

3. In testimony before Congress, George Greenspan reported that one method he used to audit the insurance restoration contracts was to verify that his client actually received payment on those jobs. How can such apparently reliable evidence lead an auditor to an improper conclusion?

4. What is the purpose of predecessor–successor auditor communications? Which party, the predecessor or successor auditor, has the responsibility for initiating these communications? Briefly summarize the information that a successor auditor should obtain from the predecessor auditor.

5. Did the confidentiality agreement that Minkow required Ernst & Whinney to sign improperly limit the scope of the ZZZZ Best audit? Why or why not? Discuss general circumstances under which confidentiality concerns on the part of a client may properly affect audit planning decisions. At what point do client-imposed audit scope limitations affect the type of audit opinion issued?

6. What procedures, if any, do professional standards require auditors to perform when reviewing a client's pre-audit but post-year-end earnings press release?

9. *Ibid.*

10. *CFO Magazine*, "Ten Questions for Barry Minkow," CFO.com, 1 January 2005.

United States Surgical Corporation

Leon Hirsch founded United States Surgical Corporation (USSC) in 1964 with very little capital, four employees, and one product: an unwieldy mechanical device that he intended to market as a surgical stapler. In his mid-30s at the time and lacking a college degree, Hirsch had already tried several lines of business, including frozen foods, dry cleaning, and advertising, each with little success. In fact, the dry cleaning venture ended in bankruptcy. No doubt, few of Hirsch's friends and family members believed that USSC would become financially viable. Despite the long odds against him, in a little more than one decade Hirsch had built the Connecticut-based USSC into a large and profitable public company whose stock was traded on a national exchange. More importantly, the surgical stapler that Hirsch invented revolutionized surgery techniques in the United States and abroad.

During the early years of its existence, USSC dominated the small surgical stapling industry that Hirsch had established in the mid-1960s. By 1980, several companies were encroaching on USSC's domestic and foreign sales markets. USSC's principal competitor at the time was a company owned by Alan Blackman. Blackman's company sold its products primarily in foreign countries but was attempting to significantly expand its U.S. sales. Hirsch alleged that Blackman, who was a former friend and associate, had infringed on USSC's patents by "reverse-engineering" the company's products.

In the early 1980s, USSC began an aggressive counterattack to repel Blackman's intrusion into its markets. First, USSC adopted a worldwide litigation strategy to contest Blackman's right to manufacture and market his competing products. Second, the company embarked on a large research and development program to create a line of new products technologically superior to those being manufactured by Blackman. Each of these initiatives required multimillion-dollar commitments by USSC—commitments that threatened the company's steadily rising profits and Hirsch's ability to raise additional capital that USSC desperately needed to finance its rapid growth.

Hirsch overcame the major challenges facing his company. USSC maintained its dominant position in the surgical stapling industry, while continuing to report record profits and sales each year. Ironically, those record profits and sales eventually spelled trouble for the company. Mounting suspicion that USSC's reported operating results were too good to be true prompted the Securities and Exchange Commission (SEC) to launch an investigation of the company's financial affairs. In 1983, the SEC leveled several charges of misconduct against key USSC officers, including Leon Hirsch. Within a short time, USSC's audit firm, Ernst & Whinney, resigned and withdrew the unqualified audit opinions it had issued on the company's 1980 and 1981 financial statements. In 1985, the SEC released a report on its lengthy investigation of USSC. The SEC ruled that the company had used a "variety of manipulative devices to overstate its earnings in its 1980 and 1981 financial statements."[1] (Exhibit 1 contains USSC's original balance sheets and income statements for the period 1979 to 1981.)

---

1. This and subsequent quotations, unless indicated otherwise, were taken from Securities and Exchange Commission, *Accounting and Auditing Enforcement Release No. 109A,* 6 August 1986.

EXHIBIT 1

UNITED STATES
SURGICAL
CORPORATION'S
1979–1981
FINANCIAL
STATEMENTS

U.S. Surgical Corporation
Consolidated Balance Sheets 1979–1981 (000s omitted)

	1981	December 31, 1980	1979
Current Assets:			
Cash	$ 426	$ 1,243	$ 596
Receivables (net)	36,670	30,475	22,557
Inventories:			
Finished Goods	29,216	9,860	5,685
Work in Process	5,105	2,667	1,153
Raw Materials	20,948	18,806	7,365
	55,269	31,333	14,203
Other Current Assets	7,914	1,567	1,820
Total Current Assets	100,279	64,618	39,176
Property, Plant, and Equipment:			
Land	2,502	2,371	1,027
Buildings	32,416	18,511	13,019
Molds and Dies	32,082	15,963	8,777
Machinery and Equipment	40,227	23,762	12,362
	107,227	60,607	35,185
Allowance For Depreciation	(14,953)	(9,964)	(6,340)
	92,274	50,643	28,845
Other Assets	14,786	3,842	2,499
Total Assets	$207,339	$119,103	$70,520
Current Liabilities:			
Accounts Payable	$ 12,278	$ 6,951	$ 6,271
Notes Payable	—	—	1,596
Income Taxes Payable	—	1,685	—
Current Portion of Long-Term Debt	724	666	401
Accrued Expenses	5,673	5,130	5,145
Total Current Liabilities	18,675	14,432	13,413
Long-Term Debt	80,642	47,569	33,497
Deferred Income Taxes	7,466	2,956	1,384
Stockholders' Equity:			
Common Stock	1,081	930	379
Additional Paid-in Capital	72,594	34,932	10,736
Retained Earnings	32,665	20,881	13,189
Translation Allowance	(1,086)	—	—
Deferred Compensation—from Issuance of Restricted Stock	(4,698)	(2,597)	(2,078)
Total Stockholders' Equity	100,556	54,146	22,226
Total Liabilities and Stockholders' Equity	$207,339	$119,103	$70,520

EXHIBIT 1—
continued

UNITED STATES
SURGICAL
CORPORATION'S
1979–1981
FINANCIAL
STATEMENTS

U.S. Surgical Corporation
Consolidated Income Statements 1979–1981 (000s omitted)

	December 31,		
	1981	1980	1979
Net Sales	$111,800	$86,214	$60,876
Costs and Expenses:			
Cost of Products Sold	47,983	32,300	25,659
Selling, General, and Administrative*	45,015	37,740	23,935
Interest	5,898	4,063	3,403
	98,896	74,103	52,997
Income Before Income Taxes	12,904	12,111	7,879
Income Taxes			
Federal and Foreign	795	3,406	2,279
State and Local	325	820	471
	1,120	4,226	2,750
Net Income	$ 11,784	$ 7,885	$ 5,129
Net Income per common share and common share equivalent	$1.13	$.89	$.68
Average number of common shares and common share equivalents outstanding	10,403,392	8,816,986	7,555,710

*Included in the amounts for this line item are the following research and development expenses: 1981—$1,337, 1980—$3,020, 1979—$2,289.

To settle the SEC charges, USSC officials signed an agreement with the federal agency that forced the company to reduce its previously reported earnings by $26 million. Additionally, senior executives of USSC, including Hirsch, agreed to return to the company large bonuses they had been paid during 1980 and 1981. Following the signing of the agreement with the SEC, Hirsch reported that the criticism of his company and his management decisions was undeserved. Hirsch implied that cost considerations motivated him to accept the SEC sanctions: "It was our opinion that the settlement [with the SEC] was preferable to long, costly and time-consuming litigation."[2]

USSC's Abusive Accounting Practices

The enforcement release that disclosed the key findings of the SEC's investigation of USSC charged the company with several abusive accounting and financial reporting practices. A focal point of the SEC's investigation was an elaborate scheme that USSC executives implemented to charge inventoriable production costs to a long-term asset account, molds and dies. This scheme, which required the cooperation of several of USSC's vendors, was deliberately concealed from the company's audit firm, Ernst & Whinney.[3]

2. K. B. Noble, "U.S. Surgical Settlement to Restate Earnings," *The New York Times*, 28 February 1984, B2.

3. A subsequent section of this case discusses the details of this scheme, including the measures that USSC executives took to conceal it from Ernst & Whinney.

The SEC investigation also revealed that USSC recorded inventory shipments to its sales force as consummated sales transactions. Until the mid-1970s, USSC had marketed its products through a network of independent dealers. Historically, inventory shipments to these dealers had been treated as arm's length transactions and thus reportable as revenue. By 1980, the company marketed its products almost exclusively through a sales staff consisting of full-time employees working on a commission basis. Each member of the sales staff maintained an inventory of USSC products, which they transported from client to client. When USSC shipped products to a salesperson, the company recorded the inventory as having been sold, although employees could return unsold items for full credit.

In 1980 and 1981, USSC's management began intentionally shipping excessive amounts of inventory to its sales staff. A former USSC sales manager later testified regarding this practice. "It was nothing to come home and find $3,000 worth of product sitting in a box on your front porch from UPS and a note saying, 'We thought you needed a little more product.'"[4] According to the SEC, USSC's policy of recognizing inventory shipments to its sales staff as consummated sales transactions inflated the company's 1980 and 1981 pretax profits by $1,150,000 and $750,000, respectively.

The SEC also charged that USSC abused the accounting rule that permits the capitalization of legal expenditures incurred to develop and successfully defend a patent. In 1980, the company capitalized less than $1 million of such expenditures; the following year, that figure leaped to $5.8 million. The SEC investigation disclosed that a significant portion of the 1981 litigation expenditures stemmed from Australian lawsuits filed against Alan Blackman and his company. Because USSC did not have any registered patents in Australia, these expenditures should have been immediately charged to operations instead of being deferred in an asset account. Approximately $3.7 million of USSC's 1981 litigation expenditures involved efforts to defend the company's U.S. patents. However, USSC chose to amortize these costs over a 10-year period even though the 17-year legal life of most of the patents would expire in 1983 or 1984.

USSC leased, rather than sold, many of its surgical tools. The company's accounting staff recorded the cost of these assets in a subsidiary fixed asset ledger, leased and loaned assets. USSC periodically retired such assets and removed their accounts from the sub-ledger. However, SEC investigators discovered that in many cases the costs associated with these assets were not removed from the sub-ledger but instead debited to the accounts of other assets still in service. In 1981, USSC also understated depreciation expense on several fixed assets by arbitrarily extending their useful lives and establishing salvage values for them for the first time.

Allegations of Audit Deficiencies

The SEC's investigation of USSC uncovered several alleged flaws in Ernst & Whinney's audits of the company, particularly the 1981 audit. An important risk factor present during the 1981 USSC audit that Ernst & Whinney may have overlooked was the company's strong incentive to reach targeted sales and profit goals. If those targeted figures were not reached, USSC would have had difficulty raising the additional capital needed for expansion purposes. A former USSC vice president later revealed that Hirsch often made firm commitments to security analysts regarding the company's future sales and profits.[5] This individual maintained that many of USSC's abusive

---

4. N. R. Kleinfeld, "U.S. Surgical's Checkered History," *The New York Times,* 13 May 1984, F4.
5. *Ibid.*

accounting practices sprang from Hirsch's efforts to deliver the promised sales and earnings figures. USSC's management bonus plan provided another incentive for USSC officials to misrepresent the company's financial data.

> Surgical's executive officers could earn bonuses ranging from 15 percent to 75 percent of their base salaries, if the earnings per share growth ranged from 15 percent to 30 percent over the previous year. Management therefore had powerful personal incentives to keep the earnings per share high.

The SEC also suggested that Ernst & Whinney failed to properly apply analytical procedures during the planning phase of the 1981 audit. Ernst & Whinney apparently overlooked the important implications for its 1981 audit of several material changes in USSC account balances between December 31, 1980, and December 31, 1981. For example, the balance of the molds and dies account more than doubled from the end of 1980 to the end of 1981. According to the SEC, "This unusually large increase should have caused the auditors to scrutinize carefully the nature and source of the additions, and whether certain costs were properly identified and capitalized under GAAP."

Research and development expenses and patents were two other USSC accounts whose balances changed materially from 1980 to 1981. USSC reported a greater than 50 percent decrease in research and development expenses in 1981 as compared with the previous year. This decrease occurred even though USSC undertook a large product development campaign during 1981. USSC's accounting records for 1981 also reflected a significant increase in litigation expenditures that were deferred in its patents account. (USSC included the patents account in noncurrent "Other Assets" on its balance sheet. See Exhibit 1.)

The SEC maintained that the unusually large changes in key USSC account balances between 1980 and 1981 should have placed Ernst & Whinney on alert that the 1981 USSC audit would have a higher-than-normal degree of risk associated with it. "The heightened audit attention was particularly important since the aggregate effect of the changes was material to Surgical's 1981 financial statements . . . [and] the changes all had the effect of increasing income."

According to the SEC, Ernst & Whinney made three critical errors when considering the question of whether USSC should be allowed to record inventory shipments to its sales staff as valid sales transactions. First, the SEC pointed out that Ernst & Whinney failed to recognize that "sales" of inventory to employees generally do not qualify as arm's length transactions. "Because the potential for abuse is so great when a 'sale' transaction is between a company and its employee, the presumption is that no 'true' sale has taken place." Second, the SEC maintained that USSC's repurchase of significant amounts of inventory from its salespeople during 1981 should have alerted Ernst & Whinney that the original inventory shipments to these employees were not bona fide sales transactions. This oversight by Ernst & Whinney particularly troubled the SEC since the audit firm's 1980 and 1981 workpapers clearly documented these repurchases.

Finally, the SEC criticized Ernst & Whinney for failing to investigate a client executive's assertion that USSC was not obligated to repurchase inventory from employees who resigned or were terminated. Ernst & Whinney's 1981 audit program included a procedure to obtain and review a copy of the employment contract signed by USSC's sales employees and to incorporate that contract in the permanent workpaper file. Although the Ernst & Whinney audit program indicated that this procedure had been completed, there was no evidence to this effect in the firm's 1981 workpapers. The SEC ruled that if the employment contract had been obtained and reviewed, Ernst & Whinney would have learned that USSC not only had a policy of re-purchasing inventory from former employees but had a contractual obligation to do so.

The SEC reserved its harshest criticism of Ernst & Whinney for the firm's failure to prevent USSC from capitalizing a material amount of production expenses in the molds and dies account. During the last few months of 1980, USSC began systemati-cally charging production costs to that noncurrent asset account, resulting in a sig-nificant overstatement of assets and a corresponding understatement of cost of goods sold. Company executives used several methods to conceal this illicit scheme. The most common of these methods was instructing the company's vendors, who did most of the production work on USSC's products, to describe generic production costs as capitalizable expenditures on invoices submitted for payment to USSC.

One of USSC's primary vendors was Lacey Manufacturing Company, a division of Barden Corporation—which also happened to be an Ernst & Whinney audit client. In late 1980, USSC officials instructed Barden Corporation to begin using the phrase "tool-ing modifications" to describe the work performed for USSC by Lacey Manufacturing. Previously, these invoices had described the expenditures incurred for USSC as generic production costs. This change in the description of the incurred costs was critical since all tooling costs for new or redesigned products were capitalizable expenditures.

Chronology of USSC–Ernst & Whinney Disagreement Regarding Capitalization of Alleged Tooling Costs

For many years, accounting educators have maintained that the imbalance of power in the auditor–client relationship impairs the quality of audits.[6] This imbalance of power favors the client, largely because client executives retain and compensate their company's independent auditors. When technical disputes arise during an audit, client executives may use their leverage on auditors to extract important con-cessions from them.

A classic example of an audit conflict arose during Ernst & Whinney's 1981 audit of USSC. This conflict stemmed from USSC's illicit scheme to charge production costs to the noncurrent asset account molds and dies. The following chronology lists the key events in this dispute:

1/27/82   The Ernst & Whinney audit team completes its fieldwork on the USSC engagement.

2/2/82   Paul Yamont, senior vice president and treasurer of Barden Corporation, makes an unsolicited telephone call to William Burke, the Ernst & Whinney audit engagement partner on the Barden audit. Yamont informs Burke that Barden accountants have discovered numerous USSC purchase orders and corresponding Barden invoices that do not accurately describe the work that Lacey Manufacturing (a division of Barden Corporation) has been performing for USSC. According to Yamont, these invoices and purchase orders, totaling approximately $1 million, indicate that the Lacey work for USSC has been for "tooling modifications." In fact, Lacey has simply been producing and assembling products for USSC. Burke immediately visits Barden to discuss this issue with Yamont.

---

6. A. Goldman and B. Barlev, "The Auditor-Firm Conflict of Interests: Its Implications for Independence," *Accounting Review* 49 (October 1974), 707–718; D. R. Nichols and K. Price, "The Auditor-Firm Conflict: An Analysis Using Concepts of Exchange Theory," *Accounting Review* 51 (April 1976), 335–346; M. C. Knapp and B. H. Ward, "An Integrative Analysis of Audit Conflict: Sources, Consequences and Resolution," *Advances in Accounting* 4 (1987), 267–286.

2/3/82	Ernst & Whinney approves the issuance of a press release by USSC management that reports the company's sales and earnings for 1981. (At this point, Michael Hope, the USSC audit engagement partner, is unaware of the problem brought to William Burke's attention by Paul Yamont.)
2/5/82	Burke again visits Yamont to discuss the alleged mislabeled invoices.
2/8/82	Barden Corporation's board of directors votes to retain Ernst & Whinney to formally investigate the mislabeled invoices.
2/10/82	Burke contacts Norman Strauss, regional director of accounting and auditing for Ernst & Whinney's New York region, and informs him of Yamont's concerns. Strauss immediately informs Bruce Dixon, the Ernst & Whinney partner in charge of the New York region, of the Barden situation. Shortly thereafter, Dixon calls Hope and instructs him not to sign off on the USSC audit until the questionable invoice charges have been fully investigated. Dixon also informs Robert Neary, Ernst & Whinney's chief technical partner, of the problem.
2/13/82	Burke sends an Ernst & Whinney audit manager to Barden Corporation to investigate the invoices and purchase orders in question.
2/15/82	Burke joins the Ernst & Whinney audit manager at Barden Corporation to tour the Lacey Manufacturing facility and to discuss the questionable invoices and purchase orders with Robert More, the Lacey general manager. More informs Burke that nearly all of the invoiced charges being reviewed were for generic production work performed for USSC rather than for tooling modifications.
2/18/82	Burke meets with the Barden board of directors and reports that the results of the Ernst & Whinney investigation demonstrate that the USSC purchase orders and the corresponding Barden invoices misrepresent the nature of the work performed by Lacey Manufacturing for USSC. The chairman of Barden's board of directors then reports that an independent investigation by an outside law firm has yielded the same conclusion. The Barden directors vote to require that all future work performed for USSC be properly described in invoices submitted for payment to the company.
2/20/82 (approximately)	Hope and Dixon are unsure how to proceed on the USSC audit, given the results of Burke's investigation. Because of confidentiality concerns, Hope cannot raise the issue directly with USSC officers. Barden officers are concerned that if USSC perceives that their company has brought the problem to the attention of Ernst & Whinney, USSC may terminate its relationship with Barden. Finally, Hope and Dixon decide to send a confirmation letter to Yamont and More that asks them to confirm that the disputed $1 million in charges was for tooling modifications. (Hope and Dixon realize that Yamont and More will refuse to sign the confirmation letter.)
2/25/82	Yamont contacts Hope and informs him that he cannot sign the confirmation letter since he is aware that the disputed charges are not for tooling modifications. Following the refusal of Yamont and, subsequently, More to sign the confirmation letter, Ernst & Whinney officials discuss the problem with the management of both USSC and Barden. Eventually, executives of each company agree to allow auditors from the two Ernst & Whinney teams to have mutual access to their company's accounting records.
3/3/82	Hope meets with top USSC executives and asks them to relate their understanding of the costs incurred by Lacey Manufacturing on behalf of

USSC. The USSC officials inform Hope that in early 1981, they had instructed More, the Lacey general manager, to make certain tooling changes that would result in improved efficiency in the production of USSC products. The executives then provided an elaborate and confusing explanation as to why the tooling modifications were charged out on a per-unit basis. (Earlier, Ernst & Whinney representatives had noted that the disputed costs were billed to USSC based upon the number of units of product manufactured by Lacey. Intuitively, costs associated with tooling modifications should have been billed in one lump sum or in installments. The fact that the costs were billed on a per-unit basis suggested that they were production costs.)

Hope asks USSC's controller for purchase orders that the company had placed with outside contractors other than Barden (Lacey). Hope is searching for evidence of additional mislabeled costs. In the files that Hope is allowed to review, he finds charges billed to USSC that are similar to the disputed tooling modification costs billed to USSC by Barden. USSC officials assure Hope that the costs incurred on USSC's behalf by these vendors were, in fact, for tooling modifications.

3/5/82   Hope and Burke meet with senior USSC executives and More of Lacey Manufacturing. In More's presence, one of the USSC executives again explains that the disputed costs involved tooling changes requested by USSC in early 1981. More indicates that he agrees with that characterization of the costs. (Of course, More had previously maintained that the disputed amounts were production, not tooling, costs. More justifies his change in opinion by stating that earlier he "hadn't thought it through.")

3/10/82   Hope and Burke tour the Lacey Manufacturing facility to obtain a better understanding of the firm's production process. More is asked to act as a guide for the Ernst & Whinney partners on the tour. Shortly before the tour is scheduled to begin, a senior executive with USSC arrives unexpectedly at Lacey and asks permission to accompany the others on the tour. During the tour, More explains that production personnel charge their time to either tooling jobs or production jobs. He also notes that personnel often inadvertently charge tooling costs to production jobs.

3/11/82   During a conference call involving Hope, Burke, top technical partners of Ernst & Whinney, and the firm's internal and external legal counsel, Hope explains the additional audit procedures performed to analyze the disputed tooling costs. He then reports his conclusion that the disputed costs involved tooling modifications, not generic production work. The other Ernst & Whinney personnel agree with Hope.

3/14/82   To support the conclusion that the disputed costs were for tooling
(approx-   modifications, Hope is instructed to obtain a signed confirmation letter from
imately)   Yamont of Barden Corporation to that effect. When asked to sign the letter, Yamont refuses, as he had done in late February.

3/15/82   Hope decides not to investigate further the questionable tooling costs that he discovered on March 3—tooling costs charged to USSC by vendors other than Lacey Manufacturing. Regarding these items, Hope makes the following entry in the USSC workpapers: "Discussed with [another audit partner] on 3/15/82. Although explanations are incomplete, amounts are immaterial."

3/16/82   More signs the Ernst & Whinney confirmation letter regarding the tooling modification costs that Yamont had refused to sign.

3/17/82   Hope signs Ernst & Whinney's unqualified audit opinion on USSC's 1981 financial statements, which are issued shortly thereafter.

The SEC's investigation of USSC's 1981 financial statements and Ernst & Whinney's audit of those financial statements revealed that Hope and the other Ernst & Whinney auditors had been lied to extensively by USSC personnel. The mislabeled purchase orders and invoices that Ernst & Whinney uncovered were elements of a fraudulent scheme USSC's management had concocted to make production expenditures appear to be capitalizable tooling costs. The scheme originated in 1980 when USSC executives tried to force several vendors to take back a significant amount of inventory that had been rendered obsolete by technological changes. When the vendors refused, the USSC executives devised a "compromise." The executives would inflate the amount of future purchase orders for production work to include the cost of the obsolete inventory and then indicate in the purchase orders that these amounts were for tooling modifications rather than for production expenses. The USSC executives also instructed the vendors to describe these amounts on subsequent invoices as charges for tooling modifications. This agreement required USSC to pay for the obsolete inventory; however, the company benefited since the cost of that inventory was not expensed immediately but rather capitalized in the molds and dies account and depreciated over several years.[7]

Although the SEC's investigation revealed that USSC officials had lied repeatedly to Michael Hope, the federal agency still censured the audit partner.[8] The SEC ruled that Ernst & Whinney, and Hope in particular, had sufficient opportunity to discover, and should have discovered, that USSC executives were misrepresenting their firm's financial condition and results of operations.

The auditors failed to design proper audit procedures, test critical assertions, resolve material conflicts in the audit evidence, and reconcile with the other evidence what they should have recognized were implausible client representations, in violation of GAAS. The bulk of the evidence available to the auditors was so inconsistent with their client's position that the auditors should have realized the [disputed] billings were not properly capitalizable as tooling and that Surgical's representations were false and not made in good faith.

EPILOGUE

USSC recovered from the problems it experienced in the early 1980s. Impressive growth rates in revenues and earnings sent USSC's stock price spiraling upward during the latter part of that decade. By 1996, USSC reported a net income of $109 million on sales of $1.1 billion and total assets exceeding $1.5 billion. Leon Hirsch also recovered nicely from his close and unpleasant encounter with the SEC. Hirsch ranked as the third-highest paid corporate executive in the nation in 1991, earning more than $23 million.[9] In September 1997, Hirsch's

7. In some instances, the SEC found that USSC and its vendors simply fabricated phony purchase orders and invoices for tooling modifications to "convert" the obsolete inventory costs to capitalizable expenditures.

8. The SEC also filed a civil complaint against Barden Corporation and Robert More. The SEC alleged that Barden and More "provided substantial cooperation and assistance in furthering and concealing practices" that USSC employed to misrepresent its financial condition and results of operations. Barden and More settled the SEC complaint without admitting guilt or denying any wrongdoing by agreeing to abide by a court order prohibiting them from engaging in any future violations of federal securities laws.

9. "Executive Pay at New Highs," *The New York Times*, 11 May 1992, D5.

nearly five million shares of USSC stock had a market value surpassing $200 million.

Leon Hirsch made headlines once again in October 1997. In the midst of a takeover bid for a rival, Circon Corporation, Hirsch chastised certain executives of that company. Hirsch charged that the executives were not focusing sufficient attention on the economic interests of their stockholders and attempted to replace two of the company's directors with his own nominees to Circon's board. Hirsch justified his action by stating that his nominees "can make some of the other [Circon] directors understand their responsibilities to shareholders."[10] A leading stockholder rights activist was apparently not convinced that Hirsch, given his prior history, was motivated by a desire to improve Circon's corporate governance. This activist bluntly stated that Hirsch "is like the devil of corporate governance."[11]

USSC withdrew its takeover bid for Circon in mid-1998 after announcing that it had agreed to be acquired by the large conglomerate Tyco International Ltd. Analysts pegged the value of the takeover package at approximately $3.3 billion. Following the merger, Tyco executives reported that Leon Hirsch would continue to oversee USSC's operations.

Several years after Tyco acquired USSC, Tyco found itself the target of a massive class-action lawsuit filed by its stockholders and former stockholders. The lawsuit resulted from allegations that Tyco executives, most notably the company's former CEO and CFO, Dennis Kozlowski and Mark Swartz, respectively, had used a variety of accounting gimmicks to grossly misrepresent Tyco's operating results and financial condition from at least 1998 through 2003. In June 2005, Kozlowski and Swartz were convicted on more than 20 counts of fraud, grand larceny, and conspiracy.[12] Two years later, in May 2007, Tyco agreed to pay nearly $3 billion to settle the pending class-action lawsuit. That settlement is apparently the largest ever paid by a single defendant to settle a civil lawsuit.[13]

Questions

1. Identify audit procedures that, if employed by Ernst & Whinney during the 1981 USSC audit, might have detected the overstatement of the leased and loaned assets account that resulted from the improper accounting for asset retirements.

2. In 1981, USSC extended the useful lives of several of its fixed assets and adopted salvage values for many of these same assets for the first time. Are these changes permissible under generally accepted accounting principles? Assuming these changes had a material effect on USSC's financial condition and results of operations, how should the changes have been disclosed in the company's financial statements? How should these changes have affected Ernst & Whinney's 1981 audit opinion? (Assume that the current audit reporting standards were in effect at the time.)

3. Prepare common-sized financial statements for USSC for the period 1979–1981. Also compute key liquidity, solvency, activity, and profitability ratios for 1980 and 1981. Given these data, identify what you believe were the high-risk financial statement items for the 1981 USSC audit.

10. "U.S. Surgical's Rx for Circon: Corporate Governance," *The Wall Street Journal*, 6 October 1987, B4.

11. *Ibid.*

12. M. Maremont, "Kozlowski, Swartz Are Found Guilty in Tyco Fraud Retrial," *The Wall Street Journal* (online), 17 June 2005.

13. C. Forelle, "Tyco Accord May Spell Trouble for Auditor," *The Wall Street Journal* (online), 16 May 2007.

4. What factors in the auditor–client relationship create a power imbalance in favor of the client? Discuss measures that the profession could take to minimize the negative consequences of this power imbalance.

5. Regarding the costs incurred for USSC by Barden, identify (a) the evidence Hope collected that supported USSC's claim that the costs involved tooling modifications and (b) the audit evidence that supported the position that the costs were generic production expenses. What do generally accepted auditing standards suggest are the key evaluative criteria that auditors should consider when assessing audit evidence? Given these criteria, do you believe Hope was justified in deciding that the costs in question were for tooling modifications? Why or why not?

6. In your opinion, did Hope satisfactorily investigate the possibility that there were additional suspicious tooling charges being paid and recorded by USSC? If not, what additional steps should he have taken to further explore this possibility? If Hope believed there was some likelihood that his client had committed an illegal act, what additional audit procedures, if any, would have been appropriate? (Assume that current auditing standards were in effect at the time.)

7. When a CPA firm has two audit clients that transact business with each other, should the two audit teams be allowed to share information regarding their clients? Why or why not?

New Century Financial Corporation

It is well enough that people of the nation do not understand our banking and monetary system, for if they did, I believe there would be a revolution before tomorrow morning.

Henry Ford

From 1962 to 1992, Ed McMahon served as the quintessential sidekick and straight man to Johnny Carson on the long-running and popular television program *The Tonight Show*. After leaving that program, McMahon stayed in the television spotlight for 12 years by serving as the host of *Star Search*, a syndicated talent show. McMahon's resume also includes long stints as cohost of *TV Bloopers and Practical Jokes*, the annual *Macy's Thanksgiving Day Parade*, and the *Jerry Lewis Labor Day Telethon* and as commercial spokesperson for such companies as Budweiser and American Family Publishing.

McMahon's 50-year-plus career in television made him one of the most recognized celebrities in that medium. Understandably then, the American public was shocked when press reports in June 2007 revealed that McMahon was more than $600,000 past due on his home mortgage payments. The $5 million mortgage on McMahon's Beverly Hills mansion was held by Countrywide Financial Corporation.

Unfortunately, millions of everyday Americans with mortgage balances only a fraction of Ed McMahon's have recently faced the unhappy prospect of losing their homes owing to the worst financial crisis to strike the United States economy since the Great Depression. As that crisis quickly worsened and spread to the global economy, the search began for the parties responsible for it. Among the potential culprits identified by the press was the accounting profession, in particular, independent auditors.

Mortgage Mess

Nearly one-half of recent mortgage foreclosure victims in the United States obtained their loans from so-called subprime lenders that became dominant forces in the mortgage industry over the past two decades. The largest of those lenders were Countrywide, HSBC, New Century Financial Corporation, and Wells Fargo, but more than a dozen other large companies provided loans to borrowers with suspect credit histories. The implosion of the lucrative but high-risk subprime sector of the mortgage industry in 2007 and 2008 ignited a financial crisis in the United States that would quickly engulf the global economy.

The origins of the subprime mortgage debacle in the United States can be traced to the collapse of New Century, the nation's second largest subprime lender. New Century was founded in 1995 by three friends who had previously worked together at a mortgage banking company. New Century, which was based in Irvine, California, grew dramatically over its brief existence. In 1996, New Century reported total revenues of $14.5 million and total assets of $4.4 million. Nine years later, the company reported total revenues of $2.4 billion and total assets of $26 billion.

During the heyday of subprime mortgage lending in 2005 and 2006, New Century funded $200 million of new mortgage loans on a typical business day. In early February 2007, just a few months after company executives insisted that New Century was financially strong, those same executives unsettled Wall Street when they re-vealed that the company would be restating previously released financial statements as a result of the misapplication of generally accepted accounting principles (GAAP).

Two months later, New Century declared bankruptcy. A court-appointed bank-ruptcy examiner summarized the far-reaching implications that New Century's down-fall had for the global economy.

> The increasingly risky nature of New Century's loan originations created a ticking time bomb that detonated in 2007 . . . The demise of New Century was an early con-tributor to the subprime market meltdown. The fallout from this market catastrophe has been massive and unprecedented. Global equity markets were rocked, credit markets tightened, recession fears spread, and losses are in the hundreds of billions of dollars and growing.[1]

In fact, New Century would be just the first of many high-profile companies brought down by the turmoil in the Unites States's mortgage industry. Longtime stalwarts of the nation's financial services industry that fell victim to that turmoil included Bear Stearns, Lehman Brothers, and Merrill Lynch.

In September 2008, the federal government assumed control of the Federal Na-tional Mortgage Association and the Federal Home Loan Mortgage Company, two "government-sponsored" but publicly owned companies better known as Fannie Mae and Freddie Mac, respectively. At the time, the two organizations owned or guaran-teed nearly one-half of the approximately $12 trillion of home mortgages in the United States. For decades, the federal government had used Fannie Mae and Freddie Mac to create an orderly and liquid market for homeowner mortgages, but the enor-mous losses each suffered in 2007 and 2008 undercut that role and forced the U.S. Department of the Treasury to take over their operations.

Angry investors lashed out at a wide range of parties who they believed bore some measure of responsibility for the massive financial crisis. Those parties included the major subprime mortgage lenders in the United States, such as New Century, and the politicians, regulatory authorities, ratings agencies, and independent auditors who had failed to prevent or rein in the imprudent business practices of those lending institutions.

Only a few years removed from the sweeping reforms prompted by the Enron and WorldCom scandals, the accounting profession was once again forced to defend it-self from a wide range of angry and often self-righteous critics. Among these critics was *The New York Times*. The prominent newspaper castigated the auditors of sub-prime lenders for stamping those institutions' financial statements with the account-ing profession's equivalent of the Good Housekeeping Seal of Approval. "While ac-counting firms don't exert legal or regulatory authority over their clients, they do bestow seals of approval, the way rating agencies do. People in the financial industry, as well as investors, have reason to believe that a green light from an auditor means that a company's accounting practices have passed muster."[2]

The following section of this case provides a historical overview of subprime mort-gage lending in the United States. Next, the history and operations of New Century

---

1. "Final Report of Michael J. Missal, Bankruptcy Court Examiner," In re: New Century TRS Holdings, Inc., a Delaware corporation, *et al.*, U.S. Bankruptcy Court for the District of Delaware, Case No. 07-10416 (KJC), 29 February 2008. Unless indicated otherwise, the quotations appearing in this case were taken from this source.

2. V. Bajaj and J. Creswell, "A Lender Failed. Did Its Auditor?" *The New York Times* (online), 13 April 2008.

Financial Corporation are reviewed with a particular focus on the company's major role in the subprime mortgage fiasco. The case then examines the criticism of KPMG, New Century's longtime independent audit firm, by the federal bankruptcy examiner appointed to investigate the company's sudden collapse in early 2007.

Subprime Lending: A Historical Perspective

Like all businesses, mortgage companies struggle to achieve a proper balance between "risk" and "return" in their operations. The major risk historically faced by mortgage lenders is the possibility that their clients will be unable or unwilling to pay the principal and interest on their mortgage loans.

Prior to the 1980s, individuals who were poor credit risks effectively had only two choices for obtaining a mortgage to purchase a home. Those alternatives were obtaining a home loan insured by either the Federal Housing Administration (FHA) or the Department of Veteran Affairs (VA). Borrowers with good credit histories, so-called prime borrowers, would typically seek financing for a new loan directly from a bank, savings and loan, or other financial institutions.

The deregulation of the lending industry beginning in the 1980s made it much easier for subprime borrowers to obtain mortgage loans to finance the purchase of a new home. The Depository Institutions Deregulation and Monetary Control Act of 1980 did away with restrictions that imposed a ceiling on the interest rates lending institutions could charge on new mortgage loans. Subsequent legislation allowed mortgage lenders to create a wide array of financing alternatives to compete with the standard 30-year, fixed interest rate mortgage loan that had long been the industry's principal product. Most notably, these nontraditional mortgage loans included ARMs, or adjustable rate mortgages, that would become particularly popular with mortgage borrowers who had impaired or "subprime" credit histories or profiles.

Despite the deregulatory legislation of the 1980s, the subprime sector of the mortgage industry did not experience explosive growth until the "securitization" of mortgage loans became increasingly common following the turn of the century. Wikipedia defines securitization as "a structured finance process in which assets, receivables, or financial instruments [such as mortgage loans] are acquired, classified into pools, and offered as collateral for third-party investment."

The securitization option caused many mortgage lenders to adopt an "originate to distribute" business model. This new business model meant that the credit risk posed by new mortgages was no longer exclusively absorbed by lending institutions but rather was shared with investors worldwide who purchased so-called mortgage-backed securities or MBS. By 2006, nearly one-fourth of all new residential mortgage loans in the United States were made to subprime borrowers; three-fourths of those mortgages were securitized and sold to investors in the United States and around the world.

The insatiable demand for high-yield MBS among investors, particularly institutional investors such as large banks and hedge funds, caused subprime lenders to ratchet up their marketing efforts. To persuade individuals who were high credit risks to obtain mortgage loans, the subprime lenders developed new products designed specifically for that sector of the mortgage market.

Among the most popular mortgage products developed for the subprime lending market were "stated-income" and "interest-only" mortgages. An applicant for a stated-income loan was simply asked to report his or her annual income during the application process for the loan. The applicant's self-reported income was used by the lender to determine the size of the loan that the individual could afford. Not surprisingly, many applicants for stated-income loans, commonly known as "liars' loans" in the mortgage industry, grossly overstated their annual incomes so that they could purchase a larger home than was economically feasible, given their actual annual incomes.

A borrower who obtained an interest-only or IO mortgage loan was required to pay only interest on his or her loan balance for a fixed period of the mortgage term. The IO feature of an IO loan typically extended over either the first 5 or the first 10 years of the mortgage term. Similar to other mortgage loans, the most common term of an IO loan was 30 years.

Housing prices in those regions of the country where subprime lending was particularly prevalent—such as Arizona; California; south Florida; and Las Vegas, Nevada—rose steeply during the late 1990s and into the early years of the new century. Many subprime borrowers in those housing markets purchased a home with the express intention of reaping a short-term windfall profit. An individual who obtained a 100 percent loan to acquire a $2 million home could realize a more than $400,000 "profit" on that home in two years if housing prices rose 10 percent each year. After two years, the borrower could extract that profit by refinancing his or her mortgage. That profit could then be used to make the monthly payments on the new mortgage. Or, that individual could sell the home and use the resulting profit to purchase a much larger home—with a much larger mortgage—that he or she could also "flip" in a few years.

Housing prices generally reached their peak in the United States in mid-2006, although they had been declining in some regions of the country over the previous twelve months. By late 2007, prices in several major regional housing markets had declined by 10 percent from their peak levels. By mid-2008, housing prices in those same markets had declined by 20 percent, or more, from their high watermarks.

As housing prices steadily fell, a growing number of subprime borrowers began defaulting on their monthly mortgage payments. In fact, many of those individuals quickly became "upside down in their homes," that is, the unpaid balances of their mortgages exceeded the market values of their homes. By early 2008, an estimated 9 million U.S. homeowners had a negative equity in their homes.

The sharp downturn in the housing market had an immediate and drastic impact on mortgage lenders, particularly subprime mortgage lenders such as New Century. Many of the subprime loans originated and packaged for sale by New Century included repurchase clauses. If the default rate on those packages of loans exceeded a certain rate, New Century could be forced to repurchase those loans. As the housing market weakened, New Century and other subprime lenders were flooded with loan repurchase requests.

The financial problems facing the mortgage industry soon spread to other sectors of the economy because of the securitization of subprime mortgage loans. Many high-profile companies in the financial services industry, such as Merrill Lynch, that had no direct connection to the large subprime lenders, suffered huge losses as the market value of MBS plunged. Making matters worse, a large proportion of MBS that originated in the United States was sold worldwide. As one observer of the mortgage market noted, the securitization process effectively "spread the cancer of subprime mortgages to investors throughout the U.S. and the rest of the world."[3]

New Century: Poster Child for Subprime Mortgage Lending

Bob Cole, Ed Gotschall, and Brad Morrice found themselves without jobs in 1995 when the company for which they had worked for several years, Plaza Home Mortgage, was purchased by a much larger competitor. The three friends decided to pool

3. K. Amadeo, "Understanding the Subprime Mortgage Crisis," *About.com* (online), 9 October 2008.

their resources and establish their own mortgage company, a company that would focus on the "low-end" or subprime sector of the mortgage market. While Cole served as New Century Financial Corporation's chief executive officer (CEO) and Gotschall as the company's chief financial officer, Morrice became the chief operating officer (COO), a role in which he oversaw New Century's lending operations. Morrice would eventually replace Cole as New Century's CEO. In June 1997, the company went public by listing its stock on the NASDAQ—New Century's stock would be switched to the New York Stock Exchange in late 2004.

Cole, Gotschall, and Morrice earned relatively modest annual salaries throughout their tenure with the company. For example, in 2005, each of them received a salary of $569,250. However, New Century's incentive compensation plan rewarded the three cofounders handsomely with significant bonuses and stock option grants when the company met or exceeded its financial goals. During 2005, the three executives received total compensation of approximately $15 million each. In addition, *The New York Times* reported that, collectively, they realized more than $40 million in trading profits on the sale of New Century stock between 2004 and 2006.[4]

New Century thrived from its inception thanks largely to three key factors. First, mortgage interest rates, which had spiked during the mid-1990s, stabilized and then generally trended downward for more than a decade. Second, the economic and regulatory environment at the time made subprime lending the most lucrative sector of the mortgage industry. Finally, the booming housing market in Orange County, California, where the company was located, gave New Century a large and easily accessible market to tap.

Once New Century was well established in Orange County, the company's ruling troika of Cole, Gotschall, and Morrice began pursuing expansion opportunities for their company in other "hot" real estate markets in the United States. At its zenith, New Century operated more than 200 retail mortgage offices in the United States from which company employees originated new mortgage loans. The company's wholesale division, which produced the bulk of its loan originations, operated through a far-flung network of more than 35,000 independent mortgage brokers.

New Century's 2003 Form 10-K filed with the Securities and Exchange Commission (SEC) provided a concise summary of the company's business model.

> *We offer mortgage products designed for borrowers who generally do not satisfy the credit, documentation or other underwriting standards prescribed by conventional mortgage lenders and loan buyers, such as Fannie Mae and Freddie Mac. We originate and purchase loans on the basis of the borrower's ability to repay the mortgage loan, the borrower's historical pattern of debt repayment and the amount of equity in the borrower's property (as measured by the borrower's loan-to-value ratio, or LTV). We have been originating and purchasing these types of loans since 1996 and believe we have developed a comprehensive and sophisticated process of credit evaluation and risk-based pricing that allows us to effectively manage the potentially higher risks associated with this segment of the mortgage industry.*

In 2004, New Century's management reorganized the company as a real estate investment trust (REIT), so that it would qualify for favorable tax treatment under the Internal Revenue Code. This organizational change had little impact on the company's operations or the underlying nature of its principal line of business, that is, originating subprime mortgage loans.

---

4. V. Bajaj, "Report Assails Auditor for Work at Failed Home Lender," *The New York Times* (online), 26 March 2008.

New Century experienced impressive growth from its founding in 1996 through 2001; however, a significant increase in subprime lending activity quadrupled New Century's revenues from fiscal 2002 to fiscal 2005. In the latter year, New Century originated or purchased more than $56 billion of mortgage loans and securitized $17 billion of those loans, resulting in net earnings of $411 million for the company.

The decision by New Century's management to focus the company's marketing efforts principally on stated-income and IO loans contributed significantly to its remarkable growth in revenues beginning in 2002. By 2005, approximately three-fourths of the company's loan originations involved one of those two products.

Throughout the period that New Century's revenues were increasing dramatically, company spokespeople repeatedly insisted in press releases and public filings with the SEC that the company had a strong and sophisticated system of internal controls. That contention was subsequently questioned by the bankruptcy examiner appointed to investigate the collapse of New Century.

> Several interviewees told the Examiner that they thought New Century's information technology and data entry and processing systems were not "state of the art" and were not sufficient for a business of the size and nature of New Century's. In particular, New Century's loan production processes were apparently manual and people-intensive through the fall of 2005. Up until that time, New Century apparently used an outdated DOS-based loan underwriting and appraising operating system, which according to one Management interviewee, allowed users to "finagle anything."

The bankruptcy examiner's report went on to note that the company's accounting system was particularly lax with regard to tracking "loan repurchase claims." According to the examiner, New Century did not develop an "automated system or protocol" for tracking such claims until late 2006. By that time, the company was being swamped by loan repurchase requests owing to the weakening housing markets in the principal geographical areas that it served. Besides failing to properly track loan repurchase requests throughout most of its history, New Century "did not have a formal policy spelling out exactly how to calculate reserves it might need to repurchase [rejected] loans."[5]

By late 2005, several members of New Century's board of directors were openly challenging top management's high-risk business strategies as well as questionable accounting and financial reporting decisions made by the company. The most vocal of these critics was Richard Zona, an outside director who also served on the company's audit committee.

Earlier in his long and distinguished career, Zona had been a senior partner with Ernst & Young (E&Y) and had served for a time as E&Y's National Director of Financial Services, a position in which he oversaw the firm's audit, tax and management consulting services. In the late 1990s, Zona had also served on an advisory council to the Federal Reserve Board.

In late 2005, Zona drafted a resignation letter, which he addressed to New Century's board of directors. In that letter, Zona suggested that company management was manipulating reported earnings, employing "aggressive" revenue recognition methods, and failing to provide an adequate allowance for loan losses.[6] Excerpts from Zona's letter are included in Exhibit 1.

---

5. Bajaj and Creswell, "A Lender Failed."

6. Zona eventually rescinded the 2005 resignation letter and remained on the company's board until September 2007.

EXHIBIT 1

EXCERPTS FROM
DRAFT OF 2005
RESIGNATION
LETTER SUBMITTED
BY RICHARD ZONA
TO NEW CENTURY'S
BOARD

At the October 25th and 26th [2005] Board meeting, Management informed the Board that its current forecast and analyst consensus for third quarter EPS of $2.24 per share could not be achieved unless Management reversed $.26 per share of loan loss reserves . . . Obviously, Management's desire to reverse reserves in the third quarter smacked of earnings manipulation.

Management use of off balance sheet gain on sale accounting substantially overstates earnings when compared to cash flows, thus generating extremely aggressive income recognition.

Our largest shareholder has questioned the appropriateness of our accounting for loan losses.

As to accounting for loan losses, it is a long standing accounting maxim that accounting should be designed and applied to match revenues with expenses. Management's methodology to provide for loan losses based upon their estimate of charge offs over the next 18 months does not accomplish that objective . . . Management's methodology does not result in a proper matching of revenues with costs, (loan loss provisions), because charge offs are back ended.

Source: "Final Report of Michael J. Missal, Bankruptcy Court Examiner," In re: New Century TRS Holdings, Inc., a Delaware corporation, *et al.*, U.S. Bankruptcy Court for the District Delaware, Case No. 07-10416 (KJC), 29 February 2008.

Throughout 2006, New Century's financial condition and operating results deteriorated rapidly. To quell concerns regarding the company's health, New Century management repeatedly assured Wall Street that the company was financially sound. In August 2006, New Century reported a significant increase in its earnings for the second quarter of the year compared with that for the same period in the prior year. A company spokesperson noted that those operating results were "evidence of the strength and stability of our franchise." New Century's third-quarter earnings' press release for 2006 admitted that subprime lenders faced "challenging" market conditions because of increasing loan delinquencies. Nevertheless, the press release assured the investing public that New Century was "adequately reserved for the expected higher level of loan losses."

On January 31, 2007, New Century's management team met with the company's board of directors and audit committee. At that meeting, management told the board and audit committee that New Century had understated its reserve for loan repurchase losses for each of the first three quarterly reporting periods of 2006. New Century's controller, David Kenneally, attributed those understatements to an "inadvertent oversight" in the method used to compute the reserve. Members of New Century's board and audit committee testified that they were "shocked" by this revelation and described the January 31 meeting as "ugly" and "very emotional."

On February 7, 2007, New Century filed a Form 8-K with the SEC, which publicly disclosed the prior understatements of the loan repurchase loss reserve. The 8-K indicated that the understatements were due to the company failing "to account for expected discounts upon the disposition of repurchased loans" and due to its failure to "properly consider the growing volume of repurchase claims outstanding that resulted from the increasing pace of repurchase requests." The 8-K filing did not disclose to what extent the loan repurchase loss reserve had been understated but instead simply indicated that the previously reported earnings for the first three quarters of 2006 "should no longer be relied upon."

On March 2, 2007, New Century informed the SEC that its 2006 Form 10-K would be delayed and that it would eventually report a loss for the entire year. At the same time, New Century disclosed that KPMG was considering issuing a going-concern opinion on the company's 2006 financial statements—KPMG resigned as New Century's auditor a few weeks later without having issued an opinion on those financial statements. On April 2, 2007, New Century filed for bankruptcy in a U.S. federal court. At the time, New Century was the ninth largest company to file for bankruptcy in the U.S. history.[7] In May 2008, company management announced that New Century's audited financial statements for 2005 should no longer be relied upon.

Within a few days of New Century's bankruptcy filing, the company's stock price fell to less than $1 per share, down from more than $30 per share two months earlier—the stock had reached its all-time high of $66 per share in 2004. Not surprisingly, stockholders and other parties were enraged by the company's sudden collapse that mimicked the downfall of Enron and WorldCom. Exhibit 2 presents a sarcastic commentary on New Century's collapse by one of the company's many critics. This commentary was in the form of a fictitious letter addressed to the readers of an online banking forum.

EXHIBIT 2

FICTITIOUS LETTER
SUPPOSEDLY
WRITTEN BY
FORMER NEW
CENTURY CEO
FOLLOWING THE
COMPANY'S
BANKRUPTCY FILING

Dear BankNet360 Readers:

Hi, my name is Brad Morrice and I've just bailed out of my sinking ship, the SS New Century Financial.

But don't feel bad for me; I'll be doing just fine. I may have bankrupt the company, treated mortgage underwriting like a bad cold, and helped cause more layoffs than a recession, but I should still bank about $25 million. To the creditors I say, "nanee-nanee billy goat."

Regrets? Sure, I've got some. I should have cashed in more of my options when the NEW stock was on a rocket ship fueled by option ARMs and I.O. loans from heaven. Ah, those were the days, when loans fell from the sky—and into the laps of subprime borrowers who can more easily discern Britney from J-Lo than understand all the conditions of their upcoming loan repricings.

You know, I wonder also how I can walk away from New Century with so much dough. This Chief Restructuring Officer, Holly Etlin, I don't know what planet she is from, but she can come over to my palace, er, place, anytime.

Oh, look at the time. That money's going to hit my account any moment now, and I've got shopping to do. Well, my regards to the subprime mortgage industry. All you Wall Street guys—hope you can handle the risk.

Sincerely yours,

Brad A. Morrice
Founder (ret.)
New Century Financial Corp. (bankrupt)

Source: BankNet360.com (http://www.banknet360.com/viewpoints/Discussion.do?discussion_id=191), 13 June 2007.

---

7. The five largest companies to file for bankruptcy in 2007 were mortgage lenders. Four of those five companies were subprime lenders.

"Go-to Auditor"

The New York Times characterized KPMG as the "go-to auditor" for the subprime sector of the mortgage industry.[8] KPMG's audit clients in that sector included the largest subprime lenders, namely, Countrywide, HSBC, New Century, and Wells Fargo. KPMG served as New Century's auditor from the company's inception in 1995 until its resignation in April 2007.

New Century's bankruptcy filing resulted in heated criticism of KPMG. *The New York Times* drew a parallel between Arthur Andersen's audits of Enron Corporation that had failed to expose the huge energy company's aggressive accounting treatments and KPMG's audits of New Century. According to the newspaper, KPMG had failed to warn investors that New Century's "mortgage freight train was about to run off the rails."[9]

> *New Century's accounting methods let it prop up profits, charming investors and allowing the company to continue to tap a rich vein of Wall Street cash that it used to underwrite more mortgages. Without the appearance of a strong bottom line, New Century's financial lifeline could have been cut earlier than it was.*[10]

The federal bankruptcy examiner appointed for New Century carried out an exhaustive investigation of the large subprime lender's sudden failure. A major focus of that investigation was KPMG's 2005 audit of New Century and the accounting firm's reviews of the financial statements included in the company's Form 10-Qs for the first three quarters of 2006. KPMG was required to provide the bankruptcy examiner with nearly 2 million pages of documents relating to those engagements. Exhibit 3 presents KPMG's audit report on New Century's 2005 financial statements.

In his 560-page report, the bankruptcy examiner alleged that KPMG had failed to perform its New Century engagements "in accordance with professional standards." The examiner's specific allegations included charges that the 2005 New Century audit was improperly staffed and that the independence of certain KPMG auditors may have been impaired. The examiner also maintained that KPMG failed to adequately consider serious internal control problems evident in New Century's accounting and financial reporting system and failed to properly audit the company's critically important loan repurchase loss reserve.

Staffing Issues on the New Century Engagement

In the spring of 2005, shortly after KPMG completed the 2004 audit of New Century, an almost entirely new team of auditors, approximately 15 KPMG employees in total, was assigned to that client. The only two members of the 2004 audit engagement team "held over" for the 2005 audit were two first-year associates. The two key members of the 2005 audit team, the audit engagement partner and the senior manager, had just joined the Los Angeles office of KPMG, the practice office responsible for servicing New Century.

John Donovan, the engagement partner for the 2005 New Century audit, had served for 17 years as an audit partner with Arthur Andersen prior to that firm being forced to disband in 2002. After Andersen's demise, Donovan became an audit partner with (E&Y), which he left in early 2005 to take a similar position with KPMG.

New Century's audit committee was unhappy with KPMG's decision to appoint Donovan as the audit engagement partner for the 2005 audit. Members of the audit

---

8. Bajaj and Creswell, "A Lender Failed."

9. *Ibid.*

10. *Ibid.*

EXHIBIT 3

NEW CENTURY
FINANCIAL
CORPORATION AND
SUBSIDIARIES
REPORT OF
INDEPENDENT
REGISTERED
CERTIFIED PUBLIC
ACCOUNTING FIRM

KPMG's 2005 Audit Report on New Century's Financial Statements

The Board of Directors

New Century Financial Corporation

We have audited the accompanying consolidated balance sheets of New Century Financial Corporation and subsidiaries as of December 31, 2005, and 2004, and the related consolidated statements of income, comprehensive income, changes in stockholders' equity, and cash flows for each of the years in the three-year period ended December 31, 2005. These consolidated financial statements are the responsibility of Company's Management. Our responsibility is to express an opinion on these consolidated financial statements based on our audits.

We conducted our audit in accordance with the standards of the Public Company Accounting Oversight Board (United States). Those standards require that we plan the audit to obtain reasonable assurance about whether the financial statements are free of material misstatement. An audit includes examining, on a test basis, evidence supporting the amounts and disclosures in the financial statements. An audit also includes assessing the accounting principles used and significant estimates made by management, as well as evaluating the overall financial statement presentation. We believe that our audits provide a reasonable basis for our opinion.

In our opinion, the consolidated financial statements referred to above present fairly, in all material respects, the financial position of New Century Financial Corporation and subsidiaries as of December 31, 2005 and 2004, and the results of their operations and their cash flows for each of the years in the three-year period ended December 31, 2005, in conformity with U.S. generally accepted accounting principles.

We have also audited, in accordance with the standards of the Public Company Accounting Oversight Board (United States), the effectiveness of the Company's internal control over financial reporting as of December 31, 2005, based on criteria established in Internal Control—Integrated Framework issued by the Committee of Sponsoring Organizations of the Treadway Commission (COSO), and our report dated March 15, 2006 expressed an unqualified opinion on management's assessment of, and the effective operation of, internal control over financial reporting.

KPMG LLP
Los Angeles, California
March 15, 2006

Source: New Century's 2005 10-K.

committee believed that Donovan's lack of experience with the mortgage industry made him a poor choice to supervise that audit and asked KPMG to appoint another partner to oversee the audit. When KPMG refused, the audit committee considered dismissing KPMG and retaining a different audit firm. "Ultimately, the Audit Committee determined that a switch to a new accounting firm would be tremendously disruptive and would send a bad signal to its lenders."

Mark Kim accepted a position with KPMG in May 2005, shortly before being assigned to serve as the senior manager on the 2005 New Century audit engagement. Kim had several years of prior experience as an auditor and had served for three years as the assistant controller of a small mortgage lending company.

During his tenure on the New Century audit team, Mark Kim complained to John Donovan that it was difficult to recruit a "good team" of auditors to work on the engagement. In an e-mail to Donovan, an exasperated Kim remarked, "We will never get a good team out here because of the reputation that the engagement has." Another e-mail sent by a New Century accountant to the company's controller, David Kenneally, seemed to corroborate Kim's opinion. This latter e-mail noted that KPMG had not assigned the "A team" to the New Century audit.

In fact, Kenneally, a former KPMG employee, was apparently the key reason that the New Century engagement had a negative reputation within KPMG's Los Angeles office. Evidence collected by the New Century bankruptcy examiner suggested that the company's accounting function was "weak" and was overseen by Kenneally who was "domineering" and "difficult, condescending, and quick-tempered." One KPMG subordinate on the New Century audit team testified that Kenneally often berated Donovan and Kim. In another e-mail sent by Kim to Donovan, the KPMG senior manager indicated that "Dave [Kenneally] seems to know the answers for everything and anything and the rest of the accounting department is on almost the same boat as the audit team is—little knowledge of what's going on. This intimidates everyone on the engagement team."

The tense relationship between the KPMG audit engagement team and New Century's management, particularly Kenneally, worsened as the 2005 audit neared completion. Two individuals with KPMG's Financial Derivatives Resource (FDR) group were brought in to review New Century's accounting for certain hedges and other financial derivatives during the final phase of the audit. They requested various documents from New Century that were needed to complete their review of the aforementioned items. When New Century failed to provide that documentation, the two specialists refused to "sign off" on the company's relevant accounting decisions. This refusal prevented Donovan from releasing the opinion on New Century's financial statements that were to be included in the company's 2005 10-K.

Hours before the SEC filing deadline for New Century's 2005 10-K, an angry Donovan e-mailed one of the FDR specialists, "I am very disappointed we are still discussing this. As far as I am concerned, we are done. The client thinks we are done. All we are going to do is p___ everybody off." Later that same day, a high-ranking KPMG partner in the firm's New York headquarters office instructed Donovan to release the unqualified opinion on New Century's 2005 financial statements. Donovan was instructed to release the opinion even though the two FDR specialists had not approved the company's accounting decisions for its financial derivatives.[11]

The following day, New Century's audit committee called a meeting with Donovan and Kim. In that meeting, members of the audit committee reportedly "yelled" and "screamed" at the two KPMG auditors. Later, Kenneally told the New Century bankruptcy examiner that he had been "furious" over the "near-disaster"—that is, the fact that New Century's filing of its 2005 10-K with the SEC had almost been delayed. Because of the incident, New Century's audit committee deferred the decision of whether to reappoint KPMG as the company's auditor for the 2006 fiscal year. Donovan later testified that he had been concerned that the audit committee would dismiss KPMG.

Over the following two months, Donovan assured New Century's audit committee that "a situation like this will never happen again." After receiving that assurance, the audit committee reappointed KPMG as New Century's audit firm.

---

11. The FDR specialists were allowed to dissociate themselves from the decision to issue the audit opinion on New Century's 2005 financial statements in a "disagreement memorandum" included in the 2005 workpapers. The following month, New Century finally provided the documentation that had been requested by those specialists. A review of that documentation revealed that New Century had improperly accounted for certain of its derivatives, resulting in "a misstatement of several million dollars." However, KPMG ruled that those errors were immaterial, meaning that it was not necessary to restate the 2005 financial statements.

The bankruptcy examiner speculated that the 2005 10-K incident impaired KPMG's independence during the remainder of the firm's tenure with New Century. "In particular, it is possible that Donovan and Kim were not as skeptical as they might otherwise have been with regard to critical assumptions [underlying New Century's accounting decisions]." The examiner went on to suggest that "Donovan and Kim may have looked for ways to add unique value in order to salvage KPMG's reputation, such as by providing proactive (though erroneous) advice in connection with the repurchase reserve calculation methodology."

In a subsequent interview with *The New York Times*, the bankruptcy examiner further questioned KPMG's independence when he maintained that the New Century auditors had been eager to please the company's management team. "They acquiesced overly to the client, which in the post-Enron era seems mind-boggling."[12] In another interview with the Reuters news agency, the examiner expressed a similar point of view. "In the post-Enron era, one of the lessons should have been that accountants need to be skeptical, strong, and independent. You didn't have any of those attributes here."[13]

Inadequate Consideration of Internal Control Problems

Section 404 of the Sarbanes-Oxley Act requires auditors of public companies to audit the effectiveness of their clients' internal controls over financial reporting.[14] In both 2004 and 2005, KPMG concluded that New Century maintained effective internal control over its financial reporting function.

During the 2004 internal control audit, the KPMG auditors identified five "significant deficiencies" in internal controls that they reported to New Century's audit committee. Since the KPMG auditors concluded that those deficiencies did not qualify as "material weaknesses," the audit firm was able to issue an unqualified opinion on New Century's internal controls for 2004. No significant deficiencies or material weaknesses in internal controls were identified by KPMG during the 2005 internal control audit.

New Century's bankruptcy examiner challenged KPMG's conclusion that the company's internal controls over financial reporting were effective during 2004 and 2005. The examiner pointed out that throughout its existence New Century did not have an "effective mechanism for tracking, processing and handling [loan] repurchase claims." This internal control weakness prevented the company from determining the magnitude of loan repurchase requests at any point in time, which, in turn, prevented the company from properly considering those requests in arriving at the period-ending balances of the loan repurchase loss reserve.

A related internal control weakness was New Century's failure to adopt "formal policies and procedures" for calculating the loan repurchase loss reserve at the end of each accounting period. The lower-level accountants who were assigned the task of computing the reserve balance each reporting period testified that they simply followed the instructions passed down to them by the individual who had previously been responsible for the reserve computation.

---

12. Bajaj, "Report Assails Auditor."

13. A. Beck, "KPMG Allowed Fraud at New Century, Report Says," *Reuters.com*, 27 March 2008.

14. KPMG's 2004 and 2005 audits of New Century were completed while PCAOB *Auditing Standard No. 2*, "An Audit of Internal Control Over Financial Reporting Performed in Conjunction with an Audit of Financial Statements" was in effect. That standard has subsequently been replaced by PCAOB *Auditing Standard No. 5*, "An Audit of Internal Control Over Financial Reporting That Is Integrated with an Audit of Financial Statements." The two standards are very similar.

During both the 2004 and 2005 audits, the KPMG auditors discovered the internal control weaknesses related to New Century's loan repurchase loss reserve. The bankruptcy examiner noted that those control weaknesses had particularly critical implications for New Century in 2005 when the volume of loan repurchase requests was increasing rapidly. Despite those implications, KPMG characterized those weaknesses as "inconsequential" during the 2005 audit. Since the internal control problems were not deemed significant deficiencies or material weaknesses, KPMG did not communicate them to New Century's audit committee.

The bankruptcy examiner insisted that for at least the 2005 audit, the inadequate accounting procedures for loan repurchase requests qualified as a material weakness in internal control that should have caused KPMG to issue an adverse opinion on New Century's internal controls. In fact, New Century's management reached a similar conclusion in early 2007.

> The material weaknesses identified [by New Century's management in early 2007] were: (1) the failure to maintain effective controls over the interpretation and application of the accounting literature relating to the Company's critical accounting policies (specifically as to the calculation of repurchase reserves); and (2) the failure to maintain effective controls to provide reasonable assurances that the Company collected, analyzed, and used information relating to outstanding purchase claims when establishing the allowance for repurchase losses.

Debbie Biddle was the KPMG audit senior principally responsible for the 2005 internal control audit. Similar to John Donovan and Mark Kim, Biddle had joined KPMG's Los Angeles office shortly before the 2005 New Century audit began. Biddle had transferred to the Los Angeles office from a KPMG affiliate in the United Kingdom. Prior to being assigned responsibility for the 2005 New Century internal control audit, Biddle had "virtually no experience auditing U.S. clients and no prior SOX experience."

The bankruptcy examiner reported that Biddle and her colleagues failed to thoroughly review the 2004 audit workpapers for New Century. As a result, they may have been unaware of the internal control problems discovered by KPMG auditors the prior year and thus failed to properly consider those problems in planning and carrying out the 2005 audit.

> The Examiner found no evidence that the KPMG [2005] engagement team engaged in a formal process to compare year over year deficiency findings in connection with the 2005 SOX 404 audit. Conducting this analysis would have been prudent given the wholesale turnover in the KPMG engagement team. This failure is significant, as it impacted the planning for the 404 audit in 2005, the evaluation of findings in 2005, and the planning for the year-end audits.

Failure to Properly Audit New Century's Loan Repurchase Loss Reserve

In early 2005, the quality of New Century's loan portfolio, as measured by such objective criteria as delinquency and default rates, began declining rapidly. Internal data collected by New Century revealed that the delinquency rate on loans originated during 2005 was approximately double that of loans originated during the previous year. The delinquency rate continued to rise throughout 2006 as conditions within the housing market deteriorated.

The increasing delinquency and default rates on loans originated by New Century caused a large increase in the number of loan repurchase claims filed by investors that had purchased large blocks of those loans. Because of the inadequate accounting procedures and internal controls for loan repurchase claims, New Century's accounting staff failed to record the needed increases in the loan repurchase loss reserve throughout 2005 and beyond. For example, despite the large increase in loan repurchase requests in 2005, New Century's loan repurchase loss reserve actually declined from the end of 2004 to the end of 2005.

New Century's bankruptcy examiner estimated that the understatement of the loan repurchase loss reserve and errors in related accounts inflated New Century's reported pretax earnings for fiscal 2005 by 14.3 percent or approximately $64 million. The examiner determined that errors in those same accounts overstated New Century's reported pretax earnings for the first three quarters of 2006 by approximately $200 million or 59 percent.

New Century's accountants used a 90-day "look-back" period in determining the adequacy of the loan repurchase loss reserve each financial reporting period. That is, only repurchase requests for loans sold in the 90 days immediately preceding the balance sheet date were considered in arriving at the reserve balance. In fact, the company often received repurchase requests for loans sold more than three months earlier.

The bankruptcy examiner criticized KPMG for not insisting that New Century use a longer than 90-day "window" in computing the loan repurchase loss reserve. However, a KPMG workpaper suggested that policy was reasonable. "Based on the review of the Company's repurchase log and discussions with management, it appears reasonable that the most recent 3 months sales are at risk for repurchase." The bankruptcy examiner contested the assertion that KPMG had reviewed the log of loan repurchase requests, since that accounting record indicated that loans were being reacquired by New Century as long as three years after the date they were sold. The examiner also uncovered evidence suggesting that a New Century executive had informed a KPMG auditor that a significant number of loans older than 90 days were being repurchased by the company.

KPMG's audit workpapers documented the ominous increase in loan repurchase requests received by New Century beginning in late 2004. In 2005, New Century repurchased $332 million of loans, compared with $135 million the prior year. Despite this large increase, the bankruptcy examiner reported that KPMG "failed to perform any increased procedures or testing of New Century's repurchase reserves" during the 2005 audit.

A secondary factor that contributed to the understatement of New Century's loan repurchase loss reserve was the company's failure to consider an "interest recapture" element in computing that reserve each reporting period. The bankruptcy examiner found this obvious oversight by the company's accountants "perplexing."

> The failure to include Interest Recapture in the repurchase reserve calculation from the outset is perplexing because the Examiner understands that it was a long time requirement under loan repurchase agreements for New Century to pay investors the amount of interest that the borrower had failed to pay.

In fact, the workpaper memorandum that summarized the audit tests KPMG applied during the 2005 audit to the loan repurchase loss reserve indicated that interest recapture was a component of the reserve.

> A KPMG workpaper from January 2006 notes that estimated losses on future repurchases "include accrued interest the investor [loan purchaser] would have collected from the borrower, if the loan had performed, that New Century must pay to the investor at the time of repurchase."

The evidence that KPMG relied on to reach that erroneous conclusion was a statement made by David Kenneally. The bankruptcy examiner criticized the KPMG auditors for not corroborating Kenneally's assertion with other audit evidence. "If KPMG had performed adequate tests and calculations, it would have determined that Interest Recapture was omitted from the repurchase reserve calculation."

During early 2006, New Century changed the method used to compute the period-ending balance of the loan repurchase loss reserve.[15] This change resulted in large increases in the understatements of that account at the end of each subsequent quarterly reporting period—by the third quarter the reserve was understated by approximately 1,000 percent.

Kenneally testified that the change in accounting for the reserve account was recommended by Mark Kim, the KPMG senior audit manager. Kim would later testify that he did not explicitly remember making that recommendation. Nevertheless, evidence collected by the bankruptcy examiner caused him to conclude that a KPMG auditor "almost certainly" recommended the change in accounting for the reserve account.

> At a time when KPMG was aware, as evidenced by its own workpapers, that market conditions were worsening and repurchases were increasing, KPMG made a recommendation to New Century to remove a component of the repurchase reserve that had the effect of decreasing the reserve . . . and then failed to inform the Audit Committee of the change in this critical accounting policy.

In November 2006, New Century hired a new chief financial officer (CFO) who had 30 years of prior experience in the mortgage industry. The CFO immediately questioned the adequacy of the company's loan repurchase loss reserve and asked KPMG to provide him with a written statement that the reserve was properly stated. KPMG refused to provide that written assurance.

As a result of the new CFO's persistent inquiries, New Century's accounting staff eventually recognized that the accounting change made in early 2006 for the loan repurchase loss reserve had been improper and had materially understated the reserve for each of the first three quarterly reporting periods of 2006. That realization led to the February 7, 2007, 8-K filing in which New Century reported those understatements. That 8-K disclosure triggered the series of events that resulted in New Century filing for bankruptcy less than two months later.

In Defense of KPMG

Representatives of KPMG responded forcefully to the allegations against their firm in the report prepared by New Century's bankruptcy examiner. Particularly galling to the large accounting firm was the suggestion that KPMG auditors had "deferred excessively"[16] to client executives during the course of the New Century engagements. In response to that allegation, a KPMG spokesperson told a reporter with *The New York Times*, "There is absolutely no evidence to support that contention."[17] In a subsequent interview with the *Times*, that same individual suggested that the bankruptcy examiner's report was unfair and "one-sided."

---

15. The change in the method of computing the loss reserve involved deleting the "inventory severity" component of that reserve. That component involved those losses expected to be incurred by New Century on loans that had already been reacquired as of the given balance sheet date. Kim allegedly suggested dropping this component because he believed that it was considered by New Century in arriving at the balance of a related valuation account for the company's portfolio of outstanding loans. In fact, that was not the case.

16. Bajaj, "Report Assails Auditor."

17. *Ibid.*

> *The examiner was appointed by the court to identify potential lawsuits in a bankruptcy case. Consistent with that charge, he has prepared an advocacy piece, which has many one-sided statements and significant omissions. In the end, the examiner concluded that the bankruptcy estate may be able to file a lawsuit against KPMG for negligence—a claim we strongly dispute—and a claim even the examiner notes in his report for which KPMG has strong defenses.*[18]

Several other parties also came to KPMG's defense. An accounting professor at the University of Chicago maintained that KPMG was not at fault in the New Century case and instead attributed the company's bankruptcy to its high-risk business model. "The business model of New Century depended on real estate values that would continue to go up and certainly not go down. The economic model here is what is at fault. It's the cause of what happened, not anything that KPMG did."[19]

At a minimum, the New Century bankruptcy report served to sustain a string of embarrassing public relation incidents for KPMG. In 2005, KPMG had faced potential criminal charges for a series of questionable tax shelters that it had marketed to well-heeled tax clients. In that same year, KPMG had agreed to pay the SEC $22.5 million to settle charges that audits of one of its largest clients, Xerox, had been flawed. Subsequent to that announcement, KPMG paid $80 million to settle civil litigation stemming from its Xerox audits.

Even before the New Century bankruptcy report was released, KPMG had been linked to the ongoing crises and scandals in the mortgage industry. Charges of large-scale earnings manipulation by Fannie Mae called into the question the quality of KPMG's audits of that organization, which for decades had played such a large role in the mortgage industry. Finally, in early January 2008, KPMG had been named a codefendant in a large class-action lawsuit that charged Countrywide, another KPMG audit client, with perpetrating an accounting fraud.

EPILOGUE

In August 2008, Ed McMahon revealed that he had finally found a buyer for his Beverly Hills mansion that would allow him to pay off his large mortgage. A key factor that helped McMahon sell his home was that someone reportedly wanted Britney Spears as their next-door neighbor. Most individuals snared by the financial crisis that overwhelmed the mortgage industry and housing market in the United States did not share McMahon's good fortune. By the end of 2008, more than 1.5 million Americans would face foreclosure proceedings on their homes, easily the largest number of residential foreclosures in U.S. history.

In an effort to thwart the nationwide financial panic caused by the meltdowns in the mortgage and housing industries, the U.S. Congress passed a massive bailout plan in October 2008. The price tag for that rescue effort, intended to shore up the nation's crumbling financial infrastructure, was measured in hundreds of billions of dollars. Even if the rescue effort proved successful, most experts expected that the U.S. economy, as well as the global economy, would suffer adverse lingering effects for years, if not decades, to come.

---

18. Bajaj and Creswell, "A Lender Failed."
19. *Ibid.*

Questions

1. KPMG served as the independent audit firm of several of the largest subprime mortgage lenders. Identify the advantages and disadvantages of a heavy concentration of audit clients in one industry or subindustry.

2. As noted in the case, there was an almost complete turnover of the staff assigned to the New Century audit engagement team in 2005. What quality control mechanisms should accounting firms have in such circumstances to ensure that a high-quality audit is performed?

3. Section 404 of the Sarbanes-Oxley Act requires auditors of a public company to analyze and report on the effectiveness of the client's internal controls over financial reporting. Describe the responsibilities that auditors of public companies have to discover and report (a) *significant deficiencies* in internal controls and (b) *material weaknesses* in internal controls. Include a definition of each item in your answer. Under what condition or conditions can auditors issue an unqualified or clean opinion on the effectiveness of a client's internal controls over financial reporting?

4. One of New Century's most important accounts was its loan repurchase loss reserve. Each accounting period, New Century was required to estimate the ending balance of that account. What general principles or procedures should auditors follow when auditing important "accounting estimates"?

5. New Century's bankruptcy examiner charged that KPMG did not comply with applicable "professional standards" while auditing the company. List specific generally accepted auditing standards (GAAS) that you believe KPMG may have violated on its New Century engagements. Briefly defend each item you list.

6. Mortgage-backed securities (MBS) produced by New Century and other major subprime lenders have been a focal point of attention during the recent financial crisis. Many parties have maintained that the mark-to-market rule for securities investments such as MBS has contributed significantly to that crisis and that the rule should be modified, suspended, or even eliminated. Briefly summarize the principal arguments of those parties opposed to the mark-to-market rule. Do you believe that those arguments are legitimate? Why or why not?

7. Identify what you consider to be the three most important "takeaways" or learning points in this case. Rank these items in order of importance (highest to lowest). Justify or defend each of your choices.

SECTION 2

AUDITS OF HIGH-RISK ACCOUNTS

CASE 2.1

Jack Greenberg, Inc.

Auditors commonly find themselves facing situations in which they must persuade client executives to do something they absolutely and resolutely do not want to do. When all else fails, auditors may be forced to use a tactic that clinical psychologists, marriage counselors, parents of toddlers, and other interpersonal experts typically frown upon; namely, the old-fashioned "if-you-don't-cooperate, I-will-punish-you" threat. In the mid-1990s, an exasperated team of Grant Thornton auditors resorted to threatening a stubborn client executive to goad him into turning over key documents that had significant audit implications. The executive eventually capitulated and turned over the documents—which resulted in even more problems for the Grant Thornton auditors.

The Brothers Greenberg

For decades, Jack Greenberg oversaw a successful wholesale meat company, a company that he eventually incorporated and named after himself.[1] Jack Greenberg, Inc., marketed a variety of meat, cheese, and other food products along the eastern seaboard of the United States from its Philadelphia headquarters. Jack Greenberg's failing health in the early 1980s prompted him to place his two sons in charge of the company's day-to-day operations. After their father's death, the two brothers, Emanuel and Fred, became equal partners in the business. Emanuel assumed the title of company president, while Fred became the company's vice president. The two brothers and their mother made up the company's three-person board of directors. Several other members of the Greenberg family also worked in the business.

Similar to many family-owned and -operated businesses, Jack Greenberg, Inc. (JGI), did not place a heavy emphasis on internal control. Like their father, the two Greenberg brothers relied primarily upon their own intuition and the competence and integrity of their key subordinates to manage and control their company's operations. By the mid-1980s, when the privately owned business had annual sales measured in the tens of millions of dollars, Emanuel realized that JGI needed to develop a more formal accounting and control system. That realization convinced him to begin searching for a new company controller who had the expertise necessary to revamp JGI's outdated accounting function and to develop an appropriate network of internal controls for the growing company. In 1987, Emanuel hired Steve Cohn, a CPA and former auditor with Coopers & Lybrand, as JGI's controller. Cohn, who had extensive experience working with a variety of different inventory systems, immediately tackled the challenging assignment of creating a modern accounting and control system for JGI.

Among other changes, Cohn implemented new policies and procedures that provided for segregation of key responsibilities within JGI's transaction cycles. Cohn also integrated computer processing throughout most of JGI's operations, including the payroll, receivables, and payables modules of the company's accounting function.

---

1. The facts of this case and the quotations included in it were taken from the following court opinion: *Larry Waslow, Trustee for Jack Greenberg, Inc. v. Grant Thornton LLP*; United States Bankruptcy Court for the Eastern District of Pennsylvania, 240 B.R. 486; 1999 Bankr. LEXIS 1308.

One of the more important changes that Cohn implemented was developing an internal reporting system that produced monthly financial statements the Greenbergs could use to make more timely and informed decisions for their business. Cohn's new financial reporting system also allowed JGI to file more timely financial statements with the three banks that provided the bulk of the company's external financing. By the early 1990s, JGI typically had a minimum of $10 million in outstanding loans from those banks.

One area of JGI's operations that Cohn failed to modernize was the company's accounting and control procedures for prepaid inventory. Since the company's early days, imported meat products had accounted for a significant portion of JGI's annual sales. Because foreign suppliers required JGI to prepay for frozen meat items, the company maintained two inventory accounts, Prepaid Inventory and Merchandise Inventory. Prepayments for imported meat products were charged to the Prepaid Inventory account, while all other merchandise acquired by the company for resale was debited to the Merchandise Inventory account. Prepaid inventory typically accounted for 60 percent of JGI's total inventory and 40 percent of the company's total assets.

Long before Cohn became JGI's controller, Jack Greenberg had given his son Fred complete responsibility for the purchasing, accounting, control, and other decisions affecting the company's prepaid inventory. Following their father's death, the two brothers agreed that Fred would continue overseeing JGI's prepaid inventory. When Cohn attempted to restructure and computerize the accounting and control procedures for prepaid inventory, Fred refused to cooperate. Despite frequent and adamant pleas from Cohn over a period of several years, Emanuel refused to order his younger brother to cooperate with Cohn's modernization plan for JGI's accounting system.

Accounting for Prepaid Inventory

Fred Greenberg processed the purchase orders for meat products that JGI bought from foreign vendors. The items purchased were inspected by the appropriate authority in the given country and then loaded into refrigerated lockers to be transported by boat to the United States. When a vendor provided documentation to JGI that a shipment was in transit, Fred Greenberg approved payment of the vendor's invoice. These payments, as noted earlier, were charged or debited to JGI's Prepaid Inventory account. Fred Greenberg maintained a handwritten accounting record known as the prepaid inventory log to keep track of the items included in the Prepaid Inventory account at any point in time.

When a shipment of imported meat products arrived at a U.S. port, a customs broker retained by JGI arranged for the individual items to be inspected and approved for entry into the United States by customs officials. After a shipment had cleared customs, the customs broker sent a notification form to that effect to Fred Greenberg. When the product arrived by truck at JGI's warehouse, a U.S. Department of Agriculture (USDA) official opened and inspected the items included in the order. The USDA official completed a document known as Form 9540-1 to indicate that the items had passed inspection. Each Form 9540-1 also indicated the date that the given products had arrived at JGI's warehouse.

Upon completion of the USDA inspection process, the prepaid inventory items were turned over to the manager of JGI's warehouse. The warehouse manager stamped the items to indicate that they had passed the USDA inspection and then completed a document known as a delivery receipt that listed the date of arrival, the vendor, the type of product, and the quantity of the product. The warehouse manager sent the delivery receipt form to Fred Greenberg, who matched the form with the appropriate vendor invoice. Fred then deleted the given inventory items from the prepaid inventory log and forwarded the matched invoice and delivery receipt to Steve Cohn, who processed an accounting entry that transferred the product from the Prepaid Inventory account to the Merchandise Inventory account. At the end of each year, JGI took a physical inventory of the company's warehouse and adjusted the balance of the Merchandise Inventory account to agree with the results of the physical inventory.

Because of the accounting procedures used for JGI's two inventory accounts, there was some risk that certain inventory items would be "double-counted" at year-end. That is, certain inventory items might be included in both the Prepaid Inventory and Merchandise Inventory accounts if there was any delay in processing the delivery receipt forms. For example, suppose that a shipment of imported meat products arrived at JGI's warehouse on December 29, two days before the close of the company's fiscal year. If Fred Greenberg failed to delete the items in the shipment from the prepaid inventory log and failed to forward the delivery receipt and invoice for the shipment to Steve Cohn on a timely basis, the items in the shipment could be included in both inventory accounts at the end of the year.[2] To reduce the risk of such errors, Cohn reconciled the prepaid inventory log maintained by Fred to the year-end balance of the Prepaid Inventory account. Cohn also asked Fred to allow him to review any delivery receipts that arrived during the last few days of the fiscal year.

Fred's Fraud

Steve Cohn realized that the accounting procedures for prepaid inventory increased the risk that JGI's year-end inventory would be misstated. In early 1992, Cohn, who by this time had been given the title of chief financial officer (CFO), designed a computerized accounting system for JGI's prepaid inventory. Cohn then called a meeting with the two Greenberg brothers to illustrate the system and demonstrate the important information and control advantages that it would provide over the "sloppy" manual system that Fred had used for years to account for prepaid inventory. Several years later, Cohn would recount how the Greenberg brothers reacted to his proposal.

I told Fred how this was a great idea and how I believed that this would be a big step forward in being able to monitor the [prepaid] inventory and determine what was open. . . . And I showed it to Fred, looked at it and said, "Isn't this great? We can do this." And I said, "Don't you want to do this?" And he looked at me and said, "No."

I was flabbergasted. I looked over to Manny [Emanuel]. He just sat there. And I was furious. I didn't talk to Fred for weeks. I was—I was having a hard time dealing with it. I couldn't imagine why he wouldn't want me to do this. It was such a good thing for the company. And he didn't want to do it.

Later in 1992, the persistent Cohn decided to personally collect the information needed to maintain a computerized accounting system for JGI's prepaid inventory. Cohn would watch for delivery trucks arriving at JGI's warehouse, which was adjacent to the company's administrative offices. When a truck arrived, either he or a subordinate would go to the shipping dock and make copies of the delivery receipt and other documents for each shipment of imported meat products. "We used to run

2. Because such items would be present during the year-end physical inventory of JGI's warehouse, the book-to-physical inventory adjustment would cause them to be included in the December 31 balance of the Merchandise Inventory account.

back and forth trying to get these receivings [delivery receipts] that [the warehouse manager] was preparing and it became a game. I became a laughingstock because it was a joke that I was trying to get this information." After several weeks, an exasperated Cohn gave up his futile effort.

Fred Greenberg had reason not to cooperate with Cohn's repeated attempts to overhaul the accounting and control procedures for JGI's prepaid inventory. Since the mid-1980s, Fred had been intentionally overstating the company's prepaid inventory. Those overstatements had materially understated JGI's annual cost of goods sold as well as overstated the company's gross profit and net income each year. In subsequent court testimony, Fred reported that his father's failing health had compelled him to begin manipulating JGI's reported operating results. "To avoid aggravating his illness, I started the practice [inflating prepaid inventory] so he would feel better about his business."

Fred also testified that following his father's death "significant changes occurring in the market which adversely affected us" caused him to continue his fraudulent scheme. During the late 1980s and early 1990s, Fred and his brother found it increasingly difficult to compete with larger wholesalers that were encroaching on their company's market. To compete with these larger companies, JGI was forced to reduce the gross margins on the products that it sold. To mitigate the impact of this competitive pressure on JGI's operating results, Fred routinely overstated prepaid inventory to produce gross margins that approximated those historically realized by the company.

> Fred manipulated the dates upon which the prepaid inventory was received in order to make it appear that the company's operations generated the same general financial performance from period to period. He did this by determining how much inventory needed to be prepaid inventory so that the percentages of gross profit and net income would remain consistent.

To overstate prepaid inventory, Fred destroyed delivery receipts forwarded to him by JGI's warehouse manager and neglected to update the prepaid inventory log for the given shipments. Weeks or even months later, he would prepare new delivery receipts for those shipments, delete the items in the shipments from the prepaid inventory log, and then forward the receipts along with the corresponding vendor invoices to Cohn. This practice caused the affected prepaid inventory items to be included in both inventory accounts, Prepaid Inventory and Merchandise Inventory, for extended periods of time.

Auditing Prepaid Inventory

Grant Thornton served as JGI's independent audit firm from 1986 through 1994. Because prepaid inventory was JGI's largest asset and because it posed significant audit risks, the engagement audit team allocated a disproportionate amount of audit resources to that item. Several weeks before the end of each fiscal year, Grant Thornton provided Steve Cohn with an "Engagement Compliance Checklist" that identified the documents and other information needed by the audit engagement team to complete the audit. Many of these requested items involved JGI's prepaid inventory, including "government forms, bills of lading, insurance information, and the delivery receipts prepared by the warehouse personnel evidencing the date upon which the [prepaid] inventory was received at the warehouse." Each year, Grant Thornton also requested a copy of Fred Greenberg's prepaid inventory log and Cohn's reconciliation of the information in that record to JGI's general ledger controlling account for prepaid inventory.

One key item that Grant Thornton did not request from Cohn was the Form 9540-1 prepared for each shipment of imported meat products delivered to JGI's warehouse. Grant Thornton auditors later testified that they became aware in 1988 that a Form 9540-1 was prepared for each prepaid inventory shipment received by JGI. However, the audit team did not learn until 1993 that the USDA official who completed the 9540-1 gave a copy of that document to a JGI warehouse clerk.

Each year, Cohn diligently collected the information requested by Grant Thornton and gave it to the accounting firm well before the date the audit was to begin, with one exception. Because Fred Greenberg failed to give the prepaid inventory log, delivery receipts, and other information he maintained for JGI's prepaid inventory to Cohn on a timely basis, Grant Thornton received that information well after the audit had begun each year.

Grant Thornton audited all of JGI's prepaid inventory transactions each year. "Grant Thornton tested 100 percent of the prepaid inventory transactions, which meant that Grant Thornton examined every invoice for prepaid inventory and reviewed the delivery receipts to confirm if and when a delivery had been made." By examining the invoices and delivery receipts, the auditors could determine which prepaid inventory purchases were apparently "still open" at year-end, that is, the prepaid inventory shipments that were properly included in JGI's year-end Prepaid Inventory account.

Because Fred Greenberg had destroyed many of the delivery receipts prepared by the warehouse manager, the Grant Thornton auditors failed to discover that much of JGI's year-end prepaid inventory was "double-counted." A critical issue in subsequent litigation stemming from this case was whether Grant Thornton was justified in relying on the delivery receipts to audit JGI's year-end prepaid inventory. Members of the audit engagement team maintained that because JGI's warehouse manager prepared the delivery receipts independently of the company's accounting function for prepaid inventory, those documents provided sufficient competent evidence to corroborate prepaid inventory. "Grant Thornton believed it was acceptable to rely on the Delivery Receipt to verify the date of delivery because JGI's internal control procedures for inventory were based on a system of 'segregation of duties.'" A Grant Thornton representative provided the following explanation of exactly what was implied by the phrase "segregation of duties."

Question: *You speak of segregation of duties. What do you mean by that?*

Answer: *Somebody is separate—you know, the purchasing function is separate from the receiving function and the approval function is different from the person who executes the transactions.*

Question: *Does that mean that there are separate people that do these different functions?*

Answer: *Yes. Separate people or departments.*

1993 and 1994 JGI Audits

During the 1992 JGI audit, members of the Grant Thornton audit team told Steve Cohn and Emanuel Greenberg they were concerned by the large increase in prepaid inventory over the previous three years.[3] The auditors also expressed concern regarding the haphazard accounting procedures applied to prepaid inventory. These concerns caused the auditors to include the following comments in a report entitled

---

3. The dollar value of JGI's prepaid inventory increased by 303 percent from the end of 1989 to the end of 1992.

"Internal Control Structure Reportable Conditions and Advisory Comments" that was submitted to Emanuel Greenberg at the conclusion of the 1992 audit. "Prepaid inventory should be set up on a personal computer and updated daily from purchases. This would identify a problem much sooner and reduce the risk of loss should such a problem occur." Cohn later testified that he had encouraged Grant Thornton to include this recommendation in the report filed with Emanuel Greenberg. Despite this recommendation, Emanuel would not pressure his brother to cooperate with Cohn's effort to strengthen the accounting procedures for prepaid inventory.

Grant Thornton auditors had access to the notification forms JGI's customs broker sent to Fred Greenberg when a prepaid inventory shipment arrived in a U.S. port. During the 1993 audit, a Grant Thornton auditor noticed that for several prepaid inventory shipments an abnormally long period of time had elapsed between the date the customs broker inspected the merchandise and the date that merchandise arrived at JGI's warehouse. When asked about this issue, Fred Greenberg explained that "floods in the Midwest" had slowed down many shipments en route to the East Coast from ports on the West Coast. A Grant Thornton auditor contacted JGI's customs broker regarding Fred's explanation. The customs broker told the auditor that Fred's explanation was valid.

Near the end of the 1993 audit, a Grant Thornton auditor stumbled across a large stack of Form 9540-1 documents in the receiving office of JGI's warehouse. Following this discovery, the Grant Thornton audit team attempted to match individual delivery receipts with the corresponding Form 9540-1 documents to verify the dates reported on the delivery receipts. Because the latter documents were in no particular alphabetical, chronological, or numerical order, the "task proved insurmountable and was abandoned." In explaining why the auditors did not insist on JGI providing those forms in a usable condition, a Grant Thornton representative noted that the 1993 audit program did not require the delivery receipts to be matched with the Form 9540-1 documents. "However, Grant Thornton decided that since JGI had access to the forms, it wanted them produced for the 1994 audit so that it could use them to verify the date recorded on the delivery receipts."

Following the completion of the 1993 audit, Grant Thornton once again submitted a report entitled "Internal Control Structure Reportable Conditions and Advisory Comments" to Emanuel Goldberg. In this report, Grant Thornton included several specific recommendations regarding improvements needed in the accounting procedures applied to prepaid inventory. One of these recommendations was to maintain an orderly file of the Form 9540-1 documents that could be used for internal control purposes and during the annual independent audit. A second recommendation called for JGI to begin using a specific set of computer-based accounting and internal control procedures and documents for prepaid inventory. These latter items were the same procedures and documents that Steve Cohn had developed and presented to the Greenberg brothers in 1992.

Throughout 1994, Fred Greenberg continued to refuse to adopt Grant Thornton's recommendations for improving the accounting for, and control over, prepaid inventory. In the fall of 1994, Cohn contacted Grant Thornton and told members of the audit engagement team that Fred had not complied with their recommendations. A Grant Thornton representative then met with Fred and told him that, at a minimum, JGI would have to provide the Form 9540-1 documents to Grant Thornton if the accounting firm was to complete the 1994 audit. Still, Fred refused to comply.

Shortly after Grant Thornton began the 1994 audit, a senior member of the audit engagement team advised Fred that unless the Form 9540-1 documents were provided, the accounting firm would likely resign as JGI's independent auditor. Within a few days, Fred turned over the documents to Grant Thornton. "However, before he did so, he altered the dates on them. Apparently, the alterations were so obvious that after reviewing the forms for only 10 seconds, Grant Thornton knew there was a problem. Grant Thornton informed Emanuel and Cohn that the dates were falsified and terminated the audit." When Emanuel confronted his brother regarding the altered documents, the suddenly remorseful Fred "admitted everything."

Following Fred's confession, JGI retained Grant Thornton to determine the impact of the fraudulent scheme on the company's prior financial statements and to develop a set of current financial statements that were reliable. The Greenbergs provided this information to their company's three banks. Within six months, JGI filed for bankruptcy and ceased operations.

EPILOGUE

JGI's sudden collapse sparked a spate of lawsuits. In February 1997, JGI's court-appointed bankruptcy trustee filed a civil action that contained eight specific charges against Grant Thornton. These charges included, among others, breach of contract, negligence, and fraud. A primary defense Grant Thornton used in attempting to rebut those allegations was contributory negligence on the part of JGI and its management.

Grant Thornton argued that JGI had a responsibility to implement internal controls that would have been effective in uncovering Fred Greenberg's fraudulent scheme. In particular, Grant Thornton contended that Emanuel Greenberg should have required his brother to adopt the computer-based accounting and control procedures initially proposed by Steve Cohn in 1992. The accounting firm also maintained that Emanuel Greenberg had been negligent in failing to discover Fred's subterfuge since he had never taken any steps to check or verify his brother's work for the all-important Prepaid Inventory account.

The federal judge who presided over the lawsuit filed against Grant Thornton by JGI's bankruptcy trustee responded to the firm's contributory negligence defense by first suggesting that the accounting firm, rather than JGI's management, had more "leverage" to force Fred Greenberg to adopt Cohn's recommendations. "Cohn could not insist that Fred implement tighter controls over the prepaid inventory, but Grant Thornton, as JGI's auditor, could. Indeed, that is how the fraud was finally discovered in 1994."

Additionally, the judge pointed out that Grant Thornton had failed to present any compelling evidence that Emanuel Greenberg had suspected his brother was misrepresenting JGI's prepaid inventory. "Accordingly, Emanuel had no reason to check or verify his brother's work in matching up the delivery receipts with the other prepaid inventory documentation." The judge went even further in absolving Emanuel of responsibility for his brother's misconduct by suggesting that independent auditors are the parties primarily responsible for discovering such schemes.

> Given Fred's equal ownership in the company and his apparent control, not only is there no evidence that Emanuel was "slipshod," there is no evidence that he could have prevented Fred's wrongful acts. Rather, in the unique circumstances where a corporation is owned and operated by family members, the goal of deterring wrongdoing is best served by subjecting the auditors to potential liability, thereby encouraging greater diligence by them in such situations in the future.

After responding to Grant Thornton's arguments, the federal judge criticized several aspects of the firm's JGI audits. Although Grant Thornton identified the large increase in prepaid inventory during the late 1980s and early 1990s as an audit risk factor, the judge suggested that the accounting firm did not thoroughly investigate the underlying cause of that dramatic increase. Likewise, the judge maintained that during the 1993 audit Grant Thornton did not adequately investigate the abnormally long time lag between the date that certain imported meat shipments arrived at a U.S. port and the date they were delivered to JGI's warehouse.[4] The judge also referred to criticism of Grant Thornton that was included in a report prepared by an expert witness retained by JGI's bankruptcy trustee. Among other issues, this report criticized Grant Thornton for not discovering until 1993 that JGI had copies of the Form 9540-1 documents. According to the expert witness, if the auditors had performed a routine "walk-through" audit procedure to document their understanding of JGI's important accounting and control procedures, they would have immediately discovered that "third-party documentation [Form 9540-1] existed to verify the arrival dates of the inventory."

The federal judge was most critical of Grant Thornton's decision near the end of the 1993 audit to continue relying on the internally generated delivery receipts when the firm had access to externally generated documentation to vouch the prepaid inventory transactions and year-end balance. In the judge's opinion, that decision could be construed as "reckless."

According to Grant Thornton, although it now knew that third-party verification of the delivery dates existed, it considered it unnecessary to have the USDA forms for the 1993 audit because of its reliance on JGI's segregation of duties. Yet, Grant Thornton refused to rely upon JGI's segregation of duties for its 1994 audit. Rather, it demanded that JGI produce the USDA forms for the 1994 audit.... If Grant would not issue an unqualified opinion in 1994 relying solely upon JGI's segregation of duties, then why did it do so in 1993?

In October 1999, the federal judge issued a 36-page opinion weighing the merits of the allegations filed by JGI's trustee against Grant Thornton and the validity of the accounting firm's rebuttals of those allegations. After striking down one of the charges filed against Grant Thornton, the judge ruled that the other charges would be addressed in a subsequent trial. Since no further mention of this case can be found in public records, Grant Thornton and JGI's bankruptcy trustee apparently settled the case privately.

Questions

1. Identify important audit risk factors common to family-owned businesses. How should auditors address these risk factors?

2. In your opinion, what primary audit objectives should Grant Thornton have established for JGI's (a) Prepaid Inventory account and (b) Merchandise Inventory account?

3. Assess Grant Thornton's decision to rely heavily on JGI's delivery receipts when auditing the company's prepaid inventory. More generally, compare and contrast the validity of audit evidence yielded by internally prepared versus externally prepared client documents.

4. Describe the general nature and purpose of a "walk-through" audit procedure. Are such tests required by generally accepted auditing standards?

5. Identify audit procedures, other than a walk-through test, that might have resulted in Grant Thornton discovering that Fred Greenberg was tampering with JGI's delivery receipts.

6. Once an audit firm has informed client management of important internal control weaknesses, what further responsibility, if any, does the audit firm have regarding those items? For example, does the audit firm have a responsibility to insist that client management correct the deficiencies or address them in some other way?

4. Recall that JGI's customs broker had confirmed Fred Greenberg's assertion that floods in the Midwestern states during 1993 were responsible for this time lag. Apparently, that assertion was not valid.

CASE 2.2

Golden Bear Golf, Inc.

Jack Nicklaus electrified sports fans worldwide in 1986 when he won the prestigious Masters golf tournament at the ripe old age of 46. Over the previous several years, the "Golden Bear" had been struggling to remain competitive with the scores of talented young players who had earned the right to play in the dozens of golf tournaments sponsored each year by the Professional Golfers' Association (PGA).

Regaining his golden touch on the golf course was not the only challenge that Nicklaus faced during the mid-1980s. In 1985, Richard Bellinger, an accountant employed by Golden Bear International, Inc. (GBI), the private company that oversaw the famous golfer's many business interests, mustered the courage to approach his employer. Bellinger told Nicklaus that his company was on the verge of bankruptcy. Nicklaus, who had allowed subordinates to manage his company's operations, was startled by the revelation. In a subsequent interview with the *The Wall Street Journal*, Nicklaus admitted that after a brief investigation he realized that he had allowed his company to become a tangled knot of dozens of unrelated businesses. "We were an accounting nightmare. . . . I didn't know what any of them did and neither did anyone else."[1]

Nicklaus immediately committed himself to revi[ving his com]pany. The first step that he took to turn around his company was [naming himself c]hief executive officer (CEO). Nicklaus then placed Bellinger [in charge of day-to-]day operations. Within a few years, the two men had r[eturned GBI to profitable con]dition by focusing its resources on lines of busine[ss . . . su]ch as golf course design, golf schools, and the licer[sing . . .]

In the late 1990s, Jack Nicklaus once ag[ain faced] an "accounting nightmare." This time, Nicklaus could n[ot blame himself for th]e predicament he faced. Instead, the responsibility for the new [. . . squ]arely on the shoulders of two of Nicklaus's key subordinates, who [. . . orchest]rated a fraudulent accounting scheme that jeopardized their employer's corporate empire.

Player of the Century

Jack Nicklaus began playing golf as a young boy and had mastered the game by his mid-teens. After graduating from high school, the golf prodigy accepted a scholarship to play collegiately for Ohio State University in his hometown of Columbus. At the age of 21, Nicklaus joined the professional golf tour and was an instant success, racking up more than one dozen victories within a few years.

Shortly after joining the professional golf tour, the business-minded Nicklaus realized that winning golf tournaments was not the most lucrative way to profit from his enormous skills. At the time, the undisputed "king" of golf was Arnold Palmer, who endeared himself to the golfing public with his easy smile and affable manner on the golf course. Adoring legions of fans known as "Arnie's Army" tracked Palmer's every move during a tournament. Palmer's popularity with the public translated into a series of high-profile and profitable endorsement deals. On the

---

1. R. Lowenstein, "A Golfer Becomes an Executive: Jack Nicklaus's Business Education," *The Wall Street Journal*, 27 January 1987, 34.

other hand, golf fans generally resented Nicklaus's no-nonsense approach on the golf course. Those same fans resented Nicklaus even more when it became evident that the burly Ohioan with the trademark crew cut would likely replace Palmer as the world's best golfer, which he did. Nicklaus would ultimately win a record 18 major golf championships and edge out Palmer for the "Player of the Century" award in the golfing world.

With the help of a professional sports agent, Nicklaus worked hard to develop a softer, more appealing public image. By the mid-1970s, Nicklaus's makeover was complete and his popularity rivaled that of Palmer. As his popularity with the public grew, Nicklaus was able to cash in on endorsement deals and other business opportunities. Eventually, Nicklaus founded GBI to serve as the corporate umbrella for his business interests.

In 1996, Nicklaus decided to expand his business operations by spinning off a subsidiary from GBI via an initial public offering (IPO). Nicklaus named the new public company Golden Bear Golf, Inc. (Golden Bear). One of Golden Bear's principal lines of business would be the construction of golf courses. GBI would remain a privately owned company that would continue to manage Nicklaus's other business ventures. Because Nicklaus planned to retain more than 50 percent of Golden Bear's common stock, he and his subordinates would be able to completely control the new company's operations.

Nicklaus chose his trusted associate Richard Bellinger to serve as Golden Bear's CEO. Bellinger then appointed John Boyd and Christopher Curbello as the two top executives of Paragon International, Golden Bear's wholly owned subsidiary that would be responsible for the company's golf course construction business. Boyd became Paragon's president and principal operating officer, while Curbello assumed the title of Paragon's vice president of operations. On August 1, 1996, Golden Bear went public. The company's stock traded on the NASDAQ exchange under the ticker symbol JACK.

Triple Bogey for Golden Bear

Shortly after Golden Bear's successful IPO, Paragon International's management team was inundated with requests to build Jack Nicklaus–designed golf courses. In a few months, the company had entered into contracts to build more than one dozen golf courses. Wall Street analysts, portfolio managers, and individual investors expected these contracts to translate into sizable profits for Golden Bear. Unfortunately, those profits never materialized.

Less than one year after Golden Bear's IPO, Boyd and Curbello realized that they had been much too optimistic in forecasting the gross profit margins Paragon would earn on its construction projects. Instead of earning substantial profits on those projects, Paragon would incur large losses on many of them. To avoid the embarrassment of publicly revealing that they had committed Paragon to a string of unprofitable construction projects, the two executives instructed Paragon's accounting staff to embellish the subsidiary's reported operating results.

A key factor that may have contributed to Boyd and Curbello's decision to conceal Paragon's financial problems was the incentive compensation package each had received when they signed on with the company. The two executives could earn sizable bonuses if Paragon met certain operating benchmarks. In addition, Boyd had been granted a large number of Golden Bear stock options.

Because Paragon's construction projects required considerably more than one year to complete, the company used percentage-of-completion accounting to recognize the revenues associated with those projects. Initially, Paragon applied the widely used "cost-to-cost" percentage-of-completion method that requires a company to determine the percentage of a project's total estimated construction costs incurred in a given accounting period. Then, the same percentage of the total revenue (and gross profit) to be earned on the project is booked for that period.

During the second quarter of fiscal 1997, Boyd and Curbello determined that Paragon would have a large operating loss if the cost-to-cost method was used to recognize revenue on the golf course construction projects. At that point, the two executives instructed Paragon's controller to switch to what they referred to as the "earned value" percentage-of-completion accounting method. "In developing its percentage-of-completion estimates under the earned value method, Paragon relied not on objective criteria, such as costs incurred, but instead relied on management's subjective estimates as to its [a project's] progress."[2]

Throughout the remainder of fiscal 1997 and into fiscal 1998, Paragon's management routinely overstated the percentage-of-completion estimates for the company's golf course construction projects each quarter. To further enhance Paragon's operating results, the company's accounting staff inflated the contractual revenue amounts for most of the company's construction projects. These increased revenue amounts were allegedly attributable to "change orders" that amended the original construction contracts between Paragon and the company's clients. A final window-dressing scheme used by Paragon was recording revenue for *potential* construction projects.

> *In some cases, Paragon recognized revenue in connection with potential projects that Paragon had identified while looking for new work, even though Paragon had no agreements in connection with these projects. In other cases, Paragon recognized revenue in connection with projects where the project's owners were either entertaining bids from Paragon and other contractors or were negotiating with Paragon regarding a project yet to be awarded.*[3]

During the spring of 1998, John Boyd and several of his top subordinates, including Christopher Curbello, attempted to purchase Paragon International from Golden Bear. When that effort failed, Boyd and Curbello resigned their positions with Paragon. After their departure, Paragon's new management team quickly discovered that the subsidiary's operating results had been grossly misrepresented.

A subsequent investigation carried out jointly by Arthur Andersen & Co. (Paragon's audit firm), PricewaterhouseCoopers, and Golden Bear's external legal firm resulted in Golden Bear issuing restated financial statements in October 1998 for fiscal 1997 and for the first quarter of fiscal 1998. For fiscal 1997, Golden Bear had initially reported a $2.9 million net loss and golf course construction revenues of $39.7 million; the restated amounts included a $24.7 million net loss for fiscal 1997 and golf course construction revenues of only $21.8 million. For the first quarter of fiscal 1998, Golden Bear had reported an $800,000 net loss and golf course construction revenues of $16.0 million. Those amounts were restated to a $7.2 million net loss and golf course construction revenues of $8.3 million.

"Audit Failures"

The Securities and Exchange Commission (SEC) launched its own investigation of Golden Bear shortly after the company issued the restated financial statements. A primary target of the SEC investigation was Michael Sullivan, the Arthur Andersen

---

2. Securities and Exchange Commission, *Accounting and Auditing Enforcement Release No. 1604,* 1 August 2002.

3. Securities and Exchange Commission, *Accounting and Auditing Enforcement Release No. 1603,* 1 August 2002.

audit partner who served as the Golden Bear engagement partner. Sullivan had been employed by Andersen since 1970 and had been a partner in the firm since 1984.

The SEC enforcement release that disclosed the results of its investigation of Andersen's Golden Bear audits included a section entitled "Sullivan's Audit Failures." According to the SEC, Sullivan was well aware that the decision to use the earned value method "accelerated revenue recognition by material amounts" for Paragon.[4] In fact, Sullivan was very concerned by Paragon's decision to switch from the cost-to-cost method to the "new and untested" earned value method. This concern prompted him to warn Paragon's management that he expected the earned value method to produce operating results approximately in line with those that would have resulted from the continued application of the cost-to-cost method. To monitor the impact of the earned value method on Paragon's operating results, Sullivan required the client's accounting staff to "provide detailed schedules showing Paragon's project-by-project results under both methods for each reporting period from the second quarter of 1997 through the first quarter of 1998."

By the end of fiscal 1997, the comparative schedules prepared by Paragon's accountants clearly revealed that the earned value method was allowing Paragon to book much larger amounts of revenue and gross profit on its construction projects than it would have under the cost-to-cost method. When Sullivan questioned Paragon's executives regarding this issue, those executives maintained that "uninvoiced" construction costs had caused the cost-to-cost method to significantly understate the stages of completion of the construction projects. To quell Sullivan's concern, in early fiscal 1998 Paragon's management recorded $4 million of uninvoiced construction costs in a year-end adjusting entry for fiscal 1997. These costs caused the revenue that would have been recorded under the cost-to-cost method to approximate the revenue that Paragon actually recorded by applying the earned value method. Unknown to Sullivan, the $4 million of uninvoiced construction costs booked by Paragon were fictitious.[5]

The SEC criticized Sullivan and his subordinates for failing to adequately investigate the $4 million of uninvoiced construction costs that materialized at the end of fiscal 1997. According to the SEC, Sullivan relied almost exclusively on management's oral representations to corroborate those costs.

> *Sullivan knew that Paragon booked costs for which no invoices had been received and which were not reflected in the company's accounts payable system, and that recording these uninvoiced costs would have substantially reduced the gap between the results produced by the two estimation methods. . . . While procedures with respect to invoiced and paid costs were performed, Sullivan did not employ any procedures to determine whether the uninvoiced costs had actually been incurred as of year-end.*

Paragon's scheme to overstate its reported revenues and profits by applying the earned value method resulted in a dramatic increase in unbilled revenues by the end of 1997. Approximately 30 percent of the revenues reported in Golden Bear's 1997 income statement had not been billed to its customers. When Paragon's executives switched to the earned value method, they had assured Sullivan that they

---

4. The remaining quotations in this case were taken from Securities and Exchange Commission, *Accounting and Auditing Enforcement Release No. 1676*, 26 November 2002.

5. Recognize that the $4 million of uninvoiced construction costs that were accrued in the adjusting entry did not reduce Golden Bear's gross profit that it had recognized for fiscal 1997 under the earned value method. The $4 million of construction costs simply replaced an equal amount of expenses that had been recorded to produce the "proper" amount of gross profit under the earned value method.

would bill their customers on that basis. Despite that commitment, Paragon continued to bill their customers effectively on a cost-to-cost basis. (Paragon could not bill customers for the full amount of revenue that it was recording on the construction projects since those customers were generally aware of the *actual* stages of completion of those projects.)

The SEC maintained that Sullivan and his subordinates should have rigorously tested Paragon's large amount of unbilled revenues at the end of 1997. "A significant unbilled revenue balance requires adequate testing to determine the reason that the company is not billing for the work it reports as complete and whether unbilled amounts are properly recognized as revenue." Instead, the SEC charged that Sullivan relied "excessively" on oral representations from Paragon management to confirm the unbilled revenues and corresponding receivables.

In at least one case, the SEC reported that members of the Golden Bear audit team asked the owner of a Paragon project under construction to comment on the reasonableness of the $2 million unbilled receivable that Paragon had recorded for that project at the end of 1997. The owner contested that amount, alleging that Paragon had overestimated the project's stage of completion. "Despite this significant evidence that a third party with knowledge of the project's status disputed Paragon's estimated percentage-of-completion under the contract, the audit team did not properly investigate this project or otherwise expand Andersen's scope of testing of Paragon's unbilled revenue balances." According to the SEC, Sullivan did not believe the unbilled revenue posed major audit issues but instead was a "business issue" that Paragon had to resolve with its clients.

A second tactic Paragon used to inflate its reported profits was to overstate the total revenues to be earned on individual construction projects. During the 1997 audit, Andersen personnel selected 13 of Paragon's construction projects to corroborate the total revenue figures the company was using in applying the earned value percentage-of-completion accounting method to its unfinished projects. For 11 of the 13 projects selected, the Andersen auditors discovered that the total revenue being used in the percentage-of-completion computations by Paragon exceeded the revenue figure documented in the construction contract. Paragon's management attributed these differences to unsigned change orders that had been processed for the given projects "but could not produce any documents supporting these oral representations." Sullivan accepted the client's representations that the given revenue amounts were valid. "In each instance, Sullivan failed to properly follow up on a single undocumented amount; instead, Sullivan relied solely on Paragon management's oral representations that the estimated revenue amounts accurately reflected the economic status of the jobs."

Another scam used by Paragon to inflate its revenues and profits was to record revenue for nonexistent projects. In the enforcement release that focused on Sullivan's role in the Paragon scandal, SEC officials pointed out that the publication *AICPA Audit and Accounting Guide—Construction Contracts* is clearly relevant to the audits of construction companies such as Paragon. This publication recommends that auditors visit construction sites and discuss the given projects with project managers, architects, and other appropriate personnel. The purpose of these procedures is to assess "the representations of management (for example, representations about the stage of completion and estimated costs to complete)." Despite this guidance, the Andersen auditors did not visit any project sites during the 1997 audit.[6]

---

6. As a point of information, most of Paragon's golf construction projects were outside of the United States. During 1996, auditors employed by foreign affiliates of Andersen visited some of these sites.

Such visits may have resulted in Andersen discovering that some of Paragon's projects were purely imaginary. In addition, Andersen would likely have determined that Paragon was overstating the stages of completion of most of its existing projects.

The SEC reprimanded Andersen for not visiting any of Paragon's job sites or discussing those projects with knowledgeable parties. "Failing to discuss project status, including percentage-of-completion estimates, with project managers and other on-site operating personnel was, under the circumstances, a reckless departure from GAAS."

The SEC also criticized Sullivan for not insisting that Golden Bear disclose in its 1997 financial statements the change from the cost-to-cost to the earned value method of applying percentage-of-completion accounting. Likewise, the SEC contended that Sullivan should have required Golden Bear to disclose material related-party transactions involving Paragon and Jack Nicklaus, Golden Bear's majority stockholder.

Finally, the SEC noted that Sullivan failed to heed his own concerns while planning the 1997 Golden Bear audit. During the initial planning phase of that audit, Sullivan had identified several factors that prompted him to designate the 1997 Golden Bear audit a "high-risk" engagement. These factors included the subjective nature of the earned value method, Paragon's large unbilled revenues, the aggressive revenue recognition practices advocated by Golden Bear management, and severe weaknesses in Paragon's cost accounting system. Because of these factors, the SEC maintained that Sullivan and his subordinates should have been particularly cautious during the 1997 Golden Bear audit and employed a rigorous and thorough set of substantive audit procedures.

EPILOGUE

In August 1998, angry Golden Bear stockholders filed a class-action lawsuit against the company, its major officers, and its principal owner, Jack Nicklaus. That same month, the NASDAQ delisted the company's common stock, which was trading for less than $1 per share, considerably below its all-time high of $20. Richard Bellinger resigned as Golden Bear's CEO two months later to "pursue other interests." In December 1999, Golden Bear announced that it had reached an agreement to settle the class-action lawsuit. That settlement required the company to pay its stockholders $3.5 million in total and to purchase their shares at a price of $0.75. In 2000, Golden Bear, by then a private company, was folded into Nicklaus Companies, a new corporate entity that Jack Nicklaus created to manage his business interests.

In November 2002, Michael Sullivan was suspended from practicing before the SEC for one year. Sullivan's employer, Andersen, had effectively been put out of business a few months earlier when a federal jury found it guilty of obstruction of justice for destroying audit documents pertaining to its bankrupt client Enron Corporation.[7] In August 2002, Paragon's former controller received a two-year suspension from practicing before the SEC. At the same time, the SEC sanctioned three former Golden Bear executives by ordering them to "cease and desist" from any future violations of the federal securities laws. One of those executives was Richard Bellinger. The SEC maintained that Bellinger approved Paragon's change from the cost-to-cost to the earned value method. Additionally, the SEC charged that Bellinger knew

---

7. As discussed in Case 1.1, Andersen's conviction was subsequently overturned by the U.S. Supreme Court.

the change would materially increase Golden Bear's reported revenues and gross profit but failed to require that the change be disclosed in the company's financial statements.

Finally, in March 2003, a federal grand jury indicted John Boyd and Christopher Curbello on charges of securities fraud and conspiracy to commit securities fraud. Curbello was arrested in San Antonio, Texas, on March 14, 2003, while Boyd was apprehended in Bogota, Columbia, a few days later by Secret Service and FBI agents who immediately flew him to the United States. In June 2003, Curbello pleaded guilty to conspiracy to commit securities fraud and was sentenced to three and one-half years in prison. A few months later, Boyd pleaded guilty to similar charges and was given a five-year prison sentence.

Questions

1. *SAS No. 106*, "Audit Evidence," identifies the "management assertions" that commonly underlie a set of financial statements. Which of these assertions were relevant to Paragon's construction projects? For each of the assertions that you listed, describe an audit procedure that Arthur Andersen could have employed to corroborate that assertion.

2. The SEC referred to several "audit failures" that were allegedly the responsibility of Michael Sullivan. Define what you believe the SEC meant by the phrase *audit failure*. Do you believe that Sullivan, alone, was responsible for the deficiencies that the SEC noted in Andersen's 1997 audit of Golden Bear? Defend your answer.

3. Sullivan identified the 1997 Golden Bear audit as a "high-risk" engagement. How do an audit engagement team's responsibilities differ, if at all, on a high-risk engagement as compared with a "normal" engagement? Explain.

4. The AICPA has issued several *Audit and Accounting Guides* for specialized industries. Do auditors have a responsibility to refer to these guides when auditing clients in those industries? Do these guides override or replace the authoritative guidance included in *Statements on Auditing Standards*?

5. Was the change that Paragon made in applying the percentage-of-completion accounting method a "change in accounting principle" or a "change in accounting estimate"? Briefly describe the accounting and financial reporting treatment that must be applied to each type of change.

Happiness Express, Inc.

Executives in the multibillion-dollar toy industry constantly search for the next big "hit," a magical toy that will trigger a nationwide frenzy among youngsters comparable to the mania sparked in recent decades by the Cabbage Patch Kids and Tickle Me Elmo. In more "ancient" times, silly putty, the slinky, and the hoola hoop prompted shouting matches and elbow-to-elbow combat among small armies of short-tempered parents intent on acquiring the latest must-have and hard-to-find toy as a birthday gift or Christmas present for little Suzie or tiny Tommy.

During the mid-1990s, the popular television program that featured the Mighty Morphin Power Rangers produced a windfall of revenues and profits for Happiness Express, Inc., a small New York–based company. Happiness Express had purchased licensing rights that allowed the company to market a wide range of Mighty Morphin Power Rangers toys and other merchandise. Unfortunately, similar to most toy fads, the Power Rangers craze soon subsided. To find a replacement source of revenue for his company, Joseph Sutton, Happiness Express's chief executive officer (CEO), turned to a member of the British royal family, Sarah Ferguson, the Duchess of York.

Following her divorce from Prince Andrew, the second son of Queen Elizabeth II, the Duchess decided to try her hand at writing children's books. Among the characters she created was Budgie the Little Helicopter. Joseph Sutton acquired U.S. licensing rights for toys and other merchandise featuring Budgie. Sutton believed that Budgie would be a huge hit in the United States and generate large sales of toys and related merchandise linked to him and his small squadron of friends. In announcing his company's relationship with Sarah Ferguson, the ever-optimistic and buoyant Sutton proclaimed that, "Happiness is proud to represent Budgie the Little Helicopter and to help him make his flight to America."[1]

"In Kids We Trust"

Joseph Sutton and his older brother, Isaac, worked for years as sales representatives for various toy manufacturers. In 1989, the two brothers organized their own toy company, which they named Happiness Express, Inc. Joseph assumed the title of CEO, while his brother became the company's chief operating officer (COO). Despite an initial investment of only $10,000, the Sutton brothers' company quickly gained a toehold in the fiercely competitive toy industry. Happiness Express catapulted from a few hundred thousand dollars of sales in its first year of operation to total revenues of more than $40 million for its fiscal year ended March 31, 1994.

The Suttons' business model involved identifying trendy characters introduced to children in the United States by television programs, major movies, books, and other publications. The brothers then purchased merchandise-licensing rights for those characters from Disney, Nickelodeon, Universal Studios, Warner Brothers, and major publishing companies. Licensed merchandise manufactured by Happiness Express included plastic figurines, stuffed dolls, shoelaces, battery-operated toothbrushes,

---

1. *Business Wire* (online), "Happiness Express Gets Product License for Her Royal Highness the Duchess of York's 'Budgie the Little Helicopter,'" 14 February 1994.

night-lights, bedside lamps, and a wide range of "back-to-school" items such as pencils, notebooks, and binders. Happiness Express marketed its merchandise to FAO Schwartz, J. C. Penney, Kmart, Target, Toys "R" Us, Wal-Mart, and other major retailers. Central to the early success of Happiness Express was the Suttons' heavy reliance on market research that tracked children's interest in new media characters and toys. In fact, Joseph Sutton coined the motto "In Kids We Trust" to express his company's commitment to the results of that research.

The Little Mermaid and Barney, the purple dinosaur, were two of the earliest characters for which the Suttons obtained licensing rights. The impressive sales spawned by those two lines of merchandise allowed Happiness Express to establish itself in the toy industry. To acquire the capital needed to expand the company's operations, the Suttons took Happiness Express public in July 1994 with an initial public offering (IPO) that was well received by Wall Street and individual investors. Within a few months, the company's stock price nearly doubled from its initial selling price of $10. In the spring of 1995, *Business Week* named Happiness Express the "#1 Hot Growth Company" in the United States and featured the company on its front cover. According to *Business Week*, over the previous three years Happiness Express had realized annual growth rates in sales, profits, and return on capital of 112 percent, 439 percent, and 68 percent, respectively.

For fiscal 1994, merchandise linked to Barney accounted for approximately 55 percent of Happiness Express's total revenues. In fiscal 1995, Barney-related revenues evaporated, accounting for less than 5 percent of the company's sales that year. Fortunately, the Mighty Morphin Power Rangers stepped into the vacuum created by the sudden decline in children's affection for Barney—or, at least, Barney-related merchandise. For fiscal 1995, Power Rangers merchandise produced 75 percent of Happiness's revenues.

Despite the gaudy financial results posted by Happiness Express during the mid-1990s, many Wall Street analysts questioned whether the company could sustain that level of financial performance. Those analysts doubted that the Sutton brothers could continue their phenomenal winning streak of identifying the next "hot" children's character. One financial analyst and self-appointed critic of Happiness Express asked Joseph Sutton, "What will replace Power Rangers when they fade?"[2] The self-assured Sutton replied: "We've proved to the industry that we know how to go where the action is."[3] In Sutton's mind, the coming "action" in the toy industry would revolve around Budgie the Little Helicopter and Dudley the Dragon, a Barney-type character that had his own children's television program. Sutton's enthusiasm for those two characters did not placate his critic, who pointed out that toy companies that become heavily dependent on one or a few lines of merchandise often experience severe financial problems due to sudden and unexpected shifts in children's taste for toys.

Budgie Crashes, Dudley Is a Dud

In the spring of 1995, shortly before the close of Happiness Express's 1995 fiscal year, a Wall Street investment firm projected a "precipitous" drop in the company's earnings during fiscal 1996.[4] The firm predicted that declining interest in the Mighty

---

2. L. Bongiorno, "Happiness Is a Hot Toy," *Business Week*, 22 May 1995, 70.

3. *Ibid.*

4. *Business Wire* (online), "Happiness Express 'Comfortable' with Fiscal 1995, '96 Projections," 7 March 1995.

Morphin Power Rangers television program would quickly translate into falling sales of licensed merchandise featuring those characters. Joseph Sutton responded to that grim prediction by referring to another earnings forecast for Happiness Express released at approximately the same time by Donaldson, Lufkin & Jenrette (DLJ), a prominent Wall Street firm. This latter forecast projected a sizable increase in revenues and profits for Happiness Express during fiscal 1996.

To support this second forecast, Sutton revealed that his firm's backlog of toy orders in the spring of 1995 was nearly three times larger than the company's backlog 12 months earlier. While admitting that sales of Power Rangers merchandise would likely decline in fiscal 1996, Sutton insisted that the company's new products would more than make up for those lost sales. Bolstering Sutton's point of view regarding his company's future were the record operating results that Happiness Express reported in the late spring of 1995 for the fiscal year ended March 31, 1995. The company's net income for fiscal 1995 of $7.5 million was nearly double the figure reported the previous year, while its 1995 revenues rose to $60 million, a 50 percent increase over the previous 12 months. Approximately one-half of the latter increase was attributable to Happiness Express's fourth-quarter sales. During the fourth quarter of fiscal 1994, the company reported sales of $2.3 million; that figure was dwarfed by the $12.8 million of sales the company reported for the fourth quarter of fiscal 1995.

Despite Joseph Sutton's rosy outlook for his company, fiscal 1996 proved to be a difficult year for Happiness Express. By the fall of 1995, sales of Power Rangers merchandise had fallen off drastically. Making matters worse for Happiness Express, Budgie the Little Helicopter failed to capture the imagination of children in the United States despite intense promotional efforts by the company and the Duchess of York. Likewise, children's response to Dudley the Dragon was underwhelming. In early September 1995, the price of Happiness Express common stock plunged when Joseph Sutton publicly admitted that DLJ's earnings forecast for fiscal 1996 had been too optimistic. The day following that announcement, the company was rocked by the filing of a large class-action lawsuit that named Happiness Express and its key officers as defendants. The lawsuit charged that Happiness Express's previous financial statements had been distorted by fraudulent misrepresentations and that certain company executives had engaged in "insider trading." As those executives were touting the company's promising prospects earlier in the year, they were allegedly selling large blocks of the company's stock that they owned.

As the end of fiscal 1996 approached, Happiness Express's sales continued to sag, which caused management to issue an earnings release indicating that the company would report a loss of $14 to $17 million for the year. That news sent the company's stock price plummeting to less than $2 per share. A few days later, a company spokesperson revealed that federal authorities, including representatives of the Securities and Exchange Commission (SEC), had seized certain accounting records and documents of Happiness Express and were launching an investigation of financial irregularities within the company. More bad news arrived on May 31, 1996, when Happiness Express's audit firm, Coopers & Lybrand, withdrew the audit opinion it had issued a few weeks earlier on the company's 1996 financial statements. Exhibit 1 presents the letter Coopers & Lybrand sent to Joseph Sutton to notify him of that decision.

Throughout the summer of 1996, the financial condition of Happiness Express worsened. On September 25, the company's board of directors filed for bankruptcy and fired Isaac Sutton; two days later, Joseph Sutton resigned as CEO. In May 1999, the SEC filed a criminal complaint against Joseph Sutton, Isaac Sutton, and Happiness

EXHIBIT 1

COOPERS &
LYBRAND LETTER
RESCINDING 1996
AUDIT OPINION

May 31, 1996

Mr. Joseph Sutton
Chief Executive Officer
Happiness Express, Inc.
One Harbor Park Drive
Port Washington, NY 11050

Dear Mr. Sutton:

In connection with the investigation into the financial irregularities recently discovered with respect to the financial statements and accounting records of Happiness Express, Inc., certain information has come to our attention regarding the Company's financial statements as of and for the year ended March 31, 1996, that indicates a revision of those statements is necessary.

Please notify persons who are known to be relying or who are likely to rely on the financial statements and the related auditors' report that they should not be relied upon, and that revised financial statements and auditors' report will be issued upon completion of the investigation.

Also, you should discuss with the Securities and Exchange Commission, appropriate stock exchanges, and other regulatory authorities the disclosures to be made or other measures to be taken in the circumstances.

Very truly yours,

Coopers & Lybrand L.L.P.

Express's former chief financial officer (CFO), Michael Goldberg. The complaint also named Goldberg's close friend and Goldberg's former landlord as defendants.

The SEC charged the Suttons and Goldberg with inflating Happiness Express's sales and net income for fiscal 1995 and 1996. For fiscal 1995, the SEC revealed that the company had actually incurred a net loss of $1 million rather than the $7.5 million net income it had reported. Happiness Express's executives had apparently booked phony sales and receivables to conceal the company's deteriorating financial condition and operating results from Wall Street analysts, investors, and other parties. The primary source of the company's financial problems that had prompted the fraudulent scheme was the sudden drop in sales of Mighty Morphin Power Rangers merchandise.

The SEC alleged that Michael Goldberg had sold Happiness Express common stock during 1995 before the fraudulent scheme was revealed, allowing him to earn "illicit" trading profits of approximately $310,000. Additionally, the SEC's investigation indicated that Goldberg had provided "material nonpublic information concerning Happiness Express's poor financial condition" to two other individuals, his close friend and his landlord. Reportedly, the close friend had used this information to earn large trading profits by "shorting" the common stock of Happiness Express. The nonpublic information that the landlord received from Goldberg caused him to sell his Happiness Express stock before the company's true financial condition and operating results were publicly reported.

Class-Action Lawsuit Targets Coopers & Lybrand

Coopers & Lybrand was the principal target of the multimillion-dollar, class-action lawsuit filed by Happiness Express's stockholders in the fall of 1995. Plaintiff attorneys in that lawsuit alleged that Coopers & Lybrand had recklessly audited Happiness Express's financial statements for fiscal 1995, which prevented the firm from uncovering millions of dollars of bogus sales and corresponding receivables in the company's accounting records. Approximately $6 million of the bogus revenues involved fictitious sales to Wow Wee International, Ltd. and West Coast Liquidators that had been booked by Happiness Express's accounting staff near the end of fiscal 1995.

The allegations included in the class-action lawsuit focused almost exclusively on the audit procedures Coopers & Lybrand had applied to Happiness Express's 1995 sales and to the company's 1995 year-end receivables. Plaintiff attorneys charged that the Coopers & Lybrand audit team had failed to obtain a thorough understanding of Happiness Express's operations and internal controls and, as a result, failed to properly plan the 1995 audit. For example, the plaintiff attorneys identified several red flags linked to Happiness Express's year-end receivables that the Coopers & Lybrand auditors had apparently overlooked or ignored. These red flags included a significant change in the nature of Happiness Express's accounts receivable between the end of 1994 and the end of 1995.

Historically, Happiness Express had "factored" most of its accounts receivable. A finance company typically approved or authorized Happiness Express's credit sales before shipments were made to given customers and then provided cash advances for the resulting receivables. This practice significantly reduced the credit risk that Happiness Express faced on its outstanding receivables. At the end of fiscal 1994, approximately 88 percent of Happiness Express's receivables were factored. Because of the bogus sales (and receivables) entered in the company's accounting records near the end of fiscal 1995, only 19 percent of its receivables were factored at the end of that year. The Coopers & Lybrand auditors apparently never learned of this change in the nature of Happiness Express's accounts receivable, and, consequently, failed to make the appropriate modifications in their planned audit procedures for that important financial statement line item.

> *The allegation here is that Coopers was reckless when it relied on a previous year's information without bothering to independently assess the current year's data, which were vastly different. . . . Coopers' [fiscal 1995] workpapers are replete with inaccurate references to conditions which did not exist at March 31, 1995. For example, in assessing Happiness's controls over its revenues, Coopers noted in its workpapers that: "Accounts receivable are predominantly factored (credit risk is not an issue) and the Company obtains credit authorizations from the factor company prior to shipping."[5]*

Another red flag Coopers & Lybrand allegedly ignored in planning the 1995 audit was the suspicious nature of the large receivables from Wow Wee and West Coast Liquidators that resulted from credit sales recorded by Happiness Express in late fiscal 1995. In fact, Happiness Express booked $2.4 million of fictitious sales to Wow Wee, alone, on the final day of fiscal 1995. The majority of the bogus sales to West Coast Liquidators were recorded in the final month of fiscal 1995. In their civil complaint,

---

5. This and all subsequent quotations, unless indicated otherwise, were taken from the following source: *Jacobs and Sbordone, et al. v. Coopers & Lybrand, et al.*, 1999 U.S. Dist. LEXIS 2102; Fed. Sec. L. Rep. (CCH) P90, 443.

the attorneys for Happiness Express's stockholders pointed out that Coopers & Lybrand's policy and procedures manual alerted the firm's personnel to the risk posed by such transactions. "Unusually large increases in year-end sales to a single or a few customers is an indicator of the risk of potential material misstatements in financial statements."

Plaintiff legal counsel also pointed out that Coopers & Lybrand should have doubted the integrity of *any* credit sales made to Wow Wee since that company was a toy manufacturer and one of Happiness Express's largest suppliers. An audit procedure performed by Coopers & Lybrand involved obtaining and testing a Happiness Express report listing the company's "Top 25 Customers" for the period April 1, 1994–March 31, 1995. The $3.2 million of sales allegedly made to Wow Wee during fiscal 1995 should have placed that company among Happiness Express's five largest customers. However, Wow Wee did not appear on the "Top 25" list, nor did the Coopers & Lybrand auditors apparently question client personnel regarding this noticeable omission from that report.

During the fiscal 1995 audit, the Coopers & Lybrand auditors performed a sales cutoff test. Included in this test were the $2.4 million of bogus credit sales to Wow Wee recorded by Happiness Express on the final day of fiscal 1995. Plaintiff attorneys contended that carelessness on the part of the auditors caused them to overlook glaring irregularities evident in the accounting documents for those sales.

> *In the performance of the sales cutoff test, Coopers purportedly examined invoices and bills of lading associated with approximately $2.4 million of approximately $3.2 million of phony Wow Wee sales. However, the invoices and bills of lading purportedly examined by Coopers in the performance of this test were highly suspicious on their face. For example, none of these Wow Wee invoices contained customer purchase order numbers. In addition, at least one of the three bills of lading associated with the fictitious Wow Wee sales purportedly examined by Coopers in the performance of the sales cutoff test was, illogically, purportedly signed by the shipping company's representative on March 29, 1995, two days prior to the date of the bill of lading. Obviously, it would have been impossible for someone to sign a bill of lading before it was generated. Yet, Coopers did not question the legitimacy of the bill of lading.*

Coopers & Lybrand mailed accounts receivable confirmations to selected customers of Happiness Express at the end of fiscal 1995. The auditors informed Michael Goldberg that the Wow Wee receivable was included in the accounts chosen for confirmation. Because Goldberg provided the auditors with an incorrect address for Wow Wee, the confirmation was never returned to Coopers & Lybrand. After the auditors discussed this matter with Goldberg, he offered to contact the appropriate individual at Wow Wee to ensure that the confirmation was returned. The auditors accepted Goldberg's offer. Goldberg then forged a confirmation and had it faxed to Coopers & Lybrand. The auditors apparently accepted the confirmation without performing any follow-up procedures.

The large receivable from West Coast Liquidators accounted for approximately 13 percent of Happiness Express's accounts receivable at the end of fiscal 1995.[6] However, that receivable was not among the accounts Coopers & Lybrand selected for confirmation. In the civil complaint they filed against Coopers & Lybrand, plaintiff attorneys also pointed out that Coopers & Lybrand's sales cutoff test did not include

---

6. Happiness Express had total receivables of almost $11 million at the end of fiscal 1995, accounting for approximately one-third of the company's total assets.

any of the bogus sales to West Coast Liquidators during the final month of fiscal 1995. The attorneys maintained that even a cursory investigation of those transactions would have revealed that they were suspicious in nature.

In fact, had Coopers even performed the perfunctory procedure of examining Happiness's invoices associated with the year-end receivables from West Coast Liquidators, it would have discovered that they also were highly suspicious on their face. For example, such invoices representing $1,346,598 of purported sales to West Coast Liquidators did not contain any bills of lading or purchase order numbers.

EPILOGUE

Coopers & Lybrand contested each of the allegations included in the class-action lawsuit. At one point, the firm's legal counsel charged that the allegations involved no more than "nitpicking attacks" by the plaintiff attorneys. However, U.S. District Judge Robert P. Patterson ruled that the allegations were sufficient to allow the case to proceed to trial. In particular, the federal judge ruled that, if proven, the plaintiffs' allegations would support a finding of "scienter" under the federal securities laws.

Based on the facts as alleged, a trier of fact could find Coopers' audit so reckless that Coopers should have had knowledge of the underlying fraud and acted in blind disregard that there was a strong likelihood that Happiness was engaged in the underlying fraud. Proving this will be plaintiffs' burden at trial, but they have alleged facts sufficient to support a finding of scienter on the part of Coopers and so Coopers' motion to dismiss is denied.

After several years of legal wrangling, an out-of-court settlement was reached to resolve the class-action lawsuit stemming from the Happiness Express fraud. In January 2002, the parties to the lawsuit filed a legal notice describing the details of the proposed settlement with the federal district court in which the case would have been tried. The proposed settlement required Coopers & Lybrand to contribute $1.3 million to a settlement fund. Happiness Express's former stockholders would receive $715,000, or

55 percent, of the settlement fund, while the stockholders' attorneys would receive the remaining $585,000.

In the legal notice filed with the federal court, the plaintiff attorneys were required to state why they supported the settlement. The attorneys noted that a major problem they would have to surmount in pursuing the case was proving that Coopers & Lybrand had a motive to issue a false audit opinion on Happiness Express's financial statements. Additionally, the plaintiff attorneys admitted that they would have to overcome the contention by Coopers & Lybrand that the Happiness Express auditors had no actual knowledge of the falsifications in the company's accounting records and financial statements. Finally, even if the jury ultimately ruled in favor of Happiness Express's former stockholders, the plaintiff attorneys pointed out that the jury might decide that Coopers & Lybrand was responsible for only a small portion of the losses suffered by the stockholders. As a result, the stockholders might receive only a nominal judgment from the accounting firm.[7]

The SEC settled the charges pending against Michael Goldberg by requiring him to pay a $150,000 civil fine and to forfeit the $310,000 of insider trading profits that he had earned while serving as Happiness Express's CFO. Goldberg also agreed not to violate federal securities laws in the future, although under the terms of the SEC settlement he neither admitted nor

7. No further public comment or report regarding the proposed settlement was found. Most likely, the parties agreed to the proposed settlement. As a point of information, the settlement payment would have been made by the successor firm to Coopers & Lybrand, PricewaterhouseCoopers.

denied the charges that the SEC had filed against him. In February 2003, the SEC issued a litigation release that reported the settlement of the charges pending against Michael Goldberg's close friend who had received "material nonpublic information" from Goldberg regarding Happiness Express's deteriorating financial condition. Goldberg's friend was required to forfeit the $79,000 of trading profits he had earned by "shorting" Happiness Express's common stock and to pay a civil fine in the same amount. The SEC also announced that it had settled the insider trading claim filed previously against Goldberg's former landlord but did not reveal the nature of that settlement.

In 2003, Joseph Sutton pleaded guilty to conspiracy to commit bank fraud and securities fraud and was sentenced to 30 months in federal prison. His brother, Isaac, refused to plead guilty to similar charges pending against him and instead opted for a jury trial. On September 29, 2004, a New York jury found Isaac Sutton innocent of all the fraud charges filed against him by the SEC.

Questions

1. Identify the primary audit objectives that auditors hope to accomplish by (a) confirming a client's year-end accounts receivable, (b) performing year-end sales cutoff tests.

2. Identify and briefly describe any mistakes or errors in judgment that Coopers & Lybrand may have made in its effort to confirm the Wow Wee receivable at the end of fiscal 1995. In your opinion, did these apparent mistakes or errors in judgment involve "negligence" on the part of the given auditors? Would you characterize the mistakes or errors as "reckless" or "fraudulent"? In each case, justify your answer.

3. Should the Coopers & Lybrand auditors have confirmed the receivable from West Coast Liquidators at the end of fiscal 1995? Why or why not? Should the auditors have included one or more sales to West Coast Liquidators in their year-end sales cutoff tests for fiscal 1995?

4. What alternative audit procedures can be applied to a large receivable of an audit client when a confirmation of that receivable cannot be obtained for whatever reason? Compare and contrast the evidence provided by these procedures with the evidence yielded by a confirmation.

5. The SEC charged certain executives of Happiness Express with "insider trading." Do auditors have a responsibility to consider or investigate the possibility that client executives have engaged in insider trading activities? Defend your answer.

CASE 2.4

CapitalBanc Corporation

In 1975, Carlos Cordova and several other investors founded Capital National Bank (CNB) in Bronx, New York.[1] Cordova was appointed the bank's chief executive officer and chairman of the board. Over the next several years, the bank opened five branch offices in the New York City metropolitan area. CNB catered primarily to the banking needs of Hispanic-American and immigrant communities in New York City. In 1986, Cordova and the other owners of CNB formed CapitalBanc Corporation, a publicly owned bank holding company registered with the Securities and Exchange Commission (SEC). Throughout its entire existence, the principal operating entity controlled by CapitalBanc was CNB. Cordova assumed the titles of president, chief executive officer, and chairman of the board of the new bank holding company.

In the fall of 1987, CapitalBanc retained Arthur Andersen & Co. as its independent audit firm. Andersen's first engagement for CapitalBanc was to audit the bank holding company's consolidated financial statements for the fiscal year ending December 31, 1987. Thomas Curtin, an Arthur Andersen partner since 1979, served as the engagement partner for the 1987 CapitalBanc audit. Curtin delegated the responsibility for much of the audit planning to James Lukenda, an audit manager with Arthur Andersen since 1983. Lukenda also supervised the staff auditors assigned to the CapitalBanc engagement.

On December 29, 1987, several Arthur Andersen staff auditors accompanied members of CNB's internal audit staff to the bank's 177th Street Branch. The Arthur Andersen auditors intended to observe and participate in a surprise count of the branch's cash funds by the internal auditors. Related audit objectives included testing CNB's compliance with certain control procedures and evaluating the competence of the bank's internal audit staff.

The accounting personnel at each CNB branch maintained a "vault general ledger proof sheet" that reconciled the cash on hand to the balance of the branch's general ledger cash account. During the surprise cash count at the 177th Street Branch, the Arthur Andersen auditors discovered a $2.7 million reconciling item listed on the branch's proof sheet. That amount equaled 61 percent of the branch's general ledger cash balance and 45 percent of the branch's total cash funds that were supposed to be available on the date of the surprise count. When the staff auditors asked to count the $2.7 million of cash represented by the reconciling item, bank employees told them that Cordova had segregated those funds in a locked cabinet within the bank's main vault. Three keys were required to unlock the cabinet. Cordova, who was out of the country at the time, maintained custody of one of those keys.

Stymied temporarily, one of the staff auditors telephoned Lukenda. The staff auditor relayed to Lukenda the information regarding the $2.7 million of segregated cash. After considering the matter and discussing it with Curtin, Lukenda instructed the

---

1. The facts of this case were drawn from the 1987 annual report of CapitalBanc Corporation and the following source: Securities and Exchange Commission, *Accounting and Auditing Enforcement Release No. 458*, 28 June 1993.

staff auditor to count the cash upon Cordova's return. Lukenda also reportedly told the staff auditor that it would not be necessary to place audit seals on the doors of the cabinet or to secure it in any other way given the three-key security system used by the branch. Following the telephone conversation with Lukenda, the staff auditor advised bank personnel that Arthur Andersen auditors would count the cash on the date Cordova returned from his trip.

CNB's practice of segregating a large amount of cash in the locked cabinet was clearly not a normal banking procedure. In a subsequent investigation, the SEC commented on this practice:

> It is an unusual circumstance for a substantial portion of a bank's cash to be inaccessible for an extended period of time. It is also unusual for a substantial portion of a bank's assets not to be invested and earning interest for an extended period of time.[2]

In early January 1988, an employee of the 177th Street Branch notified Arthur Andersen that Cordova would return on January 14. On that date, the Arthur Andersen staff auditors arrived at the branch to complete their count of the cash funds. Cordova opened the locked cabinet in the main vault in the presence of the staff auditors. The auditors then proceeded to count the $2.7 million that had not been counted on December 29, 1987. All of the cash was present. None of the other cash funds of the 177th Street Branch or other CNB branches was counted by the Arthur Andersen auditors on January 14, 1988.

After counting the segregated cash, the staff auditors asked Cordova why he kept those funds in the locked cabinet. Cordova explained that a customer who had cashed a large certificate of deposit insisted on having the funds available on demand at all times. According to Cordova, the customer intended to use the funds to buy foreign currencies when market conditions became favorable. The volatility of the foreign currency market dictated that the customer have immediate access to the funds on a daily basis.

Near the completion of the 1987 CapitalBanc audit, Lukenda reviewed the workpaper that documented Cordova's explanation for the $2.7 million of segregated cash. Lukenda then discussed that explanation with Curtin. After considering the matter, Curtin instructed Lukenda to have the staff auditors confirm that there was an offsetting liability to the given customer in CNB's accounting records equal to the amount of the segregated funds. The staff auditors obtained the documentation for this liability directly from CNB personnel. This information was not confirmed with the customer or independently verified by the auditors in any other way. The staff auditors also did not obtain documentation confirming that the customer had cashed a large certificate of deposit. Finally, the staff auditors neglected to obtain any evidence to corroborate Cordova's assertion regarding the customer's planned use of the funds.

Following the completion of the CapitalBanc audit in March 1988, Arthur Andersen issued an unqualified opinion on the firm's 1987 financial statements. Those financial statements reported a net income of $701,000, total cash funds of $14.1 million, and total assets of $143.2 million. CapitalBanc included the audited financial statements in its 1987 Form 10-K registration statement filed with the SEC.

2. Securities and Exchange Commission, *Accounting and Auditing Enforcement Release No. 458*, 28 June 1993.

EPILOGUE

In July 1990, the Office of the Comptroller of the Currency declared CapitalBanc Corporation insolvent and placed it under the control of the Federal Deposit Insurance Corporation (FDIC). The following year, Banco Popular de Puerto Rico purchased the assets of CNB from the FDIC.

In late 1991, Carlos Cordova pleaded guilty to three counts of bank fraud and conspiracy to commit bank fraud. Two of Cordova's associates pleaded guilty to similar charges. Earlier in 1991, Cordova had agreed to an order issued by the SEC that permanently banned him from serving as an officer or director of a public company. A federal investigation of CNB's financial affairs revealed that Cordova misappropriated at least $400,000 of the $2.7 million allegedly stored in the locked cabinet in the 177th Street Branch's main vault. Cordova, with the help of his subordinates, had intentionally concealed this shortage from the Arthur Andersen auditors during the 1987 audit. Cordova secretly returned to the 177th Street Branch on January 9, 1988, and placed cash obtained from other CNB branches in the locked cabinet to replace the funds that he had embezzled.

The description of the three-key security system relayed to the Arthur Andersen auditors by employees of the 177th Street Branch was a subterfuge. The fast-thinking employees conceived that hoax to deter the auditors from gaining access to the locked cabinet on the day of the surprise cash count. Cordova's explanation regarding why he kept the large amount of cash segregated in the locked cabinet was also a fabrication.

In 1993, the SEC reported the results of its investigation of Arthur Andersen's 1987 CapitalBanc audit, an investigation that focused on the audit of the 177th Street Branch's cash funds. In that report, the SEC disclosed the following sanctions imposed on Thomas Curtin and James Lukenda:

> *It is hereby ordered, that Respondents [Curtin and Lukenda] are censured and must be duly registered and in good standing as certified public accountants in the states in which they each reside or their principal office is located and they must each become a member of or be associated with a member firm of the SEC Practice Section of the AICPA's Division for CPA Firms as long as they practice before the Commission.*[3]

Questions

1. When auditing cash, which of the management assertions discussed in *SAS No. 106*, "Audit Evidence," are of primary concern to an auditor? Why?

2. Identify audit procedures that should be applied to cash funds maintained by a client on its business premises.

3. Identify mistakes or oversights made by Arthur Andersen personnel while auditing the cash funds at the 177th Street Branch.

---

3. *Ibid.*

CASE 2.5

SmarTalk Teleservices, Inc.

Arthur Levitt served as the chairman of the Securities and Exchange Commission (SEC) from 1993 to 2001, the longest tenure of any head of that federal agency. Throughout his eight-year term with the SEC, Levitt campaigned against "earnings management" practices that public companies used to embellish their financial statements. "Restructuring reserves" were a principal target of Levitt's campaign. During the 1990s, many public companies established a large restructuring reserve after acquiring another company. The items credited to these reserves typically included postacquisition "exit" expenditures, such as severance payments to laid-off employees, that the given companies would allegedly incur in future years to eliminate redundant operating units or activities.

Levitt claimed that many companies overstated restructuring reserves by including in them routine operating expenses of future reporting periods. This accounting scam caused these companies to take a "big bath" or earnings reduction in the current period but gave them an opportunity to post impressive "turnaround" profits in future periods. Because Wall Street analysts realized that restructuring reserves would augment a company's future earnings, they often responded favorably to them. "One of the reasons for the popularity of restructuring charges may be that announcements of restructuring are often rewarded by Wall Street. . . . Analysts quickly update future earnings estimates and a jump in the company's stock price often results."[1]

Favorable stock market reactions to announced restructuring reserves apparently goaded a growing number of corporate executives to use such reserves to manage or manipulate their companies' reported earnings. Hundreds of public companies, including many blue-chip firms, booked restructuring reserves during the 1990s. General Motors shocked its stockholders by recording a $3 billion restructuring reserve, a "record" that was easily topped by an $8.9 billion restructuring reserve announced by IBM. Among the most prolific users of restructuring reserves was AT&T, which established four such reserves in the late 1980s and early 1990s.

In the mid-1990s, regulatory authorities and rule-making bodies began taking measures to deal with the growing prevalence of restructuring reserves in corporate financial statements. In 1995, the SEC warned 300 public companies that their most recent financial statements had contained questionable restructuring reserves. A few months earlier, the Emerging Issues Task Force (EITF) of the Financial Accounting Standards Board (FASB) had issued EITF 94-3, "Liability Recognition for Certain Employee Termination Benefits and Other Costs to Exit an Activity (including Certain Costs Incurred in a Restructuring)." EITF 94-3 was the first of a series of technical pronouncements that clarified the conditions under which companies could establish restructuring reserves and the specific items that could be properly included in them. Among other stipulations, EITF 94-3 requires companies to have a definitive "exit plan" before establishing a restructuring reserve. This document "must specifically identify all significant actions to be taken to complete the exit plan, activities

---

1. *World Accounting Report* (online), "SEC Warning over Restructuring Charges," 1 April 1994.

that will not be continued, including the method of disposition and location of those activities, and the expected date of completion."[2]

Despite EITF 94-3 and related pronouncements, public companies continued to include restructuring reserves in their financial statements during the late 1990s. One such company was Los Angeles–based SmarTalk Teleservices, Inc., a leading provider of prepaid calling services and prepaid wireless services. In 1997, SmarTalk acquired six other prepaid telephone card companies. SmarTalk's 1997 financial statements included a $25 million restructuring reserve for future expenditures that the company would incur to "exit certain activities." The largest item in SmarTalk's restructuring reserve was $13.5 million of "contract termination fees" that the company would absorb in 1998 for changing from one service carrier, WorldCom, to another, Frontier Communications. SmarTalk's projected exit expenditures also included inventory write-downs, severance benefits for employees who would be laid off, and various other 1998 expenditures that the company lumped into a "general reserve" component of its restructuring reserve.

A subsequent SEC investigation revealed that SmarTalk's 1997 restructuring reserve and the related restructuring charges were invalid since the company did not have a formal exit plan as required by EITF 94-3. In fact, the largest component of the restructuring reserve, the contract termination fees, did not involve an "exit activity." SmarTalk's decision to switch service carriers was not prompted by the six acquisitions the company made in 1997 but instead was simply a strategic business decision made by the company's top executives. The SEC also found fault with each of the other components of SmarTalk's restructuring reserve. For example, much of the inventory write-down included in that reserve involved prepaid calling cards that the company continued to sell well into 1998. Likewise, the SEC pointed out that GAAP expressly prohibit companies from booking "general reserves" under any circumstances.

The restructuring charges that SmarTalk included in its 1997 income statement contributed significantly to the nearly $62 million net loss that the company incurred for that year. Nevertheless, in SmarTalk's press release that reported its 1997 operating results, company management chose to stress the fact that SmarTalk's "earnings before one-time charges" for 1997 were nearly $2.8 million, reflecting a large increase from the comparable amount reported the prior year.[3] Wall Street also apparently chose to focus on SmarTalk's 1997 earnings before one-time charges. In late February 1998, shortly after SmarTalk reported its 1997 operating results, Credit Suisse First Boston Corporation, a major Wall Street investment firm, issued a "buy" recommendation on the company's stock. The end result of the positive "spin" placed on SmarTalk's 1997 earnings report was that the company sustained an impressive upward trend in its stock price. From mid-August 1997 through March 1998, SmarTalk's stock price nearly doubled, rising from less than $19 per share to more than $34 per share over that time frame.

The SEC's investigation of SmarTalk's 1997 financial statements was triggered by an August 10, 1998, press release issued by the company. That press release revealed that PricewaterhouseCoopers (PwC), SmarTalk's audit firm, was reviewing the

---

2. This and all remaining quotations in this case, unless indicated otherwise, were taken from Securities and Exchange Commission, *Accounting and Auditing Enforcement Release No. 1787*, 22 May 2003.

3. *Coven v. SmarTalk Services, Inc., et al.*, United States District Court for the Eastern District of New York (1998). In addition to the $25 million of restructuring charges, SmarTalk's 1997 income statement also included a $39 million "acquisition-related charge."

company's 1997 restructuring reserve. PwC had issued an unqualified opinion on SmarTalk's 1997 financial statements in the spring of 1998.[4] However, over the next several months, the company's increasingly aggressive accounting and financial reporting decisions caused the relationship between PwC and SmarTalk's management to become "contentious." On July 18, 1998, PwC initiated a "post-audit review" of the 1997 SmarTalk audit workpapers for the purpose of deciding whether to remain the company's audit firm. The major focus of that review was the $25 million restructuring reserve. Complicating the review was the fact that Philip Hirsch, the audit partner who had supervised the 1997 SmarTalk audit, had left PwC shortly after completing that engagement.

Ironically, SmarTalk's August 10, 1998, press caused the SEC to investigate PwC's 1997 audit of SmarTalk. As a result of that investigation, the SEC criticized Hirsch and his subordinates for failing to properly audit SmarTalk's restructuring reserve. The SEC charged that the PwC auditors should have discovered that the contract termination fees included in the reserve were not true "exit" costs. Likewise, the auditors were apparently aware that during 1998 SmarTalk continued to sell the prepaid calling cards that were the basis for the inventory write-down included in the 1997 restructuring reserve. The federal agency also pointed out that the PwC audit team should have realized that GAAP forbid the accrual of "general reserves." Finally, and most importantly, the SEC reported that Hirsch knew SmarTalk's management team had failed to "commit the enterprise to an exit plan" by the end of fiscal 1997. The absence of such a commitment meant that SmarTalk had been precluded from establishing a restructuring reserve for that year.

Despite the SEC's extensive criticism of PwC's 1997 audit of SmarTalk, the federal agency's harshest criticism of the accounting firm was reserved for its post-audit review of the 1997 audit workpapers. Shortly after that review was initiated, PwC learned of a large class-action lawsuit being filed by SmarTalk's stockholders. That lawsuit apparently prompted PwC to make "undocumented changes in" and "revisions to" the 1997 SmarTalk audit workpapers.

> *During the period from the end of July through early August 1998, with the knowledge of several PwC partners with firm-wide responsibilities, PwC made revisions to its [1997 SmarTalk] working papers. Those revisions were not documented. Language in the working papers was revised, added, and deleted. Documents were removed from the working papers and discarded, and documents were also added to the working papers. The post-audit revisions were not dated or otherwise distinguished to indicate that they had been made as part of a post-audit review and PwC discarded most of the notes containing a second post-audit reviewer's instructions.[5]*

The SEC contacted PwC in February 1999 and asked the firm to produce its 1997 SmarTalk audit workpapers. PwC complied but did not inform the SEC that those workpapers had been altered. When the SEC discovered that some of the electronic workpapers for the 1997 audit had been accessed following the completion of the audit, PwC officials admitted that the workpapers had been altered.

In May 2003, the SEC sanctioned PwC and Philip Hirsch for engaging in "improper professional conduct." The SEC banned Hirsch from practicing before it for one year

---

4. Technically, Price Waterhouse, not PwC, audited SmarTalk's 1997 financial statements. PwC was created on July 1, 1998, when Price Waterhouse and Coopers & Lybrand merged. For purposes of clarity, the SEC referred to PwC as SmarTalk's auditor in the enforcement release that it issued for this case.

5. As a point of information, at the time that PwC altered the audit workpapers, the firm was not under investigation by the SEC for its 1997 SmarTalk audit.

and fined PwC $1 million. In addition, the SEC required PwC to "establish and maintain policies and procedures to preserve working papers intact following the archiving of working papers and also during the course of, and following the conclusion of, any post-audit review." PwC was also required to retain an independent consultant to prepare and submit a report to the SEC and the Public Company Accounting Oversight Board confirming that such policies and procedures had been implemented.

Several months prior to announcing the penalties imposed on PwC, the SEC had sanctioned SmarTalk's former chief financial officer (CFO), who was the individual responsible for making the key accounting decisions for the $25 million restructuring reserve. In addition to ordering him to cease and desist from future violations of federal securities laws, the SEC fined the CFO $50,000.

The August 10, 1998, press release that revealed PwC's decision to review SmarTalk's restructuring reserve sent the company's stock price into a freefall from which it never recovered. In January 1999, SmarTalk filed for bankruptcy. A few days following that bankruptcy filing, SmarTalk ceased operations when AT&T purchased the company's remaining assets.[6]

Questions

1. Suppose that you are supervising a future audit engagement involving a public company that has recently established a large restructuring reserve. What audit objectives would you establish for that reserve? For each audit objective you list, identify audit evidence that you would collect to help achieve that objective.

2. What is the role of the FASB's Emerging Issues Task Force? Are pronouncements issued by the EITF considered generally accepted accounting principles?

3. Federal prosecutors filed "obstruction of justice" charges against Arthur Andersen & Co. for destroying documents that pertained to that firm's audits of Enron Corporation. Why was PwC not charged with obstruction of justice in this case? What professional standards, if any, do you believe PwC violated by altering the SmarTalk audit workpapers during its post-audit review?

---

6. PwC was eventually named as a codefendant in the class-action lawsuit filed by SmarTalk's stockholders. In 2002, PwC agreed to pay $15 million to be dismissed from that lawsuit.

CBI Holding Company, Inc.

During the 1980s, CBI Holding Company, Inc., a New York–based firm, served as the parent company for several wholly owned subsidiaries, principal among them Common Brothers, Inc. CBI's subsidiaries marketed an extensive line of pharmaceutical products. The subsidiaries purchased these products from drug manufacturers, warehoused them in storage facilities, and then resold them to retail pharmacies, hospitals, long-term care facilities, and related entities. CBI's principal market area stretched from the northeastern United States into the upper Midwest.

In 1991, Robert Castello, CBI's president and chairman of the board, sold a 48 percent ownership interest in his company to Trust Company of the West (TCW), a diversified investment firm. The purchase agreement between the two parties gave TCW the right to appoint two members of CBI's board; Castello retained the right to appoint the three remaining board members. The purchase agreement also identified several so-called "control-triggering events." If any one of these events occurred, TCW would have the right to take control of CBI. Examples of control-triggering events included CBI's failure to maintain certain financial ratios at a specified level and unauthorized loans to Castello and other CBI executives.

Castello engaged Ernst & Young as CBI's independent audit firm several months before he closed the TCW deal. During this same time frame, Castello was named "Entrepreneur of the Year" in an annual nationwide promotion cosponsored by Ernst & Young. From 1990 through 1993, Ernst & Young issued unqualified opinions on CBI's annual financial statements.

Accounting Gimmicks

Castello instructed several of his subordinates to misrepresent CBI's reported operating results and financial condition for the fiscal years ended April 30, 1992 and 1993.[1] The misrepresentations allowed Castello to receive large, year-end bonuses to which he was not entitled for each of those fiscal years. CBI actively concealed the fraudulent activities from TCW's management, from TCW's appointees to CBI's board, and from the company's Ernst & Young auditors because Castello realized that the scheme, if discovered, would qualify as a control-triggering event under the terms of the 1991 purchase agreement with TCW. Several years later in a lawsuit prompted by Castello's fraud, TCW executives testified that they would have immediately seized control of CBI if they had become aware of that scheme.

Understating CBI's year-end accounts payable was one of the methods Castello and his confederates used to distort CBI's 1992 and 1993 financial statements. At any point in time, CBI had large outstanding payables to its suppliers, which included major pharmaceutical manufacturers such as Burroughs-Wellcome, Schering, and FoxMeyer. At the end of fiscal 1992 and fiscal 1993, CBI understated payables due to its large vendors by millions of dollars. Judge Burton Lifland, the federal magistrate who presided over the lawsuit stemming from Castello's fraudulent scheme, ruled that the intentional understatements of CBI's year-end payables were very material to the company's 1992 and 1993 financial statements.

---

1. Due to a change in CBI's fiscal year, the company's 1992 fiscal year was only 11 months.

Ernst & Young's 1992 and 1993 CBI Audits

In both 1992 and 1993, Ernst & Young identified the CBI audit as a "close monitoring engagement." The accounting firm's audit manual defined a close monitoring engagement as "one in which the company being audited presents significant risk to E&Y...there is a significant chance that E&Y will suffer damage to its reputation, monetarily, or both."[2] Ernst & Young's workpapers for the 1992 and 1993 audits also documented several "red flags" suggesting that the engagements posed a higher-than-normal audit risk.

Control risk factors identified for the CBI audits by Ernst & Young included the dominance of the company by Robert Castello,[3] the absence of an internal audit function, the lack of proper segregation of duties within the company's accounting department, and aggressive positions taken by management personnel regarding key accounting estimates. These apparent control risks caused Ernst & Young to describe CBI's control environment as "ineffective." Other risk factors identified in the CBI audit workpapers included the possible occurrence of a control-triggering event, an "undue" emphasis by top management on achieving periodic earnings goals, and the fact that Castello's annual bonus was tied directly to CBI's reported earnings.

For both the 1992 and 1993 CBI audits, the Ernst & Young engagement team prepared a document entitled "Audit Approach Plan Update and Approval Form." This document described the general strategy Ernst & Young planned to follow in completing those audits. In 1992 and 1993, this document identified accounts payable as a "high risk" audit area. The audit program for the 1992 audit included two key audit procedures for accounts payable:

a. Perform a search for unrecorded liabilities at April 30, 1992, through the end of field work.

b. Obtain copies of the April 30, 1992, vendor statements for CBI's five largest vendors and examine reconciliations to the accounts payable balances for such vendors as shown on the books of CBI.

The 1993 audit program included these same items, although that program required audit procedure "b" to be applied to CBI's 10 largest vendors.

During the 1992 audit, the Ernst & Young auditors discovered numerous disbursements made by CBI in the first few weeks of fiscal 1993 that were potential unrecorded liabilities as of April 30, 1992. The bulk of these disbursements included payments to the company's vendors that had been labeled as "advances" in the company's accounting records. CBI personnel provided the following explanation for these advances when questioned by the auditors: "When CBI is at its credit limit with a large vendor, the vendor may hold an order until they receive an 'advance.' CBI then applies the advance to the existing A/P balance."

In truth, the so-called advances, which totaled nearly $2 million, were simply payments CBI made to its vendors for inventory purchases consummated on, or prior to, April 30, 1992. Castello and his confederates had chosen not to record these transactions in order to strengthen key financial ratios of CBI at the end of fiscal 1992 and

---

2. This and all subsequent quotations were taken from the following court opinion: *In re CBI Holding Company, Inc., et al., Debtors; Bankruptcy Services, Inc., Plaintiff—against—Ernst & Young, Ernst & Young, LLP, Defendants;* 247 B.R. 341; 2000 Bankr. LEXIS 425.

3. The CBI audit engagement partner noted during the 1993 audit that the company's CFO appeared to be "afraid of his boss, Castello." When questioned by an auditor regarding an important issue, the CFO typically responded by telling the individual to "ask Castello." In the audit partner's view, this raised an "integrity red flag."

otherwise embellish the company's apparent financial condition. Because of concern that Ernst & Young would discover that CBI had grossly understated its accounts payable at year-end, Castello developed the "advances" ruse.

Subsequent court testimony revealed that after reviewing internal documents supporting the advances explanation—documents that had been prepared to deceive Ernst & Young—the Ernst & Young auditors readily accepted that explanation and chose not to treat the items as unrecorded liabilities. This decision prompted severe criticism of Ernst & Young by Judge Lifland.

The federal judge pointed out that the auditors had failed to rigorously investigate the alleged advances and to consider the veracity of the client's explanation for them. For example, the auditors did not investigate the "credit limit" feature of that explanation. The Ernst & Young auditors neglected to determine the credit limit that the given vendors had established for CBI or whether CBI had "maxed out" that credit limit in each case as maintained by client personnel. Nor did the auditors attempt to analyze the given vendors' payable accounts or contact those vendors directly to determine if the alleged advances applied to specific invoice amounts, particularly invoice amounts for purchases made on or before April 30, 1992. Instead, the auditors simply chose to record in their workpapers the client's feeble explanation for the advances, an explanation that failed to address or resolve a critical issue. "The advance explanation recorded in E&Y's workpapers, even if it were true, did not tell the E&Y auditor the essential fact as to whether the merchandise being paid for by the advance had been received before or after April 30, 1992."

Because of the lack of any substantive investigation of the advances, the Ernst & Young auditors failed to determine "whether a liability should have been recorded for each such payment as of fiscal year-end, and whether, in fact, a liability was recorded for such payment as of fiscal year-end." This finding caused Judge Lifland to conclude that Ernst & Young had not properly completed the search for unrecorded liabilities. The judge reached a similar conclusion regarding the second major audit procedure for accounts payable included in the 1992 audit program for CBI.

The 1992 audit program required the Ernst & Young auditors to obtain the year-end statements sent to CBI by the company's five largest vendors and to reconcile the balances in each of those statements to the corresponding balances reported in CBI's accounting records. Ernst & Young obtained year-end statements mailed to CBI by five of the company's several hundred vendors and completed the reconciliation audit procedure. However, the vendors involved in this audit test were not the company's five largest suppliers. In fact, Ernst & Young never identified CBI's five largest vendors during the 1992 audit. The federal judge scolded Ernst & Young for this oversight and maintained that the "minimal" amount of testing applied by Ernst & Young to the small sample of year-end vendor statements was "not adequate."

The audit procedures that Ernst & Young applied to CBI's year-end accounts payable for fiscal 1993 suffered from the same flaws evident during the firm's 1992 audit. Similar to the previous year, CBI's management attempted to conceal unrecorded liabilities at year-end by labeling subsequent payments of those amounts as "advances" to the given vendors. Once more, Judge Lifland noted that the "gullible" auditors readily accepted the explanation for these advances that was relayed to them by CBI personnel. As a result, the auditors failed to require CBI to prepare appropriate adjusting entries for approximately $7.5 million of year-end payables that the client's management team had intentionally ignored.

The 1993 audit program mandated that Ernst & Young obtain the year-end statements for CBI's 10 largest vendors and reconcile the balances in those statements to the corresponding accounts payable balances in CBI's accounting records. Again, Ernst & Young failed to identify CBI's largest vendors and apply this procedure to their year-end payable balances. Instead, the auditors simply applied the reconciliation procedure to a sample of 10 CBI vendors.[4]

One of CBI's 10 largest vendors was Burroughs-Wellcome. If the Ernst & Young auditors had reconciled the balance due Burroughs-Wellcome in its year-end statement with the corresponding account payable balance in CBI's accounting records, the auditors would have discovered that a $1 million "advance" payment made to that vendor in May 1993 was actually for an inventory purchase two weeks prior to April 30, 1993. This discovery would have clearly established that the $1 million amount was an unrecorded liability at year-end.

Ernst & Young Held Responsible for CBI's Bankruptcy

In March 1994, Ernst & Young withdrew its opinions on CBI's 1992 and 1993 financial statements after learning of the material distortions in those statements that were due to Castello's fraudulent scheme. Almost immediately, CBI began encountering difficulty obtaining trade credit from its principal vendors. A few months later in August 1994, the company filed for bankruptcy. In early 2000, Judge Lifland presided over a 17-day trial in federal bankruptcy court to determine whether Ernst & Young would be held responsible for the large losses that CBI's collapse inflicted on TCW and CBI's former creditors. Near the conclusion of that trial, Judge Lifland ruled that Ernst & Young's conduct during the 1992 and 1993 CBI audits was the "proximate cause" of those losses.

> The demise of CBI was a foreseeable consequence of E&Y's failure to conduct its audits in fiscal 1992 and 1993 in accordance with GAAS, which was the cause of its failure to detect the unrecorded liabilities, which in turn foreseeably caused it to withdraw its opinions in March 1994. As direct and reasonably foreseeable consequences thereof, CBI's vendors restricted the amount of credit available, CBI's inventory and sales declined, its revenues declined, its value as a going concern diminished, and ultimately it filed for bankruptcy and was liquidated.

Judge Lifland characterized Ernst & Young's conduct as either "reckless and/or grossly negligent" and identified several generally accepted auditing standards that the accounting firm violated while performing the 1992 and 1993 CBI audits. Although the bulk of the judge's opinion dealt with the audit procedures Ernst & Young applied to CBI's accounts payable, his harshest criticism focused on the firm's alleged failure to retain its independence during the CBI engagements.

Several circumstances that arose during Ernst & Young's tenure as CBI's audit firm called into question its independence. For example, Judge Lifland referred to an incident in 1993 when Robert Castello demanded that Ernst & Young remove the audit manager assigned to the CBI engagement. Apparently, Castello found the audit manager's inquisitive and probing nature disturbing. The CBI audit engagement partner "submissively acquiesced" to Castello's request and replaced the audit manager.

Shortly after the completion of the 1993 audit, Castello hired a new chief financial officer (CFO). This individual resigned eight days later. The CFO told members of the Ernst & Young audit team he was resigning because of several million dollars of "grey accounting" he had discovered in CBI's accounting records. Judge Lifland chided

---

4. The court opinion that provided the background information for this case did not indicate what criteria, if any, Ernst & Young used to select the vendor accounts to which the reconciliation procedure was applied in the 1992 and 1993 audits.

Ernst & Young for being slow to pursue this allegation. Nearly five months passed before the CBI audit engagement partner contacted the former CFO. By that point, Ernst & Young had already discovered Castello's fraudulent scheme and withdrawn its 1992 and 1993 audit opinions.

In February 1994, the audit engagement partner met with Castello to discuss several matters. Ernst & Young's unpaid bill for prior services provided to CBI was the first of those matters, while the second issue discussed was Ernst & Young's fee for the upcoming audit. The last topic on the agenda was the allegation by CBI's former CFO regarding the company's questionable accounting decisions. According to Judge Lifland, the audit partner "wanted to speak to [the former CFO] in order to ask him whether his leaving the post of chief financial officer and his allegations of 'grey accounting' had anything to do with the financial statements that E&Y had just certified; however, [the audit partner] obligingly allowed himself to be put off." In Judge Lifland's opinion, the Ernst & Young audit partner was "more concerned about insuring E&Y's fees than he was about speaking to [the former CFO]."

The final matter Judge Lifland discussed in impugning Ernst & Young's independence was the accounting firm's effort to retain CBI as an audit client after discovering that the 1992 and 1993 audits had been deficient. Judge Lifland charged that Ernst & Young officials realized when they withdrew the audit opinions on CBI's 1992 and 1993 financial statements that the CBI audits had been flawed. In the days prior to withdrawing those opinions, two individuals, a former CBI accountant and CBI's controller at the time, informed Ernst & Young that the "advances" discovered during the 1992 and 1993 audits had been for payment of unrecorded liabilities that existed at the end of CBI's 1992 and 1993 fiscal years. After investigating these admissions, Ernst & Young determined that they were true. Ernst & Young also determined that the CBI auditors "had failed to detect the unrecorded liabilities because they had failed to properly perform the search [for unrecorded liabilities]."

Ernst & Young failed to notify CBI's board of directors of the flaws in the 1992 and 1993 audits.[5] According to Judge Lifland, Ernst & Young did not inform the board members of those flaws because the accounting firm realized that doing so would lower, if not eliminate, its chance of landing the "reaudit" engagement for CBI's 1992 and 1993 financial statements. "E&Y's egocentric desire to get the reaudit work is illustrated by the fact that it prepared an audit program for the reaudit two days before E&Y met with the CBI board of directors and one day before they withdrew their opinion."

CBI's board ultimately selected Ernst & Young to reaudit the company's 1992 and 1993 financial statements. Given the circumstances under which Ernst & Young obtained that engagement, Judge Lifland concluded that the accounting firm's independence was likely impaired. "Thus, E&Y knew prior to agreeing to perform the reaudit work that it had not complied with GAAS. E&Y also knew that CBI's board of directors did not know of E&Y's failure to comply with GAAS. It is reasonable to infer that if CBI's board of directors knew of such failure, E&Y and CBI would be in adversarial positions."[6]

---

5. At this point, the TCW representatives on CBI's board were apparently the company's principal decision makers.

6. After ruling that Ernst & Young was principally responsible for the losses resulting from CBI's bankruptcy, Judge Lifland ordered that the trial be resumed on the issue of damages. The judgment imposed by Judge Lifland or the out-of-court settlement ultimately reached by the parties was not publicly reported.

Questions

1. Most of Judge Lifland's criticism of Ernst & Young focused on the audit procedures Ernst & Young applied to CBI's accounts payable. Generally, what is an auditor's primary objective in auditing a client's accounts payable? Do you believe that the two principal audit tests applied to CBI's accounts payable would have accomplished that objective if those tests had been properly applied? Why or why not?

2. Do you believe that the Ernst & Young auditors should have used confirmations in auditing CBI's year-end accounts payable? Defend your answer. Briefly explain the differing audit objectives related to accounts receivable and accounts payable confirmation procedures and the key differences in how these procedures are applied.

3. In early 1994, Ernst & Young officials discovered that the CBI auditors had failed to determine the true nature of the "advances" they had uncovered during the 1992 and 1993 audits. In your view, did Ernst & Young have an obligation to inform CBI management of this oversight prior to seeking the "reaudit" engagement? More generally, does an auditor have a responsibility to inform client management of mistakes or oversights made on earlier audits?

4. Under what circumstances, if any, should an audit engagement partner acquiesce to a client's request to remove a member of the audit engagement team?

5. Ernst & Young officials believed that the CBI audits were high-risk engagements. Under what general circumstances should an audit firm choose not to accept a high-risk engagement?

Campbell Soup Company

Campbell Soup easily qualifies as one of the most recognizable brand names across the globe. Founded shortly before the start of the Civil War, Campbell Soup Company long had a reputation as having one of the most rigid corporate cultures in the United States. An unwritten but strictly enforced company dress code required Campbell executives and other management personnel to wear starched white shirts and conservative business suits. While hard at work in their offices on production budgets, sales forecasts, or new promotional campaigns, those executives and office managers were expected to maintain an air of formality and decorum by wearing their suit jackets. Even the company's marketing department was known for its traditionalist views. Nearly 100 years would pass before Campbell's cautious marketing executives redesigned the company's standard red and white label introduced in the early 1900s.

By the late 1990s, Campbell's stifling corporate culture had relaxed somewhat. This more easygoing mindset apparently extended to the company's accounting and financial reporting practices. In early 2000, Campbell found itself snared in a contentious legal battle with a large contingent of its stockholders. The stockholders charged that accounting gimmicks applied by Campbell's accounting staff had misrepresented the company's reported operating results and ultimately led to a sharp decline in the price of its common stock.

"Never Underestimate the Power of Soup"

In 1860, Abraham Anderson organized a small canning business in Camden, New Jersey, located a few miles east of Philadelphia across the Delaware River. Several years later, Anderson took on a partner, Joseph Campbell, who sold produce in the communities surrounding Camden. The two men merged their business backgrounds to begin manufacturing canned vegetables and fruit preserves that they marketed in Philadelphia and southwestern New Jersey. When Anderson decided to leave the business in 1876, Campbell bought out his interest in the partnership and renamed the firm the Joseph Campbell Preserving Company. Campbell's company struggled financially until he found a well-heeled investor, Arthur Dorrance, to become his new partner. Several years later, Dorrance persuaded Campell to hire his nephew, John Dorrance, who was a chemist by training. The younger Dorrance would be responsible for the breakthrough event that catapulted the Camden-based business to the top of the prepared food market in the United States.

In 1899, John Dorrance came up with a cost-effective method of canning condensed soup. Within a span of months, condensed soup products replaced canned vegetables and preserves as the Campbell company's primary product line. By the early 1920s, John Dorrance was the sole owner of the Campbell Soup Company, which easily reigned as the nation's largest producer of canned soup products. More than eight decades later, Campbell still dominates the soup industry, maintaining a steady two-thirds market share within the industry. Likewise, the Dorrance family continues to control the now publicly owned company, thanks to the large block of Campbell common stock that John Dorrance's descendants collectively own.

Throughout most of the twentieth century, the conservative polices of Campbell's management produced steady but not spectacular growth in revenues and profits for the blue chip company. Unlike most of its competitors, Campbell was slow to diversify its product offerings. A corporate policy requiring a new venture to earn a profit during its initial year of operation stymied most proposals to diversify the company's short product line. In 1980, Campbell's new management team surprised the business world by selling debt securities, the first time the company had raised funds by borrowing in the debt market. Even more startling was the company's announcement that the borrowed funds would be used to finance an aggressive expansion program.

During the early and mid-1980s, Campbell's new management team released more than 300 new products. The new product offerings doubled Campbell's revenues over the next several years but their impact on the company's bottom line was less than impressive. In fact, despite several billion dollars of sales in 1989, the company registered an anemic profit of only $4.4 million.

Another overhaul of top management in 1990 resulted in a new company slogan, "Never Underestimate the Power of Soup," that underscored a renewed focus by Campbell on its core product line. Campbell's new management team restructured the company's operations and eliminated many of the product offerings introduced the previous decade. Unfortunately, as the twentieth century was coming to a close, the nation's appetite for condensed soup products was waning. The weakening demand for what Campbell insiders refer to as "red and white" prompted the company's executives to take a more direct, if less palatable, approach to improving their company's earnings.

Red and White Window Dressing

Campbell stockholders filed a series of lawsuits in the late 1990s that were eventually consolidated into one large, class-action lawsuit. The stockholders claimed that Campbell and its key executives had used an assortment of questionable business practices and accounting schemes to enhance the company's reported earnings. These scams were intended to ensure that Campbell met or surpassed the quarterly and annual profit forecasts issued by Wall Street analysts who tracked the company's common stock. The alleged scams included *trade loading*, *improper accounting for loading discounts*, *shipping to the yard*, and *guaranteed sales*.

Campbell and its competitors have historically offered sizable trade discounts near the end of accounting periods to entice customers to make product purchases that they would otherwise defer. So-called "trade loading" is particularly prevalent when a company appears to be falling short of a critical revenue or earnings target. To make up for significant revenue and earnings shortfalls in the late 1990s, Campbell's management "maintained a practice of offering steep discounts, often as much as 15 to 20 percent, to its customers at each quarter's end."[1] Understandably, this excessive trade loading made it increasingly difficult for Campbell to reach its revenue and earnings targets each successive period.

The large, period-ending trade discounts offered by Campbell's management posed another problem for the company. Wall Street analysts monitored not only Campbell's quarterly revenue and profit figures but also paid close attention to the

---

1. This and all subsequent quotes, unless indicated otherwise, were taken from the following source: *Denise L. Nappier et al., Plaintiffs v. PricewaterhouseCoopers LLP, Defendant*, 227 F. Supp. 2d 263; 2002 U.S. Dist. LEXIS 18781; Fed. Sec. L. Rep. (CCH) P91,991.

company's gross margins. Any deterioration in Campbell's gross profit percentage from one period to the next might signal that the company was using price concessions to prop up its reported revenues and profits. To maintain reasonable gross profit margins, Campbell executives reportedly instructed the company's accountants to record the large, period-ending trade discounts as selling, general and administrative (SG&A) expenses instead of treating them as reductions of gross revenues. The plaintiffs in the class-action lawsuit conceded that it was customary in Campbell's industry to treat certain sales discounts as SG&A expenses. However, sales discounts charged off as SG&A expenses generally involve price concessions granted to customers for their participation in certain promotional activities, such as agreeing to erect product displays in high-traffic areas of retail stores. The plaintiffs also pointed out that these "performance-related" discounts rarely exceed 3 percent of the invoiced sales.

As Campbell executives became increasingly concerned with maintaining their company's good standing with Wall Street, they resorted to increasingly desperate methods to achieve their company's financial goals, including "shipping to the yard" and "guaranteed sales." The plaintiffs in the class-action lawsuit maintained that near the end of accounting periods Campbell began recording large sales of product that had not been ordered by customers. Instead of delivering this product, Campbell shipped it to a company warehouse or loaded it on trucks that were then parked at various Campbell distribution facilities around the nation. "Guaranteed sales" involved large sales recorded near the end of an accounting period for which Campbell's customers had an unconditional right to return the product. Although this practice was clearly not fraudulent, the plaintiffs insisted that Campbell had a responsibility to record a reserve or allowance in anticipation of the substantial customer returns likely to result from these "sales." Despite the fact that a large percentage of product sold under guaranteed sales contracts was eventually returned by Campbell's customers, the company's accounting staff apparently never recorded appropriate reserves for those sales returns.

In 1999, Campbell's management team decided to discontinue the questionable business practices and accounting gimmicks that had been used to embellish the company's operating results. Management then issued a press release indicating that Campbell would fall far short of Wall Street's earnings forecast for the company's next quarterly reporting period. In that press release, company officials attributed the shortfall to "inefficiencies in the supply chain" and "warm weather"—sultry weather apparently curtails the public's appetite for soup. The press release made no mention of the four aggressive methods management had used to enhance Campbell's reported profits for the past several periods.

The somber press release triggered a sharp sell-off of Campbell's common stock over the following weeks. In fact, the company's stock price would trend downward over the following four years, eventually declining by more than 65 percent. The press release also resulted in the large class-action lawsuit filed against Campbell by disgruntled investors who believed they had been shortchanged by the company's management.

"Reckless" Auditors?

The plaintiffs in the class-action lawsuit filed against Campbell Soup Company and its top executives eventually added PricewaterhouseCoopers (PwC), Campbell's independent auditor, as a defendant in the case. According to the complaint filed against PwC, the prominent accounting firm had "recklessly" aided the accounting schemes used by Campbell's executives to misrepresent their company's reported operating results in the late 1990s. The bulk of the allegations leveled at PwC stemmed from the firm's 1998 audit of Campbell. That audit covered Campbell's fiscal year for the 12-month period ended August 2, 1998.

Judge Joseph E. Irenas, a federal judge assigned to the Third Circuit of the U.S. District Court system, was chosen to preside over the Campbell class-action lawsuit. Since the lawsuit was filed under the Securities and Exchange Act of 1934, one of Judge Irenas' first tasks was to decide whether the allegations against each defendant satisfied the new "pleading standard" included in the Private Securities Litigation Reform Act (PSLRA) of 1995, a federal statute that amended the 1934 Securities Act. The PSLRA established a "uniform and stringent pleading standard" to protect corporate executives, independent auditors, and other parties associated with financial statements filed under the 1934 Securities Act from so-called "strike suits" intended to obtain a quick, if not modest, settlement from such defendants.[2] Because of the PSLRA's pleading standard, federal judges must dismiss any defendants if there appears to be insufficient justification for including them in a given lawsuit.

To allow a lawsuit filed under the 1934 Securities Act to proceed against a defendant, a federal judge must find that the plaintiffs have alleged or "pleaded" facts "to support a strong inference of scienter" on the part of that defendant. Generally, "scienter" means "intent to deceive," but the federal courts have varying interpretations of how to apply that term in securities lawsuits. The Third Circuit of the U.S. District Court has generally ruled that to satisfy the PSLRA pleading standard, plaintiffs must allege, at a minimum, that defendants acted with "recklessness." The Third Circuit defines recklessness as follows: "Highly unreasonable conduct involving not merely simple, or even inexcusable negligence, but an extreme departure from the standards of ordinary care … which presents a danger of misleading buyers or sellers [of securities] that is either known to the defendant or is so obvious that the actor must have been aware of it."

To determine whether PwC would remain a defendant in the Campbell lawsuit, Judge Arenas reviewed PwC's 1998 audit workpapers that the plaintiffs had relied upon in filing their complaint against the accounting firm. If Judge Arenas concluded after reviewing those workpapers that there was a "strong inference" PwC had been aware of the improper business practices and/or accounting irregularities employed by Campbell, the firm would remain a defendant in the case. The plaintiffs' legal counsel would then have the opportunity to prove in court that PwC had acted with at least recklessness in auditing Campbell's annual financial statements.

PwC Goes Four for Four

While reviewing PwC's audit workpapers, Judge Arenas considered one by one the four questionable business practices or accounting irregularities allegedly perpetrated by Campbell. For purposes of his analysis, the judge worked under the assumption that those allegations were valid.

Trade Loading

The plaintiffs in the class-action lawsuit alleged that PwC's 1998 audit workpapers demonstrated that the auditors were well aware of the excessive trade loading by their client. Campbell's large period-ending sales, according to the plaintiffs, should

---

2. Refer to Case 1.4, "Health Management, Inc.," for a more in-depth discussion of the PSLRA and its implications for independent auditors.

have been a "red flag" that prompted the PwC auditors to investigate the possibility that their client was fraudulently misrepresenting its operating results.

Judge Arenas agreed with the plaintiffs that PwC's workpapers revealed the firm was aware of Campbell's disproportionately large sales near the end of quarterly reporting periods. However, the judge disagreed with the assertion that PwC should have considered those heavy sales a red flag. Instead, the judge pointed out that PwC's audit workpapers referred to the large, period-ending sales as a "traditional" trend in Campbell's operating results. Nowhere in PwC's workpapers did the firm's auditors characterize the sales as suspicious or even "unusual," characterizations that would have required the auditors to further investigate those sales. According to Judge Irenas, because PwC, rightly or wrongly, had not perceived the trade loading practices as a red flag, the plaintiffs could not allege that the audit firm had recklessly failed to investigate those practices.[3]

Improper Accounting for Loading Discounts

The second issue addressed by Judge Irenas in assessing whether PwC would remain a defendant in the Campbell lawsuit was whether the audit firm realized that the large trade discounts granted on period-ending sales were routinely recorded as SG&A expenses. PwC was aware that only "performance-related" discounts qualified for SG&A treatment. During the 1997 audit, PwC auditors learned that Campbell was booking some trade discounts as SG&A expenses. When PwC raised this issue with client executives, those officials pledged that in the future Campbell would provide "proper accounting for non-performance-related discounts." In fact, Campbell's accounting staff did not fully implement those measures. Nevertheless, Judge Irenas ruled that PwC's at least token investigation of the questionable accounting decisions for the large, period-ending sales discounts undercut any allegation that the auditors had been "reckless" with regard to auditing those items.

Shipping to the Yard

The third complaint levied against PwC revolved around Campbell's alleged practice of "shipping to the yard" at the end of accounting periods. According to the plaintiffs, while completing their year-end inventory inspections PwC auditors must have observed the unusually large number of fully loaded Campbell trucks parked at the company's warehouses and other distribution facilities. Judge Irenas rejected this allegation because the plaintiffs failed to identify specific facts supporting the allegation, as mandated by the PSLRA. To eliminate so-called fishing expeditions by plaintiffs in securities lawsuits, the PSLRA requires plaintiffs to "plead with particularity" specific facts supporting each allegation filed against a defendant.

Although Judge Irenas quickly rejected the third complaint, he did address a related issue raised by the plaintiffs. The plaintiffs pointed out that Campbell Soup had historically recorded all customer sales on an FOB shipping point basis, meaning that the company recorded a sale when the given product was loaded on a delivery truck at a Campbell distribution facility. In fact, the actual shipping terms for many of Campbell's sales were FOB destination, meaning that the legal title to such goods did not transfer to the customer until they arrived at the customer's place of business.

---

3. One could argue that PwC was negligent in failing to fully grasp the potential audit issues posed by the large, period-ending sales booked by Campbell. But, because negligence is not a sufficient basis for a civil claim filed under the 1934 Securities Act, the plaintiffs in this case were prevented from pursuing that line of reasoning.

In reviewing PwC's 1998 audit workpapers, the judge found that PwC was aware of this practice. After discussing the matter with client officials during the 1998 audit, PwC auditors had decided that since Campbell used the sales cutoff policy consistently, it would not have a material effect on Campbell's 1998 operating results.[4] The judge found this conclusion reasonable and did not pursue the matter any further.

Guaranteed Sales

The plaintiffs in the class-action lawsuit charged that because of PwC's "long history as Campbell's auditor and consultant," the firm "must have known" about Campbell's practice of booking "guaranteed sales" near the end of accounting periods. According to the plaintiffs, the PwC auditors either "reviewed" or "recklessly ignored" Campbell accounting documents that revealed the existence of the allegedly bogus sales. Once more, Judge Irenas quickly quashed this complaint by ruling that the plaintiffs' legal counsel had failed to produce specific evidence pertinent to the allegation. "PwC's role as Campbell's auditor is insufficient, by itself, to permit an inference that PwC knew of these allegedly deceptive practices."

After completing his review of PwC's audit workpapers, Judge Irenas ruled that individually and collectively the plaintiffs' allegations did not provide a sufficient basis to justify including the accounting firm as a defendant in the Campbell class-action lawsuit. "Thus, while plaintiffs' allegations might provide some indication that PwC's 1998 audit was inadequate, they fall short of creating a strong inference of scienter." In his opinion, Judge Irenas also cautioned future plaintiffs intending to file legal actions against audit firms under the 1934 Securities Act. The judge warned those parties that any "red flags" allegedly overlooked by an auditor must be "closer to 'smoking guns' than mere warning signs."

EPILOGUE

In October 2002, Judge Irenas dismissed PwC as a defendant in the Campbell class-action lawsuit but gave the plaintiffs 60 days to file an amended complaint properly supporting their claim that the audit firm had acted at least recklessly during the 1998 Campbell audit. Apparently, the plaintiffs chose not to file an amended complaint. In February 2003, Campbell Soup Company revealed that it had reached an agreement to settle the class-action lawsuit stemming from its allegedly deceptive business and accounting practices.

Campbell executives agreed to pay the plaintiffs $35 million to settle their claims but denied that they or their company were guilty of any wrongdoing.

In March 2000, Campbell's CEO who had led the firm through the turbulent late 1990s abruptly resigned his position. In the coming months, Campbell announced a broad-based "corporate renewal" program. Among the five objectives of that program were "revitalizing" the company and "improving organization excellence and vitality."

---

4. For any one year, the impact of the improper sales cutoff policy for FOB destination sales was a net amount. For example, FOB destination sales booked as revenue at the end of fiscal 1998 that should have been recorded in fiscal 1999 were offset by the FOB destination sales booked at the end of fiscal 1997 that should have been recorded in fiscal 1998. As a result, the net impact on the 1998 operating results was immaterial.

Questions

1. Identify legitimate business practices that corporate executives can use for the primary purpose of manipulating or "managing" their company's reported operating results. Are such practices ethical? Defend your answer.

2. Suppose that a company uses one or more of the practices that you identified in responding to the previous question. What implications, if any, do those practices have for the company's independent auditors?

3. What auditing standard, if any, requires auditors to determine whether their clients have properly classified key amounts in their periodic income statements? Identify three methods that audit clients can use to put a favorable "spin" on their reported operating results without changing their "bottom line" or net income.

4. What audit procedures might have resulted in the discovery of the "shipping to the yard" and "guaranteed sales" schemes allegedly used by Campbell?

5. After reviewing PwC's audit workpapers, Judge Irenas ruled that there was insufficient evidence to support a strong inference of scienter or "reckless" conduct on the part of the audit firm. Do you believe that PwC was "negligent" in performing the 1998 Campbell audit? Defend your answer. Provide a hypothetical example related to the facts of this case under which PwC would have been guilty of "recklessness."

6. Identify the parties affected by the PSLRA. Briefly explain how that federal statute affects each of those parties.

Rocky Mount Undergarment Company, Inc.

Employees involved in the accounting and control functions of organizations often face ethical dilemmas. Typically, at some point in each of these dilemmas an employee must decide whether he or she will "do the right thing." Consider the huge scandal involving Equity Funding Corporation of America in the early 1970s. In that scandal, dozens of the life insurance company's employees actively participated in a fraudulent scheme intended to grossly overstate Equity Funding's revenues and profits. These employees routinely prepared phony insurance applications, invoices, and other fake documents to conceal the fraud masterminded by the firm's top executives. When questioned by a reporter following the disclosure of the fraud, one of Equity Funding's employees meekly observed, "I simply lacked the courage to do what was right."[1]

In early 1986, several employees of Rocky Mount Undergarment Co., Inc. (RMUC), came face to face with an ethical dilemma. RMUC, a North Carolina–based company, manufactured undergarments and other apparel products. Approximately one-half of the company's annual sales were to three large merchandisers: Kmart (29 percent), Wal-Mart (11 percent), and Sears (9 percent). RMUC employed nearly 1,300 workers in its production facilities and another 40 individuals in its administrative functions. Between 1981 and 1984, RMUC realized steady growth in revenues and profits. In 1981, RMUC reported a net income of $378,000 on net sales of $17.9 million. Three years later, the company reported a net income of $1.5 million on net sales of $32 million.

Unfortunately, RMUC failed to sustain its impressive profit trend in 1985, as reflected by the financial data presented for the firm in Exhibit 1. Disproportionately high production costs cut sharply into the company's profit margin during that year. These high production costs resulted from cost overruns on several large customer orders and from significant start-up costs incurred due to the opening of a new factory.

A subsequent investigation by the Securities and Exchange Commission (SEC) revealed that the company's senior executive and another high-ranking officer had refused to allow the firm to report its actual net income of $452,000 for 1985. To inflate the company's 1985 net income, these executives instructed three of their lower-level subordinates to overstate the firm's year-end inventory and thereby understate its cost of goods sold. When the three subordinates were reluctant to participate in the scheme, the two executives warned them that unless they cooperated, the company might "cease operations and dismiss its employees."[2] After much prodding, the three subordinates capitulated and began systematically overstating the firm's 1985 year-end inventory.

---

1. H. Anderson, "12 More Ex-Equity Officials Get Jail, Fine or Probation," *Los Angeles Times*, 25 March 1975, Sections 3, 9, and 11.

2. This and all subsequent quotations were taken from Securities and Exchange Commission, *Accounting and Auditing Enforcement Release No. 212*, 9 January 1989.

EXHIBIT 1

RMUC, INC.,
SELECTED FINANCIAL
DATA, 1981–1985

RMUC, Inc. Selected Financial Data, 1981–1985 (000s omitted)					
	1985	**1984**	**1983**	**1982**	**1981**
Net sales	$39,505	$32,167	$25,697	$21,063	$17,851
Cost of sales	32,415	24,199	19,700	16,590	14,358
Selling, general & administrative expenses	5,791	4,523	3,405	2,694	2,454
Net income	452	1,529	1,153	756	378
Total assets	24,808	14,745	11,134	6,916	5,529
Stockholders' equity	11,263	6,999	3,510	3,469	2,714
Current assets	20,924	12,678	9,648	5,779	4,639
Accounts receivable	7,115	4,725	3,734	2,608	1,290
Inventory	12,158	7,507	5,694	2,869	3,045
Current liabilities	7,302	6,999	3,510	3,469	2,714

Following [the two executives'] specific instructions, the three RMUC employees inflated quantity figures on selected count sheets by adding numerals to the accurate quantity figures per item which had been previously recorded thereon during the physical inventory count. The three RMUC employees then multiplied the inflated quantity figures per item on the count sheets by the actual unit cost per item and recorded the resulting false and inflated cost figures on the count sheets.

While the three lower-level employees were overstating RMUC's inventory, the two company executives who concocted the scheme periodically telephoned them to check on their progress. At one point, the three subordinates indicated that they were unwilling to continue falsifying RMUC's year-end inventory quantities. However, after additional coaxing and cajoling by the two executives, they resumed their fraudulent activities. Eventually, the three employees "manufactured" more than $900,000 of bogus inventory. After RMUC's senior executive reviewed and approved the falsified inventory count sheets, the count sheets were forwarded to the company's independent audit firm.

To further overstate RMUC's December 31, 1985, inventory, the company's senior executive instructed another RMUC employee to obtain a false confirmation letter from Stretchlon Industries, Inc. Stretchlon supplied RMUC with most of the elastic needed in its manufacturing processes. At the time, RMUC had an agreement to purchase 50 percent of Stretchlon's common stock at net book value. On December 31, 1985, Stretchlon had in its possession only a nominal amount of RMUC inventory. Nevertheless, a Stretchlon executive agreed to supply a confirmation letter to RMUC's independent auditors indicating that his firm held approximately $165,000 of RMUC inventory at the end of 1985. As a condition for providing the confirmation, the Stretchlon executive insisted that RMUC prepare and forward to him a false shipping document to corroborate the existence of the fictitious inventory. After receiving this shipping document, the Stretchlon executive signed the false confirmation and mailed it to RMUC's independent audit firm.

The fraudulent schemes engineered by RMUC's executives overstated the firm's December 31, 1985, inventory by approximately $1,076,000. Instead of reporting inventory of $12,158,000, in its original December 31, 1985, balance sheet, RMUC reported inventory of $13,234,000. The overstatement of inventory boosted RMUC's reported net income for 1985 to $1,059,000, which was more than $600,000 higher than the actual figure.

EXHIBIT 2

Footnote
Disclosure of
RMUC's Inventory
Fraud

> Subsequent to the issuance of its financial statements for the year ended December 31, 1985, the Company determined that inventory as reported was misstated. The accompanying financial statements have been restated to reflect correction of such misstatement. The significant effects of restatement were to reduce inventories $1,076,000, increase cost of sales $1,140,000, increase selling, general and administrative expenses $40,000, and reduce net income $607,000 from the amounts previously reported.

Near the completion of the 1985 audit, RMUC's auditors asked the company's senior executive to sign a letter of representations. Among other items, this letter indicated that the executive was not aware of any irregularities [fraud] involving the company's financial statements. The letter also stated that RMUC's financial statements fairly reflected its financial condition as of the end of 1985 and its operating results for that year. Shortly after receiving the signed letter of representations, RMUC's audit firm issued an unqualified opinion on the firm's 1985 financial statements.

Following the SEC's discovery of the fraudulent misrepresentations in RMUC's 1985 financial statements, the federal agency filed civil charges against the firm's two executives involved in the fraud. The SEC eventually settled these charges by obtaining a court order that prohibited the executives from engaging in any further violations of federal securities laws. RMUC also issued corrected financial statements for 1985. Exhibit 2 presents a footnote included in those financial statements. That footnote describes the inventory-related misstatements in the company's original 1985 financial statements.

Questions

1. Did the overstatement of RMUC's inventory at the end of 1985 materially affect the company's reported financial data for that year? Defend your answer.

2. What audit procedures might have prevented or detected the overstatements of RMUC's inventory quantities at the end of 1985?

3. How did RMUC's buyout option for Stretchlon affect the quality of the evidence provided by the inventory confirmation letter, if at all? Explain.

4. Refer to Exhibit 2. In your view, did the footnote included in that exhibit adequately describe the misrepresentations in RMUC's original financial statements for 1985? Why or why not?

5. How would you have reacted if you had been one of the employees pressured by RMUC's executives to misrepresent the company's 1985 year-end inventory? Before responding, identify the alternative courses of action that would have been available to you.

SECTION 3

INTERNAL CONTROL ISSUES

3

CASE 3.1

The Trolley Dodgers

In 1890, the Brooklyn Trolley Dodgers professional baseball team joined the National League. Over the following years, the Dodgers would have considerable difficulty competing with the other baseball teams in the New York City area. Those teams, principal among them the New York Yankees, were much better financed and generally stocked with players of higher caliber.

After nearly seven decades of mostly frustration on and off the baseball field, the Dodgers shocked the sports world by moving to Los Angeles in 1958. Walter O'Malley, the flamboyant owner of the Dodgers, saw an opportunity to introduce professional baseball to the rapidly growing population of the West Coast. More important, O'Malley saw an opportunity to make his team more profitable. As an inducement to the Dodgers, Los Angeles County purchased a goat farm located in Chavez Ravine, an area two miles northwest of downtown Los Angeles, and gave the property to O'Malley for the site of his new baseball stadium.

Since moving to Los Angeles, the Dodgers have been the envy of the baseball world: "In everything from profit to stadium maintenance ... the Dodgers are the prototype of how a franchise should be run."[1] During the 1980s and 1990s, the Dodgers reigned as the most profitable franchise in baseball with a pretax profit margin approaching 25 percent in many years. In late 1997, Peter O'Malley, Walter O'Malley's son and the Dodgers' principal owner, sold the franchise for $350 million to media mogul Rupert Murdoch. A spokesman for Murdoch complimented the O'Malley family for the longstanding success of the Dodgers organization: "The O'Malleys have set a gold standard for franchise ownership."[2]

During an interview before he sold the Dodgers, Peter O'Malley attributed the success of his organization to the experts he had retained in all functional areas: "I don't have to be an expert on taxes, split-fingered fastballs, or labor relations with our ushers. That talent is all available."[3]

Edward Campos, a longtime accountant for the Dodgers, was a seemingly perfect example of one of those experts in the Dodgers organization. Campos accepted an entry-level position with the Dodgers as a young man. By 1986, after almost two decades with the club, he had worked his way up the employment hierarchy to become the operations payroll chief.

After taking charge of the Dodgers' payroll department, Campos designed and implemented a new payroll system, a system that only he fully understood. In fact, Campos controlled the system so completely that he personally filled out the weekly payroll cards for each of the 400 employees of the Dodgers. Campos was known not only for his work ethic but also for his loyalty to the club and its owners: "The Dodgers trusted him, and when he was on vacation, he even came back and did the payroll."[4]

---

1. R. J. Harris, "Forkball for Dodgers: Costs Up, Gate Off," *The Wall Street Journal*, 31 August 1990, B1, B4.

2. R. Newhan, "Dodger Sale Heads for Home," *Los Angeles Times*, 5 September 1997, C1, C12.

3. Harris, "Forkball for Dodgers," B1.

4. P. Feldman, "7 Accused of Embezzling $332,583 from Dodgers," *Los Angeles Times*, 17 September 1986, Sec. 2, 1, 6.

Unfortunately, the Dodgers' trust in Campos was misplaced. Over a period of several years, Campos embezzled several hundred thousand dollars from his employer. According to court records, Campos padded the Dodgers' payroll by adding fictitious employees to various departments in the organization. In addition, Campos routinely inflated the number of hours worked by several employees and then split the resulting overpayments 50–50 with those individuals.

The fraudulent scheme came unraveled when appendicitis struck down Campos, forcing the Dodgers' controller to temporarily assume his responsibilities. While completing the payroll one week, the controller noticed that several employees, including ushers, security guards, and ticket salespeople, were being paid unusually large amounts. In some cases, employees earning $7 an hour received weekly paychecks approaching $2,000. Following a criminal investigation and the filing of charges against Campos and his cohorts, all the individuals involved in the payroll fraud confessed.

A state court sentenced Campos to eight years in prison and required him to make restitution of approximately $132,000 to the Dodgers. Another of the conspirators also received a prison sentence. The remaining individuals involved in the payroll scheme made restitution and were placed on probation.

Questions

1. Identify the key audit objectives for a client's payroll function. Comment on objectives related to tests of controls and substantive audit procedures.

2. What internal control weaknesses were evident in the Dodgers' payroll system?

3. Identify audit procedures that might have led to the discovery of the fraudulent scheme masterminded by Campos.

Howard Street Jewelers, Inc.

Lore Levi was worried as she scanned the March 1983 bank statement for the Howard Street Jewelers.[1] For more than four decades, she and her husband, Julius, had owned and operated the small business. Certainly the business had experienced ups and downs before, but now it seemed to be in a downward spiral from which it could not recover. In previous times when sales had slackened, the Levis had survived by cutting costs here and there. But now, despite several measures the Levis had taken to control costs, the business's cash position continued to steadily worsen. If a turnaround did not occur soon, Mrs. Levi feared that she and her husband might be forced to close their store.

Mrs. Levi had a theory regarding the financial problems of Howard Street Jewelers. On more than one occasion, she had wondered whether Betty the cashier, a trusted and reliable employee for nearly 20 years, might be stealing from the cash register. To Mrs. Levi, it was a logical assumption. Besides working as a part-time sales clerk, Betty handled all of the cash that came into the business and maintained the cash receipts and sales records. If anybody had an opportunity to steal from the business, it was Betty.

Reluctantly, Mrs. Levi approached her husband about her theory. Mrs. Levi pointed out to Julius that Betty had unrestricted access to the cash receipts of the business. Additionally, over the previous few years, Betty had developed a taste for more expensive clothes and more frequent and costly vacations. Julius quickly dismissed his wife's speculation. To him, it was preposterous to even briefly consider the possibility that Betty could be stealing from the business. A frustrated Mrs. Levi then raised the subject with her son, Alvin, who worked side by side with his parents in the family business. Alvin responded similarly to his father and warned his mother that she was becoming paranoid.

Near the end of each year, the Levis met with their accountant to discuss various matters, principally taxation issues. The Levis placed considerable trust in the CPA who served as their accountant; for almost 40 years he had given them solid, professional advice on a wide range of accounting and business matters. It was only natural for Mrs. Levi to confide in the accountant about her suspicions regarding Betty the cashier. The accountant listened intently to Mrs. Levi and then commented that he had noticed occasional shortages in the cash receipts records that seemed larger than normal for a small retail business. Despite Julius's protestations that Betty could not be responsible for any cash shortages, the accountant encouraged the Levis to closely monitor her work.

Embezzlements are often discovered by luck rather than by design. So it was with the Howard Street Jewelers. In the spring of 1985, a customer approached the cash register and told Alvin Levi that she wanted to make a payment on a layaway item.

---

1. Most of the facts of this case were reconstructed from information included in several legal opinions. The following two articles served as additional sources for this case: *Securities Regulation and Law Report,* "Accounting & Disclosure: Accounting Briefs," Vol. 23, No. 21 (24 May 1991), 814; *Securities Regulation and Law Report,* "Accounting & Disclosure: Accounting Briefs," Vol. 24, No. 19 (8 May 1992), 708.

Alvin, who was working the cash register because it was Betty's day off, searched the file of layaway sales tickets and the daily sales records but found no trace of the customer's layaway purchase. Finally, he apologized and asked the customer to return the next day when Betty would be back at work.

The following day, Alvin told Betty that he was unable to find the layaway sales ticket. Betty expressed surprise and said she would search for the ticket herself. Within a few minutes, Betty approached Alvin, waving the sales ticket in her hand. Alvin was stumped. He had searched the layaway sales file several times and simply could not accept Betty's explanation that the missing ticket had been there all along. Suspicious, as well, was the fact that the sale had not been recorded in the sales records—a simple oversight, Betty had explained.

As Alvin returned to his work, a troubling and sickening sensation settled into the pit of his stomach. Over the next several weeks, Alvin studied the daily sales and cash receipts records. He soon realized that his mother had been right all along. Betty, the trusted, reliable, longtime cashier of the Howard Street Jewelers, was stealing from the business. The estimated embezzlement loss suffered by Howard Street Jewelers over the term of Betty's employment approached $350,000.

Questions

1. Identify the internal control concepts that the Levis overlooked or ignored.

2. When Mrs. Levi informed the CPA of her suspicions regarding Betty, what responsibilities, if any, did the CPA have to pursue this matter? Alternately, assume that, in addition to preparing tax returns for Howard Street Jewelers, the CPA (a) *audited* the business's annual financial statements, (b) *reviewed* the annual financial statements, and (c) *compiled* the annual financial statements.

3. Assume that you have a small CPA firm and have been contacted by a husband and wife, John and Myrna Trubey, who are in the final stages of negotiating to purchase a local jewelry store. John will prepare jewelry settings, size jewelry for customers, and perform related tasks, while Myrna will be the head salesclerk. The Trubeys intend to retain four of the current employees of the jewelry store— two salesclerks, a cashier, and a college student who cleans the store, runs errands, and does various other odd jobs. They inform you that the average inventory of the jewelry store is $200,000 and that annual sales average $800,000, 30 percent of which occur in the six weeks prior to Christmas.

    The Trubeys are interested in retaining you as their accountant should they purchase the store. They know little about accounting and have no prior experience as business owners. They would require assistance in establishing an accounting system, monthly financial statements for internal use, annual financial statements to be submitted to their banker, and all necessary tax returns. John and Myrna are particularly concerned about control issues—given the dollar value of inventory that will be on hand in the store and the significant amount of cash that will be processed daily.

    You see this as an excellent opportunity to acquire a good client. However, you have not had a chance to prepare for your meeting with the Trubeys because they came in without an appointment. You do not want to ask them to come back later, since that may encourage them to check out your competitor across the street.

Required: Provide the Trubeys with an overview of the key internal control issues they will face in operating a jewelry store. In your overview, identify at least five control activities you believe they should implement if they acquire the store. You have never had a jewelry store as a client but you have several small retail clients. Attempt to impress the Trubeys with your understanding of internal control issues for small retail businesses.

Saks Fifth Avenue

Attracting customers and closing sales are challenges that face all retailers ranging from a Piggly Wiggly grocery in a small southern town to the Giorgio Armani boutique nestled among the elegant shops lining Rodeo Drive in Beverly Hills. Besides the never-ending need to produce revenues, retailers wrestle daily with many other challenges and problems that pose serious threats to their operations. Theft of cash and inventory by employees historically ranks as one of the most common threats to retail operations. Increasing numbers of employee lawsuits—lawsuits predicated on sexual harassment, racial discrimination, and related charges—also jeopardize the financial health of many retailers. Strong internal controls can significantly reduce the likelihood of losses from employee theft and from lawsuits filed by employees. Saks Fifth Avenue, an upscale merchandiser based in New York, learned that lesson firsthand in the late 1990s.

Promotions, Pay Raises, and Pilfering

In late 1993, Joseph Fierro accepted a part-time sales position with a Saks Fifth Avenue store in New York City.[1] Fierro was assigned to the Men's Polo Department of that store, a department supervised by Robert Perley. Fierro's hard work and ingenuity produced sizable sales and impressed his superior. Within a few months, Perley hired Fierro as a full-time salesperson at an annual salary of $30,000. A few months later, Perley created a new position for Fierro, "Clothing Specialist," so that he could give his star employee a 20 percent raise. By early 1996, Fierro's annual salary had risen to $46,000 on the strength of strong performance appraisals consistently given to him by Perley.

In late August 1996, Joseph Fierro purchased a shirt from another department of the Saks store in which he worked. To obtain an employee discount for the shirt, a discount that he was not entitled to receive, Fierro forged two signatures on a document used to authorize employee sales discounts. The signatures he forged were those of Robert Perley and Donna Ruffman, a coworker. Fierro also entered the transaction in one of his department's electronic cash registers using Ms. Ruffman's employee identification number. The discount saved Fierro $9.85.

Approximately one week later, two auditors from Saks' Loss Prevention Department reviewed the August transactions entered in the electronic cash registers of the Men's Polo Department. The auditors noticed the employee sales transaction entered by Ms. Ruffman. After examining the documentation for the transaction, they suspected that someone had forged the authorization signatures for the related discount. The auditors questioned several employees in the department regarding the suspicious sale, including Joseph Fierro. Fierro initially denied that he had entered the transaction in his department's cash register. When the auditors suggested that they could easily determine who initiated the transaction, Fierro recanted. He admitted originating the transaction and forging the signatures of both Perley and Ms. Ruffman. In a written statement, Fierro later apologized for the incident. "I realize

---

1. The facts and quotations appearing in this case were drawn from the following legal opinion: *Fierro v. Saks Fifth Avenue,* 13 F. Supp. 2d 481 (1998).

it was wrong to do this. I exercised poor judgment and I am truthfully sorry for what I did. I realize that something like this is wrong and it will never happen again."

After being questioned by the Loss Prevention auditors, Fierro returned to his department and discussed the matter with Perley. Perley told Fierro that he had no influence on the Loss Prevention Department's decisions but pledged to help him in any way he could. Perley later testified that he telephoned both the Loss Prevention Department and the Human Resources Department and appealed to them not to terminate Fierro.

On September 13, 1996, two representatives of Saks' Human Resources Department notified Fierro that he was being dismissed for violating company policy. They referred Fierro to Saks' employee handbook that lists specific examples of prohibited employee conduct. The preface to that section of the employees' handbook read as follows: "The following list of prohibited conduct represents essential guidelines that are so fundamental to Saks Fifth Avenue's operations that such violations must result in immediate dismissal." Saks charged Fierro with engaging in the following three acts that mandated the dismissal of an employee.

1. Theft of Saks Fifth Avenue or another associate's merchandise, property, or services;
5. Forging a signature;
28. Ringing a transaction under another associate's number or on a dummy date line when doing so results in an unauthorized or unwarranted benefit to the associate ringing the transaction.

Saks' Human Resources Department conducted an exit interview with Fierro on the date he was terminated. During this interview, Fierro again apologized for the poor judgment he had exercised. He also expressed disbelief that an "exceptional employee" could be fired for such a "trivial transgression."

He Called Me Buttafucco!

After losing his job at Saks Fifth Avenue, Fierro searched for employment in the New York City area. Among the jobs he applied for was a position with a financial services company. This company insisted on contacting Fierro's former employers. Before the prospective employer contacted Saks, Fierro called a Saks employee in the Human Resources Department who had conducted his exit interview. This individual had allegedly indicated during the exit interview that the reason Fierro was dismissed would not be disclosed to prospective employers. However, when Fierro telephoned this individual, she informed him that if asked, she would reveal the circumstances that had led to his dismissal.

Shortly after Fierro's telephone conversation with the human resources employee, he filed a discrimination lawsuit against Saks Fifth Avenue with the Equal Employment Opportunity Commission (EEOC). Fierro filed the lawsuit pursuant to Title VII of the Civil Rights Act of 1964 and the New York Human Rights Law. In his lawsuit, Fierro claimed that he was subjected to a "hostile work environment" during his employment with Saks. Fierro also claimed that Robert Perley, his supervisor, had discriminated against him because of his Italian-American heritage and that Perley had fired him in retaliation for his decision to stand up to that discriminatory treatment.

Fierro predicated his charge of discriminatory treatment upon inappropriate remarks allegedly made to him by Perley. He claimed that Perley had referred to him on occasion by a three-letter term commonly used as a slur against Italian-Americans.[2] Fierro also claimed that Perley had occasionally called him "Joey Buttafucco."[3] Finally, Perley had allegedly made an insensitive racial remark that alluded to Fierro's Hispanic wife. After Perley made the latter remark, Fierro told him that the remark was unacceptable. At that point, according to Fierro, Perley "commenced a plan to terminate him."

Fierro maintained that the discriminatory remarks allegedly made to him by Perley caused him to have low personal esteem and severely damaged his career. Those remarks also reportedly caused him to suffer "permanent psychological damage." Fierro insisted that he was haunted by images of the three-letter slur that Perley had used in referring to him: "Every time I look in the mirror I see those three letters above my head and it really hurts."

District Court Settles Fierro's Lawsuit

Federal district judge Charles Brieant presided over Fierro's lawsuit against Saks Fifth Avenue. Judge Brieant quickly rejected Fierro's claim that Perley discriminated against him. The judge also dismissed the related allegation that Saks fired Fierro for "standing up" to Perley's discriminatory treatment. Evidence presented by both Fierro and Saks suggested that rather than discriminating against Fierro, Perley considered him a valued employee and gave him glowing job performance appraisals. The evidence reviewed by Judge Brieant also suggested that Perley was not involved in Fierro's dismissal. That decision apparently was made by the Human Resources Department with considerable input from the Loss Prevention Department. In fact, as noted earlier, Perley made two telephone calls to intercede on Fierro's behalf.

Judge Brieant concluded that Saks' dismissal of Fierro was not a discriminatory action but simply a consistent application of the company's zero-tolerance policy for employee theft. The judge admitted that the theft loss Saks suffered was "relatively trivial." But he went on to note that retailers have a "strong business interest in deterring employee pilfering." Neither the Civil Rights Act of 1964, nor the New York Human Rights Law, the judge observed, prohibits employers from being "overly rigid or even harsh" in punishing employee theft. Saks' employment records demonstrated that the company consistently punished employee theft with the harsh measure of termination. For example, Saks immediately dismissed a former coworker of Fierro who was caught "booking credits to his own account."

Judge Brieant considered more seriously Fierro's claim that he was subjected to a hostile work environment. The judge invoked the following definition of a hostile work environment:

A hostile work environment exists when the workplace is permeated with discriminatory intimidation, ridicule, and insult, that is sufficiently severe or pervasive to alter the conditions of the victim's employment.

An employer can assert several defenses in an employee lawsuit that alleges a hostile work environment. Among the most credible defenses, Judge Brieant noted, is the existence of an explicit antiharassment policy. Saks had such a policy during Fierro's employment. The company also had a related complaint procedure that

2. Perley testified that he was of English, Irish, and Scandinavian descent.

3. Joey Buttafucco rose—or plunged—to infamy in the early 1990s for a highly publicized affair with an underage woman who later attempted to murder his wife. For several months, the travails of Buttafucco provided headline material for the tabloids and were the source of countless jokes for late-night comedians.

allowed employees to file a grievance against a superior or coworker for engaging in "hostile" behavior. Judge Brieant noted that Fierro never filed a grievance against Perley or his coworkers during his three years with Saks. When asked why he did not take such action, Fierro testified that "I was afraid of repercussions. If you start to conflict with your manager, before you know it it's not a very pleasant outcome." Judge Brieant found Fierro's inaction unsatisfactory.

> At some point, employees must be required to accept responsibility for alerting their employers to the possibility of harassment. Without such a requirement, it is difficult to see how Title VII's deterrent purposes are to be served, or how employers can possibly avoid liability in Title VII cases. Put simply, an employer cannot combat harassment of which it is unaware.

Fierro presented evidence supporting his contention that references to individuals' racial orientation, sexual orientation, and religious affiliation were common in his former department. However, his former coworkers testified that they intended such references to be humorous or self-deprecating. Perley denied participating "in this intended humor" of his subordinates. After reviewing the evidence presented in Fierro's lawsuit, Judge Brieant observed that Perley's department "did not adhere to the highest standards of decorum."[4] Nevertheless, he suggested that the department's work environment was not hostile but "merely offensive."

> Conduct that is merely offensive and not severe enough to create an objectively hostile or abusive work environment—an environment that a reasonable person would find hostile or abusive—is beyond Title VII's purview. Thus, for racist comments, slurs, and jokes to constitute a hostile work environment, there must be more than a few isolated incidents of racial enmity, meaning that instead of sporadic racial slurs, there must be a steady barrage of opprobrious racial comments.

In July 1998, Judge Brieant dismissed Fierro's allegation that he was subjected to a hostile work environment at Saks Fifth Avenue. The judge noted that Fierro did not make such a claim during his employment with Saks or during his exit interview. Instead, that allegation and the related discrimination charges apparently originated near the time Saks refused to give Fierro a "clean" employment reference. Judge Brieant concluded that the timing of Fierro's allegations and Saks' refusal to provide the employment reference was "hardly a coincidence."

Questions

1. In your opinion, was Saks' zero-tolerance policy for employee theft reasonable? Was the policy likely cost-effective? Defend your answers.

2. Did Saks' antiharassment policy and the related complaint procedure qualify as internal controls? Explain.

3. Identify five control activities that you would commonly find in a men's clothing department of a major department store. Identify the control objective associated with each of these activities.

4. Should a company's independent auditors be concerned with whether or not a client provides a nonhostile work environment for its employees? If your answer is "yes," identify the specific audit issues that would be relevant in this context.

---

4. Despite this observation, Judge Brieant complimented Perley for a department that "had an enviable record of diversity." The department included "men and women of African-American, Hispanic, Irish, Jewish, and Italian descent, as well as homosexuals."

Triton Energy Ltd.

Bill Lee retired in the mid-1990s from Triton Energy after leading the Dallas-based oil and gas exploration firm through three turbulent decades. During Lee's tenure, Triton discovered large oil and gas deposits in several remote sites scattered around the globe. Although adept at finding oil, Triton's small size hampered the company's efforts to exploit its oil and gas properties. Major oil firms, large metropolitan banks, and other well-heeled investors often refused to participate in the development of promising oil and gas properties discovered by Triton. Why? Because they were unnerved by Bill Lee's reputation as a run-and-gun, devil-may-care "wildcatter."

To compensate for Triton's limited access to deep-pocketed financiers, Lee resorted to less conventional strategies to achieve his firm's financial objectives. In the early 1980s, Triton struck oil in northwestern France at a site overlooked by many major oil firms. To expedite its drilling efforts and to gain an advantage over competitors that had begun snapping up leases on nearby properties, Triton formed an alliance with the state-owned petroleum firm, *Compagnie Francaise des Petroles*. This partnership proved very beneficial for Triton since it gave the firm ready access to the governmental agency that regulated France's petroleum industry. A business journalist commented on Triton's political skills as a key factor in its successful French venture. "Triton's success is due not just to sound geology but also to good politics. It has established a close relationship with the all-powerful French energy administration, which issues all new drilling permits."[1]

Triton's policy of working closely with government agencies and bureaucrats landed the company in trouble with U.S. authorities during the 1990s. Charges that Triton bribed foreign officials to obtain favorable treatment from governmental agencies led to investigations of the company's overseas operations by the U. S. Department of Justice and the Securities and Exchange Commission (SEC). These investigations centered on alleged violations of the Foreign Corrupt Practices Act of 1977 (FCPA), including the accounting and internal control stipulations of that federal statute.

A Brief History of a Texas Wildcatter

L. R. Wiley founded Triton Energy Corporation, the predecessor of Triton Energy Ltd., in 1962. At the time, industry analysts estimated that there were approximately 30,000 businesses involved in oil and gas exploration, most of which were small "Mom and Pop," or simply "Pop," operations. The volatile ups and downs of the petroleum industry dramatically thinned the ranks of oil and gas producers during the 1960s and 1970s. The oil bust of the 1980s wiped out most of the surviving firms in the industry. Less than 20 significant "independent" oil and gas producers remained in business by 1985.[2] Triton Energy was one of those firms.

---

1. P. Kemezis and W. Glasgall, "A Texas Wildcatter Cashes In on French Oil," *Business Week*, 13 May 1985, 106–107.

2. The dominant companies in the oil and gas industry include such firms as ExxonMobil and ConocoPhillips. These firms are often referred to as the "majors" or simply as "Big Oil."

Bill Lee joined Triton in the early 1960s and was promoted to chief executive officer (CEO) in 1966. Under Lee, Triton competed in the rough-and-tumble business of oil and gas exploration by employing a rough-and-tumble business strategy. Lee recognized that the large domestic oil firms in the U.S. had already identified the prime drilling sites in this country. So Lee decided that Triton should focus its exploration efforts in other oil-producing countries, particularly in regions of those countries largely overlooked by "Big Oil." During Lee's tenure with Triton, the company launched exploration ventures in Argentina, Australia, Canada, Columbia, France, Indonesia, Malaysia, New Zealand, and Thailand.

In the early 1970s, Triton discovered a large oil and gas field in the Gulf of Thailand. Recurring disagreements and confrontations with the Thai government stymied Triton from developing that field for more than 10 years. Lee's experience with the Thai government taught him an important lesson: if Triton's exploration ventures were to be successful in foreign countries, the company had to foster good relationships with key governmental officials in those countries.

Lee created Triton Indonesia, Inc., a wholly owned subsidiary of Triton Energy, to develop an oil field that the company acquired in Indonesia in 1988. This oil field, located on the island of Sumatra and known as the Enim Field, belonged to a Dutch firm in the 1930s. At the time, Sumatra was a protectorate of the Netherlands. When the Japanese invaded Indonesia during World War II, retreating Dutch soldiers dynamited the Enim Field to render it useless to Japan. Over the next four decades, the dense jungles of Sumatra reclaimed the oil field. In the mid-1980s, Lee learned of the potential oil reserves still buried in the Enim Field. A small Canadian company owned the drilling rights for those reserves. Triton wrested control of the drilling rights from that company in a protracted legal battle. After investing several million dollars and several years of hard work in the Enim Field, Triton began pumping thousands of barrels each day from the long dormant oil reservoir.

Triton's strategy of working closely with officials of the Indonesian government contributed greatly to the success of the Enim Field project. To strengthen Triton's ties to those officials, the company hired a French citizen, Roland Siouffi, as a consultant. Siouffi, who had resided in Indonesia for nearly three decades, served as Triton's liaison with Indonesian tax authorities and with governmental agencies that oversaw the country's oil and gas industry.

In 1991, Triton struck black gold again, this time in Columbia. Several large firms had drilled exploratory wells in the foothills of the Andes Mountains that stretch across Columbia. Those wells came up dry. Nevertheless, geological reports convinced Lee and other Triton executives that the region contained large but well-hidden oil reservoirs. Lee and his colleagues were right. In 1991, Triton pinpointed huge oil and gas deposits trapped in complex geological structures lying beneath the Columbian jungles. These reservoirs were the largest discovered in the western hemisphere since the 1968 Prudhoe Bay discovery in Alaska. Again, Triton established close working relationships with governmental officials, this time in Columbia, to develop the new oil field.

On the strength of Triton's Indonesian and Columbian oil strikes, the company's stock skied from a few dollars per share in the late 1980s to more than $50 per share in 1991.[3] Triton's common stock ranked as one of the 10 best performing stocks on the New York Stock Exchange in 1991. Despite the company's obvious knack for finding oil, many Wall Street analysts refused to recommend Triton's common stock. Rumors of the bribing of foreign officials, allegations of creative accounting methods,

---

3. D. Galant, "The Home Runs of 1991," *Institutional Investor*, March 1992, 51–56.

and intimations of other corporate wrongdoings soured these analysts on Triton. One Wall Street portfolio manager succinctly summed up his view of Triton. "Bill Lee is not a guy I'd like to see running an oil company I had invested in."[4]

The allegations of abusive management practices and creative accounting caught up with Triton in the mid-1990s. Those allegations persuaded the U.S. Department of Justice and the SEC to probe Triton's ties to government officials in foreign countries. The principal focus of this investigation was the relationships that Triton executives had cultivated with Indonesian officials during the development of the Enim Field.

The central issue addressed by U.S. authorities while investigating Triton was whether the company had violated a seldom-enforced federal statute, the Foreign Corrupt Practices Act of 1977 (FCPA). The FCPA was a by-product of the scandal-ridden Watergate era of the 1970s. During the Watergate investigations, the Office of the Special Prosecutor uncovered numerous bribes, kickbacks, and other payments made by U.S. corporations to officials of foreign governments to initiate or maintain business relationships. Widespread public disapproval compelled Congress to pass the FCPA, which criminalizes most such payments. The FCPA also requires U.S. companies to maintain internal control systems that provide reasonable assurance of discovering improper foreign payments.

> *The accounting provisions [of the FCPA] were enacted by Congress along with the anti-bribery provisions because Congress concluded that almost all bribery of foreign officials by American corporations was covered up in the corporations' books and that the requirement for accurate records and adequate internal controls would deter bribery.*[5]

Exhibit 1 summarizes the FCPA's key anti-bribery and internal control requirements.

EXHIBIT 1

KEY PROVISIONS OF THE FOREIGN CORRUPT PRACTICES ACT

Anti-Bribery Provisions:

Section 30 (A) of the Securities Exchange Act, the anti-bribery provision of the FCPA, prohibits any issuer . . . or any officer, director, employee, or agent of an issuer from making use of instruments or interstate commerce corruptly to pay, offer to pay, promise to pay, or to authorize the payment of any money, gift, or promise to give, anything of value to any foreign official for purposes of influencing any act or decision of such foreign official in his official capacity, or inducing such foreign official to do or omit to do any act in violation of the lawful duty of such official, or inducing such foreign official to use his influence with a foreign government or instrumentality thereof to affect or influence any act or decision of such government or instrumentality, in order to assist such issuer in obtaining or retaining business for or with, or directing business to, any person.

Recordkeeping and Internal Control Provisions:

Section 13(b)(2) of the Securities Exchange Act is comprised of two accounting provisions referred to as the "books and records" and "internal controls" provisions. These accounting provisions were enacted as part of the FCPA to strengthen the accuracy of records and to "promote the reliability and completeness of financial information that issuers are required to file with the Commission or disseminate to investors pursuant to the Securities Exchange Act." Section 13(b)(2)(A) requires issuers to make and keep books, records, and accounts that accurately and fairly reflect the transactions and dispositions of their assets. Section 13(b)(2)(B)

---

4. T. Mack, "Lucky Bill Lee," *Forbes*, 14 October 1991, 50.

5. This quotation and the remaining quotations in this case, unless indicated otherwise, were drawn from the following source: Securities and Exchange Commission, *Accounting and Auditing Enforcement Release No. 889*, 27 February 1997.

EXHIBIT 1—
continued

KEY PROVISIONS
OF THE FOREIGN
CORRUPT PRACTICES
ACT

requires issuers to devise and maintain a system of internal accounting controls sufficient to provide reasonable assurances that, among other things, transactions are executed in accordance with management's general or specific authorization and that transactions are recorded as necessary to permit presentation of financial statements in conformity with GAAP and to maintain accountability for assets.

Source: Securities and Exchange Commission, *Accounting and Auditing Enforcement Release No. 889,* 27 February 1997.

Indonesian Charges

Triton Energy's former controller sued the company in 1991, claiming that he had been fired in 1989 after refusing to sign off on the company's Form 10-K registration statement. The controller refused to sign off on the 1989 10-K because it failed to disclose "bribery, kickbacks, and payments to government officials, customs officials, auditors, inspectors and other persons in positions of responsibility in Indonesia, Columbia, and Argentina."[6] The controller acknowledged that Triton's senior management had not authorized the payments but insisted that the FCPA required such payments to be disclosed in the company's 10-K. Before the case went to trial, Triton officials dismissed the charges, suggesting that they were "totally without merit."[7] During the trial, considerable evidence surfaced supporting the controller's allegations. A memo written by Triton's former internal audit director contained the most damaging of this evidence.

In late 1989, Triton management sent the company's new internal audit director to review and report on Triton Indonesia's operations. Upon returning, the internal audit director filed a lengthy memorandum with several Triton executives, including the company's president and at least two key vice presidents. Exhibit 2 presents selected excerpts from that memo. The memo documented extensive wrongdoing by employees and officials of Triton Indonesia. At one point, the frustrated internal audit director complained that the subsidiary's accounting records were so misleading it was impossible "to tell a real transaction from one that has been faked."[8]

EXHIBIT 2

SELECTED EXCERPTS
FROM THE INTERNAL
AUDIT MEMO
REGARDING
OPERATIONS OF
TRITON INDONESIA

"In Indonesia, I found myself in a country of state supported corruption."

"I was told that we pay between $1,000 and $1,900 per month just to get our invoice to Pertamina [the state-owned Indonesian oil company] paid."

"We must pay people in customs in order to get our equipment off the dock so that it can be used in operations."

"What is worse, and this is extremely confidential, is that we paid the auditors in order to have their audit exceptions taken care of. . . . This part is particularly bad to me. I had hoped that at least the Indonesian auditors were honest."

Source: A. Zipser, "Crude Grab?" *Barron's,* 25 May 1992, 12–15.

---

6. A. Zipser, "Crude Grab?" *Barron's,* 25 May 1992, 15.

7. Mack, "Lucky Bill Lee."

8. A. Zipser, "Trials of Triton," *Barron's,* 26 July 1993, 14–15.

After reading the memo, the alarmed Triton executives ordered that all copies be collected and destroyed. Despite these instructions, one copy of the memo survived and became a key exhibit in the lawsuit filed against Triton by its former controller.

Another former Triton accountant also corroborated many of the former controller's allegations. This individual, who had previously served as a Price Waterhouse auditor, joined Triton Indonesia's accounting staff in early 1989. Almost immediately, the accountant discovered serious internal control deficiencies in the subsidiary's operations. Inadequate segregation of key accounting and control responsibilities created an environment in which individuals could easily perpetrate and then conceal fraudulent transactions. The accountant's most serious charge regarding his former employer involved an admission made by his superior. The superior told the accountant that auditors from Pertamina, the state-owned Indonesian oil firm, had been "bought" by Triton. Among other responsibilities, these auditors regularly reviewed Triton Indonesia's tax records. "I understood the words 'buy the audit' to mean bribe Pertamina auditors. To me, it represented an illegal transaction, the proposal of an illegal transaction."[9]

Coworkers reportedly shunned the accountant after he objected to such conduct. A few weeks later, the accountant resigned. Because he was concerned that his brief tenure with Triton Indonesia might blight his professional career, the accountant filed a 37-page report with the U.S. embassy in Indonesia. That report documented questionable transactions, events, and circumstances he had encountered during his employment with Triton Indonesia. In the report, the accountant described his former superiors as "unprincipled, unethical liars."[10]

Peat Marwick served as Triton Energy's audit firm over a span of more than two decades beginning in 1969. During the planning phase for the 1991 audit, Peat Marwick learned of the memorandum written by Triton's former internal audit director. A Peat Marwick auditor questioned client management concerning the unlawful activities allegedly documented in that memo. Company officials convinced Peat Marwick that all copies of the memo had been destroyed. A Triton executive then prepared a memo responding to Peat Marwick's inquiries. This second memo omitted many key details of questionable activities documented by the internal audit director. At a subsequent meeting with Peat Marwick representatives, Triton management directly refuted the principal allegation reportedly included in the internal audit memo. Several Triton officials told Peat Marwick that there was no evidence Triton Indonesia officers or employees had bribed Indonesian auditors.[11]

In the summer of 1992, the jury that heard the lawsuit filed by Triton's former controller ruled in his favor and awarded him a $124 million judgment. That judgment ranks as one of the largest wrongful termination awards ever handed down by a U.S. court.[12] Following the trial, the surviving copy of the memo written by Triton's former internal audit director became a road map for federal authorities to follow while investigating Triton's abusive management and accounting practices.

---

9. Zipser, "Crude Grab?" 13.

10. *Ibid.*, 14.

11. In 1992, Triton Energy retained Price Waterhouse to serve as its audit firm, replacing Peat Marwick.

12. The judgment was subsequently reduced in a private, out-of-court settlement involving the former controller, Triton, and Triton's insurer. The former controller received approximately $10 million from Triton and an undisclosed additional sum from Triton's insurer. Shortly before the jury verdict was announced, the former controller had offered to settle the case for $5 million.

Results of SEC Investigation

Triton Indonesia negotiated a contract with the Indonesian government for the right to develop the Enim Field. This contract made the nation's state-owned oil company, Pertamina, a partner in the project. The agreement gave the Triton subsidiary operational and financial control over the joint venture but allowed Pertamina to review and override all-important decisions involving the project. Another feature of the agreement required Triton Indonesia to transport oil recovered from the Enim Field through Pertamina's pipelines. Finally, the agreement obligated Triton Indonesia to pay significant taxes to the Indonesian government on the basis of the Enim Field's production.

Two Indonesian audit teams periodically examined Triton Indonesia's accounting and tax records. Pertamina auditors reviewed the accounting records to ensure that the Triton subsidiary complied with its contractual obligations to Pertamina. Auditors from the Indonesian Ministry of Finance and Pertamina auditors inspected the tax records to ensure that the proper taxes were being paid to the Indonesian government. The Ministry of Finance auditors were known as the "BPKP" auditors since they worked for the agency's audit branch, *Badan Pengawasan Keuangan Dan Pembangunan*.

Pertamina and BPKP auditors concluded a joint tax audit of a Triton Indonesia operating unit in May 1989. The audit revealed that the unit owed approximately $618,000 of additional taxes. Of this total, $385,000 involved taxes levied by Pertamina auditors, while the remaining $233,000 were taxes assessed by BPKP auditors. Two officers of Triton Indonesia discussed this matter with Roland Siouffi, the longtime Indonesian resident hired the year before to serve as a liaison with government officials. Siouffi then met with two key members of the Pertamina audit team. Siouffi arranged to pay these two individuals $160,000 to eliminate the additional tax assessment of $385,000 proposed by the Pertamina auditors. Triton Indonesia paid $165,000 to a company controlled by Siouffi in August 1989.[13] A few weeks later, that company paid $120,000 and $40,000, respectively, to the two Pertamina auditors. Triton Indonesia's controller prepared false documentation for the payment made to Siouffi's company. The documentation indicated that the payment was for seismic data purchased for the Enim Field.

In August 1989, a BPKP auditor reminded Triton Indonesia officials that their firm still owed $233,000 of taxes. An executive of Triton Indonesia discussed this matter with Siouffi. After meeting with the BPKP auditor, Siouffi told Triton Indonesia's management that in exchange for $20,000 the auditor would reduce the $233,000 tax bill to $155,000. Triton Indonesia processed a $22,500 payment to another company controlled by Siouffi, who then paid the BPKP auditor $20,000. Triton Indonesia's controller prepared false documentation indicating that the payment to Siouffi's company was for equipment repairs at the Enim Field made by Siouffi's employees. Following the payments made to the Pertamina and BPKP auditors by Siouffi, Triton Indonesia received letters from the two audit teams indicating that they had resolved the issues raised during the tax audit.

Throughout 1989 and 1990, Triton Indonesia continued to channel improper payments to various government officials through Roland Siouffi. Triton Indonesia fabricated false documentation to "sanitize" each payment for accounting purposes. The SEC identified $450,000 of such payments recorded in Triton Indonesia's accounting records.

Triton Indonesia officers periodically briefed key members of Triton Energy's management regarding the payoffs funneled through Siouffi. In these briefings, the Triton

---

13. Triton Indonesia paid Siouffi a "commission" for the illegal payments he funneled to government officials. In this case, the commission was $5,000.

Energy officers also learned of the false accounting entries and documentation prepared to conceal the true nature of the payments. "The Triton Energy officers expressed concern about such practices which they had neither directed nor authorized, but failed to require Triton Indonesia to discontinue those practices." At one point, a Triton Indonesia officer directly told Triton Energy's president that illicit payments were being made to Siouffi. The president responded "that he had worked in another foreign country and understood that such things had to be done in certain environments."[14]

SEC Sends a Message

In 1997, the SEC climaxed a four-year investigation of Triton Indonesia and its parent company by issuing a series of enforcement releases. Those releases charged Triton and its executives with violating the anti-bribery, accounting, and control requirements of the FCPA. Without admitting or denying these charges, six officers of Triton Energy and Triton Indonesia signed consent decrees that prohibited them from violating federal securities laws in the future. The consent decrees also imposed a $300,000 fine on Triton Energy and fines of $35,000 and $50,000 on two former Triton Indonesia officers. Exhibit 3 presents the footnote appended to Triton Energy's 1996 financial statements that described the company's settlement with the SEC.

Although Triton Energy did not authorize the improper payments and the bogus accounting for the payments, the SEC sharply criticized two executives who were aware of the practices and allowed them to continue unchecked:

> The senior management of Triton Energy, ____ and ____, simply acknowledged the existence of such practices and treated them as a cost of doing business in a foreign jurisdiction. The toleration of such practices is inimical to a fair business environment and undermines public confidence in the integrity of public corporations.

The SEC publicly conceded that it intended the Triton case to send a "message" to corporate managers. SEC officials noted that the case "underscored the responsibilities of corporate management in the area of foreign payments"[15] and impressed upon U.S. companies that "it's not O.K. to pay bribes as long as you don't get caught."[16]

EXHIBIT 3

TRITON ENERGY'S DISCLOSURE OF SEC SETTLEMENT IN 1996 FINANCIAL STATEMENT FOOTNOTES

In February 1997, the Company and the Securities and Exchange Commission (SEC) concluded a settlement of the SEC's investigation of possible violations of the Foreign Corrupt Practices Act in connection with Triton Indonesia, Inc.'s former operations in Indonesia. The investigation was settled on a "consent decree" basis in which the Company neither admitted nor denied charges made by the SEC that the Company violated the Securities Exchange Act of 1934 when Triton Indonesia, Inc. made certain payments in 1989 and 1990 to a consultant advising Triton Indonesia, Inc. on its relations with the Indonesian state oil company and tax authority, misbooked the payments and failed to maintain adequate internal controls. Under the terms of the settlement, the Company's subsidiary, TEC, was permanently enjoined from future violations of the books and records and internal control provisions of the Securities Exchange Act of 1934 and paid a civil monetary penalty of $300,000. In 1996, the Company was advised that the Department of Justice had concluded a parallel inquiry without taking any action.

---

14. Apparently, the attention drawn to the illicit payments by the lawsuit filed by Triton Energy's former controller caused Triton Indonesia to stop making those payments.

15. *Securities Regulation and Law Report*, "SEC Official Predicts More FCPA Cases in Near Future," Vol. 29, No. 18 (2 May 1997), 607.

16. L. Eaton, "Triton Energy Settles Indonesia Bribery Case for $300,000," *The New York Times*, 28 February 1997, D2.

Prior to the Triton case, more than 10 years had elapsed since the SEC had filed FCPA-related charges against a public company. During the late 1990s, frequent allegations of improper foreign payments by U.S. corporations prompted the SEC to initiate several FCPA investigations. The SEC attributes the apparent increase in such payments to the increasingly global nature of U.S. corporations.[17] Each year, additional U.S. companies attempt to establish footholds in emerging markets. Funneling unlawful payments to officials of foreign countries is often the most effective method of breaking down entry barriers to those markets.

The growing sophistication of illicit foreign payment schemes complicates the SEC's efforts to rigorously enforce the FCPA. In fact, critics of the FCPA suggest that it is practically unenforceable except in the most blatant cases. As one journalist noted, the days of "bulky cash payments in large sealed envelopes" are long past.

> *Now the bribes, kickbacks, and "facilitating payments," such as those described in Triton Energy's internal memorandum, more often get channeled through expensive "consultants," dummy charities, and construction projects that never seem to materialize.*[18]

Many corporate executives have lobbied against enforcement of the FCPA. These executives maintain that the federal law places U.S. multinational companies at a significant competitive disadvantage relative to other multinational firms. A member of President Clinton's administration supported this point of view when he observed that the U.S. is the only country that has "criminalized bribery of foreign officials."[19,20]

EPILOGUE

Bill Lee was never directly implicated in the Indonesian payments scandal and retired as Triton Energy's CEO in January 1993. The SEC sanctioned the Triton executives involved in that scandal. All of those executives subsequently resigned their positions with the company. Thomas Finck, who came to Triton after the Indonesian scandal, replaced Lee as Triton's CEO. In 1996, a journalist noted that Triton's new CEO seemed to be employing some of his predecessor's "old tricks."[21] One of Finck's first major decisions was to reorganize Triton Energy as a subsidiary of an offshore holding company headquartered in the Cayman Islands. Finck reported that moving Triton's headquarters to the Cayman Islands would significantly reduce the company's tax burden. Critics placed a different spin on the decision. They suggested that the company's desire "to avoid scrutiny under the U.S. Foreign Corrupt Practices Act"[22] likely motivated the move to the Caymans.

Triton Energy sold its Indonesian subsidiary in 1996 but under Finck continued its high-risk strategy of searching for obscure and overlooked oil fields across the globe. Depressed oil prices caused the value of Triton's sizable oil reserves to fall dramatically during the 1990s, leaving the company in a financial lurch

---

17. *Securities Regulation and Law Report*, "SEC Official Predicts More FCPA Cases."

18. A. Zipser, "A Rarely Enforced Law," *Barron's*, 25 May 1992, 14.

19. *Ibid.*

20. The FCPA was initially unclear regarding whether or not so-called "facilitating payments" qualified as bribes and thus were illegal under that federal statute. Generally, bribes are significant amounts paid to foreign governmental officials to secure or retain business, while facilitating payments are relatively modest and routine payments typically made to lower-ranking governmental officials to expedite or "facilitate" business transactions. In 1988, the FCPA was amended to address that issue. As amended, facilitating payments made to encourage "routine governmental action" are not covered by the FCPA.

21. A. Zipser, "New Management, Old Tricks as Oil Firm Heads for Caymans," *Barron's*, 25 March 1996, 10.

22. *Ibid.*

in early 1998. Company officials announced that Triton was for sale and retained an investment banking firm to find a potential buyer. When a buyer could not be found, Triton announced plans to restructure its operations and to continue as an independent entity. That announcement caused Triton's stock to plummet to its lowest level in several years and prompted Thomas Finck to resign as the company's CEO. A few years later, in the summer of 2001, Triton Energy's tumultuous history as an independent firm ended when Amerada Hess purchased the company for a reported $2.7 billion.

Questions

1. Identify the key factors that complicate the audit of a multinational company.

2. Identify specific control activities that Triton Energy could have implemented for Triton Indonesia and its other foreign subsidiaries to minimize the likelihood of illegal payments to government officials. Would these control activities have been cost-effective?

3. Does an audit firm of a multinational company have a responsibility to apply audit procedures intended to determine whether the client has complied with the FCPA? Defend your answer.

4. If a company employs a high-risk business strategy, does that necessarily increase the inherent risk and control risk components of audit risk for the company? Explain.

5. What responsibility, if any, does an accountant of a public company have when he or she discovers that the company has violated a law? How does the accountant's position on the company's employment hierarchy affect that responsibility, if at all? What responsibility does an auditor of a public company have if he or she discovers illegal acts by the client? Does the auditor's position on his or her firm's employment hierarchy affect this responsibility?

6. If the citizens of certain foreign countries believe that the payment of bribes is an acceptable business practice, is it appropriate for U.S. companies to challenge that belief when doing business in those countries? Defend your answer.

CASE 3.5

Goodner Brothers, Inc.

"Woody, that's $2,400 you owe me. Okay? We're straight on that?"

"Yeah, yeah. I got you."

"And you'll pay me back by next Friday?"

"Al. I said I'd pay you back by Friday, didn't I?"

"Just checkin'."

Borrowing money from a friend can strain even the strongest relationship. When the borrowed money will soon be plunked down on a blackjack table, the impact on the friendship can be devastating.

Woody Robinson and Al Hunt were sitting side by side at a blackjack table in Tunica, Mississippi. The two longtime friends and their wives were spending their summer vacations together as they had several times. After three days loitering in the casinos that line the banks of the Mississippi River 20 miles south of Memphis, Woody found himself hitting up his friend for loans. By the end of the vacation, Woody owed Al nearly $5,000. The question facing Woody was how would he repay his friend.[1]

Two Pals Named Woody and Al

Woodrow Wilson Robinson and Albert Leroy Hunt lived and worked in Huntington, West Virginia, a city of 60,000 tucked in the westernmost corner of the state. The blue-collar city sits on the south bank of the Ohio River. Ohio is less than one mile away across the river, while Kentucky can be reached by making a 10-minute drive westward on Interstate 64. Woody and Al were born six days apart in a small hospital in eastern Kentucky, were best friends throughout grade school and high school, and roomed together for four years at college. A few months after they graduated with business management degrees, each served as the other's best man at their respective weddings.

Following graduation, Al went to work for Curcio's Auto Supply on the western outskirts of Huntington, a business owned by his future father-in-law. Curcio's sold lawnmowers, bicycles, and automotive parts and supplies that included tires and batteries, the business's two largest revenue producers. Curcio's also installed the automotive parts it sold, provided oil and lube service, and performed small engine repairs.

Within weeks of going to work for Curcio's, Al helped Woody land a job with a large tire wholesaler that was Curcio's largest supplier. Goodner Brothers, Inc., sold tires of all types and sizes from 14 locations scattered from southern New York to northwestern South Carolina and from central Ohio to the Delaware shore. Goodner concentrated its operations in midsized cities such as Huntington, West Virginia; Lynchburg, Virginia; Harrisburg, Pennsylvania; and Youngstown, Ohio, home to the company's headquarters. Founded in 1969 by two brothers, T. J. and Ross Goodner,

---

1. The central facts of this case were drawn from a legal opinion issued in the 1990s. The names of the actual parties involved in the case and the relevant locations have been changed. Additionally, certain of the factual circumstances reported in this case are fictionalized accounts of background material disclosed in the legal opinion.

nearly three decades later Goodner Brothers' annual sales approached $40 million. The Goodner family dominated the company's operations. T. J. served as the company's chairman of the board and chief executive officer (CEO), while Ross was the chief operating officer (COO). Four second-generation Goodners also held key positions in the company.

Goodner purchased tires from several large manufacturers and then wholesaled those tires to auto supply stores and other retailers that had auto supply departments. Goodner's customers included Sears, Wal-Mart, Kmart, and dozens of smaller retail chains. The company also purchased discontinued tires from manufacturers, large retailers, and other wholesalers and then resold those tires at cut-rate prices to school districts, municipalities, and to companies with small fleets of automobiles.

Goodner Brothers hired Woody to work as a sales representative for its Huntington location. Woody sold tires to more than 80 customers in his sales region that stretched from the west side of Huntington into eastern Kentucky and north into Ohio. Woody, who worked strictly on a commission basis, was an effective and successful salesman. Unfortunately, a bad habit that he acquired during his college days gradually developed into a severe problem. By the mid-1990s, a gambling compulsion threatened to wreck the young salesman's career and personal life.

Woody bet on any and all types of sporting events, including baseball and football games, horse races, and boxing matches. He also spent hundreds of dollars each month buying lottery tickets and lost increasingly large sums on frequent gambling excursions with his friend Al. By the summer of 1996 when Woody, Al, and their wives visited Tunica, Mississippi, Woody's financial condition was desperate. He owed more than $50,000 to the various bookies with whom he placed bets, was falling behind on his mortgage payments, and had "maxed out" several credit cards. Worst of all, two bookies to whom Woody owed several thousand dollars were demanding payment and had begun making menacing remarks that alluded to his wife, Rachelle.

Woody Finds a Solution

Upon returning to Huntington in early July 1996, Woody struck upon an idea to bail him out of his financial problems: he decided to begin stealing from his employer, Goodner Brothers. Other than a few traffic tickets, Woody had never been in trouble with law enforcement authorities. Yet, in Woody's mind, he had no other reasonable alternatives. At this point, resorting to stealing seemed the lesser of two evils.

One reason Woody decided to steal from his employer was the ease with which it could be done. After several years with Goodner, Woody was very familiar with the company's sloppy accounting practices and lax control over its inventory and other assets. Goodner's executives preached one dominant theme to their sales staff: "Volume, volume, volume." Goodner achieved its ambitious sales goals by undercutting competitors' prices. The company's dominant market share in the geographical region it served came at a high price. Goodner's gross profit margin averaged 17.4 percent, considerably below the mean gross profit margin of 24.1 percent for comparable tire wholesalers. To compensate for its low gross profit margin, Goodner scrimped on operating expenses, including expenditures on internal control measures.

The company staffed its 14 sales outlets with skeletal crews of 10 to 12 employees. A sales manager supervised the other employees at each outlet and also worked a sales district. The remaining staff typically included two sales representatives, a receptionist who doubled as a secretary, a bookkeeper, and five to seven employees who delivered tires and worked in the unit's inventory warehouse. Goodner's Huntington location had two storage areas, a small warehouse adjacent to the sales office and a larger storage area two miles away that had previously housed a discount grocery store. Other than padlocks, Goodner provided little security for its tire inventory, which typically ranged from $300,000 to $700,000 for each sales outlet.

Instead of an extensive system of internal controls, T. J. and Ross Goodner relied heavily on the honesty and integrity of the employees they hired. Central to the company's employment policy was never to hire someone unless that individual could provide three strong references, preferably from reputable individuals with some connection to Goodner Brothers. Besides following up on employment references, Goodner Brothers obtained thorough background checks on prospective employees from local detective agencies. For more than two decades, Goodner's employment strategy had served the company well. Fewer than 10 of several hundred individuals employed by the company had been terminated for stealing or other misuse of company assets or facilities.

Each Goodner sales outlet maintained a computerized accounting system. These systems typically consisted of an "off-the-shelf" general ledger package intended for a small retail business and a hodgepodge of assorted accounting documents. Besides the Huntington facility's bookkeeper, the unit's sales manager and two sales representatives had unrestricted access to the accounting system. Since the large volume of sales and purchase transactions often swamped the bookkeeper, sales representatives frequently entered transactions directly into the system. The sales reps routinely accessed, reviewed, and updated their customers' accounts. Rather than completing purchase orders, sales orders, credit memos, and other accounting documents on a timely basis, the sales reps often jotted the details of a transaction on a piece of scrap paper. The sales reps eventually passed these "source documents" on to the bookkeeper or used them to enter transaction data directly into the accounting system.

Sales reps and the sales manager jointly executed the credit function for each Goodner sales outlet. Initial sales to new customers required the approval of the sales manager, while the creditworthiness of existing clients was monitored by the appropriate sales rep. Sales reps had direct access to the inventory storage areas. During heavy sales periods, sales reps often loaded and delivered customer orders themselves.

Each sales office took a year-end physical inventory to bring its perpetual inventory records into agreement with the amount of inventory actually on hand. One concession that T. J. and Ross Goodner made to the policy of relying on their employees' honesty was mandating one intra-year inventory count for each sales office. Goodner's management used these inventories, which were taken by the company's two-person internal audit staff, to monitor inventory shrinkage at each sales outlet. Historically, Goodner's inventory shrinkage significantly exceeded the industry norm. The company occasionally purchased large shipments of "seconds" from manufacturers; that is, tires with defects that prevented them from being sold to major retailers. The tires in these lots with major defects were taken to a tire disposal facility. A sales office's accounting records were not adjusted for these "throwaways" until the year-end physical inventory was taken.

Selling Tires on the Sly

Within a few days after Woody hatched his plan to pay off his gambling debts, he visited the remote storage site for the Huntington sales office. Woody rummaged through its dimly lit and cluttered interior searching for individual lots of tires that apparently had been collecting dust for several months. After finding several stacks of tires satisfying that requirement, Woody jotted down their specifications in a small notebook. For each lot, Woody listed customers who could potentially find some use for the given tires.

Later that same day, Woody made his first "sale." A local plumbing supply dealer needed tires for his small fleet of vehicles. Woody convinced the business's owner that Goodner was attempting to "move" some old inventory. That inventory would be sold on a cash basis and at prices significantly below Goodner's cost. The owner agreed to purchase two dozen of the tires. After delivering the tires in his large pickup, Woody received a cash payment of $900 directly from the customer.

Over the next several months, Woody routinely stole inventory and kept the proceeds. Woody concealed the thefts in various ways. In some cases, he would charge merchandise that he had sold for his own benefit to the accounts of large-volume customers. Woody preferred this technique since it allowed him to reduce the inventory balance in the Huntington facility's accounting records. When customers complained to him for being charged for merchandise they had not purchased, Woody simply apologized and corrected their account balances. If the customers paid the improper charges, they unknowingly helped Woody sustain his fraudulent scheme.

Goodner's customers frequently returned tires for various reasons. Woody completed credit memos for sales transactions voided by his customers, but instead of returning the tires to Goodner's inventory, he often sold them and kept the proceeds. Goodner occasionally consigned tires to large retailers for promotional sales events. When the consignees returned the unsold tires to Goodner, Woody would sell some of the tires to other customers for cash. Finally, Woody began offering to take throwaways to the tire disposal facility in nearby Shoals, West Virginia, a task typically assigned to a sales outlet's delivery workers. Not surprisingly, most of the tires that Woody carted off for disposal were not defective.

The ease with which he could steal tires made Woody increasingly bold. In late 1996, Woody offered to sell Al Hunt tires he had allegedly purchased from a manufacturer (by this time, Al owned and operated Curcio's Tires). Woody told Al that he had discovered the manufacturer was disposing of its inventory of discontinued tires and decided to buy them himself. When Al asked whether such "self-dealing" violated Goodner company policy, Woody replied, "It's none of their business what I do in my spare time. Why should I let them know about this great deal that I stumbled upon?"

At first reluctant, Al eventually agreed to purchase several dozen tires from his good friend. No doubt, the cut-rate prices at which Woody was selling the tires made the decision much easier. At those prices, Al realized he would earn a sizable profit on the tires. Over the next 12 months, Woody continued to sell "closeout" tires to his friend. After one such purchase, Al called the manufacturer from whom Woody had reportedly purchased the tires. Al had become suspicious of the frequency of the closeout sales and the bargain basement prices at which Woody supposedly purchased the tires. When he called the manufacturer, a sales rep told Al that his company had only one closeout sale each year. The sales rep also informed Al that his company sold closeout merchandise directly to wholesalers, never to individuals or retail establishments.

The next time Al spoke to Woody, he mentioned matter-of-factly that he had contacted Woody's primary supplier of closeout tires. Al then told his friend that a sales rep for the company had indicated that such merchandise was only sold to wholesalers.

"So, what's the point, Al?"

"Well, I just found it kind of strange that, uh, that ..."

"C'mon, get to the point, Al."

"Well, Woody, I was just wondering where you're getting these tires that you're selling."

"Do you want to know, Al? Do you really want to know, Buddy? I'll tell you if you want to know," Woody replied angrily.

After a lengthy pause, Al shrugged his shoulders and told his friend to "just forget it." Despite his growing uneasiness regarding the source of the cheap tires, Al continued to buy them and never again asked Woody where he was obtaining them.

Internal Auditors Discover Inventory Shortage

On December 31, 1996, the employees of Goodner's Huntington location met to take a physical inventory. The employees treated the annual event as a prelude to their New Year's Eve party. Counting typically began around noon and was finished within three hours. The employees worked in teams of three. Two members of each team climbed and crawled over the large stacks of tires and shouted out their counts to the third member who recorded them on preformatted count sheets.

Woody arranged to work with two delivery workers who were relatively unfamiliar with Goodner's inventory since they had been hired only a few weeks earlier. Woody made sure that his team was one of the two count teams assigned to the remote storage facility. Most of the inventory he had stolen over the previous six months had been taken from that site. Woody estimated that he had stolen approximately $45,000 of inventory from the remote storage facility, which represented about 10 percent of the site's book inventory. By maintaining the count sheets for his team, Woody could easily inflate the quantities for the tire lots that he and his team members counted.

After the counting was completed at the remote storage facility, Woody offered to take the count sheets for both teams to the sales office where the total inventory would be compiled. On the way to the sales office, he stopped in a vacant parking lot to review the count sheets. Woody quickly determined that the apparent shortage remaining at the remote site was approximately $20,000. He reduced that shortage to less than $10,000 by altering the count sheets prepared by the other count team.

When the year-end inventory was tallied for Goodner's Huntington location, the difference between the physical inventory and the book inventory was $12,000, or 2.1 percent. That percentage exceeded the historical shrinkage rate of approximately 1.6 percent for Goodner's sales offices. But Felix Garcia, the sales manager for the Huntington sales office, did not believe that the 1996 shrinkage was excessive. As it turned out, neither did the accounting personnel and internal auditors at Goodner's corporate headquarters.

Woody continued "ripping off" Goodner throughout 1997. By midyear, Woody was selling most of the tires he stole to Al Hunt. On one occasion, Woody warned Al not to sell the tires too cheaply. Woody had become concerned that Curcio's modest prices and its increasing sales volume might spark the curiosity and envy of other Huntington tire retailers.

In October 1997, Goodner's internal audit team arrived to count the Huntington location's inventory. Although company policy dictated that the internal auditors count the inventory of each Goodner sales outlet annually, the average interval between the internal audit inventory counts typically ranged from 15 to 20 months. The internal auditors had last counted the Huntington location's inventory in May 1996, two months before Woody Robinson began stealing tires. Woody was unaware that the internal auditors periodically counted the entire inventory of each Goodner operating unit. Instead, he understood that the internal auditors only did a few test counts during their infrequent visits to the Huntington sales office.

After completing their inventory counts, the two internal auditors arrived at an inventory value of $498,000. A quick check of the accounting records revealed a book inventory of $639,000. The auditors had never encountered such a large difference between the physical and book inventory totals. Unsure what to do at this point, the auditors eventually decided to take the matter directly to Felix Garcia, the Huntington sales manager. The size of the inventory shortage shocked Garcia. He insisted that the auditors must have overlooked some inventory. Garcia, the two internal auditors, and three delivery workers spent the following day recounting the entire inventory. The resulting physical inventory value was $496,000, $2,000 less than the original value arrived at by the auditors.

Following the second physical inventory, the two internal auditors and Garcia met at a local restaurant to review the Huntington unit's inventory records. No glaring trends were evident in those records to either Garcia or the auditors. Garcia admitted to the auditors that the long hours required "just to keep the tires coming and going" left him little time to monitor his unit's accounting records. When pressed by the auditors to provide possible explanations for the inventory shortage, Garcia erupted. "Listen. Like I just said, my job is simple. My job is selling tires. I sell as many tires as I can, as quickly as I can. I let you guys and those other suits up in Youngstown track the numbers."

The following day, the senior internal auditor called his immediate superior, Goodner's chief financial officer (CFO). The size of the inventory shortage alarmed the CFO. Immediately, the CFO suspected that the inventory shortage was linked to the Huntington unit's downward trend in monthly profits over the past two years. Through 1995, the Huntington sales office had consistently ranked as Goodner's second or third most profitable sales outlet. Over the past 18 months, the unit's slumping profits had caused it to fall to the bottom one-third of the company's sales outlets in terms of profit margin percentage. Tacking on the large inventory shortage would cause the Huntington location to be Goodner's least profitable sales office over the previous year and one-half.

After discussing the matter with T. J. and Ross Goodner, the CFO contacted the company's independent audit firm and arranged for the firm to investigate the inventory shortage. The Goodners agreed with the CFO that Felix Garcia should be suspended with pay until the investigation was concluded. Garcia's lack of a reasonable explanation for the missing inventory and the anger he had directed at the internal auditors caused Goodner's executives to conclude that he was likely responsible for the inventory shortage.

Within a few days, four auditors from Goodner's independent audit firm arrived at the Huntington sales office. Goodner's audit firm was a regional CPA firm with six offices, all in Ohio. Goodner obtained an annual audit of its financial statements because one was demanded by the New York bank that provided the company with a line of credit. Goodner's independent auditors had never paid much attention to the internal controls of the client's sales offices. Instead, they performed a "balance sheet" audit that emphasized corroborating Goodner's year-end assets and liabilities.

During their investigation of the missing inventory, the auditors were appalled by the Huntington unit's lax and often nonexistent controls. The extensive control weaknesses complicated their efforts to identify the source of the inventory shortage. Nevertheless, after several days, the auditors' suspicions began settling on Woody Robinson. A file of customer complaints that Felix Garcia kept in his desk revealed that over the past year an unusually large number of customer complaints had been filed against Woody. During that time, 14 of his customers had protested charges included on their monthly statements. Only two customers serviced by the other sales rep had filed similar complaints during that time frame.

When questioned by the auditors, Garcia conceded that he had not discussed the customer complaints with Woody or the other sales rep. In fact, Garcia was unaware that a disproportionate number of the complaints had been filed against Woody. When Garcia received a customer complaint, he simply passed it on to the appropriate sales rep and allowed that individual to deal with the matter. He maintained a file of the customer complaints only because he had been told to do so by the previous sales manager whom he had replaced three years earlier.

After the independent auditors collected other incriminating evidence against Woody, they arranged for a meeting with him. Also attending that meeting were Goodner's CFO and Felix Garcia. When the auditors produced the incriminating evidence, Woody disclaimed any knowledge of, or responsibility for, the inventory shortage. Woody's denial provoked an immediate and indignant response from Goodner's CFO. "Listen, Robinson, you may have fooled the people you've been working with, but you're not fooling me. You'd better spill the beans right now, or else." At this point, Woody stood, announced that he was retaining an attorney, and walked out of the meeting.

EPILOGUE

Goodner Brothers filed a criminal complaint against Woody Robinson two weeks after he refused to discuss the inventory shortage at the Huntington sales office. A few weeks later, Woody's attorney reached a plea bargain agreement with the local district attorney. Woody received a five-year sentence for grand larceny, four years of which were suspended. He eventually served seven months of that sentence in a minimum-security prison. A condition of the plea bargain agreement required Woody to provide a full and candid written summary of the fraudulent scheme that he had perpetrated on his employer.

Woody's confession implicated Al Hunt in his theft scheme. Over the 15 months that Woody had stolen from Goodner, he had "fenced" most of the stolen inventory through Curcio's Tires. Although the district attorney questioned Al Hunt extensively, he decided not to file criminal charges against him.[2]

Goodner Brothers filed a $185,000 insurance claim to recoup the losses imposed on them by Woody Robinson. The company's insurer eventually paid Goodner $130,000, which equaled the theft losses that Goodner could document. After settling the claim, the insurance company sued Curcio's Tires and Al Hunt to recover the $98,000 windfall that Curcio's allegedly realized due to Al Hunt's involvement in the theft ring. The case went to federal district court where a judge ordered Hunt to pay $64,000 to Goodner's insurer. Al Hunt then sued Woody Robinson to recover that judgment. The judge who presided over the earlier case quickly dismissed Al Hunt's lawsuit. According to the judge, Al Hunt's complicity in the fraudulent scheme voided his right to recover the $64,000 judgment from his former friend.

---

2. Ironically, Woody's confession also implicated his wife, Rachelle. After Woody revealed that Rachelle had typically deposited the large checks written to him by Al Hunt, the district attorney reasoned that Rachelle must have been aware of Woody's fraudulent scheme and was thus an accessory to his crime. However, Woody insisted that he had told his wife the checks were for gambling losses owed to him by Al. After interrogating Rachelle at length, the district attorney decided not to prosecute her.

Questions

1. List what you believe should have been the three to five key internal control objectives of Goodner's Huntington sales office.

2. List the key internal control weaknesses that were evident in the Huntington unit's operations.

3. Develop one or more control policies or procedures to alleviate the control weaknesses you identified in Question 2.

4. Besides Woody Robinson, what other parties were at least partially responsible for the inventory losses Goodner suffered? Defend your answer.

Troberg Stores

"Checker needed up front."

"Kirby Jacobson placed a final can on the shelf in front of him and then turned and headed for the checkout stand at the front of the store. Kirby worked for Troberg Stores, a chain of small grocery stores located in a cluster of small towns in northern Minnesota. After graduating from high school in 1980, Kirby accepted a job as a stocker with Troberg's Sixth Street store in his hometown. Fifteen years later, Kirby had risen to the position of assistant store manager.

Although technically a management position, Kirby's job required him to be a jack-of-all-trades for the Sixth Street store. He worked as a stocker and checker when needed, prepared purchase orders for three departments, closed the store several days per week, and trained new employees. Kirby was a quiet and introverted individual who was known for his punctuality and work ethic. Coworkers always called Kirby first if they needed someone to fill in for them.

"I'll help you over here at register three, Ma'am," Kirby said politely to a young woman nearly hidden behind an overloaded shopping cart. The Sixth Street store had four checkout stands. During the day, the store's three full-time cashiers staffed checkout stands one through three. Kirby, the two other assistant store managers, the produce manager, and the dairy manager served as relief checkers. Relief checkers typically manned register four. On this afternoon in early May 1995, Kirby opened checkout stand number three because the cash register in checkout stand four was being repaired. Violet Rahal, the cashier assigned to register three, had taken her lunch break a few minutes earlier at 1 p.m.

After checking out several customers, Kirby closed register three and resumed his stocking duties. Thirty minutes later, Violet Rahal returned from her lunch break. Because she noticed that several items at her work station had been rearranged, Violet asked Roma Charboneau, the cashier at register two, if someone had used register three during her lunch break. Roma replied that Kirby had checked out several customers at register three. Violet then counted her cash till. Then she counted it again. Each time, she arrived at the same total. Her cash till was short by $210. Violet immediately reported the shortage to Angelo Velotti, the store manager.[1]

Who Stole the Cash?

Cash shortages had been a recurring problem for Troberg's Sixth Street store. Over the previous 12 months, Angelo Velotti had reported four cash shortages, each exceeding $200, to the owner of Troberg Stores, Elliott Paulsen. The cash shortage Violet Rahal discovered was the first that could be tracked to a specific cash register and a specific time of day.

When Violet reported the missing $210 to Angelo Velotti, the frustrated store manager slammed his fist on his desk. "What is going on here?" he shouted.

---

1. This case was developed from a legal opinion written in the late 1990s. The names of the actual parties involved in the case and the relevant locations have been changed. In addition, certain of the factual circumstances reported in this case are fictionalized accounts of the facts disclosed in the legal opinion.

"I counted my till when I left for lunch. Just like I always do," Violet responded timidly. "Then, when I got back—"

"Violet, I'm not accusing you. But this has to stop."

A shaken Violet regained her composure and continued. "When I got back, I noticed that someone had been using register three. Roma said that it was Kirby."

"Kirby," Angelo muttered under his breath in disgust.

"So, I counted my till. Twice. Each time, I came up short by $210."

"Stay here, Violet. I'm getting to the bottom of this right now."

Velotti marched to aisle four where Kirby was stocking and brusquely told the assistant store manager to come to his office. When Kirby asked why, Velotti snapped, "You'll find out soon enough."

Velotti's frustration stemmed from mounting pressure that Paulsen was applying on him to tighten the internal controls of the Sixth Street store. Each time Velotti reported a cash shortage, Paulsen exploded. "We're barely making ends meet as it is!" Paulsen had bellowed on the previous occasion that Velotti had reported an apparent theft of cash.

Increasing competition from nationwide grocery chains had been slicing away at Troberg's revenues and profits for several years. Residents of the small towns in which Troberg's stores were located often drove to metropolitan areas to take advantage of the lower prices and greater variety of merchandise offered by the large grocery chains. By the spring of 1995, Troberg's gross profit percentage hovered at an anemic 10 percent, meaning that the Sixth Street store needed to produce $2,000 of revenues to replace the gross profit lost due to a $200 theft. The gross profit percentage for comparable grocery chains ranged from 18 to 25 percent.

At the same time Paulsen was demanding that Velotti eliminate the Sixth Street store's theft losses, he was slashing the store's operating budget. During the past year, Velotti had trimmed the store's payroll from 30 to 24 employees. Velotti realized that reducing the store's staff during each work shift and assigning more job responsibilities to each employee provided dishonest subordinates a greater opportunity to take advantage of the business. But when he tried to make that argument to Paulsen, the owner refused to listen. "Doesn't matter how many or how few employees you have since honesty is a part of everybody's job description," Paulsen had once barked at Velotti.

After returning to his office with Kirby Jacobson in tow, Angelo Velotti told Violet and Kirby that he was calling the local police department. Velotti asked the police department to immediately dispatch an officer to the Sixth Street store to investigate the apparent theft. Next, Velotti telephoned Elliott Paulsen. As expected, the unpleasant news detonated Paulsen's notoriously quick temper.

A few weeks earlier, Paulsen and Velotti had spent several hours studying the previous four thefts of cash at the Sixth Street store. Three of those shortages had been discovered at the end of the day when an assistant store manager prepared the daily cash deposit. On each of those occasions, the assistant store manager who discovered the cash shortage had been Kirby Jacobson. The fourth shortage occurred at register four one busy Saturday afternoon. Kirby had worked as a relief checker during the shift in which that cash shortage arose, along with three other individuals. Since the exact time that the cash shortage occurred could not be pinpointed, the shortage could not be traced to a specific individual.

Paulsen and Velotti concluded that Kirby's connection with the four thefts was not a coincidence. The two men later testified that their investigation caused them to "lose trust and confidence" in Kirby, although they had never previously questioned his integrity. They also testified that prior to the May 1995 theft they had discussed changing Kirby's job responsibilities so that he would not have access to the store's cash.

Elliott Paulsen, who lived in a nearby community, and Officer Jessica Burnett arrived at the Sixth Street store within one hour after Violet Rahal discovered the $210 cash shortage. Officer Burnett first spoke privately with Paulsen. The owner told the police officer about the Sixth Street Store's rash of cash thefts over the previous 12 months and Kirby's link to each of those thefts. Officer Burnett then interviewed the Troberg employees on the scene, including Velotti. Although Roma Charboneau reported seeing three "suspicious characters" milling around the candy counter near register three while it was unattended, Officer Burnett quickly concluded that the theft was likely an "inside job." The officer then decided that Kirby Jacobson and Violet Rahal should take polygraph examinations.

Officer Burnett followed the required procedures for administering polygraph examinations in the case of a suspected employee theft. The Employee Polygraph Protection Act (EPPA), a federal statute enacted by Congress in 1988, dictates the procedures to be followed in such circumstances. First, Officer Burnett obtained the permission of Elliott Paulsen, the victim of the crime, to conduct the polygraph examinations. Next, the officer met with the two suspects, Kirby Jacobson and Violet Rahal. Officer Burnett advised the two employees that they were not required to take a polygraph test. When she was certain that Jacobson and Rahal understood their legal rights, the officer asked each of them to take a polygraph test at a later date.

Truth and Consequences

Both Kirby and Violet agreed to submit to a polygraph examination regarding their involvement in, or knowledge of, the May 1995 theft at Troberg's Sixth Street store. Kirby later testified that he consented to take the polygraph because he believed it was the only way to "clear his name." At the time, Kirby was unaware that Elliott Paulsen and Angelo Velotti suspected he was responsible for all five thefts at the Sixth Street store. When Kirby agreed to take a polygraph test, Paulsen and Velotti decided that they would await the outcome of that test before making a final decision regarding his employment status.

In early June 1995, the state Department of Criminal Investigation administered polygraph tests to Kirby Jacobson and Violet Rahal. Violet easily "passed" the test. The polygrapher reported finding no signs of undue anxiety or other inappropriate physiological responses in Violet's polygraph results.[2] Analysis of Kirby's polygraph printout revealed indications of emotional distress and deception, suggesting that he was not being truthful regarding his alleged lack of involvement in the theft. After reviewing the polygraph results, Officer Burnett told Elliott Paulsen that she believed Kirby had stolen the $210. Despite that belief, the officer declined to file criminal charges against Jacobson. She informed Paulsen that there was insufficient evidence to prove beyond a reasonable doubt that Kirby had stolen the cash.

---

2. The legal opinion from which this case was developed provided the following description of a polygraph: "The basic theory underlying the polygraph is that a subject's honesty, dishonesty, or guilty knowledge can be judged from those physical responses that are scientifically related to emotional upset.... The tension associated with the inner conflict of choosing between willful dishonesty and truthfulness is presumed to be measurable by recording changes in inherent body functions. The polygraph does not measure whether the subject is either lying or telling the truth. Rather it merely records the physiological changes that occur as the subject responds to a series of questions requiring simple 'yes' or 'no' answers."

Shortly after receiving the polygraph results, Paulsen met with Velotti. The two men decided not to dismiss Kirby. They later testified that they chose not to fire Kirby because he had been a valued employee of the Sixth Street store for so many years. Instead, they chose to demote him from assistant store manager to stocker, the lowest employment position at the Sixth Street Store. They also decided to forbid Kirby from handling any cash in the store. Despite the demotion, Paulsen and Velotti did not reduce Kirby's salary or his other employment benefits.

The day following his meeting with Paulsen, Velotti called Kirby into his office. Velotti notified Kirby of his demotion and informed him that he would never again be considered for a managerial position with the company. Shocked by the news, Kirby did not question Velotti regarding the decision but instead quietly walked out of the office. A few days later, Velotti, who had remained angry at Kirby since the May 1995 theft, privately told Kirby that he would "never forget" the incident. Velotti also told Kirby he should consider accepting another employment opportunity if one became available.

The weeks following Kirby's demotion were very unpleasant for him. Kirby later testified that the demotion "devastated and humiliated" him. Worst of all was the treatment he received from the management personnel in the store. His former peers openly gossiped about his alleged involvement in the May 1995 theft and made jokes regarding his demotion. Kirby soon found his work environment intolerable and resigned his job with the Sixth Street store. After leaving Troberg Stores, Kirby lapsed into a depression and eventually sought psychological counseling.

Kirby Fights Back

Two years following his resignation, Kirby Jacobson filed a civil complaint against Troberg Stores, Elliott Paulsen, and Angelo Velotti. Kirby's lawsuit charged that during and following the investigation of the May 1995 theft, Troberg Stores violated his civil rights under the EPPA. Kirby's lawsuit contained the following specific allegations:

1. Troberg Stores caused him to take the polygraph examination.
2. Troberg improperly used the polygraph results.
3. Troberg disciplined him on the basis of the polygraph results.
4. He was constructively discharged by Troberg on the basis of the polygraph results.

The federal judge who presided over Kirby's lawsuit found that few legal cases had been filed by individuals under the EPPA since it was passed in 1988. To provide a sound basis for his opinion in the case, the judge reviewed the history of the polygraph and dissected the requirements of, and legislative rationale underlying, the EPPA.

The polygraph was invented in the late 1920s. During the latter part of the twentieth century, businesses began routinely using polygraph examinations to screen new employees, to investigate apparent incidents of theft and embezzlement by employees, and for related purposes. The absence of statutory guidelines for, and restrictions on the use of, polygraph examinations resulted in many employers abusing polygraph tests, including using them to justify discriminatory employment practices. To remedy such abusive practices, Congress passed the EPPA.

Exhibit 1 presents a key excerpt from the EPPA. That passage seemingly eliminates the use of polygraph tests for employment purposes within the private sector. However, a subsequent section of the EPPA allows employers under certain restrictive conditions to request an employee to submit to a polygraph examination. Exhibit 2

EXHIBIT 1

KEY EXCERPT FROM
EMPLOYEE
POLYGRAPH
PROTECTION ACT

Except as provided in Sections 2006 and 2007 of this title, it shall be unlawful for any employer engaged in or affecting commerce or in the production of goods for commerce—

(1) directly or indirectly, to require, request, suggest, or cause any employee or prospective employee to take or submit to any lie detector test;
(2) to use, accept, refer to, or inquire concerning the results of any lie detector test of any employee or prospective employee;
(3) to discharge, discipline, discriminate against in any manner, or deny employment or promotion to, or threaten to take any action against—
    (a) any employee or prospective employee who refuses, declines, or fails to take or submit to any lie detector test, or
    (b) any employee or prospective employee on the basis of the results of any lie detector test.

EXHIBIT 2

"ONGOING
INVESTIGATION
EXEMPTION"
INCLUDED IN
EMPLOYEE
POLYGRAPH
PROTECTION ACT

Subject to Sections 2006 and 2009 of this title, this chapter shall not prohibit an employer from requesting an employee to submit to a polygraph test if

(1) the test is administered in connection with an ongoing investigation involving economic loss or injury to the employer's business, such as theft, embezzlement, misappropriation, or an act of unlawful industrial espionage or sabotage;
(2) the employee had access to the property that is the subject of the investigation;
(3) the employer had a reasonable suspicion that the employee was involved in the incident or activity under investigation; and
(4) the employer executes a statement, provided to the examinee before the test, that
    (a) sets forth with particularity the specific incident or activity being investigated and the basis for testing particular employees;
    (b) is signed by a person (other than a polygraph examiner) authorized to legally bind the employer;
    (c) is retained by the employer for at least 3 years; and
    (d) contains at a minimum
        (i)   an identification of the specific economic loss or injury to the business of the employer,
        (ii) a statement indicating that the employee had access to the property that is the subject of the investigation, and
        (iii) a statement describing the basis of the employer's reasonable suspicion that the employee was involved in the incident or activity under investigation.

presents this exception, referred to as the "ongoing investigation exemption."[3] Since Troberg Stores failed to follow all the steps outlined in Exhibit 2, the federal judge overseeing Kirby's lawsuit ruled that the company could not invoke the ongoing investigation exemption to the EPPA in preparing a defense to Kirby's charges.

> *The EPPA contemplates the situation in which [Troberg Stores] found itself with [Kirby Jacobson] and provides explicit instructions as to how [Troberg Stores] could have protected its business and acted in response to results of a polygraph test that implicated its employee in the store theft. [Troberg Stores], however, had to comply with all of the requirements specified in Sections 2006 and 2007 in order to invoke use of the ongoing investigation exemption.*

---

3. Even if an employer invokes the ongoing investigation exemption to the EPPA, the employer may not rely exclusively on polygraph results to make an adverse employment decision regarding an employee suspected of theft.

In his legal opinion, the federal judge responded to each allegation that Kirby Jacobson filed against Troberg Stores. Regarding the first allegation, the judge ruled that the company had not required or effectively caused Kirby to take the polygraph examination. Instead, the judge ruled that Officer Burnett, on her own initiative, had asked Kirby to take the polygraph test. The judge found in favor of Kirby on the remaining three allegations. First, the judge ruled that Troberg Stores and its management improperly used the polygraph results in evaluating Kirby's employment status. Second, evidence presented by Kirby's legal counsel clearly demonstrated that Paulsen and Velotti relied on the polygraph results in deciding to demote Kirby. Finally, the judge agreed that Kirby faced an intolerable work environment following his demotion, which effectively forced him to resign his job. Since Troberg Stores and its management were ultimately responsible for creating the hostile work environment, the judge ruled that the company had constructively discharged Kirby.

The federal judge awarded Kirby Jacobson approximately $40,000 in damages from Troberg Stores and its management. Included in those damages was $15,000 for "emotional distress" inflicted on Kirby by his former employer and approximately $25,000 for lost wages and employment benefits.

In awarding the judgment to Kirby Jacobson, the judge acknowledged that Kirby "may well have committed the theft from the cash register." The judge then went on to point out that Troberg Stores bungled two opportunities to dismiss Kirby. First, the company could have dismissed Kirby immediately following the May 1995 theft. Circumstantial evidence collected by Paulsen and Velotti clearly implicated Kirby in the previous thefts at the Sixth Street store. According to the judge, the additional suspicion cast on Kirby's integrity by the May 1995 theft provided Troberg Stores sufficient justification to fire him with little risk of any legal repercussions. Second, Troberg Stores could have taken advantage of the "ongoing investigation exemption" of the EPPA. That option was available to the company since Paulsen and Velotti had initiated an investigation of the previous thefts at the Sixth Street store prior to the May 1995 incident. By invoking this exemption to the EPPA, the company could have used the polygraph test results, along with the other available incriminating evidence, to dismiss Kirby, again with little risk of any legal reprisal.[4]

Questions

1. The management of Troberg Stores was unfamiliar with the EPPA. Should a business's internal control process address its need to comply with all relevant state and federal statutes? Or is such compliance beyond the scope of an entity's internal control process? Defend your answer.

2. The legal opinion on which this case is based did not elaborate on the internal controls Troberg Stores had in place for its cash processing activities. Visit a local grocery store and unobtrusively observe one or more checkout stands. Develop a list of policies and procedures apparently used by the store to maintain control over its checkout stand operations. For each of these items, identify the apparent control objective.

---

4. Troberg's financial problems worsened following Kirby Jacobson's resignation. In the late 1990s, a large competitor purchased all of Troberg's stores.

3. What types of duties should typically be segregated or separated across employees of a small business? What measures can a small business implement if adequate segregation of duties is not economically feasible?

4. What ethical responsibilities do a business's managers and owners have when they suspect an employee of theft? Should such ethical considerations be integrated into a business's internal control policies and procedures? Explain.

5. Do you believe the EPPA improperly limits retail businesses' ability to investigate and prosecute potential incidents of employee theft? Defend your answer. Identify other laws and regulations that have potential control implications for retail businesses.

SECTION 4

ETHICAL RESPONSIBILITIES OF ACCOUNTANTS

Creve Couer Pizza, Inc.

Imagine this scenario. A few years after graduating from Appalachian State University, Boise State University, or Boston College with an accounting degree, you find yourself working as an audit senior with an international accounting firm. Your best friend, Rick, whom you have known since kindergarten, is a special agent with the Internal Revenue Service (IRS). Over lunch one day, Rick mentions the IRS's informant program.

"You know, Jess, you could pick up a few hundred dollars here and there working as a controlled informant for us. In fact, if you would feed us information regarding one or two of those large corporate clients of yours, you could make a bundle."

"That's funny, Rick. Real funny. Me, a double agent, spying on my clients for the IRS? Have you ever heard of the confidentiality rule?"

Sound farfetched? Not really. Since 1939, the IRS has operated an informant program. Most individuals who participate in this program provide information on a one-time basis; however, the IRS also retains hundreds of "controlled informants" who work in tandem with one or more IRS special agents on a continuing basis. Controlled informants provide the IRS with incriminating evidence regarding individuals and businesses suspected of cheating on their taxes. In the early 1990s, the IRS revealed that more than 40 of these controlled informants were CPAs.

Now consider this scenario. You, the audit senior, are again having lunch with your friend Rick, the IRS special agent. Rick knows that the IRS is investigating you for large deductions taken in recent years on your federal income tax returns for a questionable tax shelter scheme. The additional tax assessments and fines you face significantly exceed your net worth. Your legal costs alone will be thousands of dollars. To date, you have been successful in concealing the IRS investigation from your spouse, other family members, and your employer, but that will not be possible much longer.

"Jess, I know this investigation is really worrying you. But I can get you out of this whole mess. I talked to my supervisor. She and three other agents are working on a case involving one of your audit clients. I can't tell you which one right now. If you agree to work with them as a controlled informant and provide them with information that you can easily get your hands on, they will close the case on you. You will be off the hook. No questions. No fines or additional taxes. Case closed ... permanently."

"Rick, come on, I can't do that. What if my firm finds out? I'd lose my job. I would probably lose my certificate."

"Yeah, but face these facts. If the IRS proves its case against you, you are going to lose your job and your certificate ... and probably a whole lot more. Maybe even your marriage. Think about it, Jess. Realistically, the agency is looking at a maximum recovery of $50,000 from you. But if you cooperate with my supervisor, she can probably squeeze several million out of your client."

"You're sure they would let me off ... free and clear?"

"Yes. Free and clear. Come on, Jess, we need you. More important, you need us. Plus, think of it this way. You made one mistake by becoming involved in that phony tax shelter scam. But your client has been ripping off the government, big time, for years. You would be doing a public service by turning in those crooks."

Returning to reality, consider the case of James Checksfield. In 1981, Checksfield, a Missouri CPA, became a controlled informant for the IRS. The IRS special agent who recruited Checksfield had been his close friend for several years and knew that Checksfield was under investigation by the IRS. Reportedly, Checksfield owed back taxes of nearly $30,000 because of his failure to file federal income tax returns from 1974 through 1977. At the same time the IRS recruited Checksfield, the federal agency was also investigating a Missouri-based company, Creve Couer Pizza, Inc. The IRS believed that the owner of this chain of pizza restaurants was "skimming receipts" from his business—that is, failing to report on his federal income tax returns the total sales revenue of his eight restaurants. Checksfield had served as Creve Couer's CPA for several years, although both the IRS and Checksfield denied that he was recruited specifically to provide information regarding that company.

From 1982 through 1985, Checksfield funneled information to the IRS regarding Creve Couer Pizza. Based upon this information, federal prosecutors filed a six-count criminal indictment against the owner of that business in 1989. This indictment charged the owner with underreporting his taxable income by several hundred thousand dollars. The owner faced fines of nearly $1 million and a prison term of up to 24 years if convicted of the charges. Meanwhile, the IRS dropped its case against Checksfield. Both the IRS and Checksfield maintained that there was no connection between the decision to drop the case against him and his decision to provide the IRS with information regarding Creve Couer Pizza.

Following the indictment filed against the owner of Creve Couer Pizza, the owner's attorneys subpoenaed the information that the IRS had used to build its case against him. As a result, the owner discovered the role played by his longtime friend and accountant in the IRS investigation. Quite naturally, the owner was very upset. "What my accountant did to me was very mean and devious. He sat here in my home with me and my family. He was like a member of the family. On the other hand, he was working against me."[1] In another interview, the owner observed, "A client has the right to feel he's getting undivided loyalty from his accountant."[2] Contributing to the owner's anger was the fact that he had paid Checksfield more than $50,000 in fees for accounting and taxation services during the time the CPA was working undercover for the IRS.

The print and electronic media reported the case of the "singing CPA" nationwide, prompting extensive criticism of the IRS. The case also caused many clients of CPAs to doubt whether they could trust their accountants to protect the confidentiality of sensitive financial information. When questioned concerning the matter, the IRS expressed no remorse for using Checksfield to gather incriminating evidence regarding the owner of Creve Couer Pizza. An IRS representative also rejected the contention that communications between accountants and their clients should be "privileged" under federal law similar to the communications between attorneys and their clients.

The IRS says the claim of a privileged [accountant-client] relationship is nonsense. "To the contrary," says Edward Federico of the IRS's criminal-investigation division in St. Louis, "the accountant has a moral and legal obligation to turn over information."[3]

The accounting profession was appalled by the Checksfield case and tried to minimize the damage it had done to the public's trust in CPAs. In particular, the profession condemned the actions of the IRS.

1. "Accountant Spies on Client for IRS," *Kansas City Star*, 18 March 1992, 2.
2. "The Case of the Singing CPA," *Newsweek*, 17 July 1989, 41.
3. *Ibid.*

Rarely has there been such a case of prosecutorial zeal that violated rudimentary standards of decency.... Turning the client-accountant relationship into a secret tool for government agents is an abominable practice. It demeans the service. It erodes trust in the accounting profession.[4]

EPILOGUE

In August 1990, the Missouri State Board of Accountancy revoked James Checksfield's CPA license for violating a state law that prohibits CPAs from disclosing confidential client information without the client's permission. In November 1991, the U.S. Department of Justice suddenly announced that it was dropping the tax evasion charges against the owner of Creve Couer Pizza, although pretrial arguments had already been presented for the case. The Justice Department had little to say regarding its decision. Legal experts speculated that federal prosecutors dropped the charges because the judge hearing the case was expected to disallow the evidence that the IRS had collected with the assistance of Checksfield.

Despite the negative publicity produced by the Creve Couer case, the IRS continues to use accountants both in public practice and private industry as informants. In the late 1990s, *Forbes* magazine reported a case in which a disgruntled controller of a retail electronics chain got even with his boss.[5] Shortly before leaving the firm, the controller copied accounting and tax records documenting a large-scale tax fraud perpetrated by the chain's owner. Thanks to this information, the IRS collected a nearly $7 million fine from the owner and sent him to jail for 10 months. The former controller received a significant but undisclosed "finder's fee" from the IRS for his "cooperation."

Questions

1. Do CPAs who provide accounting, taxation, and related services to small businesses have a responsibility to serve as the "moral conscience" of those clients? Explain.

2. In a 1984 opinion handed down by the U.S. Supreme Court, Chief Justice Warren Burger noted that "the independent auditor assumes a public responsibility transcending any employment relationship with the client." If this is true, do auditors have a moral or professional responsibility to turn in clients who are cheating on their taxes or violating other laws?

3. Assume that you were Jess in the second hypothetical scenario presented in this case. How would you respond to your friend's suggestion that you become a controlled informant for the IRS? Identify the parties that would be affected by your decision and the obligations you would have to each.

4. "IRS Oversteps with CPA Stoolies," *Accounting Today*, 6 January 1992, 22.
5. J. Novack, "Boomerang," *Forbes*, 7 July 1997, 42–43.

F&C International, Inc.

Alex Fries emigrated to the United States from Germany in the early nineteenth century.[1] The excitement and opportunities promised by the western frontier fascinated thousands of new Americans, including the young German, who followed his dreams and the Ohio River west to Cincinnati. A chemist by training, Fries soon found a job in the booming distillery industry of southern Ohio and northern Kentucky. His background suited him well for an important need of distilleries, namely, developing flavors to make their often "sour" products more appealing to the public. Alex Fries eventually established his own flavor company. Thanks largely to Fries, Cincinnati became the home of the small but important flavor industry in the United States. By the end of the twentieth century, the flavor industry's annual revenues approached $5 billion.

Alex Fries' success in the flavor industry became a family affair. Two of his grandsons created their own flavor company, Fries & Fries, in the early 1900s. Several decades later, another descendant of Alex Fries, Jon Fries, served as the president and chief executive officer (CEO) of F&C International, Inc., a flavor company whose common stock traded on the NASDAQ stock exchange. F&C International, also based in Cincinnati, reigned for a time during the 1980s as Ohio's fastest-growing corporation. Sadly, the legacy of the Fries family in the flavor industry came to a distasteful end in the early 1990s.

The Fraud

Jon Fries orchestrated a large-scale financial fraud that led to the downfall of F&C International. At least 10 other F&C executives actively participated in the scam or allowed it to continue unchecked due to their inaction. The methods used by Fries and his cohorts were not unique or even innovative. Fries realized that the most effective strategy for embellishing his company's periodic operating results was to inflate revenues and overstate period-ending inventories. Throughout the early 1990s, F&C systematically overstated sales revenues by backdating valid sales transactions, shipping customers product they had not ordered, and recording bogus sales transactions. To overstate inventory, F&C personnel filled barrels with water and then labeled those barrels as containing high-concentrate flavor products. The company also neglected to write off defective goods and included waste products from manufacturing processes in inventory. Company officials used F&C's misleading financial statements to sell equity securities and to obtain significant bank financing.

As F&C's fraud progressed, Jon Fries and his top subordinates struggled to develop appropriate sales and inventory management strategies since the company's accounting records were unreliable. To help remedy this problem, F&C created an imaginary warehouse, Warehouse Q.

---

1. The facts of this case were developed from several SEC enforcement releases and a series of articles that appeared in the *Cincinnati Enquirer*. The key parties in this case neither admitted nor denied the facts reported by the SEC. Those parties include Jon Fries, Catherine Sprauer, Fletcher Anderson, and Craig Schuster.

Warehouse Q became the accounting repository for product returned by customers for being below specification, unuseable or nonexistent items, and items that could not be found in the actual warehouses.[2]

Another baffling problem that faced Fries and his confederates was concealing the company's fraudulent activities from F&C's independent auditors. The executives continually plotted to divert their auditors' attention from suspicious transactions and circumstances uncovered during the annual audits. Subversive measures taken by the executives included creating false documents, mislabeling inventory counted by the auditors, and undercutting subordinates' attempts to expose the fraud.

The size and complexity of F&C's fraud eventually caused the scheme to unravel. Allegations that the company's financial statements contained material irregularities triggered an investigation by the Securities and Exchange Commission (SEC). The investigation revealed that F&C had overstated its cumulative pretax earnings during the early 1990s by approximately $8 million. The company understated its pretax net loss for fiscal 1992 alone by nearly 140 percent, or $3.8 million.

The Division Controller

Catherine Sprauer accepted an accounting position with F&C International in July 1992, shortly after the June 30 close of the company's 1992 fiscal year. Sprauer, a CPA, drafted the Management's Discussion and Analysis (MD&A) section of F&C's 1992 Form 10-K registration statement. In October 1992, the 28-year-old Sprauer became the controller of F&C's Flavor Division. Following that promotion, Sprauer continued to help prepare the MD&A sections of F&C's periodic financial reports submitted to the SEC.

In early January 1993, an F&C employee told Sprauer that he saw company employees filling inventory barrels with water in the final few days of June 1992. This individual also advised Sprauer that he had documentation linking two F&C executives to that incident, which was apparently intended to overstate the company's year-end inventory for fiscal 1992. According to the SEC, Sprauer abruptly ended the conversation with this employee and did not discuss his allegations with anyone.

Later that same day, another F&C employee approached Sprauer and confessed that he was involved in the episode recounted to her earlier in the day. This individual told Sprauer that he had acted under the direct instructions of Jon Fries. The employee then attempted to hand Sprauer a listing of inventory items affected by the fraud. Sprauer refused to accept the list. The persistent employee placed the list in Sprauer's correspondence file. The document detailed approximately $350,000 of nonexistent inventory in F&C's accounting records. Sprauer reportedly never showed the list of bogus inventory to her superiors, to other F&C accountants, or to the company's independent auditors. However, she subsequently warned F&C's chief operating officer (COO), Fletcher Anderson, that the company had "significant inventory problems."

The Chief Operating Officer

Fletcher Anderson became the COO of F&C International in September 1992 and joined the company's board of directors a few days later. On March 23, 1993, Anderson succeeded Jon Fries as F&C's president and CEO. During the fall of 1992,

---

2. Securities and Exchange Commission, *Accounting and Auditing Enforcement Release No. 605,* 28 September 1994. All subsequent quotations are taken from this source.

Anderson stumbled across several suspicious transactions in F&C's accounting records. In late September 1992, Anderson discovered sales shipments made before the given customers had placed purchase orders with F&C. He also learned that other sales shipments had been delivered to F&C warehouses rather than to customers. Finally, in early October 1992, Anderson uncovered a forged bill of lading for a customer shipment. The bill of lading had been altered to change the reported month of shipment from October to September. Each of these errors inflated F&C's reported earnings for the first quarter of fiscal 1993, which ended September 30, 1992.

More direct evidence that F&C's financial data were being systematically distorted came to Anderson's attention during the second quarter of 1993. In November, a subordinate told Anderson that some of the company's inventory of flavor concentrate was simply water labeled as concentrate. The following month, Anderson learned of Warehouse Q and that at least $1.5 million of the inventory "stored" in that warehouse could not be located or was defective.

Catherine Sprauer submitted her resignation to Fletcher Anderson in late January 1993. Among the reasons Sprauer gave for her resignation were serious doubts regarding the reliability of the company's inventory records. Anderson insisted that Sprauer not tell him why she believed those records were unreliable because he wanted to avoid testifying regarding her concerns in any subsequent litigation.

In February 1993, shortly before Anderson replaced Jon Fries as F&C's top executive, an F&C cost accountant warned him that the company had an inventory problem "in the magnitude of $3–4 million." Anderson later told the SEC that although the cost accountant had access to F&C's inventory records and its actual inventory, he believed the accountant was overstating the severity of the company's inventory problem.

The Chief Financial Officer

Craig Schuster served as the chief financial officer (CFO) of F&C International during the early 1990s. As F&C's CFO, Schuster oversaw the preparation of and signed the company's registration statements filed with the SEC, including the company's 10-K reports for fiscal 1991 and 1992. Throughout 1992, Schuster became aware of various problems in F&C's accounting records, most notably the existence of Warehouse Q. In March 1992, Schuster learned that his subordinates could not locate many items listed in F&C's perpetual inventory records. A few months later, Schuster discovered that customer shipments were being backdated in an apparent attempt to recognize sales revenue prematurely. In late 1992, Schuster determined that approximately $1 million of F&C's work-in-process inventory was classified as finished goods.

On December 17, 1992, a frustrated Schuster prepared and forwarded to Fletcher Anderson a 23-page list of $1.5 million of inventory allegedly stored in Warehouse Q. The memo indicated that the inventory could not be located or was defective. The SEC's enforcement releases focusing on the F&C fraud did not reveal how or whether Anderson responded to Schuster's memo.

Because he supervised the preparation of F&C's financial reports filed with the SEC, Schuster knew that those reports did not comment on the company's inventory problems. On January 1, 1993, Craig Schuster resigned as the CFO of F&C International. The final F&C registration statement Schuster signed was the company's 10-Q for the first quarter of fiscal 1993, which ended September 30, 1993.

The Rest of the Story

In a September 28, 1994, enforcement release, the SEC criticized Catherine Sprauer, Fletcher Anderson, and Craig Schuster for failing to ensure that F&C's financial reports "filed with the Commission and disseminated to the investing public were accurate." The federal agency also chastised the three individuals for not disclosing in F&C's financial reports "significant accounting problems of which they were aware." Finally, the SEC scolded Anderson and Schuster for not establishing adequate internal controls to provide for the proper recognition of revenue and the proper valuation of inventory. In an agreement reached with the SEC to settle the allegations pending against them, the three former F&C executives pledged to "permanently cease and desist" from committing or causing violations of federal securities laws.

A second enforcement release issued by the SEC on September 28, 1994, contained a series of allegations directed at Jon Fries and seven other senior F&C executives. The SEC charged that these executives were primarily responsible for F&C's fraudulent earnings scheme. To settle these charges, each executive pledged not to violate federal securities laws in the future. The settlement agreement permanently banned Jon Fries from serving as an officer or director of a public company. Several of the individuals agreed to forfeit proceeds received from earlier sales of F&C securities. Fries relinquished more than $2 million he had realized from the sale of F&C common stock. Finally, the SEC imposed civil fines on four of the executives that ranged from $11,500 to $20,000.

F&C International filed for bankruptcy in April 1993 shortly after the fraud became public. The following year, a competitor purchased F&C's remaining assets. In March 1995, Jon Fries began serving a 15-month sentence in a federal prison for his role in the F&C fraud.

Questions

1. Jon Fries (CEO), Fletcher Anderson (COO), Craig Schuster (CFO), and Catherine Sprauer (division controller) were the four central figures in this case. Identify the key responsibilities associated with the professional roles these individuals occupied. Briefly describe the type and extent of interaction each of these individuals likely had with F&C's independent auditors.

2. Using the scale shown below, evaluate the conduct of the four key individuals discussed in this case. Be prepared to defend your answers.

$$-100 \ldots \ldots \ldots \ldots \ldots \ldots 0 \ldots \ldots \ldots \ldots \ldots \ldots 100$$

| Highly | Highly |
| Unethical | Ethical |

3. For a moment, step into the shoes of Catherine Sprauer. What would you have done during and following each of the confrontations she had with the two employees who insisted that F&C executives were involved in a fraudulent scheme to misrepresent the company's financial statements?

4. Craig Schuster resigned as F&C's CFO on January 1, 1993. Apparently, Schuster did not reveal to any third parties the concerns he had regarding F&C's accounting records and previous financial statements. In your opinion, did Schuster have a responsibility to inform someone of those concerns following his resignation? Defend your answer.

5. Assume that you, rather than Fletcher Anderson, were F&C's COO in December 1992. What would you have done upon receiving the list of Warehouse Q inventory from Craig Schuster?

Suzette Washington, Accounting Major

Suzette Washington financed her college education by working as an inventory clerk for Bertolini's, a clothing store chain located in the southeastern United States.[1] Bertolini's caters primarily to fashion-conscious young men and women. The company's stores carry a wide range of clothing, including casual wear, business suits, and accessories. The Bertolini's store for which Suzette worked is located a few blocks from the campus of the large state university that she attended. Except for management personnel, most of Bertolini's employees are college students. Suzette's best friend and roommate, Paula Kaye, worked for Bertolini's as a sales clerk. Paula majored in marketing, while Suzette was an accounting major.

During Suzette's senior year in college, Bertolini's began experiencing abnormally high inventory shrinkage in the store's three departments that stocked men's apparel. Suzette's supervisor, an assistant store manager, confided in her that he believed one or more of the sales clerks were stealing merchandise. Over lunch one day in the student union, Suzette casually mentioned the inventory problem to Paula. Paula quickly changed the subject by asking Suzette about her plans for the weekend.

"Paula, rewind for just a second. Do you know something that I don't?"

"Huh? What do you mean?"

"Missing inventory . . . shrinkage . . . theft?"

After a few awkward moments, Paula stopped eating and looked squarely into her friend's eyes. "Suzette, I don't know if it's true, but I've heard a rumor that Alex and Matt are stealing a few things each week. Polo shirts, silk ties, jeans. Occasionally, they take something expensive, like a hand-knit sweater or sports jacket."

"How are they doing it?"

"I've heard—and don't repeat any of this now—I've heard that a couple of times per week, Alex stashes one or two items at the bottom of the trash container beneath the number two cash register. Then Matt, you know he empties the trash every night in the dumpster out in the alley, takes the items out and puts them in his car."

"Paula, we can't let them get away with this. We have to tell someone."

"No 'we' don't. Remember, this is just a rumor. I don't know that it's true. If you tell a manager, there will be questions. And more questions. Maybe the police will be brought in. You know that eventually someone's going to find out who told. And then . . . slashed tires . . . phone calls in the middle of the night."

"So, don't get involved? Don't do anything? Just let those guys keep stealing?"

"Suze, you work in inventory. You know the markup they put on those clothes. They expect to lose a few things here and there to employees."

"Maybe the markup wouldn't be so high if theft wasn't such a problem."

Now, there was no doubt in Paula's mind that Suzette was going to report the alleged theft scheme to management. "Two months, Suze. Two months till we graduate.

---

1. This case was developed from information provided by a former college student who is now a CPA. The names, location, and certain other background facts have been changed.

Can you wait till then to spill the beans? Then we can move out of state before our cars are spray-painted."

One week following Suzette and Paula's conversation, a Bertolini's store manager received an anonymous typed message that revealed the two-person theft ring rumored to be operating within the store. Bertolini's immediately retained a private detective. Over a four-week period, the detective documented $500 of merchandise thefts by Alex and Matt. After Bertolini's notified the police, the local district attorney filed criminal charges against the two young men. A plea bargain agreement arranged by their attorneys resulted in suspended prison sentences for Alex and Matt. The terms of that agreement included making restitution to Bertolini's, completing several hundred hours of community service, and a lengthy period of probation.

Questions

1. What would you do if you found yourself in a situation similar to that faced by Suzette in this case?

2. Do you believe that it was appropriate for Suzette to report the alleged theft ring to a store manager? Would it have been unethical for Suzette *not* to report the rumored theft ring?

3. Accounting majors are preparing to enter a profession recognized as having one of the strongest and most rigorously enforced ethical codes. Given this fact, do you believe that accounting majors have a greater responsibility than other business majors to behave ethically?

4. Briefly discuss internal control activities that might have prevented the theft losses suffered by Bertolini's.

Oak Industries, Inc.

Oak Industries began operations in the early 1930s as a manufacturer of car radio components. The California-based company struggled financially through its first few years but managed to emerge from the Depression, unlike many of its competitors. In the late 1960s, Oak expanded into the cable television industry. Technological innovations developed by the company contributed to the tremendous growth of that industry during the latter part of the twentieth century. In 1977, Oak began marketing subscription television services. Within four years, Oak ranked as the largest operator of subscription television systems in the United States. Oak's subscription television subsidiary also generated the majority of the company's annual revenues by the early 1980s.

Rainy Day Reserves

Exhibit 1 presents selected financial data for Oak Industries for the period 1978–1981. Oak established new sales and profit records each successive year during this period. In fact, in both 1980 and 1981 the company's *actual* net income was greater than the figure reported by the company. In 1980, Oak's top executives became concerned that the company could not indefinitely sustain its impressive growth rate in annual profits. To help the company maintain this trend, the executives began creating reserves that could be used to boost Oak's reported profits in later years.

> *To report a smooth upward earnings trend and to provide a "cushion" of profits to be used in periods of lower actual earnings, Oak implemented a policy during 1980 and 1981 of establishing unneeded reserves to be released (reversed) in later periods, if needed.*[1]

These "rainy day reserves" included overstatements of the company's allowances for inventory obsolescence and uncollectible receivables.

Unfortunately, Oak needed to "dip" into its rainy day reserves much sooner than expected. In 1981, Oak established subscription television operations in the Dallas-Fort Worth and Phoenix metropolitan areas. Almost immediately, the company began encountering major financial problems in these new operations due principally to unexpectedly low sales. Based upon its sales forecasts for these two new market areas, Oak had stockpiled a large quantity of television decoder boxes. Because of the significant shortfall in subscribers, much of this inventory was not needed. To make matters worse, rapid technological changes soon rendered the excess inventory obsolete. Oak also had an unusually high rate of sales returns for a new model of a decoder box that it sold to new subscribers. Quality control problems in Oak's manufacturing processes caused this model to be unreliable. Finally, Oak experienced a higher-than-normal rate of uncollectible receivables in the Dallas-Fort Worth and Phoenix market areas.

---

1. Securities and Exchange Commission, *Accounting and Auditing Enforcement Release No. 63*, 25 June 1985.

EXHIBIT 1

OAK INDUSTRIES,
INC., SELECTED
FINANCIAL DATA,
1978–1981

Oak Industries, Inc., Selected Financial Data, 1978–1981				
	1981	**1980**	**1979**	**1978**
Net Sales*	$507,119	$385,586	$281,348	$192,181
Gross Profit	168,437	125,163	86,060	51,402
Net Income	30,350	20,082	11,170	4,850
Earnings Per Share	2.23	1.85	1.36	0.72

*Net sales, gross profit, and net income are expressed in thousands of dollars.

Source: Oak Industries, Inc., 1982 Form 10-K filed with the Securities and Exchange Commission.

Reversal of the Rainy Day Reserves

In the first quarter of fiscal 1982, Oak's senior management instructed the company's accountants to "release" several million dollars of the reserves established during 1980 and 1981. The reversal of these reserves significantly reduced Oak's reported expenses and allowed the company to sustain its smooth upward earnings trend by reporting a record quarterly profit. If the reserves had not been reversed, the company's net income for the first quarter of 1982 would have been nearly 50 percent lower than the reported figure of $7.5 million. Oak's top executives boasted in the company's financial report for the first three months of 1982 that "first-quarter sales and net income were greater than in any first quarter in the Company's history."

As fiscal 1982 progressed, Oak's financial problems worsened. At year-end, the management of Oak's subscription television subsidiary notified corporate headquarters of $40 million of asset write-offs and increases in loss reserves needed for that subsidiary. Oak's senior executives realized that if they booked the $40 million of additional expenses, the company's consolidated income statement for 1982 would reflect a large loss. Instead of reporting that loss, the executives decided to report earnings per share of $0.25 for 1982, which translated to a net income of approximately $4.1 million.

To "manufacture" the desired net income for fiscal 1982, Oak's senior executives turned to the company's chief financial officer (CFO), who oversaw the company's accounting department. The senior executives instructed the CFO to take the necessary steps to produce the target earnings figure. In response to that directive, the CFO instructed the firm's controller to determine how much of the $40 million of unrecorded expenses could be booked if the company were to report earnings per share of $0.25 for 1982. After the controller arrived at that figure, the CFO instructed him to arbitrarily allocate that amount between the company's reserves for bad debts and inventory obsolescence. The controller complied, which resulted in Oak reporting the management-mandated $0.25 earnings per share for 1982.

SEC Investigation Focuses on Oak's Controller

A principal focus of the Securities and Exchange Commission (SEC) investigation that uncovered Oak Industries' accounting fraud was the company's controller, a CPA with impressive credentials that included several years of experience with Arthur Andersen & Co., Oak's independent audit firm. According to the SEC, the controller often questioned his superiors' judgment, at least initially, when they instructed him to misrepresent the company's financial data. For example, the controller recommended disclosing in Oak's financial statements for the first quarter of 1982 that the company had reversed several million dollars of the illicit rainy day reserves.

When his superiors rejected that recommendation, he relented and subsequently helped prepare the misleading financial statements for that quarter.

Later in 1982, Oak's controller received a series of memos from the CFO of the firm's subscription television subsidiary. Among other financial problems being experienced by that unit, these memos notified the controller that the subsidiary's inventory obsolescence reserve was significantly understated. At the end of the fourth quarter of 1982, the subsidiary's CFO reported that his unit's inventory should be written down by nearly $10 million. When Oak's senior executives disagreed with that assessment, the controller "accepted [their] judgment and failed to take steps necessary to cause Oak to record the necessary reserves."[2]

The SEC also reported that Oak's controller knew that key accounting documents were being withheld from the company's independent auditors, Arthur Andersen & Co. Oak often prepared two sets of loss exposure analyses: one set to be used for internal decision-making purposes and another set to be forwarded to Arthur Andersen. The loss exposure analyses given to the independent auditors understated the severity of Oak's inventory obsolescence and bad-debt problems.

During Oak's 1982 audit, the firm's controller received a memorandum written by one of the company's internal auditors. This memorandum suggested that the independent auditors be given an "edited version" of an earlier memo that analyzed the status of Oak's reserve for uncollectible receivables. This edited version of the earlier memo significantly understated Oak's estimated uncollectible receivables at the end of 1982.

We [the internal audit staff] would like to issue the edited version of the . . . memo to Arthur Andersen to avoid any additional suspicions on their part as to the content. We believe the revised memo has been toned down sufficiently to be issued to them.

The controller did not prevent the internal audit staff from forwarding the misleading memo to the independent auditors. As a result, Oak's independent auditors received an inaccurate analysis of the year-end status of the client's uncollectible receivables.

Near the end of Arthur Andersen's 1982 audit of Oak Industries, the company's controller signed a letter of representations addressed to the audit firm. Among other assertions, this letter indicated that company officials had provided all of Oak's financial records and related information to Arthur Andersen. The letter of representations also stated that Oak's financial statements had been prepared in accordance with generally accepted accounting principles (GAAP).

EPILOGUE

In June 1985 and March 1986, the SEC issued enforcement releases documenting Oak Industries' abusive accounting and financial reporting practices. These releases also reported the sanctions imposed on the company and its executives involved in the fraudulent scheme. The SEC permanently banned Oak's chief executive officer (CEO) from serving as an officer or director of a publicly owned firm.

Four other Oak officers, including its CFO and controller, settled charges filed against them by agreeing not to violate federal securities laws in the future. The SEC also required Oak to establish an audit committee that would assume an active role in the company's accounting and financial reporting function.

In early 1985, Oak voluntarily reissued its financial statements for 1982 and 1983. Collectively,

---

2. This and subsequent quotations, unless indicated otherwise, are taken from Securities and Exchange Commission, *Accounting and Auditing Enforcement Release No. 93*, 26 March 1986.

these financial statements reduced Oak's previously reported net income for those years by approximately $44 million, or $2.70 per share. The company also disclosed in early 1985 that it would be discontinuing its subscription television operations.

One of the SEC's enforcement releases in the Oak Industries case focused exclusively on the firm's controller. In this release, the SEC noted that the controller clearly was not a "primary decision-maker" within the firm or a member of its senior management. As a result, the controller was not directly responsible for the company's earnings manipulation scheme. Nevertheless, the SEC maintained that the controller failed to fulfill his professional responsibilities when he became aware of that scheme:

> Although [the controller] may have made the appropriate recommendations to his corporate supervisors, when those recommendations were rejected, [he] acted as the "good soldier," implementing their directions which he knew or should have known were improper.

The SEC's refusal to recognize the "good soldier" defense as a valid justification for questionable conduct by mid-level corporate executives was debated by the business press following the public disclosure of the Oak Industries fraud. Most parties who commented on this issue supported the SEC's position. However, one individual warned, "It's unrealistic to place a burden on mid-level [corporate] managers to discharge obligations that they're not in a position to discharge."[3]

Often complicating the role of a corporate controller is the fact that his or her immediate superior lacks an accounting background. This was true in the Oak Industries case. Oak's controller was a CPA, but his immediate superior, the company's CFO, was not. The chief accountant of the SEC's enforcement division at the time, Robert Sack, observed that "added pressure" is often placed on a controller when his or her superior is not a CPA.[4] Sack recommended in such cases that a controller develop a relationship with the firm's board of directors, legal counsel, and independent auditors. These parties can serve as allies for the controller if his or her superior makes unreasonable demands at some point regarding accounting or financial reporting issues.

Questions

1. Is it unethical for a company to intentionally understate its earnings? Why or why not?

2. Should auditors be equally concerned with potential understatements and potential overstatements of a client's revenues and expenses? Identify audit techniques that may be particularly helpful in uncovering understatements of revenues and overstatements of expenses.

3. Place yourself in the position of Oak's controller when the company's senior executives rejected his recommendation to disclose the reversal of the rainy day reserves. What would you have done at that point?

4. What responsibilities do a company's controller and other accounting employees have when interacting with the firm's independent auditors? Do these responsibilities conflict with other job-related responsibilities of a company's accounting employees? Explain.

5. Should the SEC and other regulatory bodies hold corporate accountants who are CPAs to a higher standard of conduct than corporate accountants who are not CPAs? Defend your answer.

---

3. K. Victor, "Tough-Minded SEC Takes Aim at Corporate 'Good Soldiers'," *Legal Times*, 7 April 1986, 1.

4. *Securities Regulation and Law Reports*, "Internationalization Raising Questions on SEC Disclosure System, Peters Says," 12 December 1986, 1773.

Wiley Jackson, Accounting Major

Wiley Jackson spent three months as an audit intern with a local practice office of a major accounting firm while he was earning an undergraduate accounting degree at the University of Wisconsin–Milwaukee.[1] Wiley thoroughly enjoyed the three-month internship. He made several friends and, more importantly, gained valuable work experience and insight into the nature and work environment of independent auditing. On the final day of his internship, Wiley had an exit interview with the office managing partner (OMP). The OMP told Wiley that he had impressed his superiors and coworkers. Wiley's performance reviews indicated that he had strong technical and interpersonal skills and always conducted himself in a professional and ethical manner. At the end of the exit interview, the OMP offered Wiley a full-time position with the firm once he completed his master's degree in accounting at UWM. Wiley was thrilled by the offer and accepted it immediately.

While working on his graduate degree, Wiley received a packet of documents from his future employer that he was to complete and return. The packet contained standard insurance forms, 401-K elections, a W-4 form, a personal investments worksheet for independence-compliance purposes, and a "Statement of Arrests and Convictions" form. Wiley recalled having completed an earlier version of the latter document before beginning his internship. Among the questions included in this form was the following:

> *Have you ever been convicted of a misdemeanor (excluding minor traffic violations) or a felony, or driving while intoxicated in this or any other state, or are criminal charges currently pending against you?*

The form required a full explanation if this question was answered "Yes." Wiley had previously responded "No" to this question because, at the time, he had had a "clean" record, except for a few parking tickets and one speeding violation. But now, as he sat at his desk staring at the form, he was not sure how to respond to the question.

After completing his internship, Wiley had been invited to a graduation party at an off-campus location. Although he was not a "party animal," Wiley had decided to accept the invitation since it would likely be his final opportunity to see many of his friends who were graduating from UWM. When he arrived at the site of the party, Wiley was surprised by the large number of people there. In fact, because the older, two-story home could not accommodate all the party-goers, several dozen of them were congregated in the front yard and on the residential street on which the house was located.

As he made his way through the boisterous crowd, Wiley suddenly came face to face with Sally Jones. Sally, a UWM alumnus, had been the audit senior assigned to Wiley's largest client during his internship. While Wiley was talking to Sally, an acquaintance thrust a cold beer into his hand and slapped him on the shoulder. "No talking business here, Dude. It's party time!" As luck would have it, just a few minutes later, the party was "busted" by the local police. Before Wiley realized exactly what

---

1. This case was written by Brian Daugherty, Assistant Professor at the University of Wisconsin–Milwaukee. The facts of this case were developed from an actual series of events. Certain background information has been changed to conceal the identities of the individuals involved in the case.

was happening, a policeman approached him and asked for his I.D. As he handed over his driver's license, Wiley, who was three days short of his 21st birthday, realized that he was in trouble. Moments later, the stone-faced policeman began writing out a minor-in-possession citation. The citation ordered Wiley to appear before a local judge the following month.

Wiley was distraught and had a difficult time sleeping that night. The next morning, he called an attorney and told him what had happened. The attorney informed Wiley that he had dealt with many similar situations involving college students and that Wiley should not be "stressed out" by the incident. For first-time offenders, like Wiley, the attorney had always been successful in persuading a judge to approve "deferred adjudication." As long as Wiley stayed out of trouble over the following two years, the minor-in-possession charge would be expunged from his record, "just like it never happened," according to the attorney.

Questions

1. Place yourself in Wiley's position. How would you respond to the "Arrests and Convictions" question? Before responding, identify the decision alternatives available to you.

2. Suppose that Wiley does not disclose the citation he received. A few weeks after going to work for his new employer, Wiley is called into the OMP's office. The OMP tells Wiley that he has recently learned of the minor-in-possession citation that Wiley had been given. The OMP then hands Wiley a copy of the Arrest and Convictions form that he completed after receiving the job offer from the firm. How should the OMP deal with this matter? How, if at all, should Wiley be disciplined? Defend your answer.

3. Assume that Sally Jones was the individual who told the OMP that Wiley had been given a police citation at the graduation party. Do you believe Sally had a moral or ethical responsibility to inform the OMP of that matter? Why or why not?

CASE 4.6

Arvel Smart, Accounting Major

Arvel Ray Smart was born in Lebanon, Missouri, and grew up in the small town of Bolivar 40 miles west of Lebanon in southeastern Missouri.[1] Arvel's mother and father graduated from the University of Missouri with accounting degrees in the mid-1970s. The Smarts spent three years working on the tax staff of a Big Eight practice office in Kansas City before deciding to establish their own accounting firm in Bolivar. Arvel helped out in his parents' office during high school, especially when they were facing tax deadlines. He enjoyed the work, which is why he decided to major in accounting when he enrolled at the University of Missouri following graduation from high school. Arvel realized that he most likely would have the opportunity to take over his parents' accounting firm when they retired. His only sibling, an older sister, was a performing arts major at Washington University in St. Louis and had no interest in becoming involved in the family business.

During his junior year at Mizzou, Arvel was admitted into the five-year program in the School of Accountancy. After completing the 150-hour program, Arvel would receive Bachelor of Science and Master of Accountancy degrees. After completing his junior year, Arvel accepted an internship with a Big Four practice office in Kansas City. Because he wanted to gain a better understanding of auditing, Arvel chose to intern on the audit staff of that office. Arvel was surprised by the number of interesting assignments he was given that summer. In fact, by the end of the summer he was reconsidering the decision he had made earlier to choose the tax track of Mizzou's five-year accounting program.

On the final day of Arvel's internship, the office managing partner met with him and offered him an entry-level auditing position. Arvel thanked the partner for the job offer and told him that he would seriously consider accepting it. He explained to the partner that he had not yet made a final decision about whether to focus on auditing or taxation early in his career. The partner was very understanding and told Arvel that he had plenty of time to make up his mind and then added that the job offer would remain open for 12 months, until the end of the following summer.

Arvel enrolled in the undergraduate auditing course during the spring semester of his fourth year in college. He enjoyed the course so much that he made up his mind to begin his career as an auditor and to accept the job offer from the firm with which he had interned the previous summer. He planned to delay accepting that offer, however, until the end of the summer. Arvel's girlfriend, who was also an accounting major at Mizzou, had accepted an offer for a summer internship with a Big Four practice office in St. Louis. Arvel was hoping to spend the summer in St. Louis, so he had interviewed earlier in the year with two regional accounting firms based in that city. Both of the firms had offered him an internship.

During the final week of the spring semester of his fourth year, Arvel accepted an internship offer from one of the two St. Louis–based accounting firms. Arvel realized that both regional and national accounting firms use internships as a tool to recruit permanent employees and that they typically offer internships to students they

---

1. This case is based on factual circumstances involving a recent accounting graduate. Key facts, including the individual's name and relevant locations, have been changed to obscure his or her identity.

believe have an interest in eventually accepting a permanent position with them. That realization caused Arvel to experience some degree of guilt when he called and accepted the internship with the St. Louis firm. He quickly cleared his guilty conscience by convincing himself that there was some remote chance he would change his mind and accept a job with the St. Louis accounting firm. In fact, in Arvel's mind, that firm had a responsibility to prove to him that it offered more opportunities than the Big Four accounting firm from which he had already received an outstanding job offer.

Questions

1. Before interviewing with the two St. Louis accounting firms, did Arvel have an obligation to inform them that he had an outstanding job offer from a Big Four practice office in Kansas City? Why or why not?

2. Did Arvel Smart behave unethically by accepting the internship with the St. Louis accounting firm when he intended to accept the outstanding job offer from the Big Four accounting firm at the completion of that internship? Defend your answer.

David Quinn, Tax Accountant

We have all had "that" friend, an individual who attaches himself or herself to us without our encouragement—or approval, for that matter.[1] For Debbie Woodruff, *that* friend was David Quinn. Debbie met David in the very first college accounting class that either of them took at the large public university they attended. Shortly before the instructor entered the room, David had rushed in and taken the seat to Debbie's left. Moments later, an out-of-breath David had leaned over and asked Debbie, "Is this Accounting 201?" That question was the beginning of a relationship that would last for decades.

Debbie had little trouble grasping the revenue recognition rule, accrual accounting, straight-line depreciation, and the other fundamental concepts and topics in the introductory financial accounting course. David, on the other hand, struggled to earn a "B" in the course. Debbie never questioned David's intelligence. The problem was that David simply had too many outside interests—campus politics, his social fraternity, and weekend parties—to devote sufficient time to studying for the rigorous departmental exams in ACCT 201.

Before each exam, David would ask Debbie if they could study together. Debbie was not particularly fond of David, but she agreed to tutor him while she prepared for each exam because explaining an accounting concept or principle to someone else made the given item "gel" in her own mind. During two of these tutoring sessions, David asked Debbie for a date. The second time, Debbie told him that she did not mind studying together but that their "chemistry" made dating out of the question. David's outspoken and opinionated manner was the principal source of the chemistry problem between the two accounting majors. On most subjects—politics and economics, in particular—David had an opinion, an expert opinion, which he was more than willing to share with anyone who would listen. Debbie was much more reserved and preferred to spend her time focusing on her studies rather than debating whatever happened to be the front- page issue of the day.

Over the remainder of their college careers, Debbie and David sat side by side in most of their accounting courses and several other business courses, as well. Eventually, Debbie came to accept David's brash personality and considered him a friend—just not a close friend. Debbie maintained a near-perfect 3.9 average in her accounting courses, while David finished with a 3.2 in his accounting major. During her final year of college, Debbie accepted an audit staff position with the nearby office of a Big Eight accounting firm. As fate would have it, David accepted a job on the tax staff of that same office.

Debbie wasn't thrilled by the fact that she and David would be working for the same firm. However, she expected that they would seldom see each other since she would be working primarily at client locations, while David would likely be "stuck" in the office completing tax returns and doing tax research. Debbie was right. During their first year in public accounting, she saw David only on the rare occasions that

---

1. The key facts of this case were provided by a former public accountant who is now an accounting professor. The names of all parties and locations have been changed.

she was in the office, which was typically during the wrap-up phase of an audit to which she had been assigned.

Each time she was in the office, David would ask Debbie to go to lunch with him. Debbie always accepted. She didn't like to admit it, but the lunches served a useful purpose, namely, catching up on all the office scuttlebutt. David seemingly made it his business to know everyone else's business. He would joyfully tell Debbie which tax manager had not received a recommendation for promotion, which audit senior was interviewing for a position on a client's accounting staff, and which intra-office relationship was not "working out."

One Friday in early April, Debbie and David met for lunch to celebrate the end of her second busy season. Debbie was in the office tying up loose ends on the soon-to-be-completed audit of her largest client. She was looking forward to the lunch because she hadn't spoken to David since the office Christmas party almost four months earlier.

On their way to a nearby restaurant, David told Debbie that three of his friends on the tax staff of another Big Eight accounting firm would be meeting them for lunch. Debbie realized that the presence of those individuals would likely divert David's attention and deprive her of the latest news from the office grapevine. So, she resigned herself to having a boring lunch. She could not have been more wrong.

During lunch, the four tax professionals swapped war stories regarding the latest returns on which they had worked. Debbie found the topic of the conversation inappropriate. In her mind, it was best to never discuss professional engagements, audit or otherwise, over lunch in a public setting. You just never knew who might be eavesdropping at an adjoining table. Debbie became particularly uncomfortable when David began discussing the tax return of a wealthy local businessman who had previously served several terms on the city council.

"Yeah, you wouldn't believe the investments this guy has," David said to the friend on his left. "The guy is loaded. And I mean . . . loaded!" Debbie cringed. Anyone within 20 feet could have heard David's emphatic pronouncement. She attempted to change the subject of the conversation, but David refused to yield the floor.

"No, wait, Debbie, I gotta tell these guys about the latest racket this dude is running." Debbie cringed once more. "You wouldn't believe what he wants us to do. He wants to write off the cost of his daughter's wedding as an entertainment expense. And, you know what? I think we are going to let him do it!"

Debbie couldn't take it anymore. "David, you shouldn't be talking about this at lunch. You don't know who is listening."

"Come on, Debbie. No one's listening."

"David. I'm serious. This is inappropriate."

"What?" David was obviously surprised that his normally meek friend was challenging him. Over the five years that he had known Debbie, she had never behaved in this manner. He was not only surprised but also somewhat miffed that Debbie was running the risk of embarrassing him in front of three fellow tax professionals. "Look around us, Debbie. These people aren't listening to us. Besides, they are all strangers."

"David, that's the point. These people are strangers. And how do you know that they aren't listening? Isn't it possible that one of them might call up your client and tell him what they heard?"

David leaned back in his chair and shook his head. "Oh yeah, I'm sure Grandma over there wrote down every word I just said."

Debbie was flabbergasted at her friend's flippant attitude toward what she considered a very important topic. "David, does the phrase 'client confidentiality' mean anything to you? Surely you tripped across it when studying for the CPA exam?"

"Oh, so you are going to bring up the CPA exam? I guess you *are* trying to embarrass me in front of my friends. Just because you passed that stupid thing the first time and I am still working on it doesn't make you an expert on ethics issues."

"David. You know that's not what I meant," Debbie responded indignantly. "Even if 'Grandma' isn't listening, you are talking about sensitive issues regarding a tax client with three guys from a competing office."

"Oh, I see. My buddies here are going back to their office to report me to the state board, right?" David was no longer miffed; he was angry. "Now, you've gone too far, Debbie. My friends would never do anything to get me into trouble." He then added in a sarcastic tone, "If anyone 'reports me' it will be you, Miss Self-righteous."

Debbie reached into her purse and counted out the money for her part of the bill. She then laid the cash on the table in front of her and, without speaking to David or his friends, left the restaurant.

David and Debbie did not speak again until their office's annual July Fourth golf tournament. To his credit, David approached Debbie and said that he hoped they could put their unpleasant encounter behind them.

"I'm sorry it happened. Why don't we just forget it, Debbie? We've been friends for a long time. There's no reason we can't get over this."

Debbie stepped forward and gave David a light hug and told him that they could be friends once more. Despite the nice overture by David, in the future Debbie made every effort to avoid him when she was working in the office.

EPILOGUE

Debbie sat waiting in the college placement office to meet the managing partner of the practice office where she had worked as a staff accountant and senior auditor. After almost five years in that office, Debbie had decided that public accounting was not for her. Instead, she had decided to pursue a Ph.D.—with the eventual career objective of becoming an accounting professor. Debbie subsequently spent five years earning her doctoral degree, including a stressful 18 months fretting over her dissertation. Ten years later, after accumulating an impressive portfolio of publications, she returned to her alma mater to accept a tenured position in its accounting department. After 15 years at her alma mater, Debbie was a full professor and just a few years away from retirement.

Each fall semester, representatives of the major accounting firms came to Debbie's campus to interview the latest crop of soon-to-be accounting graduates. Today was her former employer's opportunity to attempt to impress her students. Debbie realized that she had a responsibility to interact with the recruiters who came to campus—but she always dreaded meeting with the recruiters from her former employer. She knew that throughout lunch David Quinn, her old friend who was now the managing partner of the office in which she had worked, would tell story after story of their college and coworker days, stories that she had heard repeatedly, stories that became more embellished each year.

In Debbie's mind, the annual lunch with David and his subordinates was a small price to pay to help her students land a job with her former employer. Besides, this year, she had a course to teach immediately after lunch, so she had an excuse to leave early. As she sat waiting for David, she suddenly realized that her course that afternoon was in the same classroom where she had met him for the first time more than 30 years earlier.

Questions

1. Explain the meaning of the phrase "client confidentiality" in the context of a CPA's ethical responsibilities. In your opinion, did David Quinn violate the accounting profession's client confidentiality rule?

2. Assume the role of Debbie Woodruff. How would you have handled the situation that arose in the restaurant?

3. Did Debbie have a responsibility to report David's behavior to a superior in her practice office or to anyone else? Why or why not? Did Debbie have a responsibility to determine whether her firm's tax department was providing appropriate professional advice regarding the deductibility of the entertainment expenses being claimed by David's client?

Jack Bass, Accounting Professor

Jack Bass grew up on a large farm in the Palouse region of southeastern Washington.[1] Jack observed firsthand the challenges associated with earning a livelihood by "working the land" and he wanted no part of it. Instead of spending each day working outside in the elements, Jack wanted to become a professional. He discussed various careers with his high school counselor, including law, medicine, and accounting. Because Jack had always enjoyed numbers, the counselor suggested that he enroll in a bookkeeping course. Despite the fact that most of his friends disliked the course, Jack enjoyed it. He enjoyed the course so much that he decided that after graduating from high school he would major in accounting at nearby Washington State University.

After four years at Wazoo, Jack graduated with a degree in accounting and accepted a position with a Big Eight accounting firm in Seattle. Initially, Jack, like many of his colleagues, planned to pursue a partnership position with his firm. But each year that he worked in public accounting, Jack became less and less enamored with his job.

One of Jack's largest clients required him to spend six weeks per year in a small city in central Idaho. Staff training courses and other work assignments resulted in Jack spending another six to eight weeks away from home, meaning that he was "on the road" approximately three months per year. Another facet of his job that Jack disliked was the dreaded busy season. From November 1 through mid-March, Jack could count on working varying amounts of overtime each week. In college, Jack had always prided himself on his time management skills. By his fourth year in public accounting, however, Jack constantly felt as if he were "running to catch up." Even during the supposedly "slow" summer months, Jack never seemed to have sufficient time to complete his job assignments without putting in a few extra hours in the evenings or on the weekends. In fact, the harder he worked, the more work he seemed to be given by his superiors.

In the weeks prior to his fourth busy season, Jack decided that public accounting was not for him and began exploring other employment opportunities. During a recruiting trip to the Washington State campus, Jack met privately with one of his former accounting professors whom he had always admired. Jack trusted the professor to provide him with a candid and objective assessment of the various career paths that he might consider pursuing. During their conversation, the professor suggested that Jack consider a career in academics. Over the next several months, Jack investigated the opportunities available in academics and discussed the matter with family members and another accounting professor. The more he found out about the work role and lifestyle of a professor, the more that career path appealed to him. After considering and dismissing several other options (including a job offer from a client to become its assistant controller), Jack decided that he would pursue a doctorate in business with the eventual career goal of becoming an accounting professor.

---

1. The key facts of this case were provided by a college professor. The names of all parties and locations have been changed.

After taking the Graduate Management Admission Test (GMAT), Jack applied to several doctoral programs in accounting and eventually enrolled in a program at a Big Ten school. Five years later, he completed his degree and accepted a position as an assistant professor at a large private university on the West Coast. As an assistant professor, Jack's principal responsibility was to complete research projects that would yield papers considered for publication in the major accounting research journals. Each semester, Jack's teaching responsibilities included one section of the undergraduate auditing course and one large section of the introductory financial accounting course.

The "megasection" of the introductory financial accounting course that Jack was assigned to teach typically had more than 300 students. For that reason, the examinations for that section consisted of objective—multiple-choice and true/false—questions. Jack saw no reason to change that policy. During the fifth week of his first semester as an accounting professor, Jack and his two teaching assistants proctored the first exam in the megasection. After the exam was completed, the teaching assistants used the accounting department's Scantron machine to grade the exams. The graded Scantrons were then returned to the students during the next meeting of the class.

While reviewing the exam with his students, Jack told them to identify any test items that had been graded incorrectly by the Scantron machine. If there were grading errors on a Scantron, the students were instructed to return the Scantron to a teaching assistant at the end of class so that the appropriate change in the student's test score could be recorded. Past experience with Scantrons had made Jack aware that erasures and stray marks or smudges could cause individual exam items to be incorrectly graded by the Scantron machine. At the end of the class, Jack was surprised when nearly 30 students turned in their Scantrons. After reviewing those returned Scantrons, Jack suspected that some of the students had changed their answers. Because he had not instructed his teaching assistants to make copies of the Scantrons before they were returned to the students, there was no way for him to confirm his suspicions.

Four weeks later, Jack and his teaching assistants administered the second midterm exam. For this exam, Jack instructed his teaching assistants to copy each of the more than 300 Scantrons. When the Scantrons were returned to the students during the next class session, neither Jack nor his teaching assistants revealed that the Scantrons had been copied. As he had done when discussing the answer key for the first exam, Jack instructed his students to identify exam items that had been incorrectly graded and to return those Scantrons to his teaching assistants to be corrected. At the end of the class session, 35 students returned their Scantrons and indicated that they had not received credit for one or more correct answers. Six of these students identified five or more exam items, out of a total of 100, that had been incorrectly graded by the Scantron machine.

When Jack compared the Scantrons returned by students with the copies of those Scantrons made by his teaching assistants, he found that 15 students had changed one or more answers on their Scantrons. Each of the six students who had identified five or more grading errors had changed all of those items; in other words, there were no actual grading errors on their Scantrons. Of the remaining nine students who returned Scantrons that had been changed, three changed three incorrect answers to correct answers, two changed two answers, and four changed only one incorrect answer. Jack checked his grade book to ascertain which, if any, of these 15 students had indicated after the first exam that their Scantrons contained grading errors. Ten of these students had reported Scantron errors on the first exam. Six of these 10 students were the individuals who had changed five or more incorrect answers on the second exam.

Among the students who made changes to their Scantrons was D. R. Street, III. Prior to each of the two midterm exams, D. R. had dropped by Jack's office during his office hours to review important topics that would be tested on those exams. Because of those visits, D. R. was one of the few students in Jack's large megasection whom he actually knew by name. During the second of those visits, Jack had asked D. R. about his major and his career plans. D. R., who was a sophomore at the time, planned to enroll in law school after completing a dual major in accounting and finance. His long-term career goal was to join his father's law firm, a prominent firm based in Washington, D.C., that specialized in securities litigation.

After identifying the students who had changed answers on their Scantrons for the second exam, Jack immediately went to his department chairperson, Juliette Kasulis, to discuss the matter. Because Jack was a new faculty member and not familiar with the protocol to follow in such situations, Dr. Kasulis explained the alternative ways he could handle the matter. According to Dr. Kasulis, the university's policies and procedures manual gave Jack considerable leeway in dealing with an episode of academic dishonesty. For example, Jack could assign each student who had changed a Scantron answer an "F" for the course and include an official sanction for the incident in the student's academic folder maintained by the university's admissions and records office. Among the least harsh alternatives available to Jack would be requiring each of the students to withdraw from the course with a "WP" (withdrawal while passing). This alternative would force them to retake the course in a subsequent semester but would not result in any official sanction being included in their academic folder.

After discussing the matter at length with Dr. Kasulis, Jack decided to impose the penalty that she suggested. Dr. Kasulis's suggestion was to require each student to withdraw from the course with a WP and to place a temporary sanction letter in their academic folder. If the students were not involved in any further incidents involving academic dishonesty during the following three semesters, the sanction letter would be removed from their academic folders. Dr. Kasulis told Jack that each of the students would be asked to schedule an appointment with the dean of students the following week. During these meetings, which Jack would attend, each student would be informed individually of the sanction he or she was being given for the incident.

Although he knew that he had a responsibility to do so, Jack did not look forward to meeting with the students involved in the cheating incident. Jack regretted that the incident had occurred but believed that he had acted appropriately in the matter. In his mind, academic dishonesty was a very important issue. As a professor, he realized that he had a responsibility to protect the integrity of the grades that he assigned in his courses.

One by one, Jack and the dean of students met with the 15 students who had changed Scantron answers on the second exam. The typical session lasted no more than 10 minutes. After the dean of students explained the matter and the proposed sanction to each student, the student was given an opportunity to respond. The typical response was an admission of guilt and an apology to both Jack and the dean of students. Only three students believed that the sanction imposed on them was unfair. Two of these students maintained that they had been entrapped. In their view, Jack should have forewarned his class that his teaching assistants had copied the scantrons for the second exam. The dean of students informed these two students that they could appeal the sanction imposed on them. Eventually, both students grudgingly accepted the sanction.

The one student who refused to accept the recommended sanction for the cheating incident was D. R. Street, III. D. R. had changed two answers on his Scantron for the second exam but was not among the students who had reported grading errors on the first exam. In his meeting with Jack and the dean of students, an emotional D. R. insisted he had not cheated and, instead, had simply been a victim of a misunderstanding. According to D. R., he thought that Jack had instructed the students to change any wrong answers on their Scantrons to correct answers and then give them to a teaching assistant at the end of the class in which the key for the second exam was discussed.

"Why would Professor Bass ask you to do that, D. R.? What purpose would be served by changing the incorrect answers and then returning the Scantron to a teaching assistant?"

"I don't know. I guess I wasn't paying much attention," was D. R.'s tearful response to the dean's question.

"If that was what you believed were Professor Bass's instructions, why didn't you return your Scantron for the first exam? Didn't Professor Bass follow the exact same procedure when discussing the answer key for the two exams?"

"That was a month earlier. I didn't remember what he had instructed us to do after the first exam."

The dialogue between the dean and D. R. continued for several minutes as Jack sat silently. Each time that the dean suggested that D. R.'s explanation for his behavior was less than logical, D. R. maintained his innocence. Jack had been uncomfortable during each of the previous sessions with the students involved in the cheating incident, but the session with D. R. was extremely unpleasant since he knew and liked the young man.

Finally, the exasperated dean stopped questioning D. R. who, by this point, was sobbing nonstop. After an extended pause, the dean told D. R. that his only option was to appeal the sanction. A few moments later, D. R. regained his composure and told the dean that he wanted to resolve the matter immediately.

"Well, what do you suggest?"

"What if I just withdraw from Professor Bass's course without any sanction letter being placed in my file?"

"D. R., I don't believe that would be fair to the other students involved in this matter," the dean replied. "Besides, as I explained, the sanction letter will be removed from your file within three semesters if you are not charged with any other incidents of academic dishonesty."

"But, sir, I plan to apply to law school next year. My dad wants me to apply to the Ivy League schools. If that sanction is in my file, they may not consider me."

Jack and the dean now fully understood why D. R. was so resistant to the proposed sanction.

"Well, D. R., I'm not sure what else I can say. Professor Bass and I believe that the proposed sanction is fair and we plan to stand by it. Again, if you want, you can file an appeal. I'm sorry."

One week following the session with D. R., the dean of students called Jack and asked that he come by his office. The dean informed Jack that D. R.'s father had spoken directly with the chancellor of the university. D. R.'s father had told the chancellor that since there was no explicit evidence that demonstrated his son was guilty of academic dishonesty, he believed that D. R. should be allowed to withdraw from the accounting course without a letter of sanction being placed in his file. The chancellor had agreed with D. R.'s father and asked the dean of students to reconsider the matter.

"Jack, I am inclined to put this behind us by simply allowing D. R. to withdraw from your class." The dean paused for a moment and then added, "What do you think?"

Jack did not believe the resolution to the matter was fair or appropriate. But, in his mind, he did not have much of a choice. So, he agreed to allow D. R. to withdraw from the course without placing a temporary letter of sanction in his file.

Questions

1. Do you believe that Jack Bass "entrapped" his students by not informing them that the Scantrons for the second exam had been copied? Explain.

2. In your opinion, should the students who were possible repeat offenders, that is, those students who had improperly changed answers on the second exam and reported Scantron errors on the first exam, have been dealt with more harshly than the other students involved in the cheating incident? Defend your answer.

3. Should the number of incorrect answers changed by the students involved in the cheating incident have been considered in determining what punishment they would receive? Why or why not?

4. Do you believe that the decision to allow D. R. to simply withdraw from the accounting course was the proper decision? Was it a fair decision? Explain. How would you have suggested that the dean of students and Jack respond to the chancellor's request that D. R.'s punishment be reconsidered?

Thomas Forehand, CPA

Act I

Thomas Forehand spent the early years of his professional career in a large city working on the auditing staff of a major accounting firm and then serving as an assistant controller for a municipal hospital.[1,2] In 1995, Forehand and his wife decided they wanted a different lifestyle for themselves and their three young children. After several months of searching for a new job, Forehand decided to accept an offer made to him by a CPA with whom he had become acquainted at local professional meetings. Forehand agreed to purchase the CPA's accounting practice that was located in a small suburb approximately 30 miles from the downtown business district where Forehand had worked for more than a decade. The purchase agreement required the former sole practitioner to remain with the firm during a three-year transitional period to minimize client turnover. In 1998, when Forehand assumed complete ownership of the firm, he had six full-time employees, including a receptionist and five accountants, three of whom were CPAs. Tax, compilation, and bookkeeping services accounted for the bulk of Forehand's revenues.

Computer manufacturers, e-commerce start-ups, and other high-tech businesses dominated the greater metropolitan area in which Forehand's firm was located. As a result, the economy of that area was hit hard by the recession that rocked the nation's high-tech sector shortly after the turn of the century. In a span of 18 months, Forehand lost nearly one-third of his clients, forcing him to lay off two of his professional employees. Making matters worse, over that same time frame, Forehand lost more than 80 percent of his personal savings. He had invested those funds in the stocks of major e-commerce firms whose prices "tanked" in late 2000 and early 2001.

On a late Friday afternoon in June 2001, while Forehand sat at his desk contemplating his seemingly bleak future, his receptionist brought a potential client to his door. "Hello, Mr. Forehand. I'm John Jones." Jones was a tall man with a sturdy physique and a firm handshake. He was wearing a starched white shirt, blue jeans, and a frayed baseball cap. Immediately catching Forehand's attention were large, diamond-encrusted rings in the shape of a horseshoe that Jones wore on the pinkie finger of each hand.

"What can I do for you, Mr. Jones?"

"I'm looking for some accounting help."

1. This case was originally published by the American Accounting Association in *Issues in Accounting Education*, Vol. 19, November 2004, 529–538. The case was coauthored by Carol A. Knapp. I would like to thank Tracey Sutherland, Executive Director of the American Accounting Association, for granting permission to include this case in this edition of *Contemporary Auditing: Real Issues and Cases*. An instructional grant provided by Glen McLaughlin funded the development of this case. I would like to thank Mr. McLaughlin for his generous and continuing support of efforts to integrate ethics into business curricula.

2. The central facts of this case were drawn from a recent legal opinion. The names of the actual parties involved in the case have been changed. Additionally, key factual circumstances reported in this case are fictionalized accounts of background material disclosed in the legal opinion.

"Well, you certainly came to the right place. I am the most helpful accountant you will find in this area."

Jones proceeded to tell Forehand that he had recently inherited "a good deal of money" from his grandmother and planned to set up a business in his hometown that was some 60 miles away, on the other side of the metropolitan area. When Forehand seemed surprised that Jones was searching for an accounting firm a considerable distance from his proposed business, Jones quickly added that he planned to visit several accounting firms in the metropolitan area before choosing one.

Because he had worked several years for an electrical contractor, Jones believed that he had sufficient experience and contacts in that field to quickly develop a profitable electrical contracting business. "Coleman Services" was the name he intended to use for his new company. Jones had settled on the generic name—Coleman was his grandmother's maiden name—because he hoped to expand into other lines of business in the future.

As soon as Jones paused, an anxious Forehand seized the opportunity to "sell" his firm to the prospective client. Forehand described the types of services he could offer a new business, including taxation, bookkeeping, and general consulting services. He also stressed the importance of a new entrepreneur having a close relationship with his accountant. Because of his firm's small size, Forehand assured Jones that he would receive prompt and personalized service.

Jones listened politely to Forehand's sales pitch, put the business card Forehand offered him in his shirt pocket, and then excused himself. As Jones walked out the door, Forehand decided that he would likely never see Jones again. Since Jones had failed to ask any questions about Forehand's services or fees, he had obviously been unimpressed with the small accounting firm. Forehand realized that Jones had likely sensed that he was desperate to acquire new clients, which he was. A few minutes later, the disconsolate Forehand told his employees they could begin their weekend early—there was little for them to do anyway.

Act II

When Thomas Forehand walked into his office the following Monday morning, he had a voice mail message waiting for him. John Jones had selected his firm over several others. In the brief message, Jones told Forehand that he would drop by the office that afternoon "to get the ball rolling."

During their conversation later that day, it soon became apparent to Forehand that Jones had little understanding of what steps were necessary to set up a new business. Most of the questions Forehand directed to Jones produced either a blank stare or an indifferent shrug of the shoulders. Finally, Forehand decided to take the initiative.

"John, I think we should start by developing a business plan for you." Jones seemed bored by the lengthy explanation of the nature and purpose of a business plan and only glanced momentarily at the example that Forehand spread out on his desk.

When Forehand attempted to goad him into talking about the specific services his firm would provide, the restless Jones finally spoke. "We don't need to talk about that. What you really need to know is that I want to put together a business big enough to clear about $20,000 per month."

Forehand was surprised by the naïve nature of Jones' remark. "I'm not sure what you mean, John. Do you mean $20,000 of revenues per month or $20,000 of profits per month or $20,000 of net cash flow per month?"

"I mean $20,000 of cash, cash money, each month. I expect to operate on a cash basis and I want to know how much business I have to bring in every month to clear that much cash."

Even more confused now, Forehand responded, "You mean you aren't going to extend credit to your customers?"

"No. No credit. Just cash. I'm going to make them pay hard, cold cash."

Now, Forehand was just as frustrated as Jones, but for a different reason. Over the previous few minutes, Forehand had realized that this promising new client was not so promising after all. Clearly, Jones had no idea what was involved in operating a business, any type of business.

"Are you sure that you have the background necessary to start a business, John?"

"Yep. All I know is that the key to having a successful business is having customers willing to pay cash. And I have a lot of customers lined up who are willing to pay me cash."

Forehand put down his pen and leaned back in his chair for several moments before responding. "Well, exactly what do you want me to do to help you? I'll have to rely on you to tell me because I have to admit, I'm a little confused at this point."

"Okay, that's fair. Why don't we start like this." Finally, Jones seemed interested in the proceedings. "Over the next couple of days, you can set up a business on paper that would produce $20,000 of cash, or what did you say, 'net cash flow' per month. Why don't you fix up a set of financial statements or whatever you call them for a company that size that does electrical contracting work. And, I think you should put together a list of documents that the company would need to have and the types of reports that it would have to file with the IRS and any other of those government-type organizations."

"Aren't you going about this backward? Shouldn't we . . ."

Jones cut off Forehand in mid-sentence. "Now wait a minute. You asked me what I wanted, didn't you?" Forehand reluctantly nodded, which prompted Jones to speak again. "Somewhere, you can find information on a typical electrical contracting business. And you already know what types of documents and reports that a business like that would have to prepare every year. Soon as you get all of that information put together, then we can go from there."

"Go? Go where?" a flustered Forehand asked.

"Go about gettin' the business started," Jones shot back quickly. "Now, what's so hard about that? You said you're a CPA. I know you can put together all of that stuff."

"Well . . . you're right. I can do what you asked. I just hope that is what you really need."

"Good," the suddenly upbeat Jones replied. "Now, what do you charge for your services?"

"Well, for this type of work . . . I would have to charge $100 an hour." Forehand expected that the first mention of his hourly fee would stop Jones in his tracks and possibly bring their awkward discussion to an abrupt conclusion.

"Sounds fair to me," Jones replied nonchalantly. "How about I start out by paying you $2,500 up front. It's called a retainer, isn't it?"

As Forehand sat dumbfounded and silent at his desk, Jones stood and reached into his right front pocket and extracted a large roll of crisp $100 bills. He then counted out 25 of the bills and laid them in a neat pile in front of Forehand. "There you are. I'll be back on Friday afternoon around one to get that report." Without offering to shake Forehand's hand, Jones turned and left, leaving his newly hired accountant gawking at the stack of money in front of him.

Act III

The always prompt Jones returned to Forehand's office at 1 p.m. on Friday. "Thomas, do you have my report?"

"Yes I do. Here you are."

Jones spent several minutes thumbing through the 15-page report after Forehand had completed his explanation of the key items included in it. He then shook his head and tossed the report on the corner of Forehand's desk. "Whew, I didn't know that starting a business involved this much stuff."

"It gets more complicated all the time," Forehand responded.

After taking off his baseball cap and scratching his head for several moments, Jones stood and closed the door to Forehand's office. Jones then sat down and leaned forward as he began speaking in a forceful and unapologetic tone. "Listen here, Thomas. I'm going to come clean with you." Over the next several minutes, Jones explained that the money he had inherited from his grandmother had been in the form of cash—cash that she had literally hidden under a mattress, buried in cans in her backyard, and stashed in remote corners of remote cubbyholes of her large home. "Dang it, she had told me where it was all hid. But, I may have forgotten some of the spots. I spent the better part of two days tearing that old house apart. I just hope I got it all." After a brief pause, Jones shook his head and smiled. "That old lady was quite a hoot. Didn't trust bankers a lick."

Forehand was too shocked to interrupt his new client or to provide any commentary on the sudden and unexpected revelation.

"Anyway, why don't we just forget about you helping me set up the business. I think I can do that myself. And, I really don't need an accountant. My brother has a friend who knows how to keep the books for a cash business." Jones paused for a moment as if to allow Forehand to recover. "Are you with me now? Thomas, you with me?" Forehand's gape-mouthed expression didn't change, but when he blinked his eyes and took a breath, Jones continued. "What I really need to do is run my money through a business. Any business. Here's my plan."

The "plan" was for Forehand to loan Jones $120,000 on a one-year promissory note. Jones would use the cash flow from his "business" to make 12 monthly payments of $11,000, meaning that Forehand would earn approximately 10 percent interest on the loan. The loan agreement would indicate that the assets of Jones' business would serve as the collateral for the loan. But, to persuade Forehand to go along with the plan, Jones would give him cash of $135,000 as the true collateral for the loan. When the loan was paid off, Forehand would return only $120,000 of the cash; he would keep the remaining $15,000 as a "loan origination fee."

By the time Jones had finished laying out his proposal, Forehand felt like he had been struck by a tidal wave. His head was spinning. Finally, he mustered enough breath to speak. "John, I can't go along with this…."

"C'mon, Thomas. There's nothing wrong here. Uncle Sam will be taken care of since I'll be paying a lot of taxes on my money. And, you are going to make out like a bandit. You'll get $12,000 in interest plus another $15,000. For what? For nothing. You're not taking any risk whatsoever. If I don't pay off the loan, you keep the cash collateral." Again, Jones waited to allow Forehand's brain to catch up. "And then, after one year, we can do it all over again. You'll be making nearly $30,000 a year for the next several years. I know you can use it. I know your business isn't doing well. You basically admitted that the other day."

During the tedious pause that followed, Forehand stared blankly at the wall to his left. He then leaned forward, propped his elbows on his desk, and clasped his hands together as if he were seeking divine guidance. At that point, Jones stood and took his wad of $100 bills out of his pocket. He slowly and deliberately counted out 50 of the bills. "Here you are, Thomas. Here's a bonus for doing the deal. That's $5,000. Now. Do we have a deal?"

After studying the large stack of bills for several moments, Thomas Forehand extended his right hand to John Jones and meekly said, "Deal."

Act IV

Thomas Forehand liquidated his remaining investments and borrowed $25,000 from his parents to finance the $120,000 "loan" to John Jones. True to his word, Jones delivered a large bundle of $100 bills held together with rubber bands as collateral for the loan. For nine months, Jones made the monthly payments on the first day of each month. But, in the spring of 2002, two FBI agents arrived at Forehand's firm to tell him that Jones would not be making any further payments on the loan since he had been arrested for selling a variety of illegal drugs including marijuana and methamphetamines. The agents then informed Forehand that he was being charged with conspiracy to commit money laundering and aiding and abetting money laundering. Forehand was then handcuffed, read his Miranda rights, and taken to the local county courthouse to be arraigned.

The principal witness against Forehand during his criminal trial was John Jones. With the coaxing of federal prosecutors, Jones recounted the series of meetings between himself and Forehand that had eventually led to the loan agreement between the two men. Under cross-examination by Forehand's legal counsel, Jones testified that he had never told Forehand the actual source of his cash "inheritance." When given the opportunity to testify on his own behalf, Forehand insisted repeatedly that he did not know or suspect that Jones was attempting to launder money from an illicit drug operation but did admit that he had failed to report the receipt of more than $10,000 in cash to the IRS as required by a federal statute. Forehand's denials had little impact on the jury. Forehand was convicted on both federal charges filed against him. He was sentenced to six years in federal prison, fined $19,000, and was required to forfeit $70,000 of cash he had received from Jones that had been confiscated by law enforcement authorities.

Questions

1. What professional standards are relevant to client acceptance decisions? What general principles do these standards suggest accounting firms should apply in arriving at client acceptance decisions? Identify specific measures that accounting firms should take before deciding to accept a potential client.

2. Assume that you were Thomas Forehand. How would you have responded to the "loan" proposition laid out by John Jones? Do CPAs have a professional or moral responsibility to report illegal acts committed by clients or potential clients?

3. Identify the parties who were affected by Forehand's decision to cooperate with John Jones. What responsibility, if any, did Forehand have to each of those parties? Indicate how each of those parties was affected by Forehand's decision.

4. Thomas Forehand did not intend to become involved in criminal activity when he met John Jones. Instead, Jones goaded Forehand into becoming an active participant in his money-laundering scheme. What strategies can CPAs and businesspeople use to prevent themselves from stepping onto a "slippery slope" that may eventually result in them becoming involved in unethical, immoral, and possibly criminal conduct?

SECTION 5

ETHICAL RESPONSIBILITIES OF INDEPENDENT AUDITORS

Cardillo Travel Systems, Inc.

If virtue is not its own reward,
I don't know any other stipend attached to it.

Lord Byron

ACT 1

Russell Smith knew why he had been summoned to the office of A. Walter Rognlien, the 74-year-old chairman of the board and chief executive officer (CFO) of Smith's employer, Cardillo Travel Systems, Inc.[1] Just two days earlier, Cardillo's in-house attorney, Raymond Riley, had requested that Smith, the company's controller, sign an affidavit regarding the nature of a transaction Rognlien had negotiated with United Airlines. The affidavit stated that the transaction involved a $203,000 payment by United Airlines to Cardillo but failed to disclose why the payment was being made or for what specific purpose the funds would be used. The affidavit included a statement indicating that Cardillo's stockholders' equity exceeded $3 million, a statement that Smith knew to be incorrect. Smith also knew that Cardillo was involved in a lawsuit and that a court injunction issued in the case required the company to maintain stockholders' equity of at least $3 million. Because of the blatant misrepresentation in the affidavit concerning Cardillo's stockholders' equity and a sense of uneasiness regarding United Airlines' payment to Cardillo, Smith had refused to sign the affidavit.

When Smith stepped into Rognlien's office on that day in May 1985, he found not only Rognlien but also Riley and two other Cardillo executives. One of the other executives was Esther Lawrence, the firm's energetic 44-year-old president and chief operating officer (COO) and Rognlien's wife and confidante. Lawrence, a longtime employee, had assumed control of Cardillo's day-to-day operations in 1984. Rognlien's two sons by a previous marriage had left the company in the early 1980s following a power struggle with Lawrence and their father.

As Smith sat waiting for the meeting to begin, his apprehension mounted. Although Cardillo had a long and proud history, in recent years the company had begun experiencing serious financial problems. Founded in 1935 and purchased in 1956 by Rognlien, Cardillo ranked as the fourth-largest company in the travel agency industry and was the first to be listed on a national stock exchange. Cardillo's annual revenues had steadily increased after Rognlien acquired the company, approaching $100 million by 1984. Unfortunately, the company's operating expenses had increased more rapidly. Between 1982 and 1984, Cardillo posted collective losses of nearly $1.5 million. These poor operating results were largely due to an aggressive franchising strategy implemented by Rognlien. In 1984 alone that strategy more than doubled the number of travel agency franchises operated by Cardillo.

Shortly after the meeting began, the overbearing and volatile Rognlien demanded that Smith sign the affidavit. When Smith steadfastly refused, Rognlien showed him the first page of an unsigned agreement between United Airlines and

---

1. The events discussed in this case were reconstructed principally from information included in Securities and Exchange Commission, *Accounting and Auditing Enforcement Release No. 143*, 4 August 1987. All quotations appearing in this case were taken from that document.

Cardillo. Rognlien then explained that the $203,000 payment was intended to cover expenses incurred by Cardillo in changing from American Airlines' Sabre computer reservation system to United Airlines' Apollo system. Although the payment was intended to reimburse Cardillo for those expenses and was refundable to United Airlines if not spent, Rognlien wanted Smith to record the payment immediately as revenue.

Not surprisingly, Rognlien's suggested treatment of the United Airlines payment would allow Cardillo to meet the $3 million minimum stockholders' equity threshold established by the court order outstanding against the company. Without hesitation, Smith informed Rognlien that recognizing the United Airlines payment as revenue would be improper. At that point, "Rognlien told Smith that he was incompetent and unprofessional because he refused to book the United payment as income. Rognlien further told Smith that Cardillo did not need a controller like Smith who would not do what was expected of him."

ACT 2

In November 1985, Helen Shepherd, the audit partner supervising the 1985 audit of Cardillo by Touche Ross, stumbled across information in the client's files regarding the agreement Rognlien had negotiated with United Airlines earlier that year. When Shepherd asked her subordinates about this agreement, one of them told her of a $203,000 adjusting entry Cardillo had recorded in late June. That entry, which follows, had been approved by Lawrence and was apparently linked to the United Airlines–Cardillo transaction:

Dr Receivables—United Airlines	$203,210	
Cr Travel Commissions and Fees		$203,210

Shepherd's subordinates had discovered the adjusting entry during their second-quarter review of Cardillo's 10-Q statement. When asked, Lawrence had told the auditors that the entry involved commissions earned by Cardillo from United Airlines during the second quarter. The auditors had accepted Lawrence's explanation without attempting to corroborate it with other audit evidence.

After discussing the adjusting entry with her subordinates, Shepherd questioned Lawrence. Lawrence insisted that the adjusting entry had been properly recorded. Shepherd then requested that Lawrence ask United Airlines to provide Touche Ross with a confirmation verifying the key stipulations of the agreement with Cardillo. Shepherd's concern regarding the adjusting entry stemmed from information she had reviewed in the client's files that pertained to the United Airlines agreement. That information suggested that the United Airlines payment to Cardillo was refundable under certain conditions and thus not recognizable immediately as revenue.

Shortly after the meeting between Shepherd and Lawrence, Walter Rognlien contacted the audit partner. Like Lawrence, Rognlien maintained that the $203,000 amount had been properly recorded as commission revenue during the second quarter. Rognlien also told Shepherd that the disputed amount, which United Airlines paid to Cardillo during the third quarter of 1985, was not refundable to United Airlines under any circumstances. After some prodding by Shepherd, Rognlien agreed to allow her to request a confirmation from United Airlines concerning certain features of the agreement.

Shepherd received the requested confirmation from United Airlines on December 17, 1986. The confirmation stated that the disputed amount was refundable through 1990 if certain stipulations of the contractual agreement between the two parties were not fulfilled.[2] After receiving the confirmation, Shepherd called Rognlien and asked him to explain the obvious difference of opinion between United Airlines and Cardillo regarding the terms of their agreement. Rognlien told Shepherd that he had a secret arrangement with the chairman of the board of United Airlines. "Rognlien claimed that pursuant to this confidential business arrangement, the $203,210 would never have to be repaid to United. Shepherd asked Rognlien for permission to contact United's chairman to confirm the confidential business arrangement. Rognlien refused. In fact, as Rognlien knew, no such agreement existed."

A few days following Shepherd's conversation with Rognlien, she advised William Kaye, Cardillo's vice president of finance, that the $203,000 amount could not be recognized as revenue until the contractual agreement with United Airlines expired in 1990. Kaye refused to make the appropriate adjusting entry, explaining that Lawrence had insisted that the payment from United Airlines be credited to a revenue account. On December 30, 1985, Rognlien called Shepherd and told her that he was terminating Cardillo's relationship with Touche Ross.

In early February 1986, Cardillo filed an 8-K statement with the Securities and Exchange Commission (SEC) notifying that agency of the company's change in auditors. SEC regulations required Cardillo to disclose in the 8-K statement any disagreements involving technical accounting, auditing, or financial reporting issues with its former auditor. The 8-K, signed by Lawrence, indicated that no such disagreements preceded Cardillo's decision to dismiss Touche Ross. SEC regulations also required Touche Ross to draft a letter commenting on the existence of any disagreements with Cardillo. This letter had to be filed as an exhibit to the 8-K statement. In Touche Ross's exhibit letter, Shepherd discussed the dispute involving the United Airlines payment to Cardillo. Shepherd disclosed that the improper accounting treatment given that transaction resulted in misrepresented financial statements for Cardillo for the six months ended June 30, 1985, and the nine months ended September 30, 1985.

In late February 1986, Raymond Riley, Cardillo's legal counsel, wrote Shepherd and insisted that she had misinterpreted the United Airlines–Cardillo transaction in the Touche Ross exhibit letter filed with the company's 8-K. Riley also informed Shepherd that Cardillo would not pay the $17,500 invoice that Touche Ross had submitted to his company. This invoice was for professional services Touche Ross had rendered prior to being dismissed by Rognlien.

ACT 3

On January 21, 1986, Cardillo retained KMG Main Hurdman (KMG) to replace Touche Ross as its independent audit firm. KMG soon addressed the accounting treatment Cardillo had applied to the United Airlines payment. When KMG personnel discussed the payment with Rognlien, he informed them of the alleged secret arrangement with United Airlines that superseded the written contractual agreement. According to Rognlien, the secret arrangement precluded United Airlines from demanding a refund of the $203,000 payment under any circumstances. KMG refused to accept this explanation. Roger Shlonsky, the KMG audit partner responsible for the Cardillo engagement, told Rognlien that the payment would have to be

---

2. Shepherd apparently never learned that the $203,000 payment was intended to reimburse Cardillo for expenses incurred in switching to United Airlines' reservation system. As a result, she focused almost exclusively on the question of when Cardillo should recognize the United Airlines payment as revenue. If she had been aware of the true nature of the payment, she almost certainly would have been even more adamant regarding the impropriety of the $203,000 adjusting entry.

recognized as revenue on a pro rata basis over the five-year period of the written contractual agreement with United Airlines.[3]

Cardillo began experiencing severe liquidity problems in early 1986. These problems worsened a few months later when a judge imposed a $685,000 judgment on Cardillo to resolve a civil suit filed against the company. Following the judge's ruling, Raymond Riley alerted Rognlien and Lawrence that the adverse judgment qualified as a "material event" and thus had to be reported to the SEC in a Form 8-K filing. In the memorandum he sent to his superiors, Riley discussed the serious implications of not disclosing the settlement to the SEC: "My primary concern by not releasing such report and information is that the officers and directors of Cardillo may be subject to violation of rule 10b-5 of the SEC rules by failing to disclose information that may be material to a potential investor."

Within 10 days of receiving Riley's memorandum, Rognlien sold 100,000 shares of Cardillo stock in the open market. Two weeks later, Lawrence issued a press release disclosing for the first time the adverse legal settlement. However, Lawrence failed to disclose the amount of the settlement or that Cardillo remained viable only because Rognlien had invested in the company the proceeds from the sale of the 100,000 shares of stock. Additionally, Lawrence's press release underestimated the firm's expected loss for 1985 by approximately 300 percent.

Following Lawrence's press release, Roger Shlonsky met with Rognlien and Lawrence. Shlonsky informed them that the press release grossly understated Cardillo's estimated loss for fiscal 1985. Shortly after that meeting, KMG resigned as Cardillo's independent audit firm.

EPILOGUE

In May 1987, the creditors of Cardillo Travel Systems, Inc., forced the company into involuntary bankruptcy proceedings. Later that same year, the SEC concluded a lengthy investigation of the firm. The SEC found that Rognlien, Lawrence, and Kaye had violated several provisions of the federal securities laws. These violations included making false representations to outside auditors, failing to maintain accurate financial records, and failing to file prompt financial reports with the SEC. In addition, the federal agency charged Rognlien with violating the insider trading provisions of the federal securities laws. As a result of these findings, the SEC imposed permanent injunctions on each of the three individuals. The SEC also attempted to recover from Rognlien the $237,000 he received from selling the 100,000 shares of Cardillo stock in April 1986. In January 1989, the two parties resolved this matter when Rognlien agreed to pay the SEC $60,000.

Questions

1. Identify the accountants in this case who faced ethical dilemmas. Also identify the parties who would be potentially affected by the outcome of each of these dilemmas. What responsibility did the accountant in each case owe to these parties? Did the accountants fulfill these responsibilities?

---

3. Cardillo executives also successfully concealed from the KMG auditors the fact that the United Airlines payment was simply an advance payment to cover installation expenses for the new reservation system.

2. Describe the procedures an auditor should perform during a review of a client's quarterly financial statements. In your opinion, did the Touche Ross auditors who discovered the $203,000 adjusting entry during their 1985 second-quarter review take all appropriate steps to corroborate that entry? Should the auditors have immediately informed the audit partner, Helen Shepherd, of the entry?

3. In reviewing the United Airlines–Cardillo agreement, Shepherd collected evidence that supported the $203,000 adjusting entry as booked and evidence that suggested the entry was recorded improperly. Identify each of these items of evidence. What characteristics of audit evidence do the profession's technical standards suggest auditors should consider? Analyze the audit evidence that Shepherd collected regarding the disputed entry in terms of these characteristics.

4. What are the principal objectives of the SEC's rules that require 8-K statements to be filed when public companies change auditors? Did Shepherd violate the client confidentiality rule when she discussed the United Airlines–Cardillo transaction in the exhibit letter she filed with Cardillo's 8-K auditor change statement? In your opinion, did Shepherd have a responsibility to disclose to Cardillo executives the information she intended to include in the exhibit letter?

5. Do the profession's technical standards explicitly require auditors to evaluate the integrity of a prospective client's key executives? Identify the specific measures auditors can use to assess the integrity of a prospective client's executives.

Mallon Resources Corporation

At some point in their careers, every public accountant reaches that crossroads where they must answer the important question: Should I stay in public accounting or should I accept a job offer in the "outside" world? Duane Knight, a CPA employed by the Denver-based accounting firm Hein + Associates (HA), reached that point in his career in February 1994.[1] Knight graduated with an accounting degree from Colorado State University in 1983 and accepted a job three years later with HA. By 1994, Knight had risen to the position of audit manager, one step from becoming a partner with his firm. On February 15, 1994, George Mallon, the president and chief executive officer (CEO) of Mallon Resources Corporation, telephoned Knight. Mallon asked Knight if he would be interested in becoming the treasurer and principal accounting officer of Mallon Resources, a publicly owned company that operated a gold mine and owned several large oil and gas properties.

Knight was well acquainted with Mallon Resources since HA had served as the company's audit firm for several years. In fact, Knight had been assigned to the audit engagement team for that client since 1991. In February 1994, when George Mallon contacted him, Knight was supervising the fieldwork on the 1993 audit of Mallon Resources' financial statements.

Following his conversation with George Mallon, Knight became concerned that he had an "independence problem." This concern caused Knight to discuss the matter with a fellow audit manager at HA. After reviewing the applicable professional standards, the two men concluded that Knight indeed had an independence problem. However, Knight did not immediately bring this matter to the attention of his superiors at HA.

George Mallon formally offered Knight the position of treasurer and chief accounting officer of Mallon Resources on February 17, 1994. Knight promptly notified a senior HA audit partner of the job offer. The two men decided that Knight should dissociate himself from the Mallon Resources audit while the job offer was pending. One week later, on February 24, 1994, Knight accepted the job offer extended by George Mallon. Knight immediately informed his superiors at HA of his decision and told them that he would terminate his position with the accounting firm on March 31 and assume his new position with Mallon Resources on April 1. Within the next few days, HA assigned another audit manager to oversee the Mallon Resources audit. Despite the decision to remove Knight from the Mallon Resources audit, he continued to be involved in that engagement during his last few weeks of employment with HA.

Knight's involvement in the Mallon Resources audit after February 24, 1994, included developing several "prepared-by-client" schedules for the company. Among these schedules were analyses of Mallon Resources' tax deferrals. HA audited these schedules and filed them in the Mallon Resources workpapers. Knight also prepared unaudited exhibits included in the 1993 10-K registration statement that Mallon Resources submitted to the Securities and Exchange Commission (SEC). Knight's

---

1. Most of the facts presented in this case and all of the quotations appearing within it were taken from Securities and Exchange Commission, *Accounting and Auditing Enforcement Release No. 798,* 2 July 1996.

former subordinates on the HA engagement team reviewed these exhibits. Finally, during March 1994 Knight spent considerable time in the Mallon Resources corporate offices. At least some of this time he spent working on matters related to the company's 1993 audit. For example, on March 28, Knight reviewed the Management Discussion and Analysis (MD&A) section that accompanied Mallon Resources' 1993 audited financial statements. He also discussed the content of the MD&A section with the company's legal counsel.

Clarence Hein contacted Knight on March 29, 1994, two days before Knight formally joined Mallon Resources. Hein, HA's managing partner, served as the audit engagement partner for the 1993 Mallon Resources audit. Hein asked Knight to review several important and unresolved issues on the audit, which was nearing completion. Eventually, Hein arranged a conference call with SEC personnel to discuss one of those issues. Knight, Hein, and the new audit manager assigned to the Mallon Resources audit participated in that conference call. During the telephone conversation, Knight was identified simply as a "future Mallon employee."

> Although Hein knew that Knight was still a Hein + Associates employee, he told Knight that he should represent Mallon's perspective in the telephone call with the [SEC] staff.

Following the conference call, Hein asked Knight to write a memo on behalf of Mallon Resources that documented the resolution of the issue discussed with the SEC. Two weeks later, after Knight had begun working for Mallon Resources, he sent the memorandum to Hein. The memo was then included in the workpaper file for the 1993 Mallon Resources audit.

Mallon Resources filed its 1993 10-K with the SEC on April 4, 1994. The 10-K contained the company's audited financial statements for 1993 and HA's unqualified audit opinion on those statements. During the first two weeks of April, Knight, now an employee of Mallon Resources, continued to work on assignments for HA. Knight eventually billed HA for 55 hours of work he performed as an "independent contractor" for the accounting firm during those two weeks.

In June 1994, the SEC began investigating Duane Knight's relationship with HA and Mallon Resources during the company's 1993 audit. The SEC questioned Knight's status after reviewing documents Mallon Resources had submitted to the federal agency. Those documents suggested that Knight had served in dual and conflicting roles during the 1993 Mallon Resources audit. (Note: Exhibit 1 contains a timeline that summarizes the key events in this case and the dates of those events.)

EXHIBIT 1

TIMELINE, MALLON
RESOURCES CASE

December 31, 1993	1993 fiscal year of Mallon Resources ends.
January 1994	Duane Knight, an audit manager with Hein + Associates (HA), is assigned to the 1993 Mallon Resources audit. The audit engagement partner is Clarence Hein, HA's managing partner. Knight drafts an audit planning memorandum, the audit budget, and the client engagement letter.
January 27, 1994	Representatives of HA and Mallon Resources sign the audit engagement letter.
Early February 1994	Knight supervises fieldwork on the Mallon Resources audit.

EXHIBIT 1—
continued

TIMELINE, MALLON
RESOURCES CASE

February 15, 1994	George Mallon, president and CEO of Mallon Resources, telephones Knight. The two men discuss Knight becoming Mallon Resources' treasurer and principal accounting officer.
February 15, 1994	Following his conversation with Mallon, Knight tells another HA audit manager that he may have an "independence problem." After reviewing the AICPA's professional standards, the two audit managers conclude that Knight does have an independence problem. Knight does not immediately inform his superiors at HA of his telephone conversation with George Mallon.
February 17, 1994	Knight receives a written offer of employment from Mallon. Knight informs a senior audit partner with HA of the offer. The two men agree that Knight cannot work on the Mallon Resources audit while the offer is pending.
February 24, 1994	Knight accepts the employment offer from Mallon and agrees to a start date of April 1, 1994. Knight informs his superiors at HA of his decision.
Late February, 1994	Another audit manager is assigned to the Mallon Resources audit to replace Knight.
February 24–March 28, 1994	Knight, who is still employed by HA, drafts several "prepared-by-client" schedules analyzing Mallon Resources' tax deferrals. These schedules are then audited by HA and included in the 1993 workpapers for the Mallon Resources engagement. Knight also prepares unaudited exhibits included in Mallon Resources' 1993 10-K registration statement. HA auditors review these exhibits.
March 28, 1994	Knight discusses the content of the MD&A section of Mallon Resources' 1993 annual report with the company's general counsel.
March 29, 1994	Clarence Hein asks Knight to review several important accounting and auditing issues that remain unresolved on the Mallon Resources audit. Knight, Hein, and the new audit manager assigned to the Mallon Resources audit conduct a telephone conference call with the SEC to discuss one of those issues. During this conference call, Knight is identified simply as a "future Mallon employee."
March 30, 1994	Hein asks Knight to write a memorandum documenting Mallon Resources' position regarding the accounting issue discussed with the SEC.
April 1, 1994	Knight formally becomes an employee of Mallon Resources.
April 4, 1994	Mallon Resources files its 1993 10-K with the SEC. The 10-K includes an unqualified audit opinion issued by HA on the company's 1993 financial statements.
April 14, 1994	Knight sends the memo that Hein requested on March 30 to HA. That memo is included in the workpapers for the 1993 Mallon Resources audit.

(continued)

EXHIBIT 1—
continued

TIMELINE, MALLON
RESOURCES CASE

April 15, 1994	Knight sends a bill to HA for 55 hours of work he performed for the firm as an "independent contractor" during the first two weeks of April.
Mid-June 1994	Documents submitted by Mallon Resources to the SEC raise questions in the minds of SEC personnel regarding Knight's relationship with HA and Mallon Resources during the company's 1993 audit.
June 21, 1994	The SEC begins a formal inquiry regarding the relationships between and among Knight, HA, and Mallon Resources during the company's 1993 audit.
July 5, 1994	HA informs the SEC that Knight left the firm on April 15 to begin his employment with Mallon Resources. HA also informs the SEC that Knight did not work on the 1993 Mallon Resources audit following his February 15 telephone conversation with George Mallon.
July 11, 1994	The SEC requests additional information from HA regarding Knight's involvement with the 1993 Mallon Resources audit. HA acknowledges that Knight actually began working for Mallon Resources on April 1 but that he continued to perform limited work for HA through April 15. Clarence Hein reveals that Knight participated, at Hein's request, in the March 29 conference call with the SEC.
July 15, 1994	Knight confirms to the SEC that he participated in the March 29 conference call.
July 20, 1994	The SEC notifies Mallon Resources that HA was not independent during its 1993 audit of the company. Mallon Resources must retain another accounting firm to audit the financial statements included in its 1993 10-K.
August 1, 1994	Knight, Hein, HA's legal counsel, and Mallon Resources' legal counsel meet with SEC representatives. At this meeting, the SEC is told that other than Knight's participation in the March 29 conference call he had no significant involvement in the preparation or audit of Mallon Resources' 1993 financial statements following February 15.
August 2, 1994	The SEC interviews the audit manager who replaced Knight on the Mallon Resources audit. This individual reveals that Knight prepared certain schedules for Mallon Resources in late March that were then audited by HA and included in the Mallon Resources workpaper file.
December 5, 1994	Mallon Resources submits an amended 10-K for 1993 to the SEC. That 10-K includes an unqualified audit opinion issued by Price Waterhouse.
July 2, 1996	The SEC issues an enforcement release that announces sanctions imposed on Duane Knight and Hein + Associates for their conduct during the 1993 audit of Mallon Resources.

On July 5, in response to an SEC inquiry, HA informed the agency that Knight had left the firm on April 15 to begin his employment with Mallon Resources. HA also informed the SEC that Knight did not work on the 1993 audit of Mallon Resources following his February 15 conversation with George Mallon. On July 11, in response to a second SEC inquiry, HA disclosed that Knight actually had begun employment with Mallon Resources on April 1. HA also disclosed that Knight had continued to perform limited work for the accounting firm through April 15. This latter work reportedly did not involve the Mallon Resources engagement. Finally, HA revealed that Knight had participated in the March 29 conference call at the request of Clarence Hein. Knight also independently confirmed to the SEC that he had been involved in the March 29 conference call.

On July 20, the SEC notified Mallon Resources that its 1993 10-K registration statement was deficient. The SEC ruled that HA was not independent of Mallon Resources and thus the company had not met its obligation to obtain an independent audit opinion on its 1993 financial statements. Following this ruling, Mallon Resources dismissed HA and retained Price Waterhouse as its new audit firm. In early December 1994, Mallon Resources submitted an amended 1993 10-K to the SEC. An unqualified audit opinion issued by Price Waterhouse accompanied the financial statements in that 10-K.

SEC representatives met with Knight, Hein, HA's legal counsel, and Mallon Resources' legal counsel on August 1. At that meeting, the SEC representatives were told that, other than the March 29 conference call, Knight had no substantive involvement with the preparation or audit of Mallon Resources' 1993 financial statements following February 15. The next day, August 2, the SEC interviewed the audit manager who had replaced Knight on the Mallon Resources audit. This individual contradicted the information the SEC had obtained the previous day by testifying that Knight had prepared certain schedules "on behalf of" Mallon Resources during March 1994. This audit manager also revealed that HA had audited those schedules and included them in the client's 1993 audit workpaper file.

Without admitting or denying the facts of this case as reported by the SEC, Knight and HA agreed to sanctions imposed on them by the federal agency. Those sanctions included a public censure of Knight and his former employer. The SEC also required HA to retain an independent reviewer. This individual would study HA's quality controls for safeguarding the firm's independence on audit engagements and make recommendations for improvements in those controls. The settlement agreement between HA and the SEC obligated the accounting firm to implement the independent reviewer's recommendations.

In the enforcement release that announced the sanctions imposed on Knight and HA, the SEC stressed the critical importance of auditor independence to the investing and lending public. The federal agency noted that auditors "must avoid even an appearance of impropriety" to ensure that the public has confidence in audited financial statements. Later in the enforcement release, the SEC explained its rationale for disqualifying the 1993 audit opinion that HA had issued on Mallon Resources' financial statements.

> *When an auditor accepts employment with an issuer, any work subsequently performed by the auditor taints the entire audit, regardless of the nature of that work. Knight's participation in the audit tainted the entire auditing process, thereby requiring a re-audit of Mallon's financial statements.*

Questions

1. Define auditor independence. Why is independence often referred to as the cornerstone of the auditing profession?

2. Identify the specific violations of the profession's ethical rules by the parties involved in this case. Relying on the timeline included in Exhibit 1, indicate when each of these violations occurred.

3. Do you agree with the SEC that Knight's conduct following his acceptance of the job offer from George Mallon "tainted" the entire 1993 audit of Mallon Resources? Why or why not?

4. Should auditors be allowed to become employees of their former clients? Defend your answer. What problems does this practice pose for (a) the auditing profession, (b) audit firms, and (c) audit clients?

The North Face, Inc.

Executives of The North Face, Inc., faced a troubling dilemma during the 1990s.[1] For decades, those executives had struggled to develop and maintain an exclusive brand name for their company's extensive line of outdoor apparel and sporting equipment products. By positioning those products for the "high-end" segment of the retail market, North Face's management had consciously chosen to ignore the much larger and more lucrative mainstream market. This decision kept the company's primary customers happy. Those customers, principally small, independent specialty sporting goods stores, did not want North Face to market its merchandise to major discount retailers such as Wal-Mart and Costco.

Economic realities eventually forced North Face's executives to begin selling the company's products to the mainstream market via backdoor marketing channels. Unfortunately, the company's relatively high-priced merchandise did not compete effectively with the mass-market brands sold by the major discount retailers. Making matters worse, as the company's merchandise began appearing on the shelves of discount retailers, those products quickly lost their exclusive brand name appeal, which caused North Face's sales to its principal customers to drop sharply.

North Face's change in marketing strategies, a decision to spend millions of dollars to relocate the company's headquarters from northern California to Colorado, and other gaffes by the company's management team caused *Chief Executive* magazine to include North Face among the nation's five "worst-managed" corporations. A short time later, North Face's public image and reputation on Wall Street would be damaged even more by public revelations that the company's reported operating results had been embellished with various accounting and marketing gimmicks.

Adventurers, Inc.

Hap Klopp founded North Face in the mid-1960s to provide a ready source of hiking and camping gear that he and his many free-spirited friends and acquaintances needed to pursue their "back to nature" quest. Initially, the business operated from a small retail store in San Francisco's North Beach neighborhood. The company quickly added a mail-order sales operation. In 1970, North Face began designing and manufacturing its own line of products after opening a small factory in nearby Berkeley.

Over the next decade, North Face endeared itself to outdoor enthusiasts by sponsoring mountain-climbing expeditions across the globe, including successful attempts to scale Mount Everest, Mount McKinley, China's K-2, and the highest peaks in South America. The name recognition and goodwill generated by these expeditions allowed North Face to establish itself as the premier supplier of top-quality parkas, tents, backpacking gear, and other apparel and equipment demanded by "professional" mountain climbers. Adding even more credibility to North Face's merchandise was the lifetime warranty that Hal Klopp attached to each item his company sold and the fact that the United States Marine Corps purchased tents and other bivouac supplies from North Face.

1. The development of this case was funded by Glen McLaughlin. I would like to thank Mr. McLaughlin for his generous and continuing support of efforts to integrate ethics into business curricula.

North Face's sterling reputation for rugged and durable hiking, camping, and mountaineering gear prompted company management to begin marketing related lines of apparel and sporting equipment for skiers, whitewater daredevils, and other outdoor types. Among the most popular items marketed by the company were its Mountain Jacket, Snow Leopard Backpack, and Tadpole Tent. The company's expanding product line triggered rapid sales growth during the 1970s and 1980s. Similar to the management teams of many growth companies, North Face's executives confronted several imposing challenges that could undermine their company's financial success. The most critical of those challenges was maintaining quality control in North Face's cramped production facilities.

Company executives prided themselves on producing only the highest-quality outdoor sporting equipment and apparel. To maintain the quality of that merchandise, they insisted on manufacturing all of North Face's products in-house, rather than outsourcing some of the company's manufacturing operations to third parties. By the mid-1980s, North Face's overburdened manufacturing facilities could not satisfy the steadily growing demand for the company's merchandise or maintain the high-quality production standards established by management. North Face's limited production capacity and mounting quality control problems caused the company to routinely deliver merchandise to retail stores after the peak selling seasons for its highly seasonal products. The quality control problems also caused North Face to accumulate a large inventory of "seconds," that is, merchandise items having minor flaws.

In the late 1980s, North Face's management made a decision it would soon regret. The company opened several outlet stores to dispose of obsolete and second-grade merchandise. This decision angered the specialty sporting goods stores that had been North Face's primary customers since the company's inception. To pacify those customers, North Face did a quick about-face and closed the outlet stores.

Over the next several years, North Face continued to struggle with maintaining its image as the leading producer of high-quality outdoor apparel and sporting equipment, while at the same attempting to gradually ease into the mainstream retail market. By this time, Hap Klopp had left the company to become an author—one of his books was entitled *The Complete Idiot's Guide to Business Management*. In fact, the company experienced several changes in company management and ownership during the late 1980s and throughout the 1990s.

In July 1996, a new management team took North Face public, listing the company's common stock on the NASDAQ exchange. Sold initially at $14 per share, the company's stock price peaked at nearly $30 per share in February 1998, fueled by the company's steadily increasing sales and profits. In fiscal 1994, North Face reported total sales of $89 million; four years later in fiscal 1998, the company's sales had nearly tripled, rising to approximately $250 million.

Despite the company's strong operating results, by early 1999 North Face's stock price had plunged from its all-time high. Persistent rumors that North Face's management had enhanced the company's reported revenues and profits by "channel stuffing" and other questionable, if not illegal, practices caused the sharp decline in the stock price. To squelch those rumors, North Face's board of directors attempted to purchase the company in a leveraged buyout underwritten by a large investment banking firm. That effort failed in March 1999 when NASDAQ officials halted public trading of North Face's stock following an announcement that the company would be restating its previously reported operating results due to certain "bad bookkeeping."[2]

---

2. D. Blount, "Shares of Colorado-Based Outdoor Clothing Maker Slump," *Denver Post* (online), 11 May 1999.

In May 1999, North Face officials publicly revealed that their company's audited financial statements for 1997 and the company's pre-audited operating results for 1998, which had been released in January 1999, had been distorted by fraudulent accounting schemes. The principal schemes involved violations of the revenue recognition principle. For 1997, North Face's reported revenues of $208.4 million had been overstated by approximately $5 million, while the company's net income of $11.2 million had been overstated by $3.2 million. In January 1999, the company had reported unaudited revenue and net income of $263.3 million and $9.5 million, respectively, for fiscal 1998. The company's actual 1998 revenues were $247.1 million, while the company's actual net income for the year was $3.6 million.

Bartering for Success at North Face

The management team that took over North Face in the mid-1990s established a goal of reaching annual sales of $1 billion by 2003. Many Wall Street analysts believed North Face could reach that goal, given the company's impressive operating results over the previous several years. When the actual revenues and profits of North Face failed to meet management's expectations, the company's chief financial officer (CFO) and vice president of sales took matters into their own hands, literally.

In December 1997, North Face began negotiating a large transaction with a barter company. Under the terms of this transaction, the barter company would purchase $7.8 million of excess inventory North Face had on hand near the end of fiscal 1997. In exchange for that inventory, North Face would receive $7.8 million of trade credits that were redeemable only through the barter company. Historically, companies have used such trade credits to purchase advertising or travel services.

Before North Face finalized the large barter transaction, Christopher Crawford, the company's CFO, asked North Face's independent auditors how to account for the transaction. The auditors referred Crawford to the appropriate authoritative literature for nonmonetary exchanges. That literature generally precludes companies from recognizing revenue on barter transactions when the only consideration received by the seller is trade credits. To circumvent the authoritative literature, Crawford restructured the transaction. The final agreement with the barter company included an oral "side agreement" that was concealed from North Face's independent auditors.

> Crawford, however, structured the transaction to recognize a profit on the trade credits. First, he required the barter company to pay a portion of the trade credits in cash. Crawford agreed that The North Face would guarantee that the barter company would receive at least 60 percent recovery of the total purchase price when it resold the product. In exchange for the guarantee, the barter company agreed to pay approximately 50 percent of the total purchase price in cash and the rest in trade credits. This guarantee took the form of an oral side agreement that was not disclosed to the auditors.[3]

To further obscure the true nature of the large barter transaction, Crawford split it into two parts. On December 29, 1997, two days before the end of North Face's fiscal 1997 fourth quarter, Crawford recorded a $5.15 million sale to the barter company. For this portion of the barter deal, North Face received $3.51 million in cash and trade credits of $1.64 million. Ten days later, during North Face's first quarter of fiscal 1998, the company's accounting staff booked the remaining $2.65 million portion of

3. U.S. District Court, Northern District of California, *Securities and Exchange Commission v. Christopher F. Crawford and Todd F. Katz*, February 2003.

the barter transaction. North Face received only trade credits from the barter company for this final portion of the $7.8 million transaction. North Face recognized its normal profit margin on each segment of the barter transaction.

Crawford, who was a CPA, realized that Deloitte & Touche, North Face's independent auditors, would not challenge the profit recognized on the $3.51 million portion of the barter transaction recorded during the fourth quarter of fiscal 1997. There was no reason for the Deloitte auditors to challenge the recognition of profit on that component of the transaction since North Face was being paid in cash. Of course, the side agreement with the barter company that Crawford concealed from Deloitte should have caused North Face to defer the recognition of the profit on that portion of the barter transaction.

Crawford also realized that Deloitte would maintain that no profit should be recorded on the $1.64 million balance of the December 29, 1997, transaction with the barter company for which North Face would be paid exclusively in trade credits. However, Crawford was aware of the materiality thresholds that Deloitte had established for North Face's key financial statement items during the fiscal 1997 audit. He knew that the gross profit of approximately $800,000 on the $1.64 million portion of the December 1997 transaction fell slightly below Deloitte's materiality threshold for North Face's collective gross profit. As a result, he believed that Deloitte would propose an adjustment to reverse the $1.64 million transaction but ultimately "pass" on that proposed adjustment since it had an immaterial impact on North Face's financial statements. As Crawford expected, Deloitte proposed a year-end adjusting entry to reverse the $1.64 million transaction but then passed on that adjustment during the wrap-up phase of the audit.

In early January 1998, North Face recorded the remaining $2.65 million portion of the $7.8 million barter transaction. Again, Crawford instructed North Face's accountants to record the full amount of profit margin on this "sale" despite being aware that accounting treatment was not consistent with the authoritative literature. Crawford did not inform the Deloitte auditors of the $2.65 million portion of the barter transaction until after the 1997 audit was completed.

The barter company ultimately sold only a nominal amount of the $7.8 million of excess inventory that it purchased from North Face. As a result, in early 1999, North Face reacquired that inventory from the barter company.

In the third and fourth quarters of fiscal 1998, Todd Katz, North Face's vice president of sales, arranged two large sales to inflate the company's revenues, transactions that were actually consignments rather than consummated sales. The first of these transactions involved $9.3 million of merchandise "sold" to a small apparel wholesaler in Texas. During the previous year, this wholesaler had purchased only $90,000 of merchandise from North Face. The terms of this transaction allowed the wholesaler to return any of the merchandise that he did not resell and required North Face to pay all of the storage and handling costs for that merchandise. In fact, North Face arranged to have the large amount of merchandise stored in a warehouse near the wholesaler's business. Katz negotiated a similar $2.6 million transaction with a small California wholesaler a few months later.

During a subsequent internal investigation, North Face's audit committee questioned the validity of the large transaction with the Texas wholesaler. North Face paid for the Texas customer to fly to North Face's new corporate headquarters in Aspen, Colorado, to discuss that transaction with members of the audit committee and the company's CEO, who were not aware of the true nature of the transaction. The night before the customer met with North Face officials, Katz went to his hotel room and had him sign a fake purchase order for the $9.3 million transaction—a purchase order had not been prepared for the bogus sale when it was originally arranged by Katz.

Several months later, Katz instructed a North Face sales representative to ask the Texas customer to sign an audit confirmation letter sent to him by Deloitte. By signing that letter, the customer falsely confirmed that he owned the $9.3 million of merchandise as of December 31, 1998, North Face's fiscal year-end. The California wholesaler involved in the bogus $2.6 million sale signed a similar confirmation after having been asked to do so by a North Face sales representative. In May 1999, following the completion of North Face's 1998 audit, the Texas customer returned the $9.3 million of merchandise that he had supposedly purchased from North Face.

Erasing the Past

Richard Fiedelman served for several years as the Deloitte "advisory" partner assigned to the North Face audit engagements. Within Deloitte, an advisory partner is typically a senior audit partner who has significant industry expertise relevant to a given audit client. Fiedelman was the advisory partner on the North Face engagement team because he was in charge of Deloitte's "consumer retail group" in the firm's northern California market area. In addition to consulting with members of an audit engagement team on important issues arising during an audit, an advisory partner typically reviews the audit workpapers before the engagement is completed.[4]

Pete Vanstraten was the audit engagement partner for the 1997 North Face audit.[5] Vanstraten proposed the adjusting entry near the end of the 1997 audit to reverse the $1.64 million barter transaction that North Face had booked in the final few days of fiscal 1997. Vanstraten proposed that adjustment because he was aware that the authoritative literature generally precludes companies from recognizing revenue on barter transactions when the only consideration received by the seller is trade credits. Vanstraten was also the individual who "passed" on that adjustment after determining that it did not have a material impact on North Face's 1997 financial statements. Richard Fiedelman reviewed and approved those decisions by Vanstraten.

Shortly after the completion of the 1997 North Face audit, Pete Vanstraten transferred from the office that serviced North Face. In May 1998, Will Borden was appointed the new audit engagement partner for North Face.[6] In the two months before Borden was appointed the North Face audit engagement partner, Richard Fiedelman functioned in that role.

Fiedelman supervised the review of North Face's financial statements for the first quarter of fiscal 1998, which ended on March 31, 1998. While completing that review, Fiedelman became aware of the $2.65 million portion of the $7.8 million barter transaction that Christopher Crawford had instructed his subordinates to record in early January 1998. Recall that North Face received only trade credits from the barter company for this final portion of the large barter transaction. Despite being familiar with the authoritative literature regarding the proper accounting treatment for barter transactions involving trade credits, Fiedelman did not challenge North Face's decision to record its normal profit margin on the January 1998 "sale" to the barter company. As a result, North Face's gross profit for the first quarter of 1998 was overstated

---

4. The information regarding the nature and role of a Deloitte advisory partner was obtained from a senior audit manager with that firm.

5. "Pete Vanstraten" is a fictitious name assigned to the 1997 North Face audit engagement partner. The SEC enforcement releases issued in this case and other available sources did not identify that partner's actual name.

6. "Will Borden" is also a fictitious name.

by more than $1.3 million, an amount that was material to the company's first-quarter financial statements. In fact, without the profit margin on the $2.65 million transaction, North face would have reported a net loss for the first quarter of fiscal 1998 rather than the modest net income it actually reported that period.

In the fall of 1998, Will Borden began planning the 1998 North Face audit. An important element of that planning process was reviewing the 1997 audit workpapers. While reviewing those workpapers, Borden discovered the audit adjustment that Pete Vanstraten had proposed during the prior-year audit to reverse the $1.64 million barter transaction. When Borden brought this matter to Fiedelman's attention, Fiedelman maintained that the proposed audit adjustment should not have been included in the prior-year workpapers since the 1997 audit team had *not* concluded that North Face should *not* record the $1.64 million transaction with the barter company. Fiedelman insisted that, despite the proposed audit adjustment in the 1997 audit workpapers, Pete Vanstraten had concluded that it was permissible for North Face to record the transaction and recognize the $800,000 of profit margin on the transaction in December 1997.

Fiedelman could not offer any viable explanation to Borden as to why the 1997 workpapers included the proposed audit adjustment for the $1.64 million transaction. Clearly, either Fiedelman or Borden could have easily addressed that issue by simply contacting Vanstraten; however, neither apparently chose to do so. Nor did either of the two partners refer to the authoritative literature to determine whether North Face was entitled to record that transaction. Instead, Borden simply accepted Fiedelman's assertion that North Face was entitled to recognize profit on a sales transaction in which the only consideration received by the company was trade credits. Borden also relied on this assertion during the 1998 audit. As a result, Borden and the other members of the 1998 audit team did not propose an adjusting entry to require North Face to reverse the $2.65 million sale recorded by the company in January 1998. Recall that North Face had received only trade credits from the barter company for that portion of the $7.8 million transaction.

After convincing Borden that the prior-year workpapers misrepresented the decision that Pete Vanstraten had made regarding the $1.64 million barter transaction, Fiedelman "began the process of documenting this revised conclusion in the 1997 working papers."[7] According to a subsequent investigation by the Securities and Exchange Commission (SEC), Deloitte personnel "prepared a new summary memorandum and adjustments schedule reflecting the revised conclusion about profit recognition, and replaced the original 1997 working papers with these newly created working papers." The Deloitte personnel who revised the 1997 workpapers did not document the revisions in those workpapers. "In the end, the 1997 working papers, as revised, did not indicate that the 1997 audit team had originally reached a different conclusion concerning the company's accounting for the 1997 barter transaction."

The SEC requires that a partner not assigned to an engagement team review the audit workpapers for an SEC registrant. The Deloitte "concurring" partner who reviewed the 1998 workpapers questioned Will Borden's decision to allow North Face to recognize revenue on a sales transaction for which it had been paid exclusively in trade credits. The partner then referred to the prior-year workpapers and discovered that the workpapers pertaining to the December 1997 transaction with the barter company had been altered.

---

7. This and all remaining quotes in this case were taken from the following source: Securities and Exchange Commission, *Accounting and Auditing Enforcement Release No. 1884*, 1 October 2003, 2.

Because of concerns raised by the concurring partner, Deloitte investigated the 1997 and 1998 North Face transactions with the barter company. The concurring partner's concerns also prompted North Face's audit committee to retain a second accounting firm to investigate the company's 1997 and 1998 accounting records. These investigations ultimately revealed the true nature of the transactions with the barter company, including the previously undisclosed "side agreement" that Christopher Crawford had made with officials of that company. The investigations also led to the discovery of the two bogus consignment sales that Crawford had arranged during 1998.

EPILOGUE

The SEC sanctioned Richard Fiedelman for failing to document the changes that his subordinates had made in the 1997 North Face workpapers. In commenting on the North Face case, the federal agency stressed the important function of audit workpapers and the need for any *ex post* changes in those workpapers to be clearly and fully documented.

> The auditor's working papers provide the principal support for the auditor's report, including his representation regarding the observance of the standards of field work, which is implicit in the reference in his report to generally accepted auditing standards. It therefore follows that any addition, deletion, or modification to the working papers after they had been finalized in connection with the completion of the audit may be made only with appropriate supplemental documentation, including an explanation of the justification for the addition, deletion, or modification.

The SEC also criticized Fiedelman for failing to exercise due professional care while reviewing North Face's financial statements for the first quarter of 1998. According to the SEC, Fiedelman allowed North Face to record the January 1998 barter transaction "directly contrary to the conclusion reached by Deloitte in its 1997 year-end audit." In October 2003, the SEC imposed a three-year suspension on

Fiedelman that prevented him from being involved in the audits of SEC clients.

In February 2003, the SEC suspended Christopher Crawford for five years, which prohibited him from serving as an officer or director of a public company or being associated with any financial statements filed with the federal agency over that time frame. The SEC also fined Crawford $30,000 and required him to disgorge approximately $30,000 of trading profits he had earned on the sale of North Face stock. The SEC also denied Todd Katz, the former vice president of sales who had helped Crawford manipulate North Face's reported operating results, the privilege of serving as an officer of a public company for five years and fined him $40,000. The two former North Face customers involved in the bogus consignment sales arranged by Katz were reprimanded by the SEC.

In May 2000, VF Corporation, the world's largest apparel company, more commonly known as Vanity Fair, made North Face a wholly owned subsidiary by purchasing the company's outstanding common stock for $2 per share. VF immediately installed a new management team to take over North Face's operations. Under the leadership of that new management team, North Face quickly returned to profitability and reestablished itself as one of the nation's premier suppliers of outdoor equipment and apparel.

Questions

1. Should auditors insist that their clients accept all proposed audit adjustments, even those that have an "immaterial" effect on the given financial statements? Defend your answer.

2. Should auditors take explicit measures to prevent their clients from discovering or becoming aware of the materiality thresholds used on individual audit engagements? Would it be feasible for auditors to conceal this information from their audit clients?

3. Identify the general principles or guidelines that dictate when companies are entitled to record revenue. How were these principles or guidelines violated by the $7.8 million barter transaction and the two consignment sales discussed in this case?

4. Identify and briefly explain each of the principal objectives that auditors hope to accomplish by preparing audit workpapers. How were these objectives undermined by Deloitte's decision to alter North Face's 1997 workpapers?

5. North Face's management teams were criticized for strategic blunders that they made over the course of the company's history. Do auditors have a responsibility to assess the quality of the key decisions made by client executives? Defend your answer.

NextCard, Inc.

In the late 1990s, the investing public's fascination with Internet-based companies prompted the cyberspace equivalent of the Oklahoma Land Rush, according to one prominent Wall Street analyst. "In a land rush, you suspend rules because your perception is that time is of the essence."[1] That perception caused many anxious investors who feared missing out on a once-in-a-lifetime investment opportunity to bid the prices of Internet stocks to ever-higher levels. Those investors readily discounted the fact that most Internet companies were reporting minimal revenues and sizable, if not staggering, operating losses. Over a 15-month stretch between late 1998 and March 2000, the dot-com-laced NASDAQ stock exchange rose by more than 150 percent. By comparison, over the same time frame, the largely "Old Economy" Dow Jones Industrial Average managed a much less impressive 15 percent gain.

Dot-com fever caused many investment services and publications to create new stock indices dedicated strictly to Internet companies. On June 30, 1999, *USA Today* launched the *Internet 100* to track the stock prices of 100 high-profile companies whose primary lines of business were directly or exclusively related to the Internet. Within a few months, the collective value of that index had risen by more than 60 percent. Other Internet stock indices realized similar increases. By early March 2000, the 300 companies included in the *Forbes Internet Index* had a collective market value of $1.2 trillion, which was approximately equal to the total value of all publicly traded U.S. stocks a little more than one decade earlier.

The public's feeding frenzy on Internet stocks produced numerous paper billionaires among dot-com bigwigs. Dot-com billionaires making appearances in the *Forbes 400*, a list of the 400 "richest people in America," included, among several others, Jeff Bezos (Amazon), Stephen Case (AOL), Mark Cuban (Broadcast.com), Andrew McKelvey (Monster.com), Pierre Omidyar (eBay), Jay Walker (Priceline), David Wetherell (CMGI), and Jerry Yang and David Filo (Yahoo!). As you might expect, the surging prices of Internet stocks added an even larger number of new members to the millionaires' club. By early 2000, one publication reported that in northern California's Silicon Valley alone, the Internet revolution was creating 64 new millionaires each day.[2] Among these millionaires were Jeremy and Molly Lent, a husband-and-wife team that founded the Internet-based NextCard, Inc., in 1997.

Credit on the Fly

Jeremy Lent served as the chief financial officer (CFO) of Providian Financial Corporation during the early 1990s. At the time, Providian ranked among the largest financial services companies in the United States. Experts in the financial services industry attributed Providian's success to the direct-mail marketing methods the company used to identify and then recruit as customers, individuals who made extensive use of credit cards. In the late 1990s, Lent decided that the marketing tactics used by Providian could be easily adapted to the Internet, which prompted him and his wife

---

1. G. Ip, S. Pulliam, S. Thurm, and R. Simon, "How the Internet Bubble Broke Records, Rules, Bank Accounts," *The Wall Street Journal* Interactive Edition, 14 July 2000.
2. *The Economist* (online), "The Country-Club Vote," 20 May 2000.

to create NextCard, an online company that would offer Internet users the opportunity to obtain a credit card in a matter of moments.

Because of his tenure at Providian, Lent realized that a key metric in the credit card industry is the acquisition cost of a new customer. Lent was convinced that he could use the Internet to undercut the average acquisition cost of a new customer incurred by brick-and-mortar credit card companies, such as Providian. Likewise, Lent believed that his company would have significantly lower bad-debt losses than conventional credit card issuers since marketing research had found that Internet users were generally more affluent and, thus, better credit risks, than individuals drawn from the general population of consumers.

One of Lent's first major strategic initiatives was hiring dozens of marketing researchers to analyze a large database of "clickstream data" that documented the "surfing" habits of Internet users. After analyzing the data, the company's marketing team developed Internet-based advertising campaigns targeting Internet users who made frequent use of, and maintained large balances on, their credit cards. NextCard's online ads encouraged such individuals to apply for a credit card with NextBank, a virtual bank that was NextCard's largest operating unit, and to transfer their existing credit card balances to this new card. The key inducement used by Lent to convince potential customers to apply for a NextBank credit card was a lower interest rate than that charged by conventional credit card issuers. Lent also promised those potential customers that a decision regarding their online credit card application would be made within 30 seconds of their submitting that application.

Initially, Lent's business model for NextCard appeared to be a huge success as the company quickly became recognized as one of the leaders of the Internet Revolution that made the term *e-commerce* the hottest buzzword among Wall Street analysts and individual investors. The company's website was regularly named one of the top 50 financial websites by *Money* magazine and by 2000 had more daily "hits" or visits than any other website in the financial services industry. More importantly, for several consecutive years, NextCard issued more credit cards online than any other credit card issuer, including such large and well-established firms as American Express, Bank of America, Citibank, and MBNA. Lent used NextCard's prominent position in the Internet industry to create a network of 60,000 online "affiliates" that referred potential credit card customers to NextCard. Several of these affiliates, including Amazon.com, purchased significant ownership interests in NextCard.

By early 2000, NextCard was well on its way to achieving one of Lent's primary goals for the company: obtaining one million credit card customers. During that year, NextCard extended more than $1 billion of credit to its customers. Those impressive operating statistics did not translate into immediate profits for NextCard, a fact that Lent and other company executives frequently downplayed or simply ignored in press releases and other public disclosures. In February 2000, a NextCard executive boasted that "we continue to beat our aggressive growth targets while maintaining very strong parameters in the other core elements of our business model. Our average balance per account, which is one of the major drivers of success in the credit card business, remains approximately $2,000. Our acquisition cost, credit quality, and yield—all major drivers of profitability—continue to be strong and stable, leading to continued very strong revenue results."[3] This statement conveniently overlooked the fact that NextCard's New Age business model had produced a large loss during the company's just completed 1999 fiscal year, $77.2 million to be exact.

3. *Business Wire* (online), "NextCard Announces Significant Growth Milestones Ahead of Plan," 22 February 2000.

Despite the fact that NextCard was posting large losses each reporting period, Lent had taken the company public in 1999. On the first day NextCard's stock was traded, the stock's price rose from an initial selling price of $20 per share to more than $40, making Lent and several other NextCard executives instant multimillionaires. A few months later, the stock surged past $50 per share. When the "lock-up" period mandated by the Securities and Exchange Commission (SEC) following an initial public offering expired, Lent and his colleagues sold large chunks of their ownership interests in the company.

When NextCard reported an unexpectedly large loss of $81.9 million for fiscal 2000, company executives could no longer sidestep the recurring question posed by persistent Wall Street analysts, namely, "When would NextCard earn its first quarterly profit?" NextCard's management team insisted that the company had "turned the corner" and pledged that NextCard would report its first-ever quarterly profit by the fourth quarter of fiscal 2001. At the same time, company officials predicted that NextCard would report a net income of $150 million by fiscal 2003.

In March 2000, the NASDAQ stock index crested at an all-time high of more than 5,000. Over the following 18 months, the Internet "bubble" in the stock market burst, causing the stock prices of most Internet companies, including NextCard, to spiral downward. Many of these New Age companies survived, including such firms as Amazon.com, eBay, Monster.com, and Yahoo!. NextCard would not be among those survivors.

Loose Credit = Bad Debts

The bursting of the Internet bubble in the stock market quickly cut off NextCard's access to the debt and equity markets. Without the ability to raise additional debt or equity capital, NextCard suddenly faced the need to raise capital the "old-fashioned way," namely, via profitable operations.

Despite the promises and predictions of NextCard's executives, the company never reported a profit, principally because two of the key premises on which Jeremy Lent had predicated NextCard's business model proved to be invalid. First, the average acquisition cost NextCard incurred to obtain new customers proved to be much higher than the figure Lent had originally projected. NextCard spent huge amounts on Internet advertising campaigns to recruit customers only to find that Internet users routinely ignored, if not treated with contempt, most efforts of online advertisers to attract their attention. In fact, the "click-through" rate for most Internet advertisements hovered at a fraction of 1 percent, considerably lower than the response rate to direct or "junk" mail advertisements used by conventional credit card issuers.

Lent's other major miscalculation had even more serious consequences for NextCard. Internet users, at least the subpopulation of Internet users who signed up for a NextBank credit card, proved to be much higher credit risks than Lent had expected. A large proportion of the Internet users who took advantage of NextCard's liberal credit policies were individuals who could not obtain credit from any other source. For these desperate and shallow-pocketed consumers, NextCard effectively served as the "lender of last resort." These individuals eventually produced the large balances that Lent had expected Internet users to carry on their credit cards but they often allowed those balances to go unpaid, resulting in large credit losses for NextCard.

In sum, instead of incurring minimal marketing expenditures to acquire "good" credit card customers, NextCard spent large amounts to acquire "bad" credit card customers. Making matters worse, many of NextCard's competitors, including American Express, "went to school" on NextCard's mistakes. These competitors learned from those mistakes and developed more cost-effective—and ultimately profitable—Internet marketing strategies to expand their market shares in the intensely competitive credit card industry.

Early in NextCard's history, the company's executives apparently realized that their business model contained serious flaws. Despite that realization, those executives continued to pursue Jeremy Lent's dream of creating one of the dominant companies in the credit card industry. To shore up the company's stock price and to maintain credibility on Wall Street and among private investors, NextCard's executives chose to conceal the extent and source of the company's financial problems. The principal means used to accomplish this goal was understating NextCard's massive credit losses by refusing to provide sufficient allowances each period for expected bad debts.

Because NextBank was subject to federal banking regulations, the Office of the Comptroller of the Currency (OCC) regularly reviewed the company's accounting records and operating policies and procedures. During 2001, OCC auditors forced NextCard to significantly increase its allowance for bad debts. When NextCard publicly reported the OCC's decision, company management denied that the larger allowance for bad debts was due to unexpectedly high credit losses. Instead, NextCard officials insisted that the increase in the allowance for bad debts was necessary because the company had suffered large losses as a result of fraudulent schemes perpetrated by hackers and other Internet miscreants. In November 2001, a skeptical Wall Street analyst questioned how such a massive problem could "pop up" so unexpectedly and without any previous warning from company officials.[4] In fact, subsequent investigations would reveal that NextCard officials had routinely and materially understated the company's allowance for credit losses.

In late 2001, angry NextCard investors filed a large class-action lawsuit against the company and its executives. Among other charges, that lawsuit alleged that NextCard's management team had intentionally concealed the extent and nature of the company's financial problems. In addition, the plaintiffs charged that the NextCard executives had engaged in insider trading by selling off large portions of their ownership interests in the company before NextCard's true financial condition became apparent. This large class-action lawsuit and widespread concerns regarding the integrity of NextCard's publicly reported financial data caused various federal regulatory authorities, including the SEC, to launch investigations of the company's financial affairs.

Suspicious Audit Trails

Discovering that your largest client is the subject of a series of federal investigations for tampering with its accounting records and issuing materially misleading financial statements is, no doubt, among the life events feared most by audit partners of major accounting firms. Thirty-six-year-old Robert Trauger found himself facing that disturbing scenario in the fall of 2001. Trauger, a partner in the San Francisco office of Ernst & Young, had served for several years as the audit engagement partner for NextCard. In March 2001, Trauger had authorized the unqualified opinion issued on NextCard's 2000 financial statements.

After considering his options, including doing nothing and simply awaiting the outcome of the various federal investigations of NextCard, Trauger decided to take matters into his own hands. His first decision was to contact his top subordinate on the 2000 NextCard audit, Oliver Flanagan.

Like most accounting professionals, Oliver Flanagan enjoyed challenging assignments. A native of Ireland, Flanagan accepted an entry-level position on the auditing staff of the London, England, office of Ernst & Young in the mid-1990s. Flanagan left

4. J. Graham, "What's the Next Move for Troubled NextCard?" *Investor's Business Daily*, 1 November 2001, 6.

E&Y in late 1999 to accept a position in the banking industry but quickly discovered that he missed working as an independent auditor. So, Flanagan asked E&Y for his job back. In the late 1990s, the Internet bubble had created a huge demand for the services of public accounting firms, which caused E&Y to be more than happy to re-hire Flanagan. Among the locations having the greatest need for auditors at the time was the booming Silicon Valley region near San Francisco. Given his interest in the banking industry and the "adventure" of going stateside, Flanagan quickly accepted the opportunity to move to San Francisco and become a member of the NextCard audit engagement team.

Despite the fact that he had only a few years of auditing experience, Flanagan was assigned to serve as the senior audit manager on the NextCard engagement, a position in which he would report directly to Robert Trauger. Flanagan realized that Trauger was a "fast track" partner in the San Francisco office of E&Y since he was in charge of the prestigious NextCard engagement. As a result, Flanagan hoped that Trauger would serve as his mentor and help him advance quickly within E&Y.

In early November 2001, more than six months after the 2000 NextCard audit was completed, Robert Trauger left a message instructing Oliver Flanagan to meet him in the E&Y office the following Saturday morning. Flanagan was probably not surprised by the request since weekend work was nothing unusual with a major accounting firm. Plus, the planning phase for the 2001 audit of the financially troubled NextCard was nearing completion. If Flanagan expected Trauger to discuss the 2001 audit during the weekend meeting, he was wrong. Instead, when Flanagan contacted Trauger, the audit partner told him to gather all of the workpapers for the 2000 NextCard audit and "have them ready for revisions"[5] during that meeting. Flanagan knew that it was not common to revise prior-year audit workpapers once they had been archived. Almost certainly, NextCard's well-documented financial problems and the insinuations of an accounting scandal within the company caused Flanagan to wonder what types of "revisions" Trauger intended to make to the NextCard workpapers.

Before meeting with Flanagan, Trauger contacted the other audit manager on the NextCard engagement team, Michael Mullen. Mullen had not been involved in the 2000 NextCard audit because he had only been assigned to the engagement team since June 2001. Trauger instructed Mullen to determine whether it was possible to "manipulate E&Y's computer system so that he [Trauger] could alter electronically archived working papers without being discovered."[6] Trauger wanted to revise the original NextCard workpapers without leaving any evidence that they had been altered. For the conventional "hard copy" workpapers, this goal did not pose any particular challenge. But accomplishing that same goal for the electronic workpapers meant that Trauger had to change the electronic "time stamps" on those files.

Mullen complied with Trauger's request and eventually learned from another E&Y employee that it was possible to "de-archive" previously completed electronic audit workpapers and thereby change the time stamps posted on those workpapers. Mullen sent this information to both Trauger and Flanagan. During their weekend meeting, Trauger and Flanagan reviewed the 2000 NextCard audit workpapers and made numerous additions and deletions to those workpaper files. The principal items changed were the "Summary Review Memorandum" and the receivables workpapers. In a subsequent enforcement release that focused on the conduct of Oliver Flanagan, the SEC described the process used by Trauger and Flanagan to alter the

5. Securities and Exchange Commission, *Accounting and Auditing Enforcement Release No. 1871*, 25 September 2003.

6. *Ibid.*

NextCard workpapers. (Note: In this enforcement release, the SEC referred to Trauger as simply the "audit partner.")

> *The audit partner marked up printed versions of the documents and gave them to Flanagan for Flanagan to input using Flanagan's laptop computer. In order to ensure that the revised documents appeared to have been created as part of the original working papers, the audit partner instructed Flanagan to reset the date on his computer so that any documents bearing computer-generated dates would reflect a date in early 2001. Some documents went through more than one edit, as Flanagan input the audit partner's changes and then printed out the revised version for the audit partner's further review."[7]*

NextCard's deteriorating financial condition in late 2001 and the increasing scrutiny of the company by federal regulatory authorities apparently prompted Trauger to ask Flanagan to meet with him once more to make additional alterations to the 2000 NextCard workpapers. Trauger also asked Michael Mullen to attend this second meeting, which took place in late November 2001. The SEC provided the following overview of what transpired during this second meeting:

> *The audit partner marked up printed versions of the memoranda he was revising and then the other audit manager [Mullen] input the changes. At the audit partner's direction, the other audit manager deleted charts, portions of tables, and discussion sections that indicated problems with NextCard's charge-off numbers and trends. The audit partner also added information and altered the tone of certain sections. One of the documents altered during this meeting was a memorandum entitled "Analysis for Loan Losses." Flanagan remained involved in the process by proofreading the other audit manager's work to ensure that all of the audit partner's changes were made.[8]*

The SEC issued multiple enforcement releases that documented the improper professional conduct of Robert Trauger, Oliver Flanagan, and Michael Mullen. In those enforcement releases, the SEC noted on several occasions that Trauger's intent in revising the 2000 NextCard audit workpapers was to "make it appear that there was a more satisfactory basis" for the key E&Y conclusions reached during that engagement. *The New York Times* reported that "Mr. Trauger told Mr. Flanagan that he wanted to 'beef up' the workpapers to make it appear as if the auditing team had been 'right on the mark' all along."[9] During the course of the federal investigations of NextCard, the FBI retrieved e-mails that Trauger had sent to his subordinates. Those e-mails provided a more pointed statement of Trauger's intent in modifying the NextCard workpapers. According to an FBI affidavit, in one e-mail message Trauger stated that he did not want "some smart-ass lawyer"[10] second-guessing the decisions that he had made during the 2000 NextCard audit.

Following the two meetings in which the E&Y auditors had altered the NextCard workpapers, Trauger instructed Flanagan "to scour his hard drive and delete documents or e-mails inconsistent with the altered versions of the working papers."[11] Once more, Flanagan followed his mentor's instructions. Approximately three months later, E&Y received a subpoena from the OCC that instructed the firm to give the

---

7. *Ibid.*

8. *Ibid.*

9. K. Eichenwald, "U.S. Charges Ernst & Young Ex-Partner in Audit Case," *The New York Times,* 26 September 2003, 1.

10. J. Hoppin, "Snared by SOX," *Corporate Counsel,* December 2003, 24.

11. Securities and Exchange Commission, *Accounting and Auditing Enforcement Release No. 1871,* 25 September 2003.

federal agency certain NextCard workpapers. At that time, Trauger discovered that Michael Mullen had kept a computer diskette containing some of the original NextCard workpapers that had been altered in November 2001. Trauger ordered Flanagan to obtain that diskette and destroy it. Flanagan obtained the diskette and told Trauger that he had destroyed it. In fact, Flanagan kept the diskette and subsequently gave it to federal authorities.

EPILOGUE

The computer diskette that Oliver Flanagan turned over to federal authorities investigating NextCard ultimately resulted in the FBI arresting Robert Trauger in September 2003. The U.S. Department of Justice filed criminal charges against Trauger for obstructing the federal investigations of NextCard. Trauger was the first partner of a major accounting firm to be prosecuted for destroying audit-related documents under the criminal provisions of the Sarbanes-Oxley Act of 2002. Those provisions were included in the Sarbanes-Oxley Act as a direct consequence of the widely publicized scandal involving Enron Corporation. During an SEC investigation of Enron, Andersen, the company's audit firm, had shredded certain Enron workpapers. The subsequent felony conviction handed down against Andersen by a federal court effectively put the prominent accounting firm out of business.[12] Ironically, Trauger and his subordinates were altering the NextCard workpapers in November 2001, the same time frame during which Andersen personnel were shredding the Enron workpapers.

Shortly after being arrested in September 2003, Robert Trauger insisted that he was innocent of the charges filed against him. When Trauger was released after posting a $1 million bail, his attorney issued the following public statement defending his client: "He's a good man, a well-respected accountant, and I'm confident he will be exonerated."[13] Despite those assertions, a little more than one year later on October 28, 2004, Robert Trauger pled guilty to one count of impeding a federal investigation. As a result of that plea, Trauger faced a prison sentence of up to 25 years and a fine of $500,000. On January 27, 2005, a federal judge sentenced Trauger to one year in prison and two years of "supervised release." The judge also ordered Trauger to pay a $5,000 fine. In his plea agreement, Trauger admitted he had failed to inform federal authorities that he and his subordinates had altered certain of the NextCard audit workpapers subpoenaed by those authorities.

Ernst & Young disavowed responsibility for the actions of Trauger, Flanagan, and Mullen. In a press release, an E&Y spokesperson pointed out that the actions of the three individuals were in clear violation of the firm's professional standards and internal policies. That spokesperson also noted that when E&Y discovered the nature of the individuals' conduct, firm officials cooperated fully with federal law enforcement authorities.

Not surprisingly, federal authorities were elated with the outcome of the Trauger case. In commenting on the case, a spokesperson for the U.S. Department of Justice observed that the proper functioning of the nation's capital markets depends, in large part, on the integrity of auditors and other professionals involved in the financial reporting process:

This is one of the first cases in the country in which an auditor has been accused of destroying key documents in an effort to obstruct an investigation. Our financial markets depend on the integrity of auditors, lawyers, and other professionals to do their jobs ethically and fairly. Where they fail to do so because of negligence, markets are compromised. Where they

---

12. The U.S. Supreme Court overturned Andersen's felony conviction in May 2005; however, by that time, the firm was in the process of being disbanded.

13. E. Iwata, "Accountant Arrested under Sarbanes-Oxley," *USA Today,* 26 September 2003, 2B.

fail to do so because of criminal intent, all of us are at risk. The U.S. Attorney's Office will bring those professionals to justice who join in criminal acts they are supposed to uncover and expose.[14]

Stephen Cutler, the SEC's Director of Enforcement, echoed these sentiments and stressed the importance of auditors' maintaining the integrity of the audit process:

> *Complete and accurate workpapers are critical to the integrity of the audit process and the efficacy of our investigative work. We will aggressively pursue auditors who alter or destroy workpapers or otherwise undermine the financial reporting process, and will work closely with criminal authorities to ensure that those who engage in such conduct are held accountable.*[15]

Finally, an FBI spokesperson observed: "We look to certified public accountants to maintain the integrity of publicly traded companies. The criminal acts of auditors who abuse their authority, act in their own self-interest, and violate the sacred trust of shareholders will not be tolerated."[16]

In October 2004, Michael Mullen pled guilty to lying to an FBI agent involved in the NextCard investigation. Mullen was sentenced to one year of probation and ordered to pay a $100 fine. As a result of his guilty plea, Mullen's right to practice before the SEC was suspended. In August 2003, Oliver Flanagan pled guilty to one count of criminal obstruction of justice. After cooperating with federal authorities in the prosecution of Robert Trauger, Flanagan was allowed to return to his native Ireland. Flanagan's attorney noted that "Oliver has made peace with our [U.S.] government."[17] The attorney then added that Flanagan's only wish is that Robert Trauger had been a "better mentor."[18]

NextCard's financial problems steadily worsened following the announcement in late 2001 that federal law enforcement authorities were investigating the company's financial affairs. In February 2002, the OCC ruled that NextBank was operating in an "unsafe and unsound" manner and placed the bank under the control of the Federal Deposit Insurance Corporation (FDIC). At the time, NextCard's stock was trading for $0.14 per share, down from its all-time high of $53.12. In the summer of 2003, a federal bankruptcy court liquidated the company. NextCard had total liabilities of nearly $470 million, which far exceeded its realizable assets of approximately $20 million.

In November 2006, the SEC announced that it had reached an agreement to settle fraud charges filed in 2004 against five former NextCard executives, including Jeremy Lent. In total, the SEC required the executives to pay $1.4 million of fines and other monetary damages. Approximately $900,000 of that amount was paid by Lent. The SEC allowed the five executives to consent to the settlement "without admitting or denying" the charges that had been filed against them.[19] One year earlier, in December 2005, the class-action lawsuit filed against NextCard and its former executives had been settled out of court. Ernst & Young contributed $23.5 million to the settlement pool, while Jeremy Lent contributed $635,000.

---

14. Securities and Exchange Commission, "Former Ernst & Young Audit Partner Arrested for Obstruction Charges and Criminal Violations of the Sarbanes-Oxley Act," *Release No. 2003-123*, 25 September 2003.

15. *Ibid.*

16. *Ibid.*

17. V. Colliver, "FBI Arrests Suspect in Fraud," *San Francisco Chronicle*, 26 September 2003, B1.

18. *Ibid.*

19. Securities and Exchange Commission, *Litigation Release No. 19903*, November 2006.

Questions

1. Should auditors evaluate the soundness of a client's business model? Defend your answer.

2. Identify and briefly describe the specific fraud risk factors present during the 2000 NextCard audit. How should these factors have affected the planning and execution of that engagement?

3. What are the primary objectives an audit team hopes to accomplish by preparing a proper set of audit workpapers?

4. Identify the generally accepted auditing standards violated by the E&Y auditors in this case. Briefly explain how each standard was violated.

5. When he became a member of the NextCard audit engagement team, Oliver Flanagan hoped that Robert Trauger would serve as his mentor. What responsibility, if any, do senior audit personnel have to serve as mentors for their subordinates?

6. Assume the role of Oliver Flanagan in this case. What would you have done when Robert Trauger asked you to help him alter the 2000 NextCard audit workpapers? In answering this question, identify the alternative courses of action available to you. Also identify the individuals who may be affected by your decision and briefly describe how they may be affected.

Koger Properties, Inc.

Becoming a partner with one of the large international accounting firms easily ranks among the most common career goals of accounting majors.[1] Michael Goodbread staked out that career goal three decades ago. After graduating from college, Goodbread made the first step toward reaching his objective when he accepted an entry-level position with Touche Ross & Company. In February 1973, Goodbread received his CPA license in the state of Florida after passing the CPA exam. Eight years later, the partners of Touche Ross selected Goodbread to join their ranks.

In December 1989, Goodbread accomplished his career goal a second time by becoming a partner with Deloitte & Touche, the firm created by the merger of Deloitte, Haskins & Sells and Touche Ross. Before the merger, Goodbread served as an audit partner in the Jacksonville, Florida, office of Touche Ross. Goodbread assumed an identical position with the newly formed Jacksonville office of Deloitte & Touche following the merger.

The six-digit salaries earned by partners of large international accounting firms provide them ample discretionary funds for investment purposes. Like many investors, Goodbread often considered local companies when making investment decisions. One local firm that caught Goodbread's attention during the late 1980s was Koger Properties, Inc., a real estate development company headquartered in Jacksonville. Koger's claim to fame was originating the concept of an office park. According to a Koger annual report, the company opened the nation's first office park in 1957 in Jacksonville. By the early 1990s, Koger operated nearly 40 office parks in two dozen metropolitan areas scattered across the southern United States.

In December 1988, Goodbread purchased 400 shares of Koger's common stock at a price of $26 per share. At the time, Koger had approximately 25 million shares of common stock outstanding.

Following the December 1989 merger that created Deloitte & Touche, one of Goodbread's first assignments with his new firm was supervising the audit of Koger Properties for its fiscal year ending March 31, 1990. Koger had previously been an audit client of Deloitte, Haskins & Sells. In his role as audit engagement partner, Goodbread oversaw all facets of the Koger audit. On February 21, 1990, Goodbread signed the "audit planning memorandum" that laid out the general strategy Deloitte & Touche intended to follow in completing the Koger audit. Several months later, on June 27, 1990, Goodbread signed the "audit report record" for the Koger engagement. The signing of that document by the audit engagement partner formally completes a Deloitte & Touche audit.

Goodbread dated the unqualified opinion issued on Koger's 1990 financial statements as of June 11, 1990. Almost exactly one month earlier, on May 10, 1990, Goodbread had sold the 400 shares of Koger stock that he had owned since December 1988. Goodbread sold the stock at a price of $20.75 per share.

---

1. The events discussed in this case were reconstructed principally from information included in Securities and Exchange Commission, *Accounting and Auditing Enforcement Release No. 861*, 10 December 1996.

The Securities and Exchange Commission (SEC) eventually learned that Goodbread had held an ownership interest in Koger Properties while he supervised the company's 1990 audit. The SEC charged that Goodbread's ownership interest in Koger violated its independence rules, the *Code of Professional Conduct* of the American Institute of Certified Public Accountants (AICPA), and generally accepted auditing standards(GAAS). Most important, the SEC charged that Goodbread caused Deloitte & Touche to issue an improper opinion on Koger's 1990 financial statements. Instead of the unqualified opinion Deloitte & Touche issued on those financial statements, the SEC maintained that a disclaimer of opinion had been required given the circumstances. Following its investigation of the matter, the SEC publicly censured Goodbread.

The embarrassing revelation of Michael Goodbread's ownership interest in Koger Properties marked the beginning of a long series of problems that Deloitte & Touche encountered with that audit client. In September 1991, Koger filed for bankruptcy. A short time earlier, Koger's stockholders had filed a large class-action lawsuit against Deloitte & Touche. The suit alleged that the 1989 Koger audit performed by Deloitte, Haskins & Sells and the 1990 Koger audit completed by Deloitte & Touche were deficient. Those deficient audits allegedly contributed to the subsequent decline in Koger's stock price.

A federal jury agreed with the Koger stockholders and ordered Deloitte to pay the plaintiffs $81.3 million to compensate them for damages suffered because of the 1989 and 1990 audits. In July 1997, the U.S. Court of Appeals reversed the lower court's ruling and voided the huge judgment awarded to Koger's stockholders. The appellate court ruled that the stockholders failed to prove that any errors made by Deloitte during the 1989 and 1990 Koger audits caused the losses they subsequently incurred.[2]

Another of the megafirms created by a merger of two large international accounting firms encountered an independence problem similar to that experienced by Deloitte & Touche in the Koger Properties case. However, PricewaterhouseCoopers' "problem" was much more severe and embarrassing. In 1999, that firm agreed to be censured by the SEC for dozens of alleged violations of the profession's independence rules.

> *Without admitting or denying wrongdoing, PricewaterhouseCoopers has agreed to be censured by federal regulators over a dispute that ownership of client stock had compromised its independence as an auditor. The Big Five firm agreed to pay $2.5 million to establish education programs for the profession designed to improve auditor compliance.... The Securities and Exchange Commission claims it turned up 70 instances from 1996 to 1998 in which some of the partners and managers of the firm purchased client stock.[3]*

The problems experienced by Deloitte & Touche and PricewaterhouseCoopers apparently stemmed from unfamiliarity with the profession's auditor independence rules. In the late 1990s, a top SEC official revealed that personnel from the large international accounting firms frequently contacted the federal agency to inquire about its most basic ethical rules for independent auditors. According to this official, these inquiries commonly included questions regarding "such fundamental issues as the prohibition against owning stock in companies they audit."[4]

---

2. *Securities Regulation and Law Report*, "Investors' 10b-5 Claims Against Deloitte Fail in CA for Lack of Loss Causation," 18 July 1997, 1018.

3. *Accounting Today*, "PwC Censured for Owning Client Stock," 8–21 February 1999, 3.

4. E. MacDonald, "Levitt Says Wave of Accounting Mergers Could Affect Independence of Auditors," *The Wall Street Journal*, 21 October 1997, A2, A4.

Questions

1. The SEC charged that Goodbread violated its independence rules, the AICPA's *Code of Professional Conduct*, and generally accepted auditing standards (GAAS). Explain the SEC's rationale in making each of those allegations.

2. In your opinion, did Goodbread's equity interest in Koger Properties likely qualify as a "material" investment for him? Was the materiality of that investment a relevant issue in this case? Explain.

3. Given that Goodbread purchased stock of Koger Properties in 1988, under what conditions, if any, could he have later served as the audit engagement partner for that company?

4. During much of the nineteenth century in Great Britain, independent auditors were not only allowed to have an equity interest in their clients but were required to invest in their clients in certain circumstances. Explain the rationale likely underlying that rule. Would such a rule "make sense" in today's business environment in the United States? Defend your answer.

American Fuel & Supply Company, Inc.

Consider this scenario. You are the audit manager responsible for supervising the fieldwork for a major audit client. After hundreds of hours of hard work, the audit is successfully completed, the client receives a clean opinion, and you and your colleagues go on to your next assignments. Now, the bad news. Several months later, you discover that the client's financial statements contain a material error, an error not revealed by the audit. What should you do at this point? What will you do? An audit manager with Touche Ross faced these difficult circumstances in 1986.

In the mid-1980s, Wisconsin-based American Fuel & Supply Company, Inc. (AFS), was a wholesale distributor of automotive supplies, lawn and garden supplies, and related products.[1] AFS purchased merchandise from several vendors. One of the company's largest suppliers was Chevron Chemical Company, a division of Chevron Corporation. Products that AFS purchased from Chevron included insecticides and weedkillers bearing the Ortho brand label. AFS's president and sole shareholder directed the company's day-to-day operations.

AFS prepared comparative financial statements for its fiscal year ending December 31, 1985, that were accompanied by an unqualified audit opinion issued by Touche Ross on February 28, 1986. The company distributed 100 copies of the financial statements, principally to creditors such as Chevron Chemical.

Several months following the completion of the 1985 AFS audit, Touche Ross personnel discovered that the company's 1985 financial statements contained a material error. AFS had billed certain of its customers twice for merchandise they had purchased. This error caused the company's 1985 revenues to be overstated by nearly $1 million. More important, the error had converted the net loss actually suffered by AFS that year to a reported net income. Chevron Chemical and other creditors of AFS later testified that they relied on the erroneous financial statements in deciding to continue extending credit to the company.

During August and September 1986, members of the AFS audit engagement team wrestled with the question of what they should do given the dilemma they faced. A central figure in these deliberations was James Wagner, the audit manager who had supervised the field work on the 1985 AFS audit. In late August 1986, Wagner bluntly summarized the situation for his superiors: "There is a set of financial statements out being used by [AFS's] vendors and lenders that has an error in it." Two weeks later, Wagner, a Touche Ross audit partner, and the accounting firm's assistant legal counsel held a conference call to discuss the matter. During this conference call, these individuals agreed on the course of action Touche Ross would take to resolve the matter.

Unless AFS notified its creditors and vendors of the existence of the error in the financial statements, Touche would withdraw their opinion and give notice to its creditors and vendors whom they knew were relying upon the financial statements that their opinion had been withdrawn.

---

1. The principal facts of this case and the quotations appearing within it were drawn from the following legal opinion: *Chevron Chemical v. Deloitte & Touche*, 483 N.W. 2d 314 (Wis. App. 1992).

Following the conference call, Touche Ross representatives met with AFS officials and attempted to persuade them to recall the company's 1985 financial statements. The AFS officials refused to do so. Touche Ross then advised the client that it intended to withdraw its audit report on AFS's 1985 financial statements and to inform all parties known to be relying on those financial statements that the audit report had been withdrawn.

A few days later, Touche Ross personnel met again with AFS's management. The company's legal counsel also attended this meeting. AFS's attorney insisted that Touche Ross would violate the confidentiality of its contractual relationship with AFS by withdrawing its audit opinion and notifying third parties of that decision. The client's attorney then threatened legal action against Touche Ross if the accounting firm carried through on its planned course of action.

Eventually, AFS and Touche Ross hammered out a compromise. This compromise permitted Touche Ross to notify AFS's sole secured creditor (lender) that the firm's audit opinion on AFS's 1985 financial statements had been withdrawn. However, Touche Ross could not notify AFS's unsecured creditors of its decision to withdraw the audit report. These unsecured creditors included Chevron Chemical and AFS's other suppliers.

James Wagner believed the compromise was unacceptable. In a confidential memo apparently intended for his superiors, Wagner maintained that Touche Ross had an obligation to the other parties relying on the audit opinion issued on AFS's 1985 financial statements. Wagner suggested that Touche Ross should "send a letter to the vendors or creditors that we know have received the financial statements telling them that ... the opinion should no longer be relied upon."

EPILOGUE

AFS filed for bankruptcy in April 1987. The company's president filed for personal bankruptcy approximately two years later. In early 1989, Chevron Chemical sued Touche Ross, alleging that the accounting firm negligently audited AFS's 1985 financial statements. Chevron Chemical also claimed that Touche Ross had a responsibility to notify it after learning of the error in AFS's 1985 financial statements. A Wisconsin state court rejected the allegation that Touche Ross negligently audited AFS in 1985. However, the court ruled, and a Wisconsin state appellate court later agreed, that Touche Ross "was negligent as a matter of law in failing to notify plaintiff [Chevron Chemical] of the withdrawal of their opinion." The original state court awarded damages of $1.6 million to Chevron Chemical.

Questions

1. A major focus of the lawsuit that Chevron Chemical filed against Touche Ross was the auditing profession's rules regarding the "subsequent discovery of facts existing at the date of the auditor's report." Those rules distinguish between situations in which a client cooperates with the auditor in making all necessary disclosures and situations involving uncooperative clients. Briefly summarize the differing responsibilities that auditors have in those two sets of circumstances.

2. Given your previous answer, do you believe that Touche Ross complied with the applicable professional standards after learning of the error in AFS's 1985 financial statements? Explain.

3. Do you agree with the assertion of AFS's legal counsel that Touche Ross would have violated the profession's client confidentiality rule by withdrawing its 1985 audit opinion and notifying all relevant third parties of that decision? Why or why not?

4. Suppose that Touche Ross had resigned as AFS's auditor following the completion of the 1985 audit but prior to the discovery of the error in the 1985 financial statements. What responsibility, if any, would Touche Ross have had when it learned of the error in AFS's 1985 financial statements?

SECTION 6

PROFESSIONAL ROLES

Leigh Ann Walker, Staff Accountant

Leigh Ann Walker graduated from a major state university in the spring of 1989 with a bachelor's degree in accounting.[1] During her college career, Walker earned a 3.9 grade point average and participated in several extracurricular activities, including three student business organizations. Her closest friends often teased her about the busy schedule she maintained and the fact that she was, at times, a little too "intense." During the fall of 1988, Walker interviewed with several public accounting firms and large corporations and received six job offers. After considering those offers, she decided to accept an entry-level position on the auditing staff of a Big Six accounting firm. Walker was not sure whether she wanted to pursue a partnership position with her new employer. But she believed that the training programs the firm provided and the breadth of experience she would receive from a wide array of client assignments would get her career off to a fast start.

Walker spent the first two weeks on her new job at her firm's regional audit staff training school. On returning to her local office in early June 1989, she was assigned to work on the audit of Saint Andrew's Hospital, a large sectarian hospital with a June 30 fiscal year-end. Walker's immediate superior on the Saint Andrew's engagement was Jackie Vaughn, a third-year senior. On her first day on the Saint Andrew's audit, Walker learned that she would audit the hospital's cash accounts and assist with accounts receivable. Walker was excited about her first client assignment and pleased that she would be working for Vaughn. Vaughn had a reputation as a demanding supervisor who typically brought her engagements in under budget. She was also known for having an excellent rapport with her clients, a thorough knowledge of technical standards, and for being fair and straightforward with her subordinates.

Like many newly hired staff auditors, Walker was apprehensive about her new job. She understood the purpose of independent audits and was familiar with the work performed by auditors but doubted that one auditing course and a two-week staff-training seminar had adequately prepared her for her new work role. After being assigned to work under Vaughn's supervision, Walker was relieved. She sensed that although Vaughn was demanding, the senior would be patient and understanding with a new staff auditor. More important, she believed that she could learn a great deal from working closely with Vaughn. Walker resolved that she would work hard to impress Vaughn and had hopes that the senior would mentor her through the first few years of her career.

Early in Walker's second week on the Saint Andrew's engagement, Jackie Vaughn casually asked her over lunch one day whether she had taken the CPA examination in May. After a brief pause, Walker replied that she had not but planned to study intensively for the exam during the next five months and then take it in November.[2]

---

1. This case is based upon a true set of facts; however, the names of the parties involved have been changed. An employee of a job placement firm provided much of the information incorporated in this case. This firm had been retained by the student identified in this case as Leigh Ann Walker.

2. At the time, the CPA examination was offered twice annually, in November and May. In most states, including Leigh Ann's home state, an individual who sat for the exam for the first time was required to take all four parts.

Vaughn indicated that was a good strategy and offered to lend Walker a set of CPA review manuals—an offer Walker declined. In fact, Walker had returned to her home state during the first week of May and sat for the CPA exam but she was convinced that she had failed it. Fear of failure, or, rather, fear of admitting failure, caused Walker to decide not to tell her coworkers that she had taken the exam. She realized that most of her peers would not pass all sections of the exam on their first attempt. Nevertheless, Leigh Ann wanted to avoid the embarrassment of admitting throughout the remainder of her career that she had not been a "first timer."

Walker continued to work on the Saint Andrew's engagement throughout the summer. She completed the cash audit within budget, thoroughly documenting the results of the audit procedures she applied. Vaughn was pleased with Walker's work and frequently complimented and encouraged her. As the engagement was winding down in early August, Walker received her grades on the CPA exam in the mail one Friday evening. To her surprise, she had passed all parts of the exam. She immediately called Vaughn to let her know of the impressive accomplishment. To Walker's surprise, Vaughn seemed irritated, if not disturbed, by the good news. Walker then recalled having earlier told Vaughn that she had not taken the exam in May. Walker immediately apologized and explained why she had chosen not to disclose that she had taken the exam. Following her explanation, Vaughn still seemed annoyed, so Walker decided to drop the subject and pursue it later in person.

The following week, Vaughn spent Monday through Wednesday with another client, while Walker and the other staff assigned to the Saint Andrew's engagement continued to wrap up the hospital audit. On Wednesday morning, Walker received a call from Don Roberts, the office managing partner and Saint Andrew's audit engagement partner. Roberts asked Walker to meet with him late that afternoon in his office. She assumed that Roberts simply wanted to congratulate her on passing the CPA exam.

The usually upbeat Roberts was somber when Walker stepped into his office that afternoon. After she was seated, Roberts informed her that he had spoken with Jackie Vaughn several times during the past few days and that he had consulted with the three other audit partners in the office regarding a situation involving Walker. Roberts told Walker that Vaughn was very upset by the fact that she (Walker) had lied regarding the CPA exam. Vaughn had indicated that she would not be comfortable having a subordinate on future engagements whom she could not trust to be truthful. Vaughn had also suggested that Walker be dismissed from the firm because of the lack of integrity she had demonstrated.

After a brief silence, Roberts told a stunned Walker that he and the other audit partners agreed with Vaughn. He informed Walker that she would be given 60 days to find another job. Roberts also told Walker that he and the other partners would not disclose that she had been "counseled out" of the firm if they were contacted by employers interested in hiring her.

Questions

1. In your opinion, did Vaughn overreact to Walker's admission that she had been untruthful regarding the CPA exam? If so, how would you have dealt with the situation if you had been in Vaughn's position? How would you have dealt with the situation if you had been in Roberts' position?

2. Vaughn obviously questioned Walker's personal integrity. Is it possible that one can fulfill the responsibilities of a professional role while lacking personal integrity? Why or why not?

Bill DeBurger, In-Charge Accountant

"Bill, will you have that inventory memo done by this afternoon?"

"Yeah, Sam, it's coming along. I should have it done by five, or so."

"Make it three . . . or so. Okay, Bub?"

Bill responded with a smile and a nod. He had a good relationship with Sam Hakes, the partner supervising the audit of Marcelle Stores.[1]

Bill DeBurger was an in-charge accountant who had 18 months experience with his employer, a large national accounting firm. Bill's firm used the title "in-charge" for the employment position between staff accountant and audit senior. Other titles used by accounting firms for this position include "advanced staff" and "semi-senior." Typically, Bill's firm promoted individuals to in-charge after one year. An additional one to two years experience and successful completion of the CPA exam were usually required before promotion to audit senior. The title "in-charge" was a misnomer, at least in Bill's mind. None of the in-charges he knew had ever been placed in-charge of an audit, even a small audit. Based upon Bill's experience, an in-charge was someone a senior or manager expected to work with little or no supervision. "Here's the audit program for payables. Go spend the next five weeks completing the 12 program steps . . . and don't bother me," seemed to be the prevailing attitude in making work assignments to in-charges.

As he turned back to the legal pad in front of him, Bill forced himself to think of Marcelle Stores' inventory—all $50 million of it. Bill's task was to summarize in a two-page memo the 900 hours of work that he, two staff accountants, and five internal auditors had done over the past two months. Not included in the 900 hours was the time spent on eight inventory observations performed by other offices of Bill's firm.

Marcelle Stores was a regional chain of 112 specialty stores that featured a broad range of products for do-it-yourself interior decorators. The company's most recent fiscal year had been a difficult one. A poor economy, increasing competition, and higher supplier prices had slashed Marcelle's profit to the bone over the past 12 months. The previous year, the company had posted a profit of slightly less than $8 million; for the year just completed, the company's pre-audit net income hovered at an anemic $500,000.

Inventory was the focal point of each audit of Marcelle's financial statements. This year, inventory was doubly important. Any material overstatement discovered in the inventory account would convert a poor year profit-wise for Marcelle into a disastrous year in which the company posted its first-ever loss.

Facing Bill on the small table that served as his makeshift desk were two stacks of workpapers, each two feet tall. Those workpapers summarized the results of extensive price tests, inventory observation procedures, year-end cutoff tests, an analysis of the reserve for inventory obsolescence, and various other audit procedures. Bill's task

---

1. The source for this case was a former public accountant who is now a college instructor. The names of the parties involved in the case and certain other background facts have been changed.

was to assimilate all of this audit evidence into a conclusion regarding Marcelle's inventory. Bill realized that Sam Hakes expected that conclusion to include the key catch phrase "presented fairly, in all material respects, in conformity with generally accepted accounting principles."

As Bill attempted to outline the inventory memo, he gradually admitted to himself that he had no idea whether Marcelle's inventory dollar value was materially accurate. The workpaper summarizing the individual errors discovered in the inventory account reflected a net overstatement of only $72,000. That amount was not material even in reference to Marcelle's unusually small net income. However, Bill realized that the $72,000 figure was little better than a guess.

The client's allowance for inventory obsolescence particularly troubled Bill. He had heard a rumor that Marcelle intended to discontinue 2 of the 14 sales departments in its stores. If that were true, the inventory in those departments would have to be sold at deep discounts. The collective dollar value of those two departments' inventory approached $6 million, while the client's allowance for inventory obsolescence had a year-end balance of only $225,000. Earlier in the audit, Bill had asked Sam about the rumored closing of the two departments. The typically easygoing partner had replied with a terse "Don't worry about it."

Bill always took his work assignments seriously and wanted to do a professional job in completing them. He believed that independent audits served an extremely important role in a free market economy. Bill was often annoyed that not all of his colleagues shared that view. Some of his coworkers seemed to have an attitude of "just get the work done." They stressed form over substance: "Tic and tie, make the workpapers look good, and don't be too concerned with the results. A clean opinion is going to be issued no matter what you find."

Finally, Bill made a decision. He would not sign off on the inventory account regardless of the consequences. He did not know whether the inventory account balance was materially accurate, and he was not going to write a memo indicating otherwise. Moments later, Bill walked into the client office being used by Sam Hakes and closed the door behind him.

"What's up?" Sam asked as he flipped through a workpaper file.

"Sam, I've decided that I can't sign off on the inventory account," Bill blurted out.

"What?" was Sam's stunned, one-word reply.

Bill stalled for a few moments to bolster his courage as he fidgeted with his tie. "Well . . . like I said, I'm not signing off on the inventory account."

"Why?" By this point, a disturbing crimson shade had already engulfed Sam's ears and was creeping slowly across his face.

"Sam . . . I just don't think I can sign off. I mean, I'm just not sure whether the inventory number is right."

"You're . . . *just not sure*?" After a brief pause, Sam continued, this time pronouncing each of his words with a deliberate and sarcastic tone. "You mean to tell me that you spent almost 1,000 hours on that account, and you're just not sure whether the general ledger number is right?"

"Well . . . yeah. Ya know, it's just tough to . . . to reach a conclusion, ya know, on an account that large."

Sam leaned back in his chair and cleared his throat before speaking. "Mr. DeBurger, I want you to go back into that room of yours and close the door. Then you sit down at that table and write a nice, neat, very precise and to-the-point inventory memo. And hear this: I'm not telling you what to include in that memo. But you're going to write that memo, and you're going to have it on my desk in two hours. Understood?" Sam's face was entirely crimson as he completed his short speech.

"Uh, okay," Bill replied.

Bill returned to the small conference room that had served as his work area for the past two months. He sat in his chair and stared at the pictures of his two-year-old twins, Lesley and Kelly, which he had taped to the wall above the phone. After a few minutes, he picked up his pencil, leaned forward, and began outlining the inventory memo.

Questions

1. What conclusion do you believe Bill DeBurger reached in his inventory memo? Put yourself in his position. What conclusion would you have expressed in the inventory memo? Why?

2. Would you have dealt with your uncertainty regarding the inventory account differently than Bill did? For example, would you have used a different approach to raise the subject with Sam Hakes?

3. Evaluate Sam Hakes' response to Bill's statement that he was unable to sign off on the inventory account. In your view, did Sam deal with the situation appropriately? Was Sam's approach "professional"? Explain.

4. Is it appropriate for relatively inexperienced auditors to be assigned the primary responsibility for such critical accounts as Marcelle Stores' inventory? Explain.

David Myers, WorldCom Controller

Awaiting his court appearance to be charged with securities fraud, David Myers sat in a jail cell in 2002 and counted the cinder blocks again and again to distract himself.[1] In his pocket was a plastic red dog named Clifford, given to him by his young son. "He'll take care of you," the boy had said, according to his mother.

For Mr. Myers, the former controller of WorldCom Inc., the past four years have been a life-altering journey. It began when the prosperous businessman and father of three put aside his misgivings and agreed to go along with false accounting entries that eventually became part of an $11 billion fraud.

The scheme Mr. Myers participated in set off a chain of events that had a devastating impact on his company, his colleagues, and his family. The collapse of the telecommunications giant resulted in the loss of more than 17,000 jobs and billions of dollars in pensions and investments.

Hoping to win a lighter sentence, Mr. Myers, 47 years old, pleaded guilty and immersed himself in the government's investigation. He helped prosecutors identify false numbers in WorldCom's financial filings from 2000 to 2002. That evidence, and his court testimony, helped convict WorldCom Chief Executive Officer Bernard Ebbers last week for his role in one of the largest financial frauds in corporate history.

As the U.S. government rolls through a historic wave of prosecutions of business fraud, Mr. Myers is one of the executives watching a successful life come unglued. He and his family are now preparing for his sentencing set for June. Federal guidelines suggest he could serve more than 10 years in prison, though he is expected to receive a shorter sentence because of his cooperation.

"We don't know what is going to happen," says his wife, Lynn, 39. "I don't know if he's going to prison or for how long. I just want him home."

Raised in Jackson, Mississippi, Mr. Myers played basketball and was a honor student in high school. The son of civil servants, he earned degrees in marketing and accounting from the University of Mississippi. He married, had two children, and divorced in 1990.

In 1993, Mr. Myers married his second wife, Lynn, an interior designer and onetime cheerleader, who is also a Jackson native. The couple settled into a suburban life working in the yard and having dinners with friends. They had a son, Jack, now five. Mr. Myers joined WorldCom in 1995 as treasurer—just as the telecom upstart was about to hit a huge growth spurt.

As WorldCom's stock price rose through the late 1990s, the Myerses' lifestyle grew richer. They moved to a house on the edge of a large, bass-filled lake. The couple began traveling to London, Paris, and Bermuda on WorldCom business trips. When WorldCom's share price peaked in 1999, the options held by the Myerses were valued at more than $15 million, though they cashed in only about $300,000 worth. "We had a good life and knowing the options were there was nice," says Mrs. Myers. The party ended in 2000 amid the bursting of the Internet bubble and a stiff price war among telecom companies. WorldCom's business began a sharp decline.

In January 2001, Mr. Myers and Buford Yates, an accountant who worked for him, met in the office of WorldCom's chief financial officer Scott Sullivan, according to testimony from Mr. Myers. Knowing WorldCom wouldn't meet analyst expectations for the coming quarter, the three agreed, at Mr. Sullivan's behest, to reclassify some of the company's biggest expenses, according to Mr. Myers' testimony. This essentially moved expenses off WorldCom's income statement, erasing their effect on the bottom line. "I didn't think that was the right thing to do, but I had been asked by Scott to do it and I was asking him [Mr. Yates] to do it," Mr. Myers testified.

In an illustration of how huge ethical lapses often begin with small steps, he justified his actions to himself, thinking WorldCom's business would soon improve, people close to the case say. But rather than being a stopgap measure, the improper accounting continued. Mr. Myers helped direct false entries again and again. People close to Mr. Myers say he believed Mr. Sullivan's explanations that eventually the company's problems would be straightened out.

Drawing Away

In the summer of 2001, Mr. Myers realized there was no end to the company's woes. He became depressed. He considered quitting, but realized the scandal would follow him because of what he had already done. On weekends, he withdrew, begging off on evenings out with his friends, blaming the stress of work. He grew increasingly irritable and distant.

Mrs. Myers sought the advice of Buddy Stallings, a priest from their Episcopal church. "She was worried about their life," says Father Stallings. "She felt things were spiraling out of control." He told her that she and Mr. Myers shouldn't be afraid to make changes in their life.

One warm evening in 2001, Mrs. Myers stood by the lake outside their house. When Mr. Myers joined her, she began crying. "You're somewhere else," she recalls telling him. "We have a baby. You work all the time. Why not quit?" Mr. Myers, whose annual salary was about $240,000 before options, told her he wanted to earn enough to start his own business and that he didn't want to quit, out of loyalty to Mr. Sullivan, the chief financial officer. But he didn't confide that he was also worried about the accounting at WorldCom.

Mr. Myers' thoughts turned to suicide, according to investigators. He began entertaining the idea of staging his own fatal car accident. Over a period of weeks, Mr. Myers began driving his BMW faster and faster through a turn on a highway underpass between Worldcom's Clinton, Mississippi, headquarters and his home, according to a person close to the situation. Trying to determine the speed at which his car would completely lose control, Mr. Myers pushed the speedometer higher each time, reaching 115 miles an hour one night. Eventually, Mr. Myers abandoned the idea.

Mrs. Myers says she urged her husband to see a doctor. He did, and began taking an antidepressant. His depression lifted. But he still didn't share the root of his troubles, Mrs. Myers says. "I knew something was wrong but I couldn't pull out of him what it was."

On a Sunday in June 2002, the phone rang at the Myerses' house. Mr. Myers listened to a WorldCom employee who worked for Cynthia Cooper, head of internal audits. She was looking into accounting entries that she found suspicious. The employee said Ms. Cooper had focused in on certain large expense items—ones Mr. Myers knew would lead to his office.

Mr. Myers plopped on the stairs at the back of his house, watching his wife and son play in the yard. He mulled over the enormity of the problem. He vowed to come clean if Ms. Cooper confronted him.

On June 17, 2002, Ms. Cooper entered Mr. Myers' office. She peppered him with questions, according to regulatory filings. Did he know about the entries? Was there any support for them? Were other companies doing the same thing?

Mr. Myers confessed. He calmly explained that he knew about the entries but there was no support for them. An auditor accompanying Ms. Cooper asked what he had planned to tell the Securities and Exchange Commission if officials asked about the bookkeeping. He said he hoped they wouldn't ask. As the meeting broke up, Mr. Myers felt better than he had for months, as though a cloud over him had lifted, Mrs. Myers said he told her later.

Inside WorldCom, panic erupted as the company grappled with the explosive news that billions in profits had been manufactured through improper accounting. But initially, Mr. Myers was told by one WorldCom director that his job would probably be safe, people close to the situation say.

That changed a few days later, when he and Mr. Sullivan flew to Washington on the company plane for a meeting with the board's audit committee. The two men, seated at opposite ends of the plane, barely spoke. At one point, Mr. Sullivan offered Mr. Myers a chocolate-covered doughnut, telling him it was the only thing he could force himself to eat since the news broke. Mr. Myers declined.

It finally dawned on Mr. Myers that he was in trouble. He and Mr. Sullivan were excluded from a hastily called meeting of WorldCom's management and board. When Mr. Myers attempted to talk to a WorldCom lawyer, he was told he should hire his own lawyer and stop confiding in the WorldCom legal staff, people close to Mr. Myers say. On his way out that day, another WorldCom lawyer wished him the best. Mr. Myers knew he was going to lose his job.

Later that evening, Mr. Myers, staying at Embassy Suites hotel in Washington, got a call from a lawyer appointed for him by WorldCom; the lawyer told him that no one would believe Mr. Sullivan had pulled off the fraud alone. The board was offering him the chance to resign.

Mr. Myers, stricken, called his wife. He told her about his role in the bogus accounting entries. The usually restrained Mr. Myers cried as he asked what their friends and neighbors would say about him. Mrs. Myers, also crying, told him he was a good man and nothing would change that, she recalls. Mr. Myers later told her that he clung to those words in the weeks that followed. The next morning, he flew home and faxed in his letter of resignation.

In the days that followed, Mr. and Mrs. Myers drew the blinds, pulled the car in the garage and went into hiding, people close to them say. Because he had acted on orders, Mr. Myers still didn't think he would face personal liability for the fraud, Mrs. Myers says. When two agents with the Federal Bureau of Investigation showed up at the door and flashed their badges, Mrs. Myers let them in.

"I was shocked, but I thought they were there to talk about Bernie and Scott," she says. "I didn't think we were in trouble."

Mr. Myers led the agents to the sun porch. Mrs. Myers ran upstairs to call her father, a lawyer, who instructed her to tell Mr. Myers not to answer any questions without an attorney. As Mrs. Myers watched the agents drive away, she recalls thinking, "Oh my God, this is huge."

"Helpless Feeling"

During a meeting with Richard Janis, the lawyer her husband later hired, Mrs. Myers recalls sobbing as he told them political pressure was high to make an example of WorldCom employees involved in the fraud. This was the first time she realized her husband might go to prison. "It was a helpless feeling," she says, realizing her husband could miss a big part of their son's childhood.

Mr. and Mrs. Myers moved to her parents' house in another part of Jackson to escape the media throng that had begun to gather at their own home. Once, when they saw a police car cruising the neighborhood, they froze, thinking the police might be looking for them, Mrs. Myers says. Mr. Myers began looking around when he took the trash out to see if anyone was watching him, Mrs. Myers says he told her.

On July 30, 2002, Mr. and Mrs. Myers prepared to go to New York, where he would be charged with securities fraud. Mrs. Myers cried as she kissed their son goodbye. "He didn't know why I was sad," she says. Jack, clutching a small plastic "Clifford" dog, handed the toy to his father, Mrs. Myers recalls. "That was his favorite toy and he gave it to David."

In New York, the couple met with Father Stallings, their former priest, who had relocated to a church on Staten Island. During a walk, Mr. Myers said he had been told he would have to turn over his shoelaces, belt and tie when he turned himself in the next day. Father Stallings gave Mr. Myers a pair of loafers so he wouldn't have to remove any laces. Afterward, he took the couple to the church and gave them communion. He thinks that gave Mr. Myers solace. "I believe it made a difference," he says.

The next day, Mr. Myers was fingerprinted in FBI offices in Manhattan and had his mug shot taken. He was led outside and handcuffed, in what is known as a "perp walk." Wearing a blue suit and a red tie, Mr. Myers appeared emotionless as he walked to a car waiting to take him to the federal courthouse. He wasn't allowed in the car for a few minutes, as an FBI agent sat inside with the door locked. Cameras flashed. The agent unlocked the door and Mr. Myers was let in.

Before returning home, the Myerses visited the World Trade Center site and Mr. Myers placed the plastic toy dog on an informal memorial there.

On September 25, 2002, Mr. Myers was the first of four WorldCom managers to plead guilty to securities fraud. Standing under an umbrella, his lawyer said: "Myers was a reluctant participant in the events that have led us here. . . . He recognizes that as a corporate officer, those facts do not relieve him of responsibility in this matter."

The Myerses returned to Jackson and tried to pick up their lives. Mr. Myers began volunteering as a bookkeeper at their church and worked on a archaeology dig nearby. Once, while on a treadmill at his gym, he looked up to see his own image in handcuffs on television. He put his head down and moved faster, Mrs. Myers says he told her. Driving around Jackson, he often thought he was recognized at stoplights, she says.

With the support of friends, the Myerses slowly began to emerge from their isolation. They received more than 200 letters from people who sympathized with their situation, Mrs. Myers says.

A turning point for Mr. Myers came in June 2003 when he borrowed a bicycle and signed up to chaperone a 500-mile bike ride with a group of youngsters, including some from troubled homes. Mr. Myers struggled to make the long rides each day. Often alone, he contemplated the future and his past actions, Mrs. Myers says. He strained to climb one particularly steep hill—and the exhilaration of riding down the other side made him believe good times still lay ahead, she says.

He returned home more optimistic. He bought a necklace with a cross on it at the gift shop of a Jackson church and began wearing it daily. Their priest reminded him that everyone makes mistakes but it's how a person deals with them that matters, Mrs. Myers says.

Anticipating a prison sentence, Mr. Myers began preparing. The family moved to a smaller house that shared a backyard with the couple's best friends. He started a real-estate company with Mr. Yates, the accountant who worked for him and also pleaded guilty to securities fraud. They hoped the company, which buys residential real estate, would produce profits to help them tide their wives over if they were sent to prison.

Mr. Myers' work as a witness for the government increased. In December 2003, he spent most of a weekend in a New York hotel room, poring over WorldCom documents. Every five hours, he would take a break, walking across the street to grab some pizza and a soda. That Sunday, he handed prosecutors a computer disk detailing every false number he recognized in WorldCom's financial filings from 2000 to 2002.

Around that time, prosecutors were working to win a plea agreement from Mr. Sullivan, the former chief financial officer. Ultimately, they hoped to get Mr. Sullivan to testify against Mr. Ebbers, the chief executive.

On March 2, 2004, Mr. Sullivan pleaded guilty to three counts of securities fraud—and agreed to testify against Mr. Ebbers. In testimony, Mr. Sullivan said one of the reasons he decided to plead guilty was Mr. Myers' statements to investigators about him. The same day, Mr. Ebbers was indicted on fraud charges.

In January, Mr. Myers stood in the witness room at the courthouse in Manhattan, waiting to testify against Mr. Ebbers. Looking out the window at St. Andrew's church, he noticed an ornate cross on the rear peak of the roof, similar to the one he wears around his neck. As his testimony proceeded over the next several days, he often looked out at the cross at St. Andrew's while holding the one around his neck, Mrs. Myers says.

On February 3, the day after Mr. Myers completed his testimony, the couple returned to Jackson. Their son was sleeping, and Mrs. Myers laid down beside him. He woke up and asked where his father was. He raced to the bedroom and jumped into the bed with Mr. Myers, crying "my Daddy," Mrs. Myers recalls.

Mrs. Myers says she hasn't told Jack his father may have to spend time in prison. "He doesn't understand what's going on," she says. "He loves his Daddy. What do you say when Daddy doesn't come home?"[2]

Questions

1. Research online news services to identify recent developments in the WorldCom case. Briefly summarize those developments in a bullet format.

2. Does the fact that David Myers' superior, Scott Sullivan, asked him to make the false accounting entries in WorldCom's accounting records diminish Myers' responsibility for his improper conduct? Defend your answer.

3. What punishment, if any, do you believe David Myers should have been given for his role in the WorldCom fraud?

4. Is it appropriate for federal law enforcement authorities "to make an example" of individuals involved in high-profile financial frauds, such as WorldCom and Enron? Explain.

2. On August 10, 2005, a federal judge sentenced David Myers to one year and one day in federal prison for his role in the WorldCom fraud. On October 10, 2005, Myers surrendered to federal authorities to begin serving his prison term at the federal correctional facility in Yazoo City, Mississippi. Because he received credit for good behavior while in prison, Myers was released in August 2006. One month earlier, the SEC had ruled that Myers should repay more than $1 million of bonuses that he had received from WorldCom over the course of the fraud. However, the federal agency subsequently waived that repayment when Myers demonstrated that he was incapable of making it. The SEC also permanently prohibited Myers from serving as an officer, director, or accountant of a public company.

Tommy O'Connell, Audit Senior

Tommy O'Connell had been a senior with a Big Five accounting firm for less than one month when he was assigned to the audit engagement for the Altamesa Manufacturing Company.[1] Tommy worked out of his firm's Fort Worth, Texas, office, while Altamesa was headquartered in Amarillo, the "capital" of the Texas Panhandle. The young senior realized that being assigned to the tough Altamesa engagement signaled that Jack Morrison, the Altamesa audit partner and the office managing partner, regarded his work highly. Serving as the audit senior on the Altamesa job would allow Tommy to become better acquainted with Morrison. Despite the challenges and opportunities posed by his new assignment, Tommy did not look forward to spending three months in Amarillo, a five-hour drive from Fort Worth. This would be his first assignment outside of Fort Worth since his marriage six months earlier. He dreaded breaking the news to his wife, Suzie, who often complained about the long hours his job required.

Altamesa manufactured steel girders used in the construction and renovation of bridges in West Texas, New Mexico, Colorado, and Oklahoma. The company's business was very cyclical and linked closely to the funding available to municipalities in Altamesa's four-state market area. To learn more about the company and its personnel, Tommy arranged to have lunch with Casi McCall, the audit senior on the Altamesa job the two previous years. According to Casi, Altamesa's management took aggressive positions regarding year-end expense accruals and revenue recognition. The company used the percentage-of-completion method to recognize revenue since its sales contracts extended over two to five years. Casi recounted several disputes with the company's chief accountant regarding the estimated stage of completion of jobs in progress. In an effort to "front-load" as much of the profit on jobs as possible, the chief accountant typically insisted that jobs were further along than they actually were.

Speaking with Casi made Tommy even more apprehensive about tackling the Altamesa engagement. But he realized that the job gave him an excellent chance to strengthen his fast-track image within his office. To reach his goal of being promoted to manager by his fifth year with the firm, Tommy needed to prove himself on difficult assignments such as the Altamesa engagement.

An Unpleasant Surprise for Tommy

It was late May, just two weeks before Tommy would be leaving for Amarillo to begin the Altamesa audit—the company had a June 30 fiscal year-end. Tommy, Jack Morrison, and an audit manager were having lunch at the Cattleman's Restaurant in the Cowtown district of north Fort Worth.

"Tommy, I've decided to send Carl with you out to Amarillo. Is that okay?" asked Jack Morrison.

"Uhh . . . sure, Jack. Yeah, that'll be fine," Tommy replied.

---

1. The facts of this case were reconstructed from an actual series of events. Names and certain background information have been changed to conceal the identities of the individuals involved in the case.

"Of all people," Tommy thought to himself, "he would send Carl Wilmeth to Amarillo with me." Carl was a staff accountant with only a few months' experience, having been hired in the middle of the just-completed busy season. Other than being auditors and approximately the same age, the two young men had little in common. Tommy was from Lockettville, a small town in rural West Texas, while Carl had been raised in the exclusive Highland Park community of north central Dallas. Texas Tech, a large state-supported university, was Tommy's alma mater. Carl had earned his accounting degree from a small private college on the East Coast.

Tommy did not appreciate Carl's cocky attitude, and his lack of experience made him a questionable choice in Tommy's mind for the Altamesa engagement. As he tried to choke down the rest of his prime rib, Tommy recalled the complaints he had heard about Carl's job performance. Over the past three months, Carl had worked on two audits. In both cases, he had performed admirably—too admirably, in fact, coming in well under budget on his assigned tasks. On one engagement, Carl had completed an assignment in less than 60 hours when the audit budget allotted 100 hours; the previous year, 110 hours had been required to complete that same task. Both seniors who had supervised Carl suspected that he had not completed all of his assigned audit procedures, although he signed off on those procedures on the audit program. The tasks assigned to Carl had been large-scale tests of transactions that involved checking invoices, receiving reports, purchase orders, and other documents for various attributes. Given the nature of the tests, the seniors would have had difficulty confirming their suspicions.

"Boss" Tommy

Six weeks later, in early July, the Altamesa audit was in full swing. Carl had just finished his third assigned task on the job, in record time, of course. "Boss, here's that disbursements file," Carl said as he plopped a large stack of workpapers in front of Tommy. "Anything else you want me to do this afternoon? Since I'm way ahead of schedule, maybe I should take off and work on my tan out on the golf course."

"No, Carl. I think we have plenty to keep you busy right here." Tommy was agitated but he tried not to let it show. "Why don't you pull out the contracts file and then talk to Alissa Myers in the sales office. Get copies of any new contracts or proposals over the past year and put them in the contracts file."

At this point, Tommy simply did not have time to review Carl's cash disbursements workpapers. He was too busy trying to untangle Altamesa's complex method of allocating overhead costs to jobs in process. Later that afternoon, he had an appointment to meet with the chief accountant and a production superintendent to discuss the status of a large job. Tommy and the chief accountant had already butted heads on two occasions regarding a job's stage of completion. Casi had been right: the chief accountant clearly meant to recognize profit on in-progress jobs as quickly as possible. With four decades of experience, Scrooge—a nickname Casi had pinned on the chief accountant—obviously considered the young auditors a nuisance and did not appreciate their probing questions. Each time Tommy asked him a question regarding an important issue, the chief accountant registered his disgust by pursing his lips and running his hand through his thinning hair. He then responded with a rambling, convoluted answer intended to confuse rather than inform.

To comprehend Altamesa's accounting decisions for its long-term contracts, Tommy spent several hours of nonchargeable time each night in his motel room flipping through copies of job order worksheets and contracts. Occasionally, he referred to prior-year workpapers, his firm's policy and procedures manual, and even his tattered cost accounting textbook from his college days. Carl spent most of his evenings in the motel's club being taught the Texas Two-step and Cotton-eyed Joe by several new friends he had acquired.

During July and August, Tommy and Carl worked 50 to 60 hours per week on the Altamesa engagement. Several times Tommy wondered to himself whether it was worthwhile to work so hard to earn recognition as a "superstar" senior. He was also increasingly concerned about the impact of his fast-track strategy on his marriage. When he tried to explain to Suzie that the long hours and travel would pay off when he made partner, she was unimpressed. "Who cares if you make partner? I just want to spend more time with my husband," was her stock reply.

To Tell or Not to Tell

Finally, late August rolled around and the Altamesa job was almost complete. Jack Morrison had been in Amarillo for the past three days combing through the Altamesa workpapers. Nothing seemed to escape Morrison's eagle eye. Tommy had spent 12 hours per day since Morrison had arrived, tracking down missing invoices, checking on late confirmations, and tying up dozens of other loose ends. Carl was already back in Fort Worth, probably working on his golf swing. Morrison had allowed Carl to leave two days earlier after he had finished clearing the review comments in his files.

"Tommy, I have to admit that I was a little concerned about sending a light senior out to run this audit. But, by golly, you have done a great job." Morrison did not look up as he signed off on the workpapers spread before him on Altamesa's conference table. "You know, this kid Carl does super work. I've never seen cleaner, more organized workpapers from a staff accountant."

Tommy grimaced as he sat next to Morrison at the conference table. "Yeah, right. They should look clean, since he didn't do half of what he signed off on," Tommy thought to himself. Here was his opportunity. For the past several weeks, Tommy had planned to sit down with Morrison and talk to him regarding Carl's job performance. But now he was reluctant to do so. How do you tell a partner that you suspect much of the work he is reviewing may not have been done? Besides, Tommy realized that as Carl's immediate supervisor, he was responsible for that work. Tommy knew that he was facing a no-win situation. He leaned back in his chair and remained silent, hoping that Morrison would hurry through the last few workpaper files so they could make it back to Fort Worth by midnight.

EPILOGUE

Tommy never informed Jack Morrison of his suspicions regarding Carl's work. Thankfully, no problems—of a legal nature—ever arose on the jobs to which Carl was assigned. After passing the CPA exam on his first attempt, Carl left the accounting firm and enrolled in a prestigious MBA program. Upon graduation, Carl accepted a job on Wall Street with one of the large investment banking firms. Tommy reached his goal of being promoted to audit manager within five years. One year later, he decided that he was not cut out to be a partner and resigned from the firm to accept a position in private industry.

Questions

1. Compare and contrast the professional roles of an audit senior and a staff accountant. In your analysis, consider the different responsibilities assigned to each role, the job-related stresses that individuals in the two roles face, and how each role contributes to the successful completion of an audit engagement. Which of these two roles is (a) more important and (b) more stressful? Defend your choices.

2. Assume that you are Tommy O'Connell and have learned that Carl Wilmeth will be working for you on the Altamesa audit engagement. Would you handle this situation any differently than Tommy did? Explain.

3. Again, assume that you are Tommy. Carl is badgering you for something to do midway through the Altamesa job. You suspect that he is not completing all of his assigned procedures, but at the time you are wrestling with an important and contentious accounting issue. What would you do at this point? What could you do to confirm your suspicions that Carl is not completing his assignments?

4. Now, assume that Jack Morrison is reviewing the Altamesa workpapers. To date, you (Tommy) have said nothing to Morrison about your suspicions regarding Carl. Do you have a professional responsibility to raise this matter now with Morrison? Explain.

5. Assume that at some point Tommy told Morrison that he suspected Carl was not completing his assigned tasks. The only evidence Tommy had to support his theory was the fact that Carl had come in significantly under budget on every major task assigned to him over a period of several months. If you were Jack Morrison, how would you have handled this matter?

Avis Love, Staff Accountant

"Oh no, not Store 51," Avis Love moaned under her breath. For the third time, Avis compared the dates listed in the cash receipts journal with the corresponding dates on the bank deposit slips. Avis shook her head softly and leaned back in her chair. There was no doubt in her mind now. Mo Rappele had definitely held open Store 51's cash receipts journal at the end of October.[1]

Avis Love was a staff accountant with the Atlanta office of a large international accounting firm. Several months earlier, Avis had graduated with an accounting degree from the University of Alabama at Birmingham. Although she did not plan to pursue a career in public accounting, Avis had accepted one of the several offers she had received from major accounting firms. The 22-year-old wanted to take a two- or three-year "vacation" from college, while at the same time accumulating a bankroll to finance three years of law school. Avis intended to practice law with a major firm for a few years and then return to her hometown in eastern Alabama and set up her own practice.

For the past few weeks, Avis had been assigned to the audit engagement for Lowell, Inc., a public company that operated nearly 100 retail sporting goods stores scattered across the South. Avis was just completing a year-end cash receipts cutoff test for a sample of 20 Lowell stores. The audit procedures she had performed included preparing a list of the cash receipts reported in each of those stores' accounting records during the last five days of Lowell's fiscal year, which ended October 31. She had then obtained the relevant bank statements for each of the stores to determine whether the cash receipts had been deposited on a timely basis. For three of the stores in her sample, the deposit dates for the cash receipts ranged from three to seven days following the dates the receipts had been entered in the cash receipts journal. The individual store managers had apparently backdated cash receipts for the first several days of the new fiscal year, making it appear that the receipts occurred in the fiscal year presently under audit by Avis's firm.

Avis had quickly realized that the objective of the store managers was not to overstate their units' year-end cash balances. Instead, the managers intended to inflate their recorded sales. Before Avis began the cutoff test, Teddy Tankersley, the senior assigned to the Lowell audit and Avis's immediate superior, had advised her that there was a higher-than-normal risk of cash receipts and sales cutoff errors for Lowell this year. The end of Lowell's fiscal year coincided with the end of a three-month sales promotion. This campaign to boost Lowell's sagging sales included bonuses for store managers who exceeded their quarterly sales quota. This was the first time that Lowell had run such a campaign and it was a modest success. Fourth-quarter sales for the fiscal year just ended topped the corresponding sales for the previous fiscal year by 6 percent.

When Avis uncovered the first instance of backdated cash receipts, she had felt a noticeable surge of excitement. In several months of tracing down invoices and receiving reports, ticking and tying, and performing other mundane tests, the young accountant had occasionally found isolated errors in client accounting records. But this was different. This was fraud.

---

1. The facts of this case were developed from an actual series of events. Names, locations, and certain other background information have been changed to conceal the identities of the individuals involved in the case.

Avis had a much different reaction when she uncovered the second case of backdated cash receipts. She had suddenly realized that the results of her cutoff test would have "real world" implications for several parties, principally the store managers involved in the scheme. During the past few months, Avis had visited six of Lowell's retail stores to perform various interim tests of controls and to observe physical inventory procedures. The typical store manager was in his or her early 30s, married, with one or two small children. Because of Lowell's miserly pay scale, the stores were chronically understaffed, meaning that the store managers worked extremely long hours to earn their modest salaries.

No doubt, the store managers who backdated sales to increase their bonuses would be fired immediately. Clay Shamblin, Lowell's chief executive officer (CEO), was a hard-nosed businessman known for his punctuality, honesty, and work ethic. Shamblin exhibited little patience with subordinates who did not display those same traits.

When Avis came to the last store in her sample, she had hesitated. She realized that Mo Rappelle managed Store 51. Three weeks earlier, Avis had spent a long Saturday afternoon observing the physical inventory at Store 51 on the outskirts of Atlanta. Although the Lowell store managers were generally courteous and accommodating, Mo had gone out of his way to help Avis complete her tasks. Mo allowed Avis to use his own desk in the store's cramped office, shared a pizza with her during an afternoon break, and introduced her to his wife and two small children who dropped by the store during the afternoon.

"Mo, what a stupid thing to do," Avis thought to herself after reviewing the workpapers for the cutoff tests a final time. "And for just a few extra dollars." Mo had apparently backdated cash receipts for only the first two days of the new year. According to Avis's calculations, the backdated sales had increased Mo's year-end bonus by slightly more than $100. From the standpoint of Lowell, Inc., the backdated sales for Mo's store clearly had an immaterial impact on the company's operating results for the year just ended.

After putting away the workpapers for the cutoff test, a thought dawned on Avis. The Lowell audit program required her to perform cash receipts cutoff tests for 20 stores . . . any 20 stores she selected. Why not just drop Store 51 from her sample and replace it with Store 52 or 53 or whatever?

EPILOGUE

Avis brooded over the results of her cutoff test the remainder of that day at work and most of that evening. The following day, she gave the workpaper file to Teddy Tankersley. Avis reluctantly told Teddy about the backdated cash receipts and sales she had discovered in three stores: Store 12, Store 24, and Store 51. Teddy congratulated Avis on her thorough work and told her that Clay Shamblin would be very interested in her findings.

A few days later, Shamblin called Avis into his office and thanked her for uncovering the backdated sales. The CEO told her that the company's internal auditors had tested the year-end cash receipts and sales cutoff for the remaining 72 stores and identified seven additional store managers who had tampered with their accounting records. As Avis was leaving the CEO's office, he thanked her once more and assured her that the store managers involved in the scam "would soon be looking for a new line of work . . . in another part of the country."

Questions

1. Would it have been appropriate for Avis to substitute another store for Store 51 after she discovered the cutoff errors in that store's accounting records? Defend your answer.

2. Identify the parties potentially affected by the outcome of the ethical dilemma faced by Avis Love. What obligation, if any, did Avis have to each of these parties?

3. Does the AICPA's *Code of Professional Conduct* prohibit auditors from developing friendships with client personnel? If not, what measures can auditors take to prevent such friendships from interfering with the performance of their professional responsibilities?

4. Identify the key audit objectives associated with year-end cash receipts and sales cutoff tests.

5. What method would you have recommended that Avis or her colleagues use in deciding whether the cutoff errors she discovered had a material impact on Lowell's year-end financial statements? Identify the factors or benchmarks that should have been considered in making this decision.

Charles Tollison, Audit Manager

"No, that's okay, Bea. I'll write that memo this weekend and send it to Mr. Fielder. You go on home."[1]

"Are your sure, Chuck? I don't mind staying a while longer."

"Thanks, Bea, but you've already put in too much overtime this week."

After he sent his secretary home, Charles Tollison spent several minutes shuffling through the audit workpapers and correspondence stacked on his desk, trying to decide what work he would take home over the weekend. Finally, only one decision remained. Tollison couldn't decide whether to take the inventory file with him. Compulsive by nature, Tollison knew that if he took the inventory file home, he would have to complete his review of that file, which would increase his weekend workload from 6 hours to more than 12 hours. As he stewed over his decision, Tollison stepped to the window of his office and idly watched the rush-hour traffic on the downtown streets several stories below.

It was nearly 6:30 on a Friday evening in early August. Charles Tollison, an audit manager for a large international accounting firm, had suffered through a tough week. His largest audit client was negotiating to buy a smaller company within its industry. For the past two months, Tollison had supervised the fieldwork on an intensive acquisition audit of the competitor's accounting records. The client's chief executive officer (CEO) suspected that the competitor's executives had embellished their firm's financial data in anticipation of the proposed buyout. Since the client was overextending itself financially to acquire the other firm, the CEO wanted to be sure that its financial data were reliable. The CEO's principal concern was the valuation of the competitor's inventory, which accounted for 45 percent of its total assets.

The client's CEO had requested that Tollison be assigned to the acquisition audit because she respected Tollison and the quality of his work. Normally, an audit manager spends little time "in the trenches" supervising day-to-day audit procedures. However, because of the nature of this engagement, Tollison had felt it necessary to spend 10 hours per day, six and seven days per week, poring over the accounting records of the takeover candidate with his subordinates.

As Tollison stared at the gridlocked streets below, he was relieved that the acquisition audit was almost complete. After he tied up a few loose ends in the inventory file, he would turn the workpapers over to the audit engagement partner for a final review.

Tollison's tough week had been highlighted by several contentious meetings with client personnel, a missed birthday party for his 8-year-old daughter, and an early breakfast Thursday morning with his office managing partner, Walker Linton. During that breakfast, Linton had notified Tollison that he had been passed over for promotion to partner—for the second year in a row. The news had been difficult for Tollison to accept.

For more than 13 years, Tollison had been a hardworking and dedicated employee of the large accounting firm. He had never turned down a difficult assignment, never

---

1. This case was developed from information obtained from a CPA employed for many years with a large international accounting firm.

complained about the long hours his work required, and made countless personal sacrifices, the most recent being the missed birthday party. After informing Tollison of the bad news, Linton had encouraged him to stay with the firm. Linton promised that the following year he would vigorously campaign for Tollison's promotion and "call in all favors" owed to him by partners in other offices. Despite that promise, Tollison realized that he had only a minimal chance of being promoted to partner the following year. Seldom were two-time "losers" ticketed for promotion.

Although he had been hoping for the best, Tollison had not expected a favorable report from the Partner Selection Committee. In recent weeks, he had gradually admitted to himself that he did not have the profile for which the committee was searching. Tollison was not a rainmaker like his friend and fellow audit manager, Craig Allen, whose name appeared on the roster of new partners that would be formally announced the following week. Allen was a member of several important civic organizations and had a network of well-connected friends at the local country club. Those connections had served Allen well, allowing him to steer several new clients to the firm in recent years.

Instead of a rainmaker, Tollison was a technician. If someone in the office had a difficult accounting or auditing issue to resolve, that individual went first to Tollison, not to one of the office's six audit partners. When a new client posed complex technical issues, the audit engagement partner requested that Tollison be assigned to the job. One reason Tollison was a perfect choice for difficult engagements was that he micromanaged his jobs, insisting on being involved in every aspect of them. Tollison's management style often resulted in his "busting" time budgets for audits, although he seldom missed an important deadline. To avoid missing deadlines when a job was nearing completion, Tollison and the subordinates assigned to his engagements would work excessive overtime, including long weekend stints.

Finally, Tollison turned away from his window and slumped into his chair. As he sat there, he tried to drive away the bitterness that he was feeling. "If Meredith hadn't left the firm, maybe I wouldn't be in this predicament," Tollison thought to himself. Three years earlier, Meredith Olivetti, an audit partner and Tollison's closest friend within the firm, had resigned to become the chief financial officer (CFO) of a large client. Following Olivetti's resignation, Tollison had no one within the firm to sponsor him through the tedious and political partner selection process. Instead, Tollison had been "lost in the shuffle" with the dozens of other hardworking, technically inclined audit managers within the firm who aspired to a partnership position.

Near the end of breakfast Thursday morning, Walker Linton had mentioned to Tollison the possibility that he could remain with the firm in a senior manager position. In recent years, Tollison's firm had relaxed its "up or out" promotion policy. But Tollison was not sure he wanted to remain with the firm as a manager with no possibility of being promoted to partner. Granted, there were clearly advantages associated with becoming a permanent senior manager. For example, no equity interest in the firm meant not absorbing any portion of future litigation losses suffered by the firm. On the other hand, in Tollison's mind accepting an appointment as a permanent senior manager seemed equivalent to having "career failure" stenciled on his office door.

Ten minutes till seven, time to leave. Tollison left the inventory file lying on his desk as he closed his bulging briefcase and then stepped toward the door of his office. After flipping off the light switch, Tollison paused momentarily. He then grudgingly turned and stepped back to his desk, picked up the inventory file, and tucked it under his arm.

Questions

1. Do you believe Charles Tollison was qualified for a partnership position with his firm? Explain.

2. Did Tollison's firm treat him "fairly"? Why or why not?

3. Identify the criteria you believe large international accounting firms should use when evaluating individuals for promotion to partner. In your opinion, which of these criteria should be most heavily weighted by these firms? Should smaller accounting firms establish different criteria for evaluating individuals for promotion to partner? Explain.

4. Discuss the advantages and disadvantages of the "up or out" promotion policy followed by many accounting firms.

Hamilton Wong, In-Charge Accountant

After spending much of the previous three months working elbow-to-elbow with as many as six colleagues in a cramped and poorly ventilated conference room, Hamilton Wong was looking forward to moving on to his next assignment.[1] Wong was an in-charge accountant on the audit staff of the San Francisco office of a large international accounting firm, the firm that had offered him a job two years earlier as he neared completion of his accounting degree at San Jose State University. His current client, Wille & Lomax, Inc., a public company and the second largest client of Wong's office, owned a chain of retail stores in the western United States that stretched from Seattle to San Diego and as far east as Denver and Albuquerque.

Although Wille & Lomax's stores operated under different names in different cities, each stocked the same general types of merchandise, including briefcases and other leather goods, luggage and travel accessories, and a wide range of gift items, such as costume jewelry, imported from Pacific Rim countries. The company also had a wholesale division that marketed similar merchandise to specialty retailers throughout the United States. The wholesale division accounted for approximately 60 percent of the company's annual sales.

A nondescript building in downtown San Francisco, just one block from bustling Market Street, served as Wille & Lomax's corporate headquarters. The company's fiscal year-end fell on the final Saturday of January. With the end of March just a few days away, Hamilton and his fellow "Willies"—the nickname that his office assigned to members of the Wille & Lomax audit engagement team—were quickly running out of time to complete the audit. Wong was well aware that the audit was behind schedule because he collected, coded, and input into an electronic spreadsheet the time worked each week by the individual Willies. He used the spreadsheet package to generate a weekly time and progress report that he submitted to Angela Sun, the senior who supervised the field work on the Wille & Lomax audit.

In addition to Wong and Sun, another in-charge accountant, Lauren Hutchison, and four staff accountants had worked on the Wille & Lomax audit since early January. Wong and Hutchison knew each other well. They shared the same start date with their employer and the past two summers had attended the same weeklong staff and in-charge training sessions at their firm's national education headquarters. Hutchison's primary responsibility on the current year's audit was the receivables account but she also audited the PP&E (property, plant, and equipment) and leases accounts. Besides his administrative responsibilities, which included serving as the engagement timekeeper and maintaining the correspondence file for the audit, Wong supervised and coordinated the audit procedures for inventory, accounts payable, and a few smaller accounts.

Hamilton was thankful that it was late Friday afternoon. In recent weeks, with the audit deadline looming, Angela Sun had required the Willie & Lomax crew to work until at least 7 p.m. each weekday except Friday, when she allowed them to leave

---

1. This case is based upon the experiences of an individual previously employed by one of the major accounting firms. The names of the parties involved in this case and other background facts, such as locations, have been changed.

"early" at 5 p.m. The engagement team had spent three consecutive Saturdays in the client's headquarters and would be spending both Saturday and Sunday of the coming weekend hunched over their workpapers. Wong had just completed collecting and coding the hours worked during the current week by the other members of the engagement team. Now it was time for him to enter in the electronic spreadsheet his chargeable hours, which he dutifully recorded at the end of each work day in his little "black book."

Before entering his own time, Wong decided to walk across the hall and purchase a snack in the employees' break room. In fact, he was stalling, trying to resolve a matter that was bothering him. Less than 30 minutes earlier, Lauren Hutchison had told him that during the current week, which included the previous weekend, she had spent 31 hours on the receivables account, 18 hours on the leases account, and 3 hours on PP&E. What troubled Wong was the fact that he knew Hutchison had worked several additional hours on the Wille & Lomax audit during the current week.

This was not the first time Hutchison had underreported her hours worked. On several occasions, Wong had noticed her secretively slipping workpaper files into her briefcase before leaving for home. The next morning, those files included polished memos or completed schedules that had not existed the previous day. Wong was certain that Hutchison was not reporting the hours she spent working at home on her audit assignments. He was just as certain that each week she consciously chose to shave a few hours off the total number she had spent working at the client's headquarters. Collectively, Wong estimated that Hutchison had failed to report at least 80 hours she had worked on the audit.

"Eating time" was a taboo subject among auditors. Although the subject was not openly discussed, Wong was convinced that many audit partners and audit managers subtly encouraged subordinates to underreport their time. By bringing their jobs in near budget, those partners and managers enhanced their apparent ability to manage engagements. The most avid time-eaters among Wong's peers seemed to be the individuals who had been labeled as "fast-track" superstars in the office.

After Hutchison had reported her time to Wong that afternoon, he had nonchalantly but pointedly remarked, "Lauren, who are you trying to impress by eating so much of your time?" His comment had caused the normally mild-mannered Hutchison to snap back, "Hey, Dude, you are the timekeeper, not the boss. So just mind your own ___ business." Immediately, Wong regretted offending Hutchison, whom he considered his friend. But she stomped away before he could apologize.

Wong knew whom Hutchison was trying to impress. Angela Sun would almost certainly be promoted to audit manager in the summer and then become the audit manager on the Wille & Lomax engagement, meaning that there would be a vacancy in the all-important senior position on the engagement team. Both Hutchison and Wong also anticipated being promoted during the summer. The two new seniors would be the most likely candidates to take over the job of overseeing the field work on the Wille & Lomax audit.

The in-charge accountant who handled the administrative responsibilities on the Wille & Lomax engagement was typically the person chosen to take over the senior's role when it came open. But Wong worried that the close friendship that had developed between Lauren Hutchison and Sun might affect his chances of landing the coveted assignment. Almost every day, Hutchison and Sun went to lunch together without extending even a token invitation to Wong or their other colleagues to join them. John Berardo, the audit engagement partner, would choose the new senior for the Wille & Lomax engagement, but Angela Sun would certainly have a major influence on his decision.

There was little doubt in Wong's mind that Hutchison routinely underreported the time she worked on the Wille & Lomax audit to enhance her standing with Sun and Berardo. Not that Hutchison needed to spruce up her image. She had passed the CPA exam on her first attempt, had a charming personality that endeared her to her superiors and client executives, and, like both Sun and Berardo, was a Stanford graduate. Wong, on the other hand, had suffered through three attempts at the CPA exam before finally passing, was shy by nature, and had graduated from a public university.

What irritated Wong the most about his subtle rivalry with Hutchison was that during the past two weekends he had spent several hours helping her research contentious technical issues for Wille & Lomax's complex lease contracts on its retail store sites. Earlier in the engagement, Hutchison had also asked him to help analyze some tricky journal entries involving the client's allowance for bad debts. In each of those cases, Wong had not charged any time to the given accounts, both of which were Hutchison's responsibility.

Before entering his time for the week, Wong checked once more the total hours that he had charged to date to his major accounts. For both inventory and accounts payable, he was already over budget. By the end of the audit, Wong estimated that he would "bust" the assigned time budgets for those two accounts by 20 to 25 percent each. On the other hand, Hutchison, thanks to her superior "time management" skills, would likely exceed the time budget on her major accounts by only a few hours. In fact, she might even come in under budget on one or more of her accounts, which was almost unheard of, at least on the dozen or so audits to which Wong had been assigned.

After finishing the bag of chips he had purchased in the snack room, Wong reached for the computer keyboard in front of him. In a few moments, he had entered his time for the week and printed the report that he would give to Angela Sun the following morning. After briefly glancing at the report, he slipped it into the appropriate workpaper file, turned off the light in the empty conference room, and locked the door behind him as he resolved to enjoy his brief 16-hour "weekend."

Questions

1. Place yourself in Hamilton Wong's position. Would you report all of your time worked on the Wille & Lomax audit? Why or why not? Do you believe that Lauren Hutchison behaved unethically by underreporting the time she worked on that engagement? Defend your answer.

2. Academic research suggests that underreporting time on audit engagements is a common practice. What are the key objectives of tracking hours worked by individual accounts or assignments on audit engagements? What implications does the underreporting of time have for individual auditors, their colleagues, and the overall quality of independent audits?

3. What measures can accounting firms take to ensure that time budgets do not interfere with the successful completion of an audit or become dysfunctional in other ways?

4. What measures can accounting firms take to reduce the likelihood that personal rivalries among auditors of the same rank will become dysfunctional?

SECTION 7

PROFESSIONAL ISSUES

PricewaterhouseCoopers Securities, LLC

In the spring of 1998, the management of Polypipe, a British company involved in the construction materials industry, faced a critical decision. Polypipe's executives had to decide whether to accept, or attempt to fend off, a hostile takeover bid being made by one of the company's competitors. After deciding to oppose the takeover attempt, those executives faced another important decision: what M&A (mergers and acquisition) firm should they retain to help them survive the takeover bid?

Polypipe relied heavily on PricewaterhouseCoopers (PwC), the company's independent auditor for more than 25 years, for a wide range of advice regarding important business and economic issues. When asked to recommend an M&A firm, PwC representatives suggested that Polypipe hire the M&A firm with which they were most familiar, namely, PricewaterhouseCoopers Financial Advisory Services (FAS). PwC's FAS practice stretched around the globe and employed thousands of securities traders, corporate turnaround experts, and specialists in a variety of other financial services fields. The FAS unit marketed various investment banking services, including M&A consulting, business recovery, corporate valuation, and dispute resolution services. At the time, PwC reported that the primary role of its FAS practice was to "provide creative solutions and ideas that increase value to clients during critical periods and when they are making important decisions that define their future."

During the 1990s, the large international firms that dominate the accounting profession began to move aggressively into a wide range of financial services fields, including investment banking. "The Big Five say the move into investment banking is just another way of providing corporate clients with one-stop shopping for auditing, consulting, tax and other financial services."[1] In fact, by the late 1990s, PwC and the other members of the Big Five no longer viewed themselves as "accounting" firms. "PwC—as its leaders tell us ad nauseam—is a professional services firm—not an accountancy firm, not an audit firm."[2] Over the next several years, PwC and its cohorts would learn that professional firms pursuing lines of business outside their historical areas of expertise may be able to develop and exploit new and lucrative revenue streams. But these firms also learned the painful lesson that new lines of business often pose significant challenges that are not immediately obvious to industry "rookies."

Taking on Wall Street

Coopers & Lybrand surprised much of the accounting profession in 1996 when it created Coopers & Lybrand Securities, LLC (CLS), a wholly owned subsidiary that it registered as a securities brokerage firm with the Securities and Exchange Commission (SEC). Two years later, in July 1998, CLS was renamed PricewaterhouseCoopers Securities, LLC (PwCS), following the merger of Price Waterhouse and Coopers & Lybrand. PwCS was then folded into the FAS practice of the new firm.

1. M. Goldstein, "Big 5 Eye Niche Wall Street Ignores: Growing Practice in M&A Deals," *Crain's New York Business*, 23 August 1999, 3.

2. *Financial Times* (London), "Mergers and Separations: As PwC Enjoys Its First Birthday, the Issue of Auditor Independence Has Resurfaced," 1 July 1999, 12.

Investment banking services for corporate customers, not retail brokerage services, was the principal business activity of PwCS. By the turn of the century, each Big Five firm had a sizable investment banking practice. In fact, based upon one industry metric, KPMG could boast of having the world's *largest* investment banking practice. In 1998, KPMG was involved in more M&A transactions, 430 to be precise, than any other firm in the investment banking industry. Coming in a close second was PwC with 429 M&A deals, while Morgan Stanley Dean Witter & Co., a longtime and very prominent Wall Street investment banker, nailed down third place. To a layperson, those statistics suggested that the Big Five was effectively taking over the investment banking industry. But, in reality, that was not the case.

In 1998, the total dollar volume of KPMG's and PwC's M&A transactions was $1.65 billion and $1.24 billion, respectively. Those numbers paled in comparison with the annual dollar value of M&A transactions for industry giants such as Morgan Stanley and Goldman Sachs. For example, in 1998, Goldman Sachs was the financial advisor for M&A deals totaling nearly $400 billion. Goldman Sachs, Morgan Stanley, and the other behemoths of the investment banking world typically accept only "mega" or multibillion dollar M&A engagements. By contrast, the "low end" of the M&A market—in which the Big Five firms chose to compete—typically involves transactions measured in a few million dollars.

The Polypipe deal referred to earlier, which involved total corporate assets of approximately $500 million, was easily PwC's largest M&A deal in 1998. In Europe, large accounting firms have historically served as general financial advisors and business consultants to their small and midsized audit clients. This historical role allowed the new M&A divisions of the Big Five firms to quickly establish themselves in that region of the world.

Despite their early success in Europe, the Big Five firms found that "cracking" the M&A market in the United States was much more difficult. Among the biggest barriers these firms faced in acquiring M&A clients in the United States was Rule 302, "Contingent Fees," of the *AICPA Code of Professional Conduct*. Because contingent fees may result in situations in which an independent auditor's "interests are directly aligned with those of the client,"[3] the U.S. accounting profession has long banned such fee arrangements for any professional services provided to audit clients. Exhibit 1 presents the full text of Rule 302.

In the investment banking industry, contingent fee arrangements are the norm. Large companies desperate to defeat hostile takeover bids, attempting to acquire

EXHIBIT 1

RULE 302, CONTINGENT FEES, *AICPA CODE OF PROFESSIONAL CONDUCT*

Rule 302—Contingent Fees

A member in public practice shall not
(1) Perform for a contingent fee any professional services for, or receive such a fee from a client for whom the member or the member's firm performs,
    (a) an audit or review of a financial statement; or
    (b) a compilation of a financial statement when the member expects, or reasonably might expect, that a third party will use the financial statement and the member's compilation report does not disclose a lack of independence;
    or
(2) Prepare an original or amended tax return or claim for a tax refund for a contingent fee for any client.

---

3. P. Spiegel, "PwC Settles Federal Case with $5 Million Fine," *Financial Times* (London), 18 July 2002, 9.

competitors, or intending to market new securities believe that the most effective way to make their investment banker fully committed to the given engagement is to tie the firm's compensation to the eventual outcome of that engagement. Rule 302 expressly prohibits an accounting firm from charging contingent fees to an investment banking client if the firm also provides any type of audit or audit-related service to that client. Understandably, Rule 302 poses a huge problem for the Big Five firms' investment banking units in the United States. This is a "nonproblem" for those firms in Europe where they generally are not prohibited from charging contingent fees for nonaudit services sold to audit clients.

In the late 1990s, frustration posed by Rule 302 apparently prompted certain PwC officials to begin circumventing that rule. The Securities and Exchange Commission (SEC) acted quickly and harshly when it discovered that PwCS was using contingent fee arrangements for investment banking services provided to PwC audit clients.

Value-Added Fees

In July 2002, the SEC revealed that in 14 instances over the five-year period from 1996 through 2001, PwCS or its predecessor, CLS, had accepted contingent fees from investment banking clients that were also PwC or Coopers & Lybrand audit clients. The SEC reported that PwC and Coopers & Lybrand officials had been well aware that such fee arrangements were strictly banned. "Because of the broker-dealer's [PwCS/CLS] affiliation with the audit firm [PwC/Coopers & Lybrand], Respondents [PwC and PwCS] at all times recognized that the broker-dealer remained subject to auditor independence rules, understood that it therefore should not charge contingent fees to audit clients, and had written guidelines that prohibited charging contingent fees to audit clients."[4] The SEC also noted that when Coopers & Lybrand organized CLS, the firm distributed a memorandum advising its partners that because "CLS is wholly owned by the firm, it is subject to, and we intend to comply with, the rules of the AICPA and the Securities and Exchange Commission governing independence, conflicts of interest, and contingent fees."

In four of the 14 cases involving contingent fee payments to PwCS or CLS, the given firm expressly incorporated a contingent fee arrangement in the formal engagement letter obtained from the investment banking client. In the other 10 cases uncovered by the SEC, PwCS or CLS obtained "engagement letters that purported to create permissible 'value-added fee' arrangements, but issued side letters or entered into oral understandings that created forbidden contingent fee arrangements."[5,6] Exhibit 2 presents a description of one of the circumstances in which PwCS used a side letter to create a contingent fee arrangement. As a point of information, the SEC did not sanction or reveal the names of the investment banking clients that paid contingent fees to PwCS or CLS.

The SEC charged that PwC and Coopers & Lybrand lacked adequate internal controls to "identify and prevent" contingent fee arrangements that could compromise

---

4. The remaining quotations in this case, unless indicated otherwise, were taken from Securities and Exchange Commission, *Accounting and Auditing Enforcement Release No. 1596*, 17 July 2002.

5. The SEC defined "value-added fee" arrangements in the following manner: "Value-added fees are arrangements in which the client, at its unfettered discretion, determines at the end of the engagement whether the services rendered warrant an additional fee based on qualitative factors." According to the SEC, value-added fees are permissible under Rule 302.

6. Consistent with the SEC's position, the Public Company Accounting Oversight Board (PCAOB) prohibits auditors of public companies from having any contingent fee arrangements with audit clients. Likewise, the PCAOB does not prohibit value-added fee arrangements between auditors and clients as long as such fee arrangements do not include any contingent fee structure. (*PCAOB Release No. 2005-014*, 26 July 2005.)

EXHIBIT 2

CONTINGENT FEE
ARRANGEMENT USED
BY PwCS THAT
INVOLVED A "SIDE
LETTER"

In May 1999, PwCS agreed to help a PwC public audit client, Company C, sell an operating unit pursuant to an engagement letter stating that, under AICPA guidelines, "PwCS does not bill on a 'success' or 'contingent' fee basis. Rather, our fees . . . are based upon the time expended, the complexity of the services provided, the experience of PwCS team members and the value of the services provided." In a side letter bearing the same date as the engagement letter, however, PwCS created, in substance, a contingent fee arrangement by proposing a "fee structure" . . . equivalent to the market compensation for services of this nature, a minimum total fee of $155,000; plus an additional incentive fee equal to 2% of the excess of the transaction value over $7,000,000.

Source: Securities and Exchange Commission, *Accounting and Auditing Enforcement Release No. 1596*, 17 July 2002.

their independence with audit clients that were also investment banking clients. Most galling to the SEC was that, shortly before the merger that created PwC, CLS officials developed a PowerPoint marketing presentation to make Coopers & Lybrand partners aware of CLS's investment banking services. This PowerPoint presentation indicated that "the SEC allows CLS to accept 'success fees,' 'contingent fees,' and 'value-added fees.'" Apparently, the Coopers & Lybrand audit partners who attended these presentations did not report this oversight to the appropriate authorities within their firm.

From 1996 through 2001, CLS and PwCS accepted "several million dollars of contingent fees" from clients that were also audit clients of their respective parent organization. In 2002, the SEC fined PwC $5 million for the breaches of Rule 302. At the time, that fine was the second largest ever imposed on an accounting firm by the SEC. The federal agency also censured PwC and issued cease-and-desist orders against PwC and PwCS. These latter orders prohibited PwC and PwCS from violating federal securities laws in the future. Three years earlier, PwC had agreed to pay $2.5 million to establish educational programs to "improve auditor compliance" with the profession's independence standards. This payment was made to settle SEC allegations that numerous PwC managers and partners had violated the profession's independence rules by purchasing stock in the firm's audit clients.

EPILOGUE

In commenting on the contingent fee debacle involving PwC, one critic of the accounting profession charged that CPAs and CPA firms "don't seem to even recognize conflicts of interest anymore."[7] Samuel DiPiazza, the global chief executive officer (CEO) of PwC, responded to such critics by observing that his firm and other major accounting firms needed "to rebuild the public's trust in our profession and in the markets by adhering to the highest ethical standards."[8] Rebuilding the public's trust apparently did not, in DiPiazza's mind, require PwC to

7. B. Etzel, "PwC's M&A Ambitions: A Bold Move for Accountancy, or a Blatant Conflict of Interest?" *Investment Dealers Digest* (online), 19 August 2002.

8. S. Taub, "Accountants Fire Back," *CFO.com*, 22 November 2002.

place less emphasis on the provision of nonaudit services such as investment banking. One month after the SEC sanctioned PwC for accepting improper contingent fee payments, PwCS announced that it was hiring 60 new employees to increase its M&A market share in the United States.[9]

Questions

1. Do you believe the SEC's punishment of PwC and PwCS was appropriate in this case? Defend your answer.

2. In your opinion, is it appropriate for accounting firms to offer financial services, such as investment banking, that have historically been provided by other professionals? Defend your answer.

3. Do you believe that accounting firms could feasibly use value-added fee arrangements? Why or why not? (See footnote No. 5 for a definition of "value added" fees.)

9. As a point of information, the Sarbanes-Oxley Act of 2002 prohibits audit firms from providing investment banking services to audit clients that are SEC registrants. In December 2004, Ernst & Young announced that it had sold its investment banking division to Giuliani Partners, a consulting firm headed by former New York mayor Rudolph Giuliani. E&Y's chairman noted that the sale "is part of our ongoing commitment to refocus on our core businesses—auditing, tax, and transaction advisory services" (M. Aguilar, "E&Y Sheds Investment Banking Arm in Sale to Giuliani Partners," *WebCPA.com*, 3 December 2004).

Stephen Gray, CPA

During the mid-1980s, Stephen W. Gray owned and operated a small CPA firm in Columbia, Mississippi.[1] Located in south central Mississippi near the banks of the Pearl River, Columbia's population of 5,000 provided Gray with only a modest client base and limited potential for revenue growth. In 1987, Gray struck upon an idea to expand his practice.

For several years, Gray had offered financial planning services to his clients. After developing a financial plan for a customer, Gray referred the individual to a securities broker. The broker then purchased the appropriate investments for the customer. After obtaining a broker's license in June 1987, Gray became affiliated with a Texas-based investment firm, H. D. Vest Investment Securities, Inc., and began offering brokerage services to his clients.

Gray took several steps to protect the integrity of his CPA status after he began providing brokerage services. To safeguard his independence on attest engagements, he refused to provide brokerage services to clients for whom he performed audits and other attestation services. Gray also adopted a strict policy of informing clients that he would earn commissions on securities trades they placed through him. Finally, to make his customers and the general public aware of his dual professional roles, he prominently displayed his broker's license within his office.

Gray realized that accepting commissions technically violated the ethical code of the Mississippi State Board of Public Accountancy. Since 1973, the state agency had vigorously enforced a ban on the receipt of commissions by CPAs. This ban included commissions received exclusively from non-attest clients.

When he applied for a broker's license in 1987, Gray was also keenly aware of an ongoing conflict between the Federal Trade Commission (FTC) and the American Institute of Certified Public Accountants (AICPA). That conflict involved the FTC's efforts to force the AICPA to allow its members to accept commissions from non-attest clients. The FTC prevailed in 1988 when the AICPA's ruling Council voted 191 to 5 to allow members to accept commissions for certain services provided to non-attest clients.[2] Rule 503 of the *AICPA Code of Professional Conduct*, shown in Exhibit 1, expresses the AICPA's present stance regarding the receipt of commissions by its members.

In late 1990, a CPA alerted the Mississippi State Board of Public Accountancy that he had evidence Stephen Gray was accepting commissions in exchange for brokerage services. The CPA stumbled across this evidence while providing accounting services to a former client of Gray. Following a brief investigation, the state board charged Gray with violating its ban against accepting commissions. At an April 19, 1991, hearing before the state agency, Gray acknowledged that he had accepted commissions from non-attest clients. Gray then maintained that the state board had

---

1. Most of the facts and all of the quotations appearing in this case were drawn from the following legal opinion: *Mississippi State Board of Public Accountancy et al. v. Stephen W. Gray, CPA*, 674 So. 2d 1252 (1996).

2. L. Berton, "Nation's Accountants Vote to End Bans Against Certain Fees and Commissions," *The Wall Street Journal*, 31 August 1988, 33.

EXHIBIT 1

RULE 503 OF
THE *AICPA*
CODE OF
PROFESSIONAL
CONDUCT

Rule 503—Commissions and Referral Fees

A. Prohibited commissions

A member in public practice shall not for a commission recommend or refer to a client any product or service, or for a commission recommend or refer any product or service to be supplied by a client, or receive a commission, when the member or the member's firm also performs for that client

(a) an audit or review of a financial statement; or

(b) a compilation of a financial statement when the member expects, or reasonably might expect, that a third party will use the financial statement and the member's compilation report does not disclose a lack of independence; or

(c) an examination of prospective financial information.

This prohibition applies during the period in which the member is engaged to perform any of the services listed above and the period covered by any historical financial statements involved in such listed services.

B. Disclosure of permitted commissions

A member in public practice who is not prohibited from performing services for or receiving a commission and who is paid or expects to be paid a commission shall disclose that fact to any person or entity to whom the member recommends or refers a product or service to which the commission relates.

C. Referral fees

Any member who accepts a referral fee for recommending or referring any service of a CPA to any person or entity or who pays a referral fee to obtain a client shall disclose such acceptance or payment to the client.

---

exceeded its statutory authority when it adopted the ban on commissions. He also argued that the rule was not in the public interest.

The Mississippi state board patiently listened to Gray's arguments. One month later, the board voted to revoke Gray's CPA certificate and his license to practice. Gray immediately appealed that decision, an appeal heard by the Marion County Circuit Court. During the lengthy appeals process, Gray retained both his CPA certificate and license to practice.

In reviewing the state board's decision, the circuit court placed considerable weight on the AICPA rule that allowed CPAs to receive commissions from non-attest clients. The court noted that 46 state boards of accountancy, including the Mississippi state board, prohibited CPAs from receiving such commissions. But then the court went on to observe that it was even more impressive "that the national association of all CPAs specifically allows for the receipt of commissions."

The circuit court also questioned whether the ban on receiving commissions improperly infringed on CPAs' ability to earn a livelihood. CPAs who ply their trade in the more remote areas of the state, the court observed, were particularly subject to being harmed by this rule. The circuit court proposed a control procedure to mitigate conflicts of interest that might arise from allowing CPAs to accept commissions for non-attest services. This procedure would require CPAs to file a report with the state board disclosing the non-attest services they provided on a commission basis. These reports would also require disclosure of the relationship, if any, between the non-attest and attest services offered by a CPA.

On January 16, 1992, the Marion County Circuit Court released its ruling on Stephen Gray's appeal. That ruling overturned the state board's decision to revoke Gray's CPA certificate and license to practice. According to the circuit court, the state board's action was "too extreme a remedy for the facts and circumstances of this case."

The Mississippi State Board of Public Accountancy appealed the circuit court's reversal of its decision to the Supreme Court of Mississippi. Under Mississippi state law, the key issue that a state court must consider in reviewing a state agency's decision is whether that decision was arbitrary and capricious. After studying the case, the supreme court concluded that the circuit court never raised the issue of whether the state board's decision was arbitrary and capricious. Instead, the circuit court simply substituted its judgment for that of the state board in overturning the latter's decision. The supreme court ruled that the circuit court's failure to fulfill its judicial mandate invalidated the reversal of the state board's decision.

To bring closure to the Gray case, the Supreme Court of Mississippi decided to tackle the question itself of whether the state board's decision to revoke Gray's CPA certificate and license to practice qualified as arbitrary and capricious. First, the supreme court reviewed the legislative authority granted the state board. An excerpt from the relevant state statute follows:

> The Mississippi State Board of Public Accountancy is hereby authorized with the following powers and duties: to adopt and enforce such rules and regulations concerning certified public accountant examinee and licensee qualifications and practices as the board considers necessary to maintain the highest standard of proficiency in the profession of certified public accounting and for protection of the public interest.

Later sections of this statute grant the state board authority to promulgate accounting, auditing, and ethical standards for CPAs. These standards include the following rule that Stephen Gray violated:

> A licensee shall not pay a commission to obtain a client nor shall he accept a commission for a referral to a client of products or services of others. This rule shall not prohibit payments for the purchase of all, or a material part of, an accounting practice or retirement payments to individuals formerly engaged in the practice of public accounting or payments to their heirs and estates.

The supreme court then addressed the issue of whether the state board's ban on commissions qualified as arbitrary and capricious. After a thorough review of the matter, the court ruled that the ban on commissions was an appropriate professional standard for the board to adopt and enforce. In reaching that decision, the court referred to the *United States v. Arthur Young & Co.* opinion handed down in 1984 by the U.S. Supreme Court.[3] In that opinion, the Supreme Court observed that CPAs have a responsibility to maintain complete fidelity to the public interest at all times. Allowing CPAs to accept commissions could potentially cause them to place their own economic interests over their responsibilities to the public, reasoned the Mississippi supreme court. More to the point, the state supreme court questioned Gray's ability to retain his independence and objectivity while offering services on a commission basis to non-attest clients.

> Gray's dual role as a certified public accountant and a registered representative of the H. D. Vest firm creates a potential conflict of interest and raises questions of independence and objectivity with regard to whether his investment advice is motivated by the client's tax needs or the commissions those investments might generate.

---

3. *United States v. Arthur Young & Co.*, 104 S. Ct. 1495 (1984).

In May 1996, the Supreme Court of Mississippi issued its decision in the Gray case. The supreme court reversed the circuit court's ruling and thereby reinstated the state board's decision to revoke Stephen Gray's CPA certificate and license.

The Mississippi State Board of Public Accountancy was acting within its regulatory power when it revoked Gray's license. There is substantial evidence in the record to support the decision, which was not arbitrary or capricious or in violation of Gray's rights. In conclusion, we find that the circuit court improperly substituted its own judgment for that of the Board. Accordingly, we reverse the order of the circuit court and reinstate the Board's decision.

EPILOGUE

In 1996, the Mississippi State Board of Public Accountancy dropped its ban on the receipt of commissions from non-attest clients. The board effectively adopted Rule 503 of the *AICPA Code of Professional Conduct,* shown in Exhibit 1.[4] In fact, by the turn of the century, most state boards of accountancy had changed their ethical codes to allow CPAs to receive commissions from non-attest clients.

As noted earlier, Stephen Gray retained his CPA certificate and license to practice while his appeal of the state board's decision worked its way through the judicial system. Following the Mississippi supreme court's ruling in the Gray case, the state board reconsidered its original decision to revoke Gray's CPA certificate and license to practice. Instead of enforcing that decision, the state board required Gray's accounting practice to undergo one year of supervisory review. Gray successfully completed that review and at last report was a CPA in good standing with the Mississippi State Board of Public Accountancy.

Questions

1. Why do professions adopt ethical codes for their members? What factors cause professions to change these codes over time?

2. In your opinion, did the Mississippi State Board of Public Accountancy make an appropriate decision when it eventually chose not to revoke Stephen Gray's CPA certificate and license to practice? Defend your answer.

3. Suppose that a CPA's spouse holds a broker's license. Would the CPA violate Rule 503 of the *AICPA Code of Professional Conduct* if the spouse provides brokerage services on a commission basis to an attest client of the CPA?

4. Compare and contrast the oversight roles within the accounting profession of state boards of public accountancy and the AICPA. What is the role of state societies of CPAs in the accounting profession?

---

4. The complete ethical code of the Mississippi State Board of Public Accountancy can be found at that organization's website, http://www.msbpa.state.ms.us.

CASE 7.3

Scott Fane, CPA

As for most young professionals, earning a reasonable livelihood ranked as a top priority for Scott Fane, a CPA specializing in taxation services who relocated to Florida in the mid-1980s. To practice as a CPA in Florida, Scott registered with the Florida Board of Accountancy, which regulates the public accounting profession within the state of Florida. Scott soon butted heads with that state agency. A protracted legal battle ensued. In 1993, the young CPA and the Florida Board of Accountancy finally settled their differences in the hallowed chambers of the U.S. Supreme Court.

Searching for Clients in the Sunshine State

Scott Fane moved to Florida from New Jersey in 1985 with the hope that Florida's robust economy would help him quickly establish a thriving accounting practice. In New Jersey, Scott relied on direct solicitation to identify and pursue potential clients. Although businesses commonly use direct mail, telephone calls, and in-person visitations to contact potential customers, professions historically have discouraged their members from utilizing those marketing methods. In the 1970s, the Federal Trade Commission (FTC) persuaded the American Institute of Certified Public Accountants (AICPA) to eliminate its ban on direct solicitation by AICPA members. Most state boards quickly fell in line with the AICPA and repealed their bans on direct solicitation, including the New Jersey state board. Among the holdouts that continued to prohibit direct solicitation was the Florida state board.

After moving to Florida, Scott targeted his practice development efforts on individuals and small businesses. Most of these potential customers had an ongoing relationship with a CPA. In New Jersey, Scott overcame that problem by contacting potential clients directly and offering to provide them services at fees lower than those charged by their existing CPAs. Florida's ban on direct solicitation effectively undermined that strategy.[1]

> The rule . . . presented a serious obstacle, because most businesses are willing to rely for advice on the accountants or CPAs already serving them. In Fane's experience, persuading a business to sever its existing accounting relations or alter them to include a new CPA on particular assignments requires the new CPA to contact the business and explain the advantages of a change.[2]

In 1990, frustration drove Scott to sue the Florida Board of Accountancy in a U.S. District Court. Scott charged that the state agency's ban on direct solicitation was unconstitutional. Specifically, Scott alleged that the rule violated his First Amendment rights to freedom of speech.

Scott Scores Twice in the Lower Courts

The Florida Board of Accountancy mustered a vigorous defense to Scott Fane's lawsuit. First, the state board maintained that the ban on direct solicitation shielded users of accounting services from zealous, "overreaching" CPAs. Second, the state

---

1. The Florida Board of Accountancy defined "direct solicitation" as all uninvited in-person visits or conversations or telephone calls to a specific potential client.

2. *Edenfield v. Fane*, 113 S.Ct. 1792 (1993).

board claimed that the ban safeguarded auditors' independence, the cornerstone of the independent audit function. To bolster these arguments, the state board called on one of its former chairmen.

The former state board chairman testified that CPAs who solicit clients are "obviously in need of business and may be willing to bend the rules."[3] Thus, the ban on direct solicitation allegedly prevented CPAs from falling prey to their own economic (greedy) impulses. The former chairman also testified that clients obtained via direct solicitation efforts would have considerable leverage on their CPAs. A client might use this leverage to extract concessions from a newly retained accountant. In the context of independent audits, such concessions might ultimately result in improper audit opinions and, more important, in suboptimal decisions by financial statement users relying on those opinions.

The district court judge rejected the arguments made by the Florida Board of Accountancy and its former chairman. Although those arguments seemed reasonable, the judge observed that the state board had provided no concrete evidence to corroborate its claims:

> The defendant [state board] has failed to demonstrate a causal relationship between in-person, direct, uninvited solicitation, and accountant misconduct. Similarly, the defendant has failed to prove any harm to third parties as a result of the alleged misconduct.[4]

In September 1990, the district court judge ruled in Scott Fane's favor in his lawsuit against the Florida Board of Accountancy. The state board immediately appealed that ruling to the U.S. Court of Appeals. In a two-to-one decision, the appellate court sustained the district court judge's ruling. The two appellate judges who supported that decision held that the Florida state board had failed to prove there existed a "substantial need" for the ban on direct solicitation. Appellate Judge Edmondson filed a strong dissent to the majority opinion. Judge Edmondson observed that the federal government has historically allowed states significant leeway in regulating the professionals they license. Given this longstanding precedent, the judge believed that any doubt in the case should be resolved in favor of the state board's position.

Judge Edmondson also agreed with the state board's contention that direct solicitation potentially jeopardized CPAs' integrity and credibility. He noted that direct solicitation might provoke individual CPAs to engage in "fraud, undue influence, intimidation, overreaching, and other forms of vexatious conduct."[5] The other two appellate judges suggested that severe sanctions for such conduct served as an effective deterrent. Judge Edmondson disagreed, pointing out that direct solicitation efforts are, by definition, private in nature. How then could state boards monitor these efforts and discourage abusive solicitation practices?

Finally, Judge Edmondson pointed out that Florida "cloaked" CPAs practicing within its boundaries in an "aura of competence" that had the potential to intimidate or "overawe" prospective clients. As a result, Florida had a right and responsibility to take vigorous measures to protect the public from unethical CPAs. In Judge Edmondson's opinion, Florida was attempting to do just that by banning direct solicitation.

> Even if I personally questioned that the Florida rule is necessary for an ordered CPA profession, it would not be my place to second-guess state officials about the state rule's wisdom or effectiveness. What is important for me is that reasonable people,

3. *Ibid.*

4. *Fane v. Edenfield*, 945 F.2d 1514 (1990).

5. *Fane v. Edenfield*, 507 U.S. 761 (1991).

such as those that I expect comprise the Florida Board of Accountancy, could think that the rule against in-person solicitation of clients functions to assure greater competence of CPAs, more reasoned selection of CPAs by lay people, and the accuracy of audit statements upon which the public relies.[6]

Dissatisfaction with the appellate court's decision and Judge Edmondson's strong defense of its point of view prompted the Florida Board of Accountancy to appeal the Scott Fane case to the U.S. Supreme Court. The focal issue of the case, commercial speech, happened to be a topic of considerable interest to the Supreme Court in the early 1990s. Not surprisingly, then, the Fane case survived the rigorous review process for cases appealed to the Supreme Court and was placed on the high court's 1992–1993 docket.

Scott Takes His Case to the U.S. Supreme Court

The Supreme Court heard arguments in the Scott Fane case in December 1992 and released its ruling four months later. In that opinion, the Supreme Court stressed the importance of commercial speech, which is defined as "expression related exclusively to the economic interests of the speaker and audience." Prior to the twentieth century, state and federal courts did not consider commercial speech to be protected by the First Amendment, which guarantees freedom of speech for U.S. citizens. During the latter decades of the twentieth century, the federal courts, including the U.S. Supreme Court, gradually extended First Amendment protection to commercial speech.

As a general rule, federal courts protect commercial speech from governmental restraint as long as it is truthful and not misleading. The Supreme Court reaffirmed that principle in the Scott Fane case.

The commercial marketplace, like other spheres of social and cultural life, provides a forum where ideas and information flourish. Some of the ideas and information are vital, some of slight worth. But the general rule is that the speaker and the audience, not the government, assess the value of the information presented.[7]

Justice Anthony Kennedy, who wrote the majority opinion in the case, observed that a governmental agency seeking to restrict commercial speech generally has two responsibilities. First, the agency must establish that the given commercial speech poses serious harms to the public. Second, the agency must demonstrate that the restrictions it intends to impose on the commercial speech alleviate those harms to a material degree.

In the Fane case, Justice Kennedy maintained that the Florida Board of Accountancy failed to prove that direct solicitation poses a serious threat to the consumers of accounting services. Justice Kennedy noted that the state board did not offer any evidence that Fane's direct solicitation efforts in New Jersey had been damaging to his customers or potential customers. Likewise, he quickly dismissed the suggestion by the former chairman of the Florida state board that CPAs who engage in direct solicitation are more likely than other CPAs to capitulate to audit clients and thus jeopardize the integrity of the independent audit function.

It appears from the literature that a business executive who wishes to obtain a favorable but unjustified audit opinion from a CPA would be less likely to turn to a stranger who has solicited him than to pressure his existing CPA, with whom he has an ongoing, personal relation and over whom he may also have some financial leverage.[8]

---

6. *Ibid.*

7. *Edenfield v. Fane*, 113 S.Ct. 1792 (1993).

8. *Ibid.*

Eight of the nine Supreme Court justices voted to uphold the two previous rulings in Scott Fane's case. In summarizing the majority's view, Justice Kennedy observed that Florida's ban on direct solicitation did not accomplish its intended objective and actually had negative consequences for Florida citizens.

> *In denying CPAs and their clients the considerable advantages of solicitation in the commercial context, Florida's law threatens societal interests in broad access to complete and accurate commercial information that the First Amendment is designed to safeguard.*[9]

Justice Sandra Day O'Connor filed a dissenting opinion in the Scott Fane case that closely paralleled many of the arguments made previously by Judge Edmondson of the U.S. Court of Appeals. Justice O'Connor argued that individual states should be allowed to prohibit commercial speech inconsistent with a profession's public image, although that speech is not directly harmful to the parties to whom it is intended. In Justice O'Connor's view, the recent trend toward allowing professions to become more commercial has had a subtle but adverse impact on professions. "Commercialization has an incremental, indirect, yet profound effect on professional culture, as lawyers know all too well."[10]

EPILOGUE

Scott Fane's legal action against the Florida Board of Accountancy was the first of three major lawsuits the state agency faced in the 1990s. While Fane's case was working its way through the federal courts, the Florida board charged another CPA, Richard Rampell, with violating its ban on direct solicitation. Rampell immediately sued the state board. Like Fane, Rampell maintained that the board's ban on direct solicitation was unconstitutional. He made the same allegation concerning the board's rule that banned competitive bidding for attestation engagements. At the time, Florida was the only state that prohibited CPAs from seeking attest clients on a competitive-bidding basis. The Florida Supreme Court eventually settled Rampell's lawsuit.

When the U.S. Supreme Court ruled in Scott Fane's favor in April 1993, the Florida Supreme Court pronounced that the Florida Board of Accountancy's ban on direct solicitation was no longer enforceable and dropped that issue from Richard Rampell's case. In July 1993, the

Florida Supreme Court ruled in favor of Rampell on the other charge he filed against the Florida Board of Accountancy. This ruling effectively eliminated the board's ban on competitive bidding for attest engagements.

> *By prohibiting CPAs from competitive bidding, the Department [Board of Accountancy] restricts economic expression constituting commercial speech. . . . The Department may regulate the profession of accountancy in an attempt to assure quality audits, but its regulations may not restrict economic expression protected by the First Amendment.*[11]

In April 1994, the U.S. Supreme Court resolved the third major case involving the Florida Board of Accountancy in the early 1990s. This case also centered on the issue of commercial speech. In 1992, the Florida board charged Silvia Ibanez, a Florida CPA, with false, deceptive, and misleading advertising. During the 1980s, Ibanez had worked as a public accountant for two major accounting firms. After obtaining a law

9. *Ibid.*

10. *Ibid.*

11. *Department of Professional Regulation, Board of Accountancy v. Richard Rampell*, 621 So.2d 426 (Fla. 1993).

degree and the Certified Financial Planner (CFP) professional designation, Ibanez established her own law firm. Although she was practicing law, Ibanez included the CPA and CFP designations in the yellow pages listing of her law firm and on her business cards. The young attorney believed those designations enhanced her credibility in the eyes of potential clients.

The Florida Board of Accountancy charged that Ibanez's use of her CPA designation misled the public by suggesting that she was practicing public accounting, which she was not. Additionally, the state board charged that Ibanez's use of the CFP designation violated an ethical rule prohibiting Florida CPAs from using a specialty designation not specifically approved by the board.

The Supreme Court ruled in favor of Ibanez on both allegations filed against her by the Florida Board of Accountancy, demonstrating once again that it generally opposes govern-

mental restraint of commercial speech. In support of its decision, the high court referred to its ruling the previous year in the Fane case. By finding in Ibanez's favor, the Supreme Court overturned the reprimand the Florida state board had imposed on her.

The reprimand . . . is incompatible with . . . the First Amendment, because the board has not demonstrated with sufficient specificity that any member of the public could have been misled by the attorney's constitutionally protected commercial speech . . . for (1) as long as the attorney holds an active CPA license from the board, consumers cannot be misled by her truthful representation to that effect; and (2) the board's justification for disciplining the attorney for using the CFP designation is not more persuasive, where the board has failed to point to any harm to the public from such designation that is potentially real, not purely hypothetical.[12]

Questions

1. Review the "rules" presently included in the *AICPA Code of Professional Conduct*. In your opinion, do any of these rules improperly limit accountants' commercial speech?

2. How may an ethical code create economic barriers of entry to a profession? Explain.

3. How may competitive bidding affect the independent audit function? Identify the potential impact on individual audit engagements and the long-range implications for the public accounting profession.

4. In a professional services context, "lowballing" refers to the practice of underpricing one's competition to obtain clients. Identify the advantages and disadvantages of lowballing within the public accounting profession. Also identify the parties who benefit from this practice and the parties that it harms.

5. Identify the advantages and disadvantages of professions being regulated at the state, rather than federal, level.

6. In the Scott Fane opinion, Justice O'Connor alluded to "incremental commercialization" within professions. Identify examples of incremental commercialization within the public accounting profession in recent years. How, if at all, has an increasing emphasis on the commercial aspects of public accounting affected the profession?

12. *Ibanez v. Florida Department of Business and Professional Regulation, Board of Accountancy*, 114 S.Ct. 2084 (1994).

CASE 7.4

Hopkins v. Price Waterhouse

In 1978, at the age of 34, Ann Hopkins faced a dilemma that a growing number of professional women are being forced to confront. Hopkins had to make a difficult choice involving her family and her career. Although comfortable with her position at Touche Ross & Company, for which she had worked several years, Hopkins realized that either she or her husband, also a Touche Ross employee, had to leave the firm because of its nepotism rules. Otherwise, neither would be considered for promotion to partner. Hopkins chose to make the personal sacrifice. She resigned from Touche Ross and within a few days accepted a position in the consulting division of Price Waterhouse.

Four years later, Hopkins was nominated for promotion to partner with Price Waterhouse. Eighty-eight individuals were nominated for promotion to partner with Price Waterhouse that year. Hopkins, a senior manager in the firm's Washington, D.C., office, was the only woman in that group. Hopkins stood out from the other nominees in another respect. She had generated the most business for Price Waterhouse of all the partner candidates. Over the previous four years, clients obtained by Hopkins had produced $40 million of revenues for Price Waterhouse. Because client development skills generally rank as the most important criterion in partnership promotion decisions, Hopkins appeared to be a shoo-in for promotion.

Strengthening Hopkins' case even more was the unanimous and strong backing her nomination received from the seven partners in the Washington, D.C., office. The extent of home office support for a candidate's nomination was another key factor Price Waterhouse considered in evaluating individuals for promotion to partner.

Much to her surprise, Hopkins was not awarded a partnership position. Instead, the senior manager was told that she would be considered for promotion the following year. A few months later, Hopkins was surprised again when her office managing partner informed her that she was no longer considered a viable candidate for promotion to partner. The firm's top executives did invite her to remain with Price Waterhouse in a nonpartner capacity. Disenchanted and somewhat bitter, Hopkins resigned from Price Waterhouse in January 1984 and accepted a position with the World Bank in Washington, D.C. Eventually, nagging uncertainty regarding her failure to make partner caused Hopkins to file a civil lawsuit against Price Waterhouse.

Prior Criticism of Personnel Practices of Big Eight Firms

The lawsuit Ann Hopkins filed against Price Waterhouse drew attention to an issue simmering within the public accounting profession for years. During a 1976 investigation of the profession by a U.S. Senate subcommittee, several parties charged that Big Eight firms' personnel practices discriminated against females and minorities.[1] At one point during its hearings, the Senate subcommittee requested each of the Big Eight firms to disclose the average compensation of their partners and the number of females and nonwhite males in their partner ranks.

---

1. U.S. Congress, Senate Subcommittee on Reports, Accounting, and Management of the Committee on Government Operations, *The Accounting Establishment* (Washington, DC: U.S. Government Printing Office, 1977).

The Senate subcommittee's request evoked uncooperative responses from several of the Big Eight firms. Exhibit 1 presents two of these responses. Exhibit 2 contains a letter that Senator Lee Metcalf, chairman of the investigative subcommittee, wrote to Ernst & Ernst after that firm questioned the Senate's authority to investigate the personnel practices of private partnerships. Eventually, six of the Big Eight firms provided the requested information regarding the number of females and minority males among their partners. Collectively, these firms had seven female partners and four partners who were African-American males out of a total of more than 3,500 partners.

EXHIBIT 1

SELECTED
RESPONSES TO THE
U.S. SENATE
REQUEST FOR
INFORMATION
REGARDING BIG
EIGHT FIRMS'
PERSONNEL
PRACTICES

June 11, 1976

The Honorable Lee Metcalf, Chairman
Subcommittee on Reports, Accounting, and Management
Committee on Government Operations
United States Senate
Washington, D.C. 20510

Dear Senator Metcalf:

I acknowledge receipt of your letter of June 7, 1976. As you know, this firm has responded and in considerable detail to the Committee's earlier requests. However, we consider the information sought in this letter to exceed the scope of the Committee's investigative authority. Moreover, the information sought includes data proprietary to this firm and its individual members. As a result, we respectfully decline to provide the requested data.

Very truly yours,

Russell E. Palmer
Managing Partner and
Chief Executive Officer
Touche Ross & Company

June 30, 1976

The Honorable Lee Metcalf, Chairman
Subcommittee on Reports, Accounting, and Management
United States Senate
Washington, D.C. 20510

Dear Senator Metcalf:

This will acknowledge your letter of June 7 which was received during the period I was away from my office.

We find it difficult to understand why the compensation of our partners is a matter of valid interest to a subcommittee of the Committee on Government Operations. We are even more perplexed with the suggestion that this could be a matter of importance in an assessment of our professional performance.

Along with these reservations we also confess to a deep-rooted belief that members of a private partnership have a right to maintain privacy over such matters if they wish to do so. Therefore, absent an understanding of its justification, we respectfully decline to furnish the compensation information you have requested.

Two partners (.5% of the total number of our partners) are female. None of our partners are blacks.

Yours very truly,

William S. Kanaga
Arthur Young & Company

EXHIBIT 2

U.S. SENATE
RESPONSE TO ERNST
& ERNST'S
RELUCTANCE TO
PROVIDE REQUESTED
PERSONNEL
INFORMATION

June 28, 1976

Mr. R. T. Baker
Managing Partner
Ernst & Ernst
Union Commerce Building
Cleveland, Ohio 64115

Dear Mr. Baker:

In your letter of June 24, you question the authority of this subcommittee to request information from your firm on various subjects. You note that our authority is primarily directed to the accounting practices of Federal departments and agencies.

Our requests for information from your firm are based on the unusual and substantial relationship which has developed between certain Federal agencies and influential segments of the accounting profession. This relationship has led to official recognition by Federal agencies of judgments on binding standards which have been made entirely within the private sector. The Securities and Exchange Commission has even formalized its acceptance of private decision-making through Accounting Series Release 150. The Moss amendment to the Energy Policy and Conservation Act also contemplates Federal recognition of private decisions on the manner of uniform accounting to be developed for the oil and gas industry.

The substantial reliance by Federal agencies upon decisions made in the private sector represents a significant delegation of the statutory authority vested in those agencies. This arrangement involves important decisions affecting the policies of the Federal government and other segments of our society.

Decisions made by Federal agencies are subject to review by Congress and the public. Much progress has been made both in Congress and the Federal government in opening the processes of decision-making to public scrutiny. The public has a right to know the identity and interests of those who act under the public's authority to determine the directions which this nation shall take.

When public decision-making authority is delegated to the private sector, the public has an even greater interest in knowing who is directing important national policies. As you are well aware, little information is available to Congress or the public concerning the activities of accounting firms. That is why it is necessary for this subcommittee to request information on various activities of accounting firms.

Your firm is substantially involved in the private decision-making process which develops accounting standards that are recognized by Federal agencies. The information which has so far been requested by this subcommittee is only a small fraction of the information that is publicly available regarding the identity and interests of Federal officials, or even major corporate officials. Yet, the decision-making area in which your firm is involved influences public policy as much or more than do many companies for which the requested information is publicly available.

This subcommittee has a responsibility to ensure that Federal accounting practices are responsive to the public interest. We must be informed on matters which are relevant to Federal accounting practices. That is why your firm has been requested to provide information to this subcommittee.

Very truly yours,

Lee Metcalf, Chairman
Subcommittee on Reports,
   Accounting, and Management

The criticism leveled at the personnel practices of Big Eight firms by the 1976 Senate investigation spurred academic researchers and investigative reporters to begin monitoring the progress of women and minorities within Big Eight firms. By the late 1980s, when the Hopkins suit against Price Waterhouse was working its way through the courts, neither group had made significant inroads into the top hierarchy of the Big Eight firms. For instance, in 1988, women held approximately 3.5 percent of the partnership positions with Big Eight firms, although these firms had been hiring women in considerable numbers since the mid-1970s.[2]

Continued concern regarding the progress of women and minorities within Big Eight firms focused the accounting profession's attention on Ann Hopkins' civil suit against Price Waterhouse. Although the Hopkins case provides only anecdotal evidence regarding the personnel practices of large international accounting firms, it is noteworthy for several reasons. First, the case yielded revealing insights into the partnership selection process employed by large accounting firms. Second, the case pointed to the need to rid performance appraisal methods of gender-based criteria in all disciplines, including professional fields. Finally, *Hopkins v. Price Waterhouse* stimulated discussion of measures that professional firms could take to facilitate the career success of their female employees.

Price Waterhouse's Consideration of Ann Hopkins for Promotion to Partner

During the 1980s, the partners of Price Waterhouse annually identified and then nominated for promotion to partner those senior managers whom they considered to be partner "material." Price Waterhouse's admissions committee collected these nominations and then provided a list of the nominees to each partner in the firm. The admissions committee invited partners to provide either a "long form" or "short form" evaluation of the individual candidates.

Typically, a partner well acquainted with a nominee provided a long form evaluation. Partners having had little or no contact with a given nominee submitted a short form evaluation or no evaluation at all. Both forms required the partners to assess the partnership potential of the nominees on several scaled dimensions, including client development abilities, interpersonal skills, and technical expertise. After responding to the scaled items, the partners indicated whether the given individual should be promoted, whether he or she should be denied promotion, or whether the promotion decision should be deferred for one or more years. The partners also provided a brief written explanation documenting the key reasons for their overall recommendation for each candidate.

After studying and summarizing the evaluations, the admissions committee prepared three lists of candidates: those recommended for admission to partnership, those not recommended for promotion, and those who had received a "hold" recommendation. These latter candidates typically included individuals having partner potential but also one or more weaknesses that needed to be addressed before they were considered again for promotion. The admissions committee submitted its recommendations to the firm's policy board, which reviewed them and selected the final slate of candidates to be voted on by the entire partnership.[3]

---

2. E. Berg, "The Big Eight," *The New York Times*, 17 December 1977, D1; "Women Comprise Half of 1986–87 Graduates," *Public Accounting Report*, 1 February 1988, 7.

3. This description of Price Waterhouse's partnership selection process was summarized from information presented in the 1985 court opinion *Hopkins v. Price Waterhouse*, 618 F. Supp. 1109 (D.C.D.C. 1985).

The admissions committee received 32 evaluation forms commenting on Ann Hopkins' nomination for partner. Thirteen partners submitted positive recommendations, eight recommended she not be promoted, three suggested she be held over for consideration the following year, and eight did not include a recommendation in their evaluation forms.

The most common criticism of Hopkins by partners who recommended she not be promoted was that she had poor interpersonal skills and an abrasive personality. These individuals criticized her for being too demanding of her subordinates, for using profanity, and for being generally harsh and overly aggressive. Two partners used gender-specific terms when commenting on Hopkins. One partner referred to her as "macho," while another observed that "she may have overcompensated for being a woman."[4]

After reviewing Hopkins' evaluations, the admissions committee recommended that she be held over for consideration, a recommendation accepted by the policy board. The admissions committee apparently decided that her interpersonal skills needed to be strengthened to allow her to function effectively as a partner.

To improve her chances of promotion the following year, Hopkins agreed to undergo a "Quality Control Review" to identify specific aspects of her job-related skills needing improvement. Several partners indicated they would give her opportunities to demonstrate that she was remedying the deficiencies in her interpersonal skills. These partners never followed through on their commitments. Four months after Hopkins completed the Quality Control Review, her office managing partner informed her that she would not be nominated for partner that year. Hopkins was also told that she probably would never be considered again for promotion to partner.

Ann Hopkins' Civil Suit against Price Waterhouse

Ann Hopkins learned of the "hold" recommendation given to her nomination for partner in mid-1983. At that time, her office managing partner discussed with her some of the reservations partners expressed regarding her nomination. In particular, he told Hopkins that several partners believed her appearance and interpersonal manner were overtly masculine and that these traits caused her to be less appealing as a partner candidate.

The office managing partner suggested that she could improve her chances for promotion if she would "walk more femininely, wear make-up, have her hair styled, and wear jewelry." Following her resignation from Price Waterhouse, Hopkins recalled these suggestions and began to question why she had been denied promotion to partner. She began to suspect that Price Waterhouse had denied her promotion not because she was perceived as unqualified to be a partner with the firm but, rather, because she was perceived as unqualified to be a *female* partner with the firm.

Eventually, Hopkins concluded that Price Waterhouse, in fact, did apply different standards for promoting females and males to partner. This issue became the focal point of the civil trial in the *Hopkins v. Price Waterhouse* case. Hopkins included the following four specific allegations in the lawsuit she filed against Price Waterhouse:

1. The criticisms of her interpersonal skills were fabricated by the Price Waterhouse partners.
2. Even if the criticisms of her interpersonal skills were valid, Price Waterhouse had promoted male candidates to partner having similar deficiencies in their interpersonal skills.

---

4. This and all subsequent quotations, unless indicated otherwise, were taken from *Hopkins v. Price Waterhouse*, 618 F. Supp. 1109 (D.C.D.C. 1985).

3. The criticisms of her interpersonal skills resulted from sexual stereotyping by Price Waterhouse partners.
4. Price Waterhouse's partnership selection process did not discount the sexually discriminatory comments made regarding her candidacy.

The judge who presided over the civil trial dismissed Hopkins' first allegation. According to the judge, the defense counsel clearly proved that Hopkins did have poor interpersonal skills, particularly when dealing with subordinates. The judge ruled that Price Waterhouse was well within its rights to deny an individual a partnership position who did not possess adequate interpersonal skills. However, the judge then pointed to court testimony documenting that Price Waterhouse had previously promoted male partner candidates described as "crude, abrasive, and overbearing." These comments were very similar to criticisms of Hopkins' interpersonal skills made during the partner selection process.

A review of the firm's past promotion decisions also revealed that two earlier female partner candidates may have been denied admission to the partnership for reasons identical to those that cost Hopkins her promotion. Evaluation comments made for those candidates criticized them for acting like "Ma Barker" or for trying to be "one of the boys."

An earlier legal case established the precedent that an employer who evaluates a woman with an aggressive or abrasive personality differently than a man with similar personality traits is guilty of sex discrimination. After reviewing all of the evidence presented during the trial, the judge ruled that Price Waterhouse had evaluated Hopkins as a candidate for becoming a female partner rather than simply a partner with the firm.

> [Female] candidates were viewed favorably if partners believed they maintained their femininity while becoming effective professional managers. To be identified as a "women's libber" was regarded as a negative comment. Nothing was done to discourage sexually biased evaluations. One partner repeatedly commented that he could not consider any woman seriously as a partnership candidate and believed that women were not capable of functioning as senior managers—yet the firm took no action to discourage his comments and recorded his vote in the overall summary of the evaluations.

Although Hopkins was found to have been the victim of sex discrimination, the judge deemed that the discrimination was not overt or intentional. In fact, Hopkins freely admitted during the trial that she never perceived she was being discriminated against because of her gender while employed with Price Waterhouse. Instead, sexually discriminatory attitudes latent within the culture of Price Waterhouse victimized Hopkins' candidacy for partner. That is, the partners who made the sexually biased remarks regarding Hopkins were unaware that they were evaluating her unfairly relative to male candidates for partner. Nevertheless, the judge ruled that Price Waterhouse perpetuated an evaluation system that allowed sexual stereotypes to undermine the promotion opportunities of female employees.

> There is no direct evidence of any determined purpose to maliciously discriminate against women but plaintiff appears to have been a victim of "omissive and subtle" discriminations created by a system that made evaluations based on "outmoded" attitudes.... Price Waterhouse should have been aware that women being evaluated by male partners might well be victims of discriminatory stereotypes. Yet the firm made no efforts ... to discourage comments tainted by sexism or to determine whether they were influenced by stereotypes.

EPILOGUE

In May 1990, six years after Ann Hopkins filed suit against Price Waterhouse, a federal judge ordered the firm to pay her $400,000 of compensatory damages. More important, the judge ordered the CPA firm to offer Hopkins a partnership position. During a party to celebrate the court's decision, Hopkins maintained that she had no reservations joining a firm that had unfairly rejected her for partnership seven years earlier. She also joked with her male coworkers at the World Bank regarding several less-than-complimentary remarks made regarding her during the trial. In particular, she questioned the assertion of one Price Waterhouse partner that she needed to enroll in charm school. Moments later, Hopkins took a long and noisy slug of champagne—straight from the bottle.

In 1996, five years after rejoining Price Waterhouse, Ann Hopkins documented her difficult road to becoming a partner in a book published by the University of Massachusetts Press that was entitled *So Ordered: Making Partner the Hard Way.* Despite the ordeal that she experienced, Hopkins insists that she has no "hard feelings" toward her fellow partners. In fact, Hopkins' daughter joined PricewaterhouseCoopers (PwC), the successor firm to Price Waterhouse, when she graduated from college in 1998.

Growing numbers of women have obtained partnership positions with the large international accounting firms since the resolution of the *Hopkins* case. But women still remain significantly underrepresented in the partnership ranks of those firms.[5] That fact was a key issue raised by Melissa Page, a former PwC tax manager, when she filed a lawsuit against PwC in July 2004 that was reminiscent of Ann Hopkins' lawsuit two decades earlier. In her complaint, Page alleged that the firm was guilty of "systematically discriminating" against women and suggested that an "old boy network" still pervaded PwC's culture.

[Page] claims her career was derailed by a corporate culture that kept women away from the very opportunities that led to partnership—including informal networking events, golf outings, and other activities that would have given her more access to clients and company executives.[6]

Page's lawsuit prompted other women in the profession to speak out. One of those individuals was Barbara Hufsmith, who reported that she had chosen to establish her own accounting firm after being a victim of gender discrimination in a male-dominated accounting firm.

I too have been discriminated against in an old boys CPA firm. It has forced me to start my own firm, for which I am grateful, but it should not have been such a painful and expensive experience. I truly believe that only a couple of partners from my old firm knew what they were doing to me was not fair. The rest of the partners were blind, stupid, and arrogant. Hopefully, a case like Ms. Page will help change the industry to be more female-partner friendly.[7]

Questions

1. Do public accounting firms have a responsibility to facilitate the career success of female employees? Why or why not? Identify policies accounting firms could implement to increase the retention rate of female employees.

2. In business circles, one frequently hears references to the "old boy network." Many women in professional firms complain that their gender precludes them

5. In late 2006, the results of a survey by the *Public Accounting Report* indicated that approximately 16 percent of Big Four partners were women.

6. *AccountingWEB.com*, "PricewaterhouseCoopers Faces Discrimination Suit," 29 July 2004.

7. *Ibid.*

from becoming a member of the old boy network within their firm. Define, in your own terms, what is meant by the phrase *old boy network*. Should professional firms attempt to break down these networks?

3. Suppose that an audit client objects to a given auditor because of his or her gender or race. Identify the alternative courses of action the auditor's employer should consider taking in such a case. Which of these alternatives do you believe the accounting firm should take? Defend your answer.

4. The nepotism rules of many professional firms pose a major inconvenience for married couples who work for, or would like to work for, those firms. Discuss the costs and benefits of these rules in a public accounting setting. In practice, do you believe these rules are equally fair (or unfair) to both sexes?

5. Several of the large public accounting firms asked to provide information to the U.S. Senate during the 1976 investigation of the accounting profession claimed that the request was an invasion of their privacy. Do you agree or disagree with these firms' view? Why? Even if such disclosures are considered an invasion of privacy, are they justified from a public interest perspective?

Sarah Russell, Staff Accountant

Sarah Russell grew up in a small town in the flatlands of western Kansas, where she was born.[1] In high school, she was homecoming queen, valedictorian of her graduating class, point guard on her basketball team for two years, and a candy striper (volunteer) at the local hospital. Since her parents had attended the University of Kansas, Sarah was off to Lawrence at age 18.

After spending her freshman year posting straight A's in 30 hours of college courses, Sarah settled on accounting as her major after seriously considering journalism, pre-law, and finance. Although Sarah had yet to take any courses in accounting, she had been impressed by a presentation that a female partner of a large accounting firm had made at a career fair. Sarah was excited by the challenges and opportunities presented by public accounting, as described by the partner. Here was a field in which she could learn a great deal in a short period of time and advance rapidly to a position where she had important responsibilities. Plus, public accounting provided a wide range of career paths. If she really enjoyed public accounting, she could pursue a partnership position with a large accounting firm. Then again, she might "hang out her shingle" in her hometown, see the world on the internal audit staff of a large corporation, or return to college after a couple of years of real-world experience to earn an MBA.

Sarah completed the tough accounting courses at the University of Kansas with only two small blemishes on her transcript—B's in individual and corporate taxation. During the fall semester of her senior year, Sarah accepted a position as a staff accountant with a Big Eight accounting firm. Sarah considered staying in her home state but decided instead to request an assignment in her new employer's Chicago office. She believed that exposure to big-city life would allow her to arrive at a more informed decision when it was time to make a long-term commitment to a career path and a lifestyle.

During her first year on the job, Sarah served on six audit engagements. Her clients included a pipeline company, a religious foundation, and a professional sports team. She worked hard on those assignments and earned impressive performance appraisals from each of her immediate supervisors. Somehow Sarah also squeezed a CPA review course into her hectic schedule that first year. And she was glad she did. She was among the few rookies in her large office to pass the CPA exam in one attempt. With that barrier out of the way, Sarah focused her energy on being promoted to audit senior as quickly as possible.

Several individuals provided Sarah with much-needed moral support during her first year, including R. J. Bell, an audit partner. Bell was 40 years old and had been a partner for eight years. According to the office grapevine, he was in line to become the new office managing partner within the next year or so. Bell tried to get to know the new staff accountants assigned to the audit staff and to help them adjust to their jobs in any way he could. Several times during the year, Bell invited small groups of

---

1. This case was authored by Carol Knapp, an assistant professor at the University of Oklahoma. This case is based upon experiences related by a young woman previously employed by a large accounting firm. The names of the individuals involved in this case and other background facts, such as locations, have been changed.

staff accountants to his home to have dinner with him and his family. Recognizing that Sarah was new to Chicago, he made a special effort to include her in such social gatherings and to give her complimentary tickets to cultural and sporting events. When Sarah's old car from college died, Bell arranged for her to obtain a loan from a local bank. Sarah appreciated Bell's help and guidance. She considered the firm to be very lucky to have an audit partner so supportive of staff accountants.

Shortly after her first anniversary with the firm, Sarah received a telephone call from Bell at home one Saturday afternoon. At first, Sarah thought there must be a client emergency that required her assistance, but Bell did not bring up any client business during the conversation. Instead, he told Sarah that he had just called to chat. Sarah felt mildly uncomfortable with the situation but spoke with Bell for a few minutes before making up an excuse to get off the phone.

The following day, Sarah, an avid jogger, had just completed a four-mile run on her regular jogging trail in a city park when Bell pulled up as she was walking toward her car. "Hi, Sarah. How was your run?" Bell asked nonchalantly. "I was just driving by and thought you might like to get a Coke after your workout."

As Sarah approached Bell's car she felt awkward but tried to act natural, as if his unexpected appearance was only a coincidence. "Thanks, R. J. But I really need to get back to my apartment. I've got several errands to run and phone calls to make."

"You sure? I'm buying."

"Yeah, I'd better get home."

"Well, okay."

Over the next several weeks, Bell made a concerted effort to develop a personal relationship with Sarah. Eventually, Bell, who was known for working long hours, was calling her nearly every evening from his office just "to chat." Once or twice per week, he invited her to get a drink with him after work. On a couple of occasions, she accepted, hoping that by doing so he would stop asking her. No such luck. Finally, she began avoiding him in the office and stopped answering her home phone when she thought it was him calling. Twice, Bell dropped by her apartment in the evening. Panic-stricken both times, Sarah refused to answer the door, hoping he would quickly decide that she was not home.

Bell's persistence caused Sarah to feel increasing levels of stress and powerlessness. She did not know what to do or to whom she could turn. She was reluctant to discuss the matter with her friends in the office since she did not want to start a rumor mill. Embarrassment prevented her from discussing the matter with her parents or other family members. Worst of all, Sarah began wondering whether she had somehow encouraged Bell's behavior. She racked her brain to recall each time that she had spoken or met with him during her first year on the job. She could not remember saying anything that could have been misconstrued by him. But maybe she had inadvertently said something that had given him the wrong impression. Maybe he had mistaken the sense of respect and admiration she had for him as affection. Maybe she had asked him an inappropriate question. Maybe . . .

E P I L O G U E

After more than six weeks of enduring Bell's advances, Sarah summoned the courage to make an appointment with him one Friday afternoon in his office. When Sarah informed Bell that she wanted to keep their relationship on a strictly professional level, he failed to respond for several tense moments. Finally, he remarked that Sarah must have misinterpreted his actions over the past several weeks. He was simply trying to make her feel more comfortable with her job. "I go out of my way to be as friendly and sociable with as many members of the audit staff as I can." Bell then told Sarah that, given the circumstances, he would see to it that she was not assigned to any of his engagements in the future. After another few moments of tense silence, he tersely asked, "Is there anything else I can do for you, Miss Russell?" Sarah

shook her head softly and then got up and left his office.

Sarah had no further contact or conversations with Bell following that Friday afternoon meeting. A few months later, she decided to return to Kansas to be closer to her family. At last report, Sarah was the chief financial officer (CFO) of a charitable organization.

Questions

1. In your opinion, how should Sarah have handled this matter? Identify the factors that Sarah should have considered in dealing with the situation. Also, identify the professional and personal responsibilities of Sarah, R. J. Bell, and other relevant individuals in this matter.

2. What were the costs and potential costs to Sarah's employer in this case? How should accounting firms attempt to prevent these types of situations from occurring? Assume that rather than speaking to Bell, Sarah had told the office managing partner about the problem she faced. How should the office managing partner have dealt with the matter?

3. This case took place in the early 1980s. Do you believe that circumstances similar to those that took place in this case could occur now? Explain.

Bud Carriker, Audit Senior

Since childhood, Louis Armstrong Carriker had been known simply as "Bud," a nickname given to him by his paternal grandmother.[1] Bud's father, a New Orleans native, was a lifelong fan of the famous blues musician after whom he named his only son. After graduating from high school, Elliot Carriker joined the military. In April 1951, Elliot, an African-American, married Bud's mother, a Mexican-American, while he was stationed at a military base in Texas. Two years later, Bud arrived. Sadly, Bud's mother died during childbirth. As a result, Bud spent most of his childhood in New Orleans being raised by his grandmother.

When he was a young teenager, Bud was reunited with his father in Dallas, Texas. Bud's new family included a stepmother and one-year old twin sisters. In high school, Bud excelled in both academics and athletics and earned a scholarship to play basketball at a small Division 1 school. Bud realized that his athletic career would end after college, so he dedicated himself to obtaining a degree that would provide him with an opportunity to earn a good livelihood following graduation. After leaving the military, Elliot Carriker had relied on the GI Bill to earn a college degree in finance. Because of his experience in the business world as a senior loan officer for a major metropolitan bank, Elliot encouraged his son to consider majoring in either accounting or finance. After several sessions with his high school career counselor, Bud decided to take his father's advice and pursue an accounting degree in college.

During his senior year in college, Bud interviewed with several of the international accounting firms and with two large Houston-based oil companies. After discussing his multiple job offers with his father, Bud decided to begin his career in the public accounting profession. Bud realized that a few years experience on the audit staff of a major accounting firm would provide him with a strong background in financial accounting. He intended to use that background to obtain a mid-level position on the accounting staff of a bank with an eventual career goal of becoming either a corporate controller or chief financial officer (CFO) in the financial services industry.

Bud launched his career in public accounting in June 1975 and was promoted to audit senior in the late fall of 1977, just prior to the beginning of his third busy season. Typically, Bud's firm considered audit seniors for promotion to audit manager during their fifth or sixth years with the firm. Throughout the early years of his career, the ever-thoughtful and deliberate Bud frequently reviewed and revised his career plan. By the time that his fifth busy season arrived in late 1979, Bud had decided that he would begin searching for a job in the private sector when he was promoted to audit manager, which he expected would be sometime during the following 18 months. Although he enjoyed public accounting, Bud was anxious to get his "real" career started.

In mid-November 1979, Alex Saunders, the managing partner of the practice office that Bud had been assigned to throughout his career, asked Bud to meet with him one afternoon. Saunders informed Bud that the firm had unexpectedly acquired a new client. The new client was a privately owned bank in a midsized city in central Texas.

---

1. This case is based upon factual circumstances. Although the key events occurred in the approximate time frame identified in the case, the names of all parties and locations have been changed.

Since accepting a position with his employer, Bud had made it known that he wanted to be assigned to a client in the banking or financial services industries. The acquisition of the new client provided Saunders an opportunity to finally grant Bud's request.

"Bud, when we picked up this client, I immediately thought of you since you have expressed an interest in gaining some experience in the banking industry. Plus, this is one of those clients where we really need an experienced audit senior to run the engagement."

"Thank you, sir. I am looking forward to this opportunity." Bud's practice office was quite large. As a result, he did not have a close relationship with Alex Saunders. Nevertheless, Bud had considerable respect for Saunders. Saunders, a native of Lubbock, was an imposing man physically, towering well over six feet. He spoke with a distinctive West Texas twang and often wore a bolo tie and cowboy boots to work. Saunders had spent his entire 35-year career in the practice office that he now managed and was well known and respected within the business community. Bud particularly appreciated Saunders' blunt, no-nonsense management style. He had a reputation for candor with his subordinates and with clients. You always knew where you stood with "Big Alex," as he was often referred to by his subordinates.

"Eric Jones will be the audit engagement partner. But I am going to shadow Eric on this job. Just like you, Eric doesn't have any past experience with a bank client. Since I have had a slew of bank clients, he can use me as a sounding board if problems develop. K. T. Wilson will be the audit manager. He's worked on a couple of savings and loan audits."

"Okay. Of course, I have worked with Eric and K. T. on a couple of audits in the past."

"Let me give you a little background on this client," Saunders said as he leaned back in his chair and folded his arms across his chest. This guy, Jim Charles, who owns the bank, is one of those 'self-made' millionaires who is more than happy to tell you his success story. He prides himself on being a 'good ol' boy' from West Texas." Alex paused. "Kind of like me, I guess," he added with a smile. "Ya know, he doesn't have a college degree."

"That's interesting."

"Well, that's what he claims, at least. He got lucky about 15 years ago and brought in a couple of wildcat wells in the Permian Basin. He used that money to buy a small bank in his hometown. In the past few years, the bank has grown by leaps and bounds because of the deregulation of the banking industry. I have reviewed his loan portfolio and it seems to me that he specializes in funding commercial real estate projects and high-risk oil and gas ventures." Bud listened intently as Saunders continued. "That's why I want an experienced audit senior running this engagement. I want you to spend a lot of time in the field. Ya know, in the past, bank clients were always considered extremely low risk. But that has totally changed in the past few years with the new legislation."

"Well sir, I will do my best."

"I know you will, Bud. What I would like you to do is meet with Eric this afternoon. As luck would have it, the firm has a three-day seminar on bank auditing next week in Houston. I want you and Eric to attend that seminar. K. T.'s schedule won't allow him to make it."

"Okay. Sir, what about the Garrett audit? Will I continue to work on that job?" For the past three years, Bud had spent the majority of the winter months assigned to the audit engagement team for Garrett Manufacturing, a local prefabricated housing company.

"No. You're gonna be too busy with this new client. I have already made arrangements to have Zach Payne take your spot on that job."

When Bud left Saunders' office, he felt a surge of excitement. This was just the type of assignment he had been hoping to land. Given the nature of the engagement and his required hands-on role, he would learn a great deal about the banking industry in a short time. Bud realized that this experience would position him well to obtain the type of job he wanted in the banking industry when he left public accounting.

In the two weeks following his meeting with Alex Saunders, Bud attended the banking seminar with Eric Jones and spent several days reviewing copies of the new client's prior-year workpapers that had been obtained from the previous auditor. On a Monday morning in early December, Bud made his first trip to the client's headquarters location. He and K. T. Wilson planned to introduce themselves to key client personnel and to do some preliminary internal control work.

The meetings with client personnel went well, at least until they met with Jim Charles, who was not only the principal owner of the bank but also its chief executive officer (CEO). During that meeting, Charles seemed annoyed for some reason. In fact, the meeting lasted no more than a few minutes. Charles told the two auditors that he had several important phone calls to make and rushed them out of his office. Although Charles had been less than cordial, Bud quickly dismissed the episode. He realized that as the audit senior he would have little interaction with Charles.

Bud and K. T. Wilson completed their initial work at the client's location and returned to their firm's office late on Tuesday afternoon. Over the next three days, Bud planned to draft a preliminary copy of the audit program and have it ready for a meeting that the two had scheduled with Eric Jones and Alex Saunders the following Monday afternoon. Just as he was completing a draft of the audit program on Friday afternoon, Alex Saunders unexpectedly dropped by the cubicle in which Bud was working. Alex asked Bud to come to his office.

"Do you want me to bring the draft of the audit program? It's almost done."

"No. That won't be necessary," Saunders replied.

As they walked silently down the hall together, Bud suspected that something was wrong. Although he didn't know Saunders well, Bud sensed that the partner was upset. Bud's suspicions were heightened when Saunders turned and closed the door behind them after they entered his office.

"Please sit down, Bud," Saunders said quietly. "Bud, I have decided to place you back on the Garrett audit. I have already spoken with Zach Payne. Zach will be taking your place on the bank engagement."

Bud was stunned, too stunned to speak. The unexpected news was both startling and extremely disappointing. Here was the assignment that he had literally coveted and now it was being taken away from him. For several awkward moments, Bud sat facing Saunders, who refused to look at him. Not making eye contact with whomever he was speaking to was very uncharacteristic of Saunders.

When Bud realized that Saunders did not intend to provide an explanation for removing him from the bank engagement, he took the initiative. "Sir, I don't understand. I was really looking forward to this assignment. I'm not sure why you believe Zach Payne is more qualified than me to run this job."

Saunders cleared his throat as he turned to the right and gazed out the large plate window that overlooked a busy street several blocks below. Finally, Saunders turned back and faced Bud. "This is not about Zach Payne, Bud. I've just decided that you are not the right person for this engagement. I'm sorry, but that's my decision." Saunders paused momentarily and then added, "Thanks for your time, Bud," signaling that the brief meeting had ended.

Still in shock, Bud rose slowly from the chair in which he had been sitting and turned toward the door. After taking a few steps, Bud turned back toward Saunders. "Mr. Saunders, I consider myself a professional. I work hard, I enjoy my work, and I believe I do a good job. I typically don't challenge the decisions of those above me. But, I believe I deserve an explanation for why you are taking me off this job." After speaking, Bud stood his ground, staring directly at Saunders, who was shuffling papers on his desk.

After several more moments of awkward silence, Saunders rose to his feet and made direct eye contact with Bud as he spoke. "You're right, young man. You deserve an explanation. I'm sorry that I wasn't more to the point. Avoiding issues is not my style." Saunders paused and cleared his throat again before speaking. "Jim Charles called me Wednesday afternoon and told me that he wanted a different senior assigned to the audit. He said that he wouldn't be comfortable working with you." After one final pause, Saunders continued. "That's why we are taking you off the job."

"Comfortable? What does that mean?" Bud blurted out.

Saunders shoved his hands into the pockets of his trousers and shrugged his shoulders in exasperation. "You know what I mean. Charles . . . Charles wants another . . . another type of person assigned to the audit."

Now, Bud understood. He had a crystal clear understanding of why he was being removed from the bank audit. As he stood there staring at Saunders, Bud felt several emotions, principally anger. He wanted to respond to Saunders, but he wasn't sure exactly what to say. Bud had always been aware that he was different from his colleagues. He was one of a handful of non-Caucasians in his office. In fact, it had been that way throughout his career. But, he had never considered his race to be an issue of any kind. At least, not until this moment.

Finally, after an extended period of silence, Saunders turned away from Bud and walked over to his window and stared down at the Friday afternoon traffic. Bud shook his head in disgust, let out a deep breath, and then left Saunders' office. It was the last time that Bud would speak to, or meet with, Alex Saunders.

EPILOGUE

Bud Carriker spent his final busy season with his employer supervising the fieldwork on the Garrett Manufacturing engagement. Shortly after that engagement was completed, he received a brief letter from Alex Saunders congratulating him on his promotion to audit manager that would take effect a few months later on July 1. However, Bud never officially became an audit manager with the firm. In June of that year, Bud resigned from the firm and accepted a position as an assistant controller with a large healthcare facility in Dallas.

The banking empire of Jim Charles collapsed suddenly in the early 1980s. Charles' bank was one of hundreds that regulatory authorities closed down during that time period for operating in an "unsafe and unsound" manner. Charles' equity in the bank, along with that of the bank's other investors, was wiped out by huge losses in the bank's loan portfolio.

Questions

1. How do you believe Alex Saunders should have reacted when Jim Charles insisted that Bud be removed from the bank's audit engagement team? What would you have done under similar circumstances if you had been Saunders?

2. In your opinion, did Saunders' decision to comply with Charles' request violate any professional or ethical standards? Defend your answer.

3. How do you believe that Bud should have reacted when Saunders told him why he had been removed from the audit engagement team?

4. The key events in this case transpired during the late 1970s. Do you believe that such a series of events could occur now? Explain.

National Medical Transportation Network

San Diego-based National Medical Transportation Network (MedTrans) eventually became the largest ambulance services provider in the United States. Reaching that pinnacle was not an easy journey. In early 1992, MedTrans encountered cash flow problems that prompted the company's two owners to search for external financing. The co-owners located a company willing to invest $10 million in MedTrans. During negotiations with that company, MedTrans' auditor, Deloitte & Touche, uncovered problems in its client's accounting records. Those problems prevented Deloitte from issuing an unqualified opinion on MedTrans' 1992 financial statements. After several unpleasant confrontations with MedTrans' chief executive officer (CEO), Deloitte resigned as the company's audit firm.

Following Deloitte's resignation, the $10 million investment deal collapsed. Within a few months, MedTrans' two owners sold their firm to a large corporation. Unhappy with Deloitte's lack of "cooperation," MedTrans' former owners sued Deloitte to recover the sizable loss they incurred on the sale of their company. Among other charges, the former owners alleged that Deloitte acted negligently by "withdrawing prematurely" from the 1992 MedTrans audit engagement.

No doubt, Deloitte's legal counsel confidently tackled the MedTrans lawsuit. The allegation that Deloitte negligently withdrew from the 1992 MedTrans audit engagement seemed implausible since the client had adamantly refused to make several large and necessary adjustments to its 1992 financial statements. Threatening comments made to Deloitte auditors by one of MedTrans' co-owners provided even stronger justification for the audit firm's resignation. Imagine then the shock and disbelief of Deloitte's attorneys when the jury that heard the lawsuit agreed with MedTrans' former owners and awarded them a multimillion-dollar judgment against the prominent accounting firm.

MedTrans Seeks Help

MedTrans' two principal officers, Roberts and Morgan, served as the company's CEO and president, respectively, and each owned 50 percent of MedTrans' common stock. Deloitte audited the company each year from 1988 through 1991—MedTrans' fiscal year ended March 31. Each of those audits resulted in an unqualified opinion being issued on MedTrans' financial statements.

By the late spring of 1992, MedTrans needed cash, and quickly. The company owed $2 million of payroll taxes and faced a $12 million repayment to its primary lender, which had suddenly canceled its line of credit. Making matters worse, MedTrans' chief financial officer (CFO) unexpectedly resigned in early June 1992. That resignation triggered a crisis between MedTrans and the company's audit firm. Deloitte was nearing completion of its 1992 MedTrans audit and had asked the CFO to sign a letter of representations indicating that the company's financial statements were materially accurate. The CFO told Gordon Johns, the Deloitte audit engagement partner, that he could not sign the letter of representations since he did not believe MedTrans' financial statements were reliable. A few days later, the CFO met with Johns to discuss the situation.

> *At the meeting, Ensz [the CFO] alerted Johns to four or five matters relevant to the audit. Ensz said that upon informing Roberts [the CEO] that those matters were not properly entered in MedTrans' journals, Roberts told Ensz to leave the journals as they were and "let's see" if the auditors "find it." Questioning Roberts' character for honesty because of some things Roberts advocated in presenting financial information, Ensz also stated he lacked faith in the integrity of Roberts and MedTrans' financial statements.*[1]

The CFO's unsettling allegations caused Deloitte to approach the remainder of the 1992 MedTrans audit with extreme caution. By the end of June 1992, the Deloitte auditors concluded that their client's financial statements contained material errors. Those financial statements reported a net income of nearly $2 million for fiscal 1992, while Deloitte's audit suggested that MedTrans had suffered a loss of approximately $500,000. A large increase in MedTrans' allowance for bad debts proposed by Deloitte accounted for most of the difference between those two figures.

During June and July 1992, Roberts negotiated with William Blair & Company to obtain the additional capital needed by MedTrans. In exchange for a $10 million investment in MedTrans, Roberts and Morgan offered Blair a 50 percent ownership interest in the company. While mulling over this offer, Blair's executives reviewed MedTrans' unaudited financial statements for 1992. Based largely upon the $2 million profit reported in those financial statements, Blair forecasted that MedTrans' annual earnings would top $6 million by 1995. On July 27, Blair's executives tentatively agreed to invest in MedTrans. The agreement was contingent on MedTrans receiving an unqualified audit opinion on its 1992 financial statements.

Roberts' negotiations with Blair were periodically disrupted by an ongoing quarrel with Gordon Johns. Roberts and Johns feuded throughout the summer of 1992 over the large increase in the company's allowance for bad debts that Deloitte believed was necessary. During a July 9 meeting, Roberts warned Johns that MedTrans' audited financial statements would have a significant impact on whether the Blair transaction was consummated.

> *A very focused Roberts vocally and explicitly emphasized the importance of MedTrans' pretax earnings because of the potential that Blair might invest in the company. . . . Johns [then] presented Roberts with about $2.5 million in suggested adjustments involving the accounts receivable reserve account. Roberts told Johns: "You better not propose any adjustment that will _____ my deal or you'll be sorry."*

Shortly after the July 9 meeting, Johns contacted an executive Deloitte partner in the firm's New York headquarters. The executive partner told Johns that "we should not be associated with companies that threaten us." Unless Roberts accepted the proposed adjustments, the executive partner recommended that Johns resign from the engagement. Johns told the executive partner that before raising the issue again with Roberts, he wanted to give him some time to analyze MedTrans' bad-debt reserve and to reconsider the need for the proposed adjustments. On July 30, Roberts and Johns met again. During this meeting, Roberts reminded Johns of the impact Deloitte's audit would have on the proposed Blair deal. Roberts also gave Johns a memorandum prepared by MedTrans' personnel that presented a more favorable analysis of the company's bad-debt reserve than the analysis developed by Deloitte.

Roberts and Johns met a final time on August 13, 1992, to discuss Deloitte's audit and the pending Blair transaction. At this meeting, Johns presented a memorandum containing a new set of proposed adjustments to MedTrans' 1992 financial statements.

---

1. This and all subsequent quotations were taken from the following court opinion: *National Medical Transportation Network v. Deloitte & Touche*, 62 Cal. App. 4th 412 (1998).

Collectively, these adjustments would have reduced MedTrans' pre-audit net income even more than the adjustments originally proposed by Deloitte.

> *During Johns' presentation, Roberts rose, threw down the memorandum and said very angrily: "You are finished." Although Johns thought he had been fired, Roberts told Johns not to construe the situation that way. However, after MedTrans' successive rejections of proposed adjustments to its unaudited financial statements, Johns believed the parties' mutually exclusive views of those statements indicated there was no longer a basis for a relationship. Thus, Johns told Roberts that if defendants [Deloitte] had not been fired, he was resigning. Roberts told Johns that "you're going to finish this regardless, under court order or otherwise." Johns believed such threat destroyed any ability to continue as an independent auditor. Johns also believed resignation was necessary because MedTrans bullied Deloitte's personnel and defendants were put at risk by MedTrans' lack of commitment to financial statements accurately depicting the difficulties the company experienced in fiscal 1992.*

Deloitte formally resigned from the MedTrans engagement shortly after the August 13 meeting between Johns and Roberts. Four days later, Roberts sent a letter to Deloitte reminding the firm that its resignation would have serious repercussions for the pending Blair deal. Roberts also insisted once more that Deloitte complete the 1992 audit. Deloitte refused to be swayed and remained MedTrans' "former" auditor.

Desperately Seeking a Replacement Auditor

William Blair & Company learned of Deloitte's resignation in mid-August 1992. On August 25, a Blair representative told Roberts that his firm was indefinitely postponing the planned investment in MedTrans and would not reconsider that decision until MedTrans obtained an independent audit opinion on its 1992 financial statements. The Blair official suggested that MedTrans retain Blair & Company's audit firm, Ernst & Young. Roberts immediately contacted Ernst & Young. Within a few days, Roberts sent Deloitte a letter authorizing the firm to "discuss freely with E&Y the audit history of MedTrans with Deloitte, the details of Deloitte's proposed audit of MedTrans for fiscal 1992, and the facts and circumstances of Deloitte's withdrawal/resignation/disengagement as MedTrans' auditor."

Gordon Johns met with representatives of Ernst & Young on September 3, 1992. During that meeting, Johns explained why Deloitte had resigned from the MedTrans engagement. Johns also revealed that he questioned the integrity of MedTrans' senior executives. Despite the information obtained from Johns, E&Y agreed to audit MedTrans' 1992 financial statements.

Roberts concluded during late September that Blair was unlikely to invest in MedTrans regardless of the outcome of E&Y's audit. At that point, Roberts began searching for another potential investor to bail MedTrans out of the financial crisis it faced. Within a few days, a company contacted by Roberts, American Medical Response, Inc. (AMR), expressed interest in acquiring MedTrans. Like MedTrans, AMR's principal line of business was providing ambulance services. When AMR executives recommended that MedTrans retain Peat Marwick, AMR's audit firm, to audit its 1992 financial statements, Roberts dismissed E&Y and contacted Peat Marwick. Roberts also contacted Deloitte and authorized the firm to discuss with Peat Marwick the circumstances surrounding its resignation from the MedTrans audit.

After communicating with Deloitte, the San Diego office of Peat Marwick agreed to audit MedTrans' 1992 financial statements. One week after accepting the engagement, Peat Marwick resigned. Subsequent testimony revealed that a "directive" sent by Peat Marwick's headquarters office to the firm's San Diego office prompted that resignation. Peat Marwick's refusal to audit MedTrans apparently quelled AMR's interest in the company.

MedTrans finally retained another audit firm in late October 1992. This firm, identified only as "Silberman" in court transcripts, had served as MedTrans' auditor during the mid-1980s. Before accepting the engagement, Silberman discussed with Deloitte the circumstances surrounding its resignation as MedTrans' auditor. In December 1992, Silberman issued an unqualified opinion on MedTrans' 1992 financial statements. Before issuing that opinion, Silberman persuaded MedTrans to accept the large adjustments proposed by Deloitte. MedTrans' 1992 income statement reported a loss of $480,000, which was approximately the figure Deloitte had arrived at several months earlier.

Laidlaw Medical Transportation, Inc., purchased MedTrans in June 1993. Roberts and Morgan netted $3 million from the sale of their company. Under Laidlaw's ownership, MedTrans soon became the largest provider of ambulance services in the nation.

MedTrans Sues Deloitte

In August 1993, Roberts and Morgan sued Deloitte on behalf of their former company. The principal allegations against Deloitte centered on charges of professional negligence and breach of contract. Roberts and Morgan charged that Deloitte's malfeasance caused Blair not to consummate the $10 million investment deal arranged by Roberts. MedTrans' former co-owners requested damages equal to the difference between the amount they received from the sale of MedTrans and the amount the company allegedly would have been worth had Blair invested in the firm. The lawsuit was tried before a jury in a California state court in July 1995.

MedTrans' legal counsel succinctly summed up the key allegations against Deloitte in the following statement:

> What is the negligence that we contend occurred? What is the breach that we contend occurred? Very simply: they [Deloitte] contracted over a course of years, and in connection with the year of 1992, to perform an audit and to render an opinion; they did neither, and walked away after getting payment for such services.

Deloitte's defense team rebutted these allegations by insisting that the accounting firm had a right to resign from the 1992 audit when it "lost faith in the honesty of MedTrans' senior management." A CPA retained by Deloitte to serve as an expert witness testified that the firm was obligated to resign from the engagement after its independence was "compromised by Roberts' threats."

After a short trial, Judge Philip Sharp instructed the jurors on the legal matters they should consider during their deliberations. The jurors reached their decision quickly, ruling in favor of MedTrans on all key issues raised during the trial.

The jury ruled that Deloitte had acted negligently and breached its contractual obligations to MedTrans when it withdrew from the 1992 audit engagement. In addition, the jury concluded that Deloitte "negligently interfered" with and "disrupted" MedTrans' economic relationships with Blair, Ernst & Young, and Peat Marwick. This latter ruling stemmed from charges that Deloitte made defamatory statements to E&Y and Peat Marwick concerning the integrity of MedTrans' former executives. Deloitte allegedly made these statements during the predecessor–successor auditor communications with those two firms following its resignation as MedTrans' auditor. After issuing their rulings on the specific complaints filed against Deloitte, the jurors awarded MedTrans' former owners a $9.9 million judgment against the accounting firm.

Deloitte Appeals Jury Verdict

Deloitte quickly appealed the jury's verdict. The accounting firm insisted that the trial judge erred when he instructed the jury prior to its deliberations. Included in Judge

Sharp's instructions to the jury was the following statement concerning an auditor's right to resign from an engagement:

> *Once an accountant has undertaken to serve a client, the employment and duty as an accountant continues until ended by consent or request of the client or the accountant withdraws from the employment, if it does not unduly jeopardize the interest of the client, after giving the client reasonable opportunity to employ another accountant or the matter for which the person [accountant] was employed has been concluded.*

These instructions, Deloitte maintained, gave the jury only one alternative, namely, deciding the case in MedTrans' favor. The accounting firm argued that the phrase "if it [the auditor's resignation] does not unduly jeopardize the interest of the client" implies that an auditor must consider the economic impact on a client before resigning. Deloitte demonstrated during the appeal that professional auditing standards do not require auditors to consider the potential economic impact on a client of a resignation decision. The jury instructions also suggested that an auditor must give a client "reasonable opportunity" to retain another audit firm before resigning. Again, Deloitte established that professional standards do not impose such a responsibility on independent auditors.

Deloitte argued before the appellate court that an accounting firm may resign from an audit engagement whenever it has "good cause" to do so. The firm also insisted that "good cause" in this context must be defined in reference to the professional standards of the auditing discipline. Deloitte then identified three reasons why it had good cause to resign from the 1992 MedTrans audit: MedTrans management's refusal to cooperate fully with the auditors, the auditors' loss of confidence in client management's integrity, and the threats that Roberts made to Johns. Deloitte claimed that Roberts' threats, alone, provided sufficient justification for resigning since those threats undermined the auditors' independence. MedTrans' attorneys agreed that auditors could resign when they had "good cause" but attempted to persuade the appellate court to apply a more legalistic interpretation to that phrase, an interpretation independent of professional auditing standards.

Strengthening Deloitte's "good cause" argument was a "friend of the court" filing submitted by the American Institute of Certified Public Accountants (AICPA). In that filing, the AICPA reiterated Deloitte's assertion that Roberts' threats undermined the audit firm's independence. The AICPA noted that an auditor must decide as a "matter of professional judgment" whether he is independent. "An auditor's independence may be impaired whenever the member and the member's client company or its management are in threatened or actual positions of material adverse interests by reason of threatened or actual litigation." The AICPA went on to observe that "an auditor who believes independence has been impaired is forbidden from issuing an audit opinion."

After briefly contesting Deloitte's contention that it had "good cause" to resign from the 1992 audit, MedTrans' legal counsel adopted a second strategy during the appeal. MedTrans' attorneys argued that Deloitte forfeited its right to file an appeal predicated on the allegedly prejudicial jury instructions since the accounting firm had not offered the trial judge any alternate jury instructions. In fact, Deloitte initially challenged the jury instructions written by Judge Sharp. At that point, Judge Sharp offered to consider alternate instructions developed by Deloitte's legal counsel; however, the accounting firm never submitted revised jury instructions for the judge's consideration. Despite Deloitte's apparent oversight, the appellate court ruled that Deloitte did not forfeit its right to challenge the impact of Judge Sharp's jury instructions on the jury's verdict.

> *Where as here, the trial court gives a jury instruction which is prejudicially erroneous as given, i.e., which is an incorrect statement of law, the party harmed by the instruction need not have objected to the instruction or proposed a correct instruction of his own in order to preserve the right to complain of the erroneous instruction on appeal.*

Jury Verdict Overturned

In early 1998, the California Court of Appeal overturned the jury's verdict in the *MedTrans v. Deloitte* civil case. The appellate court ruled that Judge Sharp's instructions predisposed the jury to rule in MedTrans' favor.

After overturning the jury's verdict, the appellate court addressed each of the major allegations made against Deloitte by MedTrans in the original trial. First, the appellate court rejected MedTrans' contention that Deloitte acted negligently when it withdrew from the 1992 audit. The court agreed with Deloitte that the auditing profession's standards are the primary authoritative source in this context. Applying those standards, the appellate court ruled that Deloitte clearly had a reasonable basis for resigning from the 1992 audit.

Next, the appellate court discredited the breach of contract allegation lodged against Deloitte. Recall that MedTrans' management pressured Deloitte to issue an unqualified opinion on the company's original 1992 financial statements. The appellate court ruled that "Deloitte cannot be held liable to MedTrans in breach of contract for having declined to issue a false 'unqualified' audit report." The court also rejected MedTrans' claim that Deloitte's failure to issue an audit opinion of any kind constituted breach of contract. Finally, the appellate court dismissed MedTrans' assertion that Deloitte's communications with the company's successor auditors were defamatory.

> *Defamation is an intentional tort. In any event, as discussed, the record contained ample evidence that defendants' communications with potential successor auditors about their reasons for resigning from their engagement with MedTrans complied with applicable professional standards requiring open communication with potential successor auditors and were consistent with MedTrans' written authorizations requesting defendants to speak freely with those potential successor auditors.*

Questions

1. Following his resignation, MedTrans' former CFO met with Gordon Johns, the Deloitte audit engagement partner. Did the CFO have a responsibility to inform Johns of the errors in MedTrans' 1992 financial statements? Defend your answer.

2. What courses of action were available to Johns following his meeting with MedTrans' former CFO? Which of those options would you have selected? Why?

3. How did the threats Roberts made to Johns impair Deloitte's independence? The AICPA maintained that an audit firm is "forbidden" from issuing an audit opinion when it believes its independence has been impaired. Identify three circumstances, unrelated to this case, that would threaten an audit firm's independence.

4. Did Deloitte have a responsibility to be totally candid with MedTrans' prospective successor auditors? Explain. Under present auditing standards, what questions should a prospective successor auditor pose to a predecessor auditor?

5. The jury in the *MedTrans v. Deloitte* lawsuit ruled that the accounting firm negligently resigned from the 1992 audit, breached its contract with the client, and made defamatory statements regarding MedTrans' former executives during the predecessor–successor auditor communications. The appellate court reversed these rulings. Provide an example of each alleged type of misconduct for which an audit firm likely *would be* held legally at fault.

Fred Stern & Company, Inc. (*Ultramares Corporation v. Touche et al.*)

In the business world of the Roaring Twenties, the scams and schemes of flimflam artists and confidence men were legendary. The absence of a strong regulatory system at the federal level to police the securities markets—the Securities and Exchange Commission was not established until 1934—aided, if not encouraged, financial frauds of all types. In all likelihood, the majority of individuals involved in business during the 1920s were scrupulously honest. Nevertheless, the culture of that decade bred a disproportionate number of opportunists who adopted an "anything goes" approach to transacting business. An example of a company in which this self-serving attitude apparently prevailed was Fred Stern & Company, Inc. During the mid-1920s, Stern's executives duped three of the company's creditors out of several hundred thousand dollars.

Based in New York City, Stern imported rubber, a raw material demanded in huge quantities by many industries in the early twentieth century. During the 1920s alone, industrial demand for rubber in the United States more than tripled. The nature of the rubber importation trade required large amounts of working capital. Because Stern was chronically short of funds, the company relied heavily on banks and other lenders to finance its day-to-day operations.

In March 1924, Stern sought a $100,000 loan from Ultramares Corporation, a finance company whose primary line of business was factoring receivables. Before considering the loan request, Ultramares asked Stern's management for an audited balance sheet. Stern had been audited a few months earlier by Touche, Niven & Company, a prominent accounting firm based in London and New York City. Touche had served as Stern's independent auditor since 1920. Exhibit 1 presents the unqualified opinion Touche issued on Stern's December 31, 1923, balance sheet. Stern's management obtained from Touche 32 serially numbered copies of the audit report. Touche knew that Stern intended to use the audit reports to obtain external debt financing but was unaware of the specific banks or finance companies that might receive the audit reports.

After reviewing Stern's audited balance sheet, which reported assets of more than $2.5 million and a net worth of approximately $1 million, and the accompanying audit report, Ultramares granted the $100,000 loan requested by the company. Ultramares later extended two more loans to Stern totaling $65,000. During the same time frame, Stern obtained more than $300,000 in loans from two local banks after providing them with copies of the December 31, 1923, balance sheet and accompanying audit report.

Unfortunately for Ultramares and the two banks that extended loans to Stern, the company was declared bankrupt in January 1925. Subsequent courtroom testimony revealed that the company had been hopelessly insolvent at the end of 1923 when its audited balance sheet reported a net worth of $1 million. An accountant with Stern, identified only as Romberg in court records, concealed Stern's bankrupt status from the Touche auditors. Romberg masked Stern's true financial condition by making several false entries in the company's accounting records. The largest of these

EXHIBIT 1

TOUCHE, NIVEN &
COMPANY'S AUDIT
OPINION ON STERN'S
DECEMBER 31,
1923, BALANCE
SHEET

February 26, 1924

**Touche, Niven & Co.
Public Accountants
Eighty Maiden Lane,
New York**

Certificate of Auditors

We have examined the accounts of Fred Stern & Co., Inc., for the year ended December 31, 1923, and hereby certify that the annexed balance sheet is in accordance therewith and with the information and explanations given us. We further certify that, subject to provision for federal taxes on income, the said statement in our opinion, presents a true and correct view of the financial condition of Fred Stern & Co., Inc., as at December 31, 1923.

entries involved a debit of more than $700,000 to accounts receivable and an offsetting credit to sales.

Following Stern's bankruptcy, Ultramares sued Touche to recover the $165,000 loaned to Stern. Ultramares alleged that the audit firm had been both fraudulent and negligent in auditing Stern's financial records. *The New York Times* noted that the negligence claim in the *Ultramares* suit was "novel" and would likely serve as a major "test case" for third parties hoping to recover losses from audit firms.[1] The novel aspect of the negligence claim stemmed from the absence of a contractual relationship between Touche and Ultramares. Touche's contract to audit Stern's December 31, 1923, balance sheet was made solely with Stern's management. At the time, a well-entrenched legal doctrine dictated that only a party in privity with another— that is, having an explicit contractual agreement with another—could recover damages resulting from the other party's negligence.

Another interesting facet of the *Ultramares* lawsuit involved the founder of Touche, Niven & Company, Sir George Alexander Touche. George Touche, who served for two years as the sheriff of London during World War I, merged his accounting practice in the early 1900s with that of a young Scottish accountant, John B. Niven, who had immigrated to New York City. The new firm prospered, and George Touche, who was knighted in 1917 by King George V, eventually became one of the most respected leaders of the emerging public-accounting profession. John Niven also became influential within the profession. Ironically, Niven was serving as the president of the American Institute of Accountants, the predecessor of the American Institute of Certified Public Accountants, when Fred Stern & Company was declared insolvent. An issue posed by the *Ultramares* lawsuit was whether George Touche and his fellow partners who were not involved in the Stern audit could be held personally liable for any improper conduct on the part of the Touche auditors assigned to the Stern engagement. Ultramares raised that issue by naming each of the Touche partners as codefendants.

Ultramares Corporation v. Touche et al.: A Protracted Legal Battle

The *Ultramares* civil suit against Touche was tried before a jury in a New York state court. Ultramares' principal allegation was that the Touche auditors should have easily discovered the $700,000 overstatement of receivables in Stern's December 31, 1923, balance sheet. That error, if corrected, would have slashed Stern's reported net

---

1. "Damages Refused for Error in Audit," *The New York Times*, 27 June 1929, 50.

worth by nearly 70 percent and considerably lessened the likelihood that Ultramares would have extended the company a sizable loan.

A young man by the name of Siess performed most of the field work on the Stern audit. When Siess arrived at Stern's office to begin the audit in early February 1924, he discovered that the company's general ledger had not been posted since the prior April. He spent the next few days posting entries from the client's journals to its general ledger. After Siess completed that task, Stern's accounts receivable totaled approximately $644,000. Stern's accountant, Romberg, obtained the general ledger the day before Siess intended to prepare a trial balance of the company's accounts. After reviewing the ledger, Romberg booked an entry debiting receivables and crediting sales for approximately $706,000. Beside the entry in the receivables account, he entered a number cross-referencing the recorded amount to the company's sales journal.

The following day, Romberg notified Siess of the entry he had recorded in the general ledger. Romberg told Siess that the entry represented Stern's December sales that had been inadvertently omitted from the accounting records. Without questioning Romberg's explanation for the large entry, Siess included the $706,000 in the receivables balance. In fact, the receivables did not exist and the corresponding sales never occurred. To support the entry, Romberg or one of his subordinates hastily prepared 17 bogus sales invoices.

In subsequent testimony, Siess initially reported that he could not recall whether he reviewed any of the 17 invoices allegedly representing Stern's December sales. Plaintiff counsel then demonstrated that "a mere glance" at the invoices would have revealed that they were forged. The invoices lacked shipping numbers, customer order numbers, and other pertinent information. Following this revelation, Siess admitted that he had not examined any of the invoices.[2] Touche's attorneys attempted to justify this oversight by pointing out that audits involve "testing and sampling" rather than an examination of entire accounting populations.[3] Thus, it was not surprising or unusual, the attorneys argued, that none of the fictitious December sales invoices were among the more than 200 invoices examined during the Stern audit.

The court ruled that auditing on a sample basis is appropriate in most cases. But, given the suspicious nature of the large December sales entry recorded by Romberg, the court concluded that Touche should have specifically reviewed the December sales invoices.

> Verification by test and sample was very likely a sufficient audit as to accounts regularly entered upon the books in the usual course of business. . . . [However], the defendants were put on their guard by the circumstances touching the December accounts receivable to scrutinize with special care.[4]

Ultramares' attorneys noted during the trial that Touche had even more reason than just the suspicious nature of Romberg's December sales entry to question the integrity of the large year-end increase in receivables. While auditing the company's inventory, Touche auditors discovered several errors that collectively caused the inventory account to be overstated by more than $300,000, an overstatement of 90 percent. The auditors also uncovered large errors in Stern's accounts payable and discovered that the company had improperly pledged the same assets as collateral for several bank loans. Given the extent and nature of the problems revealed by the Touche audit, the

2. *Ultramares Corporation v. Touche et al.*, 255 N.Y. 170, 174 N.E. 441 (1930), 449.

3. *Ibid.*

4. *Ibid.*

court ruled that the accounting firm should have been particularly skeptical of the client's accounting records. This should have been the case, the court observed, even though Touche had not encountered any reason in previous audits to question the integrity of Stern's management.

> *No doubt the extent to which inquiry must be pressed beyond appearances is a question of judgment, as to which opinions will often differ. No doubt the wisdom that is born after the event will engender suspicion and distrust when old acquaintance and good repute may have silenced doubt at the beginning.*[5]

The jury in the *Ultramares* case dismissed the fraud charge against Touche. The jurors ruled that the company's attorneys failed to establish that the audit firm had intentionally deceived Ultramares—intentional deceit being a necessary condition for fraud. Regarding the negligence charge, the jury ruled in favor of Ultramares and ordered Touche to pay the company damages of $186,000.

The judge who presided over the *Ultramares* case overturned the jury's ruling on the negligence charge. In explaining his decision, the judge acknowledged that Ultramares' attorneys had clearly established that Touche had been negligent during its 1923 audit of Stern. Nevertheless, the judge ruled that the jury had overlooked the long-standing legal doctrine that only a party in privity could sue and recover damages resulting from a defendant's negligence.

> *Negligence is not actionable unless there is a breach of duty owing by defendants to the plaintiff. To hold that the defendants' duty extended to not only Stern but to all persons to whom Stern might exhibit the balance sheet, and who would act in reliance thereon, would compel the defendants to assume a potential liability to practically the entire world.*[6]

Ultramares' attorneys quickly appealed the trial judge's decision. The appellate division of the New York Supreme Court reviewed the case. In a 3 to 2 vote, the appellate division decided that the trial judge erred in reversing the jury's verdict on the negligence charge. As appellate Justice McAvoy noted, the key question in the case centered on whether Touche had a duty to Ultramares "in the absence of a direct contractual relation."[7] Justice McAvoy concluded that Touche did have an obligation to Ultramares, and to other parties relying on Stern's financial statements, although the accounting firm's contract was expressly and exclusively with Stern.

> *One cannot issue an unqualified statement [audit opinion] . . . and then disclaim responsibility for his work. Banks and merchants, to the knowledge of these defendants, require certified balance sheets from independent accountants, and upon these audits they make their loans. Thus, the duty arises to these banks and merchants of an exercise of reasonable care in the making and uttering of certified balance sheets.*[8]

Justice McAvoy and two of his colleagues were unwavering in their opinion that Touche had a legal obligation to Ultramares. Nevertheless, the remaining two judges on the appellate panel were just as strongly persuaded that no such obligation existed. In the dissenting opinion, Justice Finch maintained that holding Touche responsible to a third party that subsequently relied upon the Stern financial statements was patently unfair to the accounting firm.

---

5. *Ibid.*, 444.

6. "Damages Refused for Error."

7. *Ultramares Corporation v. Touche et al.*, 229 App. Div. 581, 243 N.Y.S. 179 (1930), 181.

8. *Ibid.*, 182.

> *If the plaintiff [Ultramares] had inquired of the accountants whether they might rely upon the certificate in making a loan, then the accountants would have had the opportunity to gauge their responsibility and risk, and determine with knowledge how thorough their verification of the account should be before assuming the responsibility of making the certificate run to the plaintiff.*[9]

Following the appellate division's ruling in the *Ultramares* case, Touche's attorneys appealed the decision to the next highest court in the New York state judicial system, the Court of Appeals. That court ultimately handed down the final ruling in the lengthy judicial history of the case. The chief justice of New York's Court of Appeals, Benjamin Cardozo, was a nationally recognized legal scholar whose opinions were given great weight by other courts.

Justice Cardozo and his six associate justices ruled unanimously that the judge who presided over the *Ultramares* trial had properly reversed the jury's decision on the negligence claim. Justice Cardozo reiterated the arguments made by Justice Finch. He maintained that it would be unfair to hold Touche legally responsible to a third party, unknown to Touche when its audit was performed, that happened to obtain and rely upon Stern's audited balance sheet. However, Justice Cardozo went on to suggest that had Ultramares been clearly designated as a beneficiary of the Stern–Touche contract, his ruling would have been different.

Unfortunately for the accounting profession, Justice Cardozo's opinion did not end with his commentary on the negligence question in the *Ultramares* case. After resolving that issue, he sharply criticized Touche's audit of Stern. The judge implied that Ultramares might have been successful in suing Touche on the basis of gross negligence: "Negligence or blindness, even when not equivalent to fraud, is none the less evidence to sustain an inference of fraud. . . . At least this is so if the negligence is gross. . . . [In the *Ultramares* case] a jury might find that . . . [the Touche auditors] closed their eyes to the obvious, and blindly gave assent."[10]

The *Ultramares* Decision: Implications for the Accounting Profession

In retrospect, the *Ultramares* decision had two principal implications for the public accounting profession. First, Justice Cardozo's opinion established the precedent that certain direct beneficiaries of an audit, generally referred to as primary beneficiaries, are entitled to recover damages from a negligent auditor. Subsequent to the *Ultramares* ruling, very few plaintiffs were successful in establishing themselves as primary beneficiaries of an audit.[11] Consequently, this "expansion" of the auditor's legal exposure proved to be fairly insignificant.

The second key implication of the *Ultramares* case was that it provided a new strategy for plaintiff counsel to use in suing auditors on behalf of nonprivity parties. Following the *Ultramares* ruling, attorneys representing such plaintiffs began predicating lawsuits against auditors on allegations of gross negligence. Before that ruling, nonprivity third parties faced the heavy burden of proving fraud if they wanted to recover losses resulting from auditor misconduct. Because establishing gross negligence is much easier than proving intent to defraud, the *Ultramares* decision significantly increased auditors' legal exposure to nonprivity third parties.

---

9. *Ibid.*, 186.

10. *Ultramares Corporation v. Touche et al.*, 255 N.Y. 170, 174 N.E. 441 (1930), 449.

11. Decades later, the *Credit Alliance* case established several restrictive conditions that third parties must satisfy to qualify as primary beneficiaries. See: *Credit Alliance Corporation v. Arthur Andersen & Company*, 483 N.E. 2d 110 (N.Y. 1985).

A secondary issue addressed by Justice Cardozo in the *Ultramares* case was whether Sir George Touche and his fellow partners who had no direct connection with the Stern engagement could be held liable for the deficient Stern audit. This issue was moot regarding the negligence allegation since that charge had already been dismissed. But, the issue was still pertinent to the fraud charge since Justice Cardozo ruled that Ultramares was entitled to a retrial to determine whether Touche's negligence was severe enough to infer fraudulent conduct or gross negligence.[12] Because the auditors assigned to the Stern engagement were acting as agents of the accounting firm's partners, Justice Cardozo ruled that all of Touche's partners were legally responsible for the actions of those individuals.

EPILOGUE

In the years following the *Ultramares* case, the legal exposure of public accountants to third-party financial statement users was gradually extended. The first extension came on the heels of the *Ultramares* case with the passage of the Securities Act of 1933. That federal statute imposed on auditors a very significant legal obligation to initial purchasers of new securities marketed on an interstate basis.

Under the 1933 Act, plaintiffs do not have to prove fraud, gross negligence, or even negligence on the part of auditors. Essentially, plaintiffs must only establish that they suffered investment losses and that the relevant financial statements contain material errors or omissions. If a plaintiff establishes those elements of proof, the defendant accounting firm assumes the burden of proving that its employees were "duly diligent" in performing the audit.[13] To sustain a due diligence defense, an accounting firm must show that, following a "reasonable investigation," it had "reasonable ground to believe and did believe" that the audited financial statements were materially accurate. Federal courts have not been receptive to the due diligence defense if the plaintiffs have clearly established that the financial statements in question contain material errors.[14]

Auditors' legal exposure has also expanded under the common law over the past several decades. In 1965, the American Law Institute issued *Restatement of Torts*, a legal compendium relied on heavily in many jurisdictions. This source suggests that "foreseen" beneficiaries, in addition to primary beneficiaries, should have a right to recover damages from negligent auditors.[15] Foreseen beneficiaries are members of a limited group or class of third-party financial statement users. Auditors are typically aware of this distinct group of potential financial statement users but unaware of the specific individuals or entities who make up that group.

The 1983 *Rosenblum* ruling went beyond the boundary established by the *Restatement of*

---

12. For whatever reason, Ultramares chose not to file an amended lawsuit against Touche that was predicated upon an allegation of gross negligence.

13. Accounting firms have other defenses available to them when sued under the Securities Act of 1933. These defenses include, among others, expiration of the statute of limitations, establishing that the plaintiff knew the relevant financial statements were misleading when he or she purchased the securities, and proving that the plaintiff's damages were not caused by the misleading financial statements.

14. Case 7.9, "First Securities Company of Chicago (*Ernst & Ernst v. Hochfelder et al.*)," examines the legal implications posed for public accounting firms by the Securities Exchange Act of 1934, which is the "sister" statute to the 1933 Act.

15. American Law Institute, *Restatement of the Law, Second: Torts* (Philadelphia: American Law Institute, 1965).

Torts. That judicial ruling suggested that even "reasonably foreseeable" or "ordinary" third-party financial statement users should be allowed to recover damages from negligent auditors.[16] Reasonably foreseeable third parties include a much larger population of potential financial-statement users than "foreseen" third parties. The most liberal definition of "reasonably foreseeable third parties" includes individual investors who happen to obtain a copy of audited financial statements and make a decision based upon them.

Questions

1. Observers of the accounting profession suggest that many courts attempt to "socialize" investment losses by extending auditors' liability to third-party financial statement users. Discuss the benefits and costs of such a policy to public accounting firms, audit clients, and third-party financial statement users, such as investors and creditors. In your view, should the courts have the authority to socialize investment losses? If not, who should determine how investment losses are distributed in our society?

2. Auditors' legal responsibilities differ significantly under the Securities Exchange Act of 1934 and the Securities Act of 1933. Briefly point out these differences and comment on why they exist. Also comment on how auditors' litigation risks differ under the common law and the 1934 Act.

3. The current standard audit report differs significantly from the version issued during the 1920s. Identify the key differences in the two reports and discuss the forces that accounted for the evolution of the audit report into its present form.

4. Why was it common in the 1920s for companies to have only an audited balance sheet prepared for distribution to external third parties? Comment on the factors that, over a period of several decades, resulted in the adoption of the financial statement package that most companies presently provide to external third parties.

5. When assessing audit risk, should auditors consider the type and number of third parties that may ultimately rely on the client's financial statements? Should auditors insist that audit engagement letters identify the third parties to whom the client intends to distribute the audited financial statements? Would this practice eliminate auditors' legal liability to nonprivity parties not mentioned in engagement letters?

---

16. *H. Rosenblum, Inc. v. Adler*, 461 A. 2d 138 (N.J. 1983).

First Securities Company of Chicago (*Ernst & Ernst v. Hochfelder et al.*)

Ladislas Nay immigrated to the United States from Hungary in 1921 at the age of 18. The opportunities offered by his new land excited the industrious young immigrant and he promised himself that he would make the most of them. Shortly after arriving in the United States, Nay made his way to Chicago and landed a job in the booming securities industry with a small brokerage firm. For the next several years, Nay worked long and hard hours learning the brokerage business.

Unfortunately for Nay, the Great Depression hit the securities industry particularly hard. Young stockbrokers like himself were the first to be released by their firms when personnel cuts were necessary. During the bleak 1930s, Nay, who by this time had Americanized his first name to Leston, endured several job changes and two failed marriages. In 1942, as World War II began to pull the United States out of the Depression, Nay landed a permanent job with the brokerage firm of Ryan-Nichols & Company.

Within two years of joining Ryan-Nichols, Nay was promoted to president. He eventually became the firm's principal stockholder, accumulating more than 90 percent of its outstanding common stock. In 1945, Nay renamed his firm First Securities Company of Chicago. Nay's firm also successfully applied for membership in the Midwest Stock Exchange that year. Over the next two decades, Nay's career and personal life flourished. His family settled into the upper-class neighborhood of Hyde Park, near the University of Chicago. Nay and his wife, Elizabeth, participated in a wide range of community affairs, including serving on several prominent civic boards. Nay made numerous friends among the faculty and staff of the University of Chicago. In fact, many of his best customers were associated with the prestigious school.

Nay's personal attention to the financial needs of his customers earned him their respect and admiration. One of his customers described him as a kind and considerate man, much "like an old-fashioned English solicitor who took care of a family's affairs."[1] His conservative investment strategies particularly appealed to his retired clients and those nearing retirement. Nay offered many of these customers an opportunity to invest in a lucrative fund that he personally managed. This fund was not an asset of First Securities, nor were any other First Securities personnel aware it existed. Nay referred to this fund as the "escrow syndicate."

Nay loaned funds invested in the escrow syndicate to blue chip companies that developed sudden and unexpected working capital shortages. These companies paid interest rates well above the prevailing market rates. Individuals who invested in the escrow syndicate earned 7 to 12 percent on their investments, considerably more than the interest rates paid at the time by banks on savings accounts.

One of Nay's closest friends, Arnold Schueren, entrusted him with more than $400,000 over three decades and granted him a power of attorney to make investment

---

1. J. M. Johnston, "How Broker Worked $1 Million Swindle," *Chicago Daily News*, 13 December 1968, 42, 43.

decisions regarding those funds. Nay invested a large portion of Schueren's savings in the escrow syndicate. Another individual who relied heavily on Nay for investment advice was the widow of a close associate of the famed University of Chicago scientist Enrico Fermi. This woman later testified that Nay had managed her family's investments for many years but did not offer her the opportunity to invest in the escrow syndicate until after her husband's death. Nay told her that he only offered this investment opportunity to his "nearest and dearest friends."[2] Following the death of another of his customers, Norman Moyer, Nay convinced Moyer's widow to invest her husband's estate of $90,000 in the escrow syndicate. In total, 17 of Nay's friends and/or their widows invested substantial sums in the escrow syndicate.

Dr. Jekyll and Mr. Hyde: A Tragic Ending

On the morning of June 4, 1968, Leston Nay drove to St. Luke's Hospital in Chicago to pick up his wife, who had fallen and broken her hip the previous week. Earlier that morning, Nay had telephoned his secretary to tell her that he would not be in the office that day because he had a stomach virus. Shortly before noon, as his wife, who was still on crutches, made her way to the kitchen of their apartment, Nay retrieved his 12-gauge shotgun and shot her in the upper back from close range. Nay then laid a suicide note on a dressing table in his bedroom, sat down on his bed, put the muzzle of the gun in his mouth, and pulled the trigger.

News of the murder–suicide shocked the Nays' friends and associates. These same people were shocked again when the Chicago police released the contents of Nay's suicide note. The note revealed that the kindly stockbroker had led a Dr. Jekyll–Mr. Hyde existence for decades. In the note, addressed "To whom it may concern," Nay admitted stealing from his customers for more than 30 years. The escrow syndicate in which his closest friends had invested did not exist—police speculated that Nay had lost the investors' funds in the stock market. Nay had successfully concealed the missing funds for as long as he did because he periodically mailed the investors checks for interest supposedly earned by the escrow syndicate. These periodic interest payments deterred the victims of the scam from questioning the safety of their investments.

In the suicide note, Nay displayed some remorse when he referred to the 80-year-old Mrs. Moyer, who was penniless as a result of his actions. He also explained why he had decided to take his life. After Arnold Schueren died in 1967, the executor of his estate had demanded that Nay return Schueren's investment in the escrow syndicate. Nay indicated in the suicide note that he had "stalled" as long as he could but that the executor would not be put off any longer. So he took his life. Most likely, Nay murdered his wife to "save" her from the shame she would feel when his fraudulent scheme, of which she was apparently unaware, was disclosed.

Defrauded Customers Sue to Recover Their Investments

The investors in Nay's escrow syndicate filed civil lawsuits against several parties in an effort to recover their collective investments of more than $1 million. Initially, the investors sued the Midwest Stock Exchange. In that suit, the investors alleged that the stock exchange failed to adequately investigate Nay's background before admitting his firm to membership. According to the investors, a more thorough investigation might have revealed that Nay had a history, although well concealed, of unscrupulous business practices. The investors suggested that the discovery of Nay's past

---

2. *Ibid.*

unethical conduct would have forced the exchange to deny his firm's membership application and possibly prevented him from engaging in the escrow syndicate fraud. The court hearing the suit quickly dismissed the investors' claims, concluding that the stock exchange sufficiently investigated Nay's background before approving his firm's membership application.

Nay's 17 escrow participants or their estates also sued First Securities Company of Chicago. The court ruled that the brokerage firm had clearly facilitated Nay's fraudulent activities. But, since the brokerage firm was bankrupt, the escrow investors found themselves thwarted again.

Finally, Nay's former customers filed suit against Ernst & Ernst, the accounting firm that audited First Securities Company for more than two decades. The lawsuit alleged that Ernst & Ernst's negligence had prevented the firm from detecting what became known throughout the lengthy judicial history of the *First Securities* case as Nay's "mail rule." According to the plaintiffs' legal counsel, "Nay had forbidden anyone other than himself to open mail addressed to him, and in his absence all such mail was simply allowed to pile up on his desk, even if it was addressed to First Securities for his attention."[3] Nay's mail rule allowed him to conceal the escrow syndicate scam from his subordinates at First Securities and from the brokerage's independent auditors. Had Ernst & Ernst discovered the mail rule, the plaintiffs alleged, an investigation would have been warranted. Such an investigation would very likely have led to the discovery of Nay's escrow investment scam.

Ernst & Ernst v. Hochfelder et al.

The defrauded investors filed their lawsuit against Ernst & Ernst under the Securities Exchange Act of 1934. That federal statute does not expressly provide civil remedies to stockholders of companies registered with the Securities and Exchange Commission (SEC). However, since the adoption of the 1934 Act, federal courts have allowed stockholders to use the statute as a basis for civil suits against company officers, investment brokers, auditors, and other parties associated with false financial statements filed with the SEC. Most of these suits allege one or more violations of Rule 10b-5 of the 1934 Act, shown in Exhibit 1.

In the *First Securities* case, the plaintiffs charged that Ernst & Ernst's alleged negligence in failing to discover Nay's mail rule constituted a violation of Rule 10b-5.

> *The premise [of the investors' suit] was that Ernst & Ernst had failed to utilize "appropriate auditing procedures" in its audits of First Securities. . . . Respondents [investors] contended that if Ernst & Ernst had conducted a proper audit, it would*

Employment of manipulative and deceptive devices. It shall be unlawful for any person, directly or indirectly, by the use of any means or instrumentality of interstate commerce, or of the mails or of any facility of any national securities exchange,

(a) To employ any device, scheme, or artifice to defraud,
(b) To make any untrue statement of a material fact or to omit to state a material fact necessary in order to make the statements made, in the light of the circumstances under which they were made, not misleading, or
(c) To engage in any act, practice, or course of business which operates or would operate as a fraud or deceit upon any person, in connection with the purchase or sale of any security.

EXHIBIT 1

RULE 10b-5 OF THE SECURITIES EXCHANGE ACT OF 1934

---

3. *Securities and Exchange Commission v. First Securities Company of Chicago*, 463 F. 2d 981 (1972), 985.

have discovered this "mail rule." The existence of the rule then would have been disclosed to the Exchange [Midwest Stock Exchange] and to the Commission [SEC] by Ernst & Ernst as an irregular procedure that prevented an effective audit.[4]

To support their claim that the mail rule qualified as a critical internal control weakness having important audit implications, the escrow investors submitted affidavits from three expert witnesses with impressive credentials in the accounting profession. Exhibit 2 lists a portion of one of these affidavits.

The federal district court that initially presided over the *Hochfelder et al. v. Ernst & Ernst* case quickly dismissed the lawsuit.[5] This court deemed that there was no substantive evidence to support the allegation that Ernst & Ernst had negligently audited First Securities. When the investors appealed this decision, the U.S. Court of Appeals reversed the lower court decision and ordered that the case go to trial. In its decision, the appeals court ruled that sufficient doubt existed regarding the negligence claim against Ernst & Ernst to have the case heard. The appeals court also suggested that if the plaintiffs established negligence on the part of Ernst & Ernst, the accounting firm could be held civilly liable to the defrauded investors under Rule 10b-5 of the 1934 Act.

Before the *Hochfelder* case went to trial in federal district court, Ernst & Ernst appealed the ruling of the U.S. Court of Appeals to the U.S. Supreme Court. Ernst & Ernst argued before the Supreme Court that the negligence allegation of the escrow investors was insufficient, even if proved, to constitute a violation of Rule 10b-5. This issue had surfaced in many previous civil cases filed under the Securities Exchange Act of 1934. In these earlier cases, the federal courts had generally ruled or suggested that negligence constituted a violation of Rule 10b-5. That is, fraud or gross negligence, either of which is much more difficult for a plaintiff to prove than ordinary negligence, did *not* have to be established for a defendant to be held civilly liable to a plaintiff under Rule 10b-5.

Ernst & Ernst contested these earlier rulings by arguing that Rule 10b-5, as worded, could not be construed to encompass negligent behavior. Given the longstanding controversy surrounding this issue, the Supreme Court decided to rule on the issue in the *Hochfelder* case. This ruling would then establish a precedent for future lawsuits filed under Rule 10b-5.

EXHIBIT 2

EXCERPT FROM EXPERT WITNESS TESTIMONY REGARDING NAY'S MAIL RULE

Expert Witness No. 3:

If I had discovered in making an audit of a security brokerage business that its president had established an office rule that mail addressed to him at the business address, or to the company for his attention should not be opened by anyone but him, even in his absence; and that whenever he was away from the office such mail would remain unopened and pile up on his desk I would have to raise the question whether such rule or practice could possibly have been instituted for the purpose of preventing discovery of irregularities of whatever nature; would, at a minimum, have to undertake additional audit procedures to independently establish a negative answer to the latter question; also failing such an answer either withdraw from the engagement or decline to express an opinion on the financial statements of the enterprise.

---

4. *Ernst & Ernst v. Hochfelder et al.,* 425 U.S. 185 (1976), 190.

5. *Hochfelder et al. v. Ernst & Ernst,* 503 F.2d 1100 (1974). (One of the investors defrauded by Nay was Olga Hochfelder.)

Before the Supreme Court heard Ernst & Ernst's appeal, the SEC filed a legal brief with the Court. This brief supported the defrauded investors' argument that Rule 10b-5 encompassed both fraudulent and negligent conduct. The SEC pointed out that the end result of investors' acting on false financial statements is the same whether the errors in the statements result from fraud or negligence. Because a central purpose of the federal securities laws is to ensure that investors receive reliable information, the SEC argued that the ambiguity in Rule 10b-5 should be resolved in favor of investors.

Surprisingly, the bulk of the Supreme Court's opinion in the *Hochfelder* case responded to the SEC's legal brief rather than the arguments of the defrauded investors or those of Ernst & Ernst. The Court rejected the SEC's largely philosophical argument and instead focused on the question of whether the authors of Rule 10b-5 intended it to encompass both negligent and fraudulent behavior. In addressing this issue, the Court reviewed the legislative history of the 1934 Act and did a painstaking analysis of the semantics of Rule 10b-5.

The Supreme Court eventually concluded that the key signal to the underlying meaning of Rule 10b-5 was the term *manipulative*. As shown in Exhibit 1, the heading of the rule clearly indicates that it pertains to "manipulative and deceptive" devices. According to the Court, negligence on the part of independent auditors or other parties associated with false financial statements could not be construed as manipulative behavior. The Court suggested that in most cases for behavior to qualify as manipulative, intent to deceive—the legal term being *scienter*—had to be present.

> When a statute speaks so specifically in terms of manipulation and deception, and of implementing devices and contrivances—the commonly understood terminology of intentional wrongdoing—and when its history reflects no more expansive intent, we are quite unwilling to extend the scope of the statute to negligent conduct.[6]

Two of the nine Supreme Court justices dissented to the *Hochfelder* decision, while one justice abstained. In disagreeing with the majority decision, Justice Harry Blackmun sided with the view expressed by the SEC. He noted that although the decision was probably consistent with the semantics of the Securities Exchange Act of 1934, the decision clashed with the underlying intent of that important federal statute. He wrote, "It seems to me that an investor can be victimized just as much by negligent conduct as by positive deception, and that it is not logical to drive a wedge between the two, saying that Congress clearly intended the one but certainly not the other."[7] Justice Blackmun went on to comment on the "critical importance" of the independent auditor's role and the ultimate responsibility of the auditor to serve the "public interest."[8] Given this societal mandate, Justice Blackmun argued, negligent auditors should be held accountable to investors who rely to their detriment on false financial statements.

---

6. *Ernst & Ernst v. Hochfelder et al.*, 214. A particularly troublesome issue for the Supreme Court to resolve was the underlying meaning of Subsection b of Rule 10b-5. Subsections a and c of that rule refer explicitly to fraud, implying that negligence is not a severe enough form of misconduct to constitute a violation of Rule 10b-5. However, Subsection b contains no explicit reference to fraudulent conduct. The SEC construed this omission to suggest that Subsection b covers both fraudulent and negligent misconduct. The Supreme Court rejected this argument, maintaining instead that the explicit references to fraud in Subsections a and c signaled that fraudulent conduct was the implied, although unstated, culpability standard in Subsection b as well.

7. *Ernst & Ernst v. Hochfelder et al.*, 216.

8. *Ibid.*, 218.

An Unresolved Issue

At first reading, the Supreme Court's *Hochfelder* opinion appeared to establish, once and for all, the culpability standard for determining Rule 10b-5 violations. Unfortunately, the opinion is not as precise or definitive as it first appeared. A footnote to the opinion suggests that in certain cases, scienter, or intent to deceive, may not be a necessary element of proof for a plaintiff to establish in a civil suit alleging a Rule 10b-5 violation. The Court noted that some jurisdictions equate scienter with willful or reckless disregard for the truth or, more simply, "recklessness."[9] When engaging in reckless behavior, a party does not actually possess conscious intent to deceive; that is, scienter is not present. For whatever reason, the Court specifically refused to rule on the question of whether reckless behavior would be considered equivalent to scienter and thus constitute a violation of Rule 10b-5. This omission caused subsequent plaintiffs to predicate alleged Rule 10b-5 violations by independent auditors on reckless behavior, since that type of professional misconduct is much easier to prove than actual scienter.

EPILOGUE

Congressional critics of the Supreme Court's decision in the *Hochfelder* case insisted that the alleged "flaw" in Rule 10b-5 should be corrected legislatively. In late 1978, legislators introduced a bill in the U.S. House of Representatives to hold negligent auditors civilly liable to investors who relied on false financial statements filed with the SEC. Fortunately for independent auditors, Congress rejected that bill.

Questions

1. Under present technical standards, would auditors be required to disclose a company policy similar to Nay's mail rule that they discover during an audit? Explain. Assuming such disclosure had been required at the time this case took place, would that disclosure have resulted in the mail rule being discontinued?

2. Ernst & Ernst argued that the mail rule was not relevant to its audits of First Securities since that rule only involved personal transactions of Nay and the escrow investors. Do you agree? Why or why not?

3. Define *negligence* as that term has been used in legal cases involving independent auditors. What is the key distinction between negligence and fraud? Between recklessness and fraud? For all three types of professional misconduct, provide an example of such behavior in an audit context.

4. Assume that the investors defrauded by Nay could have filed their lawsuit against Ernst & Ernst under the Securities Act of 1933. How, if at all, do you believe the outcome of their suit would have been affected?

5. Assume that the jurisdiction in which the *Hochfelder* case was filed invoked the legal precedent established by the *Rusch Factors* case. Given this assumption, would the defrauded investors have been successful in pursuing a negligence claim against Ernst & Ernst under the common law? Why or why not?

---

9. *Ibid.*, 194.

SECTION 8

INTERNATIONAL CASES

Livent, Inc.

*The structure of a play is always the story of how the
birds came home to roost.*

Arthur Miller

In 1995, Canadian native Maria Messina achieved one of the most sought-after career
goals in the public accounting profession when she was promoted to partner with
Deloitte & Touche, Chartered Accountants, the Canadian affiliate of the U.S.-based
Deloitte & Touche, LLP. In an interview she granted to an accounting trade publication shortly after receiving that promotion, Ms. Messina noted that, "Becoming a partner is exciting because you are a part of everything."[1] Messina's promotion earned
her the respect and admiration of her family, her friends, and her colleagues and catapulted her to a much higher tax bracket and a more comfortable standard of living.
But another opportunity soon arose, an opportunity that promised even more intrin-
sic and extrinsic rewards for Messina.

   Throughout the 1990s, Livent, Inc., was the only publicly owned company whose
primary line of business was live theatrical productions. Livent's cofounder and the
individual recognized as the creative genius responsible for the company's impressive string of Tony Award–winning shows was Garth Drabinsky. Livent's audit firm was
Deloitte & Touche, Chartered Accountants. Maria Messina served as the engagement
partner for the 1996 audit, after having been the audit manager on several prior audits of the company. Following the completion of the 1996 Livent audit, Drabinsky
asked Messina to leave Deloitte & Touche and become Livent's chief financial officer
(CFO). After carefully weighing the challenges, opportunities, and potential draw-
backs of making the job change, Messina gave up the partnership position with
Deloitte & Touche that she had coveted for years in exchange for a "back office"
but high-paying and high-profile position in the glitzy and glamorous world of show
business.

   Within a few weeks of signing on with Livent, Maria Messina was questioning the
wisdom of her decision. Time budgets, out-of-town travel, inexperienced subordinates, and an array of other common "stressors" faced by partners of major accounting firms had complicated Messina's professional and personal life when she was at
Deloitte. But, at Livent, the pressures she faced were much more intense, much more
difficult to manage and control, even physically debilitating at times. Each passing
month imposed a heavier emotional burden on Messina. By the late summer of 1998,
Messina's life was in complete disarray. A few months later, in January 1999, Messina
pleaded guilty to a federal felony charge for her role in a massive financial fraud
orchestrated by Livent's top executives. Following that plea, the single mother of a
10-year-old daughter faced up to five years in prison and a $250,000 fine.

There Is No Business Like Show Business

The entertainment industry had fascinated Garth Drabinsky from an early age. Unlike
many of his colleagues in the industry, Drabinsky did not benefit from a network of
family members and friends in show business. Instead, Drabinsky relied on his own

---

1. T. Frank, "Opportunity Knocks," *CA Magazine*, March 1997, 27.

drive, inspiration, and indomitable work ethic to claw his way to the top of the volatile and fickle entertainment industry. Born in Toronto in 1947, Drabinsky was struck down by polio at age 3, leaving him with a severe limp for the remainder of his life. The young Canadian refused to allow his physical limitations to prevent him from reaching his goals. In fact, Drabinsky freely admits that his physical problems and his modest upbringing—his father sold air conditioners—were key factors that motivated him to "aim for the stars."

During his college years, Drabinsky made his first foray into show business by publishing a free magazine that provided critiques of movies appearing in local theaters. After graduating from law school, where he concentrated his studies on the entertainment industry, Drabinsky became involved in real estate development. The young attorney hoped to accumulate a nest egg that he could use to begin producing movies and live plays. A successful condominium project provided him with the funds he needed to begin dabbling in motion pictures and Broadway productions. By age 30, Drabinsky had produced three feature-length movies and one Broadway musical, none of which were particularly well received by critics or the ticket-buying public.

In 1979, Drabinsky and a close friend, Myron Gottlieb, decided to enter the show business world via the "back door." The two young entrepreneurs persuaded a prominent Toronto businessman to invest nearly $1 million in a "cinema complex" project they had conceived.[2] This project involved converting the basement of a large shopping mall into a multiscreen theater. The design for the "cineplex" included plush interiors for each theater, luxurious seats, and cappuccino bars in the lobby. Drabinsky intended to make a trip to the local movie theater the captivating experience it had been several decades earlier in the halcyon days of Hollywood.

Most industry insiders predicted that Drabinsky's blueprint for his cineplex concept would fail, principally because the large overhead for his theaters forced his company to charge much higher ticket prices than competitors. But the critics were wrong. Toronto's moviegoers were more than willing to pay a few extra dollars to watch a film in Drabinsky's upscale theaters. Over the next several years, Drabinsky and Gottlieb expanded their company with the help of well-heeled investors whom they convinced to pony up large sums to finance the development of multiscreen theater complexes throughout Canada and the United States. By the mid-1980s, their company, Cineplex Odeon, controlled nearly 2,000 theaters, making it the second-largest theater chain in North America.

Several major investors in Cineplex Odeon eventually began complaining of Drabinsky's unrestrained spending practices. The company's rapid expansion and the increasingly sumptuous designs Drabinsky developed for new theaters required Cineplex Odeon to borrow enormous amounts from banks and other lenders. An internal investigation in 1989 uncovered irregularities in the company's accounting records that wiped out a large profit for the year and resulted in Cineplex Odeon reporting a significant loss instead. The controversy sparked by the discovery of the accounting irregularities gave Cineplex Odeon's major investors the leverage they needed to force Drabinsky and Gottlieb to resign. During the negotiations that led to their departure from the company, Drabinsky and Gottlieb acquired the Pantages Theatre, a large live production theater in Toronto, as well as the Canadian rights to certain Broadway plays.

Within a few weeks after severing their ties with Cineplex Odeon, Drabinsky and Gottlieb had organized Live Entertainment Corporation to produce Broadway-type

2. The key financial amounts reported in this case are expressed in Canadian dollars.

shows in their hometown of Toronto. Drabinsky's concept for this new company, which he coaxed several large investors and lenders to bankroll, was to bring "corporate management" to the notoriously freewheeling and undisciplined show business industry. Following a series of widely acclaimed productions, the company—renamed Livent, Inc.—went public in 1993.[3] In May 1995, Livent filed an application with the Securities and Exchange Commission (SEC) to sell its stock in the United States. The SEC approved that application and Livent's stock began trading on the NASDAQ stock exchange. Within two years, U.S. investors controlled the majority of Livent's outstanding stock.

By early 1998, Livent owned five live production theaters in Canada and the United States, including a major Broadway theater in New York. The company's productions, among them *Fosse, Kiss of the Spider Woman, Ragtime, Show Boat,* and *The Phantom of the Opera,* had garnered a total of more than 20 Tony Awards. Show business insiders attributed Livent's rapid rise to prominence to Garth Drabinsky. After organizing Livent, Drabinsky quickly developed a keen sense of what types of shows would appeal to the public. Even more important, he was able to identify and recruit talented directors, actors, set designers, and the array of other skilled artisans needed to produce successful Broadway shows. The single-minded and domineering Drabinsky micromanaged not only the creative realm of Livent's operations but every other major facet of the company's operations as well, although he relied heavily on his friend and confidant, Myron Gottlieb—who had an accounting background—to help him oversee the company's accounting and financial reporting functions.

Despite the artistic success enjoyed by several Livent productions and the company's growing prominence in the entertainment industry, Garth Drabinsky was dogged by critics throughout the 1990s. The enigmatic Drabinsky had a well-deserved reputation as flamboyant and charming with Wall Street analysts, metropolitan bankers, and fellow corporate executives. But critics were prone to point out that Drabinsky also had a darker side to his personality. "He is—by his own admission—complex and difficult, cranky and litigious, breathtakingly ambitious, singled-minded and self-centered."[4] According to company insiders, Drabinsky could be "tyrannical and abusive"[5] to his subordinates, berating them when they failed to live up to his perfectionist standards or when they questioned his decisions. Maria Messina subsequently revealed that Livent's accountants were common targets of verbal abuse by Drabinsky and other Livent executives. "They [Livent's accountants] were told on a very regular basis that they are paid to keep their [expletive] mouths shut and do as they are [expletive] told. They are not paid to think."[6]

Critics also charged that Drabinsky failed to live up to his pledge of bringing a disciplined style of corporate management to Broadway. In reality, Drabinsky was anything but disciplined in managing Livent's finances. Because he demanded that the company's live productions be "motion-picture perfect," most of Livent's shows, particularly those that were box-office successes, incurred huge cost overruns. By 1998,

3. Drabinsky and Gottlieb's company was not affiliated with the California-based Live Entertainment, Inc. Jose Menendez organized the latter company in 1988 but was murdered along with his wife, Kitty, in August 1989. In one of the many "trials of the century," the Menendez's sons, Lyle and Erik, were subsequently convicted of murdering their parents.

4. K. Noble, "The Comeback King: Garth Drabinsky Is Back, and Creating a Lot of Showbiz Buzz," *MacLean's* (online), 4 June 2001.

5. M. Potter and T. Van Alphen, "Livent Charges $7.5 Million Kickback Scam," *The Toronto Star* (online), 19 November 1998.

6. *Profit,* "Backstage at Livent," May 1999, 29.

Livent was buckling under the huge load of debt Drabinsky had incurred to finance the company's lavish productions. In early 1998, Roy Furman, a Wall Street investment banker and close friend, persuaded Drabinsky to accept a $20 million investment from former Disney executive Michael Ovitz to alleviate Livent's financial problems. A condition of Ovitz's proposed investment was that he be granted sufficient common stock voting rights to allow him to control the company's board of directors.

During the 1980s, Ovitz had reigned as Hollywood's top talent agent. When he became chairman of the Creative Artists Agency, show business periodicals tagged him with the title of "Hollywood's most powerful man." In late 1995, Disney chief executive officer (CEO) Michael Eisner chose Ovitz to serve as his top lieutenant and gave him the title of company president. A little more than one year later, repeated personality clashes between the two Hollywood heavyweights resulted in Eisner dismissing Ovitz. No doubt, Ovitz hoped that Livent would provide him with an opportunity to refurbish his reputation in the entertainment industry, a reputation that had been tarnished during his brief and turbulent stint with Disney. Just as important, taking control of Livent would allow Ovitz to compete head-to-head with his former boss. At the time, Disney's *The Lion King* was a colossal hit on Broadway.

Before agreeing to invest in Livent, the cautious Ovitz retained the Big Five accounting firm KPMG to scrutinize the company's accounting records. After KPMG's "due diligence" investigation yielded a clean bill of health for Livent, Ovitz became the company's largest stockholder in early June of 1998 and took over effective control of the company. Ovitz took a seat on the company's board and became chairman of the board's executive committee, while Furman assumed Drabinsky's former titles of chairman of the board and CEO. Drabinsky was given the titles of vice chairman and chief creative director. In the latter role, Drabinsky continued to oversee the all-important creative facets of Livent's operations. To provide a second opinion on artistic matters, Ovitz appointed the noted producer and songwriter Quincy Jones to Livent's board.

Ovitz also demoted Myron Gottlieb to a vice president position. A former Disney executive who left that company along with Ovitz assumed Gottlieb's former position as Livent's president. Among other changes that Ovitz made in Livent's corporate management structure was hiring former KPMG audit partner Robert Webster to serve as an executive vice president of the company. Webster, who had supervised KPMG's due diligence investigation of Livent's accounting records, was given a broad range of responsibilities but his principal role was to monitor Livent's accounting and finance functions for Ovitz's new management team.

Webster's Summer of Discontent

Like Maria Messina, Robert Webster quickly discovered that the work environment within Livent was much less than ideal. After joining Livent in the early summer of 1998, Webster found that the accounting staff, including Messina, who remained Livent's CFO, was reluctant to discuss accounting matters with him. Webster later testified that some of the Livent accountants "told him that Mr. Drabinsky had warned them not to provide certain financial information until [Drabinsky] had reviewed and approved it."[7] Even more troubling to Webster was Drabinsky's management style. Webster testified that, "I had never before experienced anyone with Drabinsky's

---

7. M. Petersen, "The Roar of the Accountants: The Strange Last Days of a Theater Impresario's Reign," *The New York Times* (online), 10 October 1998.

abusive and profane management style."[8] He was shocked to find that Livent's executives often screamed and swore at the company's accountants. Webster reported that after meeting with Drabinsky, Livent's accountants were often in tears or even nauseous. Following one such meeting, Webster recalled Messina "shaking like a leaf."[9]

When Webster demanded that Livent's accountants provide him with unrestricted access to the company's accounting records, the former KPMG partner became the target of Drabinsky's wrath. Drabinsky accused Webster of attempting to "tear the company" apart with his persistent inquiries and told him that he was there to "service his [Drabinsky's] requirements."[10] Webster refused to be deterred by Drabinsky's bullying tactics. In early August 1998, after Webster began asking questions regarding a suspicious transaction he had uncovered, Messina and four of her subordinates secretly met with him. The five accountants admitted to Webster that Livent's accounting records had been distorted by a series of fraudulent schemes initiated and coordinated by Drabinsky and other top Livent executives.

Webster relayed the disturbing revelations to Livent's board. On August 11, 1998, Roy Furman issued a press release announcing that "significant financial irregularities" adversely affecting Livent's financial statements for the past three years had been discovered. The press release also indicated that Drabinsky and Gottlieb had been indefinitely suspended pending the outcome of a forensic investigation by KPMG. During the fall of 1998, company officials issued successive press releases suggesting that the impact of the accounting irregularities would be more severe than initially thought. Adding to Livent's problems was the suspension of all trading in the company's stock and a series of large class-action lawsuits filed against the company and its officers. In August 1998 alone, 12 such lawsuits were filed.

On November 18, 1998, Livent's board announced that KPMG's forensic investigation had revealed "massive, systematic, accounting irregularities that permeated the company."[11] The press release issued by Livent's board also disclosed that Deloitte & Touche had withdrawn its audit opinions on the company's 1995–1997 financial statements. Finally, the press release reported that Drabinsky and Gottlieb had been dismissed and that Livent had simultaneously filed for bankruptcy in Canada and the United States. A few weeks later, a federal grand jury in New York issued a 16-count fraud indictment against Drabinsky and Gottlieb. When the former Livent executives failed to appear for a preliminary court hearing, a U.S. federal judge issued arrest warrants for the two Canadian citizens and initiated extradition proceedings.

A "Pervasive and Multifaceted" Fraud

Details of the massive fraud allegedly conceived by Garth Drabinsky and Myron Gottlieb were eventually revealed to the public by the SEC, the Ontario Securities Commission—a Canadian agency comparable to the SEC—and publicly available records of various court proceedings in civil lawsuits. In numerous enforcement and litigation releases, SEC officials repeatedly used the descriptive phrase "pervasive and multifaceted" when referring to the Livent fraud. One of the earliest elements of the fraud was a large kickback scheme.

8. A. Clark, "An Epic from Livent: Executive Accuses Drabinsky of Bullying Tactics," *MacLean's* (online), 1 March 1999.

9. *Ibid.*

10. *Ibid.*

11. *In re Livent, Inc. Noteholders Securities Litigation*, 151 F. Supp. 2d 371 (2001).

"As early as 1990, and continuing through 1994, Drabinsky and Gottlieb operated a kickback scheme with two Livent vendors designed to siphon millions of dollars from the company directly into their own pockets."[12] Gottlieb reportedly instructed the two vendors to include in the invoices that they submitted to Livent charges for services that they had not provided to the company. After Livent paid the inflated invoice amounts, Drabinsky and Gottlieb received kickbacks equal to the payments for the bogus services. According to the SEC, over a four-year period in the 1990s, Drabinsky and Gottlieb received approximately $7 million in kickbacks from the two Livent vendors. The fake charges billed to Livent by the vendors were capitalized in "preproduction" cost accounts for the various shows being developed by the company. Legitimate costs charged to those accounts included expenditures to produce sets and costumes for new shows, costs that were amortized over a maximum period of five years.

By the mid-1990s, the kickback scheme and large losses being registered by several of Livent's plays made it increasingly difficult for the company to achieve quarterly earnings targets that Drabinsky and Gottlieb had relayed to Wall Street analysts. The two conspirators realized that if Livent failed to reach those earnings targets, the company's credit rating and stock price would fall, jeopardizing the company's ability to raise the additional capital needed to sustain its operations. Faced with these circumstances, the SEC reported that beginning in 1994 Drabinsky and Gottlieb directed Livent's accounting staff to engage in an array of "accounting manipulations" to obscure the company's financial problems.

These manipulations included such blatant subterfuges as simply erasing from the accounting records previously recorded expenses and liabilities at the end of each quarter. A particularly popular accounting scam within Livent was transferring preproduction costs from a show that was running to a show still in production. Such transfers allowed the company to defer, sometimes indefinitely, the amortization of those major cost items. To further reduce the periodic amortization charges for preproduction costs, Livent's accountants began charging such costs to various fixed asset accounts. These assets were typically depreciated over 40 years, compared with the five-year amortization period for preproduction costs. Eventually, the company's accountants began debiting salary expenses and other common operating expenses to long-term fixed asset accounts.

The SEC estimated that the accounting manipulations understated Livent's expenses by more than $30 million in the mid-1990s. Despite the resulting favorable impact on Livent's financial statements, Drabinsky and Gottlieb eventually realized that additional efforts were needed to embellish the company's financial data. So, beginning in 1996, Drabinsky and Gottlieb organized and carried out what the SEC referred to as a "fraudulent revenue-generating" scheme.

This new scam involved several multimillion-dollar transactions arranged by Drabinsky and Gottlieb. The specific details of these transactions varied somewhat but most of them involved the sale of production rights owned by Livent to third parties. For example, Livent sold the rights to produce *Ragtime* and *Show Boat* in various U.S. theaters to a Texas-based company. The contract for this transaction indicated that the $11.2 million fee paid to Livent by the Texas company was not refundable under any circumstances. However, a secret side agreement arranged by Livent's executives shielded the Texas company from any loss on this deal and, in fact,

---

12. Securities and Exchange Commission, *Accounting and Auditing Enforcement Release No. 1095,* 19 May 1999.

guaranteed it a reasonable rate of return on its large investment. Despite the considerable uncertainty regarding the actual profit, if any, that would ultimately be earned on this and similar transactions, Livent's accounting staff included at least $34 million of revenues on those transactions in the company's 1996 and 1997 income statements.

A final Livent scam documented by the SEC involved inflating reported box-office results for key productions. In late 1997, Livent opened *Ragtime* in a Los Angeles theater. The agreement with that theater allowed it to close the show if weekly ticket sales fell below $500,000. Livent's executives planned to open *Ragtime* on Broadway in January 1998. Those executives realized that if the show fared poorly in Los Angeles, its Broadway opening could be jeopardized. To inflate *Ragtime's* ticket sales during its Los Angeles run, Livent executives arranged to have two of the company's vendors—the same individuals involved in the fraudulent kickback scheme alluded to previously—purchase several hundred thousand dollars of tickets to the show. Livent reimbursed the vendors for these ticket purchases and charged the payments to various fixed asset accounts.

The fraudulent schemes engineered by Livent's executives caused the company's periodic financial statements to be grossly misrepresented. For example, in 1992, the company reported a pretax profit of $2.9 million when the actual figure was approximately $100,000. Four years later, Livent reported a pretax profit of $14.2 million, when it actually incurred a loss of more than $20 million. By 1997, the company's total fixed assets of $200.8 million were overstated by nearly $24 million due to the various accounting schemes.

SEC officials found two features of the Livent fraud particularly disturbing. As the scope of the fraud steadily grew throughout the 1990s, the company's accounting staff found it increasingly difficult to provide meaningful financial data to top management. "Because of the sheer magnitude and dollar amount of the manipulations, it became necessary for senior management to be able to track both the real and the phony numbers."[13] Gordon Eckstein, the company's senior vice president of finance and administration and Maria Messina's immediate superior, allegedly instructed a subordinate to develop computer software that would solve this problem. This software could be used to filter the bogus data out of the company's accounting records. The secret software also served a second purpose, namely, allowing Livent's accountants to record fraudulent transactions "without leaving a paper trail that Livent's outside auditors might stumble across."[14] The accountants processed in a batch mode the fraudulent changes in the accounting records demanded by Livent's executives. When these so-called "adjustments" were processed, they replaced the initial journal entries for the given transactions, making the adjustments appear as if they were the original transactions, thus duping the company's Deloitte auditors.

The second extremely troubling feature of the Livent fraud, according to the SEC, was the matter-of-fact manner in which the company's management team organized and carried out the fraud. Reportedly, Drabinsky, Gottlieb, and Robert Topol, Livent's chief operating officer (COO), regularly met with Eckstein, Messina, and other members of the company's accounting staff to discuss the details of the fraud. At these meetings, the three top executives reviewed preliminary financial reports prepared by the accounting staff and instructed the accountants on the "adjustments" needed to improve or embellish those reports. As suggested earlier, Livent's top executives

---

13. *Ibid.*

14. M. A. Hiltzik and J. Bates, "U.S. Indicts Stage Producer Drabinsky," *Los Angeles Times* (online), 14 January 1999.

relied on coercion and intimidation to browbeat their accountants, including Messina, into accepting these illicit changes. Once the adjustments were processed, "the bogus numbers were presented to Livent's audit committee, the auditors, investors, and eventually filed with the Commission [SEC]."[15]

Keeping the Auditors in the Dark

Press reports of a large accounting fraud involving a public company often prompt scathing criticism of the company's independent audit firm. The disclosure of the Livent fraud in the late summer and fall of 1998 caused Deloitte & Touche to become a target of such criticism. A Canadian financial analyst observed that investors depend on auditors to clamp down on their clients and force them to prepare reliable financial reports. "They [auditors] are the only ones in a position to question the policies, to question the numbers, to make sure they're right."[16]

Critics could readily point to several red flags or fraud risk factors during Deloitte's tenure with Livent that should have placed the accounting firm on high alert regarding the possible existence of financial statement misrepresentations. Among those factors were an extremely aggressive, growth-oriented management team; a history of prior financial reporting indiscretions by Drabinsky and Gottlieb; a constant and growing need for additional capital; and the existence of related-party transactions. Regarding the latter, several of Livent's fraudulent "revenue-generating transactions" that were documented by the SEC involved companies or corporate executives affiliated with Livent or its management team.

In Deloitte's defense, a massive collusive fraud that involves a client's top executives and the active participation of its accountants is extremely difficult to detect. Making matters worse for Deloitte was the contemptuous attitude that Livent's executives had toward independent auditors. At one point, a top Livent officer told a subordinate that independent auditors were a "necessary evil and that it was no one's business how they [Livent's executives] ran their company."[17] Also complicating the Livent audits for Deloitte was the fact Maria Messina and Christopher Craib, two former members of the Livent audit engagement team, had accepted key accounting positions with the company. The personal relationships the auditors had with Messina and Craib may have impaired their objectivity during the Livent engagements.

Christopher Craib replaced Maria Messina as the audit manager assigned to the Livent audit engagement team following Messina's promotion to partner in 1995. After the 1996 audit was completed, Drabinsky hired Craib to serve as Livent's senior controller for budgeting. Not long after joining Livent, Craib, a chartered accountant, became involved in the ongoing effort to segregate Livent's "real" accounting data from its bogus data. In subsequent testimony, Craib recalled meeting with Gordon Eckstein to discuss Livent's schizoid accounting system. Eckstein explained to Craib why it was imperative to track both the real and bogus accounting data. "I have to keep all the lies straight. I have to know what lies I'm telling these people [outside auditors]. I've told so many lies to different people I have to make sure they all make sense."[18]

---

15. Securities and Exchange Commission, *Accounting and Auditing Enforcement Release No. 1095*.

16. J. McCarten, "Auditors Taking the Heat after Financial Scandals," *The Toronto Star* (online), 18 August 1998.

17. Securities and Exchange Commission, *Accounting and Auditing Enforcement Release No. 1096*, 19 May 1999.

18. *Ibid*.

Like Craib, Maria Messina realized that concealing the Livent fraud from the Deloitte auditors was among her primary responsibilities. During a meeting shortly after Messina joined Livent, she became aware of the adversarial attitude that Livent's top executives had toward the company's independent auditors. During this meeting, Topol became angry when Messina raised an issue involving what documents to turn over to Deloitte. Topol responded with an angry outburst. "[Expletive] you and your auditors ... I don't care what they see or don't see."[19]

Despite the efforts of Livent officials to sabotage their independent audits, the company's Deloitte auditors focused considerable attention on several suspicious transactions that they uncovered. The Deloitte auditors became increasingly skeptical of Livent's accounting records in 1996 and 1997 when Drabinsky and his colleagues were scrambling to conceal the deteriorating financial condition of their company while, at the same time, attempting to raise much needed debt and equity capital.

Near the end of the 1996 audit, Deloitte & Touche, LLP, the U.S.-based branch of the firm, initially refused to allow its Canadian affiliate to issue an unqualified audit opinion on Livent's financial statements filed with the SEC. Deloitte's top technical partners in the United States believed that Livent had been much too aggressive in recognizing revenue on a few large transactions—transactions that, unknown to partners of both the firm's Canadian and U.S. affiliates, included fraudulent elements. After a series of meetings between Livent officials and representatives of Deloitte & Touche, LLP, a compromise was reached. Livent agreed to defer the recognition of revenue on one of the two large transactions in question until 1997. In return, Deloitte allowed the company to record the full amount of the revenue for the other disputed transaction.

During 1997, a major transaction with a real estate firm triggered another conflict between Deloitte and Livent management. In the second quarter of that year, the real estate firm purchased for $7.4 million the development rights to a valuable parcel of land owned by Livent. The contract between the two companies included a stipulation or "put agreement" allowing the real estate firm to cancel the transaction prior to the date that it began developing the property. When the Deloitte audit engagement partner learned of the put agreement, he insisted that no revenue could be recorded for the transaction. Complicating matters was the fact that the transaction involved a related party since Myron Gottlieb served on the board of directors of the real estate firm's parent company.

To quell the audit partner's concern, Gottlieb arranged to have an executive of the real estate firm send the partner a letter indicating that the put agreement had been cancelled—which it had not. After receiving the letter, the Deloitte partner told Gottlieb that the revenue resulting from the transaction could be recorded during Livent's third quarter when the put agreement had allegedly been cancelled. At this point, a frustrated Gottlieb ignored the partner's decision and included the disputed revenue in Livent's earnings press release for the second quarter of 1997.

When Deloitte officials learned of the press release, they demanded a meeting with Livent's board of directors. At this meeting, Deloitte threatened to resign. After considerable discussion, Livent's board and the Deloitte representatives reached a compromise. According to a subsequent legal transcript, the board agreed to reverse the journal entry for the $7.4 million transaction in the second quarter, recording it instead during the third quarter. The board also agreed to issue an amended

---

19. Securities and Exchange Commission, *Accounting and Auditing Enforcement Release No. 1097*, 19 May 1999.

earnings release for the second quarter. In exchange for these concessions, Deloitte officials purportedly agreed to allow Livent to reverse certain accrued liabilities that had been recorded at the end of the second quarter. The reversal of those accrued liabilities and the corresponding expenses reduced by approximately 20 percent the profit "correction" reported by Livent in the amended earnings press release for the second quarter.[20]

Another serious disagreement arose between Livent executives and Deloitte auditors shortly after the dispute just described was resolved. During the third quarter of 1997, Livent's management arranged to sell for $12.5 million the naming rights for one of its existing theaters and a new theater that the company was planning to build. Neither Maria Messina nor the Deloitte auditors assigned to the Livent engagement believed that the $12.5 million payment should be recorded immediately as revenue since the contract between Livent and the other party, AT&T, was strictly an oral agreement at the time and since one of the theaters was yet to be built. Gottlieb retained Ernst & Young (E&Y) to review the matter. The report E&Y submitted to Gottlieb did not take a firm position on the revenue recognition issue. Instead, E&Y's report simply suggested that the $12.5 million payment for the naming rights could be "considered" for recording during the third quarter. After receiving a copy of E&Y's report, Deloitte hired Price Waterhouse to review the transaction. When Price Waterhouse reached the same conclusion as E&Y, Deloitte allowed Livent to book the $12.5 million as revenue during the third quarter.

Don't Blame Me, Blame . . .

Resolving the legal implications of a major accounting and financial reporting fraud can require years. However, one Canadian journalist suggested that in the Livent case the legal wrangling may continue even longer, possibly for decades.[21] A key factor complicating the resolution of this case is its "cross-border" nature. Beginning in late 1998, officials from several federal agencies in Canada and the United States became embroiled in a tedious and often unfriendly struggle to determine which agency would be the first to prosecute the key parties involved in the Livent fraud. Those agencies include the Royal Canadian Mounted Police, the Ontario Securities Commission, the SEC, and the U.S. Department of Justice, among others. Law enforcement authorities in the United States failed to win the cooperation of their Canadian counterparts in attempting to extradite Garth Drabinsky and Myron Gottlieb to face a litany of federal fraud charges filed in U.S. courts. Even more frustrating to U.S. authorities was the snail's pace at which Canadian authorities moved in pursuing legal action against the two alleged fraudsters.

While Canadian and U.S. law enforcement authorities tangled over jurisdictional matters, the leading actors in the final Livent "production" waged a public relations war against each other in major metropolitan newspapers and in the courts. Drabinsky and Gottlieb were the most vocal of these individuals. They repeatedly insisted that they were not responsible for the various fraudulent schemes that had been uncovered within Livent. At a press conference held in early 1999, Drabinsky suggested that he had been too busy overseeing Livent's creative operations to become involved in any creative bookkeeping.[22] In his typical Shakespearean manner,

20. *In re Livent, Inc. Noteholders Securities Litigation.* As a point of information, this legal transcript did not include any commentary from Deloitte's perspective regarding the nature and outcome of these negotiations.

21. Noble, "The Comeback King."

22. M. Lewyckyj, "Livent's Accounting Designed to Deceive," *Toronto Sun* (online), 15 January 1999.

Drabinsky declared: "The final act of this tragedy has yet to be played out and, when it is, Myron Gottlieb and I have complete confidence that we will be vindicated."[23]

In January 1999, Myron Gottlieb filed a civil lawsuit against Maria Messina, Christopher Craib, Gordon Eckstein, and three other former Livent accountants; the lawsuit charged those six individuals with responsibility for the Livent accounting fraud. In court documents filed with this lawsuit, Gottlieb alleged that he was not "an expert on accounting practices" and that he relied on Livent's accounting staff to ensure that the company's financial statements were accurate.[24] In responding to that lawsuit, the six named defendants, with the exception of Eckstein, claimed that they had been coerced into participating in the fraud by its principal architects.[25] These defendants also rejected Gottlieb's assertion that he was unfamiliar with accounting practices. "Gottlieb was and remains an experienced businessman with a sophisticated and comprehensive grasp of accounting and auditing issues and intimate knowledge of the details of Livent's accounting practices."[26]

When Eckstein eventually responded to Gottlieb's lawsuit, he charged the Livent cofounder with being a key architect of the accounting fraud. "Gottlieb's denial of responsibility or knowledge of the accounting irregularities at Livent is in complete disregard to the facts as they existed. . . . [He] had the requisite expertise and business acumen to create and help foster the corporate culture at Livent, which ultimately resulted in the alteration of the books and records."[27] Eckstein also claimed that he was not involved in altering Livent's accounting records, although he did admit to relaying the changes demanded by Drabinsky and Gottlieb in those records to Livent's accounting staff. Finally, Eckstein maintained that Maria Messina had played an important role in the fraudulent scheme. "Messina relied on her former position as a partner at Deloitte in dealing with the field audit team once employed at Livent, to ensure that the financial statements of Livent, as presented to the auditors, were approved."[28]

Messina answered Eckstein and other critics by maintaining that she had attempted to dissuade Livent's executives from using accounting gimmicks to boost the company's revenues and profits. She insisted that she had "begged" her former colleagues at Deloitte to crack down on the aggressive revenue recognition policies being used by Livent's management.[29] To support her claim that she had not been a willing member of the Livent conspiracy, Messina pointed out that she had refused to sign the letters of representations for the 1996 and 1997 audits, each of which indicated that there were no material inaccuracies in Livent's financial statements. In fact, near the end of the 1997 audit, Messina had redrafted Deloitte's preformatted letter of representations to remove her name from it.[30]

23. C. Brodesser and M. Peers, "U.S. Indicts Duo in Liventgate," *Variety*, 18 January 1999, 137.

24. *The Gazette* (online), "Livent Co-Founder Sues 6 Employees," 19 February 1999.

25. V. Menon, "Livent Whistle-Blowers File Defence," *The Toronto Star* (online), 1 April 1999.

26. B. Bouw, "Livent Employees Fight Back: 'Gottlieb to Blame,'" *National Post* (online), 1 April 1999.

27. B. Shecter, "Drabinsky's Assertions Refuted," *National Post* (online), 26 June 1999.

28. *Ibid.*

29. *Profit*, "Backstage at Livent." In a deposition filed in one of the many lawsuits triggered by the Livent fraud, Messina described Deloitte's audits of the company as "inadequate." See D. Francis, "Livent: A Bean Counter Scandal," *National Post* (online), 10 May 2001.

30. In a court document, Messina reported that she did not reveal the various Livent fraudulent schemes prior to August 1998 because she feared Drabinsky and Gottlieb and because she believed that she would be "implicated by association." See B. Bouw, "Livent Employees Fight Back: 'Gottlieb to Blame,'" *National Post* (online), 1 April 1999.

After firing Drabinsky and Gottlieb, Michael Ovitz and the members of the new management team he installed at Livent in June 1998 sued the company's co-founders for $325 million for their alleged role in the fraudulent accounting schemes. That lawsuit prompted Drabinsky and Gottlieb to file a $200 million defamation-of-character lawsuit against Ovitz and his colleagues.

In September 1998, Drabinsky sued KPMG, the accounting firm that Ovitz had retained to perform a due diligence investigation earlier in the year and the firm retained by Livent's board of directors in August 1998 to investigate the charges of accounting irregularities revealed by Maria Messina and her subordinates. That lawsuit, which requested damages of more than $26 million, was predicated on the fact that Drabinsky had been a client of KPMG over the past two decades. Drabinksy charged that, by agreeing to perform the forensic audit requested by Livent's board in August 1998, KPMG had placed itself in a conflict of interest between two clients.[31]

Deloitte & Touche was a primary target of the various plaintiffs attempting to hold someone responsible for the Livent debacle and the resulting financial losses. In December 1999, a U.S. federal judge dismissed Deloitte as a defendant in one of those lawsuits filed by Livent's former stockholders. The judge concluded that the plaintiffs had not made a reasonable argument that Deloitte was at least "reckless" in auditing Livent. For lawsuits filed under the Securities and Exchange Act of 1934, as amended by the Private Securities Litigation Reform Act (PSLRA) of 1995, plaintiffs must allege or "plead" that the given defendant was at least "reckless." In another class-action lawsuit filed by Livent creditors, a federal judge ruled in June 2001 that the plaintiffs had met the pleading standard of recklessness, meaning that the lawsuit could proceed. This judge observed that Livent's "accounting manipulations" were so flagrant that there was a reasonable likelihood Deloitte was reckless in failing to discover them. "Deloitte & Touche's actions and omissions in connection with Livent's manipulations of its books and records display acquiescence and passivity that, in this Court's reading of the pleadings, cross over the boundary of ordinary breaches of reasonable care into the zone of recklessness."[32]

EPILOGUE

In July 1999, SFX Entertainment purchased the remaining assets of Livent, ending the company's dramatic and turbulent existence after only 10 years. In June 2000, the disciplinary committee of the Institute of Chartered Accountants of Ontario (ICAO) sanctioned the former Livent accountants who had publicly admitted some degree of involvement in the Livent fraud. Maria Messina, who pleaded guilty to three charges of professional misconduct, was fined $7,500 and suspended from practic-

ing as a chartered accountant for two years. Christopher Craib received a six-month suspension and a $1,000 fine. In March 2007, this same body found three of the Deloitte auditors who had been assigned to the 1997 Livent audit engagement team guilty of professional misconduct and publicly reprimanded them. In October 2007, the ICAO announced that it had levied fines totaling $1.55 million against these three individuals and Deloitte.

---

31. Drabinsky and KPMG ultimately settled this lawsuit out of court. Although the settlement's financial terms were not disclosed, KPMG acknowledged that it had breached its "fiduciary duty" to Drabinsky by agreeing to perform the forensic audit requested by Livent's board.

32. *In re Livent, Inc. Noteholders Securities Litigation.* Note: At last report, the lawsuit filed against Deloitte by Livent's creditors had not been resolved.

The SEC sanctioned Craib and three other Livent accountants who admitted participating in the various facets of Livent's accounting fraud. Craib received a three-year suspension from practicing before the SEC. The SEC has not yet formally sanctioned Maria Messina for her role in the Livent fraud. Likewise, federal prosecutors in the United States have yet to make a sentencing recommendation following Messina's guilty plea to one felony count of violating U.S. federal securities laws. A key factor that federal authorities in the United States will consider in determining Messina's punishment will be whether she continues cooperating with the Canadian and U.S. authorities prosecuting the key architects of the fraud.

As predicted, Canadian law enforcement authorities have been extremely methodical in pursuing their investigation and prosecution of Garth Drabinsky, Myron Gottlieb, and the other key individuals involved in the Livent scandal. In late 2002, the Royal Mounted Canadian Police filed a fraud indictment against Drabinsky and Gottlieb that contained 19 individual charges. In 2008, 10 years after the Livent fraud was exposed, the criminal charges against the two men were still pending. To date, Gordon Eckstein is the only former senior Livent executive who has been convicted or has pled guilty in the case. In 2007, Eckstein pleaded guilty to one count of fraud and agreed to testify against Drabinsky and Gottlieb.

Despite facing a litany of pending criminal charges, Drabinsky has stayed busy working as a "theatrical consultant" around the world—with the obvious exception of the United States. In October 2007, a reality television series inspired by the popular *American Idol* television program debuted on a Canadian television network. In addition to producing the show, Garth Drabinsky serves as one of the five celebrity judges—along with his friend, the noted composer Marvin Hamlisch.

Drabinsky insists that eventually he will be cleared of all charges pending against him. The strong-willed and unrepentant Drabinsky once rebuked critics who compared him to a mythological figure who was unable to capitalize on the fame and fortune he had accumulated as a young man. In referring to that individual, Drabinsky observed, "I think the bastard just gave up too soon."[33]

Questions

1. Identify common inherent risk factors that companies involved in the entertainment industry pose for their independent auditors. List and briefly describe specific audit procedures that would not be used on "typical" audit engagements but would be required for audits of companies involved in live theatrical productions, such as Livent.

2. Compare and contrast the responsibilities of an audit partner of a major accounting firm with those of a large public company's CFO. Which work role do you believe is more important? Which is more stressful? Which role would you prefer and why?

3. Explain why some corporate executives may perceive that their independent auditors are a "necessary evil." How can auditors combat or change that attitude?

4. When auditor–client disputes arise during an audit engagement, another accounting firm is sometimes retained by the client and/or the existing auditor to provide an objective report on the issue at the center of the dispute—as happened during Deloitte's 1997 audit of Livent. Discuss an accounting firm's responsibilities when it is retained to issue such a report.

---

33. M. McDonald, "Garth Drabinsky," *USNews.com*, 11 October 2004.

5. Do you believe Deloitte & Touche should have approved Livent's decision to record the $12.5 million "naming rights" payment as revenue during the third quarter of 1997? Defend your answer. What broad accounting concepts should be considered in determining the proper accounting treatment for such transactions?

6. Maria Messina has testified that when she learned of the accounting irregularities at Livent shortly after becoming the company's CFO, she felt "guilty by association," which prevented her from revealing the fraud to regulatory or law enforcement authorities. Explain what you believe she meant by that statement. Place yourself in Messina's position. What would you have done after discovering the fraudulent schemes affecting Livent's accounting records?

7. What professional standards apply to "due diligence" investigations performed by accounting firms?

Royal Ahold, N.V.

In 1887, a young Dutchman, Albert Heijn, entered the business world by purchasing a small grocery store from his father.[1] The store was located in Oostzaan, a village on the Dutch peninsula known as North Holland, which is also one of the Netherlands' 12 provinces. Unlike his father, who was content to own and operate a small business, Albert had dreams of becoming an entrepreneur on a much larger scale. Within 10 years, the frugal and hard-working Heijn owned two dozen grocery stores scattered throughout the small country.

A key to the early success of Heijn's retail grocery chain was that he designed each of his new stores to meet the specific interests and needs of the community in which it was located. For example, the merchandise stocked by Heijn stores in fishing villages was quite different from the merchandise carried by stores located in farming communities. In metropolitan areas, such as Amsterdam and The Hague, Heijn established large stores that stocked a complete range of food products and household merchandise. In fact, Heijn's company was credited with developing the supermarket concept in the Netherlands; in later years, his company popularized the convenience-store format in his home country.

In the early 1900s, Heijn launched his own brand of baked products including cookies and assorted pastries that he sold in his grocery stores. Over the years to come, the company would develop a wide range of its own products that it marketed under the Albert Heijn brand. In 1973, management changed the company's name to Ahold. The following decade, Queen Beatrix awarded the title "Royal" to the company, a designation reserved for Dutch companies that have operated continuously—and honorably—for 100 years.[2]

By the early 1990s, Royal Ahold ranked among the most prominent and respected corporations in the Netherlands. For several years during that time frame, Royal Ahold was named the most desirable employer in the Netherlands and the company with the best reputation in that nation.[3] The company was also well known outside of the Netherlands. In 1948, the Heijn family had taken the company public. By 2000, the company's stock was registered on stock exchanges around the world, including the New York Stock Exchange.

A financial scandal shortly after the turn of the century besmirched Royal Ahold's sterling reputation, prompted a consumer boycott of the company in the Netherlands, and resulted in many critics insisting that the Dutch royal family rescind

1. This case was originally published by the American Accounting Association in *Issues in Accounting Education*, Vol. 22 (November 2007), 641–660. The case was coauthored by Carol A. Knapp. I would like to thank Tracey Sutherland, Executive Director of the American Accounting Association, for granting permission to include this case in this edition of *Contemporary Auditing: Real Issues and Cases*. An instructional grant provided by Glen McLaughlin funded the development of this case. I would like to thank Mr. McLaughlin for his generous and continuing support of efforts to integrate ethics into business curricula.

2. "N.V." is an abbreviation for "naamloze vennootschap." This phrase indicates that Royal Ahold is a limited liability company under Dutch federal law whose ownership shares are publicly traded. Within the Netherlands, the company is known as Koninklijke Ahold, N.V.; in English-speaking countries, the company is referred to as Royal Ahold, N.V.

3. A. Kolk and J. Pinske, "Stakeholder Mismanagement and Corporate Social Responsibility Crisis," *European Management Journal*, Vol. 24 (February 2006), 59–72.

the company's "royal" designation. In March 2003, *The Economist*, one of Europe's most prominent business publications, referred to the Royal Ahold scandal as "Europe's Enron."[4] The Royal Ahold scandal, along with the accounting fraud at the giant Italian firm Parmalat, caused the European Union (EU) to impose more extensive and rigorous regulation on the financial reporting system and independent audit function within its member nations. The Royal Ahold debacle also focused more attention on the question of whether uniform accounting and auditing standards should be adopted around the globe.

Going Global

By the mid-1970s, Royal Ahold's management realized that for the company to continue to grow it could not limit its operations to the Netherlands because it dominated the retail grocery market in that country. At that point, the company's top executives, who had long been known for their conservative operating and financial policies, startled the Dutch business community by announcing that Royal Ahold would expand its operations into other countries.

Royal Ahold's expansion efforts got off to a slow start but then accelerated rapidly in the 1990s after the company hired a new management team. Until the late 1980s, members of the Heijn family had occupied the key management positions within the firm. In 1987, two grandsons of Albert Heijn, Ab Heijn and Gerrit-Jan Heijn, served as Royal Ahold's two top executives. In September 1987, Gerrit-Jan Heijn was kidnapped and murdered; shortly thereafter, his older brother retired from the company.[5] The professional management team hired to replace the Heijn brothers recognized that the quickest way for Royal Ahold to gain significant market share in the grocery retailing industry outside of the Netherlands was to purchase existing grocery chains in foreign countries. To finance their growth-by-acquisition policy, Royal Ahold's new executives raised large amounts of debt and equity capital during the 1990s.

By 2000, Royal Ahold had purchased retail grocery chains in Asia, Eastern Europe, Latin America, Portugal, Scandinavia, South America, and the United States. This aggressive expansion campaign made Royal Ahold the third-largest grocery retailer worldwide by the turn of the century. At the time, only U.S.-based Wal-Mart and the French firm Carrefour SA had larger annual retail grocery sales than Royal Ahold.

Royal Ahold completed its most ambitious acquisition in 2000 when it purchased U.S. Foodservice, a large food wholesaler headquartered in Columbia, Maryland, a suburb of Washington, D.C. Although Royal Ahold had previously purchased several retail grocery chains along the eastern seaboard of the United States, including New England–based Stop & Shop, U.S. Foodservice was easily the largest U.S. company it had acquired. The U.S. Foodservice acquisition was also important because it signaled the company's commitment to becoming a significant participant in the food wholesaling industry.

In 2003, after purchasing two smaller U.S.-based food distributors, Royal Ahold ranked as the second-largest food wholesaler in the United States—Houston-based

---

4. *The Economist,* "Europe's Enron," 1 March 2003, 55–56.

5. *The Clearing,* a major motion picture released in 2004 that starred Robert Redford and Willem DaFoe, was based upon the key facts surrounding the kidnapping and murder of Gerrit-Jan Heijn, although the setting of the film was changed to the United States. Ironically, the perpetrator of the vicious crime was eventually apprehended when he attempted to purchase food in a grocery store with currency from the ransom that he had been paid by the Heijn family. After serving 12 years of a 20-year sentence, the kidnapper/murderer was released and returned to live with his family in the Netherlands. To protect the individual's privacy, the Dutch media insist on referring to him by his first name only.

Sysco Corporation was the largest. In fact, the three U.S. acquisitions caused food wholesaling to be the company's largest source of revenue, accounting for slightly more than one-half of its annual sales. The company's more than 4,000 retail grocery stores located in 27 countries accounted for the remainder of its annual sales.

Royal Ahold's aggressive expansion plan created significant and largely unexpected problems for the company. Among these problems was the impact that key differences in cultural norms and expectations had on the company's ability to manage its worldwide retail grocery operations. As the company entered new markets, particularly markets outside of Western Europe and the United States, it encountered a wide range of laws, regulations, and cultural nuances that had far-reaching implications for the management of retail grocery operations.

Human resource policies involving hiring practices, performance appraisal, and employee benefits that had been developed in the Netherlands were not necessarily well received by Royal Ahold's new managers and employees in Asia, Latin America, and South America. Likewise, because grocery shopping is a ritual significantly influenced by longstanding cultural norms across the globe, company officials found that customers in new markets often did not appreciate and sometimes flatly rejected the "Dutch" way of organizing and managing a grocery store.

Particularly problematic for Royal Ahold was the staunch opposition of consumers in certain markets to the takeover of their local grocery store by an unknown foreign "invader." Because of such problems, Royal Ahold's executives eventually decided that the best strategy to use in managing their foreign grocery chains was to allow most major decisions to be made by the management personnel of those chains who were typically retained following an acquisition.

The headaches that Royal Ahold encountered due to its rapid expansion into retail grocery markets around the world were compounded by the company's decision to become a major player in the wholesaling segment of the huge food industry in the United States. Because company officials were largely unfamiliar with that segment of the industry, they applied their new hands-off mindset to that acquisition and relied almost exclusively on U.S. Foodservice's executives to oversee the subsidiary's day-to-day operations.

There was one key exception to the hands-off policy that Royal Ahold adopted with respect to its foreign operations. The company's top executives in the Netherlands insisted that foreign operating units be held to the same rigorous performance standards that were imposed on the company's domestic operations. During the 1990s, the company's new management team established a goal of achieving a 15 percent annual growth rate in profits. That overall goal was then used by top management to establish annual earnings targets for each of the company's operating units in the Netherlands and elsewhere.

Royal Ahold's senior management pressured mid- and lower-level managers throughout the company's worldwide network to reach the earnings goal established for their individual operating units. According to a former Royal Ahold official, managers who met their unit's earnings target were rewarded with significant year-end bonuses. "Ahold was determined to maintain earnings growth of at least 15 percent annually. All of the operating units had difficult targets to meet, but the rewards [in the form of bonuses] were good if targets were met."[6] In retrospect, the earnings targets for many of Royal Ahold's newly acquired operating units were unrealistic.

---

6. A. Raghavan, A. Latour, and M. Schroeder, "Questioning the Books—A Global Journal Report: Ahold Faces Scrutiny over Accounting," *Wall Street Journal*, 26 February 2003, A2.

Intense competition and the historically modest profit margins within the food industry prevented many of those units from achieving their annual earnings goals.

Similar to most major corporations, Royal Ahold had an ethical code that discouraged executives and employees from engaging in dishonest or otherwise unethical conduct. The company's "Code of Professional Conduct" included the following section that dealt specifically with accounting and financial reporting matters:

> *The integrity and completeness of record keeping is not only Ahold policy, but also law. We properly, accurately, and fairly record our financial transactions. Preventing fraud is an important priority at Ahold, both to protect Ahold's reputation and to prevent loss. Fraud is defined as committing illicit or illegal acts involving money and/or goods to achieve financial benefit, to benefit oneself or others, at a disadvantage to the company or others.*[7]

Despite such strong statements, beginning in the late 1990s, Royal Ahold's annual financial statements were distorted by a series of fraudulent accounting schemes perpetrated by self-interested executives and their subordinates. When the company's independent auditors discovered the misrepresentations in those financial statements, the prominent corporation suffered widespread embarrassment and condemnation as well as financial problems that threatened its ability to remain a going concern.

Royal Problems

Deloitte Accountants, B.V.,[8] had served as Royal Ahold's "group auditor" since 1973. The "group auditor" designation means that the Netherlands-based Deloitte Accountants oversaw the audits of the company's annual consolidated financial statements, although accounting firms in other countries, such as the United States, participated in those audits. Deloitte shocked Royal Ahold's top executives when the accounting firm announced in early 2003 that it was suspending its fiscal year 2002 audit of the company. According to Deloitte, auditors assigned to various operating units of Royal Ahold had uncovered questionable accounting and financial reporting practices that had to be thoroughly investigated before the audit could be completed.

Deloitte's announcement sent Royal Ahold's stock price into a nosedive. Over a short period of time in early 2003, the company's stock price plummeted by approximately 70 percent. During this same time frame, Standard & Poor's and Moody's slashed Royal Ahold's credit rating, which drove down the market price of the company's outstanding debt securities and made it difficult for the company to raise additional capital in either the debt or equity markets. The problems facing Royal Ahold caused one London-based financial analyst to suggest that there was a "very real risk" that the large firm would be forced into bankruptcy.[9]

Royal Ahold's board of directors responded quickly to the crisis that engulfed the company following Deloitte's decision to suspend its 2002 audit.[10] The board's first major decision was to fire Royal Ahold's chief executive officer (CEO) and chief financial officer (CFO), each of whom had been implicated in the company's

---

7. Royal Ahold, *Code of Professional Conduct: The Basic Rules of the Game* (Zaandaam, the Netherlands: Royal Ahold), 2002.

8. "B.V." is an abbreviation for "besloten vennootschap." This phrase indicates that Deloitte Accountants is a limited liability company whose ownership shares are privately registered and thus not freely transferable.

9. V. de Boer, "Ahold Fires CEO, CFO over Inflated Profit," *Financial Post*, 25 February 2003, FP 12.

10. In fact, major Dutch companies typically have a two-tiered corporate governance structure that consists of a "supervisory board" and a "management board." For purposes of this case, Royal Ahold's two boards are simply referred to as the "board of directors."

accounting irregularities. The board also announced plans to raise much-needed capital by selling several of its foreign subsidiaries. Finally, and most importantly, Royal Ahold's board pledged that it would fully cooperate with all law enforcement and regulatory agencies investigating the company's financial affairs and take the appropriate measures to ensure that the sources of the accounting problems were identified and eliminated. These measures served to bolster the flagging confidence of investors and lenders in the company.

Accounting and Disclosure Issues at Royal Ahold

The investigative agencies that scrutinized Royal Ahold's accounting records identified three principal sources of the material misrepresentations in the company's financial statements. Royal Ahold had improperly included financial data of certain foreign joint ventures in its consolidated financial statements, which resulted in large overstatements of its consolidated revenues and assets. The company had also accounted improperly for the initial investments in many of those foreign joint ventures. Finally, a forensic investigation authorized by Royal Ahold's senior management uncovered extensive fraud in the accounting records of U.S. Foodservice, the company's large United States subsidiary.

Royal Ahold's 2001 financial statements were the final financial statements issued by the company for a complete fiscal year prior to the discovery of the accounting fraud. Exhibit 1 and Exhibit 2 present the comparative income statements and balance sheets, respectively, included in the Form 20-F registration statement filed by Royal Ahold with the Securities and Exchange Commission (SEC) for fiscal 2001. Foreign companies registered with the SEC file a Form 20-F annually with that federal agency, a registration statement comparable in most respects to the Form 10-K filed with the SEC by U.S.-based companies.

EXHIBIT 1

1999–2001 ROYAL AHOLD, N.V., CONSOLIDATED STATEMENTS OF EARNINGS

Royal Ahold, N.V.
Consolidated Statements of Earnings
(expressed in thousands of euros, except share and per share amounts)

| | Fiscal Year | | |
	2001	2000	1999
Net sales	66,593,065	51,541,601	32,824,327
Cost of sales	(51,877,136)	(39,654,486)	(24,470,282)
Gross profit	14,715,929	11,887,115	8,354,045
Selling expenses	(9,650,092)	(7,905,310)	(5,806,134)
General and administrative expenses	(2,087,536)	(1,702,476)	(1,133,239)
Goodwill amortization	(166,496)	(5,236)	—
Exceptional results	(106,413)	—	—
Operating results	2,705,392	2,274,093	1,414,672
Interest income	90,065	87,021	58,589
Interest expenses	(1,020,853)	(808,990)	(420,820)
Exchange rate differences	(101,484)	51,542	(6,479)
Other financial income/expense	(961)	1,162	2,516
Net financial expense	(1,033,233)	(669,265)	(366,194)

(continued)

EXHIBIT 1—
continued

1999–2001 ROYAL
AHOLD, N.V.,
CONSOLIDATED
STATEMENTS OF
EARNINGS

Royal Ahold, N.V.
Consolidated Statements of Earnings
(expressed in thousands of euros, except share and per share amounts)

	Fiscal Year		
	2001	**2000**	**1999**
Earnings before income taxes and minority interest	1,672,159	1,604,828	1,048,478
Income taxes	(457,364)	(401,010)	(283,001)
Earnings after income taxes and before minority interest	1,214,795	1,203,818	765,477
Income from unconsolidated companies	14,553	14,562	7,437
Minority interests	(115,827)	(102,389)	(20,807)
Net earnings	1,113,521	1,115,991	752,107
Dividend cumulative preferred financing shares	38,177	17,444	12,167
Net earnings after preferred dividends	1,075,344	1,098,547	739,940
Weighted average number of common shares outstanding (× 1,000)	857,509	737,403	657,230
Earnings per common share	1.25	1.49	1.13
Diluted earnings per common share	1.23	1.43	1.10

Source: Royal Ahold's 2001 Form 20-F filed with the Securities and Exchange Commission (SEC).

EXHIBIT 2

2000–2001 ROYAL
AHOLD, N.V.,
CONSOLIDATED
BALANCE SHEETS

Royal Ahold, N.V.
Consolidated Balance Sheets
(expressed in thousands of euros)

	December 30, 2001	December 31, 2000
Assets		
Current assets:		
Cash and cash equivalents	1,972,273	1,335,592
Receivables	3,453,869	2,849,275
Inventories	5,067,035	4,100,223
Other current assets	551,106	576,876
Total current assets	11,044,283	8,861,966
Non-current assets:		
Tangible fixed assets, net of depreciation:		
Buildings and land	7,659,768	6,855,938
Machinery and equipment and other	5,698,480	4,730,821
Under construction	713,581	645,892
Total tangible fixed assets	14,071,829	12,232,651

EXHIBIT 2—
continued

2000–2001 ROYAL
AHOLD, N.V.,
CONSOLIDATED
BALANCE SHEETS

Royal Ahold, N.V.
Consolidated Balance Sheets
(expressed in thousands of euros)

	December 30, 2001	December 31, 2000
Intangible fixed assets, net of amortization	5,648,679	3,152,688
Investments in unconsolidated companies	424,066	407,843
Loans receivable	534,157	414,055
Deferred income taxes	513,450	391,421
Total non-current assets	21,192,181	16,598,658
Total assets	32,236,464	25,460,624
Liabilities and shareholders' equity		
Current liabilities:		
Loans payable	1,848,912	2,335,345
Taxes payable	715,850	551,185
Accounts payable	6,029,505	5,185,432
Accrued expenses	1,530,520	1,418,778
Other current liabilities	945,799	710,120
Total current liabilities	11,070,586	10,220,860
Long-term liabilities:		
Subordinated loans	1,779,684	1,779,907
Other loans	9,282,752	7,183,514
Total subordinated loans & other	11,062,436	8,963,421
Capitalized lease commitments	1,512,236	1,336,567
Deferred income taxes	437,982	362,949
Other provisions	1,576,570	1,396,882
Total long-term liabilities	14,589,224	12,059,819
Commitments and contingencies (note 20)		
Minority interest	684,540	677,379
Shareholders' equity:		
Cumulative preferred shares	—	—
Cumulative preferred financing shares	64,829	64,829
Common shares	230,245	204,213
Additional paid-in capital	11,218,491	8,675,969
Revaluation reserve	20,521	26,124
Reserve shareholdings	34,668	14,589
Reserve for exchange rate differences	(189,714)	(85,270)
General reserve	(5,486,926)	(6,397,888)
Total shareholders' equity	5,892,114	2,502,566
Total liabilities and shareholders' equity	32,236,464	25,460,624

Source: Royal Ahold's 2001 Form 20-F filed with the Securities and Exchange Commission (SEC).

Until late 2007, the SEC required a foreign company such as Royal Ahold to include in its annual Form 20-F a schedule that reconciled its net income determined by accounting principles applied in its home country to the net income that would have been produced by the application of U.S. generally accepted accounting principles (GAAP). Exhibit 3 presents those reconciliations for the three-year period 1999–2001.

EXHIBIT 3

RECONCILIATION OF ROYAL AHOLD'S NET EARNINGS BASED ON DUTCH GAAP TO ITS NET EARNINGS BASED ON U.S. GAAP

Reconciliation of Royal Ahold's Net Earnings Based on Dutch GAAP to Its Net Earnings Based on U.S. GAAP (expressed in thousands of euros)			
	Fiscal Year		
	2001	2000	1999
Net earnings in accordance with dutch GAAP	1,113,521	1,115,991	752,107
Items having the effect of increasing (decreasing) reported net earnings:			
a) Goodwill	(728,210)	(300,266)	(147,378)
b) Pensions	23,811	16,596	6,552
c) Revaluation of real estate	1,882	2,175	2,263
d) Restructuring costs	33,219	(1,143)	(19,202)
e) Other provisions	(57,556)	(21,434)	(28,630)
f) Sale-leaseback of property	(137,421)	—	—
g) Derivatives	(132,549)	—	—
h) Software costs	(5,360)	(5,360)	10,109
i) Deferred taxes	46,648	4,494	9,825
Subtotal	157,985	811,053	585,646
j) Dividends on cumulative preferred financing shares	(38,177)	(17,444)	(12,167)
Net earnings in accordance with U.S. GAAP applicable to common shares	119,808	793,609	573,479

Source: Royal Ahold's 2001 Form 20-F filed with the Securities and Exchange Commission (SEC).

Joint Venture Accounting

The growth-oriented policies of the management team hired to replace Ab and Gerrit-Jan Heijn stressed the importance of not only achieving an annual earnings growth rate of 15 percent but also placed a heavy emphasis on rapidly expanding the company's annual revenues. The new management team established a goal of doubling Royal Ahold's sales every five years. Royal Ahold's growth-through-acquisition strategy allowed the company to increase its reported sales from approximately 7.7 billion euros in 1990 to 62.7 billion euros in 2002. This dramatic increase in revenues yielded important benefits for the company. Most important, the impressive revenue growth gave Royal Ahold increasing credibility in the global equity and debt markets, which, in turn, allowed the company to raise the capital needed to finance its expansion program.

During the fiscal 2002 audit of Royal Ahold, Deloitte Accountants uncovered evidence suggesting that the company's consolidated revenues had been overstated. When Royal Ahold invested in a foreign company, it often acquired exactly a 50 percent ownership interest in the given company. Nevertheless, Royal Ahold would fully consolidate the company's financial data in its annual financial statements. Dutch accounting rules at the time permitted a parent company to fully consolidate the financial data of a joint venture company if the parent could control that firm's operations. Such control could be evidenced by a more than 50 percent ownership interest in the joint venture company or by other means.

Since Royal Ahold had exactly a 50 percent ownership interest in several foreign firms, the company's executives had to persuade the Deloitte auditors that they exercised effective control over those firms' operations to include their financial data in Royal Ahold's consolidated financial statements. To accomplish this goal, the company's top executives gave the auditors letters signed by key officials of the given joint venture companies. These letters informed the auditors that despite having only a 50 percent ownership interest in the company in question, Royal Ahold exercised effective control over the company's operations. In fact, Royal Ahold's management team had goaded officials of the joint venture companies to provide these letters to the Deloitte auditors. At the same time the "control letters" were forwarded to Deloitte, Royal Ahold's management signed "side letters" addressed to the executives of the joint venture companies that negated the control letters. The side letters indicated that major decisions affecting the joint venture companies would be made mutually by Royal Ahold executives and the other owners or executives of those companies.

Because Royal Ahold did not have effective control over the joint venture companies in which it had only a 50 percent ownership interest, those companies' financial data should not have been fully consolidated in the annual Royal Ahold financial statements. For Dutch accounting purposes, the joint ventures' financial data should have been "proportionately" consolidated. For example, 50 percent of the total revenues and expenses of the joint venture companies should have been included in Royal Ahold's annual consolidated income statement.

The decision to fully consolidate the financial data of the joint venture companies resulted in material errors in Royal Ahold's consolidated financial statements. In its 2001 consolidated balance sheet, Royal Ahold reported total assets of 32.2 billion euros. That figure included 4.4 billion euros of assets that Dutch regulatory authorities required Royal Ahold to "deconsolidate" when the company subsequently issued restated financial statements. Likewise, the improper joint venture accounting overstated Royal Ahold's reported consolidated revenues of 66.6 billion euros for 2001 by 12.2 billion euros.

Besides improperly accounting for its ownership interests in numerous joint venture companies, Royal Ahold failed to disclose that it had an obligation to purchase the ownership interests of certain investors in those companies. For example, Royal Ahold had committed itself to purchasing the residual ownership interest in a joint venture company based in Argentina if that company defaulted on its outstanding debt. Because of poor economic conditions in South America, the Argentine company defaulted on its outstanding debt in 2002—resulting in Royal Ahold being required to buy out the company's other investors.

Initial Accounting for Investments in Foreign Joint Ventures

In the late 1990s, Dutch accounting principles allowed companies to charge off against stockholders' equity goodwill arising from the acquisition of another company. Under U.S. GAAP at the time, companies were required to report goodwill resulting from an acquisition as an asset and to amortize that asset to expense over a time period not to exceed 40 years.

As Royal Ahold acquired ownership interests in an increasing number of companies during the late 1990s, the company became increasingly aggressive in accounting for the initial purchase transactions. In particular, Royal Ahold inflated the amount of goodwill arising from acquisitions of other companies. The company also improperly charged off various acquisition-related expenses to stockholders' equity at the time of each acquisition. These abusive accounting practices helped Royal Ahold management meet or exceed its goal of achieving 15 percent earnings growth each year. The restated financial statements subsequently issued by Royal Ahold revealed that improper "acquisition accounting" had inflated the company's reported net income for 2001 and 2000 by 36 million euros and 8 million euros, respectively.

Fraudulent Accounting at U.S. Foodservice

Deloitte Accountants' U.S. affiliate, Deloitte & Touche, audited the financial statements of U.S. Foodservice after that company was acquired by Royal Ahold in 2000. During the fiscal 2002 audit of U.S. Foodservice, the Deloitte auditors uncovered improper accounting decisions that had a material impact on the company's reported profit for that year. The improper accounting at U.S. Foodservice also materially distorted the consolidated net income of Royal Ahold. Deloitte's subsequent investigation revealed that U.S. Foodservice had been intentionally misrepresenting its financial statements for several years prior to its acquisition by Royal Ahold.

The accounting fraud at U.S. Foodservice involved "promotional allowances." Because the food wholesaling industry is intensely competitive, the companies operating in that industry have very small profit margins on their sales. In fact, the profit margins within the industry result principally from rebates, quantity discounts, "program money," and other promotional allowances paid to food wholesalers by their suppliers or vendors. For example, if U.S. Foodservice purchased $100 million of merchandise from General Mills during 2002, General Mills may have refunded 5 percent of that amount to U.S. Foodservice. Generally, the more merchandise purchased from a vendor by a food wholesaler, the larger the promotional allowance on a percentage basis.

U.S. Foodservice had various contractual agreements with its vendors regarding the volume of promotional allowances to which it was entitled and the timing of the related payments. A common agreement involved basing the prepayment of promotional allowances to U.S. Foodservice on an expected minimum amount of purchase volume over a multiyear period. Suppose, for example, that U.S. Foodservice expected to purchase $30 million from a given vendor over the three-year period 2000–2002. The vendor may have agreed to pay U.S. Foodservice $900,000, or 3 percent, of that amount as a promotional allowance. Most likely, the payment would have been made in early 2000, within the first few weeks of the period covered by the contractual agreement between the two parties.

Despite the material effect that promotional allowances had on U.S. Foodservice's operating results, the company did not have a systematic method of accounting for those allowances. "USF had no comprehensive, automated system for tracking the amounts owed by vendors pursuant to the promotional allowance agreements."[11] The absence of proper internal controls over promotional allowances provided an opportunity for dishonest employees to overstate those allowances for accounting

---

11. Securities and Exchange Commission, *Complaint in re SEC v. Resnick et al.*, July 2004. (Available at SEC website: http://www.sec.gov).

purposes, which is exactly what occurred beginning in the late 1990s. When Royal Ahold acquired U.S. Foodservice in 2000, the improper accounting for promotional allowances escalated. Apparently, many U.S. Foodservice managers began overstating promotional allowances to ensure that their operating units reached the challenging earnings goals assigned to them by Royal Ahold.

Among the most common methods used by U.S. Foodservice managers to overstate their promotional allowances was to simply inflate the promotional allowance percentages allegedly being paid by given vendors. If a vendor had agreed to pay a 5 percent refund on purchases, U.S. Foodservice might record a promotional allowance equal to 7 percent of the purchases made from that vendor. Another common scheme was "front loading" promotional allowances. For example, suppose that a vendor paid U.S. Foodservice a $2 million promotional allowance for the three-year period 2000–2002. U.S. Foodservice might record the full amount of that allowance as a reduction in cost of sales for 2000 rather than prorating the allowance over the three-year period. Eventually, some U.S. Foodservice managers resorted to recording totally fictitious promotional allowances. These fictitious promotional allowances were typically recorded as "topside" adjustments to U.S. Foodservice's financial statements at the end of an accounting period.[12]

Of the three principal accounting frauds used by Royal Ahold to misrepresent its reported operating results, the improper accounting for promotional allowances at U.S. Foodservice easily had the most dramatic impact on the company's reported profits. In 2001, alone, the improper accounting for the promotional allowances overstated Royal Ahold's earnings by approximately 215 million euros. This amount accounted for 60 percent of the net overstatement of Royal Ahold's 2001 reported net income. As shown in Exhibit 1, the company reported a net income of 1.11 billion euros for 2001; the actual earnings figure for that year was 750 million euros.

Pinpointing Responsibility for the Royal Ahold Fiasco

In the fall of 2003, Royal Ahold issued restated financial statements for 2000, 2001, and the first three quarters of 2002. The net income figures that Royal Ahold originally reported for those three periods had been overstated by 17.6 percent, 32.6 percent, and 88.1 percent, respectively. The corresponding overstatements of the company's reported revenues for those three periods were 20.8 percent, 18.6 percent, and 13.8 percent, respectively.

Similar to other recent accounting and financial reporting scandals, the public disclosure of the Royal Ahold fraud triggered a search by regulatory agencies, law enforcement authorities, the business press, and the investment community for the parties responsible for the fraud. Among the most culpable parties were the top executives of Royal Ahold. The new management team hired by the company's board to replace Ab and Gerrit-Jan Heijn created an environment in which fraud often develops and flourishes. The pressure exerted by that management team on their subordinates to achieve unrealistic earnings and revenue goals—coupled with the significant incentive compensation that could be earned by reaching those goals—almost certainly prompted much of the self-serving behavior within Royal Ahold.

Despite the fact that Royal Ahold's Deloitte auditors were intentionally misled by the company's executives and the fact that those auditors were ultimately responsible for ending the fraud, many parties believed that Deloitte should have discovered and revealed the fraud earlier than it did. In fact, Deloitte was named as a defendant in

12. "Topside" adjustments are made directly to a company's financial statements without first being recorded in its accounting records.

several large class-action lawsuits filed subsequent to the first published reports of the fraud. In defense of the Deloitte auditors, they faced an onerous task each year in planning and coordinating an annual audit that was, in reality, audits of dozens of individual operating units loosely organized under the Royal Ahold corporate umbrella.

Many parties also held regulatory agencies and oversight bodies within the accounting profession at least partially responsible for the Royal Ahold debacle. The Royal Ahold case clearly confirmed the need for what the London-based *Financial Times* referred to as "cross-border cooperation" between and among the regulatory agencies and rule-making bodies that oversee financial reporting and independent auditing across the globe.[13] In recent years, a spirit of competition rather than cooperation has often prevailed between such organizations, particularly between those organizations in the United States and those in other developed countries.

The principal source of tension among international rule-making bodies in the accounting profession has been differing philosophies regarding what should be the fundamental nature of professional standards. The Financial Accounting Standards Board in the United States has generally insisted on issuing "prescriptive" or detailed accounting standards. On the other hand, the International Accounting Standards Board, which is responsible for issuing International Financial Reporting Standards (IFRS) that EU-based companies were required to adopt by 2005, believes that accounting standards should be general guidelines that are principles based. This philosophical difference often results in financial statements prepared for a company under U.S. and EU accounting rules that are not comparable. Such lack of comparability can result in confusion on the part of financial statement users and, ultimately, in less-than-optimal decisions on their part.

Even more tension between international oversight bodies in the accounting and auditing disciplines was spawned by the Royal Ahold case when the U.S.-based Public Company Accounting Oversight Board (PCAOB) used the case to justify one of its most controversial policies. This policy required non-U.S. accounting firms to register with the PCAOB and be subject to the PCAOB's regulatory oversight. As the Royal Ahold scandal was unfolding, the PCAOB implied that the case demonstrated that foreign accounting and auditing regulatory bodies were failing to fulfill their oversight responsibilities.[14] The PCAOB's insinuation prompted indignant responses from professional organizations within several member nations of the EU and other nations as well. For example, the Japanese Institute of Certified Public Accountants (JICPA) sent an open letter to the SEC in which it criticized the PCAOB's policy. "We believe that the oversight system [for independent audits] in Japan should be relied upon without necessitating PCAOB inspection. Japan has an oversight system which is equivalent to the oversight required of professional accountants in the U.S."[15]

Finally, many parties charged that a large measure of responsibility for the recent series of audit failures involving multinational corporations such as Royal Ahold and Parmalat should be borne collectively by the small fraternity of international accounting firms that dominate the global auditing discipline. According to the *Financial Times*, the major international accounting firms have "franchised their names like

13. P. Koster, "Europe's Auditors Should Give Us the Bad News," *Financial Times*, 19 January 2004, 13.

14. A. de Jong, D. DeJong, G. Mertens, and P. Roosenboom, "Royal Ahold: A Failure of Corporate Governance." Working paper presented at Erasmus University, Rotterdam, the Netherlands, 14 January 2005.

15. Letter addressed to Jonathan Katz, member of the SEC, dated June 27, 2003, from Akio Okuyama, President and CEO of the Japanese Institute of Certified Public Accountants. (Available at SEC website: http://www.sec.gov).

the McDonald's burger chain, but without its quality control."[16] The *Financial Times* went on to note that the major accounting firms are, in fact, only "loose confederal" organizations. As a result, users of audited financial statements of multinational corporations located across the globe have no basis for judging the quality of those audits even if they are performed by accounting firms within the same organization.

EPILOGUE

Following the public disclosure of the Royal Ahold fraud in 2003 both Dutch and U.S. law enforcement authorities filed criminal charges against the company and several of its former executives. The *Financial Times* reported that the Royal Ahold case was the "most significant white-collar criminal case"[17] ever pursued by federal authorities in the Netherlands. Shortly after criminal charges were filed in the case, a Dutch prosecutor asked the SEC not to pursue the charges that it had filed against the company and its former executives since doing so would raise a "double jeopardy" issue under Dutch law. In responding to the request, the SEC noted, "Because of the importance of the case in the Netherlands and the need for further cooperation between the SEC and regulatory authorities in other countries, the Commission has agreed to the Dutch prosecutor's request."[18]

In September 2004, the fraud charges filed against Royal Ahold by Dutch law enforcement authorities were settled. The settlement required Royal Ahold to pay a fine of approximately 8 million euros. In May 2006, a Dutch court found three of Royal Ahold's former executives guilty of fraud charges that had been filed against them. Those executives included the company's former CEO and CFO. The tribunal of judges that presided over the case gave the three former executives suspended

prison sentences ranging from four to nine months. In addition, the three men received fines ranging from 120,000 euros to 225,000 euros. One of the judges who presided over the case defended the light sentences imposed on the three individuals. This judge maintained that although the Royal Ahold fraud was unfortunate and embarrassing to the Dutch business community and Dutch citizens, it was not nearly as serious as either the Enron scandal in the United States or the Parmalat scandal in Italy.[19]

A shareholders' activist group in the Netherlands was appalled by the minimal penalties imposed on the three former Royal Ahold executives. A spokesperson for that group noted, "the judgment sends a signal to managers that no matter what they do, the risk of a heavy punishment is minimal. In the United States, a conviction on the same facts would have led to a prison term of more than 10 years. This is Holland at its smallest."[20]

In July 2004, the SEC announced that it had filed fraud charges against four former executives of U.S. Foodservice. These individuals included the company's former CFO, former chief marketing officer, and two former executives in the company's purchasing division. The two former purchasing executives settled the charges by agreeing to permanent injunctions that

16. J. Plender, "Problems at Ahold, Parmalat, and Now Adecco Raise New Questions about How Global Accounting Firms Work with Multinationals," *Financial Times*, 22 January 2004, 15.

17. I. Bickerton, "Four Ahold Directors Face Court Hearing in Accounting Scandal," *Financial Times*, 6 March 2006, 28.

18. Securities and Exchange Commission, *Accounting and Auditing Enforcement Release No. 2124*, 13 October 2004.

19. T. Sterling, "Royal Ahold Executives Fined after Conviction," *Associated Press Online*, 22 May 2006.

20. *Ibid.*

prohibited them from being officers or directors of public companies and by forfeiting stock market gains they had earned on the sale of Royal Ahold's common stock during the course of the fraud. In September 2006, the former CFO pleaded guilty to one count of conspiracy and was given three years of probation by a federal judge. In November 2006, a federal jury found U.S. Foodservice's former chief marketing officer guilty of conspiracy and federal securities fraud. The following year he was sentenced to seven years in federal prison.[21]

In February 2006, the SEC filed charges against two former auditors of U.S. Foodservice, the audit engagement partner and senior audit manager who had been assigned to the company's 1999 audit engagement team. From 1996 through the conclusion of the 1999 audit in April 2000, KPMG had served as the independent audit firm of U.S. Foodservice. When the company was acquired by Royal Ahold in 2000, Deloitte Accountants, B.V., chose Deloitte & Touche to audit the U.S. Foodservice financial statements that were to be incorporated in Royal Ahold's consolidated financial statements.

The SEC alleged that the two former KPMG auditors violated numerous generally accepted auditing standards (GAAS) during the performance of the 1999 U.S. Foodservice audit and, in fact, had identified several instances in which the company had improperly recorded promotional allowances. According to the SEC, the two auditors used white correction liquid to obscure audit exceptions that documented improper promotional allowances booked by the company. Those audit exceptions were allegedly masked with correction liquid before the U.S. Foodservice workpapers were turned over to the SEC—the federal agency had requested the workpapers during the course of its investigation of the U.S. Foodservice accounting fraud. The SEC also charged that the two auditors failed to inform U.S. Foodservice's audit committee of serious internal control problems related to promotional allowances that they discovered during the 1999 audit.

Among other allegations, the SEC charged that the two auditors frequently relied on implausible representations made to them by client officials. By failing to investigate those suspicious statements and other red flags apparent during the 1999 audit, the SEC maintained that the two auditors failed to exercise a proper degree of professional skepticism, failed to propose proper adjustments to U.S. Foodservice's financial statements, and failed to collect sufficient competent evidence to support the audit opinion rendered on those financial statements. In commenting on the case, an SEC spokesperson noted, "These auditors had evidence in their hands that could have stopped the fraud in its tracks. Instead, because they failed to exercise appropriate professional skepticism, the fraud was allowed to continue."[22,23]

In November 2005, the SEC announced that it had filed enforcement actions against several individuals who were employees or executives of major U.S. Foodservice vendors. According to the SEC, each of these individuals had signed false confirmations regarding the amount of promotional allowances owed to U.S. Foodservice by their given company. The SEC reported that several of these individuals had been pressured by U.S. Foodservice management personnel to sign and return the false confirmations to Deloitte. In one case, an executive of a food vendor signed a confirmation indicating that his company owed U.S. Foodservice $3.2 million when the actual amount was only $68,000. Each of the individuals agreed to pay a $25,000 fine to the SEC to settle the charges filed against them. In commenting on the settlement of these charges, an SEC spokesperson observed, "The use of third-party

---

21. In March 2007, Royal Ahold sold U.S. Foodservice to two U.S.-based private equity firms.

22. A. K. Walker, "SEC Faults KPMG Audits," *The Baltimore Sun*, 17 February 2006, 1E.

23. In January 2008, an administrative law judge issued an "initial decision" that cleared the two KPMG auditors of all charges filed against them by the SEC. The SEC may appeal that decision and seek to overturn it. As of May 2008, the SEC had not reported whether it intended to appeal the judge's decision. The SEC did not file any charges against members of the Deloitte & Touche audit engagement teams assigned to the 2000 and 2001 U.S. Foodservice audits.

confirmations is an important part of the audit process, and the Commission will hold accountable those who work to subvert it."[24]

Also in November 2005, Royal Ahold announced that it had reached an agreement to settle a large class-action lawsuit filed against it by the company's stockholders and former stockholders. Under the terms of the agreement, Royal Ahold contributed approximately 1.1 billion euros to a settlement pool that would be distributed to the class-action plaintiffs. Shortly after the announcement of this settlement, another class-action lawsuit was filed by Royal Ahold's U.S. stockholders against the company's Deloitte auditors. That pending lawsuit seeks damages of approximately 3 billion euros.

In responding to the controversy generated by the Royal Ahold debacle, the European Parliament, which is the legislative body of the EU, amended the "8th Directive" that includes the various guidelines and rules to be followed by accounting firms performing independent audits of EU-based companies.[25] The new 8th Directive includes a requirement that foreign accounting firms involved in the audits of EU-based companies must be registered with regulatory authorities in the EU. A European publication noted that this new requirement was an apparent "tit-for-tat response" to the comparable requirement of the PCAOB.[26]

Among other changes, the revised 8th Directive imposes greater responsibility on group auditors to review and pass judgment on the overall quality of an independent audit and mandates that member nations of the EU establish "effective investigative and disciplinary systems" for accounting firms that perform independent audits. The revised directive also establishes common rules regarding the appointment and resignation of independent auditors, requires that auditors obtain appropriate training regarding International Financial Reporting Standards and International Standards of Auditing, and requires audit clients to disclose the fees paid to their independent auditors for both audit and nonaudit services.

In March 2006, the SEC issued a document entitled *SEC Rulemaking and Other Initiatives: Accommodations*. That document outlines accommodations or concessions that the SEC had agreed to make regarding various stipulations of the Sarbanes-Oxley Act of 2002. One of those concessions involved the SEC's requirement that foreign accounting firms that "audit or provide substantial services relating to the audit of an SEC-registered entity" must register with, and be periodically inspected by, the PCAOB. According to the SEC document, the PCAOB is permitted to place "varying degrees of reliance on inspections of foreign accounting firms by the home country's oversight body, based on a sliding scale—the more independent and robust a home country system, the higher the reliance on that system." Apparently, this accommodation means that if the EU's 8th Directive is fully implemented by EU member nations, most accounting firms in those nations will be exempt from the PCAOB's oversight.[27]

Questions

1. To arrive at the U.S. GAAP-based net income figures shown in Exhibit 3, Royal Ahold fully consolidated the operating results of the companies in which it held a 50 percent equity interest. For purposes of determining its U.S. GAAP-based net income figures, what accounting method should the company have applied to

24. S. Taub, "SEC Charges Seven in Ahold Fraud," *CFO.com*, 3 November 2005.

25. When the European Parliament adopts a "directive," each member nation of the EU is committed to initiating legislation that, if enacted, would implement the requirements of that directive. However, the relevant legislative body within each EU nation may or may not fully adopt the stipulations of a new directive.

26. European Information Service, *European Report* (online), "Auditing: Commission Proposes Tough New Rules to Restore Market Confidence," 17 March 2004.

27. By 2008, more than 1,800 accounting firms had registered with the PCAOB; approximately one-third of these firms were non-U.S. accounting firms from more than 70 countries.

those investments? How would the application of this latter method have affected the U.S. GAAP-based net income amounts?

2. The application of Dutch GAAP and U.S. GAAP to Royal Ahold's financial data produced significantly different net earnings figures for the company each year. Explain what is meant by "earnings quality." Suppose that the application of IFRS to a company's financial data produces a higher net income for that company than the application of U.S. GAAP. Does this mean that the U.S. GAAP-based net income figure is of "higher quality" than the net income figure yielded by IFRS? Explain.

3. Accounting for promotional allowances in the retailing and wholesaling industries has long been a controversial topic. In 2002, the Emerging Issues Task Force (EITF) of the Financial Accounting Standards Board began studying that issue. What changes, if any, did the EITF make in the recommended accounting for such promotional allowances?

4. Identify the factors that complicate an independent audit of a multinational company. Explain how these factors affected the audits of Royal Ahold that were performed by Deloitte Accountants, B.V., and its affiliated firms.

5. Briefly describe the three elements of the "fraud triangle." Identify specific fraud risk factors that were present during the audits of Royal Ahold that were performed by Deloitte Accountants. How should those risk factors have affected Deloitte's audits?

6. What audit procedures would likely have been the most effective for detecting the fraudulent accounting for U.S. Foodservice's promotional allowances?

7. Royal Ahold's two major business segments were food wholesaling and retail grocery chains. Identify and briefly explain three key differences in the overall design of an audit for those two types of business segments.

CASE 8.3

Kansayaku

Kokai saki ni tatazu [repentance never comes first]

Japanese proverb

Satoshi Hirata served on the audit staff of Asahi, one of Japan's four largest public accounting firms.[1] Like its three principal rivals, Asahi was affiliated with one of the Big Four international accounting firms, namely, KPMG. Throughout the spring of 2003, Hirata had been assigned to the audit of Resona, a large metropolitan bank. The bank was being audited jointly by Asahi and Shin Nihon, the Japanese affiliate of Ernst & Young. On April 24, 2003, after completing his work for the day on the Resona engagement, Satoshi Hirata returned to his 12-story apartment building in central Tokyo, went to the roof of that building, and leaped to his death.

Disloyal Auditors

Although Satoshi Hirata did not leave a note explaining his decision to take his life, law enforcement authorities subsequently learned that the young auditor was distressed by his job. At the time, Resona and Japan's other major banks were experiencing major financial problems. For well over a decade, Japan's handful of "megabanks" had routinely embellished their reported financial health by, among other means, refusing to provide adequate reserves for their expected loan losses. In the spring of 2003, Resona's financial condition had deteriorated to the point that its independent auditors doubted the bank could survive without a large infusion of capital from another bank or the federal government.

Hirata, one of the subordinate auditors on Resona's joint team of Asahi and Shin Nihon auditors, knew that Resona was technically insolvent and had been for years despite the fact the bank had received unqualified audit opinions each year on its annual financial statements. Hirata was apparently concerned that his superiors would issue a similar opinion at the conclusion of the audit to which he was assigned. According to one newspaper report, Mr. Hirata's suicide was intended as a "dramatic gesture to persuade his seniors that Japan could no longer afford to keep covering over the cracks."[2] The "cracks" referred to in this quotation were the huge and unreported financial problems facing Resona and Japan's other major banks.

Following Mr. Hirata's death, Asahi withdrew from the Resona audit engagement. Asahi's resignation meant that Shin Nihon would be forced to decide the large bank's future. Resona's president, Yasuhisa Katsuta, a prominent political power broker in Japan, never doubted that Shin Nihon would give his bank a clean bill of health. But he was wrong. When the Shin Nihon auditors insisted that the bank seek outside financing to remedy its financial problems, Katsuta accused them of "betraying" his firm.[3] A few days after the auditors refused to give Resona an unqualified audit opinion, Japan's federal government announced that an emergency infusion of government funds equivalent to $17 billion was necessary to rescue the bank from imminent bankruptcy. To fully understand Mr. Katsuta's reaction to Shin Nihon's decision, it is

---

1. "Kansayaku" is a generic term for "inspector" or "auditor" in the Japanese language.

2. M. Nakamoto and D. Pilling, "Resona's Downfall," *Financial Times*, 13 June 2003, 11.

3. *Ibid.*

necessary to study the history of Japan's banking system and its independent audit function.

Okurasho

By the end of World War II, Japan's economy was practically destroyed. Over the following five years, General Douglas MacArthur of the U.S. Army supervised the post-war occupation of Japan by the Allied Powers. In carrying out his mission to convert the Japanese nation into a democracy and to establish a free market economic system within the country, General MacArthur largely succeeded in his attempt to dismantle Japan's ancient political and economic infrastructure. But one important feature of that infrastructure, the secretive and powerful Okurasho, was left largely unscathed by General MacArthur's purge.

From the seventh century A.D. through World War II, the Okurasho, or "great storehouse ministry," was responsible for overseeing the economic development and well-being of the Japanese nation. Often referred to by political insiders as the "ministry of ministries," the Okurasho was a tightly knit group of powerful and wealthy individuals who advised the Japanese emperor on all major economic decisions facing the country and who effectively controlled the nation's banking system. In the Japanese economy, the banking system has historically been very powerful because the principal source of funds for private businesses has been debt rather than equity capital. The Okurasho also played a major role in overseeing Japan's stock market when it became a significant factor in the Japanese economy during the twentieth century.

Because senior members of the Okurasho chose each successive generation of the organization's leaders, the organization was self-perpetuating. In fact, the individuals who controlled the organization pressured their children to marry only members of other Okurasho families. Because General MacArthur was unaware of the Okurasho's far-reaching influence within Japan's social structure and economic system, members of the clandestine organization resurfaced following World War II and quickly took control of the Ministry of Finance (MOF), the government agency that would be responsible for managing the country's economy when the post-war occupation of Japan ended.

Despite the democratic political system imposed on Japan by General MacArthur, the country's elected officials had only minimal input into the post-war economic policies established by the MOF. Few of those officials ever questioned the MOF's heavy-handed, if not authoritarian, policies since those policies were responsible for the rapid modernization and recovery of the Japanese economy following World War II. Within four decades, the MOF's policies created the second-largest economy in the world and produced a level of economic prosperity surpassed only by the U.S. economy.

During the 1990s, President Clinton frequently criticized the MOF for its protectionist international trade policies that resulted in the United States having a huge and unfavorable trade imbalance with Japan. President Clinton charged that the secretive agency prevented Japan from becoming a "fully modern state with fair and open trade."[4] A *Business Week* report provided a similarly blunt assessment of the MOF's role in Japan's economy. "Japan's Ministry of Finance is much more than an office of government. It is a political, economic, and intellectual force without parallel in the developed world. It enjoys a greater concentration of powers, formal and informal, than any comparable body in any other industrialized democracy. In Japan, there is no institution with more power."[5]

---

4. *Business Week* (online), "The Ministry: How Japan's Most Powerful Institution Endangers World Markets," 25 September 2006.

5. *Ibid.*

By the early 1990s, Japan faced its first major financial crisis since World War II. Various economic factors and conditions prevented Japan from sustaining the impressive growth that it had experienced over the previous decades. Suddenly, Japan's economy faced many of the same problems that have frequently plagued the U.S. economy over the past century: volatile interest rates, inflation, and surging unemployment. These problems caused Japan's stock market to decline sharply and eventually led to a startling number of business failures.

The large number of business failures during the 1990s produced huge losses in the loan portfolios of the major metropolitan banks that were the principal source of Japan's investment capital. However, the extent of the loan losses was not reported in the audited financial statements released periodically by those banks. Pressure applied by MOF officials on the auditors of Japan's large banks resulted in those banks receiving clean audit opinions despite their massive financial problems. Eventually, both the MOF and the nation's major accounting firms would be held responsible for the huge government bailouts that were necessary to rescue Resona and other large Japanese banks.

Japan's Independent Audit Function

A small number of large accounting firms have dominated Japan's accounting profession and independent audit function since World War II. In turn, the MOF effectively controlled those large accounting firms over most of that time frame, wielding power over them similar to the power that it wielded over the nation's major banks. In 1998, the founder of one of Japan's major accounting firms told a U.S. journalist that the large government agency "really controls the accounting profession in Japan."[6] So complete was the MOF's control of the accounting profession that it reportedly hand-picked the individuals who were to serve in key executive positions at the country's largest accounting firms. In the late 1990s, the chief executives of four of Japan's six largest accounting firms had previously worked in some capacity with the MOF. The close ties between the MOF and the major accounting firms meant that the top executives of those firms routinely kowtowed to the wishes and demands of MOF officials.

Japan's public accounting profession is much smaller than that of the United States. In the United States, there is one CPA for approximately every 800 citizens, while in Japan there is one CPA for approximately every 9,600 citizens. In fact, Japan has fewer CPAs per capita by far than any other major industrialized country. The relatively small number of CPAs in Japan is due in large part to the onerous requirements for becoming a CPA. Until 2006, CPA candidates in Japan were required to pass three rigorous examinations and serve a three-year internship with an accounting firm before they could become a CPA.

The large accounting firms in Japan that dominate the nation's accounting profession also audit the great majority of the country's public companies, large private companies, and other important organizations in the private and public sector. Approximately 10,000 Japanese companies must be audited each year, including the approximately 4,000 companies that have securities listed on public stock exchanges. The remaining companies that must be audited include unlisted corporations that have total capital exceeding 500 million yen and corporations that receive government subsidies.

Similar to the United States, the number of major accounting firms within Japan has been declining in recent years, principally due to mergers. By 2006, Japan's Big

---

6. L. Berton, "Japanese Accounting Bites Back," *Accounting Today* (online), 9 November 1998.

Four included ChuoAoyama—an affiliate of PricewaterhouseCoopers, Deloitte Touche Tohmatsu, Ernst & Young Shin Nihon, and KPMG AZSA & Co. The latter firm was created in 2004 when Asahi, the firm that employed Satoshi Hirata, merged with another large Japanese accounting firm.

The nature, purpose, and structure of independent audits are generally very similar in Japan and the United States. However, there is one significant difference. Audit fees in Japan are dramatically lower than in the United States. The audit fee for a large Japanese company is generally one-tenth of the fee for a similar U.S. company. The much smaller audit fees charged by Japanese accounting firms impose severe restraints on the scope of independent audits and result in audit services being considerably less profitable for Japanese accounting firms than for their U.S. counterparts.

In the United States, the business press, financial analysts, and regulatory authorities maintain that an absence of auditor independence was a key factor that contributed to the series of high-profile audit failures of such companies as Enron, WorldCom, and Adelphia Communications, among others. Allegedly, auditors' typically long tenure with their clients, personal relationships between individual auditors and client personnel, and the large consulting fees that clients paid their auditors for nonaudit services made it difficult for audit firms to objectively report on major clients' financial statements. However, parties familiar with auditing practices and norms around the world insist that Japanese auditors have historically had much closer ties to their clients than do auditors in any other country, including the United States.

The cordial relationship between Japanese auditors and their clients is at least partially a cultural phenomenon because the Japanese business community "emphasizes relationships and harmonious working practices."[7] A critic of the Japanese public accounting profession suggested that this cultural norm results in Japanese auditors subordinating their judgment to the wishes or demands of their clients. "Even when corporate clients ask the auditors to do something that isn't allowed under the law, they just do it."[8]

By the late 1990s, Japan's independent audit function faced a growing credibility crisis. "In the late 1990s, problems with the current audit system started coming to light—exposed by a series of deplorable events at many corporations, including fraudulent accounting and the abrupt failure of financial institutions once considered healthy."[9] Worsening that credibility crisis was the fact that the principal regulatory authority for the public accounting profession, the MOF, rarely imposed sanctions of any kind on auditors who had failed to fulfill their professional responsibilities. In 1999, the MOF revoked an individual CPA's license to practice for the first time in more than 20 years.

Mounting frustration with the MOF's failure to take measures to strengthen Japan's independent audit function was one of several factors that resulted in the powerful agency being stripped of much of its regulatory authority near the turn of the century. The MOF lost even more of its authority following the election of Junichiro Koizumi as Japan's prime minister in 2001. The reform-minded Koizumi hoped to revitalize Japan's stagnant economy by enhancing the "transparency" of the nation's capital markets. To accomplish that objective, Koizumi realized that the arcane regulatory structure for those markets had to be overhauled.

---

7. D. Reilly and A. Morse, "Japan Leans On Auditors to Be More Independent," *post-gazette.com*, 18 May 2006.

8. *Ibid.*

9. *The Yomiuri Shimbun* (online), "CPA–Client Collusion Must Be Severed," 10 August 2006.

Under Prime Minister Koizumi's leadership, a new federal agency, the Financial Services Agency (FSA), assumed most of the responsibility for monitoring Japan's capital markets—including the nation's banking and financial reporting systems. To assist the FSA in overseeing the independent audit function and accounting profession, the new federal agency was placed in charge of the newly created Certified Public Accountants and Auditing Oversight Board (CPAAOB), which is comparable to the United States' Public Company Accounting and Oversight Board (PCAOB). To police the securities markets, another new federal agency, the Securities and Exchange Surveillance Commission, was established and placed under the FSA's control.

In 2004, Japan's federal legislative body, the Diet, rewrote the Certified Public Accountants Law. A major purpose of revising this law was to increase the number of CPAs in Japan. Among other changes, the revised law requires CPA candidates to pass only one examination rather than three to become a CPA. The national organization of CPAs, the Japanese Institute of Certified Public Accountants (JICPA), also adopted a series of measures to strengthen the profession, many of which focused on the independent audit function. Among these latter measures was prohibiting independent auditors from having any direct financial interest in a public client. Previously, auditors of public companies had been allowed to own a limited number of shares of a public client's outstanding stock.

The first major test of Japan's new regulatory structure for the accounting profession and independent audit function was posed by a financial scandal involving a large manufacturing company, Kanebo, Ltd. The nation's business press often refers to the Kanebo fiasco as "Japan's Enron."[10]

Kanebo, Ltd: Japan's Enron

The Tokyo Cotton Trading Company was founded in 1887 on the banks of the Sumida River that flows through Tokyo. Over the following decades, the company became a large and prosperous textile and apparel manufacturer—only to have its operating facilities totally destroyed during World War II. With the help of significant bank loans, the company, renamed Kanebo, Ltd., resumed operations on a much smaller scale in the late 1940s. By the late 1990s, the company ranked among Japan's largest public corporations. Kanebo's principal operations included the manufacture and sale of a long line of cosmetics, apparel, textiles, pharmaceuticals, toiletries, and food products.

In July 2005, Japanese law enforcement authorities arrested three former Kanebo executives, including Takashi Hoashi, the company's former president. The three individuals were charged with violating the Securities and Exchange Law, the principal federal statute that established the regulatory framework for Japan's securities markets, a statute comparable to the United States' Securities Exchange Act of 1934. Allegedly, the former Kanebo executives conspired to conceal their company's deteriorating financial health beginning in the late 1990s through 2004. The company's financial statements during that time frame indicated that the company was in reasonably good financial condition. However, a criminal investigation revealed that the company was hopelessly insolvent from 1995 through 2004.

According to a representative of Tokyo's Public Prosecutor's Office, Hoashi ordered Kanebo's accounting staff to falsify the company's accounting records. Hoashi reportedly told the accountants that if they did not cooperate, the company would fail and its employees would lose their jobs. Hoashi's two subordinates (who were also indicted) gave the company's accountants specific instructions on how to distort Kanebo's reported financial data. The accountants were told to record fictitious sales

---

10. *Accountancy* (*accountancymagazine.com*), "ChuoAoyama Faces ₤100m Revenue Hit," 31 May 2005.

and to understate various expenses to improve Kanebo's operating results and to make the company appear solvent.

In March 2006, Takashi Hoashi and one of his subordinates pleaded guilty to falsifying Kanebo's financial statements.[11] In commenting on the fraud, the judge who would ultimately sentence the two former executives noted, "It was a vicious and organizational crime committed by the leaders of a major Japanese company. It was also unprecedentedly cleverly devised."[12] Despite the judge's harsh remarks, he gave the two former executives suspended prison sentences.

ChuoAoyama, the second-largest CPA firm in Japan, served for decades as the audit firm for Kanebo Ltd. Tokyo's Public Prosecutor's Office filed fraud charges against three ChuoAoyama auditors who had been assigned to the Kanebo audit engagements. Each of those auditors had worked on the annual audits of that company for more than 15 years. One of the defendants had been assigned to the Kanebo engagement team for more than 30 years. Such long tenures of Japanese auditors with audit clients were common throughout the latter half of the twentieth century. According to the prosecutors, the three ChuoAoyama auditors had not only been aware of Kanebo's true financial condition but had also recommended additional methods for concealing the company's poor financial health. Among these methods was "deconsolidating" certain Kanebo subsidiaries that were posting large operating losses each year. The defendants never admitted as much, but the prosecutors speculated that the three auditors learned of this scheme from reading published reports of the Enron accounting fraud in the United States.

In the summer of 2006, the case against the ChuoAoyama auditors went to trial in Tokyo District Court. As one journalist noted, Japan's public accounting profession was "turned on its head"[13] by the case because it represented the first time in the country's history that auditors from a major CPA firm had faced criminal charges for allegedly falsifying or helping to falsify a client's financial statements. A few years earlier, ChuoAoyama had been involved in a precedent-setting civil lawsuit in Japan. ChuoAoyama had been the longtime auditor for Yamaichi Securities, a large brokerage firm that unexpectedly collapsed in late 1997. The following year, Yamaichi's former stockholders sued ChuoAoyama, charging that the firm had negligently audited Yamaichi. The lawsuit was the first of its kind filed by Japanese stockholders against an audit firm. In 2003, ChuoAoyama settled the lawsuit by agreeing to pay the Yamaichi bankruptcy administrator an amount equal to the total audit fees it had received for its final five audits of Yamaichi. Despite the settlement, ChuoAoyama officials insisted that the firm had properly performed those audits.

During the criminal trial of the three ChuoAoyama auditors, the defendants testified that shortly before the Kanebo fraud was uncovered by law enforcement authorities they had pleaded with Hoashi and his subordinates to make the proper correcting entries in the company's accounting records. According to the three auditors, the client executives refused to make those entries. When the auditors pressed the issue, the Kanebo executives "secured their cooperation by pointing out that ChuoAoyama had long overlooked the company's window dressing and said it was pointless to start complaining after taking a complacent stance for so long."[14]

---

11. No published report could be found regarding the resolution of the criminal charges filed against the third Kanebo executive.

12. *Associated Press* (online), "Ex-Kanebo Executives Sentenced for False Information," 27 March 2006.

13. *International Accounting Bulletin* (online), "Japan Confronts Its Audit Problem," 12 August 2006.

14. *Japan Economic Newswire* (online), "Japanese Editorial Excerpts," 11 August 2006.

In August 2006, the three ChuoAoyama auditors were convicted of the charges filed against them. Before sentencing the three individuals, the presiding judge noted that they had "damaged the social trust of certified public accountants" and that their "crimes deserve to be severely criticized."[15] The judge also observed, "It is shameful that they have failed to realize the high professional morality as certified accountants and lost the true aim of auditing, which is to protect investors."[16] After berating the three convicted auditors, the judge gave each of them suspended sentences ranging from one year to 18 months. The judge defended the suspended sentences by pointing out that Kanebo's executives, not the three auditors, were primarily responsible for the fraudulent scheme. The suspended prison sentences for the three auditors meant that no one involved in the large-scale Kanebo fraud would serve any time in prison for their misdeeds.

In May 2006, the FSA announced that the three ChuoAoyama auditors involved in the Kanebo fraud would have their CPA qualifications revoked. The FSA also announced that ChuoAoyama would be forced to suspend its operations for the two-month period July 1–August 31, 2006. The announcement of the suspension stunned Japan's public accounting profession. Japan's Securities and Exchange Law requires each listed company to have an independent audit firm at all times. The suspension of ChuoAoyama meant that the firm's approximately 800 clients that had securities listed on a stock exchange would be forced to either retain a temporary auditor for the two-month suspension period or dismiss ChuoAoyama and retain a new audit firm.

EPILOGUE

To prevent Kanebo Ltd. from being forced to liquidate, the Japanese federal government placed the company in a "rehabilitation" program under the direction of the Industrial Revitalization Corporation of Japan (IRCJ). The government-sponsored and -funded IRCJ had been created in April 2003 to help financially distressed companies obtain the capital they needed to survive and to provide them with "turnaround" advice from professional business consultants. Under the leadership of the IRCJ, Kanebo sold off its large cosmetics subsidiary and received more than $1 billion in government-guaranteed loans and waivers of outstanding loans. In 2006, a large investment fund purchased a majority of Kanebo's stock and took over control of the company from the IRCJ.

ChuoAoyama lost approximately one-third of its audit clients, including more than 200 publicly listed clients, during the two-month suspension imposed by the FSA. These companies included ChuoAoyama's two highest-profile audit clients, Sony Corporation and Toyota Motor Corporation. While serving the suspension, ChuoAoyama underwent an extensive internal review to strengthen its quality control functions and changed its name to the Misuzu Audit Corporation.[17]

Shortly after the FSA announced that it was suspending ChuoAoyama's operations for two months, the accounting firm's U.S. affiliate, PricewaterhouseCoopers, revealed that it would be creating a new Japanese accounting firm known as Aarata, a name that means "new and fresh" in Japanese. Aarata commenced operations on July 1, 2006, and in the subsequent weeks acquired dozens of ChuoAoyama's former clients, including Sony and Toyota. In addition, nearly one-fourth of ChuoAoyama's employees left that firm to join Aarata.

15. J. Hong, "CPAs in Kanebo Fraud Avoid Prison," *Japan Times* (online), 10 August 2006.

16. *Agence France Presse* (online), "Ex-Accountants Found Guilty in Japanese Fraud Case," 9 August 2006.

17. In February 2007, Misuzu announced that it was disbanding. The remaining three members of Japan's former Big Four hired the majority of Misuzu's employees.

EXHIBIT 1

EXCERPT FROM THE
BUSINESS
IMPROVEMENT
ORDER ISSUED TO
CHUOAOYAMA BY
THE FINANCIAL
SERVICES AGENCY
(FSA)

As a result of inspecting ChuoAoyama PricewaterhouseCoopers, the firm-wide management to ensure audit quality control was deemed insufficient, partly due to the insufficient awareness of auditors and lack of adequate efforts made in conjunction with past incidents.

Specifically, its [measures for ensuring] compliance of laws/regulations and its implementation of the [procedures for ensuring] auditors' independence were found to be insufficient, and its system [for managing] training, etc. was deemed partially insufficient.

In addition, its risk assessments at the time of engagement acceptance/continuance, the performance of audit work by each audit team and the documentation/retention of audit working papers were deemed partially insufficient. In terms of internal reviews of audits, although a multi-tiered review system has been implemented, reviews rely on those [provided] by review partners and some are deemed to lack depth. In this context, its internal review system [for identifying] issues of each audit and [for confirming] the appropriateness of the judgments and dispositions [with regard] to such issues were partially insufficient. Its monitoring of the quality control system was deemed partially insufficient, and joint audits were deemed insufficient.

Furthermore, its control system for branch offices was deemed insufficient.

Source: Financial Services Agency (http://www.fsa.go.jp)

The Kanebo audit failure prompted the FSA to investigate the audit practices of each of Japan's four large accounting firms. These investigations were carried out by the newly created CPAAOB that had been placed under the authority of the FSA. The stated purpose of the investigations was to "regain public trust in certified public accountants damaged by ChuoAoyama auditors' involvement in Kanebo's falsification of its financial statements."[18] The CPAAOB issued a report on the six-month long investigations in July 2006. That report criticized the operating policies and procedures of the four accounting firms. As a result of the CPAAOB's report, the FSA issued "business improvement orders" to each of the four firms. Exhibit 1 includes an excerpt of the business improvement order issued to ChuoAoyama.

In the aftermath of the Kanebo audit failure, leaders of the Japanese accounting profession spoke out about the need for additional reforms to strengthen the nation's independent audit function. One such individual was Tsuguoki Fujinuma, the chairman and president of the JICPA. Fujinuma issued a public statement in which he compared the Kanebo incident to the Enron debacle in the United States.

The Enron affair was not an isolated problem of one accounting firm. To the contrary, it was regarded as a failure of the entire CPA system and provoked a barrage of criticism against audits and auditors in the U.S. public. This affair ultimately led to the passage of the Sarbanes-Oxley Act, legislation imposing severe controls on CPAs. I urge all JICPA members engaged in audits to make efforts to ensure the public confidence in auditing practices, together with the JICPA itself. As they do so, I further urge them not to regard the Enron affair as a distant or unrelated failure to the accounting system, nor to regard the Kanebo incident as an isolated problem involving only one auditing firm.[19]

18. *Japan Economic Newswire* (online), "FSA to Inspect 4 Biggest Auditing Firms," 25 October 2005.

19. T. Fujinuma, "On the Alleged Fraudulent Accounting at Kanebo," website of Japanese Institute of Certified Public Accountants (http://www.hp.jicpa.or.jp/), 16 September 2005.

Despite such statements and the actions of the FSA and other regulatory authorities in response to the Kanebo affair, many third parties doubted that there would be major changes in Japan's independent audit function. As one skeptic noted, "cultural mores" will likely prove to be "sand in the gears of change."[20]

Questions

1. Research online news services to identify recent developments impacting the accounting and auditing profession in Japan. Briefly summarize these developments in a bullet format.

2. As noted in this case, Japanese companies typically rely more heavily on debt capital than do U.S. companies. Explain how this fact may cause the independent audit functions in the two countries to differ.

3. The much higher barriers to entry for the public accounting profession in Japan (as compared with other major industrialized countries) has resulted in a relatively small number of CPAs in that nation. Identify and briefly discuss the comparative advantages and disadvantages of high barriers to entry for a given profession.

4. In both Japan and the United States, a small number of accounting firms audit the great majority of large public companies. Identify the advantages and disadvantages of this "market structure" for independent audit services.

5. In both Japan and the United States, external auditors have frequently been accused of failing to maintain a proper degree of independence from their clients. What measures have and should be taken to promote the independence of auditors from their clients?

---

20. Reilly and Morse, "Japan Leans On Auditors."

CASE 8.4

Registered Auditors, South Africa

Where the cattle stand together, the lion lies down hungry.

African Proverb

After earning a law degree from the University of Capetown in 1988, 24-year-old Brett Kebble accepted an entry-level position with a prestigious Capetown law firm. The gregarious and impetuous Kebble soon realized that it would take years, if not decades, to achieve his personal goal of "making a name for himself" if he remained in the staid legal profession. So, Kebble decided to quit practicing law and join his father in the mining industry that has dominated the Republic of South Africa's economy throughout that nation's existence. Kebble's father, a successful mining engineer, had raised his family in the mining town of Springs in northwestern South Africa, 40 miles south of Pretoria, the nation's capital.

In 1991, Kebble and his father purchased a controlling interesting in a small gold mining company. Three years later, Kebble, with the financial backing of his father and several other major investors, orchestrated the takeover of Randgold & Exploration Company Limited, one of South Africa's leading mining companies. Over the following decade, Brett Kebble would become the chief executive of Randgold and two other mining companies, all three of which were publicly owned firms.

By the turn of the century, Brett Kebble had accomplished his ultimate personal goal. Thanks to his role as the self-appointed spokesperson for South Africa's all-important mining industry, Kebble easily ranked among the nation's highest-profile corporate executives. Besides his prominent position in the South African business community, Kebble had close associations with several of South Africa's leading politicians and was a strong supporter of the arts. In 2002, Kebble, a large, heavyset man known for his quick wit and humor (and lack of modesty), established and funded the annual Brett Kebble Art Awards to recognize and reward leading South African artists, sculptors, and photographers.

A Career Cut Short

Kebble's reputation and business career were severely damaged in 2004 when Randgold & Exploration Company Limited, the crown jewel of his large business empire, reported a huge cash shortage. The missing funds were equivalent to several hundred million U.S. dollars. Stockholder revolts forced Kebble to resign in August 2005 as the chief executive of Randgold and the other two public companies for which he served in that position. One month later, in September 2005, the 41-year-old Kebble was gunned down in a wealthy section of Johannesburg while on his way to a dinner engagement in his silver Mercedes.

Johannesburg police immediately concluded that Kebble's murder had been a well-planned "hit." The widely publicized murder of the controversial businessman reinforced Johannesburg's reputation as the murder capital of the world and served to support the prevailing view in the international business community that South Africa was a high-risk and dangerous place to do business. Even more damaging to the reputation of South Africa's business community were subsequent revelations of the underhanded and illegal methods that Kebble had used to build his massive empire. One journalist characterized the late Kebble as a "cheat, manipulator, corrupter, briber, and swindler."[1] South Africa's largest newspaper would add to that sentiment: "Brett Kebble was not a good South African. He was the great corrupter, a dirty businessman who had little respect for the law or codes of good business practice."[2]

South African law enforcement authorities were investigating Kebble and his business and political allies well before he was murdered in September 2005. Those investigations continued on a larger scale following his death. Among the parties targeted by the investigations was PricewaterhouseCoopers (PwC), the audit firm of Randgold & Exploration Company Limited. Throughout Kebble's tenure as Randgold's chief executive, PwC had issued clean opinions on the company's annual financial statements even as a huge amount of the company's funds were being siphoned off by Kebble and several of his top subordinates. Randgold's board of directors dismissed PwC and retained KPMG as the company's independent audit firm shortly after the public was apprised of the missing funds.

After Brett Kebble's death, Randgold's new management team hired a consulting firm to carry out a forensic investigation of the company's accounting records and financial affairs over the previous decade. Two dozen forensic auditors from the consulting firm spent months unraveling a series of complex and multilayered "Enron-style transactions" that Kebble and his subordinates had used to divert Randgold assets into related entities that they controlled.[3] In a lengthy report issued in November 2005, the consulting firm recommended that Randgold's new management team file civil and criminal charges against PwC. The consulting firm suggested that proper audits of Randgold would have led to the discovery and termination of the massive fraud engineered by Kebble.

Doing Business, South Africa Style

In many ways, Brett Kebble's life and death epitomizes the turbulent nature of South Africa's business world following the collapse of apartheid in the early 1990s. In 1990, the South African federal government succumbed to immense international and domestic pressure when it lifted the ban on the African National Congress (ANC), the political party that for decades had struggled to eliminate apartheid in the country. The ANC drew its support from blacks, who accounted for more than three-fourths of the nation's total population. The National Party, the political party of the nation's white minority that controlled most of South Africa's economic resources (including its crucial mining industry), had dominated South Africa's federal government since the 1940s. Shortly after World War II, the National Party had implemented the segregationist social and economic policies that formed the basis for what became known as apartheid.

When the first truly multiracial elections were held in South Africa in 1994, Nelson Mandela was elected the nation's president. Mandela, the leader of the ANC, had been imprisoned by the South African government from 1963 through 1990. The democratic elections also resulted in the ANC assuming control of South Africa's Parliament. After decades of a bitter and often extremely bloody struggle, South Africa's black majority had finally taken control of the country.

Since the collapse of apartheid and the takeover of the federal government by the ANC, South Africa's economy has been characterized by uncertainty and volatility. Major institutional investors around the world have been reluctant to commit significant

1. S. Ulys, "The Mysterious Murder of Brett Kebble," http://www.ever-fasternews.com, 2 October 2005.

2. A. Meldrum, "Brett Kebble, Controversial Business Leader from the New South Africa," *The Guardian* (online), 7 October 2005.

3. "Massive Fraud Revealed at Randgold & Exploration," http://www.randgold.co.za, press release issued by Randgold & Exploration Company Limited, 1 November 2005.

investment capital to South African business ventures because of that uncertainty and volatility. A related factor that has inhibited direct foreign investment in the South African economy has been corruption. In a recent study by Ernst & Young, corporate executives from nearly 70 countries around the world identified "corruption" as the principal factor that made them hesitant to do business in South Africa.[4] According to the Ernst & Young study, the corruption in South Africa's economy is manifested in widespread bribery, payroll fraud, inventory theft, and unauthorized expenditures by corporate executives, among other abuses.

South Africa's economy and capital markets have also suffered a loss of credibility as a result of a series of high-profile financial reporting scandals that have occurred in recent years. Those scandals have involved companies such as LeisureNet, MacMed, Regal Treasury, Saambou, and, most notably, Randgold & Exploration Company Limited. Critics of South Africa's accounting profession maintain that much of the responsibility for these scandals should be borne by the accounting firms that audited those companies' financial statements and failed to uncover the fraudulent schemes carried out by Brett Kebble and other self-interested corporate executives.

Numerous journalists and political adversaries of Brett Kebble maintain that he used assets stolen from Randgold not only for his personal enrichment but also to buy political favors from leaders of the ANC. Since the early 1990s, Kebble, who was of western European descent, had been among the most vocal supporters of the black empowerment movement in South Africa and a leading figure in the ANC. One of his closest associates was Jacob Zuma who served for several years as South Africa's deputy president (vice president) before being forced to resign in June 2005 amid allegations of abuse of power. Two years later, Zuma was elected ANC's new leader and became the party's presumed presidential candidate in the next national election. The published reports of the missing funds within Randgold as well as Kebble's close ties and financial dealings with Zuma ignited the stockholder revolts that forced him to resign as the chief executive of Randgold and of the other two mining companies that he and his family had controlled since the mid-1990s.

South Africa's business press has referred to the financial scandal at Randgold & Exploration Company Limited as that nation's "Enron." Like the actual Enron debacle in the United States, the highly publicized Randgold scandal persuaded the South African Parliament to pass major legislation to combat financial fraud and strengthen the nation's financial reporting system. This new legislation was intended to convince the international investment community that South Africa's capital markets would be characterized by integrity in the future. The lynchpin of the legislative reforms was a new federal law that had pervasive implications for the nation's accounting profession.

Overview of South Africa's Accounting Profession

South Africa's accounting discipline has several professional organizations. The two most important of these organizations are the South African Institute of Professional Accountants (SAIPA), which until recently was known as the Institute of Certified Public Accountants, and the South African Institute of Chartered Accountants (SAICA). Members of the SAIPA are certified public accountants (CPAs) who typically provide tax and bookkeeping services to small South African businesses. The

---

4. M.S. Bayat, "Curbing Corruption in the Republic of South Africa," *Public Manager*, Summer 2005, 15. The results of a study by PricewaterhouseCoopers that was published in late 2007 identified South Africa as the "white-collar crime capital" of the world (Africa News [online], "South Africa: Country is White-Collar Crime Capital," 16 October 2007).

dominant organization in the South African accounting profession is the SAICA, which issues the Chartered Accountant (CA) professional designation. The CA designation is equivalent to the CPA designation in the United States.

Unlike the United States, the accounting profession in South Africa is regulated almost exclusively at the federal level. Until recently, the federal agency overseeing that profession was the Public Accountants' and Auditors' Board (PAAB). PAAB delegated much of the responsibility for overseeing the South African accounting profession to the SAICA. The working relationship between the PAAB and the SAICA was analogous to the relationship that exists in the United States between state boards of accountancy and the American Institute of Certified Public Accountants (AICPA). For example, until recently, an internal SAICA committee developed and issued South Africa's professional auditing standards, which were then routinely endorsed by the PAAB. Similarly, the PAAB adopted a condensed version of the code of professional ethics developed by the SAICA.

The abrupt change of control in South Africa's federal government in the early 1990s presented major challenges for the nation's federal agencies, such as the PAAB, and its professional organizations, among them the SAICA. Throughout its history, South Africa's accounting profession, like its other professions, had been dominated by the nation's white minority—principally white males. The ANC's takeover of the South African government in 1994 resulted in federal mandates calling for the integration of the nation's professions. Since that time, the SAICA and the nation's major accounting firms have spent considerable time and resources attempting to recruit black South Africans into the profession. Those efforts have generally produced discouraging results. In 2006, fewer than 9 percent of South Africa's 22,000 CAs were blacks and of those individuals fewer than 200 were black females. Ernst & Young reported in that same year that it was the first of the Big Four accounting firms in South Africa to have more than 25 percent black partners.

In the post-apartheid era, a large percentage of South Africa's white professionals have emigrated to other countries, including an estimated 20 to 25 percent of the nation's CAs. The emigration of white CAs and the continuing underrepresentation of blacks have resulted in a significant shortage of professional accountants within South Africa. In the United States, there is approximately one CPA for every 800 citizens. South Africa, on the other hand, has approximately one resident CA for every 3,000 citizens.

In April 2006, three Big Four firms—Deloitte, KPMG, and PwC—asked the South African federal government to relax its restrictive immigration laws to make it easier for those firms to recruit accounting professionals from other countries. The three firms maintained that the significant shortage of skilled accountants within South Africa had made it increasingly difficult for the nation's accounting profession to provide the accounting, auditing, tax, and related services needed by South African citizens and businesses. To date, the South African government has not responded to that request. The federal government's position is that allowing skilled accounting professionals to immigrate to South Africa—even if those individuals are black—will only serve to continue the underrepresentation of native South African blacks within the profession.

The most significant challenge facing South Africa's accounting profession in the post-apartheid era has been the rash of accounting and financial reporting scandals involving major companies. Many parties internal and external to the profession have suggested that the most effective way to mitigate that problem is to strengthen the nation's professional accounting and auditing standards. After considerable debate, South Africa's accounting profession decided to adopt, as of January 1, 2005, the

International Financial Reporting Standards (IFRS) issued by the International Accounting Standards Board (IASB). On that same date, the South African profession also adopted the International Standards on Auditing (ISA) issued by the International Federation of Accountants (IFAC).

The adoption of international accounting and auditing standards did not placate the most vocal critics of South Africa's accounting profession. Those critics became even more strident as the Randgold accounting and financial reporting scandal unfolded during 2005 and 2006. That scandal provided the impetus for South Africa's Parliament to pass a federal statute in 2006 that had been placed on the legislative agenda 10 years earlier. The Auditing Profession Act made sweeping changes to the nature of South Africa's financial reporting system, particularly the nation's independent audit function.

Auditing Profession Act

South Africa's Auditing Profession Act (APA) went into effect on April 1, 2006. The new federal law eliminated the PAAB and replaced it with the Independent Regulatory Board for Auditors (IRBA). The term "independent" was included in the new agency's name because, unlike its predecessor, a majority of its governing board would not be accountants. Likewise, unlike the PAAB that had been financed exclusively by the accounting profession, the APA mandated that the IRBA be funded jointly by the profession and the federal government. These two stipulations were a direct response to criticism that the PAAB had been an ineffective oversight body for South Africa's accounting profession because it had been "captured" by that profession. In particular, critics suggested that the PAAB had been overly sensitive to the interests and demands of the Big Four international accounting firms, each of which has a strong presence in South Africa. The website of the IRBA identifies six "core values" that the new federal agency will embrace and promote: independence, integrity, objectivity, commitment, transparency, and accountability.

The APA also established a new professional designation in South Africa's accounting profession: Registered Auditor (RA). Under the APA, only CAs who also hold the RA credential can perform independent audits in South Africa. According to an official of the IRBA, the new RA designation was necessary because of the large number of audit failures and alleged audit failures that had occurred in South Africa over the previous several years. "Auditors have taken a huge knock in the past few years and we need to establish a brand locally that will restore integrity."[5]

The creation of the new professional designation was generally not welcomed by the SAICA and individual CAs who realized that the RA credential would almost certainly impair the prestige and prominence of the CA credential. In fact, officials of the IRBA candidly admitted that they hoped the public would impute more credibility to the new RA designation. "We're trying to tell people [existing CAs] that if you're an RA, it will have higher regard than a CA in South Africa because of the stringent new laws and examination. We want people to strive to be RAs not CAs."[6]

Prior to the passage of the APA, the SAICA had administered the CA examination. Under the APA, the SAICA continues to administer that examination; however, to become an RA a CA candidate must successfully complete a second examination administered by the IRBA. Before receiving the CA or RA credential, candidates must complete a minimum three-year internship or "training program" within the accounting

---

5. S. Naidoo, "Auditors' Brand Set to Rival That of a CA," *Sunday Times* (online), 1 October 2006.

6. *Ibid.*

EXHIBIT 1

MISSION
STATEMENTS OF THE
SAICA AND THE
IRBA

SAICA's mission is to serve the interests of the Chartered Accountancy profession and society, by upholding professional standards and integrity, and the preeminence of South African CAs nationally and internationally, through delivering competent entry level members, providing services to assist members to maintain and enhance their professional competence thereby enabling them to create value for their clients and employers, enhancing the quality of information used in the private and public sectors for measuring and enhancing organizational performance, running and facilitating programmes to transform the profession and to facilitate community upliftment and fulfilling a leadership role regarding relevant business related issues and providing reliable and respected public commentary.

The mission of the IRBA, on the other hand, is to protect the financial interest of the South African public and international investors in South Africa, through the effective regulation of audits conducted by registered auditors, and in accordance with internationally recognized standards and processes. This is achieved by providing the means and the regulatory framework for the education and training of adequate numbers of competent and disciplined accountants and auditors, to serve the needs of South Africa. The Board [IRBA] strives constantly toward the maintenance and improvement of standards of registered auditors. The Board protects the public who rely on the services of registered auditors and supports registered auditors who carry out their duties competently, fearlessly, and in good faith.

Source: SAICA website (http://www.saica.co.za)

profession. This requirement had existed for CA candidates prior to the passage of the APA and the creation of the IRBA.

Leaders of the South African accounting profession were concerned that the creation of the IRBA and the new RA designation would lead to confusion on the part of the public regarding the nature of the CA and RA designations and the roles and responsibilities of the IRBA and the SAICA. To alleviate such confusion, the two organizations issued mission statements clarifying their roles and responsibilities and their relationship to the CA and RA credentials. Exhibit 1 presents summaries of those mission statements that were posted to the SAICA website.

The APA also made major changes in the regulatory infrastructure for South Africa's independent audit function. Under this new federal statute, the IRBA has far-reaching oversight responsibilities for that function. Individual RAs as well as accounting firms providing independent audits are required to register with the IRBA. Registered accounting firms must undergo an extensive quality review of their professional audit practices by the IRBA every three years. The IRBA also has the statutory responsibility to establish ethical standards and rules for RAs. The APA required the IRBA to establish a "committee for auditor ethics" that will "determine what constitutes improper conduct by registered auditors by developing rules and guidelines for professional ethics, including a code of professional conduct."[7] The IRBA also requires RAs to engage in continuing professional development (CPD) each year. Organizations offering CPD courses or programs must be accredited by the IRBA

By far, the most controversial and important change in the nature of independent audits and auditors' professional responsibilities brought about by the APA is a requirement that RAs immediately inform the IRBA of any "reportable irregularities"

7. *Government Gazette, The Republic of South Africa*, "Auditing Profession Act, 2005," Vol. 487, No. 28406 (16 January 2006), 26.

relating to an audit client that come to their attention. Reportable irregularities are defined by the APA as

> *any unlawful act or omission committed by any person responsible for the management of an entity, which:*
>
> *—has caused or is likely to cause material financial loss to the entity or any partner, member, shareholder, creditor or investor of the entity in respect of his/her or its dealings with that entity; or*
>
> *—is fraudulent or amounts to theft; or*
>
> *—represents a material breach of any fiduciary duty owed by such person to the entity or any partner, member, shareholder, creditor or investor of the entity under any law applying to the entity or the conduct or management thereof.*[8]

RAs must disclose a reportable irregularity (RI) "without delay" to the IRBA, meaning that these matters are not to be discussed with client management before they are communicated to the federal agency. After an RI report has been submitted to the IRBA, an RA must discuss that report with client management within three days. Over the following 30 days, client management must be given an opportunity to respond to the report. At the end of this 30-day period, the RA must send a second report to the IRBA regarding the RI. In this second report, the RA must indicate whether in his or her opinion an actual irregularity has taken place or is taking place.

Reportable irregularities also have extensive implications for the audit reports prepared by South African RAs. The APA provides specific guidance for auditors to follow in determining whether and/or how to modify their audit reports for a wide range of circumstances involving RIs. For example, if an auditor reports a potential RI to the IRBA but then determines that an actual irregularity did not take place, no modification of the audit report is necessary. On the other hand, when an auditor has filed an RI report with the IRBA and subsequently determines that an actual irregularity took place, the auditor must modify the audit report even if the RI has been dealt with appropriately by management and is adequately disclosed in an accompanying "management report." The APA identifies the specific modifications that are appropriate to the audit report in such circumstances. Management's failure to disclose an RI, whether or not the matter has been appropriately addressed, may require the auditor to issue an adverse opinion on the client's financial statements. If at the audit report date an auditor has not determined whether a potential RI is an actual RI, then the potential RI, at a minimum, must be disclosed in the audit report. Again, the APA provides specific guidance for auditors to follow in the latter situation.

The APA mandates that RAs have a responsibility to report RIs regardless of how they became aware of them. For example, anonymous tips, statements made by disgruntled former employees, or confidential communications to the auditor by client employees could each trigger an RI report to the IRBA. Likewise, an RI discovered during the course of a nonaudit services engagement for a client must be disclosed to the IRBA. Under the APA, the reporting responsibility for RIs falls on individual RAs, not accounting firms. The RA on the engagement team who has the ultimate responsibility for the successful completion of the audit—typically, the audit engagement partner—has the obligation to report an RI to the IRBA. This stipulation of the law is very important given the serious criminal penalties for willfully choosing not to report an RI. An RA who has a responsibility to report an RI and fails to do so faces a large fine and a prison sentence of up to 10 years.

---

8. *Ibid.*, 10.

In addition to exposing RAs to criminal sanctions, the APA mandates that RAs who fail to fulfill their RI-related responsibilities will be subject to civil liability, as well. This civil liability extends to any "partner, member, shareholder, creditor, or investor of an entity" for which an RA fails to report a RI.[9] One of South Africa's leading corporate law firms reported that this provision of the APA "has potentially enormous consequences for auditors' liability claims."[10]

The stated purpose of the RI provisions of the APA was to "eradicate" the large-scale frauds, such as the Randgold & Exploration Company Limited scandal, that had undermined the integrity of South Africa's capital markets within the international community and resulted in large diversions of assets by dishonest corporate executives. Although certain parties, particularly South Africa's business press, welcomed the RI provisions of the APA, many corporate executives and members of the nation's accounting profession were startled, if not shocked, by those provisions. An audit partner with one of the Big Four accounting firms maintained that the RI disclosure rule would undermine the "relationship of confidentiality between auditor and client" and create an "atmosphere in which clients will be reluctant to discuss problems with their auditors."[11]

To minimize any confusion regarding the RI disclosure requirements imposed on auditors by the APA, the SAICA has recommended that accounting firms send each of their audit clients a letter describing in detail the nature of those requirements. Exhibit 2 includes a draft of such a letter prepared by the SAICA and distributed to its members.

EXHIBIT 2

DRAFT OF LETTER THAT THE SAICA SUGGESTED RAs SEND TO THEIR AUDIT CLIENTS REGARDING THE REPORTABLE IRREGULARITIES DISCLOSURE RULE

Dear Client:

You may be aware from press and other reports that new legislation regulating auditors has been enacted during 2006.

I have a statutory obligation to report matters to a regulatory oversight body or other person, such as the Independent Regulatory Board for Auditors (IRBA). Where permissible I shall endeavor to bring such circumstances to your attention.

Without detracting from the generality of such requirements, I am writing to you to provide a brief overview of the new reporting obligations imposed by the Auditing Profession Act 2005 (Act 26 of 2005).

The new legislation brings into existence a new regulator in the form of the IRBA which supersedes the Public Accountants' and Auditors' Board (PAAB).

Section 45 of the Auditing Profession Act places a legal requirement on the auditor to report to the IRBA, without delay, details of any reportable irregularity which comes to our attention, which we are satisfied or have reason to believe has taken place or is taking place in respect of [entity name].

The Auditing Profession Act defines a reportable irregularity as "any unlawful act or omission committed by any person responsible for the management of an entity, which:

---

9. *Ibid.*, 48.

10. K. Gawith, "Reportable Irregularities," http://www.deneysreitz.co.za.

11. *Africa News* (online), "Auditors Generally Welcome New Law despite Concerns about Education Roles," 7 April 2006.

EXHIBIT 2—
continued

DRAFT OF LETTER
THAT THE SAICA
SUGGESTED RAS
SEND TO THEIR
AUDIT CLIENTS
REGARDING THE
REPORTABLE
IRREGULARITIES
DISCLOSURE RULE

—has caused or is likely to cause material financial loss to the entity or any partner, member, shareholder, creditor or investor of the entity in respect of his/her or its dealings with that entity; or

—is fraudulent or amounts to theft; or

—represents a material breach of any fiduciary duty owed by such person to the entity or any partner, member, shareholder, creditor or investor of the entity under any law applying to the entity or the conduct or management thereof."

Matters which come to my attention and meet the definition above are clearly of a serious nature. In addition to reporting such matters to you and to those charged with governance of [entity name], I am obliged to report such matters to the IRBA.

Accordingly, the South African Institute of Chartered Accountants, of which I am a member, has advised its members who practice as auditors to write to their audit clients informing them of the requirements of the section dealing with reportable irregularities and what the implications can be.

What must the auditor do?

1. In terms of the legislation, if an auditor or an entity is satisfied, or has reason to believe that a reportable irregularity has taken place or is taking place, he or she must, without delay, send a written report to the IRBA.
2. The report must give particulars of the alleged irregularity.
3. The auditor must notify the members of the management board of the entity in writing within three (3) days of sending the report.
4. The auditor must take all reasonable measures to discuss the report with the management board of the entity.
5. The auditor must afford the members of the management board an opportunity to make representations in respect of the report. The auditor must send another report to the IRBA within 30 days of the initial report to the IRBA stating in his or her opinion whether or not a reportable irregularity has taken place or is taking lace. This report should also deal with whether adequate steps have been taken for the prevention or recovery of any loss.
6. The auditor may carry out such investigations he or she may consider necessary to comply with the above requirements.
7. The auditor must refer to the alleged irregularity in his or her audit report attached to the annual financial statements.
8. It is important to note that the procedure described above must be carried out regardless of how the auditor came to know of the irregularity.

What the regulator must do?

The IRBA has a responsibility to report a reportable irregularity to the appropriate regulator (which includes any government agency) e.g. South African Revenue Services, South African Police Services, or the Financial Services Board.

Possible Penalties

I need to draw your attention to the fact that if the auditor fails to report a reportable irregularity, he or she may be guilty of an offense and may be liable to a fine of R10 million or imprisonment for a term not exceeding 10 years, or both a fine and imprisonment.

(continued)

EXHIBIT 2—
continued

DRAFT OF LETTER
THAT THE SAICA
SUGGESTED RAs
SEND TO THEIR
AUDIT CLIENTS
REGARDING THE
REPORTABLE
IRREGULARITIES
DISCLOSURE RULE

Conclusion

As mentioned previously, the auditors' responsibility with regard to reportable irregularities are well defined and can have serious consequences on the auditor if not followed appropriately.

While I am certain that you are committed to ensuring that such reportable irregularities do not exist, or if they do arise they are dealt with appropriately within applicable legal requirements, you may wish to further discuss the reporting obligations with me.

Yours Sincerely,
Registered Auditor, CA

_____

Source: SAICA website (http://www.saica.co.za)

EPILOGUE

Within the first five months that the APA was in effect, the IRBA received more than 200 RI reports from auditors. The majority of the RIs involved alleged violations of South African tax laws, apparent violations of the nation's federal securities laws, and a wide range of questionable accounting practices.[12] The regulatory agency also received informal reports from auditors that clients had threatened to dismiss them if they made an RI disclosure. These informal reports seemed to confirm that the RI reporting rule had created tension between auditors and their clients. In an interview with a newspaper reporter, the IRBA's senior executive, Kariem Hoosain, admitted that the new requirement had resulted in a "strained relationship" between auditors and their clients.[13] But Hoosain quickly added that it was simply "tough luck." In the same article in which Hoosain was quoted, an officer of the SAICA indicated that the new RI rule was "onerous" for auditors and expressed his opinion that the criminal sanctions auditors faced under that rule were un-

fair.[14] The officer went on to note that "there's not much we can do now. It is the law and our members have to abide by [it]."[15]

As the details of the Randgold fraud were reported to the public, PwC, Randgold's former audit firm, became the target of increasing criticism for its role in that scandal. One reporter noted, "When the full tale of Brett Kebble's larceny is finally told, it would be something of a crime in itself if his auditors came off unscathed."[16] In October 2006, Karien Hoosain revealed that his agency was initiating an investigation of PwC's Randgold audits. Hoosain indicated that such an investigation was warranted given the report of the forensic consulting firm that had been retained by Randgold's board to scrutinize Kebble's fraudulent schemes. That report indicated that Randgold's fiscal 2003 financial statements (on which PwC had issued an unqualified opinion), "grossly misrepresented" the company's financial condition.[17] Hoosain reported that, because of the "complexities and sensitivities" of the Randgold case,

_____

12. *Africa News* (online), "Auditors Reporting Dubious Clients," 29 August 2006.

13. Naidoo, "Auditors' Brand Set to Rival That of a CA."

14. *Ibid.*

15. *Ibid.*

16. B. Rose, "What about PwC's Role in Kebble Saga?" http://www.resourceinvestor.com/ pebble.asp?relid=17819, 13 March 2006.

17. Naidoo, "Auditors' Brand Set to Rival That of a CA."

the investigation of PwC's audits would likely take years to complete.[18]

In November 2006, South African police arrested a businessman on suspicion of involvement in the murder of Brett Kebble. The businessman, who was subsequently charged with murder and conspiracy to commit murder, is a close personal friend of the South African Police Commissioner and also reportedly a member of a South African crime syndicate. Several months after his arrest, the murder suspect confessed that he had been involved in Kebble's death *at Kebble's request*. According to the suspect, Kebble had arranged to have his "assisted suicide" appear as a murder so that his family could collect on large life insurance polices that he had purchased. In any event, given the complexity of the case, South African law enforcement authorities believe that it may be years before it is ultimately solved.

Questions

1. Research online and hardcopy databases to identify important recent developments within the South African accounting profession. Summarize these developments in a bullet format.

2. Over the history of the global accounting profession, political forces have often played a major role in the development of individual nations' independent audit function. Explain how political forces have influenced the development and evolution of the independent audit function in the United States.

3. Identify the advantages and disadvantages of having a professional credential or designation for independent auditors in addition to a professional credential for accountants.

4. In your opinion, should the United States adopt a rule similar to South Africa's "reportable irregularities" rule? Defend your answer. How do you believe such a requirement would affect the United States' independent audit function and capital markets?

5. Identify strategies that the South African accounting profession could use to encourage young black men and women in that country to choose accounting as a career. In your opinion, what party or parties should take the lead in such recruiting efforts?

---

18. *Ibid.*

Zuan Yan

Let China sleep, for when it wakes, it will shake the world.

Napoleon

Every four years, the International Federation of Accountants (IFAC) organizes the World Congress of Accountants.[1] Accountants from across the globe attend this meeting to share their views on major issues and challenges facing their profession. In November 2002, the People's Republic of China hosted the World Congress of Accountants for the first time in the nation's history. Premier Zhu Rongji, the second-highest ranking official in the Chinese government, delivered the welcoming speech during the opening ceremonies. In his remarks, Premier Zhu, long known for his candid, if not blunt, manner, spoke openly of the embarrassing series of financial scandals that had created a major credibility crisis for the worldwide accounting profession over the previous decade. Premier Zhu pointed out that many of those accounting scandals had involved Chinese firms, a fact that Western journalists had largely ignored.

Similar to political leaders in many Western countries in recent years, Premier Zhu called on the accounting profession to reform itself and restore its credibility with the investing and lending public. He reminded the participants in the conference that "honesty and trustworthiness" are the lifeblood of the accounting profession.[2] Premier Zhu also assured those present that China was committed to "the cultivation of professional ethics among accountants" and, even more importantly, to creating a modern and transparent financial reporting system.[3]

Then, Mao, and Now

For several millennia, a series of family dynasties ruled China; these included, most notably, the Han, Ming, and Qing Dynasties. The collapse of the Qing Dynasty in 1912 led to the creation of the Republic of China that was dominated by a political party known as the Kuomintang or National Party. For four years following the end of World War II, a bloody civil war ensued between forces loyal to Chiang Kai-shek, the leader of the National Party, and the increasingly popular Communist Party led by Mao Zedong and his top subordinate, Zhou Enlai. In 1949, the Communist Party gained control of the country, forcing Chiang Kai-shek and his followers into exile on the island of Taiwan. On October 1, 1949, the Communist country was renamed the People's Republic of China.

Mao immediately installed a Marxist regime in China under which the central government controlled practically all of the nation's economic resources. To revitalize China's economy that had been decimated by World War II and the Chinese civil war, Mao implemented a series of economic programs, most notably the "Great Leap Forward," that were intended to convert the nation's largely agricultural economy

---

1. "Zuan yan" is a Chinese phrase meaning "to search for the truth and hold fast to it."

2. *People's Daily*, "Cherish Integrity of Accounting Profession: Chinese Premier," http://english. peopledaily.com.cn, 21 November 2002.

3. *Ibid.*

into a modern industrial economy. These programs were dismal failures, leaving China's economy in disarray and the country's citizens with a miserable standard of living.

In 1966, Mao launched the "Great Proletarian Cultural Revolution," more commonly referred to by historians as the "Cultural Revolution." This sweeping set of social and economic reforms was intended to rid China of the "liberal bourgeoisie" that was allegedly undermining Mao's efforts to establish a utopian, Communistic society controlled by the working class.[4] In reality, the Cultural Revolution was a desperate attempt by Mao to divert attention from his failed economic policies, while at the same time reaffirming his position as China's supreme leader. From 1966 through 1976, an estimated 500,000 Chinese citizens were executed and millions more exiled and persecuted at the hands of Mao's supporters.

Following Mao's death in 1976, several political figures wrestled for control of the country. Eventually, Deng Xiaoping established himself as China's unchallenged new leader, although he never officially held the top position in China's central government. Deng renounced the economic and social policies implemented by Mao during the Great Leap Forward and the Cultural Revolution. To raise China's standard of living, Deng replaced the nation's Soviet-style "command economy" with a "socialistic market economy."

Under China's new economic system, the nation's central government, which was still controlled by the Communist Party, would allow private enterprises to compete with state-owned enterprises (SOEs) across many sectors of the economy. Another critical element of Deng's economic blueprint was encouraging foreign companies to invest in China, a complete reversal of Mao's "closed door" policy. Deng especially encouraged large multinational corporations based in the United States and other Western countries to finance joint business ventures with Chinese SOEs.

In 1980, Deng emphatically endorsed his new economic plan for China, while at the same time shocking Communist allies and democratic societies around the world, when he proclaimed that "to be rich is to be glorious." Over the next three decades, Deng's economic policies, which remained in effect after his death in 1997, triggered an explosion of economic activity within China. By 2005, state-controlled enterprises accounted for only one-third of the nation's annual gross domestic product (GDP). Although still "poor" relative to common economic benchmarks, most Chinese citizens experienced a dramatic improvement in their standard of living under their nation's new "mixed" economy. Economists predict that by 2020 China's GDP will surpass that of Japan, resulting in the second-largest economy in the world. Those same economists project that by the midpoint of the twenty-first century, China's GDP will overtake that of the United States.

Deng Xiaoping's economic policies have impacted every facet of Chinese society, including the nation's professions, which had been largely discredited and debased during the three decades that Mao Zedong imposed his Marxist ideology on the country. Among the professional groups that have benefited the most from Deng's "revolution" is China's accounting profession. In recent years, China's political leaders have come to recognize that for their country to sustain its economic revival, a wide range of parties need reliable and comprehensive financial data regarding the nation's SOEs and other business enterprises. That data can only be provided if China develops a modern financial reporting system and an army of skilled accountants and auditors.

---

4. Wikipedia, "Cultural Revolution," http://en.wikipedia.org/wiki/Cultural_Revolution.

Accounting for Profits

To fully appreciate the accounting and financial reporting issues facing the Chinese economy, it is first necessary to identify the major types of business organizations within China. Prior to 1980, SOEs were the overwhelmingly dominant form of business organization within China in terms of annual economic output. As a result of the economic reforms introduced by Deng Xiaoping, three additional types of business organizations have become well established within China: collectively owned enterprises (COEs), individually owned enterprises (IOEs), and enterprises with foreign investments (FOEs).[5] COEs are typically local cooperatives organized by the members of a small community, while IOEs are principally small businesses owned and operated by individual entrepreneurs. Because most COEs and IOEs do not obtain significant investment capital from third-party investors and lenders, external financial reporting is not a major concern or regulatory requirement of these two types of organizations.

FOEs are either joint business ventures involving Chinese companies—typically SOEs—and foreign multinational corporations, or China-based businesses that are wholly owned by foreign multinational corporations. As a result, the financial data of most FOEs are eventually integrated into the consolidated financial statements of a foreign multinational corporation domiciled in the United States, a member nation of the European Union, or another developed country, meaning that FOEs typically employ "Western-style" accounting and financial reporting systems.

Over the past three decades, the efforts to develop a modern accounting and financial reporting system within China have centered on SOEs. Although the annual economic output of SOEs as a percentage of China's GDP has been steadily decreasing over the past three decades, these organizations remain the most important business units in China. In recent years, the Chinese government has sold minority ownership interests in many SOEs to private investors, ownership interests that are traded on either the Shanghai or Shenzhen Stock Exchanges, China's two major stock exchanges. China's political leaders apparently have no intention of completely "privatizing" the large petrochemical, iron and steel, and other manufacturing enterprises that continue to make up the backbone of the nation's economic infrastructure.[6]

Despite the fact that SOEs remain under the control of China's central government, the organizational structure of these entities and their internal operating policies and procedures have changed dramatically under the economic system installed by Deng Xiaopeng. Likewise, the role of SOEs' accounting and financial reporting systems has changed radically.

> *Prior to 1978 . . . SOEs were essentially production units (factories). The managers of SOEs in the pre-reform era had little or no managerial autonomy. The state provided all financing to the factories and controlled virtually all the investment and operating decisions. . . . The factories simply served the purpose of fulfilling the production quota stipulated by the government. Consequently, the managers of these factories had neither the incentive nor the managerial authority to reduce costs and generate profits. In such a command economy, the main role of accounting was to assist the government in planning and controlling decisions.[7]*

---

5. Xiang Bing, "Institutional Factors Influencing China's Accounting Reforms and Standards," *Accounting Horizons*, June 1998, 107.

6. *Ibid.*, 109.

7. *Ibid.*

In China's present economic system, the central government has transferred the responsibility for the day-to-day operations and long-term strategic planning for most SOEs to professional management teams. So, despite being ultimately accountable to the central government, most SOEs "now significantly resemble modern corporations in the West in that they are characterized by a high degree of managerial autonomy and a separation of ownership from control."[8]

The dramatic change in the nature of SOEs over the past three decades has created a need for Western-style accounting systems for these organizations. Such accounting systems produce the data necessary to properly evaluate the operating decisions of professional management teams. Likewise, under China's new economic system, there is an explicit recognition on the part of the country's political leaders that individual SOEs are competing for a finite quantity of economic resources. Consequently, there is a need to regularly assess the extent to which individual SOEs are contributing to the overall economic productivity of the nation. Finally, the central government realizes that for SOEs to raise investment capital from external sources, they must provide those parties relevant financial data.

The Ministry of Finance (MOF) is the government agency responsible for overseeing China's economy, including the nation's financial reporting system. In 1993, the MOF adopted an accounting framework for China analogous to the "Conceptual Framework" developed by the U.S. accounting profession in the late 1980s. This framework was entitled "The Accounting Standards for Business Enterprises" (ASBE). Throughout the 1980s, the MOF and other Chinese government agencies had taken steps to revamp the outmoded accounting and financial reporting systems being used by SOEs. However, those measures had been largely ineffectual. The adoption of the ASBE suggested that China's central government was intent on requiring SOEs to adopt Western-style accounting and financial reporting practices. "The introduction of ASBE was considered the most significant achievement of China's accounting reforms since the 1980s in that it signaled the end of traditional accounting in China and brought China's accounting practices into close conformity with international standards."[9]

The ASBE required most SOEs and other large Chinese enterprises to adopt the fundamental accounting principles and financial reporting formats used in Western democracies. "Among the accounting characteristics specified in the standards [ASBE] are double-entry accrual records, consistency, conservatism, comparative financial statements...and explanatory disclosures."[10] Although the ASBE principally dealt with broad accounting and financial reporting issues, the pronouncement also introduced such specific accounting methods as LIFO/FIFO, the allowance method of accounting for bad debts, the percentage-of-completion approach to revenue recognition, accelerated depreciation methods, and consolidated financial statements. Following the issuance of the ASBE, the MOF retained Deloitte Touche Tohmatsu as a consultant to assist in developing a comprehensive set of accounting standards for the Chinese economy. Over the following decade, the MOF approved several dozen accounting standards proposed by Deloitte. These new standards were generally referred to as Chinese Accounting Standards (CAS).

---

8. *Ibid.*, 111.

9. T. Tang, B. Cooper, and P. Leung, "Accounting in China: Developments and Opportunities," in *Perspectives on Accounting and Finance in China*, edited by J. B. Black and S. Gao (London: Routledge, 1995).

10. G. M. Winkle, H. Fenwick, and X. Chen, "Accounting Standards in the People's Republic of China: Responding to Economic Reforms," *Accounting Horizons,* September 1994, 55.

As one would expect, there was almost no opposition to, or criticism of, the decision by China's authoritarian central government to adopt Western-style accounting standards. However, the MOF and other government agencies faced considerable challenges in executing that decision. The most intractable of these challenges stemmed from the fact that China's accounting profession had been dismantled under Mao Zedong's regime. As one journalist noted recently, "Grey hair and experience [in China's domestic accounting profession] are scarce because the Cultural Revolution wiped out the profession."[11]

Within Mao's Soviet-style economy, professional accountants who understood complex accounting and financial reporting issues were no longer needed and, in fact, were considered part and parcel of the "liberal bourgeoisie" that had to be eliminated. Instead of skilled accountants and auditors, China's state-controlled enterprises required only the services of bookkeepers and "bean counters" to accumulate production statistics and related data, which were then funneled to the proper authorities.

To help organize and promote China's accounting profession, the MOF created the Chinese Institute of Certified Public Accountants (CICPA) in 1988. This new government agency immediately began licensing CPAs; three years later, the agency began administering a CPA examination. In 1993, the "CPA Law" issued by China's central government provided a more coherent regulatory infrastructure for the new profession by documenting in detail the specific responsibilities of the CICPA. Although this law designated the CICPA as the principal regulatory body for the accounting profession, the powerful MOF retained the authority to override any decisions made by the CICPA.

Presently, China has approximately 150,000 CPAs; however, many of these individuals are retired government bureaucrats with minimal or even no formal training or experience in accounting. These latter individuals were granted CPA designations by the CICPA because they had administrative experience of some kind with an SOE or other significant government-related organization. Leaders of China's accounting profession estimate that the nation has fewer than 100,000 professional accountants who have formal accounting training of any kind. That figure is in contrast with the approximately 400,000 professional accountants in the United States, which has approximately one-fourth the population of China. Making matters worse, the educational programs completed by China's accountants are considerably less rigorous than the educational programs completed by professional accountants in Western economies. In fact, in 2000, fewer than 20 percent of China's CPAs held a university degree of any kind.[12]

Most of China's accounting firms were quickly organized in the early 1980s when the need for accounting services within the nation's new economy became evident. However, these new accounting firms were not equivalent to accounting firms in the United States and other developed economies. The largest and most prominent of China's new generation of accounting firms were created by various government agencies and, in reality, were simply appendages of those agencies. These "accounting firms" typically provided accounting services exclusively to the SOEs and other entities that were overseen by the agencies that had created the firms.

---

11. *The Asian Banker Journal* (online), "In Search of a Reliable Auditor," 31 August 2006.

12. Y. Tang, "Bumpy Road Leading to Internationalization: A Review of Accounting Development in China," *Accounting Horizons,* March 2000, 99.

Because the MOF and the CICPA recognized that the quality of services provided by the government agency-affiliated accounting firms was suspect, the two organizations launched a "clean-up" program in 1997 to force those firms to sever their relationships with the agencies that had created them. The MOF and CICPA also reviewed the operating policies and procedures of all Chinese accounting firms, including those not affiliated with government agencies. Over the course of the two-year clean-up program, approximately 10 percent of China's estimated 4,000 accounting firms were forced to disband, while another 30 percent were sanctioned and required to implement remedial measures of some kind.

Another principal objective of this clean-up program was to make accounting firms and individual accountants aware of their ethical responsibilities. One Chinese scholar observed that China's new accounting profession was created in a "moral vacuum" devoid of any consideration of ethical principles or issues.[13] In 1999, the CICPA issued a new authoritative pronouncement entitled "Professional Ethics" that identified the fundamental ethical responsibilities of Chinese CPAs, particularly their responsibility to perform accounting services with objectivity and integrity.

Big Four Lead the Way in Chinese Audits

During the early 1980s, the major international accounting firms recognized that the robust economy emerging in China was creating a new and potentially huge market for professional accounting services. Over the following two decades, each of the major international accounting firms established a network of practice offices in China. PricewaterhouseCoopers (PwC) invested $200 million to staff 12 offices in China with a workforce of 5,500 accountants, while Deloitte spent approximately the same amount to establish 10 China-based offices with a staff of 3,000 accountants.[14] KPMG and Ernst & Young established China practice units of comparable size to those of PwC and Deloitte. As one Chinese news service noted, the Big Four firms suddenly developed an "insatiable interest" in the Chinese market.[15] Ernst & Young's global chief operating officer seemed to confirm that point of view when he observed, "There is no greater opportunity in the world than in China in terms of our business."[16]

By 2005, the Big Four accounting firms were operating the four largest accounting practices in China. The largest domestic firm, Shu Lun Pan Certified Public Accountants, based in Shanghai, had annual revenues equal to less than one-third of KPMG's China practice, which was the smallest of the Big Four accounting practices in terms of annual revenues. As could be expected, China's major domestic accounting firms felt threatened by the Big Four's rapid growth in their country.[17] Instead of choosing to compete with the Big Four, many of the large domestic firms developed working relationships with one or more Big Four firms.

Independent auditing was a principal focus of the Big Four's practice development activities in China. Prior to Deng Xiaoping's economic reforms, there was little need for an independent audit function in China similar to that of Western economies. The SOEs that dominated China's economy did not prepare periodic financial reports

---

13. *Ibid.*

14. *SinoCast China Financial Watch* (online), "Accounting Giants Load Up on China," 28 June 2005.

15. *Ibid.*

16. W. Davies, "China Accounting Sector Makes Gains amid IPO Drive," *Global News Wire—Asia Africa Intelligence Wire*, 6 February 2007.

17. T. LeeMaster, "Cleaner Regime for China Auditors," *Global News Wire—Asia Africa Intelligence Wire*, 18 April 2005.

comparable to those prepared by large corporations in the U.S. and other free market economies. In addition, the principal users of the financial data prepared by SOEs were government bureaucrats that had access to the accounting systems of SOEs and could "audit" that data directly if they questioned its authenticity.

As China's new economy began emerging, the need for an independent audit function became readily apparent. The large FOEs that were developing in China were typically required to have their financial data audited since those data would be consolidated into another reporting entity's financial statements. Likewise, China's political leaders quickly recognized that SOEs needed annual audits to encourage foreign investors to purchase minority ownership interests in them. Those officials also realized that annual audits of SOEs would establish an important measure of accountability for their professional management teams.

China's domestic independent audit function developed slowly and haphazardly during the 1980s. Unlike in the United States and other Western economies, China's accounting firms did not initially provide audit services. In the early 1980s, organizations offering audit-type services began appearing in China's major metropolitan areas. Similar to China's first-generation accounting firms, most of the nation's early audit firms were affiliated with, or sponsored by, a government agency. These audit firms—which were overseen by the State Audit Administration (SAA)—provided principally operational, compliance, and "social" audit services. Full-scope financial statement audits were rare and when they were performed were not oriented around the rigorous professional standards used in Western economies. Eventually, many of China's larger domestic accounting firms began providing services similar to those provided by audit firms, resulting in significant competition between the two types of firms.

By the early 1990s, the Chinese audit market was a mishmash of various types of audit firms and audit-type services. Adding to the confusion was an array of often conflicting auditing rules and regulations issued by the CICPA, MOF, SAA, and other government agencies that claimed some degree of regulatory oversight for the audit services market. This chaos was a contributing factor to several large-scale accounting and auditing scandals within China during the 1990s. Among the most notorious of these scandals was the Great Wall fundraising fraud involving the Great Wall Electrical Engineering Science and Technology Company. This company's executives used financial statements "certified" by a local accounting firm to raise a large amount of funds from private investors across China, much of which they embezzled. A subsequent investigation revealed that the accounting firm had spent only one day auditing the company's financial statements. China's central government dealt quickly and harshly with the parties involved in the fraud. The chief architect of the fraud, the company president, was executed, while the company's accounting firm was disbanded.

The Great Wall fundraising scandal and mounting criticism of China's chaotic audit services market by various parties, including the major international accounting firms, were key factors that persuaded the central government to issue the 1993 CPA Law. That statute consolidated the nation's accounting and auditing professions and placed them under the regulatory supervision of the CICPA, which remained ultimately accountable to the MOF. The CPA Law also mandated that the CICPA develop independent auditing standards that would be subject to the approval of the MOF.

In late 1994, the CICPA formed a task force to begin drafting Chinese Independent Auditing Standards (CIAS). Over the next several years, the CICPA issued auditing standards dealing with such topics as materiality, internal control risks, application of analytical procedures, computer-based auditing procedures, fraud detection, and "special considerations in the audit of state-owned companies."[18] Despite the promulgation of these standards, the quality of independent audits provided by domestic firms remained questionable. Many of China's domestic firms treated the new standards as guidelines rather than mandatory rules. Even more troubling, many audit clients routinely pressured their auditors to help them conceal material errors and fraudulent misrepresentations in their accounting records. "Some clients . . . expected their auditors to help them conceal their frauds. Many companies would not reappoint their auditors if the latter were unwilling to help them cover up their wrongdoings."[19]

As the Chinese audit discipline continued to evolve in the late 1990s and into the new century, the Big Four firms became increasingly important participants in that market. According to one Asian business publication, the Big Four's growing prominence in China's audit services market was due to those firms' reputation for "professionalism, technical ability, and their independence from clients."[20] By 2006, the Big Four firms audited a large majority of China's major business organizations. A Hong Kong brokerage firm surveyed 150 large companies listed on Chinese stock exchanges and found that only six did not employ Big Four auditors. The brokerage firm referred to those companies as the "suspicious six,"[21] implying that their financial statements were suspect. A manager of a Hong Kong hedge fund expressed a similar point of view: "I don't think I'm comfortable with local [audit] firms. It's the professionalism of the people. It seems like they like to twist the rules. That bothers me."[22]

The most prized of all audit clients in China are the "Big Four" banks that serve as the cornerstones of the nation's economy. These banks include the Agricultural Bank of China, the Bank of China, the China Construction Bank, and the Industrial and Commercial Bank of China. Over the past several years, China's central government has used initial public offerings (IPOs) to sell minority ownership interests in these formerly wholly owned SOEs. For each of those IPOs, government officials retained a Big Four accounting firm to audit the given bank's financial statements. This "vote of confidence" in the Big Four accounting firms by China's political leaders suggested that those firms would likely play a significant role in the future development of the Chinese economy.

EPILOGUE

In 2005, the MOF announced that it was working with the International Accounting Standards Board (IASB) to converge CAS with International Financial Reporting Standards (IFRS). Most Chinese business organizations would be required to adopt the revised CAS as of January 1, 2007, although several large SOEs were given an additional year to make the transition to the new standards. The IASB reported that it would help Chinese officials modify certain IFRS to meet the special needs of China's economic system. Among the latter IFRS was the standard requiring disclosure of material related-party transactions.

---

18. J. Z. Xiao, Y. Zhang, and Z. Xie, "The Making of Independent Auditing Standards in China," *Accounting Horizons*, March 2000, 77.

19. *Ibid.*

20. *The Asian Banker Journal*, "In Search of a Reliable Auditor."

21. *Ibid.*

22. *Ibid.*

This is a sound principle in general and particularly appropriate for companies in countries where the government owns a piece of everything, and presses companies to take steps that may be bad for them (such as buying from troubled suppliers to protect jobs). But because overlapping ownership is so common in China (the government still owns shares in almost every large company), detailing each [related-party] transaction would overwhelm the financial report.[23]

At the same time that the MOF announced the plan to converge CAS with IFRS, the government agency also announced that as of January 1, 2007, CIAS would be converged with International Standards on Auditing (ISAs). These latter standards are issued by the International Auditing and Assurance Standards Board (IAASB), an entity sponsored by the IFAC. In February 2006, the MOF released 39 new accounting standards and 48 new auditing standards that had been converged with the respective international standards.

The decision by the MOF to converge Chinese accounting and auditing standards with international standards enhanced the already strong competitive position that the Big Four firms had established within the Chinese accounting and auditing services market. Because each of those firms had global accounting practices, they had extensive expertise in helping companies implement IFRS as well as significant experience in applying ISAs. As a result, the firms were ideally suited to help Chinese companies make the transition to the new accounting and auditing standards.

Despite the Big Four's bright prospects in China, the firms still face significant challenges in that market. These challenges include acquiring sufficient skilled accountants and auditors to staff their rapidly growing Chinese practices and coping with the nation's regulatory infrastructure that continues to be a cluttered maze of often conflicting regulations issued by several layers of the Communist bureaucracy. Two more serious and difficult-to-resolve problems

facing Big Four firms are an increasing litigation risk within China and the need to deal with an authoritarian central government that influences every facet of the Chinese society and economy.

Since the 1970s, arguably the most important challenge faced by the Big Four accounting firms in the United States has been the large number of civil lawsuits filed against them. In recent years, the Big Four firms have begun experiencing litigation problems in China. Numerous accounting frauds, embezzlement schemes, and related scams have been perpetrated by opportunists hoping to take advantage of China's new economic system. Many private investors, institutional investors, government agencies, and other parties adversely affected by these subterfuges have begun adopting a Western-style strategy to recover their losses and/or mend their wounded pride, namely, filing lawsuits against parties even remotely associated with the fraudulent activities. At least in part because of their "deep pockets" and high public profiles, Big Four firms have increasingly found themselves targets of such lawsuits.

In 2003, KPMG became the first of the Big Four accounting firms to be named as a defendant in a major securities lawsuit filed by Chinese investors. The accounting firm issued a series of unqualified opinions on the financial statements of Jinzhou Port Company Limited, a company sanctioned by the MOF for intentionally overstating its revenues over the five-year period 1996–2000. The other Big Four firms have been ensnared in similar financial scandals involving Chinese companies: Deloitte (Guangdong Kelon Electrical Holdings Company), PwC (Shanghai Waigaoqiao Free Trade Zone Development Company Limited), and Ernst & Young (Global Trend Intelligent Technologies).

The Big Four firms insist that the complaints filed against them in these and other cases are unwarranted and that the engagements in question were completed with due professional

23. *The Economist* (online), "Cultural Revolution: New Accounting Rules Have Replaced the Little Red Book as China's Guide to Self-Improvement; Can the State Handle the Truth?" 11 January 2007.

care. Nevertheless, critics suggest that the quality of independent audits in China is generally weaker than in Western countries, an allegation seemingly confirmed by a Deloitte partner. "Auditing is easier in an environment where all your clients have 25 accountants, internal controls, and independent boards. The audit process is the same in this part of the world; we follow the same methodology and document it in the same way. But, the material you're dealing with is different."[24] A KPMG partner voiced a similar opinion when he noted that within China, "the public expects too much of auditors. Audit work is one thing. The most important thing is the integrity of the owners and managers."[25]

An even more serious challenge than the increasing risk of civil litigation facing the Big Four accounting firms in China is how they will deal with their ultimate "client" in that market, namely, the authoritarian central government. No doubt, executives of the Big Four firms recognize that conflicts with officials of the Chinese government could damage their future opportunities in the lucrative Chinese market. These executives also realize that their credibility in other markets around the globe could be damaged if their firms are perceived as kowtowing or capitulating to Chinese governmental officials.

Ernst & Young was the first of the Big Four firms to have a highly publicized confrontation with China's Communist central government. In 2006, a Chinese government agency hired Ernst & Young to prepare a report on the "nonperforming loans" held by China's Big Four banks. Over the previous several years, the magnitude of China's nonperforming loans had become a major international issue. "The size of China's bad loans is a figure of immense importance, as it serves as a measure of the banking sector's financial health."[26] Many economists maintained that governmental officials routinely embellished the health of the Chinese economy by refusing to disclose that a large proportion of the Big Four banks' loan portfolios were uncollectible. Allegedly, those officials refused to recognize the magnitude of this problem because doing so would damage China's credit rating in international markets, discourage much-needed foreign investment, and undercut the impressive economic trends that the central government regularly touted in the global press.

In May 2006, Ernst & Young reported that China's Big Four banks had total nonperforming loans of more than $900 billion. That figure was several times higher than the $133 billion figure being reported by the Chinese government. Chinese officials reacted quickly and fiercely to the E&Y report, referring to it as "ridiculous and barely understandable."[27] Those officials went on to point out that if the nonperforming loans figure reported by E&Y was accurate, then the "clean" opinion E&Y had issued on a Big Four bank's financial statements was almost certainly wrong.

Within a few days of the harsh criticism by Chinese officials, Ernst & Young retracted its report. In the retraction, Ernst & Young stated that, "Upon further research, Ernst & Young Global finds that this number cannot be supported, and believes it to be factually erroneous."[28] The retraction went on to note that Ernst & Young believed that the nonperforming loans figure of $133 billion reported by the Chinese government was accurate. Skeptics immediately accused E&Y of capitulating to the Chinese government. Many economic analysts chimed in as well, insisting that the Chinese government's figure was only a fraction of the actual bad loans held by the Big Four banks.

The E&Y incident raised two concerns within the global investment and business community. First, the incident only added to widespread speculation that China's impressive economic

---

24. *The Asian Banker Journal,* "In Search of a Reliable Auditor."

25. *Ibid.*

26. *Agence France Presse* (online), "Ernst & Young Withdraws 'Erroneous' Report on Bad Loans in China," 15 May 2006.

27. J. Manthorpe, "Accountants Backtrack on China Bad-Debt Report," *The Vancouver Sun,* 23 May 2006, E5.

28. *Ibid.*

data had been intentionally inflated by the nation's Communist government. "It has become an article of faith over the past quarter of a century of China's economic opening up that numbers issued by the Beijing government are at best rose-tinted, and at worst politically motivated fabrications."[29] Second, the incident suggested that China's central government would not hesitate to use its authoritarian powers to stifle dissent or honest differences of opinion, even an objective opinion expressed by a respected international accounting firm.

Ernst & Young's unpleasant encounter with Chinese governmental officials angered many Western journalists. In commenting on that encounter, one such journalist suggested that those officials had not internalized the slogan adopted by Deng Xiaoping when he attempted to resurrect the Chinese economy after nearly 30 years of the failed policies of Mao Zedong. " 'Truth from facts' was the slogan adopted by the Chinese government after Mao's death to strip away the lies that left China a wallowing giant. Thirty years on, this remains an elusive goal."[30]

Questions

1. Research relevant databases to identify important recent developments within China's accounting profession, including the nation's independent audit function. Summarize these developments in a bullet format.

2. Since ethical and moral values vary from culture to culture and nation to nation, does this mean that a global profession, such as the accounting profession, cannot have a uniform ethical code? Explain.

3. How, if at all, do financial reporting objectives differ between a free market economy and a "socialistic market economy"? Explain. Are there specific accounting concepts or principles that are more or less relevant in a free market economy than in a socialistic market economy? If so, identify those concepts or principles and briefly explain your rationale.

4. Consider two organizations that require annual independent audits: Organization A is a Chinese SOE with a minority ownership interest of 20 percent, while Organization B is a U.S. company of similar size operating in the same industry. The common stock of both entities is traded on a domestic stock exchange and each is audited by a Big Four firm. List specific differences that you might expect in the independent audits of these two organizations. *Ceteris paribus,* would you expect more "audit failures" for SOE audit clients than for similar U.S. audit clients? Defend your answer.

5. What recommendations would you make to Big Four firms to help them (1) avoid confrontations with governmental officials in an authoritarian society and (2) deal effectively with such confrontations that do arise?

---

29. *Ibid.*

30. *The Economist* (online), "Truth from Facts," 13 January 2007, 14.

Kaset Thai Sugar Company

The black Toyota minivan made slow but steady progress down the narrow, unpaved road as it approached the village of Takhli in south central Thailand, approximately 150 miles north of Bangkok. On either side of the bumpy road were fields of sugarcane, dense thickets of scrub brush, and an occasional rice paddy. Seated in a rear window seat of the minivan was Michael Wansley, a senior partner with Deloitte Touche Tohmatsu who was based in that firm's Melbourne, Australia, practice office. The vehicle's four other occupants were Thai nationals and employees of the Kaset Thai Sugar Company. No doubt, the five weary travelers who had spent several hours in the cramped minivan were overjoyed when they finally caught a glimpse of the large sugar mill in the distance that was their final destination. The sugar mill was one of many owned and operated by the Kaset Thai Sugar Company.

For the past several weeks, Michael Wansley had been supervising a debt-restructuring engagement for the company's banks and other lenders. Kaset Thai Sugar had defaulted on nearly $500 million of loans to those lenders. Wansley and the 14 subordinates on his engagement team were to study the company's accounting records and business operations and then make recommendations about how the lenders should proceed in attempting to collect all—or at least a significant portion—of the outstanding loans.

Wansley, a well known debt-restructuring expert, had become all too familiar with remote Thailand communities such as Takhli over the previous several months because the services of debt-restructuring specialists were much in demand within Thailand during the late 1990s. In March 1999, when Wansley visited the sugar mill on the outskirts of Takhli, the nation of Thailand was mired in a financial crisis. From 1985 through 1995, Thailand had boasted the highest economic growth rate in the world, averaging almost 9 percent annually over that time span. That trend prompted billions of dollars of foreign direct investment in Thailand companies, the bulk of which was in the form of loans.

Thailand's impressive economic growth came to a jarring halt in 1997, undercut by speculative investments, mismanagement, and extensive fraud on the part of business owners and corporate executives. According to one critic of Thailand's free-wheeling economic system, "cronyism, collusion, corruption, and complacency" had long been the "four modern horsemen of the apocalypse" in that economy.[1] By the late 1990s, hundreds of Thai companies faced bankruptcy, unable to pay back the loans they had secured over the previous decade. In 1999, nearly one-half of the $150 billion in outstanding loans to large Thai companies was classified as "nonperforming"—and it was estimated that $50 billion of that total would never be collected."[2]

As Thailand's financial crisis deepened, the foreign banks and other lenders that had pumped billions of dollars of debt capital into Thai companies began retaining debt-restructuring specialists in Australia, the United States, and other developed countries to help them determine how to best deal with their mounting portfolios of

---

1. U. Parpart, "Restructuring East Asia: A Progress Report," *The Milken Institute Review*, Third Quarter 1999, 42.

2. *Ibid.*, 40.

nonperforming loans. Among the major providers of these debt-restructuring services were the large international accounting firms, including Deloitte, Michael Wansley's firm.

The nature of debt-restructuring services varies significantly but such engagements often begin with an intense study or "audit" of the given entity's accounting records. This examination is intended to uncover any evidence of embezzlement or other malfeasance by management or other parties. These engagements also commonly include an in-depth analysis of the debtor company's business model to determine whether the entity appears to be economically viable. A debt-restructuring engagement typically concludes with the engagement team developing a series of recommendations intended to help the lenders of the financially troubled company minimize their loan losses. These recommendations may involve replacing the existing management team, having the lender or lenders forgive their outstanding loans in exchange for equity interests in the given company, or liquidating the company to raise funds that can be used to repay or partially repay its outstanding loans.

Not surprisingly given their nature and purpose, debt-restructuring engagements can be rife with tension. *Business Week* noted that Thailand's financial crisis spawned "Debt Wars" in that country that pitted representatives of the large international accounting firms, such as Michael Wansley, against Thai business owners and executives.[3] Thai business owners and executives resented the probing and relentless investigations of the "farangs" (foreigners) who did not appreciate or fully understand the informal and low-key culture of the Thai business community, a culture in which "handshake" contracts were common, disagreements were considered impolite, and face-to-face confrontations were rare. Making matters worse, Thai companies were not accustomed to having their financial records and business operations scrutinized by third parties because the nation's independent audit function was still evolving and was not nearly as rigorous as in developed countries around the world.

The investigative work of debt-restructuring specialists was particularly galling to members of the wealthy Thai families that had long dominated their nation's economy. Until the late 1990s, 15 Thai families controlled networks of businesses that accounted for more than one-half of Thailand's annual gross domestic product.[4] Among these families was the Siriviriyakul family that owned the Kaset Thai Sugar Company. For centuries, these families had operated their business empires with only minimal oversight or regulation from the Thai government or other parties. Suddenly, these prominent families found themselves being forced to respond to embarrassing questions and accusations posed by a small army of foreign accountants.

In January 1999, *Business Week* interviewed the 58-year-old Wansley regarding the difficult and stressful nature of his work in Thailand. Wansley noted that the most frustrating facet of debt-restructuring engagements in Thailand was the belligerent attitude of company owners. "Once you become grossly insolvent you're not supposed to be in a position of great strength, but here they think they are."[5] In a subsequent interview, Wansley also admitted that the hostile nature of the debt-restructuring engagements caused him to sometimes question his and his subordinates' safety. That concern was not unwarranted.

As the black minivan carrying Wansley and the four employees of Kaset Thai Sugar Company rolled to a stop outside the firm's Takhli sugar mill, two men on a

---

3. F. Balfour, "Fixing Thailand's Debt Mess," *Business Week* (http://www.businessweek.com), 12 February 2001.

4. Parpart, "Restructuring East Asia," 41.

5. R. Corben, M. Clifford, and B. Einhorn, "Thailand: Bring Your Spreadsheet—and Bulletproof Vest," *Business Week* (http://www.businessweek.com), 29 March 1999.

motorcycle pulled up beside the vehicle. The man sitting on the rear of the motorcycle leaped off and within a matter of seconds fired 11 bullets from an automatic pistol into the interior of the minivan. Eight of the bullets struck Michael Wansley in the head, killing him instantly. The four other passengers in the minivan were left unharmed as the gunman and his confederate sped away on the motorcycle.

The murder of Michael Wansley triggered outrage in Australia and the international business community. Australian government officials demanded that Thailand law enforcement authorities vigorously investigate the crime and apprehend those responsible. Eventually, six individuals would face criminal charges for Wansley's murder. These individuals included the gunman, the motorcyclist, the owner of the motorcycle, two employees of Kaset Thai Sugar Company who had allegedly been involved in the conspiracy to kill Wansley, and the owner of the Takhli sugar mill who was a member of the powerful Siriviriyakul family. This latter individual was charged with masterminding Wansley's murder.

The motorcyclist, who was arrested shortly after the incident, was convicted for his role in the crime and given a life sentence. A human resources manager of Kaset Thai Sugar and the owner of the motorcycle, a retired policeman, were convicted of conspiring to murder Wansley and received death sentences. The brother of the human resources manager, who was also a Kaset Thai Sugar employee, was convicted of conspiracy to commit murder but received a life sentence. To date, the alleged gunman, who was not apprehended until 2003, has not been tried for his role in the crime. This latter individual, reportedly a professional "hit man" who was paid the equivalent of $800 to kill Wansley, must first face murder charges in two other cases.

The most controversial outcome in the criminal cases emanating from Wansley's death was the acquittal of the owner of the Takhli sugar mill despite seemingly strong evidence linking him to the crime. During this individual's trial, a witness testified that the defendant had paid him approximately $1,000 to dispose of the motorcycle used in the Wansley murder. Another individual, a senior law enforcement official, revealed that the sugar mill owner had offered him $4 million in exchange for not filing charges against him in the case. Phone records introduced as evidence during the trial documented that prior to the shooting the defendant had frequent telephone conversations with the three individuals convicted of conspiring to kill Wansley.

Court testimony also revealed that shortly before his death, Michael Wansley discovered that approximately $150 million loaned to the Kaset Thai Sugar Company had been secretly transferred to small companies controlled by the sugar mill owner and other members of his family. This testimony established that the defendant had a strong motive to harm Wansley. In fact, a Kaset Thai Sugar employee testified that following Wansley's death, the sugar mill owner had told him, "It's very good the farang is dead; now we can all live comfortably."[6] Despite such evidence, the three-judge tribunal that presided over the trial handed down a "not guilty" verdict, clearing the sugar mill owner of any involvement in Wansley's murder.[7,8]

The six individuals who faced criminal charges stemming from the murder of Michael Wansley were not the only parties blamed for his death. A journalist

---

6. J. Pollard, "Death Penalty for Aussie Auditor's Killers," *The Australian* (http://www.theaustralian.news.com.au), 6 September 2006.

7. One of the judges initially assigned to the case had been replaced when allegations surfaced that he had been paid a large bribe by the defendant's family.

8. The Siriviriyakul family maintained control of the Kaset Thai Sugar Company following Michael Wansley's death. When the debt-restructuring plan eventually developed by Deloitte was rejected by the company's creditors, a Thai court refused to liquidate the company and instead allowed the Siriviriyakul family to continue operating it.

suggested that Wansley's employer, Deloitte, should shoulder some of the blame for his untimely death. Deloitte officials "should have known that they were sending the locally inexperienced Wansley into a dangerous situation without taking precautions."[9] The journalist pointed out that among the major international accounting firms, Deloitte had established a reputation as a leader in risk assessment and risk management. "These days, expertise in risk assessment—on which D. T. T. prides itself—cannot be prudently limited to financial risk."[10]

Deloitte apparently did not respond directly to such criticism. However, several years later, Keith Skinner, the chief operating officer (COO) of Deloitte Touche Tohmatsu and a close friend of Michael Wansley, agreed to be interviewed regarding Wansley's death. In that interview, Skinner indicated that Wansley's murder "has had a lasting impact" on Deloitte's operations in regions of the world that are "culturally different."[11] When asked what specific changes Deloitte had made in response to the incident, Skinner reported that Deloitte was placing a higher priority on "security" issues for professional services engagements in high-risk countries. During this same interview, Skinner noted that his friend had not only been a well-respected professional but also an individual who was known for his extraordinary personal integrity and for being a devoted humanitarian. In particular, Wansley had devoted considerable time to working with the International Red Cross.

Questions

1. Suppose in the future you are assigned to an audit engagement that requires you to travel to a foreign country openly hostile to the United States. Because of that hostility, you are uncomfortable with the assignment. What would you do? Before responding, identify the alternatives you have.

2. Do you believe it is appropriate for a professional services firm to ask employees to serve on engagements in which their personal safety is at risk? Defend your answer.

---

9. Parpart, "Restructuring East Asia," 39.

10. *Ibid.*

11. A. Caldwell, "Murdered Accountant's Son Welcomes Sentences," http://www.abc.net.au, 5 September 2006.

Australian Wheat Board

The United States and the Commonwealth of Australia have long been strong and mutually supportive allies.[1] However, the two countries' close relationship was threatened recently by an international scandal referred to in the *Sydney Morning Herald*, Australia's oldest and most prominent newspaper, as the "worst corruption scandal in Australian history."[2] At the center of this scandal was AWB Limited, a large public company that had been granted a government monopoly over the export of all wheat from that country. During the United Nations embargo imposed on Iraq following that country's invasion of Kuwait, AWB became the largest supplier of wheat to Iraq. AWB's wheat sales to Iraq were made through the United Nations (U.N.) Oil-for-Food Program, a program intended to provide humanitarian relief to Iraqi citizens during the lengthy U.N. embargo.

Following the overthrow of Saddam Hussein's regime by U.S.-led coalition forces in 2003, allegations surfaced that AWB had secured the Iraqi wheat contracts by agreeing to pay bribes to the former dictator. The U.N. formed a task force headed by Paul Volcker, the former chairman of the United States' Federal Reserve System, to investigate those allegations. In late 2005, the task force reported that AWB had paid nearly $300 million in bribes to Saddam Hussein's regime beginning in the late 1990s. AWB management had been told by Iraqi governmental officials that if the bribes were not paid, the company would not be granted the huge wheat contracts.

A former AWB officer testified that one of his superiors approved the payment of the Iraqi bribes. In defense of those illicit payments, the superior told this individual, "We are in the business of maximizing opportunities and sales returns" and, as a result, "we shouldn't jeopardize our business with Iraq"[3] [by refusing to pay the bribes demanded by Saddam Hussein]. After the fact, some AWB stockholders defended the company's decision to capitulate to Saddam Hussein's demands. "We have had enough of this free market bulls___. When you do business with Saddam, you do business the way he tells you."[4]

The AWB scandal created a brouhaha between Australia's two leading political parties, the Liberal Party and the Labor Party. Political opponents of Prime Minister John Howard, the leader of the Liberal Party, charged that he and his subordinates had approved AWB's decision to secretly funnel bribes to Saddam Hussein to secure the lucrative Iraqi wheat contracts. In referring to those bribes, a spokesperson for the Labor Party noted that, "This is the single biggest lump of money in the world paid to the Iraqi dictator, straight out of Australia, approved by the Australian government."[5]

---

1. I would like to thank Glen McLaughlin for his generous and continuing support of efforts to develop instructional cases for use in accounting and auditing courses that highlight important ethical issues.

2. *Sydney Morning Herald* (http://www.smh.com.au), "AWB's World of Trouble," 25 November 2006.

3. Australian Government, Attorney-General's Department, "Inquiry into Certain Australian Companies in Relation to the UN Oil-for-Food Programme," Transcript 24, 2322, 9 February 2006.

4. H. Stringleman, "Aussie Farmers Fume over Single-Desk Loss," *The National Business Review*, 5 May 2006, 14.

5. *Associated Press* (online), "Australian Attorney General Defends Country's Stance on Bribery against OECD Criticism," 17 January 2006.

Criticism of Prime Minister Howard was not confined to Australia. U.S. wheat farmers and several large U.S. wheat exporters, such as Cargill, Inc., were incensed by the revelations of how AWB had obtained the Iraqi wheat contracts and insisted that the United States take appropriate measures to punish Australia. U.S. Senator Norm Coleman of Minnesota, a leading spokesperson for U.S. wheat producers, publicly criticized Prime Minister Howard and suggested that, at a minimum, the prime minister had been aware that AWB was paying the bribes. This accusation prompted an irate Prime Minister Howard, who had long been an ardent supporter of the United States and its Middle Eastern policies, to demand an apology from the U.S. government, an apology that the prime minister never received.

Wheat Socialism

The Australian government created the Australian Wheat Board in 1939 to provide economic assistance to the country's wheat farmers. Many of the nation's wheat farmers had struggled to survive the Great Depression of the 1930s that had caused just as much, if not more, economic misery in Australia as it had in the United States. For the next five decades, all wheat grown in Australia had to be sold to the Australian Wheat Board at a price established by the federal agency. In 1989, Australia's federal government deregulated the nation's domestic wheat market, but any wheat that was to be exported, which was the bulk of the nation's annual harvest, still had to be sold to the Australian Wheat Board. The Australian Wheat Board pooled the wheat purchased each year for export and then marketed it principally to developing countries around the world. Proceeds from the sale of the wheat were then distributed on a pro rata basis to Australia's wheat farmers.

In 1999, Australia's federal government converted the Australian Wheat Board into AWB Limited, a private company with two classes of common stock. AWB's Class A common stock was distributed to the country's wheat farmers. This stock is nontransferable and must be sold back to AWB if an individual stops growing wheat. In 1991, AWB's Class B common stock was sold on the Australian Stock Exchange for the first time. Class B stock can be purchased by anyone, but Australian law prohibits any individual or institution from accumulating more than 10 percent of those shares. Since 9 of the 11 seats on AWB's board of directors are chosen by the Class A stockholders, Australia's wheat farmers exercise effective control over the company.

The so-called "single desk" system implemented for Australia's wheat industry was an economic boon for the nation's wheat farmers. That market structure allowed Australia to become a major player in the intensely competitive global wheat market. By the end of the century, Australia ranked second only to the United States in that market. Although Australia produced only 3 percent of the world's wheat harvest each year, the country accounted for 15 percent of annual wheat exports. Thanks to the AWB, Australian wheat was being sold to more than 50 countries by the late 1990s.

Many wheat exporters around the world, particularly major exporters in the United States, maintained that AWB achieved its prominent role in the global wheat market by relying on bribes, kickbacks, and other illicit payments to obtain major international wheat contracts. An Australian politician suggested that such payments were necessary to compete in the "corrupt" global wheat market.[6,7] That politician was referring to the

6. D. Crawshaw, C. Brinsden, and P. Mulvey, "Tensions High as AWB Monopoly Crumbles," *Global News Wire* (online), 22 December 2006.

7. As a point of information, international wheat vendors outside of the United States have long maintained that government subsidies provide U.S. wheat growers with an unfair economic advantage over wheat exporters from other countries.

fact that bribes, kickbacks, and similar payments have long characterized that market. Allegedly, governmental officials in the developing countries that are the principal buyers of exported wheat have historically demanded such payments from international wheat vendors in exchange for granting sales contracts to them.

Foreign competitors' use of bribes, kickbacks, and other illicit payments to acquire large wheat contracts was particularly galling to U.S. wheat exporters. In 1977, the U.S. Congress adopted the Foreign Corrupt Practices Act (FCPA) that prohibits U.S. companies from paying bribes or kickbacks to officials of foreign governments to initiate or maintain business relationships in those countries. The FCPA also requires U.S. companies to establish accounting and internal control systems that provide reasonable assurance of discovering such payments.[8] In the early 1990s, a member of President Bill Clinton's administration confirmed that U.S. exporters were facing an "uneven playing field" in the markets in which they competed because the United States was the only country at the time that had "criminalized bribery of foreign officials."[9]

Bribes vs. Facilitating Payments

The Organization of Economic Cooperation and Development (OECD) is an international organization of 30 democratic governments that assists its member countries in addressing a wide range of economic issues, including economic growth and development, the sharing of new technologies, and international trade disputes. Prominent members of the OECD include Australia, Canada, France, Germany, Japan, Mexico, the United Kingdom, and the United States. Increasing concern over the integrity of international markets during the 1990s prompted the OECD to develop the *Convention Against the Bribery of Foreign Public Officials in International Business Transactions*, which was modeled after the FCPA. This convention, which the OECD adopted in 1996, obligated the organization's 30 member countries to "criminalize" bribes that are paid to foreign governmental officials by companies who wish to gain a competitive advantage.

Following the Australian Parliament's passage of legislation to adopt the OECD Convention, Australian companies involved in international trade realized that they could face criminal prosecution if they paid bribes to establish or sustain international business relationships. To address this issue, many companies, including AWB, modified their corporate codes of conduct to recognize the responsibilities imposed on them by the new law.

A major focus of AWB's effort to ensure compliance with the new law was to make their executives and employees aware of the important distinction between "bribes" and "facilitating payments." Generally, bribes are significant amounts paid to foreign governmental officials to secure or retain business, while facilitating payments are relatively modest and routine payments typically made to lower-ranking governmental officials to expedite or "facilitate" business transactions. For example, a small payment made to a government clerk to expedite the unloading of goods at a foreign port would be considered a facilitating payment and not a bribe. The OECD Convention did not require member countries to criminalize facilitating payments as long as those payments are legal in the countries in which they are made.[10]

---

8. Case 3.4, "Triton Energy Ltd.," summarizes the FCPA's key anti-bribery and internal control provisions and discusses one of the few cases prosecuted under that federal statute by U.S. law enforcement authorities.

9. A. Zipser, "A Rarely Enforced Law," *Barron's*, 25 May 1992, 14.

10. The FCPA was initially unclear regarding whether or not facilitating payments qualified as bribes and thus were illegal under that federal statute. In 1988, the FCPA was amended to address that issue. As amended, "facilitating payments" made to encourage "routine governmental action" are not covered by the FCPA.

AWB modified its Corporate Ethics and Code of Conduct Policy to acknowledge that bribes are illegal but facilitating payments are not. According to that document, facilitating payments are "used to smooth business deals or engender goodwill with customers" and thus "technically differ from bribes, which are solely associated with illegal practices."[11] More specifically, AWB defined a facilitating payment as a "small benefit to a foreign public official in order to facilitate routine government action of a minor nature."[12] AWB's corporate code also addressed hypothetical questions that employees might face regarding facilitating payments. Following is one such question and the company's response:

> Question: I am managing an operation in a country where it is accepted practice for government officials to receive facilitation fees to speed up government approvals. Should I work within the system?

> Answer: Where payment of these fees would break the law, AWB does not approve the making of the payments. If it is legal to pay facilitation fees and local business practice to pay them, you should review the matter with your line manager. You should consider if payment would be ethical if its disclosure would cause embarrassment to the company.[13]

When in Rome

During the late 1990s and beyond, top AWB executives and their key subordinates ignored the new Australian law and their company's explicit policy prohibiting the payment of bribes to acquire international business contracts. Those conspirators realized that they had to disguise those payments so that they would not be uncovered by their independent auditors, internal auditors, or board of directors. In fact, according to subsequent statements made by a former Iraqi governmental official, representatives of international wheat vendors, such as AWB, often responded to requests for the payment of bribes by stating, "I can't do it. I've got a board. How do I get around my auditors?"[14] Saddam Hussein's subordinates would then explain to those executives how the payments could be made to avoid detection.

The U.N. investigation of the bribes linked to the Oil-for-Food Program was prompted by an Iraqi newspaper reporter who revealed the scheme in January 2004 following the collapse of Saddam Hussein's government the year before. In 2006, Kofi Annan, Secretary-General of the United Nations, demanded that Australia and other countries in which companies had made illicit payments to Saddam Hussein's regime take appropriate measures to punish the parties responsible for those payments. That same year, Prime Minister Howard appointed a former Australian judge, Terence Cole, to oversee a "royal commission," or task force, to investigate the AWB scandal.

Former AWB officials who testified before the Cole Commission explained that one of the biggest challenges they and other conspirators had faced was concealing the bribery payments from the United Nations. Under the U.N.'s Oil-for-Food Program, Iraq was permitted to sell a limited amount of oil each year during the U.N. embargo to provide the funds necessary to purchase food, medical supplies, and other necessities for Iraqi citizens. The proceeds from the sale of that oil were deposited in bank accounts controlled by the U.N. After Iraqi officials had negotiated to purchase

---

11. J. Barrett, "Policy on Payments Lost from AWB Site," *The Australian*, 25 February 2006, 4.

12. D. Uren, "Tax Law Change to Curb Crimes," *The Australian*, 9 February 2006, 8.

13. Barrett, "Policy on Payments Lost."

14. C. Overington, "Probe on Wheat Sales to Iraq," *theage.com* (http://www.theage.com.au), 29 April 2004.

goods from specific foreign companies, such as AWB, the U.N. disbursed payments to those companies from those bank accounts. AWB concealed the bribery payments from the U.N., as well as from its independent auditors and other parties, by funneling them through a Jordanian trucking company that was allegedly transporting the wheat to Iraq. The Jordanian company kept a small percentage of the bribes and then forwarded the balance to Hussein's regime in Baghdad.

AWB officials also devised a plan to recoup the bribes being paid to the Iraqi government. This scheme simply involved inflating the price of the wheat sold to Iraq to include those bribes. In an intracompany AWB correspondence obtained by the Cole Commission during its hearings, a company executive told one of his subordinates that because the bribe payments were being recouped from the U.N. Oil-for-Food bank accounts, they were "no skin off our nose."[15] A journalist for the *Sydney Morning Herald* berated the conspirators for this feature of the AWB fraud. "Extraordinary chutzpah was involved here. After all, the money [bribe payments] didn't even come out of AWB's pockets. It was siphoned by the wheat trader out of U.N.-held funds in New York. The defining detail of this scandal is that these bribes were free."[16] AWB also deducted the bribe payments as normal business expenses in its annual tax returns filed with the Australian Tax Office, the Australian equivalent of the U.S. Internal Revenue Service.

The AWB official who had been responsible for overseeing wheat sales to Middle Eastern countries testified before the Cole Commission that by early 2000 there was "widespread" knowledge within AWB of the illicit payments being made to the Iraqi government.[17] Two other former AWB officials who were not involved in the decision to pay the bribes testified that they questioned the propriety of the payments to the Jordanian trucking company when they became aware of them and then retained Arthur Andersen & Co. to investigate the payments.

During the time frame that AWB was paying the bribes, Ernst & Young served as the company's independent audit firm and issued an unqualified opinion each year on the company's financial statements. Exhibit 1 presents the unqualified opinion Ernst & Young issued on AWB's fiscal year 2000 financial statements, while Exhibit 2 presents the mandatory "Directors' Declaration" that accompanied the 2000 audit opinion. Available sources do not reveal why the two AWB officials who questioned the payments being made by AWB to the Jordanian trucking company did not ask Ernst & Young to investigate those payments—or whether Ernst & Young discovered any evidence of the payments during their annual audits.

EXHIBIT 1

ERNST & YOUNG'S AUDIT OPINION ON AWB'S FISCAL 2000 FINANCIAL STATEMENTS

To the members of AWB Limited

Scope

We have audited the financial report of AWB Limited for the financial year ended 30 September 2000, as set out on pages 53 to 90, including the Directors' Declaration. The financial report includes the financial statements of AWB Limited, and the consolidated financial statements of the consolidated entity comprising the company and the entities it controlled at year's end or from time to time during the financial year. The company's

(continued)

---

15. Australian Government, Attorney-General's Department, "Inquiry into Certain Australian Companies in Relation to the UN Oil-for-Food Programme," Transcript 24, 2333, 9 February 2006.

16. *Sydney Morning Herald*, "AWB's World of Trouble."

17. *Global Newswire* (online) "Zespri Boss Didn't Know about Kickbacks until Audit," 24 February 2006.

EXHIBIT 1—
continued

ERNST & YOUNG'S
AUDIT OPINION ON
AWB'S FISCAL 2000
FINANCIAL
STATEMENTS

directors are responsible for the financial report. We have conducted an independent audit of the financial report in order to express an opinion on it to the members of the company.

Our audit has been conducted in accordance with Australian Auditing Standards to provide reasonable assurance whether the financial report is free of material misstatement. Our procedures included examination, on a test basis, of evidence supporting the amounts and other disclosures in the financial report, and the evaluation of accounting policies and significant accounting estimates. These procedures have been undertaken to form an opinion whether, in all material respects, the financial report is presented fairly in accordance with Accounting Standards, other mandatory professional reporting requirements and statutory requirements, in Australia, so as to present a view which is consistent with our understanding of the company's and the consolidated entity's financial position and performance as represented by the results of their operations and their cash flows.

The audit opinion expressed in this report has been formed on the above basis.

Audit Opinion

In our opinion, the financial report of AWB Limited is in accordance with:

(a) the Corporations Law including:

(i) giving a true and fair view of the company's and consolidated entity's financial position as at 30 September 2000 and of their performance for the year ended on that date; and

(ii) complying with Accounting Standards and the Corporations Requirements; and

(b) other mandatory professional reporting requirements.

Ernst & Young
Melbourne
29 November 2000

EXHIBIT 2

DIRECTORS'
DECLARATION
ACCOMPANYING
AWB'S FISCAL 2000
FINANCIAL
STATEMENTS

In accordance with a resolution of the directors of AWB Limited, I state that:

In the opinion of the directors:

(a) the financial statements and notes of the company and of the consolidated entity are in accordance with the Corporations Law, including:

—giving a true and fair view of the company's and consolidated entity's financial position as at 30 September 2000 and of their performance for the year ended on that date; and

—complying with Accounting Standards and Corporations Regulations; and

(b) there are reasonable grounds to believe that the company will be able to pay its debts as and when they become due and payable.

This declaration is made in accordance with a resolution of the directors on behalf of the Board.

Andrew Lindberg
Executive Director

Melbourne
29 November 2000

The report filed by Arthur Andersen with AWB identified several "red flags" and "risk factors" associated with the suspicious payments.[18] In addition, the Andersen consulting team discovered similar payments being made to a Pakistani company. A subsequent investigation revealed that AWB had paid $12 million to a Pakistani governmental official to secure a grain contract with Pakistan. In its report, Andersen recommended that AWB assess its ethical culture and create a "transparent" environment in which employees "are encouraged to report incidents, risks, and improper conduct."[19]

Andrew Lindberg, AWB's former managing director (chief executive officer) testified before the Cole Commission for several days. During his testimony, more than 200 of Lindberg's responses to questions asked of him by commission members was one of the following statements: "I can't recall; I don't recall; I'm not sure I recall; I can't precisely recall; I have no recollection of that at all; I don't know."[20]

When asked what measures he and his subordinates had taken to address the allegations and recommendations included in the Andersen report, Lindberg responded that he had "left it up to the responsible management of the area ... to see that things were done"[21] since he had a "million things to deal with"[22] at the time. The individual who oversaw AWB's wheat marketing operations during the period that the Iraqi bribes were being paid testified that he did not become "actively involved in investigating any of the issues that arose out of the Arthur Andersen report" because he had "heavy commitments in other areas"[23] at the time. This latter individual indicated that, rather than investigating the matters raised by the Andersen report, he had delegated that responsibility to one of his subordinates. An Australian journalist chided the former AWB executives for not only orchestrating the illicit scheme to acquire the Iraqi wheat contracts but also for refusing to take responsibility for that scheme *ex post* during the course of the Cole Commission hearings:

> *"When in Rome, do as the Romans do" appears to have been AWB's business credo. The company's line now and then was that it did what was necessary to protect the interests of its shareholders, though the bald truth was that it colluded in embezzling money from a fund set up to ensure that ordinary Iraqis had bread on their tables and medicines in their hospitals.*[24]

Aftermath

The U.N. investigation of the Oil-for-Food Program chaired by Paul Volcker determined that Saddam Hussein's regime had received nearly $2 billion in illicit payments during the course of that program. Volcker's report indicated that more than 2,000 companies had paid bribes or kickbacks to the Iraqi government but that AWB was responsible for considerably more of those payments than any other company. An even more extensive investigation of the huge bribery scam was initiated recently. The Iraq Supreme Board of Audit, an agency of the country's post-Hussein government, hired Ernst & Young to carry out that investigation, which is not yet completed.

---

18. *The Risk Report*, "'Kickbacks' Inquiry Hones In on RM," http://services.thomson.com.au/, Issue 222 (19 January 2006).

19. *Ibid.*

20. M. Vincent, "Ends Justifies the Means at AWB, Inquiry Told," http://www.abc.net.au, 19 January 2006.

21. *The Risk Report*, "'Kickbacks' Inquiry Hones In on RM.

22. M. Vincent, "Documents Reveal Discretionary Payments Made by AWB," http://www.abc.net.au, 20 January 2006.

23. *Global Newswire*, "Zespri Boss Didn't Know about Kickbacks."

24. *Canberra Times* (online), "Taxing Times for Corruption," 27 December 2006.

For several months after Paul Volcker publicly reported his task force's findings, AWB executives staunchly denied that they had secretly paid nearly $300 million to Saddam Hussein's regime to secure the Iraqi wheat contracts. In one press release, a company spokesperson stated: "AWB did not knowingly pay or enter into any arrangements to benefit the former [Iraqi] regime."[25] In May 2006, the company's top management did a sudden and unexpected about-face by releasing a statement confirming that those payments had been made. The statement included a contrite apology from Andrew Lindberg, AWB's former chief executive, which noted in part that "we are truly sorry and deeply regret any damage this may have caused to Australia's trading reputation, the Australian government, or the United Nations."[26] During the nearly one-year long Cole Commission inquiry, evidence surfaced that a U.S.-based "crisis management guru" had advised the company to "overapologize" for its misconduct, apparently in hopes of garnering sympathy from the public and law enforcement authorities.[27]

The Cole Commission report released in late November 2006, recommended that criminal charges be filed against 11 former AWB executives. Andrew Lindberg was not one of those individuals. Although the Cole Commission did not recommend that criminal charges be filed against Lindberg, the commission's report severely criticized AWB's former senior management team. In particular, the report noted that the management team had bred a "closed culture of superiority and impregnability" in which "no one asked, 'What is the right thing to do?'"[28]

The most shocking conclusion in the Cole Commission report was that the $300 million in payments made by AWB to Saddam Hussein's regime did not technically qualify as "bribes" since they were not unlawful in Iraq at the time. Critics of the Cole Commission report insisted that this conclusion was inconsistent with the Australian law prompted by the OECD Convention. Nevertheless, Australian law enforcement authorities relied upon the Cole Commission's conclusion in deciding that AWB's former executives could not be prosecuted under that Australian law. (Note: The charges that the Cole Commission recommended be filed against the 11 former AWB executives stemmed from their intentional violation of the U.N. trade embargo sanctions.) Likewise, because of the Cole Commission report, the Australian Tax Office permitted AWB to treat the $300 million of payments as tax-deductible expenses, a ruling that saved the company approximately $400 million in back taxes, fines, and interest payments. The Cole Commission also reported that it found no incontrovertible evidence that Prime Minister John Howard or any of his subordinates had been expressly aware of the clandestine payments.

Not surprisingly, the Cole Commission report triggered charges of a government cover-up. An Australian critic of Prime Minister Howard's administration observed, "For this, the worst corruption scandal in Australian history, the Cole Commission was effectively constructed as a ministerial cover-up."[29] Particularly incensed were representatives of the U.S. wheat industry. In 2006, a group of U.S. and Canadian wheat growers filed a civil lawsuit against AWB asking for more than $1 billion in damages. The plaintiffs alleged that AWB had used unfair trade practices to secure the Iraqi grain contracts. Ironically, the Canadian Wheat Board, a government agency similar to

---

25. *Sydney Morning Herald*, "AWB's World of Trouble."

26. *Global Newswire* (online), "Dramatic Confession Presented at Australian Iraq Bribes Probe," 19 May 2006.

27. *Ibid.*

28. *The Economist* (online), "Australians Who Bribe: The Oil-for-Food Scandal," 2 December 2006.

29. *Sydney Morning Herald*, "AWB's World of Trouble."

AWB before it became a private company, had negotiated to obtain the Iraqi wheat contracts. When Iraqi officials demanded bribes in exchange for granting those contracts, the Canadian Wheat Board refused, which resulted in an abrupt end to the contract negotiations.

Following the release of the Cole Commission report, Prime Minister Howard announced that he was revoking AWB's export monopoly for Australia's wheat market. A few weeks later, the U.S. Department of Agriculture banned AWB from seeking contracts with the U.S. government. Pressure applied by U.S. officials was apparently a factor in the decision of many other countries to prohibit AWB from receiving government contracts. These decisions angered Australian wheat farmers, many of whom, as noted earlier, believed that AWB had not acted improperly in making secret payments to obtain the Iraqi wheat contracts. Many Australian businessmen, politicians, and journalists expressed the same point of view. The *Canberra Times* noted that "many people sympathize with AWB's plight. Markets and cultures tainted by corruption and/or lax governance are the rule rather than the exception, and the competition to secure lucrative contracts is fierce."[30] In this same article, the newspaper took a swipe at what many Australians perceived as the self-righteous U.S. business community. "The view that corporations have no social responsibility beyond that of making profits for their shareholders is one which is well entrenched in certain boardrooms in Australia, and more particularly in the United States."[31]

Questions

1. Many foreign companies sell securities on U.S. stock exchanges. Do the provisions of the Foreign Corrupt Practices Act apply to those companies?

2. Under current U.S. auditing standards, what responsibility, if any, does an audit firm of a multinational company have to discover bribes that are paid by the client to obtain or retain international business relationships? In a bullet format, list audit procedures that may be effective in uncovering such payments.

3. Suppose you discover during the course of an audit engagement that the audit client is routinely making "facilitating payments" in a foreign country. What are the key audit-related issues, if any, posed by this discovery?

4. A quote in this case from an Australian newspaper suggested that many corporate boards in the United States believe that they "have no social responsibility beyond that of making profits for their shareholders." In your opinion, what level of "social responsibility," if any, do corporate boards have? Defend your answer.

5. The audit report shown in Exhibit 1 refers to "Australian Auditing Standards." What organization issues Australian Auditing Standards? What is the relationship, if any, between Australian Auditing Standards and International Standards of Auditing?

---

30. *Canberra Times* (online), "Taxing Times for Corruption."
31. *Ibid.*

OAO Gazprom

In February 2002, a lengthy *Business Week* article examined a major financial scandal swirling around one of the large international accounting firms. Key features of the scandal included the accounting firm allegedly "overlooking wildly improper deals" in its audits of a huge client that ranked among the "country's biggest energy firms," a company that had become a symbol "for the evils of crony capitalism."[1] The opening prologue for the article went on to note that the scandal involved "billions and billions" of dollars of losses as well as "leaked documents, infuriated shareholders, and threatened lawsuits."[2] Several major political figures had been caught up in the scandal, including the President. No, the article was not dissecting the sudden collapse of Enron Corporation in December 2001. Instead, the article focused on the international controversy sparked by the relationship between the largest energy producer in Russia, OAO Gazprom, and that company's independent audit firm, PricewaterhouseCoopers (PwC).

The commotion surrounding PwC's audits of Gazprom was ignited by the accounting firm's alleged failure to report candidly on a series of huge transactions involving that company and several smaller firms owned or controlled by Gazprom executives or their family members. Principal among these entities was Itera, a secretive company with U.S. connections. Criticism of PwC's audits of Gazprom became so intense that the prominent accounting firm was forced to purchase full-page ads in the major Moscow newspapers to defend itself.

Rogue Capitalism

Throughout the 1990s, the dominant international accounting firms pursued strategic initiatives to expand their worldwide operations. Many of these initiatives targeted Russia and the cluster of smaller countries carved out of the former Soviet Union when it suddenly disintegrated in 1991. *The New York Times* reported that the major accounting firms were among the first foreign firms to establish significant operations in Russia following the collapse of the Soviet Union.[3] In their "competitive rush" to establish an economic beachhead in Russia, these firms may have underestimated the many risks posed by that country's turbulent and rapidly evolving business environment.

The massive reorganization of Russia's political, social, and economic infrastructure in the 1990s produced widespread chaos within the suddenly "new" country that had a proud history centuries old. Russia's political leaders wanted to quickly embrace capitalism. To accomplish this objective, Russia's new democratic government implemented a "privatization programme" intended to convert the country from communism to capitalism in a span of a few years. The first and most important phase of this enormous project gave Russian citizens the right to acquire ownership interests in thousands of Russian firms at a nominal cost by using state-issued "privatization vouchers." These Russian firms were formerly state-owned companies or

---

1. P. Starobin and C. Belton, "Russia's Enron?" *BusinessWeek* (online), 18 February 2002.

2. *Ibid.*

3. S. Tavernise, "U.S. Auditors Find Things Are Different in Russia," *The New York Times*, 12 March 2002, Section W, 1.

agencies that had established corporate governance structures equivalent to boards of directors to oversee their operations. From 1992 through 1999, more than 75 percent of Russian companies were handed over to the private sector, although the federal government retained a sizable minority ownership interest in the nation's largest and most important companies.

The privatization program succeeded in quickly converting Russia's controlled economy into a free market economy. However, the project was flawed in many respects. For example, more than one-half of the newly created companies were technically insolvent and able to survive only with subsidies and other economic support from the federal government. Complicating everyday life for these new firms and their managers was the rampant inflation in the Russian economy that exceeded 2,000 percent annually.

Arguably the most pervasive weakness of the privatization program was that it allowed thousands of the individuals who had overseen the formerly state-owned businesses to acquire top management positions in the newly organized companies. The Russian press commonly referred to these individuals as "red directors," since most of them had been Communist Party "apparatchiks" or operatives. Not surprisingly, few of these corporate managers shared or even understood the capitalistic principles they were being asked to embrace. As *Business Week* noted, these individuals "cling to the view that the enterprise is an engine to generate wealth for themselves."[4] This pervasive attitude among the newly minted corporate executives spawned a rough-and-tumble version of capitalism in Russia that sparked widespread violence—including hundreds of murders and contract killings, kickbacks, bribes, and "organized robbery."[5] Critics of the privatization program often pointed to OAO Gazprom, a huge Russian company, as a prime example of this "rogue" capitalism.

Gazprom, a term that means "gas industry," was initially a privately owned company created by officials of the Soviet Union to assume control of the country's natural gas industry. The company's most important assets are enormous natural gas reserves discovered in Siberia following World War II. In 1993, Gazprom was one of the first publicly owned firms created by Russia's privatization program. Fifteen percent of Gazprom's common stock was given to employees and 28 percent to customers, while the federal government retained an approximately 40 percent ownership interest in the company. Most of Gazprom's remaining common stock was sold to foreign investors. The federal government limited the percentage of a company's stock that could be sold to foreign investors to a small fraction of its total stock. This policy ensured that foreign investors could not gain effective control over any major Russian companies.

Gazprom's initial stockholders' meeting was held in 1995. At that meeting, the stockholders endorsed the board of directors' selection of PwC as the company's audit firm. Rem Vyakhirev, Gazprom's top executive at the time, reported that the world's largest audit firm had been chosen to enhance the credibility of his company's financial statements and financial disclosures.[6]

During the 1990s, Gazprom was arguably the most important Russian company and the largest by most standards. The massive company accounted for nearly 10 percent of Russia's gross domestic product and 20 percent of its exports and tax revenues. Gazprom had an estimated 400,000 employees and provided directly or indirectly a

---

4. P. Starobin, "Russia's World-Class Accounting Games," *BusinessWeek* (online), 5 March 2002.

5. Tavernise, "U.S. Auditors Find Things Are Different."

6. P. Kranz, "Boris' Young Turks," *Business Week*, 28 April 1997, 52.

livelihood for more than 6 million Russians. The company's influence stretched far beyond Russia's borders. Gazprom supplied more than one-half of the natural gas used in Europe and controlled one-third of the world's natural gas reserves.

Gazzoviki

Victor Chernomyrdin was born 10 years following the Russian Revolution of 1917. Chernomyrdin's parents were peasants who worked on a Russian collective farm. As a young man faced with limited educational opportunities, Chernomyrdin decided to become a skilled craftsman, a machinist. Following World War II, he acquired a job working in his country's rapidly developing natural gas industry that was controlled by the Ministry of the Gas Industry. The Soviet Union citizens fortunate enough to have the relatively stable and lucrative jobs in this field became known as the Gazzoviki.

Chernomyrdin gradually rose through the ranks of the Gazzoviki and occupied various management positions with Gazprom. His career success was due to his hard work, dedication to the Communist Party to which he belonged, and, most important, his ability to foster mutually beneficial relationships with key superiors and subordinates. Chernomyrdin spent much of his 40-year career with Gazprom in frigid Siberian oil and natural gas fields. For most of that time he worked side by side with Rem Vyakhirev, his most trusted ally and protégé whose first name was an acronym for "Revolution Engels-Marx," a common name given to Russian males in the years following the Russian Revolution. In a retrospective article examining the history of Gazprom, a British reporter commented on the company's culture and the close relationship that developed between Chernomyrdin and Vyakhirev, the two individuals who had the greatest impact on the company during its formative years.

> Gazprom is a closed world obsessed by status and hierarchy, and disdainful of outsiders. It is dominated by the macho gazzoviki, lifelong gas workers, including Mr. Vyakhirev and Mr. Chernomyrdin, who speak an earthy slang. They are united by years of working and drinking together in production plants in Russia's most remote and inhospitable regions. "You can't believe how much they drank," says one company insider. "Life was simpler in Siberia. They knew what was expected of them."[7]

By the late 1980s, Chernomyrdin was the chief executive of Gazprom. In 1992, Boris Yeltsin became the new Russian republic's first president and chose Chernomyrdin to serve as the nation's prime minister, the second-highest-ranking position in the federal government. Before leaving Gazprom, Chernomyrdin appointed Rem Vyakhirev as the company's new chief executive. Despite being the senior member of Yeltsin's administration, Chernomyrdin kept a close watch on Gazprom's financial affairs and frequently communicated with Vyakhirev regarding the company's operations. Together, Chernomyrdin and Vyakhirev guided the company through the turbulent privatization process during the mid-1990s that culminated with the firm becoming OAO Gazprom. (The "OAO" prefix indicates that Gazprom is an open-stock or publicly owned company.)

During Yeltsin's administration, Russian journalists took advantage of their country's new freedoms to openly and harshly criticize top governmental officials. A common target of that criticism was Chernomyrdin. Gruff and terse by nature, Chernomyrdin was frequently derided by the Russian press for his unpolished social skills, his poor mastery of the Russian language, and his refusal to provide candid answers to questions posed to him by reporters.

---

7. A. Jack, "Is Time Up for the 'Secret State'?" *Financial Times* (London), 25 May 2001, 33.

Chernomyrdin's critics charged that he used his political power to grant large tax concessions and other economic benefits to Gazprom. These critics also maintained that Chernomyrdin and Vyakhirev diverted billions of dollars of Gazprom's assets to themselves and family members. Allegedly, the two men and their colleagues established a network of private companies and then channeled Gazprom assets to those companies through an array of complex and clandestine transactions. The Russian press also claimed that Chernomyrdin routinely used Gazprom funds to finance the election campaigns of political candidates in his Our Home Is Russia (NDR) political party. Likewise, although Chernomyrdin frequently insisted that he had cut all ties to his Communist background, he reportedly used Gazprom funds to finance the election campaigns of several longtime colleagues running for office under the banner of the still active and powerful Communist Party.

In responding to the persistent stream of allegations and innuendos directed at him by the Russian press, an indifferent Chernomyrdin typically resorted to a brief phrase that is the Russian equivalent of "that's nonsense."[8] Another tactic Chernomyrdin used to rebuff allegations that he and his former subordinates at Gazprom were misusing corporate funds was to point out that the company's financial affairs were being closely monitored by a prestigious CPA firm, namely, PwC.

Chernomyrdin's relationship with Boris Yeltsin deteriorated over the years. In 1998, Yeltsin forced Chernomyrdin to resign as prime minister. Later that year, Chernomyrdin failed in his bid to replace Yeltsin as Russia's president. Following Yeltsin's resignation in 2000, former KGB intelligence agent Vladimir Putin was elected the new Russian president. In the meantime, Chernomyrdin had returned to Gazprom, assuming the position of chairman of the board while his close friend Rem Vyakhirev remained the company's chief executive. Putin had campaigned as a reform candidate, promising to clean up the fraud and bribery that pervaded Russian business. Putin realized that for the Russian economy to become viable, Gazprom and other large firms had to raise large amounts of debt and equity capital from foreign investors. But as long as "red directors" controlled the leading Russian firms, foreign investors were unlikely to make major financial commitments to those companies. "Gazprom's position above the law is seen as a block along the road to reform by Western investors, whose cash is desperately needed."[9]

Putin was particularly offended by the efforts of Gazprom's executives to enrich themselves at their company's expense and at their attitude that they were "above the law" and not accountable to the Russian public. In fact, while serving as Gazprom's chief executive, Vyakhirev had his company acquire Russia's only independent television network, ostensibly to silence his critics. Vyakhirev took pleasure in bragging about the power that he exercised as Gazprom's top executive. Vyakhirev "liked to boast of dispatching flunkies in the company jet to pick special tundra grass to feed the reindeer on his private Moscow estate."[10] A British periodical claimed that such abusive practices were commonplace and carried out "under the noses" of the firm's independent auditors.

> Under... Rem Vyakhirev, Gazprom resembled a badly run country more than it did a
> publicly traded energy company: it had its own intelligence service, fleet of aircraft,
> hotels, media outlets and even a yacht club. Under the noses of its Western auditors,

8. *Global News Wire* (online), "Gazprom Denies Making Contributions to Election Campaigns," 24 January 2000.

9. *The Irish Times* (online), "Russian Gas Chieftain Pushed Out by Putin," 8 June 2001.

10. *Ibid.*

billions of dollars of cash and assets leaked to companies where ownership was at best murky, at worst startlingly close to Gazprom's chiefs.[11]

True to his word, shortly after becoming president, Putin began forcing large numbers of red directors of major Russian companies to resign. Among the first such executives to lose their lucrative positions with major Russian firms were Vyakhirev and Chernomyrdin, who both chose to "retire" from Gazprom.[12] Unlike most Russian retirees, Chernomyrdin and Vyakhirev would not have to rely on a meager government pension for their retirement income. In 2001, *Forbes* reported that the two former Russian peasants were among the 500 richest individuals in the world. *Forbes* pegged Vyakhirev's personal wealth at $1.5 billion, while Chernomyrdin's more modest fortune was estimated at $1.1 billion.[13]

Accounting and Auditing on the Fly

Banishing corrupt corporate executives was an important first step in Vladimir Putin's campaign to entice foreign investors to provide desperately needed debt and equity capital for large Russian companies. However, Putin also realized that his country's accounting and financial reporting practices had to be revamped before foreign investors would commit significant funds to those companies. The new country's existing financial reporting framework was a holdover from the system used in the Soviet Union, a system that was poorly suited for the needs of a free market economy.

> *In the chaotic early years of new Russian capitalism, accounting standards here were poorly suited to market economics. They were built around reporting to tax authorities, not gauging a company's financial health for investors. Oversight was all but nonexistent and the legal system was undeveloped, leaving room for manipulation and theft.*[14]

Russia's move toward a Western-style accounting and financial reporting system began shortly after the creation of the new Russian republic in 1991. In 1992, the new federal government approved "Regulation on Accounting and Reporting in the Russian Federation," an administrative decree intended to provide a blueprint for radically changing the nation's accounting and financial reporting system. The primary responsibility for implementing this decree would rest with the Ministry of Finance, the government agency charged with overseeing the country's financial infrastructure. Several organizations, among them the United Nations, the European Union, and the World Bank, pledged to help the Ministry of Finance implement the decree. The international accounting community, including the major international accounting firms and professional accounting organizations in leading industrialized nations, also offered to help the Ministry of Finance in its effort.

The most important feature of the plan to overhaul Russia's accounting and financial reporting system was to adopt the fundamental accounting concepts and procedures that had become generally accepted in major industrialized countries over the previous two centuries. Even before the break-up of the Soviet Union, Russian accountants had recognized the concept of "fair presentation." However, an entity's financial statements were considered to be "fairly presented" if they complied with the arcane taxation, reporting, and administrative requirements of the federal government.

---

11. *Economist.com*, "Last Night at the Gazprom," 31 May 2001.

12. Although Chernomyrdin had to give up his position with Gazprom in 2001, a few months later Putin appointed him Russia's ambassador to Ukraine. This appointment surprised foreign journalists since the two men had been fierce political rivals over the previous several years.

13. *The Russian Business Monitor* (online), "Eight Russians Put on Billionaires List," 22 June 2001.

14. Tavernise, "U.S. Auditors Find Things Are Different."

The new accounting framework introduced into Russia in the early 1990s required companies to adopt such revolutionary concepts as recognizing revenues when earned and realized, properly matching revenues and expenses each accounting period, invoking the historical cost principle for most assets, and applying the going-concern principle to discontinued operating units.

Because Russia did not have a rigorous rule-making process for the accounting domain, the major international accounting firms and other influential parties encouraged the Russian federal government to endorse the accounting standards being promulgated by international rule-making bodies. In 1999, the Ministry of Finance announced that Russian companies could apply either the loose amalgamation of "Russian accounting principles" that had developed over the previous several years or the much more comprehensive and logically consistent International Accounting Standards (IAS), which are now known as International Financial Reporting Standards (IFRS).[15] The latter standards are issued by the London-based International Accounting Standards Board (IASB), which was created in 1973 with the long-range goal of developing a uniform set of worldwide accounting and financial reporting standards. In 2001, the Ministry of Finance made another bold and progressive decision when it announced that publicly owned Russian companies would be required to adopt IFRS over a transitional period running generally from 2001 through 2005.

In addition to higher-quality accounting and financial reporting practices, Russia's market reformers also realized that their nation needed a rigorous independent audit function to enhance the credibility of publicly issued financial data. The large international accounting firms that established practice offices for the first time in Russia during the early 1990s found that most large Russian companies required so-called statutory audits. Statutory audits were effectively "compliance" audits intended to determine whether a given company's periodic financial reports and internal accounting functions complied with the various governmental decrees and regulations to which they were subject. (In the Soviet Union, "independent audits" intended to enhance the credibility of publicly released financial statements in the minds of investors and creditors had not been necessary since the federal government controlled practically all economic resources.) Exhibit 1 presents an example of a statutory audit report issued by PwC in April 2000 for one of its large Russian clients, the Joint-Stock Commercial Savings Bank of the Russian Federation. Notice that the third section of the report indicates the various rules, regulations, and standards that PwC followed in performing the given audit.

EXHIBIT 1

EXAMPLE OF A
RUSSIAN STATUTORY
AUDIT REPORT
ISSUED BY
PRICEWATERHOUSE-
COOPERS

To the Shareholders of Joint-Stock Commercial
Savings Bank of the Russian Federation (an open joint-stock company):

1. We have audited the accompanying 1999 statutory accounting reports of Joint-Stock Commercial Savings Bank of the Russian Federation (open joint-stock company) (hereinafter—the Bank). These statutory accounting reports were prepared by the management of the Bank in accordance with the Chart of Accounts for credit institutions prescribed by the Bank of Russia and other regulatory documents. These statutory accounting reports differ significantly from financial statements prepared in accordance with International Accounting Standards mainly in areas of valuation of assets and capital, period of recognition of revenues and expenses, recognition of liabilities and disclosures.

---

15. The IASB adopted the phrase "International Financial Reporting Standards" in 2001.

EXHIBIT 1—
continued

EXAMPLE OF A
RUSSIAN STATUTORY
AUDIT REPORT
ISSUED BY
PRICEWATERHOUSE-
COOPERS

2. Preparation of the statutory accounting reports is the responsibility of the management of the Bank. Our responsibility as statutory auditors is to express an opinion on the trustworthiness in all material respects of these statutory accounting reports based on our audit.

3. We conducted our statutory audit in accordance with:

> The Temporary Rules of Audit Activity in the Russian Federation adopted by Decree of the President of the Russian Federation of 22 December 1993, No. 2263;

> The Regulations on Audit Activity in the Banking System of the Russian Federation No. 64 approved by the Order of the Bank of Russia of 10 September 1997, No. 02-391;

> The Regulations of the Bank of Russia "On the order of compiling and presenting to the Bank of Russia the audit report on the results of checking the credit institution's activity for the reporting year" of 23 December 1997, No. 10-P;

> The rules and standards on auditing approved by the Commission on Audit Activity under the President of the Russian Federation;

> The standards of Banking Auditing approved by Expert Committee under the Bank of Russia;

> International Auditing Standards; and

> Internal standards of the firm.

These standards require that we plan and perform the statutory audit to obtain reasonable assurance about whether the statutory accounting reports are free of material misstatement. An audit includes examining, on a test basis, evidence supporting the amounts and disclosures in the statutory accounting reports. An audit also includes assessing the accounting principles used and significant estimates made by management, as well as evaluating the overall presentation of the statutory accounting reports in order to assess compliance with laws and current regulations of the Russian Federation. We reviewed a sample of business transactions of the Bank for compliance with the effective legislation solely to obtain sufficient assurance that statutory accounting reports are free of material misstatements. We believe that our statutory audit provides a reasonable basis for our opinion.

4. In our opinion, the audited annual statutory accounting reports are prepared in all material aspects in accordance with legislation and statutory requirements regulating the procedure of accounting and preparation of statutory accounting reports in the Russian Federation and the principles of accounting accepted in the Russian Federation. On this basis, the proper preparation of the balance sheet and of the profit and loss account is confirmed.

5. Without qualifying our opinion, we draw attention to the fact that the operations of the Bank, and those of similar credit organisations in the Russian Federation, have been affected, and may be affected for the foreseeable future by the economic instability of the company.

PricewaterhouseCoopers
28 April 2000

International accounting firms encouraged Russian federal officials to adopt an audit model patterned after the independent audit function in Western countries. These firms generally supported a move toward the British audit model, which requires independent auditors to decide whether a given client's financial statements present a "true and fair" view of its operating results and financial condition. A Moscow-based PwC audit partner reported that his firm had encountered major resistance to this radical change.

> *Companies say, "I don't need this. I want you to check our compliance with the law and regulations and that is all." If the local law does not require something, it is difficult to persuade clients to buy it. They don't understand the process of [conforming] to a true and fair view.*[16]

In 1999, the Institute of Professional Accountants of Russia (IPAR), a leading professional organization roughly comparable to the American Institute of Certified Public Accountants (AICPA), applied for admission to the New York–based International Federation of Accountants (IFAC). The IFAC's website notes that it is "an organization of national professional accountancy organizations that represent accountants employed in public practice, business and industry, the public sector, and education." More than 150 professional accountancy organizations are IFAC members, including the AICPA. A major thrust of the IFAC is developing International Standards of Auditing (ISAs) that can be readily applied in developing countries without a formal rule-making body for the auditing domain. The IFAC's auditing standards tend to be broad conceptual guidelines rather than detailed rules. Nevertheless, ISAs are generally consistent with the professional auditing standards applied in the major free market economies, including Great Britain and the United States.

The IPAR became an IFAC member in 2000. In the fall of that year, the first official Russian translation of ISAs was made available to the Russian accounting profession and the foreign accounting firms with practice units in Russia. At that point, the Big Five accounting firms, each of which had a major presence in Russia, began encouraging their clients to obtain ISA-based audits and began lobbying government officials to formally endorse the ISAs.

A key factor that impeded the spread of Western-style auditing in Russia during the 1990s was the existence of so-called "pocket auditors." Many, if not most, new Russian companies created in the early 1990s retained accounting firms run by friends and relatives of their executives to audit their financial statements and provide related professional services. These accounting firms allegedly helped their clients "cook their books" and "evade taxes and disguise asset-stripping."[17] Executives of Russian companies feared that PwC and the other international accounting firms would not be as cooperative or compliant as pocket auditors. However, the controversy spawned by PwC's audits of Gazprom caused many critics to suggest that the prestigious accounting firm was firmly "in the pockets" of Gazprom's top executives.

Wildest Dream or Worst Nightmare?

In July 1997, a reporter for the London-based *Financial Times* interviewed Bruce Edwards, the PwC audit partner who had just completed supervising his firm's first annual audit of Gazprom. The reporter noted that, "to most auditors, Gazprom would rank as their wildest dream—or their worst nightmare."[18] The "dream" feature of the

---

16. PricewaterhouseCoopers, "Russia: Hammering Out Standards, Hitting a Mindset," *WorldWatch*, March 2000, 14–15.

17. Starobin, "Russia's World-Class Accounting Games."

18. J. Thornhill, "Behind the High Walls at Gazprom," *Financial Times* (London), 11 July 1997, 24.

engagement was that it provided instant credibility for PwC in the Russian audit market. Another "dream" feature of the engagement was the $12 million annual fee that the accounting firm earned for the audit. On the downside, the Gazprom audit required the 70 PwC personnel assigned to the engagement to travel the length and breadth of Russia. To accomplish their audit objectives, the PwC auditors had to inspect many of the company's more than 1,000 operating units, which included slaughterhouses, media outlets, hospitals, a yacht club, and dozens of other ventures unrelated to the company's primary line of business.

In the *Financial Times* interview, Edwards downplayed the suggestion that audits of large Russian companies were markedly different from audits of comparable U.S. firms. "There is nothing mystical about Russian accounts. There is a huge misconception that Russia is somehow different, but I do not see it being much different to anywhere else."[19] Edwards did admit that Gazprom executives and employees were initially reluctant to share information with PwC auditors. However, that reluctance was "short-lived," Edwards assured the newspaper reporter, and then went on to maintain that the quality of financial information Gazprom personnel provided to PwC auditors "was extremely high."

One feature of the Gazprom audit on which Edwards did not comment was the company's extensive related-party transactions. During the late 1990s, major Russian newspapers and other media outlets charged that Gazprom's top executives were routinely siphoning off enormous amounts of assets to related-party entities that they or their family members controlled.

According to press reports, Gazprom officials sold a huge amount of natural gas at nominal prices to Itera, a privately owned company based in the Netherlands that has major operating units in Russia and the United States. Throughout the 1990s, Itera's top executive was Igor Makarov, a former Gazprom employee and Olympic biking champion for the Soviet Union. Makarov had been taught the intricacies of the natural gas industry by his close friend and mentor, Rem Vyakhirev. In one confirmed case, Gazprom sold a large volume of natural gas to Itera for $2 per cubic meter, which Itera then resold to European customers for more than $40 per cubic meter. In another transaction, Gazprom sold its 32 percent ownership interest in a gas-producing subsidiary, Purgas, to Itera for $1,200. Industry insiders estimated that the market price of that ownership interest was approximately $400 million. Thanks to such transactions, Itera grew from a small, unknown entity to the world's seventh-largest natural gas company in a span of only seven years during the 1990s.

Although Itera appears to be the company that has profited the most from Gazprom's generosity, several other firms have been the beneficiaries of similar sweetheart deals. Among these firms is Stroitransgaz, a pipeline construction company that landed a large number of lucrative contracts with Gazprom during the 1990s. According to the Russian press, Stroitransgaz's principal owners include Viktor Chernomyrdin's two sons and Rem Vyahkirev's daughter.

In 2001, Boris Fedorov, who had previously served as the head of the Ministry of Finance, was appointed to Gazprom's board of directors. Shortly after joining the board, Fedorov told the *Moscow Times* that Gazprom was losing the equivalent of $2 billion to $3 billion each year due to "corruption, nepotism, and simple theft."[20] That same newspaper went on to report that its own five-week investigation had uncovered evidence that Gazprom assets "have been systematically handed over to

---

19. *Ibid.*
20. *Moscow Times*, "Time to Say Farewell to Vyakhirev," 22 May 2001, 12.

company managers—including Vyakhirev, his deputy Vyacheslav Sheremet, and former Prime Minister Viktor Chernomyrdin—throughout Vyakhirev's tenure."[21]

The increasingly revealing and hostile reports focusing on Gazprom's business dealings with Itera and other related companies outraged the international investment community and foreign political officials whose countries had provided billions of dollars of aid to jumpstart the fledgling Russian economy. Even more outraged were foreign investors who owned Gazprom stock. Among these investors were the stockholders of Hermitage Capital, Russia's largest private equity fund, which held a large minority ownership interest in Gazprom's outstanding stock. Most of Hermitage's stockholders were U.S. citizens.

William Browder, Hermitage's chairman and a former partner with the Wall Street investment banker Salomon Brothers, had begun accumulating Gazprom stock for Hermitage in the mid-1990s. Browder, an American citizen whose father had served decades earlier as a top official of the Communist Party in the United States, recognized that the huge natural gas reserves owned by the company were not properly impounded into Gazprom's stock market price. He expected that the stock's market price would rise dramatically when Western investors realized the massive resources controlled by the company. Unfortunately for Browder and his fellow Hermitage investors, Gazprom's stock price stubbornly refused to move higher.

A frustrated Browder reported in 2001 that if Gazprom's petroleum reserves were valued by the stock market on approximately the same basis as the comparable reserves of Exxon Mobil, the company's stock price would be 132 times higher.[22] Browder attributed the lack of interest in Gazprom's common stock to the fact that the company was literally "giving away" huge chunks of its natural gas reserves each year to Itera and other privately owned companies controlled by Gazprom executives, their family members, and their close friends and associates.

The growing controversy surrounding Gazprom's bizarre deals with Itera, which was fueled by the Russian press, forced the company's board to call for a "special audit" of the Gazprom–Itera transactions in January 2001. Ironically, that announcement sparked even more controversy and negative publicity for the company. When Gazprom's board announced that PwC had been retained to perform the Itera audit, critics immediately charged that PwC would effectively be auditing "itself," since the firm had given its implicit approval to the suspicious Itera transactions during its prior audits of Gazprom. Most galling to critics was that PwC had failed to even require Gazprom to disclose Itera as a related party in the footnotes to the company's financial statements over the previous several years.

Boris Fedorov, the sole Gazprom board member who had voted to retain an accounting firm other than PwC to perform the special audit, publicly criticized the board's decision. "There is no way you can believe in an assignment which asks an auditor to check their own figures. It is spitting in the face of investors."[23] PwC's appointment to perform the special audit even caused dissension among the accounting firm's partners. *Business Week* reported that several senior PwC partners in the firm's Moscow office believed "that any self-review [of the Itera transactions] would lack credibility."[24]

Shortly after Gazprom's board hired PwC to investigate the company's business deals with Itera, a group of minority stockholders led by Federov appointed Deloitte &

21. *Ibid.*

22. W. Browder, "Gazprom Investors Are Sold Short," *Moscow Times,* 30 July 2001, 8.

23. A. Jack and A. Ostrovsky, "Gazprom Vote Raises Concerns," *Financial Times* (London), 24 January 2001, 32.

24. Starobin and Belton, "Russia's Enron?"

Touche to perform a parallel investigation of those same transactions. The other members of Gazprom's board squelched that effort by refusing to provide Deloitte access to the company's accounting records. Federov responded by claiming that the board's decision "showed that it [Gazprom's management] had something to hide."[25] Federov went on to demand that PwC rigorously interrogate Gazprom's executives and family members known to have ties to Itera. Within days, Federov found himself the target of anonymous threats by hostile adversaries. Accustomed to the often treacherous business environment of his country, Federov dismissed the threats and insisted that he would continue demanding that Gazprom provide more transparent and reliable financial reports to investors, creditors, and other third parties.

No Smoking Guns

PwC completed its four-month investigation of Gazprom's business dealings with Itera in the summer of 2001 and filed a 67-page confidential report of its findings with Gazprom's board. Within days, much of PwC's report had been leaked to the press. According to the *Financial Times,* PwC did not identify any "deals in which Itera benefited at the expense of Gazprom."[26] Subsequent press reports undercut the credibility of PwC's investigation. These reports indicated that PwC's investigation had been severely hamstrung by a lack of cooperation on the part of both Itera and Gazprom officials. Itera's management had refused to provide documents requested by PwC auditors, while 19 executives and former executives of Gazprom, including Rem Vyakhirev, had refused to answer questions posed to them by the auditors.

Not surprisingly, the results of the PwC investigation failed to placate Boris Federov, William Browder, and other critics of Gazprom's management. Instead, the tepid PwC report served to focus increasingly harsh criticism on the large accounting firm. In early 2002, Gazprom's board announced a "contest" to retain an accounting firm to audit the company's financial statements for the fiscal year ending June 30, 2002. Although Gazprom invited PwC to prepare a bid for the 2002 audit, the Russian and international business press indicated that there was little chance PwC would be selected given the adverse publicity that continued to plague the firm. Diminishing even further PwC's chances to retain the Gazprom engagement was a recommendation issued in early 2002 by the Russian Securities Commission, a federal agency equivalent to the U.S. Securities and Exchange Commission. That agency strongly encouraged large Russian companies to change their auditors periodically.

A few days after Gazprom announced the auditor contest, PwC purchased full-page ads in major Russian newspapers. These ads attempted to rebut much of the criticism that had been directed at the firm over the previous two years for its Gazprom audits. The ads suggested that PwC had been singled out for criticism based on "an inaccurate understanding of the roles and responsibilities of auditors."[27]

In April 2002, Hermitage Capital filed multiple civil lawsuits against PwC in Russian courts alleging, among other charges, that the accounting firm had performed "deliberately false" audits of Gazprom. At the same time, Hermitage filed a request with the Ministry of Finance to suspend PwC's license to practice in Russia. A PwC spokesperson maintained that the allegations in the lawsuits were "completely unfounded" and that the firm's audits had "met all applicable legal and professional standards."[28]

25. "Gazprom Won't Permit Audit by Deloitte," *National Post,* 21 March 2001, C2.

26. A. Jack, "Auditors Find No Evidence of Deals That Aided Itera," *Financial Times,* 6 July 2001, 22.

27. A. Jack, "PwC Acts to Defend Itself in Russia," *Financial Times* (London), 28 February 2002, 20.

28. S. Tavernise, "Shareholder in Gazprom of Russia Sues Auditor," *The New York Times,* 16 April 2002, W1.

The Hermitage lawsuits were the first such lawsuits filed against a major international accounting firm in Russia. Many legal experts questioned whether there was a valid basis for the lawsuits under the emerging but scanty Russian securities laws and legal precedents. Nevertheless, the Hermitage lawsuits startled PwC and the other major accounting firms operating in Russia. The lawsuits raised in a new context a slew of "old" issues that had pestered audit firms since the inception of the independent audit function.

> *Whatever the truth, the audit profession in Russia faces the same difficulties as elsewhere in arguing that it is "watchdog not bloodhound"—with a remit to verify information, but not to actively sniff out fraud, and not to assume greater responsibility than management itself for errors they have committed. But the profession is also caught in a conflict of interest. Each firm is nominally charged with reporting to all shareholders whether a company's financial statements are "true and fair." In reality, it is appointed, paid by, and reports to executive management, which may be involved in activities to the detriment of outside investors.*[29]

The inherently problematic nature of the auditor-client relationship is made even more problematic within Russia by two key factors. *The New York Times* reported that "fierce competition" among the major accounting firms to acquire and retain the relatively few large and lucrative Russian audit clients had resulted in auditors feeling pressured to "sign off on questionable practices by such clients to avoid alienating them."[30] A former Ernst & Young employee who had been assigned to that firm's Moscow office was more blunt. "A big client [in Russia] is god. You do what they want and tell you to do. You can play straight-laced with minor clients, but you can't do it with the big guys. If you lose the account, no matter how justified you are, that's the end of a career."[31]

The second factor complicating the quality of independent audits in Russia has been the haphazard, if not ragtag, nature of the country's auditing rules. Critics of independent auditors in Western countries have long suggested that professional auditing standards are too "flexible," which ultimately results in less rigorous audits and lower-quality financial statements. This problem has been exacerbated in Russia over the past decade by the lack of consensus on what auditing rules should be applied.

The evolving nature of Russia's professional standards have allowed auditors in that country to interpret their mission too narrowly, according to one former governmental official. Auditors "check that the paperwork was done correctly, but look right past the corrupt heart of the matter."[32] One former PwC auditor provided an example of this mindset in an interview with *The New York Times*. This individual reported that a large automobile manufacturer that was a PwC audit client effectively gave away huge amounts of inventory by routinely shipping cars to supposed "dealers" who never paid for those shipments. The former PwC auditor recalled thinking, "'What's going on? You aren't getting paid—no guarantees, no nothing. Are you stupid?' It was clear to me that it was organized robbery."[33] In its audit report, PwC commented on the fact that the client was using different methods to account for certain domestic sales and sales made to foreign customers. But, according to *The New York Times,* the firm failed to convey in its audit report "what was actually going on at the company."[34]

---

29. A. Jack, "Testing Times for Auditors in Russia," *Financial Times* (London), 17 April 2002, 27.

30. Tavernise, "U.S. Auditors Find Things Are Different."

31. *Ibid.*

32. *Ibid.*

33. *Ibid.*

34. *Ibid.*

A PwC spokesperson refused to respond directly to the charges made by his firm's former employee but did insist that PwC "stood by its audits" of the given client. *The New York Times* reporter then asked an audit partner with Arthur Andersen about an Andersen client that routinely sold merchandise to related parties at deeply discounted prices. The nature of these sales was not disclosed in the company's financial statements or in Andersen's audit reports on those financial statements. When asked why such disclosures were not made, the Andersen audit partner replied that Russian law did not require them. This attitude on the part of major international accounting firms operating in Russia has proven to be extremely detrimental to domestic and foreign investors.

> In this environment, Western auditing firms could have and should have held their Russian clients to higher standards of behavior, investors in Russian companies are now saying. But, instead...the auditors chose to play by Russian rules, and in doing so sacrificed the transparency that investors were counting on them to ensure.[35]

Profit after Stealing and Subsidies

Despite earlier reports that Gazprom would likely retain a new audit firm, in May 2002 the company issued a press release indicating that PwC would remain its independent auditor. Of 29 accounting firms that had submitted bids for the Gazprom engagement, the company's board reported that PwC was the firm that best met its "requirements." Throughout the late spring and summer of 2002, PwC received more good news as one by one the Russian courts dismissed the lawsuits filed against the company by Hermitage Capital. The Russian courts ruled that under existing Russian law only the audited entity could sue its accounting firm for defective audits. Since the majority of Gazprom's board of directors and stockholders refused to side with the plaintiffs in the lawsuits, the courts' only alternative was to rule that the lawsuits were invalid. The Ministry of Finance also denied Hermitage's request that PwC's license to practice be rescinded.

William Browder reacted angrily to the dismissal of the lawsuits his firm had filed against PwC and the news that the accounting firm would remain Gazprom's auditor. Browder argued that, at a minimum, PwC and Gazprom officials should provide more detailed disclosures regarding the company's key operating results. For example, Browder suggested that in the future the company report in its income statements, "Profit after Stealing and Subsidies" and "Profit If Stealing and Subsidies Are Eliminated."[36]

Questions

1. List the challenges that a major accounting firm faces when it establishes its first practice office in a foreign country. Identify the key factors that accounting firms should consider when deciding whether to establish a practice office in a new market.

2. Suppose that a U.S.-based accounting firm has a major audit client in a foreign country that routinely engages in business practices that are considered legal in that country but that would qualify as both illegal and unethical in the United States. What specific moral or ethical obligations, if any, would these circumstances impose on this accounting firm? Explain.

35. *Ibid.*
36. M. Waller, "Fingered," *The Times* (London), 12 July 2002, 27.

3. What responsibilities, if any, do you believe PwC had to Gazprom's minority investors?

4. In your opinion, should PwC have agreed to perform the "special audit" of the Itera transactions? Defend your answer. In your answer, identify the specific ethical issues or challenges that the engagement posed for PwC.

5. In the United States, what responsibility do auditors have to determine whether or not "related parties" exist for a given audit client? Explain.

6. Explain how the British "true and fair" audit approach or strategy differs from the audit philosophy applied in the United States. In your opinion, which of the two audit approaches is better or, at least, more defensible?

7. In recent years, there has been an ongoing debate in the accounting profession focusing on the quality of the accounting standards issued by the International Accounting Standards Board versus those issued by the Financial Accounting Standards Board. Research and briefly explain the key philosophical difference between those two important rule-making bodies that significantly affects the nature of the accounting standards promulgated by each.

Tata Finance Limited

Whoever owns the stick owns the buffalo.

Indian proverb

Prior to the Islamic conquest of the Middle East, the ancient Zoroastrian religion was the national religion of Persia. To escape persecution for their religious beliefs, a large band of Persian Zoroastrians migrated eastward during the eighth century A.D., eventually settling in modern-day India. Because of their Persian heritage, the new arrivals were referred to as *Parsis* by the Hindus who dominated the Indian subcontinent. Although warmly welcomed by the Hindus, the Parsis made every effort to retain and perpetuate their culture and religion. Largely by intermarrying within their own community and by discouraging native Indians from joining their sect, the Parsis have maintained their distinct cultural heritage and identity within India over the past 12 centuries. However, the Parsis' refusal to proselyte their religious beliefs has resulted in their numbers gradually shrinking. By the dawn of the twenty-first century, there were fewer than 100,000 Parsis within India, most of whom lived in the city of Mumbai (previously known as Bombay).

Despite their relatively small numbers, the Parsis have had a disproportionate impact on the history of India over the past millennium. The Parsis were among the most ardent supporters of India's long struggle to become independent of Great Britain. Several prominent Parsi families also contributed significantly to the development of the modern Indian economy. India's largest privately owned company is controlled by a Parsi family, as is the Tata Group, India's largest business conglomerate that consists of nearly 100 companies, two dozen of which are publicly owned.

The massive Tata business empire and the Parsi family of the same name that has overseen that empire since its inception have helped shape the economic and political history of India over the past century. In recent years, however, the Tata Group and its senior executives have faced a protracted and widely publicized accounting scandal that threatens to undercut the credibility and prestige of the prominent organization and its founding family. The scandal has also taken a toll on the reputation of India's largest accounting firm that is closely affiliated with the Tata Group.

J. N. Tata: India's Business Pioneer

In the early 1870s, Jamsetjji Nusserwanji Tata founded the Central India Spinning, Weaving and Manufacturing Company. Over the following three decades, J. N. Tata would create one new company after another. Tata gave India its first steel company, hydroelectric plant, textile factory, shipping line, and cement factory. Later generations of the Tata family would found India's first automobile manufacturer, first domestically owned bank, first chemical company, and Air India, the nation's first airline, which was later nationalized by the Indian federal government.

Among the largest companies within the Tata Group are Tata Consultancy Services, Tata Finance, Tata Motors, and Tata Steel. Arguably, the best known of the public Tata companies is Tata Consultancy Services Limited, which is Asia's largest information technology consulting firm with more than 70,000 employees worldwide. In 2006, Tata Consultancy Services reported a profit of nearly $3 billion. Collectively, the publicly owned Tata companies make Tata Group the largest Indian corporate entity in terms of total market capitalization. Likewise, the member companies of the Tata

Group are India's largest employer in the private sector and account for nearly 3 percent of the nation's annual gross domestic product (GDP). Worldwide, the Tata companies have production or marketing facilities in 40 countries and export goods and services to more than 140 countries.

In addition to being India's first major business entrepreneur, J. N. Tata was an important figure in the Indian nationalistic movement. Tata believed that for his country to become independent of Great Britain, it had to first become economically self-sufficient. To achieve that goal, Tata realized that India had to develop home-grown engineers, architects, and scientists. So, late in his life, Tata founded India's first major scientific university.

J. N. Tata's dedication to achieving India's independence was surpassed only by his commitment to his religious ideals, which he integrated into each of the businesses that he founded. The crest of the Tata Group that commonly appears on the correspondence of Tata companies includes the three-word creed of the Zoroastrian religion: Humata, Hukhta, Hvarshta. That creed translates in English to "good thoughts, good words, and good deeds." Like other Zoroastrians, Tata fervently believed that one's principal purpose in life is to serve his fellow man. Because of that belief, Tata decreed that two-thirds of all the profits generated by his businesses would be contributed to charitable organizations. More than one century later, that policy is still in effect and has resulted in billions of dollars being donated by the Tata Group to a wide range of humanitarian causes.

The Tainting of Tata

Corruption has long been a major problem within the Indian economy. Among 12 major Asian countries, one recent study found that only Indonesia has a higher level of business corruption than India.[1] Nevertheless, since the days of J. N. Tata, the Tata family has prided itself on maintaining a high level of ethics within the operations of each Tata company. The London-based *Financial Times* noted that the word "Tata" was for decades accepted as a byword for integrity"[2] within the Indian economy and Indian society as a whole. According to *Newsweek*, Tata's "rigid ethical standards are so well known that corrupt [government] officials typically don't even bother asking Tata for bribes."[3]

Tata's sterling reputation for integrity and for upholding the highest standards of ethical conduct was jeopardized in 2002 by a 900-page report issued by A. F. Ferguson & Company (AFF), India's largest accounting firm. AFF served as the independent or statutory auditor for dozens of the member companies of the Tata Group. One of the large Tata companies that AFF did not audit was Tata Finance Limited, a Tata affiliate engaged in automobile financing, mortgage lending, and consumer credit cards. Another of India's largest accounting firms, S. B. Billimoria & Co., served as Tata Finance's independent auditor.

In early 2001, senior executives of the Tata Group, which included its top officer, Ratan Tata, the corporate group's executive chairman and the great-great grandson of J. N. Tata, retained AFF to carry out an internal investigation of Tata Finance. The primary purpose of the investigation was to identify the individuals responsible for a series of fraudulent transactions that had produced large losses for Tata Finance and resulted in material misrepresentations in the company's publicly issued financial

---

1. *Reuters* (online), "India Second Only to Indonesia in Business Corruption," 2 March 2004.

2. K. Merchant, "Chairman on Defensive as Scandal Tarnishes Tata," *Financial Times,* 19 August 2002, 15.

3. G. Wehfritz, R. Moreau, and S. Chatterjee, "A New Kind of Company," *Newsweek International Edition* (online), 4 July 2006.

statements. The Tata Group executives suspected that Dilip Pendse, the former "managing director," or senior operating officer, of Tata Finance, was responsible for those transactions and believed that the results of the AFF investigation would confirm their suspicion.

Enron Gimmicks: Indian Style

The accounting scandal at Tata Finance involved a little-known subsidiary of the company, Niskalp Investment & Trading Company. During the late 1990s, the stocks of technology companies soared in stock markets around the world but then suddenly collapsed when the "Internet Bubble" in those markets burst in early 2000. Niskalp earned substantial profits for Tata Finance in the late 1990s as a result of large investments made by Dilip Pendse in technology stocks. Executives of Tata Group would subsequently allege that Pendse's investments in technology stocks had not been authorized by Tata Finance's board.

When the stock prices of technology companies plunged in early 2000, Niskalp suffered huge losses on its portfolio of technology stocks. Niskalp's mounting losses throughout 2000 and into early 2001 posed a huge financial crisis for Tata Finance. The Reserve Bank of India (RBI), a federal regulatory agency for the nation's banking system, requires companies such as Tata Finance to maintain a minimum "capital adequacy ratio" (CAR). By early 2001, Tata Finance had breached the RBI's minimum CAR. Pendse initially used a series of intercompany investments, commonly referred to as intercorporate deposits or ICDs, from other companies in the Tata Group to shore up Tata Finance's capital structure. The RBI does not prohibit ICDs but it also does not allow financial institutions to consider them when computing their CAR. A subsequent investigation would reveal that many of the ICDs made to Tata Finance by its sister companies were not equity investments but rather loans. In either case, the ICDs should not have been considered by Tata Finance when computing its CAR.

As Niskalp's losses continued to rise in 2001, Tata Finance used one final measure in a desperate attempt to resolve, or at least conceal, its rapidly deteriorating financial condition. The company chose to "desubsidiarise Niskalp, allegedly to protect its own balance sheet by not having to disclose the losses of its subsidiary any more."[4] This stopgap measure failed to remedy Tata Finance's underlying financial problem, namely, its lack of adequate equity capital. Pendse then turned to his superiors at the Tata Group who provided the equity capital needed to rescue Tata Finance. Shortly after Tata Finance's true financial condition was revealed to the public, the Tata Group dismissed Dilip Pendse and four of his key subordinates. In August 2001, the Tata Group filed a complaint with law enforcement authorities charging Pendse with criminal breach of trust. Two months later, the remaining members of Tata Finance's board resigned as did the company's audit firm, S. B. Billimoria & Co.

When the details of the Tata accounting scandal were revealed, the Indian business press immediately pointed out that the accounting gimmicks used by Tata Finance were very similar to abusive accounting methods used by Enron in the United States. Like the Enron debacle, Tata Finance's independent audit firm faced heated criticism from the business press for failing to uncover and stop those abusive accounting methods. When asked to comment on the Tata scandal, S. B. Billimoria's managing partner noted, "Operating under the constraints of time and cost, we presume full honesty from our clients. After all, an audit is not an investigation."[5]

---

4. S. Vikraman, "Time to Regulate the Auditing Profession?" *Businessline,* 11 March 2002, 1.

5. *Flashpoint,* "Financial Chicanery," http://www.capitalmarket.com, 29 January 2002.

In interviews with the media, Ratan Tata maintained that he and his top subordinates at the Tata Group had not been aware of the fraudulent Tata Finance transactions. However, Dilip Pendse staunchly insisted that he had kept Ratan Tata and other Tata Group executives informed of those transactions. According to Pendse, who was employed by Tata Finance for nearly 25 years, he had met with Ratan Tata every Wednesday to discuss Tata Finance's financial affairs. Pendse also revealed that a financial report prepared for Tata Finance had included a candid discussion of the controversial ICD transactions and their impact on the company's financial condition. However, according to Pendse, a Tata Finance board member who had close ties to key Tata Group executives had deleted that discussion before the financial report was released to the public.

"The Wrath of the Tatas"

One goal that the senior executives of the Tata Group hoped to achieve when they retained AFF to investigate the Tata Finance accounting scandal was to clear their own names. One of those executives reportedly requested that Y. M. Kale, a senior AFF partner who was in line to become the next managing partner of AFF, supervise that investigation. Kale was easily among the most respected members of Indian's accounting profession. An employee or partner of AFF for 30 years, Kale served on the International Accounting Standards Board, was a former president of the Institute of Chartered Accountants of India (ICAI), and had been elected to the ICAI's governing council five times—the ICAI is the Indian federal agency that oversees the nation's accounting profession, including its independent audit function.[6] Kale had also served as the chairman of the ICAI board responsible for issuing Indian accounting standards and at the time he was selected for the Tata Finance assignment was the chairman of the ICAI audit practices committee. Kale's prominent position within India's accounting profession and his reputation for integrity and candor were, no doubt, expected to add to the credibility of the AFF report.

AFF prepared the 900-page report on the Tata Finance accounting scandal exclusively for Ratan Tata and his top subordinates within the Tata Group. Nevertheless, by July 2002, two months after the report had been delivered by AFF to the Tata Group, large segments of the report, including AFF's major findings, had been leaked to the press. The public disclosure of AFF's principal findings reignited the Tata Finance accounting scandal and triggered a firestorm of criticism directed at the senior executives of the Tata Group. Instead of absolving those executives of any responsibility for the accounting scandal, the AFF report linked them to the fraud. One journalist relied on a sports idiom to describe the unexpected outcome of the AFF investigation when he noted that the Tata Group executives had "scored an own goal."[7]

The AFF report shocked Ratan Tata and the other senior executives of the Tata Group not only because it supported the allegation of Dilip Pendse that Mr. Tata and his subordinates had been aware of the fraudulent transactions—but also because the report criticized the quality of the Tata companies' corporate governance system. This unexpected criticism stemmed largely from the paternalistic nature of the organization's top management. Throughout the history of the organization, members of the Tata family and their close friends and business associates had dominated the operating management and boards of directors of the individual Tata companies. These

6. Case 8.11, "Institute of Chartered Accountants of India," examines the ICAI's role in the development of India's accounting profession and independent audit function.

7. V. Law and M. Goyal, "Scoring an Own Goal," *India Today*, 26 August 2002, 49.

individuals made protecting the jobs of Tata employees one of their primary objectives, even if that meant refusing to eliminate unprofitable businesses or business segments. This policy endeared the Tata family and organization to its employees but it also undermined the huge conglomerate's overall profitability. The "in-bred" corporate governance structure of the Tata Group also meant that the individual Tata companies typically did not have outside or independent board members who could provide objective analyses of the companies' operations, accounting and financial reporting decisions, and other important policies and procedures.

The AFF report and the ensuing controversy that erupted after much of the report was leaked to the press created a rift between the large accounting firm and Tata Group's senior management. On August 2, 2002, AFF startled the Indian business community and accounting profession by announcing that it was retracting the report because it was flawed. Even more startling was AFF's announcement six days later that it had dismissed the three partners responsible for writing the report, including its principal author, Y. M. Kale.

AFF's decision to retract its report and to dismiss Y. M. Kale only deepened the controversy swirling around the Tata Finance accounting fraud. A senior member of one of India's other large accounting firms suggested that Kale was being made the "scapegoat" in the unseemly affair and that the Tata organization was responsible for his dismissal.[8] The Indian business press also repeatedly implied that Kale had been fired as a result of pressure applied on AFF by the Tata Group. These media reports pointed out that the Tata Group had significant leverage on AFF because the accounting firm audited several of the largest Tata companies and because the close affiliation with the Tata organization enhanced AFF's stature and prestige within India's accounting profession.

The published reports connecting them to the firing of Y. M. Kale infuriated the senior executives of the Tata Group, including Ratan Tata. To respond to that allegation and other criticism they faced as a result of the Tata Finance accounting scandal, those executives issued a press release entitled "Tata Group Condemns Campaign of Vilification." The lengthy press release, which appeared in full-page advertisements purchased by the Tata Group in several major Indian newspapers, began with the following statement: "Sections of the media have been carrying deliberately distorted and sensationalized versions pertaining to the withdrawal of a private and confidential report prepared by A. F. Ferguson and Co. (AFF) for one of the Tata Group's companies. . . . The Group's reputation and image are being sullied deliberately by the use of half truths and untruths."[9] Subsequent sections of the press release insisted that the senior executives of the Tata Group not only had nothing to do with the Tata Finance fraud, they also had not pressured AFF to either retract its report or dismiss Y. M. Kale.

The press release also charged that the AFF report, in fact, was flawed because Kale had excluded from the report important testimony provided by the former chief accountant of the Niskalp subsidiary of Tata Finance. According to that individual, Dilip Pendse had instructed him to enter fictitious transactions in Niskalp's accounting records and to prepare false accounting documents to corroborate those entries. The purpose of the fictitious transactions, according to the former accountant, was to mitigate the large investment losses being incurred by Niskalp. Four days after the Tata Group issued the August 10th press release, the former Niskalp accountant recanted and insisted that he had made the false allegations against Pendse "under

8. V. Sridhar and A. Katakam, "L'affaire Tata Finance," *Frontline* (online), 31 August–13 September 2002.

9. Tata Group, "Tata Group Condemns Campaign of Villification." Press release issued August 10, 2002.

tremendous tension, with a disturbed frame of mind due to shock and also under threat of arrest."[10]

Following the release and retraction of the AFF report and his subsequent dismissal by AFF, Y. M. Kale refused to comment publicly on the controversy despite repeated interview requests from the media. As one journalist observed, everyone wanted to know how Kale could risk his 30-year career in public accounting by "incurring the wrath of the Tatas."[11] Many of Kale's colleagues in the accounting profession came to his defense and questioned why his former firm, AFF, did not "stand behind him" during the ordeal. India's business press also berated AFF for apparently buckling to pressure applied by its largest and most important client.

> This unprecedented withdrawal [of the AFF report] has raised the hackles of the entire accounting community.... The issue is—how can an accounting firm "withdraw" its observations just because the company was not happy with them? It is the duty of any auditing firm to point out the discrepancies; isn't that the basic objective of any auditing firm?

> What this issue highlights is that maybe auditing firms do indeed work for the companies for whom they audit. Independent views and observations are good in theory but not in practical life. Then this does nullify the entire purpose of any auditing agency, doesn't it?[12]

Criticism of AFF within India's accounting profession became even more pointed when a subsequent investigation revealed that several AFF partners had performed a detailed review of, and approved, the AFF report on the Tata Finance accounting scandal before the report was forwarded to the Tata Group. As one journalist noted, "Trust and reputation are the two biggest assets for an audit firm. A. F. Ferguson & Co. (AFF) appears to have just mortgaged them in distress."[13]

EPILOGUE

The white-collar crime unit of the Mumbai Police Department investigated the criminal complaint filed against Dilip Pendse by the Tata Group. In August 2002, that unit dropped the charges filed against Pendse, reporting that there was "insufficient evidence to support" them.[14] In a subsequent interview, a senior official of the Mumbai Police Department reported that the criminal investigation of the Tata Finance scandal had revealed that the "TFL [Tata Finance Limited] board knew everything

that Pendse did. None of these transactions could have taken place without their connivance."[15] Since certain members of the Tata Finance board were close associates of Ratan Tata and other top Tata Group executives, this conclusion appeared to corroborate Pendse's testimony that Tata Group's senior management had been aware of the financial wrongdoing at Tata Finance.

The Mumbai Police Department's decision to drop the criminal complaint filed against Dilip

10. Sridhar and Katakam, "L'affaire Tata Finance."

11. *Global News Wire* (online), "People in Glass Houses... A. F. Ferguson Report on Tata Finance Raises Storm," 26 August 2002.

12. R. Dubey, "Wave of Financial Scams Hits the Indian Shores," *Arab News* (http://www.arabnews.com), 19 August 2002.

13. R. Srinivasan, "A. F. Ferguson Holding a Tiger by the Tail," *Businessline,* 11 August 2002, 1.

14. Merchant, "Chairman on Defensive as Scandal Tarnishes Tata."

15. Sridhar and Katakam, "L'affaire Tata Finance."

Pendse angered the senior executives of the Tata Group. Shortly after the charges were dropped, the Tata Group filed a legal appeal asking an Indian court to order the Mumbai Police Department to "reinvestigate" the matter.[16] Over the next several years, the Tata Group would doggedly pursue Pendse. As a result of additional criminal complaints filed by the Tata Group, Pendse was arrested for a second time by the Mumbai Police Department in December 2003. In August 2006, India's federal law enforcement agency, the Central Bureau of Investigation (CBI), filed criminal charges against Pendse, largely as a result of information provided to it by the Tata Group. These latter charges are still pending. To date, the principal criminal sanction that has been imposed on Pendse is a fine for insider trading levied against him in January 2007 by the Securities and Exchange Board of India, the Indian federal agency that is comparable to the U.S. Securities and Exchange Commission.

After retracting its report on the Tata Finance accounting scandal, AFF disclosed that it intended to reopen its investigation of the matter and file a revised report with the Tata Group. Apparently, the second report was never completed. According to an unnamed source within the Tata Group, the senior executives of that organization informed AFF in late 2002 that a revised report would not be necessary.[17]

Public criticism of AFF's decision to withdraw its report on the Tata Finance fraud prompted the ICAI to investigate that decision. The ICAI president at the time reported that his agency was considering filing charges of "gross negligence" against AFF.[18] The ICAI also announced that it would investigate allegations that AFF had shredded key documents pertaining to the Tata Finance investigation to prevent law enforcement and regulatory authorities from accessing those documents.

After a brief investigation in late 2002, the ICAI reported that it had not found any evidence of professional misconduct by AFF in connection with its investigation of the Tata Finance fraud or its subsequent decision to retract the report regarding that fraud. Over the previous several years, the ICAI had been criticized for being a lax and ineffective regulatory agency for India's accounting profession. In fact, several parties, including representatives of the major international accounting firms, had called for the ICAI to be replaced. The ICAI's finding that AFF was not guilty of any professional misconduct in the Tata Finance case reinforced the perception that the ICAI was lax in carrying out its regulatory responsibilities and resulted in even more criticism of the federal agency.

In November 2002, Y. M. Kale accepted a management position with a large consulting firm. To date, Kale has yet to comment publicly on the Tata Finance accounting scandal, his role in investigating that scandal, or AFF's decision to dismiss him. Within India's accounting profession and business community, Kale remains a respected figure. As one journalist noted, "In the entire TFL drama, only Kale appears to have come out unscathed."[19]

Questions

1. Should the fact that a business entity or other organization embraces a specific ethical, moral, or religious code or framework be relevant in designing and carrying out an audit of that organization? Defend your answer.

16. *Global News Wire* (online), "Tata Rejoinder Seeks Criminal Charges against Dilip Pendse, Insists on Reinvestigation in TFL Case," 24 October 2002.

17. *Global News Wire* (online), "New Ferguson Report on TFL Any Time Now," 12 November 2002.

18. Sridhar and Katakam, "L'affaire Tata Finance."

19. *Ibid.*

2. Suppose that an accounting firm in the United States was retained to complete an engagement similar to the one performed by AFF for the Tata Group. What professional standards would be relevant to such an engagement? How do the latter standards differ, if at all, from those that apply to the performance of an independent audit?

3. In your opinion, why do you believe that Y. M. Kale chose not to comment publicly on the controversy that surrounded the retraction of the AFF report on the Tata Finance accounting scandal and his subsequent dismissal by AFF? Did he have an ethical or moral responsibility not to comment on those matters? Explain.

CASE 8.10

Baan Company, N.V.

In May 1998, Moret Ernst & Young Accountants resigned as the independent audit firm for Baan Company, N.V., a software company headquartered in Barneveld, the Netherlands.[1] At the time, Baan, ranked among the leading worldwide suppliers of enterprise resource planning (ERP) software packages. Press reports provided conflicting accounts of why Moret Ernst & Young (Moret), the Dutch affiliate of the U.S.-based accounting firm Ernst & Young, resigned as Baan's auditor. *The New York Times* reported that Baan management had been upset by Moret's insistence that the software maker include disclosures in its financial statement footnotes regarding certain large related-party transactions.[2] A few days later, a press release issued by Baan reported that Moret resigned because of a planned "global software consultancy agreement" between Baan and Ernst & Young. In the years to follow, an investigation by the Securities and Exchange Commission (SEC) would reveal much more about the complicated nature of Baan's relationship with Moret and the circumstances that led to that relationship coming to an end.

An Enterprising Software Company

The 1990s were a frenetic but blissful time for major software companies across the globe. A slew of Y2K (Year 2000) doomsayers warned multinational corporations, "Mom and Pop" businesses, charitable organizations, government agencies at all levels, and any other organization relying heavily on computers that those machines would likely shut down one nanosecond after midnight on January 1, 2000. The result would be disruption of practically every significant internal function of those organizations, not to mention worldwide chaos. Mounting concern caused by this doomsday scenario prompted organizations of all sizes to hire Y2K remediation experts to rid their computer code of the Y2K "bug." In the United States, businesses and government agencies spent an estimated $300 billion on Y2K remediation services. Citicorp, alone, reported spending $650 million on its Y2K project.

Opportunistic software companies and business consulting firms took advantage of the sudden and dramatic surge in IT (information technology) awareness to goad corporate executives to overhaul their organizations' IT systems. The punch line of these marketing efforts went something like this: "While we are solving your Y2K problem, why don't you allow us to revamp your IT systems to prepare your organization for the dynamic and hypercompetitive business environment of the twenty-first century?" Software vendors and business consultants promised to revolutionize business processes and make companies more efficient, more focused on their goals, and, most important, more profitable.

Such marketing efforts resulted in a huge increase in IT spending during the late 1990s and produced an array of new and impressive-sounding catch phrases. Review business archives for that period and you will find the following expressions and literally hundreds of similar ones bandied about in the business press: "business

---

1. "N.V." is an abbreviation for "naamloze vennootschap." This phrase indicates that Baan Company was a limited liability company under Dutch federal law.

2. F. Norris, "An Audit Uncovers Soft Profits in Software," *The New York Times,* 10 May 1998, Section 3, 1.

process reengineering," "mission-critical, customer-driven Web applications," "digital document-management services," and "Web-enabling software solutions." Among the most widely used, and possibly least understood, phrases coined in the late 1990s was "enterprise resource planning" (ERP). The following description of "ERP software" was provided by one major software vendor: "ERP software is generally used to automate and integrate corporate functions across the board, such as inventory control, procurement, manufacturing planning, distribution, sales forecasting, finance, human resources, EDI and project management."[3] Each of the major software companies developed and intensely marketed a broad product line of ERP software during the late 1990s. These companies included, among others, Oracle, PeopleSoft, Seibel Systems, and Baan Company.

Baan Company was founded in 1978 in the Netherlands. During the 1990s, the company's software engineers developed a family of products and services that they referred to as the "Orgware Solution." According to the company's promotional literature, these products and services were intended to help companies "depict organizational structure," "reduce the time to market," provide for "dynamic enterprise modeling," and "rapidly translate a business vision into improved business process."

To help market their products and services, each of the major software companies, including Baan, developed an extensive network of business partners that included the major firms in the financial services industries. Among the most valued of these business partners were the large international accounting firms. Software executives "covet connections to the Big Five firms because of those firms' access to the executives and decision makers at the thousands of companies that they audit."[4] Just as important, the auditing, taxation, and general business consulting services that the major accounting firms provided to their clients made them well aware of those companies' IT needs.

By the mid-1990s, the major software companies had established a working relationship with each of the international accounting firms and a much closer "partnering" relationship with at least one of those firms. For example, Oracle's principal Big Five partner was Arthur Andersen, while Microsoft had paired itself with Deloitte & Touche. Baan Company affiliated itself with both Ernst & Young and Coopers & Lybrand. In Europe, Baan developed a close working relationship with its independent audit firm, Moret.

Bonding with Your Auditor

In May 1995, Baan Company went public with an initial public offering (IPO). The company's common stock traded on both the Amsterdam Stock Exchange and the NASDAQ exchange in the United States. For purposes of the Securities and Exchange Commission (SEC), Baan was a "foreign private issuer,"[5] a status that required the company to file an annual financial report with the SEC that included a complete set of audited financial statements. Prior to Baan registering its securities for sale in the United States, the Moret partner who supervised the annual Baan audit

---

3. *Business Wire* (online), "Entrust Technologies Unveils Comprehensive Plan to Address Security Requirements of ERP Software Market," 23 November 1998.

4. M. Petersen, "Consulting by Auditors Stirs Concerns," *The New York Times*, 13 July 1998, D1.

5. The SEC defines a "foreign private issuer" as a registrant that meets the following four conditions: (1) 50 percent or less of its outstanding voting stock is held by U.S. residents; (2) the majority of the company's executive officers and directors are not U.S. citizens or residents; (3) 50 percent or more of the company's assets are located outside of the United States; and (4) the company's principal business operations are outside of the United States.

engagement obtained a summary of the SEC's auditor independence rules from an audit partner with Ernst & Young, Moret's U.S. affiliate. The Moret partner was concerned that certain joint business relationships his firm had with Baan might violate the SEC's auditor independence rules.

From 1995 through 1997, Moret personnel worked closely with Baan to help the company market its software products, complete software implementation projects, and provide technical support to Baan's clients. In early 1995, Baan and Moret signed a "partner agreement" that created a "global alliance" between the two firms. "The agreement established guidelines for coordination of the global alliance, a joint structure for managing Baan's and Moret's activities, mutual indemnification between the parties, and prohibitions against the disclosure of confidential information."[6] A proposal for a consulting project that the Moret firm made to a potential client stressed the close relationship between the two firms. "Baan and Moret have a worldwide partnership. In this partnership both parties have made concrete arrangements of working together for clients. In practice this means that Baan and Moret operate as one party toward the client. Our activities are fully integrated with and steered by the Baan project management team."

During the late 1990s, Baan's IT software business grew dramatically, causing the company's stock price to spiral upward. Within two years of the company's IPO, its stock price had increased by tenfold or 1,000 percent. Because the firm was unable to hire sufficient software consultants to work on its growing backlog of customer projects, the firm "borrowed" Moret employees to help complete many of those projects. For example, in the fall of 1996, Moret assumed full responsibility for a large Baan software implementation project that was being completed for a Turkish company: "Moret consultants signed documents and made presentations on Baan's behalf, and Moret consultants were listed in project documents as being members of the Baan implementation team." Moret billed Baan more than $300,000 for the time its employees spent on that project.[7]

In another case, Moret provided employees to help Baan complete a software implementation project for a Finnish company that was Baan's third-largest customer. One of those Moret employees served as the project director for a period of time. Moret billed Baan the equivalent of nearly $1 million for the work that its employees did on that project. Baan then added a 25 percent mark-up to the amounts billed to it by Moret when preparing the billing invoices submitted to the client. "Thus, in addition to directly helping Baan complete an implementation for an important company, Moret's furnishing of consultants contributed to Baan's profits."

From late 1996 through 1998, Moret loaned several of its professional employees to Baan to help staff the Baan Support Center, which provided technical support and assistance to the company's customers. While interacting with Baan customers in this facility, the Moret employees were required to identify themselves as Baan employees. Moret received $600,000 from Baan for the time that its employees spent working in the support center.

These and other joint business relationships that Moret had with Baan clearly violated the SEC's auditor independence rule that precluded auditors of SEC registrants from having a "direct...business relationship [with an audit client], other than as a consumer in the normal course of business . . . [that] will adversely affect the

6. The remaining quotes in this case, unless indicated otherwise, were taken from Securities and Exchange Commission, *Accounting and Auditing Enforcement Release No. 1584*, 27 June 2002.

7. Because of a dispute over the amount of the bill, Moret was never paid for the time its employees spent working on this project.

accountant's independence with respect to the client." Despite their awareness of that rule, an awareness they had acquired from Ernst & Young, Moret personnel chose to ignore the rule and forge an increasingly close and profitable association with Baan.

Ernst & Young's Dual Role at Baan USA

Baan Company had several international subsidiaries, including Baan USA. In 1995, Ernst & Young audited Baan USA's financial statements that were then incorporated into Baan's consolidated financial statements for that year. Ernst & Young resigned as the subsidiary's auditor in early 1996 to pursue joint business relationships with Baan USA, "including subcontracting on software implementations and submitting joint proposals with Baan [USA] for software sales and implementation business." Ernst & Young's resignation was prompted by the realization that the business relationships with Baan USA would cause the firm to violate the SEC's auditor independence rules.

To replace Ernst & Young, Baan retained a small accounting firm in California to audit Baan USA's 1996 financial statements. By the following year, Baan USA's explosive growth in revenues resulted in that subsidiary accounting for approximately 40 percent of Baan's total worldwide revenues. This development greatly concerned the Baan audit engagement partner with the Moret firm. The partner was not comfortable with allowing the small accounting firm to take responsibility for such a large portion of the Baan annual audit. Moret officials discussed this issue with personnel in Ernst & Young's National Office in New York City. One alternative the parties considered was having Moret retain another major accounting firm to audit Baan USA's 1997 financial statements. That alternative was quickly rejected since each of those firms also had significant business relationships with Baan USA that would impair their independence while auditing the Baan subsidiary.

After considerable discussion, Moret and Ernst & Young reached an agreement that would allow the small California accounting firm to remain Baan USA's external auditor. The key feature of this agreement was that Ernst & Young would supply internal audit services to Baan USA, meaning that the subsidiary effectively outsourced its internal audit function to Ernst & Young. The Ernst & Young personnel assigned to Baan USA would work closely with the audit engagement team from the small accounting firm. This arrangement was intended to allay the concern of the Baan audit engagement partner regarding the small accounting firm's ability to successfully complete the 1997 audit of Baan USA. During the negotiations with Ernst & Young regarding the structure and nature of the 1997 Baan USA audit, the Baan audit engagement partner made it very clear that his firm (Moret) intended to rely heavily on the work of the Ernst & Young internal auditors in deciding whether to accept the results of the Baan USA audit. "[Ernst & Young's procedures must] be adequate for us to use . . . for the external audit without having to supplement a lot of the work. So, they should be similar to a normal external audit plan, perhaps supplemented with some real internal audit stuff to further substantiate that this clearly is an internal audit."

The 1997 Baan audit went off as planned and resulted in Moret issuing an unqualified opinion on the company's consolidated financial statements. In their role as Baan USA's internal auditors, Ernst & Young personnel worked side by side with the audit engagement team from the small California accounting firm. According to the SEC, the California firm conducted a full scope audit of Baan USA. However, Moret "used and relied on E&Y's work" on that audit, "citing that work repeatedly in its audit working papers and using that work to confirm the accuracy and appropriate scope of the California firm's work."

SEC Sanctions Moret

As noted earlier, Moret resigned as Baan's auditor in May 1998, following the completion of the 1997 audit. Again, two differing accounts of the reason for Moret's resignation were reported in the business press. An undisclosed factor that may have contributed to that resignation was tension between Ernst & Young's National Office and the Baan audit engagement partner with the Moret firm. The SEC revealed that the two parties bickered over the role that the Ernst & Young auditors would play in the 1997 Baan USA audit. Ernst & Young officials resisted, and likely resented, the efforts of the Baan audit engagement partner to pressure their firm into playing an increasingly important role in that audit. At one point, frustration prompted the Baan audit engagement partner to consider not completing the engagement. "The Moret audit partner [Baan audit engagement partner] indicated that Moret might have to resign from the Baan audit if E&Y would not agree to perform internal audit work along the lines he wanted."

In 2002, the SEC issued *Accounting and Auditing Enforcement Release No. 1584* to report the results of its investigation of Moret's 1995 through 1997 audits of Baan Company. Because of the joint business relationships between Baan and Moret, the SEC ruled that Moret's independence had been impaired on each of those audits. The SEC also concluded that during the 1997 audit, "Moret improperly relied on the audit work of an affiliated firm, E&Y, which also lacked independence from Baan." According to the SEC, the Ernst & Young internal auditors assigned to Baan USA had "participated in a significant portion of the [external] audit" and been "an essential part of Moret's external audit team" at a time when they had "managerial responsibilities" with Baan USA.

The SEC fined Moret $400,000 for violating the federal agency's auditor independence rules during the 1995 through 1997 Baan audit engagements. This was the first time that the SEC had fined a foreign accounting firm and the first time that it had fined an accounting firm for having a significant business relationship with an audit client. The settlement agreement that the SEC reached with Moret required the firm to "develop and implement auditor independence policies for the firm." These policies were to include prohibitions on the types of business relationships that had impaired Moret's independence during the Baan audits. Among other stipulations, the SEC also required that Moret personnel assigned to any future audits involving SEC registrants "undergo training regarding auditor independence" at least once every 12 months.

EPILOGUE

Similar to many software vendors and consulting companies that profited enormously from the late 1990s "IT revolution," Baan Company experienced a sudden and sharp drop in business activity following the turn of the century. In 2000, a British software company, Invensys, purchased Baan. Unfortunately, Baan's operating results continued to deteriorate and Invensys sold the company for a huge loss three years later.

The SEC did not sanction Ernst & Young for the role that it played in the 1997 Baan audit. But Ernst & Young soon found itself the target of another SEC investigation involving a major software vendor, a case that was very reminiscent of the Moret-Baan debacle. From 1994 through 2000, Ernst & Young was a member of a network of business partners created by PeopleSoft. Twelve other financial services firms participated in the PeopleSoft Financials Implementation

Partnership Program, including Deloitte & Touche and Price Waterhouse. Unlike the latter two accounting firms, Ernst & Young already had a relationship with PeopleSoft since it served as the large software company's independent auditor.

In June 2002, shortly before the SEC issued its enforcement release for the Moret-Baan case, the federal agency filed a complaint against Ernst & Young. This complaint charged the firm with violating auditor independence rules by maintaining a six-year joint business relationship with PeopleSoft while simultaneously serving as the company's independent auditor. "The SEC said that during the 1990s, E&Y developed and marketed a software product called EY/GEMS for PeopleSoft, which combined a PeopleSoft product with software that was used in E&Y's tax department."[8] According to the SEC, E&Y paid PeopleSoft a minimum $300,000 royalty for each sale of that joint product. PeopleSoft and Ernst & Young "closely coordinated" the marketing efforts for the software product, "including reciprocal endorsements of each other, links to each other's websites, holding themselves out as 'business partners,' and sharing customer information, customer leads and 'target accounts.'"[9] As many as 1,000 Ernst & Young employees helped install the joint software product for hundreds of companies, including many that were Ernst & Young audit clients.

In July 2003, the SEC announced the sanctions it intended to impose on Ernst & Young for the dual and conflicting roles the accounting firm had maintained with PeopleSoft. Those sanctions required Ernst & Young to forfeit the nearly $2 million of audit fees it had received from PeopleSoft from 1994 through 2000. In addition, the SEC intended to prohibit Ernst & Young from accepting new SEC audit clients for a period of six months. In defending the harsh sanctions, the SEC noted that Ernst & Young

was a repeat offender because the firm had been involved in a similar case in the mid-1990s. In an earlier discussion of the case, the SEC had made it very clear that auditor–client joint business relationships were totally inconsistent with, and undermined the credibility of, the independent audit function. "It is crucial that accountants [auditors] be independent; when they engage in joint business practices with clients, the entire audit process is subverted."[10]

Ernst & Young officials reacted angrily to the charges that the SEC filed against their firm. Those officials pointed out that the federal agency did not allege, or even suggest, that Ernst & Young's joint business relationship with PeopleSoft had diminished the quality of its PeopleSoft audits. In addition, Ernst & Young maintained that the joint business relationship it had with PeopleSoft was "commonplace" among accounting firms and software vendors and that "it did not affect our client, its shareholders, or the investing public."[11] Finally, Ernst & Young stated that since the sanctions proposed by the SEC were an "outrageous" overreaction by the federal agency, it would vigorously contest those sanctions in the federal courts. Despite such statements that the firm made repeatedly to the press, in April 2004, Ernst & Young relented and decided not to appeal the SEC sanctions.

While we are surprised and disappointed by the harsh sanctions, we accept them. The foundation of our profession depends on our independence and the objectivity of our auditors and advisors. We are committed to delivering quality in everything we do and this requires that our people never compromise their independence or objectivity, in perception or reality.[12]

8. N. Roland, "SEC Charges Ernst & Young with Conflicts: Ran Venture with PeopleSoft While Auditing Books," *National Post*, 21 May 2002, FP1.

9. S. Taub, "Will SEC Come Down Hard on E&Y over PeopleSoft?" *CFO.com*, 14 November 2002.

10. S. Zuckerman, "Ernst & Young Faces Charges by SEC," *San Francisco Chronicle*, 21 May 2002, B1.

11. A. Rayner, "Ernst & Young Accused of Breaking SEC Rules," *The Times* (online), 22 May 2002.

12. B. Carlino, "E&Y Won't Challenge Client Ban," *Accounting Today*, 19 May–6 June 2004, 1.

Questions

1. Because Baan Company registered its common stock for sale in the United
    States, the SEC had regulatory authority over the company. Do the SEC's financial
    reporting requirements differ for foreign companies versus domestic or U.S.-
    based companies? If so, briefly describe any such differences.

2. Provide specific examples of how the joint business relationships between Baan
    and Moret may have impaired the latter's independence while it was auditing
    Baan's annual financial statements.

3. Do you believe that the SEC should have sanctioned Ernst & Young for the role
    that it played in the 1997 Baan audit? Defend your answer.

4. Ernst & Young officials indicated that the joint business relationship with
    PeopleSoft "did not affect our client, its shareholders, or the investing public." Do
    you agree or disagree with that statement? Explain. Do you believe the sanctions
    that the SEC imposed on Ernst & Young were too harsh? Why or why not?

Institute of Chartered Accountants of India

The spice trade first brought European explorers, most notably the Portuguese adventurer Vasco da Gama, to the shores of the Indian subcontinent in the late fifteenth century. In the mid-eighteenth century, Great Britain used a series of military excursions to gain control over several major Indian provinces and effectively made the country the largest colony within its far-flung empire. For almost a century, Britain's colonial rule of the country was administered through the infamous British East India Company. After Great Britain thwarted the bloody Indian Rebellion of 1857, the British East India Company was abolished and India became subject to direct rule by the British monarchy. Periodic rebellions, civil unrest, and ultimately the massive civil disobedience campaign orchestrated by Mahatma Gandhi culminated in India gaining its independence from Great Britain in August 1947.

Britain's colonial rule would leave a lasting imprint on all aspects of Indian society, including its economy, financial reporting system, and accounting profession. During the two centuries that Britain controlled India, a large number of British citizens immigrated to India seeking opportunities in banking, insurance, accounting, and other financial services industries and professions. Alexander Fletcher Ferguson arrived in India in the late 1880s. A few years later, he organized an accounting firm, A. F. Ferguson & Co., that would become one of India's most prominent professional services organizations and its largest accounting firm.

Native Indians typically did not welcome British immigrants who, like Ferguson, often took advantage of their British "connections" to further their careers and otherwise elevate their social status. Making matters worse, the new immigrants often treated Indians as second-class citizens in their own country. Not surprisingly, after India gained its independence, an isolationist mindset prevailed in the country. Because of that mindset, India's central government established protectionist policies to prevent foreign companies, professional firms, and other organizations from dominating the new nation's economy. These policies included significant tariffs on imported goods, limits on equity investments in Indian companies by foreign nationals, and, most important, the so-called "License Raj." The License Raj was an extensive set of government rules and regulations established by India's first Prime Minister, Jawaharlal Nehru, that gave India's central government effective control over the nation's economy.[1] Under the License Raj, any major business venture proposed by a domestic or foreign entity had to be approved by a central government planning commission.

India's protectionist economic policies discouraged the major international accounting firms from establishing significant operations in India. However, when India's central government announced that it planned to relax its protectionist policies in the early 1990s, those firms quickly began pursuing practice development opportunities in the world's second-largest nation. Over the following decade, a bitter controversy erupted regarding the aggressive expansion efforts of the major international

---

1. Prime Minister Nehru, an admirer of Joseph Stalin, intended to develop an economy for India patterned after the Soviet economic system.

accounting firms within India. Before examining that controversy, it will be helpful to review the recent history of the Indian accounting profession.

Birth of a Profession

Shortly after India gained its independence from Great Britain, India's Parliament passed the Companies Act to set up a regulatory infrastructure for the new nation's capital markets. That regulatory structure closely resembled the regulatory framework for Britain's capital markets that was created by the series of Companies Acts adopted by the British Parliament beginning in the mid-nineteenth century. Britain's Companies Acts also served as a blueprint for the federal securities laws enacted by the U.S. Congress in the 1930s. The regulatory agency charged with overseeing India's capital markets is the Securities and Exchange Board of India (SEBI), the equivalent of the Securities and Exchange Commission in the United States. Similar to the comparable federal statutes in Great Britain and the United States, India's Companies Act mandates that publicly owned companies issue periodic financial statements audited by an independent accounting firm.

In 1949, India's Parliament passed the Chartered Accountants Act. This statute created the New Delhi–based Institute of Chartered Accountants of India (ICAI) to oversee the nation's accounting profession. In carrying out its responsibilities, the ICAI works closely with the SEBI. Unlike such professional organizations as the American Institute of Certified Public Accountants (AICPA), the Institute of Chartered Accountants in England and Wales (ICAEW), and the Japanese Institute of Certified Public Accountants (JICPA), the ICAI is a federal agency that has a wide range of statutory authority. The ICAI's regulatory mandate includes, among other responsibilities, issuing accounting standards and ethical rules of conduct for Chartered Accountants (CAs), overseeing India's independent audit function, administering the series of examinations that must be passed to become a CA, and sanctioning CAs and public accounting firms that violate their statutory, ethical, or other professional responsibilities.

Since its inception, the ICAI has embraced Great Britain's financial reporting model that requires public companies to prepare periodic financial statements providing a "true and fair" view of their financial condition and operating results. Although not expressly defined,[2] "truth" and "fairness" in this context are generally determined in reference to the economic environment in which a company is operating, unique conditions or challenges facing the company, and accounting and financial reporting concepts relevant to the company's financial affairs. Most important, the true and fair view demands that the economic substance of transactions prevails over their legal form. The true and fair reporting model is not nearly as "prescriptive" as the "fair presentation" model that underlies the U.S.'s financial reporting system. That is, the British and Indian financial reporting model relies more heavily on general concepts to guide financial reporting and accounting decisions rather than a large number of detailed accounting standards, such as those issued by the Financial Accounting Standards Board in the United States.

Shortly after its creation, the ICAI began issuing *Statements on Accounting Standards* to provide guidance for accounting and financial reporting decisions by Indian companies. Collectively, the ICAI's accounting standards were referred to as "Indian Accounting Standards" or IAS. In late 2007, the ICAI announced that it would "fully converge" IAS with International Financial Reporting Standards (IFRS) by 2011.

---

2. "While the term *true and fair view* originated in U.K. company law, U.K. law does not spell out what the term means" [D. Alexander and S. Archer, *Miller European Accounting Guide*, 2nd ed. (San Diego: Harcourt Brace, 1995), 24–25].

India's Parliament also vested the ICAI with the authority to establish or sanction professional auditing standards. Periodically, the ICAI issues *Statements on Auditing Practices* (SAPs), which are technical pronouncements that accounting firms must comply with when planning and performing independent audits. Although considerably fewer in number than the *Statements on Auditing Standards* issued by the United States' Auditing Standards Board, SAPs address the same general issues. Examples of specific SAPs include *SAP 1, Basic Principles Governing an Audit; SAP 3, Documentation; SAP 4, Fraud and Error*; and *SAP 6, Study and Evaluation of the Accounting System and Related Internal Audit Control in Connection with an Audit*. In addition to SAPs, the ICAI occasionally issues pronouncements to provide technical guidance to CAs and accounting firms on other important auditing topics. Representative of these latter items are the following ICAI publications: *Independence of Auditors, Control on the Quality of Audit Work, Audit Engagement Letters*, and *Audit of Banks*.

Watchdogs vs. Bloodhounds

Despite the apparent similarities between India's independent audit function and that of Great Britain and, to a lesser extent, the United States, independent audits performed within India are widely viewed as being less rigorous than British or U.S. audits. One possible explanation for the less rigorous nature of Indian audits is the legal climate that Indian accounting firms face as compared with their counterparts in Great Britain and the United States.

Consider the following important legal precedent embraced by India's courts that addresses the nature of the independent auditor's role:

> *An auditor is not bound to be a detective or to approach his work with suspicion or with the foregone conclusion that something is wrong. He is a watchdog but not a bloodhound. He is justified in believing tried servants of the company, and is entitled to rely upon their representation, provided he takes reasonable care.*[3]

Because of this legal precedent, India's legal system seldom holds independent auditors responsible in civil cases for failing to detect accounting and financial reporting frauds. No doubt, this legal precedent has influenced the audit policies and procedures of India's accounting firms. In commenting on the overall audit philosophy applied by his firm, the managing partner of one of India's largest accounting firms noted, "Operating under the constraints of time and cost, we presume full honesty from our clients. After all, an audit is not an investigation."[4]

As in the United States, independent auditors in India face criminal prosecution under various federal statutes and sanctions for unethical and otherwise unprofessional conduct by various law enforcement and regulatory authorities. The principal responsibility for punishing Indian auditors has been delegated to the ICAI. However, critics of the ICAI maintain that the federal agency historically has been reluctant to act on that responsibility. "The ICAI has been singularly lax in ensuring high standards of professionalism and conduct among auditors."[5]

In fact, the ICAI is the most common target of critics who claim that India's independent audit function has lagged far behind that of other countries in terms of professionalism, rigor, and overall effectiveness. Much of this criticism has been directed at the ICAI by representatives of the major international accounting firms. In recent years, that criticism prompted a large-scale and highly publicized counterattack

---

3. P. Ravindran, "Auditors and Fraud," *Financial Daily* (online), 11 October 2001.

4. *Flashpoint,* "Financial Chicanery," http://www.capitalmarket.com, 29 January 2002.

5. P. Ravidran, "Auditors and Fraud."

against those firms by parties defending the ICAI, including the ICAI itself. These parties maintained that the major problems facing India's accounting profession were not due to ineffective regulatory oversight by the ICAI but, instead, could be traced to the major international accounting firms.

Barbarians at the Gate

A nationwide financial crisis in 1991 that threatened to bankrupt India prompted the so-called "liberalization movement" by the nation's central government. The principal thrust of the liberalization movement was ending the protectionist economic policies that had been the lynchpin of India's economy for the previous four decades. The opening of India's markets to the rest of the world resulted in record economic growth for the nation over the following decade. During the 1990s, hundreds of multinational companies invested heavily in a wide range of business ventures in India. The central government's abrupt change in its economic policy also resulted in billions of dollars of foreign direct investment (FDI) in India by individual and institutional investors around the world.

India's rapid economic growth during the 1990s triggered a significant increase in the demand for accounting, auditing, and other professional services offered by the major international accounting firms. The sudden increase in the demand for their services and the announced intention of India's central government to end its protectionist economic policies caused the Big Four accounting firms to begin vigorously pursuing expansion opportunities within India during the early 1990s.[6]

The enthusiasm of the Big Four accounting firms for the Indian market was soon blunted when they realized that the ICAI, unlike most other Indian regulatory agencies, had no intention of eliminating its protectionist policies. Over the previous four decades, the ICAI had erected numerous barriers to discourage foreign accounting firms from operating in India. The most problematic of these barriers was a regulation that prohibited foreign accounting firms from establishing branch offices in India. Two of the Big Eight firms—Deloitte, Haskins & Sells, and Price Waterhouse—had established independent branch offices in India before this regulation went into effect. But those firms were limited to operating one practice office each with a maximum of 20 partners—a restriction imposed on domestic accounting firms as well. In addition, the two firms were not allowed to rename their Indian practice offices when each merged with another international accounting firm, which meant that those offices were required to operate under an out-of-date name for each firm.

Representatives of the Big Four firms reacted angrily to the ICAI's insistence on maintaining its protectionist policies even as most Indian markets were being opened to foreign competitors. In commenting on the regulation that prevented Big Four firms from establishing new practice offices in India, one Big Four spokesperson observed that the restriction was "part of a web of ... protectionist restrictions that stifle foreign entrants and shield the indigenous audit profession from genuine competition."[7] An angry KPMG partner maintained that the ICAI was "outmoded" and suggested that its regulatory responsibilities should be assigned to other federal agencies.[8]

In the late 1990s and into the new century, the domestic business press in India also became critical of the ICAI, but for different reasons. An Indian business periodical

---

6. In fact, during the 1990s, each of the Big Five accounting firms, including Andersen & Co., pursued expansion opportunities within India. However, since Andersen effectively went out of business in 2002, "Big Four" will be used in this case when referring to the dominant international accounting firms.

7. B. Jopson and A. Yee, "Accountancy's Tangled Web," *Financial Times*, 26 July 2006, 6.

8. *Ibid.*

maintained that the rising number of accounting frauds within the country was a direct consequence of the ICAI's lax regulatory attitude.[9] The business press also criticized the ICAI for allegedly being a "captive" of the profession that it regulated since the organization's governing council consisted of CAs from domestic accounting firms. One Indian journalist suggested that the ICAI should be eliminated and replaced by a regulatory agency similar to the United States' Public Company Accounting Oversight Board (PCAOB), which is controlled by a majority of nonaccountants.[10]

Mounting criticism of the ICAI greatly irritated, if not embarrassed, the members of the organization's governing council. Eventually, that criticism goaded the ICAI and its supporters to counterattack the agency's critics, principal among them the large international accounting firms. The ICAI and its supporters acknowledged that India's accounting profession was facing major challenges but contended that those problems were a direct consequence of the aggressive practice development activities of the international accounting firms within India. Despite those firms' harsh criticism of the ICAI's protectionist policies, the ICAI maintained that each of those firms, in fact, had established large-scale operations in India during the 1990s.

According to the ICAI, the so-called "MAFs" (multinational accounting firms) had used various subtle and, in some cases, covert methods to circumvent the laws and regulations intended to prevent those firms from wresting control of India's market for accounting, auditing, and related professional services from domestic accounting firms. As a direct result of those illicit methods, the MAFs had supposedly taken control of that market and, at the same time, undermined the credibility and integrity of India's accounting profession.

In 2002, the ICAI commissioned the Chartered Accountants' Action Committee for Level Playing Field (CAAC) to investigate the impact that the MAFs were having on India's accounting profession. Several months later, the CAAC issued its findings in a 141-page report entitled "White Paper on Multinational Accounting Firms Operating in India" ("White Paper"). The prologue to that report indicated that its principal purpose was to "inform the Indian business [community], Indian finance sector, Indian Government, Indian policy makers, Indian professionals, and also the general public about the correct facts about the Multinational Accounting Firms (MAFs) and about the state of the Indian accounting profession."[11,12] The prologue went on to note that it would demonstrate that the MAFs' presence in India was "illegitimate" and document that the MAFs had "illegally and surreptitiously taken over the attestation and audit functions of the [accounting] profession in India."[13]

The large international accounting firms have frequently found themselves the target of harsh criticism in recent years, primarily as a result of their link to such financial scandals as Enron and WorldCom in the United States, Kanebo Limited in Japan, Parmalat in Italy, Royal Ahold in the Netherlands, and HIH in Australia. However, easily the harshest criticism of those firms can be found in the White Paper report issued by the CAAC.

9. T. Ramanujam, "Checking the Explosion of Corporate Fraud," *Business Line*, 14 September 2002, 1.

10. S. Vikraman, "Time to Regulate the Auditing Profession?" *Business Line*, 11 March 2002, 1.

11. The "multinational accounting firms" specifically identified by the CAAC included Andersen & Co., Deloitte Touche Tohmatsu, Ernst & Young, KPMG, and PricewaterhouseCoopers.

12. The Group on White Paper on Multinational Accounting Firms, "White Paper on Multinational Accounting Firms Operating in India," The Chartered Accountants' Action Committee for Level Playing Field (New Delhi, 2003).

13. *Ibid.*, 3.

Dirty Business

Indian critics of the Big Four accounting firms maintained that the ultimate objective of those firms within India during the 1990s was to establish significant accounting and auditing practices that could then be used as a launching pad to market a wide range of consulting services. Intensive marketing of such services had paid off handsomely for those accounting firms over the previous decade in the United States and Western Europe. By the early 1990s, the Big Four firms had developed large consulting divisions that provided a wide range of services, including systems design and implementation projects, cost containment studies, and internal audit outsourcing. Each of those firms' thousands of audit clients was the principal target market for such services.

Intense competition in the audit market over the previous several decades had resulted in paper-thin profit margins for audit services. Since the profit margins on consulting services were generally several times larger than those for audit services,[14] the Big Four firms easily compensated for the declining profitability of their audit practices by selling lucrative consulting services to their audit clients and other parties.

The major roadblock that the Big Four firms faced in gaining broader access to the professional services markets in India during the 1990s was the ICAI's ban on those firms establishing their own branch offices in India. To overcome this problem, these firms began utilizing a two-pronged strategy to "invade" the India professional services market. First, those firms began using on a much larger scale a strategy that some of them had used to enter India in the first place, namely, aligning themselves with "surrogate" domestic accounting firms. Because ICAI regulations limited an accounting firm to a maximum of 20 partners and limited the number of independent audits that could be supervised by any one audit partner, the Big Four accounting firms found it necessary to establish alliances with multiple Indian accounting firms. "Each of the Big Four firms has created a messy agglomeration of Indian businesses [accounting firms] that are legally separate but in practice work together."[15]

The second tactic the Big Four firms used to establish themselves in India during the 1990s was to obtain a license to operate a business consulting firm within India. Such a license was readily available from the Reserve Bank of India (RBI), the Indian federal agency that issues those licenses. After obtaining this license, each of the Big Four firms could establish multiple practice offices within India under their global practice name. These consulting practice offices then worked closely with the domestic accounting firms that were the Big Four's surrogates in the accounting and auditing services market.

Because the Big Four firms had considerably more economic resources than their surrogate firms, they reportedly dominated, if not controlled, the operations of those firms. As a result, the surrogate firms allegedly became "storefronts" through which the Big Four firms provided accounting and auditing services within India. In its White Paper report, the CAAC suggested that many Indian accounting firms aligned themselves with MAFs during the 1990s because they believed that doing so was an economic necessity if they were to survive.

> *The traditional Indian [accounting] firms which had large audit and other professional presence felt too insecure about their capacity to retain their position and therefore many of them began thinking in terms of becoming [MAF] affiliates or surrogates to retain the very work they were handling and to access new work through the MAFs.*[16]

---

14. N. Lakshman, "Accounting Firms: Time to Redo the Numbers," *rediff.com*, 21 September 2002.

15. Jopson and Yee, "Accountancy's Tangled Web."

16. The Group on White Paper, "White Paper," 34.

A major theme of the CAAC's White Paper report was that the MAFs use of surrogate firms to "colonize" the Indian market for accounting and auditing services was, in fact, illegal since that practice allowed those firms to provide accounting, auditing, and related professional services without being subject to the ICAI's regulatory oversight. "Because the MAFs are outside the scope of the discipline of the ICAI and for that matter any discipline, no such action [regulatory oversight] is possible."[17]

One of the most important ICAI regulations that the MAFs were able to sidestep was that agency's complete ban on advertising by accounting firms. Even though the MAFs were practicing in India under their "audit" names, they were not considered accounting or auditing firms within India. So, they could advertise and use, at will, the other marketing methods that Indian accounting firms were prohibited from using. Allegedly, the MAFs used large-scale advertising and marketing campaigns not only to lure consulting clients but also to attract audit and accounting services clients for their surrogate firms. The CAAC charged that the MAFs used a wide range of unprofessional and "dishonourable" marketing methods to sell those services and that those methods had greatly diminished the integrity and credibility of India's respected accounting profession.

> While acting and operating through their surrogates in traditional areas where Indian CAs are subject to the discipline of the ICAI . . . the MAFs began and continue to merrily advertise and brand-build their own names, and take advantage of their brand value built in defiance of the Indian CA regulations established by law. . . . This snide and devious exercise extends from holding cricket matches—to high-cost advertisements—to even higher-cost events like instituting and giving Business Leadership and Entrepreneur Awards to squeeze themselves into the high-yielding corporate and financial market for professional work.[18]

The marketing strategies and tactics used by the MAFs were reportedly so effective that those firms quickly persuaded most large Indian corporations and even government agencies that their services were superior to those offered by domestic accounting and consulting firms. As a result, in a little more than one decade, the MAFs captured the "high-end" market for business consulting services within India and, through their surrogate firms, became the *de facto* auditors for a large number of major Indian companies. According to the CAAC, the MAFs conquest of the accounting, auditing, and consulting services market within India "condemned" the country's domestic firms "to play a secondary role in their country, occupying just about the same position which Indian citizens occupied during the British rule in India."[19]

According to the CAAC, the MAFs were anything but the "skilled" and "virtuous" professional services firms that they portrayed themselves to be in their elaborate marketing campaigns. Instead, the CAAC reported that over the previous few decades, the MAFs had engaged in a wide range of predatory and "dirty" business practices. Following are examples of such practices that the CAAC identified in its White Paper report, examples supported with dozens of references to specific litigation cases, news reports, and other anecdotal evidence.[20]

> "The MAFs have become skilled lobbyists and have become the tools in the hands of business to bribe the state and regulators."

> "They have become experts in money laundering."

---

17. *Ibid.*, 35.
18. *Ibid.*, 34.
19. *Ibid.*, 37.
20. *Ibid.*, 54–56.

"The MAFs have been repeatedly caught in frauds and malpractices which have forced them to seek compromises at billions of dollars of cost."

"Driven by their lust for money by any means, MAFs are now turning into experts in shredding evidence and in suppressing facts and evidence, to escape the consequences of their fraudulent actions."

"The MAFs are guilty of thousands of violations of audit independence and ethical requirements."

"The MAFs are experts in advising tax evasion and tax fraud to their clients on a global level, causing losses to governments in the billions of dollars."

The CAAC concluded its lengthy diatribe against the MAFs by declaring that the accounting profession in India was under a state of siege and that it was in the national interest that the profession be reclaimed by the nation's chartered accountants. "Finally, this is war. This cannot be won without high national spirit and without perceiving the confluence of national interest with the collective interest of the CA profession."[21] The CAAC hoped that it would be at the forefront of the effort to accomplish that goal. "This is the agenda of the CAAC. This is its goal. 'India First' is its mantra."[22]

The CAAC prepared an impressive list of action items to be considered by the ICAI and other relevant Indian regulatory authorities. Among these recommendations, two were particularly sweeping in nature. One proposal called for the ICAI to prohibit any additional multinational accounting firms from establishing practice units in India, either through an alliance with an existing Indian accounting firm or as an independent business consulting firm. For those MAFs already operating within India as consulting firms, the CAAC recommended that those firms' business licenses be revoked.

Refutation & Denial

As could be expected, the CAAC's White Paper report prompted quick responses from representatives of the Big Four accounting firms. An Ernst & Young spokesperson defended his firm's alliances with India-based accounting firms by noting that "there is no bar on establishing an alliance with a foreign firm."[23] A few months later, the managing partner of Ernst & Young's India practice unit responded curtly to a journalist when asked why his firm should not be subject to the ICAI's regulatory oversight. "We don't even fall within the jurisdiction of the ICAI, since we are just another consulting firm like Boston Consulting Group, A. T. Kearney, or McKinsey & Co. So, why us?"[24] In responding to the allegation that the Big Four controlled their surrogate firms, a PwC representative noted, "The Indian firms that are members of the PwC network are home-grown organizations wholly owned in India, and have built a brand name for more than 100 years."[25] In responding to a similar question, a KPMG spokesperson simply observed, "KPMG has been following domestic [Indian] laws."[26]

The Big Four firms also insisted that they were not providing accounting and auditing services within India. However, the CAAC's White Paper report had documented that the websites of the MAFs "proudly proclaim that they do accounting, audit, and

---

21. *Ibid.*, 139.

22. *Ibid.*, 141.

23. *Business India* (online), "This Ain't GATS," August 4, 2003.

24. *Business Today*, "Four Under Peril," *indiatodaygroup.com,* 23 November 2003.

25. *Business India* (online), "This Ain't GATS."

26. *Ibid.*

assurance services through their Indian associates."[27] When questioned regarding the independent audits performed by one of Ernst & Young's Indian affiliates, an Ernst & Young partner reported that the affiliate was "100 percent Indian-owned and Indian-managed" and "does all the audit work" on its audit engagements.[28]

Parties other than the Big Four firms were angered and concerned by the CAAC White Paper report. In the United States, the National Association of State Boards of Accountancy (NASBA) collectively regulates the practice of accountancy. The NASBA reported that if the ICAI took action against the Big Four accounting firms, it might take measures to "retaliate" against Indian accounting firms.[29] Representatives of important international accounting organizations also voiced their opinion on the controversy generated by the CAAC report. For example, the president of the International Federation of Accountants (IFAC) encouraged the ICAI to "refrain from embracing protectionist policies in the accountancy and auditing sector."[30]

Finally, not all Indian CAs and accounting firms joined with the CAAC in condemning the Big Four accounting firms. In particular, several executive partners of Big Four–affiliated firms came to the defense of their practice partners. A partner of an Indian accounting firm aligned with PricewaterhouseCoopers (PwC) reported that the staff members of his firm benefited greatly from working alongside PwC professionals and from being allowed to participate in PwC training programs.[31]

EPILOGUE

The highly publicized release of the CAAC's White Paper report in July 2003 and the ensuing criticism of that report by a wide range of parties placed tremendous pressure on the ICAI. Both supporters and critics of the report expected the ICAI to respond quickly and decisively to the report's key findings and recommendations. But that did not happen.

At the time the White Paper report was released, the ICAI was mired in two controversies. First, the Indian business press had reported that the wife of the ICAI president was a part-owner of a private business that provided "coaching" courses for the series of examinations that had to be successfully completed to earn the CA designation within India. The press questioned whether the CA candidates enrolled in that business's coaching courses received an unfair advantage over other candidates. To quell that controversy, the ICAI purchased newspaper advertisements insisting that the integrity of the CA examination process was not being compromised.

The second controversy facing the ICAI in the summer of 2003 involved what had become known as "India's Enron." India's largest business conglomerate is the Tata Group, which consists of approximately two dozen public companies and 80 privately owned businesses. Collectively, the Tata companies account for nearly 3 percent of India's gross domestic product and employ several hundred thousand Indian citizens. India's largest accounting firm, A. F. Ferguson & Co. (AFF), audits several of the largest Tata companies.

In 2001, the Tata Group hired AFF to complete an investigation of an alleged accounting and financial reporting fraud within Tata Finance

27. The Group on White Paper, "White Paper," 126.

28. *Business India* (online), "This Ain't GATS."

29. *Ibid.*

30. K. R. Srivats, "India Must Avoid Protectionism in Accountancy," *Business Line*, 16 March 2004, 1.

31. *Business India* (online), "This Ain't GATS."

Limited, a Tata company that was not audited by AFF. In 2002, AFF released a 900-page report documenting the results of its investigation of the Tata Finance fraud. That report shocked the Tata Group, the Indian business press, and the general public by implicating several of Tata's top executives, including the chairman of the Tata Group, Ratan Tata, in the fraud. Ratan Tata purchased full-page advertisements in major Indian newspapers insisting that the report was inaccurate. AFF eventually withdrew the report and dismissed the three partners responsible for writing it. One of those partners was Y. M. Kale, who was among the most prominent members of the Indian accounting profession. Kale served on the International Accounting Standards Board, was a former president of the ICAI, and reportedly was in line to become AFF's next managing partner.

The business press, leaders of the accounting profession, and various other parties demanded that the ICAI investigate the Tata scandal and the role of AFF within that scandal. After a brief investigation, the ICAI failed to file charges against anyone involved in the matter, which renewed allegations that the ICAI was a lax and ineffective watchdog agency for India's accounting profession.[32]

Finally, in late 2004, the ICAI responded to the CAAC White Paper report. The ICAI identified several proposals to strengthen the competitive position of Indian accounting firms that were not affiliated with MAFs. Among these proposals was a recommendation encouraging such firms to create cooperative networks that would allow them to pool their manpower, technological, and financial resources. The ICAI also announced that it planned to increase from 20 to 50 the maximum number of partners that accounting firms could have and that it would allow accounting firms to establish consulting divisions. Over the past decade, the so-called surrogate firms had established de facto consulting divisions as a result of their affiliations with MAFs. The ICAI's new policy meant that "nonaffiliated" firms would have an opportunity to participate in the booming business consulting market within India.

A major problem that nonaffiliated firms had faced during the 1990s was attracting qualified professionals. India's surging economy had resulted in a large increase in the demand for accounting and accounting-related services; however, there had not been a parallel increase in the number of CAs within India. In 2004, there were only 120,000 CAs in India, meaning that on a per capita basis India had considerably fewer professional accountants than any other major country, with the exception of Japan. Making matters worse for nonaffiliated firms was a large increase in the hiring of CAs by surrogate firms during the 1990s. Because the surrogate firms offered considerably higher salaries than other Indian firms, the nonaffiliated firms found it increasingly difficult to hire sufficient CAs to staff their professional engagements. To mitigate this problem, the ICAI shortened the minimum time required to obtain a CA license from nearly five and one-half years to approximately four years.

Supporters of the CAAC's more radical proposals were disappointed by the ICAI's decision not to pursue the imposition of sanctions or other operating constraints on the MAFs or their surrogate firms. The ICAI did report that it would ask other Indian regulatory agencies to review MAFs' operations in India to ensure that those firms were not violating the terms of their business licenses or other relevant federal rules or regulations. In responding to the allegation that MAFs were indirectly providing audit and attestation services in India, the ICAI reported it had found no direct evidence supporting that allegation but would continue to investigate that possibility.

The most important policy initiative the ICAI pursued as a result of the CAAC White Paper report was seeking reciprocity agreements with regulatory agencies overseeing the accounting professions of other countries. The ICAI's president noted that, "while global [accounting] firms may be keen on becoming Indian, we at the ICAI are keen on making Indian firms global."[33] Reciprocity agreements with foreign countries that are signed by the ICAI would allow Indian CAs to be recognized as qualified

---

32. For a more complete discussion of the Tata Finance scandal, see Case 8.9, "Tata Finance Limited."

33. D. Murali, "ICAI Is Not Averse to Opening Up of the Accounting Sector," *Business Line* (online), 14 September 2006.

professional accountants in those countries. For example, a reciprocity agreement with the United States would permit Indian CAs to practice public accounting in the United States—and U.S. CPAs to practice in India.

The ICAI's pursuit of reciprocity agreements was generally met with a lukewarm response by the relevant regulatory agencies of major developed countries. For decades, India had such a reciprocity agreement with Great Britain. However, Great Britain unilaterally canceled that agreement in the early 1990s, a decision that surprised and offended the ICAI. The United States has a reciprocity agreement that allows professionally registered accountants in certain countries to practice in the United States after successfully passing the IQEX—International Uniform CPA Qualification—examination administered by the NASBA. However, presently, the NASBA only allows certain professionally registered accountants from Australia, Canada, Ireland, and Mexico to sit for the IQEX examination.

A major reason that the ICAI decided to pursue reciprocity agreements with other nations was the large outsourcing industry for accounting services that quickly developed within India following the turn of the century. Thanks to the Internet, thousands of small Indian accounting firms found a new market for their services in other countries, in particular the United States. By 2004, an estimated 200,000 individual tax returns for U.S. citizens were being prepared by Indian accounting firms, a number that was expected to grow dramatically in the following years.[34] Indian accounting firms were also providing a large amount of rudimentary accounting services such as "write-up" work or

bookkeeping for small U.S. businesses. U.S. accounting firms were outsourcing such work to India because Indian firms could perform that work much more cheaply. To make Indian accountants "globally competitive" and, in particular, better prepared to address accounting issues faced by their U.S. "clients," the ICAI added the study of U.S. generally accepted accounting principles (GAAP) to the required curriculum for the CA licensing program in 2006.[35]

Ironically, the sudden growth in the outsourcing of accounting and taxation services to India caused the AICPA to consider taking steps to protect the U.S. market for such services from Indian accounting firms. The AICPA was also troubled by the fact that U.S.-based accounting firms could not always ensure that outsourced services were being performed in compliance with the standards of the U.S. accounting profession. Many parties within the U.S. profession insisted that, at a minimum, U.S. accounting firms had an ethical responsibility to notify their clients when they were outsourcing the services for those clients to accounting firms in foreign countries. An article in *The CPA Journal* succinctly summarized this controversy.

Clearly, firms that outsource the preparation of income tax returns are likely to achieve significant cost savings. But at what cost? The profession does not need more scandals, and one must wonder why many CPA firms have an unspoken rule that the client does not need to know about outsourcing. Deep down, we know taxpayers entrusting their return with a CPA are likely to respond negatively if their tax returns are prepared in India without their knowledge or consent.[36]

Questions

1. Research online and hardcopy databases to identify important recent developments within the Indian accounting profession. Summarize these developments in a bullet format.

34. K. Vandruff, "Accounting for India," *Wichita Business Journal* (online), 23 June 2006.

35. *International Accounting Bulletin* (online), "The Price of Audit on Rise in India Again after Two Years," 12 August 2006.

36. R. Brody, M. Miller, and M. Rolleri, "Outsourcing Income Tax Returns to India: Legal, Ethical, and Professional Issues," *The CPA Journal* (online), December 2004.

2. In the United States, the accounting profession is regulated at the state level, while in India the accounting profession is regulated by a federal agency. Identify and briefly discuss the comparative advantages and disadvantages of each regulatory structure.

3. In India, independent auditors are considered to be "watchdogs" but not "bloodhounds." How, if at all, does that concept of the auditor's role differ from the prevailing concept of the independent auditor's role in the United States? Explain.

4. Do you believe it was appropriate for the major international accounting firms to establish networks of "surrogate" firms in India for the purpose of gaining wider access to the professional services market in that country? Was that decision "ethical"? Defend your answers.

5. State boards of accountancy in the United States have allowed accounting firms and individual CPAs to advertise for approximately three decades. Identify the pros and cons of allowing professionals to advertise. In your opinion, should professional accountants be allowed to advertise and otherwise market their services?

6. In a bullet format, identify the parties impacted by regulatory policies designed to protect domestic professionals from foreign competitors. Briefly explain how each of these parties is affected by such policies. In your opinion, are such policies justified or appropriate? If so, under what circumstances?

7. What are the principal issues that organizations such as the ICAI and NASBA should consider in deciding whether or not to establish reciprocity agreements with other countries?

8. When CPAs outsource professional services to accountants in other countries do they have an ethical responsibility to disclose this fact to their clients? Does your answer change depending on the type of professional service being outsourced?

INDEX

SUMMARY OF TOPICS BY CASE

The following index lists the auditing-related topics addressed directly or indirectly in each case included in Contemporary Auditing: Real Issues and Cases, Seventh Edition. Those topics followed by the letter "Q" are the subject of a case question.

Enron Corporation, Case 1.1, 3–22

1. "Scope of services" issue facing audit firms (Q)
2. Involvement of auditors in client accounting and financial reporting decisions (Q)
3. Preparation and retention of audit workpapers (Q)
4. Recent "crisis of confidence" facing the public accounting profession (Q)
5. Recent recommendations to strengthen the independent audit function (Q)
6. Evolution of concept of "professionalism" in public accounting discipline over past several decades (Q)
7. Auditors' responsibilities regarding a client's quarterly financial statements (Q)
8. History of public accounting profession in the United States
9. Roles and responsibilities of key regulatory and rule-making bodies in the public accounting profession
10. Corporate culture as a key determinant of an audit client's control environment
11. Criminal liability faced by auditors and audit firms

Just for Feet, Inc., Case 1.2, 23–36

1. Use of analytical procedures to identify high-risk financial statement items (Q)
2. Identifying internal control risk factors (Q)
3. Determining impact of control risk factors on audit planning decisions (Q)
4. Identifying inherent risk factors (Q)
5. Determining impact of inherent risk factors on audit planning decisions (Q)
6. Identifying the most critical audit risk factors for a given audit engagement (Q)
7. Resolution of ethical dilemma faced by a corporate executive (Q)
8. Importance of considering economic health of client's industry in audit planning decisions
9. Nature, purpose, and importance of accounts receivable confirmation procedures
10. Role of the SEC in policing financial reporting process and independent audit function
11. Importance of investigating unusual and/or suspicious client transactions

Jamaica Water Properties, Case 1.3, 37–44

1. Responsibility of corporate executives to investigate potential misrepresentations in their company's accounting records (Q)
2. Measures needed to encourage "whistleblowing" by corporate employees (Q)
3. Encouraging and rewarding ethical behavior by corporate executives and employees (Q)
4. Problems posed by close relationships between client personnel and independent auditors (Q)
5. Contractual arrangements between auditors and clients (Q)
6. Accounting firms' litigation resolution strategies (Q)
7. Need for auditors to thoroughly investigate suspicious items uncovered during an audit

Health Management, Inc., Case 1.4, 45–61

1. Problems posed by close relationships between client personnel and independent auditors (Q)
2. Audit-related implications of a job offer made by a client to one of its independent auditors during the course of an audit (Q)
3. Performance of inventory roll back and roll forward procedures (Q)
4. Weighing the cost of an audit procedure against the quantity and quality of audit evidence it yields (Q)
5. Documenting audit test results in audit workpapers (Q)
6. Identifying "red flag" fraud risk factors and determining their impact on each phase of an audit (Q)
7. Auditors' responsibilities for discovering and reporting illegal acts by clients (Q)
8. Historical overview of class-action lawsuits and their impact on public accounting firms
9. Impact of PSLRA of 1995 on auditors' legal exposure under the Securities Exchange Act of 1934
10. Proportionate vs. joint and several liability for auditors
11. Resolution of proposed audit adjustments
12. Nature of GAAS and the responsibilities they impose on independent auditors
13. Definition of "recklessness" and its implications for auditors' legal exposure under the Securities Exchange Act of 1934

The Leslie Fay Companies, Case 1.5, 63–73

1. Use of analytical procedures to identify high-risk financial statement items (Q)
2. Financial information needed for audit planning decisions (Q)
3. Non-financial information needed for audit planning decisions (Q)
4. Control environment issues pertinent to independent audits (Q)
5. Impact on auditor independence of litigation that names client and audit firm as co-defendants (Q)
6. Audit implications of important changes and developing trends in a client's industry
7. Identifying "red flag" fraud risk factors and determining their impact on each phase of an audit

Star Technologies, Inc., Case 1.6, 75–84

1. Importance of industry knowledge for auditors (Q)
2. Identification of high-risk financial statement items (Q)
3. Impact on audit planning decisions of a client's cash-flow data (Q)
4. Identifying violations of financial statement assertions (Q)
5. Financial statement classification and disclosure issues for liabilities (Q)
6. Nature and purpose of audit review process (Q)
7. Resolution of disagreements between members of an audit engagement team (Q)
8. Wrap-up phase of an audit engagement
9. Withdrawal of an audit opinion
10. Career advancement issues facing auditors

Lincoln Savings and Loan Association, Case 1.7, 85–97

1. Substance over form concept in accounting and its audit implications (Q)
2. Threats to auditor independence (Q)
3. Audit implications of related party transactions (Q)
4. Assessment of a client's control environment (Q)
5. Determination of when gains resulting from the disposition of assets can be recognized (Q)
6. Identification of critical management assertions (Q)
7. Audit evidence needed to support management assertions (Q)
8. Identifying appropriate audit procedures to collect desired types of audit evidence (Q)
9. Audit implications of close auditor-client personnel relationships (Q)
10. Collegial responsibilities of auditors (Q)
11. Auditors' responsibility for detection of fraud (Q)
12. Societal role of independent auditor
13. SEC's oversight role for the independent audit function

Crazy Eddie, Inc., Case 1.8, 99–107

1. Use of financial ratios and other financial measures to identify high-risk financial statement items (Q)
2. Audit procedures used to detect fraudulent misstatements of inventory, accounts payable, and sales (Q)
3. Effect of important changes in a client's industry on audit planning decisions (Q)
4. Potential impact of "lowballing" on the quality of audit services (Q)
5. Objective of year-end inventory cutoff tests (Q)
6. Implications for the independent audit function of audit clients hiring former auditors (Q)
7. Impact of collusion among client executives and employees on auditors' ability to detect fraudulent misrepresentations in a client's accounting records
8. Importance of assessing the integrity of client management
9. Incentive for companies to retain large audit firms when going public

ZZZZ Best Company, Case 1.9, 109–122

1. Key differences between audits and review engagements (Q)
2. Identification of critical management assertions (Q)
3. Audit evidence needed to support management assertions (Q)
4. Identifying appropriate audit procedures to collect desired types of audit evidence (Q)
5. Limitations of audit evidence (Q)
6. Predecessor-successor auditor communications (Q)
7. Auditors' responsibility for a client's earnings press release (Q)
8. Client-imposed restrictions on the scope of an audit (Q)
9. Content of an audit engagement letter
10. Overview of SEC's 8-K auditor change disclosure rules

United States Surgical Corporation, Case 1.10, 123–133

1. Audit procedures applied to asset retirements (Q)
2. Accounting for changes in estimates and the related disclosure requirements (Q)
3. Effect of changes in estimates and improper accounting changes on an audit opinion (Q)
4. Use of analytical procedures to identify high-risk financial statement items (Q)
5. Imbalance of power in the auditor-client relationship and its impact on audits (Q)
6. Key characteristics of audit evidence (Q)
7. Evaluation of conflicting audit evidence (Q)
8. Auditors' responsibility for detection of illegal acts (Q)
9. Client confidentiality when auditing two clients that transact business with each other (Q)
10. Criteria for determining when a sale is consummated
11. Effect of a management bonus plan on the inherent risk posed by an audit client
12. Chronology of an auditor-client conflict

New Century Financial Corporation, Case 1.11, 135-151

1. Concentration of audit clients in specific industries (Q)
2. Quality control considerations for independent audits (Q)
3. Section 404 of the Sarbanes-Oxley Act (Q)
4. Auditors' responsibility to discover and report significant deficiencies and material weaknesses in internal controls (Q)
5. Auditing accounting estimates (Q)
6. Violations of generally accepted auditing standards (Q)
7. Mark-to-market rule for securities investments (Q)
8. Auditor independence
9. Impact of auditor-client conflicts on audit engagements
10. Audit implications of accounting changes
11. Auditor reviews of quarterly financial statements

Jack Greenberg, Inc., Case 2.1, 155–162

1. Audit risk factors commonly posed by family-owned businesses (Q)
2. Key audit objectives for inventory (Q)
3. Quality of audit evidence yielded by internal versus external documents (Q)
4. Nature and purpose of a walk-through audit procedure (Q)
5. Auditors' responsibility to inform client management of significant internal control weaknesses (Q)
6. Whether or not auditors have a responsibility to insist that client management correct significant internal control deficiencies (Q)
7. Segregation of duties concept and its impact on a client's internal controls
8. Need for auditors to thoroughly investigate suspicious transactions and circumstances

Golden Bear Golf, Inc., Case 2.2, 163–169

1. Identifying relevant management assertions for individual financial statement items (Q)
2. Choosing appropriate audit procedures to corroborate specific management assertions (Q)
3. Meaning of the phrase "audit failure" (Q)
4. Auditors' responsibilities on "high-risk" audit engagements (Q)
5. Nature and purpose of AICPA industry accounting and audit guides (Q)
6. Changes in accounting estimates versus changes in accounting principles (Q)
7. Proper application of the percentage-of-completion accounting method
8. Need for auditors to thoroughly investigate suspicious transactions and circumstances
9. Limitations of management representations as audit evidence

Happiness Express, Inc., Case 2.3, 171–178

1. Audit objectives associated with receivables confirmation procedures and year-end sales cutoff tests (Q)
2. Selection of receivables for confirmation purposes (Q)
3. Alternative audit procedures for receivables selected for confirmation (Q)
4. Distinguishing between, and among, auditor negligence, recklessness, and fraud (Q)
5. Auditor responsibility to investigate the possibility of illegal acts perpetrated by client executives (Q)
6. Need for auditors to identify and consider impact of industry risk factors on a client's financial health
7. Need for auditors to document key changes in clients' business practices
8. Need for auditors to thoroughly investigate large and unusual year-end transactions

CapitalBanc Corporation, Case 2.4, 179–181

1. Key management assertions related to cash (Q)
2. Audit procedures applied to cash maintained on a client's premises (Q)
3. Supervision of staff accountants assigned to an audit engagement
4. Internal auditor involvement in independent audits
5. Need to follow up on suspicious client transactions and implausible client representations

SmarTalk Teleservices, Inc., Case 2.5, 183–186

1. Audit objectives related to a restructuring reserve (Q)
2. Appropriate evidence to collect when auditing a restructuring reserve (Q)
3. Determining what pronouncements and other items are included in generally accepted accounting principles (Q)
4. Auditors' responsibility to preserve integrity of audit workpapers (Q)
5. Audit implications of earnings management by client executives

CBI Holding Company, Inc., Case 2.6, 187–192

1. Key audit objectives for accounts payable (Q)
2. Proper application of the search for unrecorded liabilities and reconciliation of year-end payables balances to vendor statements (Q)
3. Differences and similarities in accounts payable and accounts receivable confirmation procedures (Q)
4. Responsibility of auditors when they identify mistakes or other oversights they made in prior year audits (Q)
5. Client requests to remove specific auditors from audit engagement team (Q)
6. Considerations relevant to the acceptance of "high-risk" audit clients
7. Need to identify critical audit risk factors and consider those factors in planning an audit engagement
8. Need to thoroughly investigate suspicious transactions and circumstances identified during an audit

Campbell Soup Company, Case 2.7, 193–199

1. Methods that corporate executives can use to "manage" earnings (Q)
2. Ethical issues posed by earnings management by corporate executives (Q)
3. Audit implications of earnings management by client executives (Q)
4. Proper classification of key items in financial statements (Q)
5. Audit procedures appropriate to uncover potential violations of the revenue recognition rule (Q)
6. Distinguishing between auditor negligence and auditor recklessness (Q)
7. Impact of the Private Securities Litigation Reform Act on auditor-related litigation (Q)
8. Need for auditors to consider recent developments in a client's industry when planning an audit

Rocky Mount Undergarment Company, Inc., Case 2.8, 201–203

1. Assessing the materiality of financial statement errors (Q)
2. Audit procedures that may detect inventory overstatements (Q)
3. Factors affecting quality of audit evidence (Q)
4. Ethical responsibilities of accountants when being pressured to misrepresent their employer's financial data (Q)

The Trolley Dodgers, Case 3.1, 207–208

1. Tests of controls and substantive tests for the payroll transaction cycle (Q)
2. Identifying internal control weaknesses in a payroll transaction cycle (Q)
3. Audit procedures useful in detecting payroll fraud (Q)
4. Control environment issues

Howard Street Jewelers, Case 3.2, 209–211

1. Importance of internal controls for small retail businesses (Q)
2. Responsibility of a small business's CPA when alerted to potential control problems facing the client (Q)
3. Measures CPAs can take to acquire clients (Q)
4. Control environment issues

Saks Fifth Avenue, Case 3.3, 213–216

1. Cost-effectiveness issues for internal controls (Q)
2. Scope of internal controls (Q)
3. Control objectives and related control activities in a retail environment (Q)
4. Audit implications of client control policies and procedures (Q)

Triton Energy Ltd., Case 3.4, 217–225

1. Factors that complicate audits of multinational companies (Q)
2. Control activities intended to prevent violations of the Foreign Corrupt Practices Act (Q)
3. Effectiveness of control activities (Q)
4. Auditors' responsibilities to detect client violations of the Foreign Corrupt Practices Act (Q)
5. Impact on audit risk components of a client's high-risk business strategies (Q)
6. Accountants' responsibilities when they discover illegal acts perpetrated by their employer (Q)
7. Auditors' responsibilities when they discover illegal acts perpetrated by a client (Q)
8. Cultural differences in business practices and ethical issues posed by such differences for auditors and accountants (Q)
9. Regulatory policies and procedures of the Securities and Exchange Commission (Q)

Goodner Brothers, Inc., Case 3.5, 227–234

1. Identifying internal control objectives for a wholesale business (Q)
2. Identifying and remedying internal control weaknesses (Q)
3. Importance of an effective control environment for a business (Q)
4. Impact of management style and operating policies on an entity's internal controls
5. Role of internal auditors in an entity's internal control process
6. Need for auditors and client management to investigate suspicious transactions

Troberg Stores, Case 3.6, 235–241

1. Scope of an entity's internal control process (Q)
2. Identifying control objectives and control activities for a retail business (Q)
3. Need to segregate key functional responsibilities within a small business (Q)
4. Compensating controls for a small business (Q)
5. Ethical responsibilities of management when subordinates are suspected of engaging in theft or other illicit activities (Q)
6. Impact of laws and other regulations on a business's internal control process (Q)
7. Control environment issues

Creve Couer Pizza, Inc., Case 4.1, 245–247

1. CPAs serving as the moral conscience of small business clients (Q)
2. Conflict between auditors' responsibility to the public interest and the obligations imposed on them by the client confidentiality rule (Q)
3. Resolution of ethical dilemmas by auditors (Q)
4. Privileged communications between auditors and clients (Q)

F&C International, Inc., Case 4.2, 249–252

1. Professional responsibilities of a business's financial executives and high-ranking accountants (Q)
2. Nature of the interaction between client management and independent auditors (Q)
3. Ethical responsibilities of management when they suspect subordinates are engaging in theft or other illicit activities (Q)
4. Need for an entity's executives and financial managers to thoroughly investigate suspicious transactions and events coming to their attention (Q)
5. Common methods used to misrepresent an entity's reported profits
6. SEC's oversight role for the accounting and financial reporting domain

Suzette Washington, Accounting Major, Case 4.3, 253–254

1. Resolution of ethical dilemma faced by an accounting student (Q)
2. Ethical responsibilities of private accountants (Q)
3. Responsibility of accountants to report unethical conduct by their colleagues (Q)
4. Internal controls for a retail merchandiser (Q)

Oak Industries, Inc., Case 4.4, 255–258

1. Intentional understatements of earnings by audit clients (Q)
2. Audit procedures intended to uncover revenue understatements and expense overstatements (Q)
3. Ethical responsibilities of accountants when being pressured to misrepresent their employer's financial data (Q)
4. Corporate accountants' responsibilities when interacting with independent auditors (Q)

5. Ethical responsibilities of non-CPAs (accountants) vs. CPAs (Q)
6. SEC's view regarding the responsibilities of corporate accountants who are aware of fraudulent misrepresentations in their employer's financial statements
7. Letter of representations as a form of audit evidence

Wiley Jackson, Accounting Major, Case 4.5, 259–260
1. Resolution of ethical dilemma by an accounting student (Q)
2. Proper disciplining of accountants who engage in unethical behavior (Q)
3. Responsibility of accountants to report unethical conduct by their colleagues (Q)

Arvel Smart, Accounting Major, Case 4.6, 261–262
1. Resolution of an ethical dilemma by an accounting student (Q)
2. Ethical issues accounting majors may face when they have multiple job offers outstanding (Q)
3. Internship opportunities available to accounting majors

David Quinn, Tax Accountant, Case 4.7, 263–266
1. Nature and purpose of the client confidentiality rule (Q)
2. Identifying violations of the client confidentiality rule (Q)
3. Resolution of disputes with fellow professionals regarding ethical issues (Q)
4. Responsibility of accountants to report unethical conduct by their colleagues (Q)

Jack Bass, Accounting Professor, Case 4.8, 267–271
1. Ethical responsibilities of accounting professors to their students (Q)
2. Proper disciplining of accounting students who engage in unethical behavior (Q)
3. Resolution of an ethical dilemma by an accounting professor (Q)

Thomas Forehand, CPA, Accounting Major, Case 4.9, 273–277
1. Professional standards relevant to client acceptance decisions (Q)
2. Specific procedures to apply when considering whether or not to accept a potential client (Q)
3. Parties affected by the resolution of ethical dilemmas facing accountants (Q)
4. Responsibility of accountants to report criminal activity by others (Q)
5. Strategies accountants can use to manage evolving ethical dilemmas (Q)
6. Criminal liability of accountants
7. Nature and implications of money laundering activities

Cardillo Travel Systems, Inc., Case 5.1, 281–285
1. Ethical dilemmas that accountants and auditors must resolve (Q)
2. Parties affected by the resolution of ethical dilemmas facing accountants and auditors (Q)
3. Auditors' responsibilities when reviewing a client's interim financial statements (Q)
4. Importance of communication among members of an audit engagement team (Q)
5. Key characteristics of audit evidence (Q)
6. Evaluation of conflicting audit evidence by an auditor (Q)
7. SEC's 8-K auditor change disclosure rules (Q)
8. Importance of auditors' assessing the integrity of client management (Q)
9. Methods for assessing integrity of client management (Q)
10. Audit implications of significant auditor-client disputes

Mallon Resources Corporation, Case 5.2, 287–292
1. Auditor independence as the cornerstone of the auditing profession (Q)
2. Audit-related implications of an auditor discussing potential employment opportunities with an audit client during an ongoing audit (Q)
3. Ethical responsibilities of auditors who discuss and/or receive an employment offer from an audit client (Q)
4. SEC's oversight role for financial reporting and auditing domains

The North Face, Inc., Case 5.3, 293–300
1. Proper treatment of proposed audit adjustments that have an immaterial effect on a client's financial statements (Q)
2. Preventing client from gaining access to materiality thresholds for an audit (Q)

3. Identifying violations of the revenue recognition principle (Q)
4. Principal objectives of audit workpapers (Q)
5. Whether competence of client management should affect planning and performance of independent audits (Q)
6. Role of a concurring audit partner on an SEC engagement

NextCard, Inc., Case 5.4, 301–309

1. Auditors' consideration of a client's business model (Q)
2. Identifying fraud risk factors posed by a client (Q)
3. Objectives of audit workpapers (Q)
4. Identifying violations of generally accepted auditing standards (Q)
5. Responsibility of audit partners to serve as mentors for their subordinates (Q)
6. Ethical responsibilities of an auditor who is instructed to violate professional standards by his or her superior (Q)

Koger Properties, Inc., Case 5.5, 311–313

1. Financial independence rules for auditors (Q)
2. Material vs. immaterial financial interests in audit clients (Q)
3. Rationale for financial independence rules (Q)
4. Audit practice implications of mergers between large accounting firms

American Fuel & Supply Company, Inc., Case 5.6, 315–317

1. Auditors' responsibilities regarding the "subsequent discovery of facts existing at audit report date" (Q)
2. Client confidentiality rule (Q)
3. Resolution of ethical dilemmas by the members of an audit engagement team (Q)
4. Disagreements between members of an audit engagement team

Leigh Ann Walker, Staff Accountant, Case 6.1, 321–322

1. Need for auditors to possess personal integrity (Q)
2. Dealing with a lack of personal integrity on the part of staff accountants (Q)
3. Nature of staff accountant's work role and responsibilities

Bill DeBurger, In-Charge Accountant, Case 6.2, 323–325

1. Nature of in-charge accountant's work role and responsibilities (Q)
2. Assimilation of audit evidence to reach an overall audit conclusion (Q)
3. Resolution of conflict between members of an audit engagement team (Q)
4. Performance of major audit assignments by relatively inexperienced auditors (Q)

David Myers, Controller, Case 6.8, 327–331

1. Ethical responsibilities of an accountant who is instructed to make false entries in his or her company's accounting records by a superior (Q)
2. Proper punishment of corporate accountants who intentionally misrepresent their employer's financial health (Q)
3. Role of regulatory authorities in policing the accounting and financial reporting domain (Q)
4. Nature of a corporate controller's work role and responsibilities
5. Impact of involvement in an accounting and financial reporting fraud on an individual's professional and personal life

Tommy O'Connell, Audit Senior, Case 6.4, 333–336

1. Key differences between the professional roles of audit seniors and staff accountants (Q)
2. Implications for independent audits of interpersonal conflicts between members of an audit engagement team (Q)
3. Auditor's responsibility when he or she suspects that a colleague is not completing assigned audit procedures (Q)
4. Audit partner's responsibility when a subordinate reports that a member of the audit engagement team is not completing assigned audit procedures (Q)
5. Need for public accountants to achieve a proper balance between their personal and professional lives
6. Impact of a lack of client cooperation on the performance of an audit

Avis Love, Staff Accountant, Case 6.5, 337–339

1. Parties potentially affected by ethical dilemmas facing auditors (Q)
2. Auditors' ethical obligations to third-party financial statement users (Q)

3. Auditors' responsibility to document and investigate errors revealed by audit procedures (Q)
4. Potential impact on an audit of personal relationships between auditors and client personnel (Q)
5. Audit objectives of year-end cash receipts and sales cutoff tests (Q)
6. Assessing materiality of financial statement errors (Q)

Charles Tollison, Audit Manager, Case 6.6, 341–343

1. Requisite skills for promotion to partner in a major accounting firm (Q)
2. Partner promotion criteria in large vs. small accounting firms (Q)
3. "Up or out" promotion policy of many accounting firms (Q)
4. Need for public accountants to achieve a proper balance between their personal and professional lives
5. Need for a public accountant to actively plan and manage his or her professional career

Hamilton Wong, In-Charge Accountant, Case 6.7, 345–347

1. Ethical issues related to the underreporting of time worked by auditors (Q)
2. Effect of underreporting time worked on quality of independent audits (Q)
3. Measures needed to mitigate the underreporting of time worked (Q)
4. Potentially dysfunctional effects of competitive promotion system within accounting firms on quality of independent audits (Q)
5. Nature of in-charge accountant's work role and responsibilities

PricewaterhouseCoopers Securities, LLC, Case 7.1, 351–355

1. Nature and purpose of SEC sanctions imposed on accounting firms (Q)
2. Types of non-traditional services that accounting firms should be allowed to provide (Q)
3. Fee arrangements between accounting firms and their clients (Q)
4. Provision of services by accounting firms on a contingent fee basis

Stephen Gray, CPA, Case 7.2, 357–360

1. Purpose of professional codes of ethics (Q)
2. Dynamic nature of professional codes of ethics (Q)
3. Role of state boards of accountancy in regulating public accounting profession (Q)
4. Circumstances under which CPAs can accept commissions (Q)
5. Regulatory infrastructure of the public accounting profession (Q)

Scott Fane, CPA, Case 7.3, 361–365

1. Impact of existing ethical rules on CPAs' "commercial speech" (Q)
2. Economic barriers of entry created by a profession's code of ethics (Q)
3. Impact on independent audit function of competitive bidding for audit engagements (Q)
4. Impact of "lowballing" on independent audit function (Q)
5. Advantages and disadvantages of professions being regulated at the state rather than federal level (Q)
6. Impact of "creeping commercialization" on public accounting profession (Q)
7. Practice development activities used by CPAs
8. Regulatory infrastructure of the public accounting profession

Hopkins v. Price Waterhouse, Case 7.4, 367–374

1. Responsibility of public accounting firms to facilitate the career success of their female employees (Q)
2. Informal employee networks within public accounting firms and related personnel and professional implications (Q)
3. Nepotism rules of public accounting firms (Q)
4. Acceptance of female and minority public accountants by clients (Q)
5. Governmental regulation of private partnerships (Q)
6. Partnership promotion process of large public accounting firms
7. Requisite skills for promotion to partner in a major public accounting firm

Sarah Russell, Staff Accountant, Case 7.5, 375–377

1. Interpersonal conflict between an employee and partner of a CPA firm (Q)
2. Responsibilities of public accountants to respect personal rights of colleagues (Q)
3. Office managing partner's responsibility to protect the personal rights of each office member (Q)
4. Nature of staff accountant's work role and responsibilities

Bud Carriker, Audit Senior, Case 7.6, 379–382

1. Client management effort to influence staffing of audit engagement team (Q)
2. Racial discrimination within the auditing discipline (Q)
3. Responsibility of senior members of an audit practice office and/or audit engagement team to protect the civil rights of their subordinates (Q)
4. Resolution of an ethical dilemma by an audit partner (Q)
5. Issues relevant to staffing of audit engagement teams

National Medical Transportation Network, Case 7.7, 383–388

1. Responsibility of client executives to disclose financial statement errors to auditors (Q)
2. Auditors' responsibility when client personnel allege that client's financial statements contain material errors (Q)
3. Impact on auditor independence of client management threats to sue auditors (Q)
4. Circumstances threatening auditor independence (Q)
5. Predecessor-successor auditor communications (Q)
6. Circumstances under which auditors may properly resign from an audit engagement (Q)
7. Impact of questionable management integrity on an independent audit (Q)

Fred Stern & Company, Inc. (Ultramares), Case 7.8, 389–395

1. Implications for the public accounting profession of the apparent move by the courts to socialize investment losses (Q)
2. Auditors' legal exposure under the Securities Act of 1933 and the Securities Exchange Act of 1934 (Q)
3. Auditors' legal exposure under the common law versus the federal securities laws (Q)
4. Evolution of the standard audit report form (Q)
5. Evolution of standard financial statement package prepared by most companies (Q)
6. Effect on audit planning decisions of the number and type of third-party financial statement users (Q)
7. Purpose of an audit engagement letter (Q)
8. Effect of audit engagement letters on auditors' legal liability (Q)
9. Joint and several liability of partners of public accounting firms for their subordinates' malfeasance

First Securities Company of Chicago (Hochfelder), Case 7.9, 397–402

1. Responsibility of auditors to discover and disclose serious internal control deficiencies (Q)
2. Audit implications of significant internal control deficiencies (Q)
3. Key distinctions between and among negligence, gross negligence, and fraudulent conduct in an audit context (Q)
4. Differences in auditors' legal exposure under the Securities Act of 1933, the Securities Exchange Act of 1934, and the common law (Q)
5. Objectives of the federal securities laws and the independent audit function
6. Need for auditors to be skeptical even when the integrity of client management appears to be beyond reproach

Livent, Inc., Case 8.1, 405–418

1. Identification of inherent risk factors (Q)
2. Role and responsibilities of audit partners (Q)
3. Client attitudes toward auditors (Q)
4. Reports prepared by accounting firms on the application of accounting principles by non-audit clients (Q)
5. Revenue recognition issues (Q)
6. Responsibilities of corporate accounting personnel to investigate potential misrepresentations in their employer's accounting records (Q)
7. Potential conflict-of-interests faced by auditors who accept accounting positions with former clients (Q)
8. Accounting firms' responsibilities in due diligence investigations (Q)
9. Forensic investigations by accounting firms
10. Identifying "red flags" indicative of financial statement fraud
11. Audit firms' legal exposure under the Securities Exchange Act of 1934

Royal Ahold, N.V., Case 8.2, 419–434

1. Impact on a multinational corporation's reported net income when applying accounting principles other than U.S. GAAP (Q)
2. U.S. GAAP vs. IFRS: impact on earnings quality (Q)
3. Accounting for promotional allowances (Q)
4. Factors that complicate the audit of multinational corporations (Q)

5. Components of the fraud triangle (Q)
6. Identification of fraud risk factors (Q)
7. Audit procedures effective in uncovering fraudulent accounting (Q)
8. Nature of audit planning across different types of business operations (Q)
9. Accounting for intercorporate investments
10. Conflict between and among the accounting profession's international regulatory bodies
11. Need for major international accounting firms to enhance quality and consistency of their independent audits across the globe

Kansayaku, Case 8.3, 435–443

1. Impact of macroeconomic variables on a nation's independent audit function (Q)
2. Impact of differing barriers to entry on the accounting professions of individual nations (Q)
3. Advantages and disadvantages of an oligopolistic market structure for independent audit services (Q)
4. Measures necessary to promote and protect auditor independence (Q)
5. Impact of cultural norms and nuances on the performance of independent audits and the overall nature of a nation's independent audit function
6. Common challenges and problems faced by independent auditors around the globe
7. Nature and structure of regulatory oversight for the accounting profession and auditing discipline across different nations
8. Criminal and civil liability of audit firms and auditors

Registered Auditors, South Africa, Case 8.4, 445–455

1. Impact of political forces on the development of a nation's independent audit function (Q)
2. Advantages and disadvantages of a separate professional credential for independent auditors (Q)
3. Nature and purpose of South Africa's "reportable irregularities" rule (Q)
4. Impact of South Africa's reportable irregularities rule on that nation's independent audit function (Q)
5. Measures necessary to persuade individuals from underrepresented groups to pursue careers in the accounting profession (Q)
6. Impact of recurring audit failures on the international reputation and credibility of a nation's capital markets
7. Nature and structure of regulatory oversight for the accounting profession and auditing discipline across different nations
8. Criminal and civil liability of accounting firms and individual auditors

Zuan Yan, Case 8.5, 457–467

1. Impact of differing cultural norms across the globe on the ability of the worldwide accounting profession to reach a consensus on important ethical principles (Q)
2. Impact of differing economic systems on the nature of financial reporting objectives (Q)
3. Relevance of fundamental accounting concepts and principles within differing economic systems across the globe (Q)
4. Impact of differing economic systems across the globe on the nature and purpose of independent audits (Q)
5. Challenges and problems faced by accounting firms when performing audits in countries with authoritarian central governments (Q)
6. Impact of political forces on the development and evolution of a nation's accounting profession and independent audit function
7. Unique challenges and problems faced by the accounting profession of the People's Republic of China
8. Nature and structure of regulatory oversight for the accounting profession and auditing discipline across different nations
9. Civil liability of accounting firms

Kaset Thai Sugar Company, Case 8.6, 469–472

1. Problems faced by accountants when performing independent audits and other professional services in hostile countries (Q)
2. Responsibility of accounting firms to provide for the safety of their employees (Q)
3. Impact of a given nation's cultural norms and nuances on the performance of professional services engagements

Australian Wheat Board, Case 8.7, 473–481

1. Relevance of Foreign Corrupt Practices Act to foreign companies that sell securities on U.S. stock exchanges (Q)
2. Responsibility of auditors to detect bribes and related payments by clients to obtain and retain international business relationships (Q)

3. Audit procedures designed to detect bribes and other fraudulent payments (Q)
4. Bribes vs. "facilitating payments" (Q)
5. "Social responsibility" mandate of corporate boards (Q)
6. Australian Auditing Standards vs. International Standards of Auditing (Q)
7. Professional and business risks posed for accounting firms by high-profile clients

OAO Gazprom, Case 8.8, 483–496

1. Challenges that accounting firms face when they establish practice offices in foreign countries (Q)
2. Impact of cultural differences on business practices and ethical norms (Q)
3. Responsibilities of auditors to client stockholders (Q)
4. Threats to auditor independence (Q)
5. Auditors' responsibility to identify related parties and related party transactions (Q)
6. British "true and fair" audit philosophy vs. the U.S. philosophy of "fairly presented" (Q)
7. Philosophical differences between IASB and FASB and resulting impact on standards promulgated by those two organizations (Q)
8. Impact of social and governmental influences on the development of accounting and auditing practices
9. Legal exposure faced by accounting firms in foreign countries
10. Professional and business risks faced by accounting firms that audit high-profile clients

Tata Finance Limited, Case 8.9, 497–504

1. Impact on the design and performance of an independent audit when the client has a unique culture and ethical or moral code (Q)
2. Professional standards relevant to consulting engagements (Q)
3. Similarities and differences between auditing standards and standards for consulting engagements (Q)
4. Responsibilities imposed on accountants by the client confidentiality standard (Q)
5. Auditor independence issues

Baan Company, N.V., Case 8.10, 505–511

1. SEC's financial reporting requirements for domestic versus foreign companies (Q)
2. Impact of joint business relationships between auditors and their clients on auditor independence (Q)
3. Nature and purpose of SEC sanctions imposed on accounting firms (Q)
4. Oversight role of SEC for the independent audit function
5. Challenges accounting firms face in coordinating audits of multinational clients

Institute of Chartered Accountants of India, Case 8.11, 513–524

1. Comparative advantages and disadvantages of a centralized vs. a decentralized regulatory infrastructure for a nation's public accounting profession (Q)
2. Philosophical differences regarding the purpose of the independent audit function that impact the nature of that function across different cultures (Q)
3. Strategic initiatives used by major international accounting firms to enter new markets (Q)
4. Ethical issues that the major international accounting firms have faced when entering new markets (Q)
5. Ethical and competitive issues posed by allowing accounting firms to advertise their professional services (Q)
6. Nature, purpose, and propriety of protectionist economic policies intended to shield a nation's domestic accounting firms from foreign competition (Q)
7. Nature and purpose of reciprocity agreements between national regulatory organizations within the global accounting profession (Q)
8. Ethical, competitive, and regulatory issues posed by the increasing trend of international outsourcing of professional accounting services (Q)
9. Impact of political and social forces on the development and evolution of a nation's accounting profession and independent audit function
10. International criticism of operating philosophy, policies, and procedures of major international accounting firms
11. Conflict between and among the accounting profession's international regulatory bodies

SUMMARY OF CASES BY TOPIC

Advertising by Accounting Firms: ICAI.

Analytical Procedures: Just for Feet, Leslie Fay, U.S. Surgical, Crazy Eddie, Royal Ahold.

Assessment of Client Management Competence: ZZZZ Best, Lincoln, Crazy Eddie, North Face.

Audit Evidence—General: Health Management, SmarTalk, Jack Greenberg, Golden Bear, Happiness Express, U.S. Surgical, Cardillo, New Century Financial Corporation.

Audit Evidence—Limitations: Health Management, U.S. Surgical, ZZZZ Best, Lincoln, Golden Bear, CBI Holding, Rocky Mount, Bill DeBurger, Royal Ahold.

Audit Implications of Control Deficiencies: Health Management, Leslie Fay, Crazy Eddie, Jack Greenberg, Saks, Goodner, First Securities.

Audit Planning Issues: Just for Feet, Leslie Fay, ZZZZ Best, Crazy Eddie, Star Technologies, Royal Ahold.

Audit Reporting Issues: U.S. Surgical, NMTN, AWB, Gazprom, New Century Financial Corporation.

Audit Review Process: Star Technologies, North Face, Tommy O'Connell.

Audit Risk (and/or its components): Livent, U.S. Surgical, Triton.

Audit Sampling: Stern.

Audit Staffing issues: New Century Financial Corporation.

Audit Time Budgets/Audit Deadlines: Tommy O'Connell, Charles Tollison, Hamilton Wong.

Audit Workpapers: Enron, Health Management, Leslie Fay, NorthFace, NextCard, SmarTalk.

Auditing Accounting Estimates: New Century Financial Corporation.

Auditing a Multinational Company: Triton, Livent, Royal Ahold, Zuan Yan, AWB, Gazprom, Baan.

Auditing Accounts Payable (and other liabilities): Crazy Eddie, Star Technologies, CBI Holding.

Auditing Cash: CapitalBanc, Avis Love.

Auditing Contingencies: SmarTalk, Cardillo.

Auditing Contracts and Commitments: Enron, ZZZZ Best, Golden Bear, SmarTalk, Cardillo.

Auditing Intercorporate Investments: Royal Ahold.

Auditing Inventory: Just for Feet, Health Management, Leslie Fay, Crazy Eddie, Star Technologies, Jack Greenberg, Goodner, Rocky Mount, F&C.

Auditing Receivables: Just for Feet, Health Management, Star Technologies, Happiness Express, NextCard.

Auditing Revenues: Livent, U.S. Surgical, Lincoln, Crazy Eddie, Golden Bear, Campbell Soup, North Face, Oak, Avis Love, Stern.

Auditor Independence: Enron, Health Management, Leslie Fay, Lincoln, Crazy Eddie, PWCS, Jamaica, Koger, Mallon, Avis Love, NMTN, Kansayaku, South Africa, Zuan Yan, Gazprom, Tata Finance, Baan, ICAI, New Century Financial Corporation.

Auditor-Client Interaction Issues: Enron, Livent, Health Management, U.S. Surgical, Lincoln, Jack Greenberg, CBI Holding, North Face, CapitalBanc, Howard Street, Jamaica, Oak, F&C, Cardillo, Tommy O'Connell, Avis Love, NMTN, Bud Carriker, Kansayaku, South Africa, Zuan Yan, Kaset Thai, New Century Financial Corporation.

Bankruptcy Examination: New Century Financial Corporation.

"Big Four" Accounting Firms and International Practice Development Issues: Kansayaku, South Africa, Zuan Yan, Kaset Thai, Gazprom, ICAI.

Career Development Issues: Livent, Star Technologies, Wiley Jackson, Arvel Smart, David Quinn, Jack Bass, NextCard, Thomas Forehand, Leigh Ann Walker, Bill DeBurger, Sarah Russell, Tommy O'Connell, Charles Tollison, Hamilton Wong, Hopkins, Bud Carriker.

Client Acceptance/Retention Issues: Lincoln, Jack Greenberg, CBI, Thomas Forehand, Bud Carriker, Kansayaku, Zuan Yan, Kaset Thai, Gazprom, Tata Finance, Baan.

Client Confidentiality: U.S. Surgical, David Quinn, Creve Couer, American Fuel & Supply, South Africa, ICAI.

Client Management Integrity Issues: Enron, Health Management, Leslie Fay, U.S. Surgical, ZZZZ Best, Lincoln, Crazy Eddie, Star Technologies, Jack Greenberg, Golden Bear, Happiness Express, CBI Holding, Campbell Soup, SmarTalk, North Face, NextCard, David Myers, CapitalBanc, Triton, Jamaica, Oak, F&C, Cardillo, Tommy O'Connell, NMTN, First Securities, Bud Carriker, Livent, Royal Ahold, Kansayaku, South Africa, Zuan Yan, Kaset Thai, AWB, Gazprom, Tata Finance, New Century Financial Corporation.

Client-imposed Audit Scope Limitations: Health Management, ZZZZ Best, Jack Greenberg.

Collegial Responsibilities of Auditors: ZZZZ Best, Lincoln, David Quinn, Baan, North Face, NextCard, Leigh Ann Walker, Bill DeBurger, Sarah Russell, Tommy O'Connell, Charles Tollison, Hamilton Wong, Bud Carriker, Gazprom, ICAI.

Comfort Letter/Due Diligence Engagements: Livent.

Commercialism within Public Accounting Profession: Enron, PWCS, Scott Fane, Stephen Gray, Zuan Yan, Gazprom, Baan, ICAI.

Competition in U.S. Public Accounting Profession: Lincoln, Scott Fane.

Compilation Engagements: Howard Street.

Confirmation Procedures: Just for Feet, Happiness Express, CBI Holding, Royal Ahold.

Conflict in Auditor and Consultant Roles: Enron, PWCS, Gazprom, Baan, ICAI, New Century Financial Corporation.

Contingent Fees: PWCS.

Control Environment: Enron, Health Management, Leslie Fay, U.S. Surgical, ZZZZ Best, Lincoln, Crazy Eddie, Jack Greenberg, Golden Bear, Happiness Express, CBI Holding, Campbell Soup, SmarTalk, North Face, CapitalBanc, Trolley Dodgers, Howard Street, Saks, Triton, Goodner, Rocky Mount, Jamaica, Oak, F&C, Cardillo, Stern, First Securities, Livent, Royal Ahold, Kansayaku, South Africa, Zuan Yan, AWB, Gazprom, Tata Finance, New Century Financial Corporation.

Convergence of International Accounting and/or Auditing Standards: Royal Ahold, Kansayaku, South Africa, Zuan Yan, AWB, Gazprom, ICAI.

CPAs in Non-audit Roles: Livent, Health Management, PWCS, Howard Street, Creve Couer, Jamaica, Thomas Forehand, Kaset Thai, AWB, Gazprom, Tata Finance, Baan, ICAI.

Detection, Disclosure, or Audit Implications of Illegal Acts: Enron, Health Management, Happiness Express, Triton, South Africa, AWB, Gazprom, Tata Finance.

Disagreements between Auditors: Star Technologies, American Fuel & Supply, Bill DeBurger, Bud Carriker, Gazprom.

Disclosure of Internal Control Deficiencies: First Securities, Jack Greenberg, New Century Financial Corporation.

Engagement Letter: ZZZZ Best, Jamaica, Stern.

Ethical Issues Involving Accounting Majors: Suzette Washington, Wiley Jackson, Arvel Smart, Jack Bass.

Ethical Issues Faced by U.S. Accounting Firms in International Markets: Triton, Kansayaku, South Africa, Zuan Yan, Kaset Thai, AWB, Gazprom, ICAI.

Ethical Responsibilities of Accountants in Private Industry: Enron, Livent, Health Management, Leslie Fay, Jack Greenberg, Golden Bear, Trolley Dodgers, Triton, Jamaica, Jack Bass, David Myers, Suzette Washington, Rocky Mount, Oak, F&C, Cardillo, Mallon, Tata Finance, New Century Financial Corporation.

Expanding Product Line of Accounting Firms: Enron, PWCS, Stephen Gray, Kaset Thai, AWB, Baan, ICAI.

Expert Opinions as Audit Evidence: Lincoln.

Foreign Corrupt Practices Act: Triton, AWB.

Fraud Detection and/or Disclosure: Enron, Livent, Health Management, Leslie Fay, U.S. Surgical, ZZZZ Best, Lincoln, Crazy Eddie, Jack Greenberg, Golden Bear, Happiness Express, CBI Holding, SmarTalk, North Face, NextCard, Capital-Banc, Triton, Oak, Jamaica, Cardillo, Stern, First Securities, Royal Ahold, Kansayaku, South Africa, AWB, Gazprom, Tata Finance, New Century Financial Corporation.

Hiring of Auditors by Former Clients: Livent, Health Management, Lincoln, Crazy Eddie, Oak, Jamaica, Mallon.

History of Accounting Profession in Nations Other Than U.S.: Kansayaku, South Africa, Zuan Yan, Gazprom, ICAI.

History of U.S. Public Accounting Profession: Enron.

Identification of Inherent Risk Factors: Just for Feet, Leslie Fay, Star Technologies, Crazy Eddie, U.S. Surgical, Jack Greenberg, Livent, Royal Ahold.

Identification of Internal Control Objectives: Trolley Dodgers, Howard Street, Saks, Goodner, Troberg, Jack Greenberg.

Identification of Internal Control Risk Factors: Just for Feet, Lincoln.

Identification of Management Assertions: ZZZZ Best, Lincoln, Golden Bear, CapitalBanc.

Impact of Cultural Norms and Values on Independent Audit Function: Kansayaku, South Africa, Zuan Yan, Gazprom, ICAI.

Internal Control Deficiencies: Health Management, Leslie Fay, Jack Greenberg, Trolley Dodgers, Howard Street, Triton, Goodner, Troberg, First Securities, New Century Financial Corporation.

Internal Controls for Small Businesses: Howard Street, Troberg, Suzette Washington.

International Accounting Issues: Royal Ahold, South Africa, Zuan Yan, Gazprom.

International Markets, Competitive Issues: Kansayaku, Zuan Yan, Gazprom, ICAI.

Issues Related to the Global Accounting Profession: Royal Ahold, Kansayaku, South Africa, Zuan Yan, Kaset Thai, Gazprom, Baan, ICAI.

Lack of Definitive Guidelines for Client Transactions: Enron, Livent.

Legal Liability—Common Law: Stern, First Securities.

Legal Liability—Criminal: Enron, NextCard, Thomas Forehand. Kansayaku.

Legal Liability—General: Leslie Fay, Lincoln, American Fuel & Supply, Jamaica, Hopkins, Stern, First Securities, New Century Financial Corporation.

Legal Liability—International Markets: Royal Ahold, Kansayaku, South Africa, Zuan Yan, Gazprom, ICAI.

Legal Liability—1933 Act: Stern, First Securities.

Legal Liability—1934 Act: Livent, Health Management, Campbell Soup, Stern, First Securities.

Letter of Representations: Rocky Mount, Oak, NMTN.

"Lowballing" Phenomenon: Crazy Eddie, Scott Fane.

Materiality Issues: U.S. Surgical, North Face, Rocky Mount, Avis Love, New Century Financial Corporation.

Mortgage Lending: New Century Financial Corporation.

Need to Follow-up on Suspicious or Unusual Client Transactions: Enron, Just for Feet, Livent, Health Management, U.S. Surgical, ZZZZ Best, Lincoln, Jack Greenberg, Golden Bear, Happiness Express, CBI Holding, Campbell Soup, North

Face, NextCard, SmarTalk, CapitalBanc, Triton, Goodner, Jamaica, Cardillo, Avis Love, David Myers, NMTN, Stern, Royal Ahold, Gazprom, New Century Financial Corporation.

Opinion Shopping: Livent, Lincoln, Cardillo, NMTN, Royal Ahold.

Outsourcing of Accounting Services: ICAI.

Personal Integrity of Auditors: Enron, Health Management, Jamaica, SmarTalk, Wiley Jackson, Arvel Smart, David Quinn, North Face, Cardillo, Koger, Mallon, North Face, NextCard, Leigh Ann Walker, Bill DeBurger, Sarah Russell, Tommy O'Connell, Avis Love, Hamilton Wong, Bud Carriker, Royal Ahold, Kansayaku, South Africa, New Century Financial Corporation.

Personal Lives vs. Professional Work Roles: Health Management, Wiley Jackson, Thomas Forehand, Leigh Ann Walker, Bill DeBurger, Sarah Russell, Tommy O'Connell, Avis Love, Charles Tollison, Hamilton Wong, David Myers, Hopkins, Kansayaku.

Personnel Issues within Audit Firms: Mallon, NextCard, Leigh Ann Walker, Bill DeBurger, Sarah Russell, Tommy O'Connell, Charles Tollison, Hamilton Wong, Hopkins, Bud Carriker, South Africa, Kaset Thai, KPMG, New Century Financial Corporation.

Practice Development Issues—International Markets: Royal Ahold, Kansayaku, South Africa, Zuan Yan, Kaset Thai, Gazprom, Baan, ICAI.

Predecessor-Successor Auditor Communications: ZZZZ Best, Lincoln, NMTN.

Premature Signoff of Audit Procedures: Tommy O'Connell, New Century Financial Corporation.

Privileged Communications for Auditors: Creve Couer.

Professional Roles of Auditors: Enron, Jamaica, NextCard, Leigh, Ann Walker, Bill DeBurger, Sarah Russell, Tommy O'Connell, Avis Love, Charles Tollison, Hamilton Wong, Bud Carriker, New Century Financial Corporation.

Professional Skepticism: Enron, Health Management, Golden Bear, Happiness Express, CBI Holding, SmarTalk, North Face, Jamaica, New Century Financial Corporation.

Quality Control Issues for Audit Firms: Lincoln, CBI Holding, Baan, PWCS, SmarTalk, North Face, NextCard, Cardillo, Koger, Leigh Ann Walker, Bill DeBurger, Tommy O'Connell, Hamilton Wong, Hopkins, Bud Carriker, South Africa, Zuan Yan, ICAI, New Century Financial Corporation.

Receipt of Commissions by CPAs: Stephen Gray.

Reciprocity Agreements between International Regulatory Bodies: ICAI.

Regulation Issues Related to Global Accounting Profession: Livent, Royal Ahold, Kansayaku, South Africa, Zuan Yan, Kaset Thai, AWB, Gazprom, Baan, ICAI.

Regulation of the U.S. Accounting Profession: Enron, PWCS, Oak, Mallon, North Face, NextCard, Scott Fane, Stephen Gray.

Related Party Transactions: Enron, Livent, Lincoln, Star Technologies, Gazprom.

Resolution of Ethical Dilemmas: Just for Feet, Livent, Health Management, PWCS, Triton, Creve Couer, Jamaica, Suzette Washington, Wiley Jackson, Arvel Smart, David Quinn, Jack Bass, Thomas Forehand, Rocky Mount, Cardillo, American Fuel & Supply, Mallon, Leigh Ann Walker, Bill DeBurger, Tommy O'Connell, Avis Love, Hamilton Wong, David Myers, NMTN, Bud Carriker, Kansayaku, South Africa, Gazprom, Baan, ICAI.

Review of Interim Financial Statements: Enron, ZZZZ Best, North Face, Cardillo, New Century Financial Corporation.

Rule-Making Processes: Scott Fane, Stephen Gray, Royal Ahold, Kansayaku, South Africa, Zuan Yan, Gazprom, ICAI.

Scope of Internal Controls: Saks, Troberg.

Scope of Services (provision of non-audit services): Enron, PWCS, Stephen Gray, Tata Finance, Baan.

Securities and Exchange Commission: Just for Feet, Enron, Livent, Health Management, Leslie Fay, U.S. Surgical, ZZZZ Best, Lincoln, Crazy Eddie, Star Technologies, North Face, NextCard, PWCS, CapitalBanc, Triton, Jamaica, Oak, F&C, Cardillo, Koger, Mallon, First Securities, Royal Ahold, Baan, New Century Financial Corporation.

SEC's 8-K Auditor Change Rules: ZZZZ Best, Cardillo.

Societal Role of Audit Function: Enron, Lincoln, Scott Fane, Stern, First Securities, Kansayaku, South Africa, Zuan Yan, Gazprom, Baan, ICAI, New Century Financial Corporation.

Subprime Lending Issues: New Century Financial Corporation.

Subsequent Discovery of Errors: Star Technologies, North Face, American Fuel & Supply, New Century Financial Corporation.

Substance over Form Concept: Enron, Lincoln, Campbell Soup, SmarTalk, Gazprom.

Supervision of Staff Accountants: CapitalBanc, Leigh Ann Walker, Tommy O'Connell.

Understanding the Client's Industry: Enron, Just for Feet, Livent, Leslie Fay, ZZZZ Best, Lincoln, Crazy Eddie, Star Technologies, Jack Greenberg, Happiness Express, Campbell Soup, North Face, NextCard, Triton, Royal Ahold, New Century Financial Corporation.

U.S. GAAP vs. IFRS: Royal Ahold.

Walk-through Audit Procedure: Jack Greenberg.

Withdrawal of an Audit Report: Leslie Fay, Star Technologies, American Fuel & Supply, New Century Financial Corporation.